Shield of Empire

Shield of Empire

The Royal Navy and Scotland

BRIAN LAVERY

BIRLINN

First published in 2007 by
Birlinn Limited
10 Newington Road
Edinburgh
EH9 1QS

www.birlinn.co.uk

ISBN10: 1 84158 513 0
ISBN13: 978 1 84158 513 0

British Library Cataloguing-in-Publication Data
A catalogue record for this book is available from the British Library

Typeset by Hewer Text UK Ltd, Edinburgh
Printed and bound by Creative Print and Design, Wales

Contents

List of Illustrations

PLATE SECTION

The Dutch Fleet hove to off Buchan Ness

Argyll's campaign, 1685

The Bass Rock

Eilan Donan Castle as a ruin in the 1880s

Captain Lord George Graham in his cabin

A young man is introduced to the midshipmen's berth

Napoleon boards the *Bellerophon*

Captain Francois Thurot

Murdoch Mackenzie's survey of the West Coast

Seamen in 1807

Acknowledgements

Perhaps my first thanks should go to Don Hind and the crew of the *Lorne Leader*, who introduced me to the delights of sailing in the Western Isles and inspired me to look at the richness of Scottish maritime history. Secondly, I am grateful to Dr Eric Grove, now of the University of Salford, who read over the nineteenth- and twentieth-century parts of the work and made many helpful comments about my first attempts to write about these periods.

I should mention many past and present colleagues in the National Maritime Museum who have made contributions or provided ideas on one way or another – Professor Roger Knight, Chris Ware, Bob Todd, Jeremy Michell, Liza Verity, Nigel Rigby, Simon Stephens, Robert Blyth and many others; the staff of the Royal Naval Museum, Portsmouth including Campbell McMurray, Colin White and Matthew Sheldon; Robert Prescott and many others in the Scottish Institute of Maritime Studies at St Andrews University; Jim Tildesley at the Scottish Maritime Museum, Irvine; and Chris Page, Jock Gardiner, Malcolm Llewellyn-Jones, Jenny Wraight and Iain Mackenzie of the Naval Historical Branch. Two late colleagues, David Lyon and David Syrett, are sadly missed as friends and critics.

Any research in British maritime history must rely heavily on past work done by the Navy Records Society and the Society for Nautical Research. I am proud to have served on the Councils of these bodies, and exchanged many ideas with their members. The bulk of the research was done in the Public Record Office, now the National Archives, at Kew. Unusually among public bodies, it seems to have gained in efficiency over the years, if anything. There are also many vital collections in the National Maritime Museum, including models, charts, manuscripts, ships plans and the underestimated pamphlet collection.

John Tuckwell has supported the project over a number of years, and at Birlinn I am grateful to Laura Esselmont and Andrew Simmons. I am also grateful to Sarah and Alice Lavery for support and encouragement.

Brian Lavery
March 2007

Preface

This is not intended as a naval history of Scotland. That would require a much broader canvas and an earlier starting point. In his monumental work *Safeguard of the Seas*, N.A.M. Rodger is particularly fair to the non-English elements in British naval history and credits one of the greatest naval milestones to Scotland. The Lords of the Isles, he says, were one of three sources of naval power in the British Isles at the beginning of the sixteenth century. Another was Henry VIII's fleet in England and the third was James IV of Scotland's fleet, which mounted a campaign against the Lords of the Isles with some of the world's first gun-armed warships. As Rodger says, 'it is not fanciful to suggest that this obscure campaign, not anything done by English ships, marks the real end of Medieval warfare in northern waters and the first hesitant beginnings in the British Isles of what was eventually to become an entirely new style of sea fighting.'[1]

When I was writing the book, one English naval officer said to me, 'What's it about – Cochrane, Cochrane, Cochrane?' He had spent some time at Faslane, so perhaps he should have known better. Even then, I had relatively modest expectations about the size of the book, but as so often happens, it expanded as work progressed. Aspects such as the importance of Scottish officers in Nelson's navy, the role of training bases in the Second World War and the secret history of the Holy Loch base all came to light and yielded far more than I had expected.

We live in an age when many people tend to ignore the importance of the sea, and much of its lore is almost forgotten. I was once contacted by a journalist who asked me about a particular ship. We established that the ship had been built in Glasgow and launched in 1944. She then asked me where the launch had taken place. She thought it was like a book launch, which can take place anywhere. No-one who lived on Clydeside in the 1950s could ever have made that mistake, but subsequent generations have already begun to see things in a different way.

There is no question about the importance of the sea in Scottish history. The eminent historian Gordon Donaldson begins one of his major works with the statement, 'The two most conspicuous features on the map of Scotland are mountains and the sea.'[2] Mountains have tended to be barriers rather than assets, but the sea has always been hugely important, providing routes for immigrants and emigrants as well as trade, and supplying resources in the form of fish and oil. The sea has always been a source of beauty and hope and also of fear and wonder.

Scotland has two very different coastlines in east and west, which have helped to create two distinct cultures, with Glasgow looking toward the West Highlands and islands, Ireland and America, and Edinburgh towards England and Europe. No two cities in the United Kingdom are so far apart culturally despite being so close together geographically. The British are proud of the fact that that no-one lives more than 80 miles from the sea, but in Scotland that distance can be halved. Scotland has never aspired to 'rule the waves' or have 'mastery of the sea', but Scots have often played a central role in the story of British sea power, just as they have in other aspects of the British Empire.

From a strategic point of view, Scotland is important as the northern end of an island which has the potential to dominate the seas of northern Europe and to restrict movements out of Germany, the Netherlands, Russia and Scandinavia. In addition, it had many fine harbours, often underused for civilian purposes, and due to its geographical position, has suffered less than other parts of the United Kingdom from privateering, bombing and the threat of invasion. Even a spot as isolated as Scapa Flow can become the hub of naval history, for a few wartime years at least.

In *Shield of Empire* I hope I have made it clear that, among other things, the role of the navy in Scotland raises fundamental questions about Scottish identity. Despite the activities of the Lords of the Isles, James IV and the Scottish privateers, most naval history as it relates to Scotland is inextricably linked with the Union of 1707. Most of the Scots involved (except pressed seamen) have been happy to participate in a United Kingdom navy, though the English have not always been sensitive to the needs and wishes of Scots - a fact which is not unique to naval history. The Scot within the navy has always faced the classic dilemma, whether to retain his national identity or to merge into the largely English-dominated whole.

No great naval battle has ever been fought within Scottish waters (unless one includes Bloody Bay in 1481 between John Lord of the Isles and his son), but the ships which fought at Jutland in 1916 all sailed from Scottish bases and the survivors returned there. Anyway, naval historians have long been aware that naval history is about much more than battles. Scottish naval bases have been vital to the Royal Navy since the beginning of the twentieth century, and are just as important as ever today, though places such as Helensburgh and Dunfermline, for example, have never showed any signs of becoming like Chatham, Portsmouth or Plymouth – towns whose whole history is tied up with the navy and where the navy permeates every aspect of the local economy and culture.

I have not found space to say much about the contribution by Scottish shipbuilders. In a sense that is a story on its own, and I feel that its omission does not seriously detract from the main narrative. Even if all the navy's ships had been built elsewhere, Scotland's role in naval history would not have been very different.

Since the great bulk of naval records are in the National Archive at Kew, this book seemed a natural course for a naval historian of Scottish origin living in London. One of the great pleasures of writing it has been to revisit scenes from the past and see them in a historical context. The Reserve Fleet in the Gareloch, the controversy over the Holy Loch and Faslane bases, the former naval reserve training ships *Carrick* and *Unicorn* – all appear in a different light after reading about them in the archives.

The story of the Royal Navy in Scotland has always been one of an uneasy and sometimes violent relationship with England, starting from the time when Cromwell's fleet appeared in the Forth. It covers the brutal suppression of the Jacobites, the introduction of the press gang and the building of unpopular bases such as Faslane. It also has its positive side, including the role of Scottish officers in the wars with France, the opportunities of employment and travel it created over the centuries and the pride that Scotland can take in its role in the Second World War. I leave it to readers to conclude what messages it has for Scotland and the United Kingdom in the future.

Brian Lavery
Greenwich, March 2007

1. *Safeguard of the Seas*, London, 1997, p. 168.
2. *Scotland, the Shaping of a Nation*, Newton Abbot, 1980, p. 9.

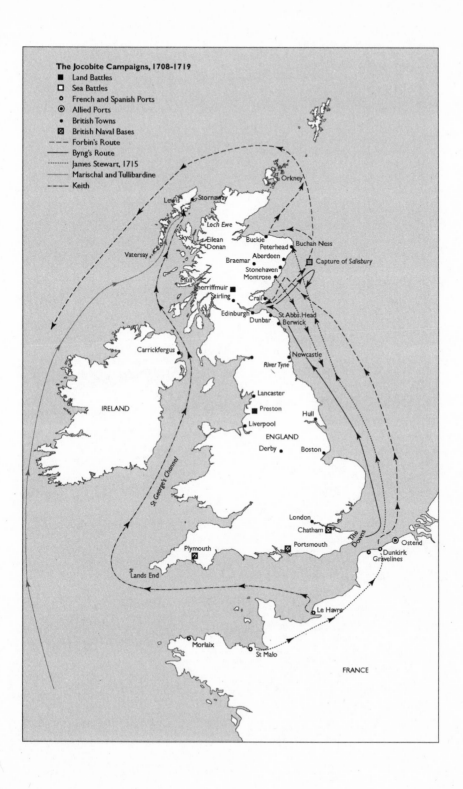

The Jocobite Campaigns, 1708-1719

- ■ Land Battles
- □ Sea Battles
- ○ French and Spanish Ports
- ◉ Allied Ports
- • British Towns
- ⊠ British Naval Bases
- --- Forbin's Route
- —— Byng's Route
- ········ James Stewart, 1715
- —— Marischal and Tullibardine
- —·—· Keith

Orkney

Lewis Stornaway
Loch Ewe
Skye Eilean
Donan
Vatersay

Buckie
Peterhead Buchan Ness
Braemar Aberdeen
Stonehaven
Montrose ☐ Capture of *Salisbury*
Mull Sherriffmuir
Stirling Crail
Edinburgh St Abbs Head
Dunbar Berwick

Carrickfergus Newcastle
River Tyne

Lancaster
IRELAND ■ Preston Hull
Liverpool
ENGLAND
Derby • Boston

St George's Channel

London
Chatham ⊠
Plymouth Portsmouth The Downs
⊠ ◉ Ostend
Lands End Dunkirk
Gravelines

Le Havre

Morlaix
St Malo FRANCE

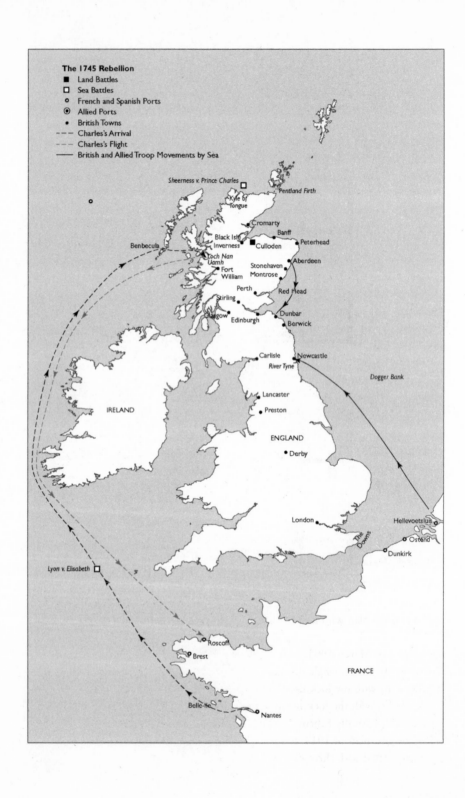

The 1745 Rebellion
- ■ Land Battles
- □ Sea Battles
- ○ French and Spanish Ports
- ◉ Allied Ports
- • British Towns
- ---- Charles's Arrival
- ---- Charles's Flight
- —— British and Allied Troop Movements by Sea

Sheerness v. Prince Charles

Pentland Firth

Kyle of Tongue

Cromarty

Black Isle   Banff
Inverness   Peterhead
Benbecula   ■ Culloden
Loch Nan Uamh   Aberdeen
Fort William   Stonehaven
Perth   Montrose
Stirling   Red Head
Glasgow   Dunbar
Edinburgh   Berwick

Carlisle   Newcastle
River Tyne   *Dogger Bank*

Lancaster
Preston

IRELAND

ENGLAND

Derby

London   Hellevoetsluis
The Downs   Ostend
Dunkirk

Lyon v. Elisabeth

Roscoff
Brest

FRANCE

Belle-Ile   Nantes

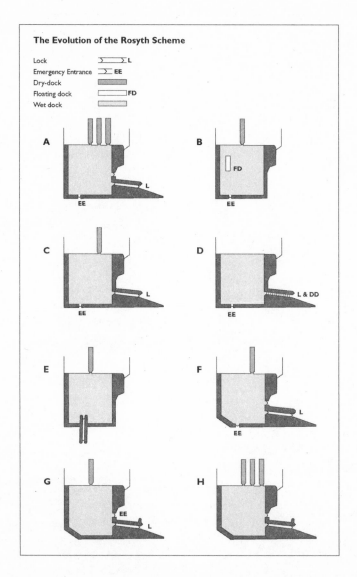

The Evolution of the Rosyth Scheme

Lock ⟩‾‾‾‾⟩ L
Emergency Entrance ⟩‾⟨ EE
Dry-dock
Floating dock ▭ FD
Wet dock

A The original plan with a square basin, three dry-docks and the emergency exit on
   the south wall
B Scheme I of March 1905, with a floating dock and the emergency exit only
C Scheme III, with a single dry-dock
D Scheme II, with the lock used as a dry-dock
E Scheme IV, with the lock in the south wall
F Scheme V, basically Scheme III with one corner cut off
G The revised plan of 1913, with the emergency exit moved to the east wall
H As completed with three dry-docks

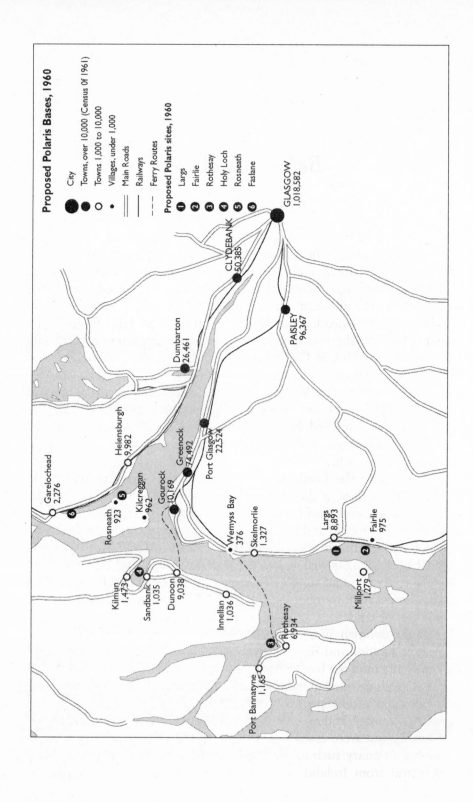

Proposed Polaris Bases, 1960

City
Towns, over 10,000 (Census 0f 1961)
Towns 1,000 to 10,000
Villages, under 1,000
Main Roads
Railways
Ferry Routes

Proposed Polaris sites, 1960
❶ Largs
❷ Fairlie
❸ Rothesay
❹ Holy Loch
❺ Rosneath
❻ Faslane

GLASGOW
1,018,582

CLYDEBANK
50,385

PAISLEY
96,367

Dumbarton
26,461

Helensburgh
9,982

Garelochead
2,276

Rosneath
923

Kilcreggan
962

Gourock
10,169

Greenock
74,492

Port Glasgow
22,524

Wemyss Bay
376

Skelmorlie
1,327

Largs
8,893

Fairlie
975

Millport
1,279

Kilmun
1,473

Sandbank
1,035

Dunoon
9,038

Innellan
1,036

Rothesay
6,934

Port Bannatyne
1,65

Chapter 1

Before the Union

The sea has always been important in Scottish history. The earliest peoples may have come from Ireland or Scandinavia around 10,000 years ago. Scotland had her first taste of organised sea power, in the modern sense, in AD 82 or 83, when a fleet of Roman galleys headed north, co-operating with land forces in an expedition to the north-east. The original Scots came to Dalriada by sea by AD 500. St Columba arrived by coracle from Ireland and set up a religious see at Iona, using boats as the only means of communication. The Vikings, the greatest seamen of their age, left an indelible mark on western and northern Scotland and the islands. As a unified Scottish Kingdom began to emerge in the early Middle Ages, seaborne trade provided its main contact with the outside world.

In the west the Lords of the Isles created a maritime domain in which the galley, a direct descendant of the Viking ship, was the predominant means of transport and warfare. The Lords were chiefs of the Clan Donald and had their headquarters in Finlaggan Castle on Islay. At their height their domains included all the Western Isles and the Isle of Man, as well as mainland areas. They also held territory in Ireland. As a feudal superior, the Lord of the Isles usually demanded the service of a number of galleys of specified size in return for a holding of land.

In the Scottish Wars of Independence, the land battles of Stirling Bridge, Falkirk and Bannockburn are commemorated in song, story and film; but in the background, sea power played an essential role. If the English invaded along the east coast, by far the easiest route, they needed ships to keep their army fed, armed and clothed in a hostile, barren country. If they operated in the west, then supplies and troops from Ireland were essential. Sea power allowed an English army to cross an estuary such as the Forth, or a sea such as the one dividing Scotland from Ireland. It could besiege coastal fortresses such as

Dunbar. It could destroy Scottish commerce and ruin her trade. Conversely, the Scots could develop sea power of their own in order to prevent these things and to raid English commerce.[1] Thus by 1307, King Robert Bruce's alliance with the western islanders gave him the use of galleys to harass English shipping. From 1310 he had the assistance of Flemish and German privateers. Eventually, English merchants became tired of the King's constant requisitioning of their ships and the interruption of trade and became less enthusiastic for the war.

The Auld Alliance between Scotland and France began in 1295. It was only possible because of the sea links between the two countries, despite the commanding position of England between them. The first Scottish naval hero was a privateer captain, Sir Andrew Wood of Largo, who served James III and James IV. In his famous ship the *Yellow Carvel*, he defeated three English vessels under Stephen Bull off the Isle of May in August 1490 and towed them into Dundee in triumph.

King James IV (1488–1513) built a fleet of galleys based at Dumbarton and used them to suppress the Lords of the Isles. He built a very different navy in the Firth of Forth. Like other kings of the age he bought, hired and requisitioned merchant ships for his fleet and he issued private men-of-war, or privateers, with 'letters of marque' which allowed them to make war on the king's enemies. The best-known captains of the reign, apart from Andrew Wood, were John, Andrew and Robert Barton of Leith, whose campaigns often strayed into piracy.

But a real 'Navy Royal' needed larger ships which the King had to build for himself, for he knew that converted merchant ships were less useful than in the past, as a new and larger type had evolved. The carrack had high castles and an armament of numerous but light guns to fire down on an enemy's decks. The only Scottish king to build a navy for more than home defence, he perhaps intended it to become a factor in European politics, to support his allies in France or Denmark. Possibly he felt that such a fleet was an essential part of the 'new monarchy' which he represented.

The most famous of all James's maritime projects was the *Great Michael*, arguably the first modern warship in the world. Her building at Newhaven took five years. The chronicler Pitscottie claims, with no exaggeration, that she 'tuik so mekill timber that scho wastit all the wodis in Fyfe except Falkland wode, by (besides) all the tymmer that was gottin out of Noroway.' Shipwrights were brought in from France to supervise the work and the ship cost the enormous sum of £30,000

Scots. She was launched in October 1511 to a fanfare of trumpets. James's great fleet was barely used. The King was killed at the Battle of Flodden and the regency which succeeded him had no interest in sea power. The *Great Michael* was sold to France and may have served for another thirty years.[2]

In May 1546, John Knox and his Protestant supporters captured St Andrews Castle and hung the body of Cardinal Beaton from a window. Royal forces besieged the castle for more than a year until seventeen French galleys came to their aid. Knox and many of his supporters had another taste of French sea power, spending two years as galley slaves.

Scottish seamen in England's wars

After James VI of Scotland inherited the English throne in 1603 and became James I, Scottish foreign policy was subjected to English needs. One of the first complaints was about the new Union Flag itself, used mainly at sea, because the 'Scottis Croce, called Sanctandrous Croce, is twyse divydit, and the Inglishe Croce, callit Sanct George, haldin haill and drawne through the Scottis Croce, whiche is thairby obscurit.'[3]

Charles I, who succeeded in 1625, soon undertook a war with Spain which his father had initiated. Without the support of Parliament and therefore without money, lacking a just cause which could appeal to the hearts of his subjects, without competent leaders, Charles's wars were almost certain to fail.

It was probably desperation which caused Charles to look north for naval recruits in 1626, for things were going very badly. The fleet sent to Cadiz had been scattered by storms and the Duke of Buckingham, Lord High Admiral and a court favourite, faced impeachment by Parliament until the King dissolved it in June. On 11 July the Privy Council in Edinburgh received a letter from the King, ten days old, ordering them to find 500 seamen to be sent south to London for the English fleet. Twenty seaport burghs were specifically ordered to provide men, including Glasgow, Dumbarton and Ayr in the west, Dundee, Aberdeen and Montrose in the east. The rest were on either side of the Firth of Forth, the main centre for Scottish shipping. All ships equipped with guns were to be detained in harbour with a view to taking them over for naval service.[4] A fortnight later, it was clear that the levy had failed. The commissioners from the twenty burghs explained the position, giving a concise account of Scottish trade and fishing at the time.

All declairit that the best of thair shippis, in respect of the long peace, were sauld, and that suche as ar unsauld being of any worth ar at thair voyageis out of the cuntrey, and the few remanent that ar within the cuntrey ar onlie small barkis unfurnished of ordonannce and unable to persew or defend. And, toucheing the mariners, it wes affirmed be thame that the grittest nomber of people of that sort within this kingdome ar in the coast syde of Fyffe, who ar fishearis and praesentlie following thair trade of fishing in the Illis, and thair returne is not looked for afore September, at whilk tyme thay will be upoun thair praeparatioun for the Bourdeous voyage.[5]

The demand on the burghs was renewed in August but their representatives, while accepting the need to defend the realm, thought it was unfair that the burden should fall on the seaport towns alone.[6]

It is not clear how many Scottish seamen actually reached the English fleet, nor how many continued to serve in the following year. But if any lasted into 1627, they saw perhaps the worst-managed and most ignominious campaign ever fought by a British fleet. One captain wrote, 'I have in the *Vanguard* above 40 men fallen down since I wrote my last letters, and the rest of our ships all in like proportion; many of our men for want of clothes are so naked that, exposed to the weather in doing their duties, their toes and feet miserably rot and fall away piecemeal with extreme cold.'[7]

The Spanish counter-attacked by raiding English and Scottish commerce from their base at Dunkirk. Late in January 1626, for example, a Leith ship called the *Maria* was taken by Dunkirkers on her way to a French port with wheat, while an admittedly exaggerated account suggested that by the end of 1626 no fewer than 200 Scottish and English vessels had been taken by 36 Dunkirk privateers. The *St John* of Leith, on her way back from Bordeaux laden with wine, was attacked by a Dunkirker off Flamborough Head in Yorkshire and defended herself for eight hours until 'schoe wes so stopped with shoit as schoe wes not able to abyde abone the watter' and the master and three of her crew had been killed. The wreck was driven ashore at Scarborough, where her owners reclaimed her. But all was not defeat; in June, William Simpson of Dysart was paid 500 marks for his courage in defending his ship and sinking a Dunkirker.[8] In March 1627, Hugh Rosse was paid expenses for securing the release of Scottish prisoners in Dunkirk, but a month later the Council was still hearing 'the pitiefull lamentationis of nomberis of poore weomen, whose husbandis, childreene, and freindis ar ather slayne or tane and detenit in miserable captivitie be the Dunkirkeris.'[9]

Although the Scottish Treasury was exhausted it was decided to commission three warships for the defence of the east coast, using £5,200 sterling put up by Sir James Baillie, a member of the Scottish Council of War. Three skippers were ordered to survey a ship called the *Unicorne* in Leith which the King bought. Two other ships, whose names are not recorded, were purchased in London. To provide crews, 'good and kindly wages' were offered, but again the east coast burghs were levied, and the number of men demanded from each might give an indication of the importance of the respective Scottish ports at the time. Leith was the largest, with twenty men, Dundee was to find sixteen, Kirkcaldy and Anstruther twelve each, St Andrews and Pittenweem ten each, Bo'ness six, Queensferry eight, Fisherrow four, and seven other ports of Fife were to provide from four to eight men each. The Earl Marischal was put in command of the force and was to fit them out in exchange for two-thirds of the value of any prizes taken. Captains Achmutie, Duglas and Murray took charge of the individual ships, but they did little; it was complained that they 'dranke and made good cheire, bot wold not offend the enimey.' While the Dunkirkers were said to 'sinck our shippis in the verrie sight of the coast', the three ships had 'lyne idle and unproffitablie in drye harboryes, without any purpois, as we conceave, to go to Sea.'[10] The crews fared little better; they refused to embark until arrears of wages were paid. In March 1627 they were ordered to convey some Scottish troops to support the King of Denmark, and Sir James Baillie again came to the rescue by agreeing to pay the arrears and to victual the ships for two months.

Scottish skippers did find one way to take advantage of the war, commanding privateers or private men-of-war, hoping to make a profit by the capture of enemy merchant ships. The first two 'Letters of Marque' giving legal status to such ships, were issued by the government in April 1626, to the *James* of Anstruther and the *Blessing* of Burntisland. Others were issued to ships of Dysart, Pittenweem, Leith and Dundee over the next few months. David Alexander, captain of the *James*, was later accused of ill-treating prisoners on board the ships he captured.[11] Though at least eight ships were granted letters of marque, it cannot be assumed that the trade was vastly profitable; it might only show that there was no other well-paid business in wartime, when ordinary trade was hazardous and payments in the King's service were unreliable.

In their urge for profit, privateer captains were often tempted to capture neutral and friendly ships. Captain Andrew Watson of Burntisland was accused of looting the cargoes of Hamburg ships and fled to England to appeal unsuccessfully to the King. Sir Robert

Gordon of Lochinvar captured a 'ship of Middleburgh, laidnit with merchandice and goods perteaning to His Majesteis freinds and confederats in the Netherlands'. After interrogation by the Council he was forced to withdraw his claims to it and pay the crew's expenses.[12]

David Alexander, one of the first privateer captains to be licensed, got involved in a complicated and bizarre legal dispute over a ship called the *Blind Fortune*. Captain Seres of that ship and his partner, Claude de la Mer, had discovered an island off Greenland where, they believed, gold and silver were just under the ice. Alexander found the ship off Shetland and boarded her, persuading the crew that if they proceeded south they would almost certainly be taken by Dunkirk privateers, who cut the ears and noses off their prisoners. They were only too glad to accept Alexander's *James* as an escort. Alexander then put ten of his own crew in the *Blind Fortune*, armed with muskets, and took an equal number of Dutchmen into his own ship.

The *Blind Fortune* was taken to Leith, where her sails were removed to prevent escape. According to Sir John Scot of Scotstarvet, a part owner of Alexander's ship, a Leith carter called Alexander Short was shown round the ship by an Inuit passenger known as 'Wikie the Savage' and found that de la Mer was involved in a conspiracy to debase the currency by false coining. This was soon disproved and Short exposed as an unreliable witness. Alexander claimed that the *Blind Fortune* was Flemish, therefore belonging to the realms of the King of Spain; in fact she was soon proved to be Dutch and neutral. David Alexander and his partners were obliged to pay the expenses of the ship while it was held in Leith, and it was released by order of the Council on 15 January 1627. The King took the opportunity to explain his attitude to privateering. While he applauded 'the endeavours and courage of suche of your subjects as by warrants have gone against the common enemie', the Dutch were His Majesty's 'speciall freinds' and were not to be molested.[13]

The Bishops' Wars

In 1638 the Scottish Lowlands, led by the Covenanters, revolted against Charles I's attempt to impose bishops on their church. Charles decided to invade the northern kingdom in the spring of 1639, though his fleet, raised by the unpopular and possibly illegal tax of ship-money, was in a poor state. His army was even worse, for it consisted mainly of untrained militias, who had no confidence in the King's cause or his ability to pay them. Nevertheless Charles planned for the main royal army of 30,000 men to march over the border, while an amphibious force of 5,000 men would sail from East Anglia under the Marquis of Hamilton to land at Aberdeen, which was held by the Marquis of Huntly on behalf of the King. On the other side of the country the Earl of Antrim was to sail from Ulster to Kintyre while the main English army, in the South of Ireland under Sir Thomas Wentworth, would sail across to Carlisle to land in the Firth of Clyde.[14]

In London, Hamilton converted colliers into troop transports and sailed to East Anglia to pick up his force of conscripts, who were surprised to find that they were to be sent north.[15] His objective was changed to the Firth of Forth after news arrived that the Covenanters had taken Aberdeen. But when the fleet arrived in the Firth on 2 May, they found that the Covenanters had hastily erected a fort at Leith, with its main battery of fourteen guns facing towards the sea. The people on both sides of the Firth 'swarmed upon the shores to behold the ships or resist their landing.'[16]

Hamilton, flying his flag in the 64-gun *Rainbow*, decided to blockade the Forth, the main area for Scottish trade. He anchored off Leith and landed his soldiers for exercise at Inchkeith and Inchcolm, which the Covenanters had failed to defend. The Royal force stopped many Scottish merchant ships, allowing them to proceed if the master swore fidelity to the King.[17] According to Sir John Pennington, the admiral in charge of the naval force, 'We have so blocked them up by sea that they cannot stir in or out with a boat but we snap them up.' A small ship called the *Bedame*, carrying about twenty Scottish officers formerly in the Swedish service, was taken and the prisoners sent to Berwick. Scottish trade had already been hit elsewhere and it was reported that twenty Scottish ships had been arrested in the Thames, that two on the way back from Spain with Segovia wool had been taken off the Isle of Wight and that 'all their traffic by sea is already cut off.' One Scottish merchant who had lived in London for some years was rash enough to fly the St Andrew's cross from his ship in the Thames and it was promptly arrested.[18] But such a blockade would take a long time to harm the Scottish economy, and was not likely to be effective against such a fanatical enemy as the Covenanters.

Because the Scottish land forces were far more efficient than the reluctant English levies raised by the King, the Scots did not feel the need for a navy to attack Hamilton's force. Of course it would have been impossible for the Scots to make long-term plans for a navy of their own in opposition to the King, and in the short term it was far more difficult to improvise a navy than an army, especially when so many Scottish merchantmen had been arrested in English ports.

Nevertheless three ships taken off Aberdeen by the King's ship *Third Whelp* were quite heavily armed, with medium-sized guns known as demi-culverins, and may have been intended to raid English forces.[19]

The Earl of Antrim, despite his lack of military and naval experience, financed the building of thirty 'long-boats' using timber from the royal forests in Derry. His shipwrights had no knowledge of mast-making, and masts ordered from naval stores at Dublin did not fit. Wentworth, in command of the most seasoned force of English troops, dragged his heels because he was aware of the risks of leaving Ireland, so no troops sailed. By June, Charles had given up the campaign before hostilities really began and made an agreement with the Covenanters.

The Second Bishops' War (1640) was a much less maritime affair. The King's servants had largely failed to collect the tax of ship-money so few Royal ships could be fitted out for sea. Those which were had to be committed to other tasks such as protecting the southern coasts against piracy and maintaining English neutrality in a war between the Dutch and the Spanish. A seaborne invasion force for the east coast failed to materialise, and the Lord High Admiral of England was pessimistic. 'If no more money, what is proposed? How then to make an offensive war, a difficulty. Whether to do nothing and let them alone and go with a vigorous war?'[20] There was an ineffective blockade of the Forth and in June a Scottish ship arrived at Leith with her rigging much damaged by an encounter with the King's ships. Plans by the Earl of Strafford (formerly Sir Thomas Wentworth), Lord Lieutenant of Ireland, to bring troops over were too late to affect the issue. Instead, the Scottish army invaded England and occupied Newcastle, discrediting the King even further and bringing the southern kingdom yet closer to civil war.

When King Charles demanded support against an Irish rebellion in November 1641, the lowland Scots were much more co-operative, for many of them had Protestant relatives in the north. Local lairds and town councils were ordered to assemble 'all ships, barks or boats betuix the Cloche ston and Irwin inclusive' to transport a hastily raised army. The date 17 February 1642 was fixed for the embarkation of the first wave of 2,500 men at Largs. George Porterfield, a burgess of Glasgow, was commissioned to provide 30,000 lb of biscuit made from white bread to feed the men. Five hundred bolls of wheat were also sent from Glasgow in sacks, two barrels of herring were provided for each vessel and 500 gallons of the best ale, each man being allowed half a gallon during the voyage.[21] Another wave of 2,500 men was sent over at the end of February, and a further 5,000 during the year, but the paying and providing of such a force led to further strains in England. The Civil War broke out there in April 1642.

The Cromwellian invasion

In 1649, following the Royalist defeat in the English Civil War, Charles I was executed and a republic proclaimed. In 1650 his son sailed for Scotland from exile in Holland, landing at Speymouth. After swallowing his pride and most of his principles, he made an alliance with the leading Scots in church and state and was proclaimed King Charles II. To crush him, Oliver Cromwell invaded Scotland in traditional fashion, using his navy to support the army in its march up the east coast. Cromwell massed his army of 16,000 men in the English-held, fortified town of Berwick, where ships could bring supplies. Twenty-three merchant ships, of 3,325 tons, were taken up for the first supply and contracts were placed for 400,000 lb of biscuit, 180 tons of cheese and 2,000 quarters of oats. Tents were ordered at a cost of just over £1 each, except for Cromwell's headquarters tent which cost £46. A squadron of eight warships of 'considerable countenance' was appointed to 'attend the motions of the army', while eight more warships were to convoy the merchantmen. The squadron was headed by Rear-Admiral Edward Hall, an outspoken anti-Royalist, in the 44-gun *Liberty* (*Charles* under the old regime). While Cromwell assembled his army, Hall used his ships to harass Scottish trade, which had no protecting warships. By 8 July, after three weeks in the area, he had captured seven ships, which, according to an English report, 'will much startle the Scots'. Spoils included a ceremonial purse carried by the Chancellor at the Coronation of the Scottish King.[22]

Cromwell's army left Berwick on 22 July and soon found the country as bare of supplies as he had expected. The Scots lit hilltop beacons and the men fled towards Edinburgh, taking their foodstuffs and cattle with them. The women stayed behind and earned a living by baking and brewing for the English, until a Scots decree forbade them. On the 26th the English reached the small port of Dunbar where in Cromwell's words they received 'some small pittance' of supplies from their ships.[23] Two days later they took Musselburgh, an even smaller port, where the ships failed to land supplies because of bad weather. Cromwell marched towards Edinburgh. David Leslie, the Scottish general, deployed his army of 26,000 men with considerable skill, keeping his forces between Cromwell and his lines of supply and

preventing him from getting to the far superior port of Leith, despite a
bombardment by the English fleet. On 27 August there was an
inconclusive battle at Gogar Loch to the west of Edinburgh, but
Cromwell was too far from his supply ships and retreated to Musselburgh and then Dunbar, arriving on 1 September.

After more than five weeks of campaigning, the New Model Army
was less than 30 miles inside Scottish territory, surrounded by superior
forces, with its men starving and falling ill because of the unfavourable
weather. A supply convoy was windbound at Harwich on the English
east coast, much to the concern of the English government. An
intelligence report suggested, 'Cromwell must fight or be gone. His
men eat nothing but bread and cheese, and lie on the ground without
huts. He has probably lost 2,000 men in killed, wounded and run
away.'[24] A plan to withdraw by sea was rejected. But the Scots
snatched defeat from the jaws of victory when the Committee of
Estates ordered Leslie to abandon his position in the hills and fight the
Battle of Dunbar on 3 September: 3,000 Scots were killed and 10,000
taken prisoner and Cromwell's position was safe.

Cromwell had much to do before Scotland was conquered. Edinburgh and Leith were soon captured, apart from the Castle, but
Stirling Castle still held out and the English were unable to send their
ships so far up the Forth with supplies and heavy artillery. Glasgow
was taken and another English force, supplied from Carlisle, was sent
up the west, but King Charles and his government remained in Perth.
In February 1651 Tantallon Castle, on the cliffs of East Lothian, was
captured with the aid of a naval bombardment and remains a
spectacular ruin to this day. On 17 July the English forces finally
crossed the Forth, sending 1,600 men of the first wave across at
Queensferry in boats; 3,500 more followed three days later. The
people of Inverkeithing blocked their harbour by 'casting great stones
in the mouth thereof and sinking of shipes and barks therein for
holding out the English'[25] but Burntisland was captured and the
English advanced on Perth, which they took on 2 August 1651.

Fifty flat boats or 'double shallops' were assembled in England,
crewed by six men each, and sent north.[26] Four battering guns and
two mortars were brought by water up the Forth to Stirling on
10 August and the Castle surrendered after four days of bombardment.[27] Three of the guns were put on a shallop for Dundee, which the
English forces were now attacking, but it broke under the weight. The
frigate *Speaker*, one of the newest and most effective ships in the
English Navy, was loaded with royal regalia and public records taken
at Stirling. In the meantime, the main Scottish Royalist army had

marched south into England, where it was heavily defeated at Worcester on 3 September. The King fled to France to begin nine years of exile.

Dundee was stormed by the English on 1 September, probably with the aid of naval forces. The looting and massacre which followed were reminiscent of the taking of Wexford in Ireland two years earlier. A Scottish warship or privateer of six guns took refuge in Aberdeen, but the inhabitants told blockading English warships that 'they would neither protect them nor deliver them up; but that if they pleased they might come and take her.' The crews of English warships went ashore and captured her. By October only four strongholds held out in the Lowlands. The Bass Rock in the Forth was blockaded by Parliamentary forces. Andrew Bennet, a ferryman of Elie in Fife, was acquitted of helping the garrison on the grounds that he had acted under duress. The Rock surrendered later in the month. Dumbarton surrendered in January 1652. Brodick Castle on Arran gave up in April after a party of troops was shipped across the Firth of Clyde from Ayr.[28] Dunottar Castle near Stonehaven was the last place in the Lowlands to surrender, in May 1652.

The Highlands remained unconquered and an army could not move far inland without dealing with the old problem of supply. A train of 400 horses, 'led by Country people laden with Bisket and Cheese', went with the army. As Major-General Deane wrote from Badenoch in July, 'We are marched up into the middle of this craggy country, where we have great difficulty to live in a body together for want of provisions both for horse and men. It is a dismal place where we scarce see a man or beast for 40 miles together.' Even the native baggage-carriers refused to continue, claiming 'that none of their forefathers ever went these ways.' The English reached Inverness, where a 40-ton pinnace was built and dragged across six miles of land to be launched into Loch Ness.[29]

An agreement was reached between the English forces and the Marquis of Argyll in August. Garrisons were established in five positions in Argyll, four of which could be supplied by sea. But when a convoy escorted by the warship *Elias* arrived in Inveraray a few days later, it was found that the clansmen had risen up and taken possession of the posts at 'Kincarn' (probably Kilchurn on Loch Awe), Tarbert and 'Lochead' (probably Castle Lachlan).[30] The English were forced to withdraw and they held only Dunolly and Dunstaffnage. There was an uneasy peace by October 1652.

In 1653 the nature of the war changed. Until then it had been a traditional defence of Scotland against the English, in a form that would have been recognisable to Edward I and Robert Bruce. It now became a war of a new kind, which anticipated the conflict between Prince Charles and the Duke of Cumberland ninety years later. The Lowlanders were reasonably content with the religious settlement and with prosperity brought about by economic union with England. An exiled Stuart prince inspired a rising in the Highlands, though he did not take part in person. The state navy was diverted by a foreign war, for conflict with the Dutch had broken out in May 1652. The navy tried to stop the rebels by patrols, blockades, troop movements by sea and by trying to prevent them crossing rivers such as the Forth.

The revolt was sparked off when a Parliamentary privateer anchored off Lewis and sent men ashore to seek fresh meat for the crew. They were seized and Lord Seaforth declared on behalf of the King, demanding that the privateer support him. Robert Lilburne, commanding the Parliamentary forces in Scotland, complained that he had very few ships to guard the coast and that 'without shipping all our fortifications in these islands signifies little or Nothing.'[31] The Earl of Glencairn led the Highland revolt until Charles's appointed leader, John Middleton, landed at Tarbartness in the north-east from his exile in Holland, with supplies of arms and ammunition. He quickly gathered support.

The rebellion was supported by the Macleans of Duart and in August 1653 a force of six government ships under Colonel Ralph Cobbett sailed from Leith and Ayr to repress them. They took Mull with no difficulty, because the Macleans had fled to Tiree. Anchored off Duart Castle, the Commonwealth ships were struck by 'a most violent storme' which lasted 16 or 18 hours. Three ships lost their masts while three others, including the *Swan* of about 200 tons, were sunk. The survivors of the disaster fled overland to Dumbarton.[32]

The English army continued to rely on support by sea, including drafts of money sent north to pay their troops. Throughout the wars, the supply of hay and straw was particularly vital and many ships were used to carry it northwards. The English could not afford to send out small forage parties to find food for their horses, for that would provide the Scottish 'moss-troopers' or guerrillas with just the opportunity they needed. When a store of hay was destroyed by fire at Leith, a Stuart agent confessed to it and was executed as a spy.[33]

General Monck, now in command of the English forces, invaded the Highlands in 1654. Knowing he would lose contact with his supply ships, he waited until May and then marched 'as soone as their is any grasse in the hills for our horse to subsist on'. It was difficult for him to arrange rendezvous with his ships. When one carrying biscuit, cheese and ammunition arrived at Inveraray from Dumbarton in September 1654, it was attacked by a party of Royalist cavalry and seized.[34] Nevertheless Monck was able to defeat Middleton at Dalnaspidal in the Grampians in July and most of the Highland chiefs made peace.

The Dutch Wars

Between 1652 and 1674, three 'Anglo-Dutch' wars were fought. All were extremely unpopular in Scotland, because most of the country's trade passed through the Staple at Veere in the Netherlands. Scotland played little part in the first war (1652–4), for the country was only half-conquered by Cromwell's forces at the time. In June 1653, fifty volunteer seamen were shipped from Leith for the English fleet, but there is no sign of any other Scottish participation.[35] In July to August 1652 the English fleet under Robert Blake went north and lay in wait in Shetland for the homeward-bound Dutch East India fleet. There was a great storm in which many Dutch ships were wrecked, while many more took refuge among the islands. 'Thus in Scalloway lay 23 ships, in the South-West bay the two East Indiamen and five ships of war, in the West bay seven ships, in Buys Haven [possibly Busta Voe] seven ships, and further north lay nine ships more – fifty-one in all.'[36] Most escaped to Holland, though a few were captured by the English.

The new English navy, like Cromwell's New Model Army, was vastly more efficient than its royal predecessors and in great battles in the North Sea it defeated the Dutch using the new tactic of 'line of battle' invented largely by General Monck, which was to dominate naval warfare for several centuries. Though the battles were fought in the English Channel or the southern end of the North Sea, there was always a fear that the Dutch warships, privateers or merchantmen might head for the north of Scotland, either as raiders or to reach the waters of the Atlantic.

After Charles II was restored to the joint thrones in 1660, rivalry with the Dutch continued. At the outbreak of the second war in 1664, the King, 'being resolved to putt out more shipes then ordinary for the security and defence of our subjects in their trade', ordered the Scottish Privy Council to 'try what number of able seamen can be raised for our service . . . even to the number of fyve hundred.' The men were promised the same pay as English seamen in the hope that this might appeal to the relatively poor Scots. But this soon turned to compulsion and in November the Privy Council demanded a levy of 291 men from 29 seaports. Again the list gives an idea of the importance attached to the different areas; though most of the men were still to come from the east coast and especially the Forth, the Clyde ports were beginning to rise in importance. Glasgow was to send ten men, Greenock and Dumbarton five each, Inverkip and Renfrew four each and Kilmacolm and Erskine two each. This was followed by another letter in December, by which the ports were required to take a census of their seamen, producing a list containing 'their age, names, and if maryed or unmaryed, if at home or abroad, and where they are at present'. Separately, the Scottish counties were ordered to produce similar lists of 'all the able seamen and seafishermen that saills in ships, boats and barkes living within any paroch of your shyre subscryed by famous men.' [37]

By January 1665 the Council had heard disturbing reports that 'many seamen intended to make saill out of this kingdome and notwithstanding of their eminent danger to be taken be the Holland shipes.' There was to be an embargo on shipping from leaving port until 12 February, in order to aid recruitment. Skippers were to give a bond of £200, or face the removal of their sails to prevent them leaving. However, the Council was prepared to be flexible. An Aberdeen ship, trapped in Bo'ness by the edict, was given permission to return home provided the owners 'conform to the tenor of the act of Council foresaid.'[38]

In February the Council ordered that 300 men be raised from among those places which had complied in sending in the list, with a further 200 from those which had not. Letters were sent to each seaport and county allocating a particular number. The men were to be in Leith by 15 March, on pain of a fine of 500 marks for every man short. Presumably the county of Kincardine had been awarded a punitive levy for failing to complete the list, for the Sheriff-Depute and heritors complained that they had been ordered to find sixty able men, 'yet there is not any in the said shyre almost any seamen except poor miserable fishermen amongst whom it will be impossible to find half of that proportion of able seamen.' The authorities refused any abatement.[39]

Prisoners who were also seamen were fair game for recruitment and in November 1664 the Council ordered that six sailors in the Edinburgh Tolbooth were to be delivered to Leith to be shipped south.[40] But this could be taken too far and by February 1665 the Privy Council was complaining about the quality of the men sent, 'His Majesties service being hiely prejudiced, and the kingdom greatly affronted in the last supply of seamen sent to his Majesty in sending a number of robbers and suchlyk insted of able seamen.'[41]

The case of Aberdeen was probably typical. In 1665 they complained that Peterhead had poached two of their seamen, James Cowie and William Scot, who had been recruited by the northern port but belonged to Aberdeen. Like Kincardineshire, they complained in 1672 that they had been over-assessed and 'Hugdlie abused'. Fourteen was the same number as Dundee and Leith, but Aberdeen 'wold not have bot about 30 seamen to put out.' Even the erratic spelling of the Privy Council warrants caused problems. It demanded that 'Fethie' provide its proportion of men. Was this 'Futtie' or Footdee near Aberdeen, or was it Findon? The magistrates of Aberdeen strongly suggested the latter. However, the provost and baillies managed to find seven men, paying them between nine and four pounds (Scots?) each, in addition to the government bounty. But other seamen went into hiding or fled abroad to evade service.[42]

Privateering was far more popular and Scottish captains were able to raid the rich commerce of the Dutch. From September 1665 the Council issued letters of marque to at least eighteen ships from Leith, Peterhead, Dundee, Glasgow and other ports, with authority to make war against the King's enemies of the time, France, the Netherlands (United Provinces) and Denmark. They were to be 'good shipes sufficiently provydit with men, armes, artileary, ammunition, and all other thinges necessary.' They had some success; Captain William Ged of the *Goodfortune* took at least one ship while Captains Gideon Murray of the *Thistle* and Wemeys of the *Wemyss* 'did take some pryses belonging to the States of the United Provinces as the Kinges enemies as being loadened with counterband goods', though they later faced a legal challenge to some of their seizures.[43]

The English and Dutch fleets both entered Scottish waters in August 1665, during a campaign centred round some homeward-bound Dutch East Indiamen in the neutral harbour at Bergen in Norway. On 7 August the main English fleet of about seventy ships under the Earl of Sandwich anchored in Bressay Sound, Shetland, to shelter from a storm. Sandwich found it 'a very barren country, mountainous and the hills all boggy . . .' The houses were 'most miserable, as bad as the dens of most beasts, I believe.'[44] He sailed south on the 13th. On the 17th the main Dutch fleet under van Tromp was off the Scottish coast looking for Sandwich and it hove to for a council of war off Buchan Ness. Neither fleet sighted the other, so a great naval battle was narrowly avoided.

While Sandwich was in Bressay Sound, plans were already being made for a fort at Lerwick to protect the anchorage from the Dutch. It was completed soon afterwards, but destroyed by the Dutch in 1673, during the Third War.

Argyll's Rebellion

In February 1685 Charles II died and was succeeded by his Catholic
brother James II. Archibald Campbell, 9th Earl of Argyll, was in exile
in Holland and already plotting a Protestant revolt in tandem with
Charles's illegitimate son the Duke of Monmouth. He raised a few
thousand pounds among the Scottish exiles and hired three ships – the
Anna of 30 guns, the *David* of 12 and the *Sophia* of 6. Evading the
half-hearted attempts of the Dutch authorities to stop them, they
sailed north intending to round Scotland and land in the Argyll
territories in the west, which had been confiscated after the Earl
was accused of treason in 1681.

Carrying 300 men and 400 sets of back armour, breast-plates and
head-pieces, the ships made a very fast passage and arrived off the
Moray Firth on 5 May. They missed the passage between Orkney and
Shetland in fog and found themselves in Scapa Flow, where they
anchored in Swanbister Bay. Spence, the Earl's chamberlain, had
connections in the islands and went ashore with Dr Blackadder, but
they were quickly arrested by the Bishop and magistrates of Kirkwall.

The leaders of the expedition were undecided about what to do.
Some wanted to land and rescue their comrades, some suggested
reprisals and a party was sent ashore and took six hostages. But the
ships sailed on without Spence and Blackadder. They spent the night
of 11 May at anchor in Tobermory Bay, then largely undeveloped,
and made a specious attempt to salvage guns from the famous Spanish
galleon wrecked there. They sailed down the Sound of Mull, unchallenged by Duart Castle, and on the 15th they arrived at Islay, on
the edge of Argyll's clan territory. The Earl expected that his authority
as chief of the Clan Campbell would instantly raise thousands of men,
but Islay had already been visited by government troops who imposed
an oath of loyalty. About eighty men were recruited to the rebellion,
but half of them soon deserted.

The *Anna* and her consorts sailed on to Campbeltown, solid clan
territory as its name suggests. On 22 May they raised the standard of
revolt, bearing the slogans 'For the Protestant Religion' and 'Against,
Popery, Prelacy and Erastianism'. Again there was indecision about
what to do next. Some wanted to develop a base in the Highlands,
others to seize what they believed was an opportunity to exploit
discontent in Ayrshire and Galloway across the firth of Clyde. Instead,
the fiery cross was sent through Argyllshire to raise the Campbells,
and Tarbert, further up the Kintyre peninsula, was chosen as the
rendezvous. The three ships sailed up the firth and the troops from

Campbeltown marched. A force of about 2,500 men was assembled at Tarbert.

Argyll wanted to move further up the coast to his former seat at Inveraray, where 500 government troops were in control and were reportedly terrorising the population. His advisers pointed out the danger of the ships being trapped in the cul-de-sac of Loch Fyne with English warships approaching. Since supplies were short at Tarbert, it was decided to land on Bute. It took three days to transport all the men to Rothesay, using the Dutch ships plus about forty local fishing boats.[45] Rothesay Castle was burnt as a reprisal for the government's burning of Argyll's castle on Loch Goil. The tiny island of Eailean Greig in the Kyles was set up as a base. It was hoped that the narrow and winding channels would prove unnavigable for English warships.

Meanwhile the government was preparing its own forces. HMS *Kingfisher* of forty guns under Captain Hamilton was in the Clyde near Dumbarton and was joined by other ships from Leith. On shore, the Earl's close relations and supporters were arrested and troops were mobilised.

The rebels landed a small party at Toward Castle opposite Rothesay while another small force sailed to Greenock, where they defeated some ineffective government opposition. They gained about thirty recruits and retired across the firth. On 11 June, the same day as Monmouth belatedly began his revolt in the south-west of England, Argyll left Eailean Greig with most of his army and crossed the mainland of Cowal. He advanced up Glendaruel and reached Ardentinny. But in the meantime the *Kingfisher* succeeded in navigating up the Kyles of Bute and the rebel base came under attack. Captain Hamilton describes events.

> We got up to them yesterday with an intention to beat his men out of the fortifications they had built there by the castle, but they did not stay for our coming up with them, but run their ships on ground and abandoned the castle. They had laid a train of matches with an intention to blow up the castle but I sent a boat on shore and prevented the blowing up.[46]

This was deeply demoralising to the rebel army, but they used local boats to cross Loch Long from Ardentinny to Coulport. They marched round the head of the Gareloch and took a circuitous route towards Glasgow, hoping to avoid conflict with government forces. The army was slowly dispersing and by the time it reached the Clyde at Kilpatrick there were only about 150 weary, dispirited men left. Argyll crossed the Clyde and was arrested by government forces at Inchinnan while trying to cross the River Cart. He was taken to Edinburgh and executed on 30 June, while Monmouth faced the same fate two weeks later.

The Scottish Navy, 1690–1707

In 1688 King James was deposed by William of Orange. For more than half a century after that James's supporters, the Jacobites, aimed to have him or his son restored to the throne. They were especially strong in Ireland and the Highlands of Scotland, where the inhabitants were unhappy about the settlement after the Revolution of 1688 which established the Presbyterian religion in Scotland, and with the central government's attempts to control them, represented most brutally by the Massacre of Glencoe in 1692.

Because of a war with France and the fear of a Jacobite revolt, the Scottish Navy was revived in March 1689, when Parliament ordered 'two frigates to be provided to cruise on the west coast of this kingdom'. The *Pelican* was hired from the Provost of Glasgow and commanded by Captain William Hamilton of Ladyland. She carried 18 guns and had a crew of 120 men, making her very small in the scale of European war, in which ships of 100 guns and 700 men were not unusual. The *Janet* of 12 guns and 80 men, commanded by Captain John Brown of Irvine, was hired from a former Dean of Guild of Glasgow.

The two captains were given wide-ranging orders to cruise between Galloway[47] and Skye, attacking any ships belonging to the former King James. Based at Ayr and Greenock, the two ships controlled communication between Scotland and the north of Ireland, where Londonderry was under siege by King James's forces. They also operated against Highland Jacobites, seizing and destroying birlinns, the descendants of the Lords of the Isles' galleys, in Kintyre and Mull. In June they captured fifty MacDonalds and McAlisters travelling from Gigha and Jura to Ireland.

Their success was short-lived. On 10 July 1689 the two ships were cruising between the Mull of Kintyre and the Irish coast when they met three ships flying the English flag and apparently of English build. They approached them but found out that they were French men-of-war, of 24, 30 and 36 guns and at least twice as powerful as the Scots. They were carrying 400 men to support the Jacobites. According to an account published in London soon afterwards, the *Janet* engaged the two smaller Frenchmen. After an hour her mainmast was shot away and the French boarded her, killing Captain Brown and all but fourteen of the crew before she surrendered. The three ships then surrounded the *Pelican,* which was already damaged. Boarders were beaten off three times and Captain Hamilton ordered the gunner to blow up the ship but was killed himself. The ship surrendered and only 30 men out of 120 were left alive. If this was indeed a 'Full and True Relation' as it claimed, then Scottish seamen were courageous to the point of fanaticism. In fact the records show that 143 men survived as prisoners, suggesting that if the ships were fully manned, then 57 were killed – an impressive enough total, implying that the Scots had fought hard by the standards of the time.

In the same month, the siege of Londonderry was relieved by King William, reducing the need for a navy on the west coast. The Scottish Jacobites had their great victory at Killiecrankie at almost the same time, but lost their leader, Graham of Claverhouse, 'Bonnie Dundee'. They were beaten at Dunkeld in August. The *Pelican* was recaptured by the English fleet off Dublin, and a year later, in 1692, she was ignominiously sunk as a breakwater to protect their dockyard at Sheerness.[48]

The Scots were expected to provide services for visiting English warships and indeed the Lowlanders did so, with a keen eye to commercial gain. In August 1689 the magistrates of Glasgow were ordered to provide four pilots 'most expert and knowing of the islands and coasts from Orkney to the mouth of the Clyde' to guide some warships from Leith to the Clyde.[49] The campaign against Highland Jacobites continued in the Western Isles during 1690 and a squadron under Captain Pottinger of the English 22-gun ship *Dartmouth* was sent there with the Scottish hired ships *Lark* and *Lamb*. In October the *Dartmouth* was anchored in the Sound of Mull near Duart Castle when she dragged her anchor in a storm and was wrecked.

In the war against the French there was less scope for privateering, for the enemy ports were further away and the French had less ocean commerce than the Dutch. Nevertheless at least ten ships were issued with letters of marque from 1689 to 1693, ranging from the *Dogarvine* of Edinburgh of 40 tons and 8 guns commanded by William Burnsyde, to the *Reid Lyon* of Queensferry of 200 tons and 14 guns commanded by John Robertsone. Other ships came from Glasgow, Kirkcaldy and Argyllshire.[50]

Seamen for England

In this war the English Navy was hungrier than ever for seamen, for it had expanded from 173 to more than 300 ships. It was, as King

William told the Scottish Privy Council, 'a war which concerns not only our kingdom of England but likewise Scotland and almost all Christendom.' A thousand men were therefore demanded from Scotland, instead of 500. As usual the recruits were offered £2 on entry and there were several new promises. Scots, if taken prisoner, would be exchanged on the same basis as Englishmen, which perhaps had been a grievance in the past. The crews of Scottish trading ships were to be immune from English press gangs, provided the 1,000 men were raised.

Though the new English government had greater financial and political credibility than recent ones, there were problems with implementing the proposals. In January 1690 the Privy Council ordered the announcement of the terms in all seaports by beat of drum in the market square, and again the burghs (forty-three in number) were ordered to provide lists of men. Dundee was reasonably successful, sending forty-four volunteers by mid-February. But two years later, numbers were still short and the Council ordered another survey. If there were not enough volunteers, then every fourth man between sixteen and sixty would be chosen by lot and would not be eligible for the 40-shilling bounty. Meanwhile, two English men-of-war were confusing the issue by recruiting in the Forth, including three men at Musselburgh; they were ordered to desist. By the beginning of March 114 volunteers had been found in the ports of the east coast, with the largest contingent, 39 men, coming from Kirkcaldy. The contribution of Leith, the largest Scottish port, is not recorded. In desperation the Council threatened the 'horning' or outlawing of any seaport or burgh which failed to deliver its list of seamen by 19 April 1692.

Yet a year later the King was still urging the Council to complete the task of recruitment. Lots were to be cast in the towns which had failed to provide men the previous year, and three men out of every eight were to be recruited, as a penalty. Each volunteer was to receive £24 bounty, an enormous increase. Perhaps this led to a number of opportunistic offers; when the men so enlisted arrived on board the *Centurion,* the English ship ordered to take them to the fleet, her captain refused to receive them because of their poor quality. There are no final figures, but it is unlikely that the full number was ever recruited.[51]

The Bass Rock

The Bass Rock on the south side of the entrance to the Firth of Forth was used as a prison for four leading Jacobites. Sergeant La Fosse, in charge of the guard, was a secret sympathiser and he noticed that when supplies arrived by boat some of the men had to leave the fort to help unload. On 15 June 1691 he and the prisoners closed the gates of the fort and turned the guns on the men outside, forcing them to flee. Over the next few months the rebels were joined by other Jacobites and eventually they numbered about twenty-five. They became a thorn in the side of the Scottish government, within sight of Edinburgh Castle.

Scotland had no navy at this stage, and very little money to create one. The first reaction of the government was to bluff the rebels with a display of medieval pageantry, to 'ordain Henry Fletcher with any one of His Majesty's heralds to pass to the said island of the Bass and, with their coats displayed, in their Majesties' name to require and command the foresaid persons, in whose hands the island presently is, to deliver up the same and also to render themselves prisoners under the pain of treason.' When that failed a small boat was hired to prevent the rebels communicating with the shore and orders were issued to prevent fishing within one and a half miles of the Rock, but vessels continued to get through. In March 1692, for example, 'a little boat went from Fisherrow and did meet with a larger one which came to the coast of Fife, and received the men and provisions out of the large boat and carried them to and livered them at the Bass.'[52] A few days later the rebels began a more active campaign when they used their own boats to seize three fishing boats from Fisherrow and steal their catches.

The government decided to try sterner methods. The English warships *Sheerness* of 32 guns, and a hired ship, the *London Merchant*, were at Leith Roads waiting for a convoy to assemble. On 13 April 1692 they moved down to the Bass and demanded the rebels' surrender, which of course was refused. They anchored alongside the fort and opened fire. They made a breach in the walls and destroyed the crane which the defenders used to hoist in supplies, but the action was not one-sided. The *Sheerness* was hit at least three times, wounding four men and doing some damage to her hull and rigging. The Scottish government replenished her powder and shot from Edinburgh Castle.

The rebels' confidence had been boosted rather than destroyed. In July a French privateer took a fishing boat and carried it to the Bass. Two longboats were kept in service against the Rock during the summer, a futile gesture which was suspended in October due to bad weather. During the winter the rebels had a supply of coals from a Dunbar boat and in February 1693 two French privateers arrived with more supplies. The Scottish Privy Council asked for help from English men-of-war, to no avail.

The usual two longboats were fitted out in the spring of 1693 but it was soon found 'that boats do come from and return to the Bass without interruption.'[53] In 1694 a third boat was added to the patrol and the Privy Council made plans to use a privateer against the Rock. In the meantime the rebels grew even bolder. In February a barque carrying wheat from Dunbar to Edinburgh was becalmed three or four miles from the Bass when eighteen of the rebels rowed out and captured her. A party of twenty-two government soldiers went out by boat in pursuit, but the rebels defended the barque. A strong wind got up and carried it out to sea. Eventually it reached Dundee, where all the rebels but three escaped ashore.

The Rock was now more than a symbolic threat and the Privy Council took decisive action. Late in February Edward Burd was commissioned as captain of the *Lyon* of 20 guns and 200 tons and in March a second ship of similar specification was put into service under Captain John Bosswell. A fireship was also to be fitted out 'for attacking, burning and destroying any such ships or vessels, one or more, as shall attempt to get to the said isle of the Bass.'[54] The defenders were now depleted in numbers after the affair of the barque and began to negotiate a surrender. It was agreed that the men on the Rock, as well as prisoners held on shore, should be taken to the French port of Le Havre and on 21 April 1694 they surrendered after holding out for nearly three years.

The Threat to Trade

Without a regular navy to defend them, Scottish merchant ships were under threat from several quarters. The official enemies, the French, were an obvious enough problem. This was exacerbated after May 1692 when the French battle-fleet was defeated at Barfleur and La Hogue. The French government now knew that they could not win great naval battles, and instead they developed the *guerre de course*, a corsair war using fast privateers based in ports such as Dunkirk and St Malo. The issue was a little more intense when a Scottish Jacobite, Robert Dunbar, commanded a privateer off his native coasts. In March 1693, off Buchan Ness, he seized a ship loaded with Spanish wine belonging to Scottish merchants and held it to ransom. English warships could be just as predatory in their breaches of Scottish sovereignty. In September 1690 the *Dartmouth* arrested two Glasgow ships, allegedly for smuggling tobacco from the English colonies in America.

In April 1691 the *Sheerness* took a neutral Danish ship in Leith Roads, amid protests from the Scottish Privy Council. Even native Scottish privateers could cause problems. In March 1693 the *Elizabeth*, owned by the Earl of Argyll, was reportedly searching ships at anchor off Greenock 'as if they were enemies'.[55]

In this lawless atmosphere, it is not surprising that in May 1695 the Committee of Trade recommended that at least five warships were needed, three of 30–40 guns and two of 20–24 guns. But as always the Treasury was hard-pressed and three ships were ordered from builders on the River Thames at a cost of £17,000, which was regarded as 'excessively dear'.[56] The first, the *Royal William*, of 32 guns, was commissioned on 1 April 1696 under Captain Edward Burd who had commanded the privateer *Lyon* at the siege of the Bass. His lieutenant was Andrew Brown and the warrant officers consisted of a master (in charge of navigation), boatswain, gunner, carpenter and surgeon. Petty officers included a cook, two master's mates, four midshipmen, five quarter-masters, a gunner's and a surgeon's mate, a coxswain and a steward. The able seamen were recruited from the Forth ports, mainly Bo'ness, and two trumpeters joined the crew in 1697. As usual, seamen were in short supply and the ship had only 100 men out of an establishment of 180. To make up the numbers, 80 soldiers were sent on board as marines.

The *Royal Mary* and *Dumbarton Castle* were commissioned in June and July. They were of 284 tons and 24 guns, with a crew of 100. But the new Scottish fleet was to see little service in this war, except that Captain Burd was sent to Orkney with the *Royal William* in January 1697, to deal with an English warship in the area. The Treaty of Ryswick ended hostilities with France in September and the three Scottish ships were laid up at Blackness and Burntisland. The Scottish government was still struggling to find money to pay the builders and the crews and in March 1703 Captain Thomas Gordon of Aberdeen was allowed to charter the *Royal William* for a commercial voyage to the East Indies.

For all the disputes, the Lowland Scots and the English had made common cause against the Jacobites, Irish and French and to a certain extent the war secured the Protestant religion in Britain and checked the ambition of the French King, Louis XIV. Though the Scottish naval contribution was tiny, Scots were beginning to appreciate the need for a strong navy in the joint kingdoms.

The Darien Scheme

Any goodwill that had been built up in wartime was soon dissipated by the events which followed the peace treaty in 1697. The Scots were still barred from trade with the English colonies by the Navigation Acts of 1660. Therefore they decided to set up their own, founding the 'Company of Scotland Trading to Africa and the Indies' to get some share of the enormous profits which the English were making in the West Indies, North America and India. Money was raised from small and large investors all over Scotland, but English backers were forced to withdraw because of pressure from their East India Company. King William refused any help to the Scottish colonists, because he did not want to offend his Spanish allies.

The Company of Scotland was not at first committed to any specific area. Since Scotland had no yard capable of building ocean-going ships, agents were sent abroad to purchase them. Some had commissions as privateers from the Privy Council. In July 1698 five ships sailed from Leith, carrying the hopes of the nation with them. Off Madeira the captains opened their sealed orders to set up a colony in the Bay of Darien in Central America. Fort St Andrew and New Edinburgh were established but soon the colonists were skirmishing with the Spanish and falling prey to dysentery and fever. The attempt was abandoned, but only the flagship, the *Caledonia*, completed the journey home.

A second expedition left from Greenock in May 1699, unaware that the colony had been abandoned. They arrived in November, but in March 1700 they had to surrender to the Spanish. The whole Darien Scheme had cost Scotland several hundred lives and about £200,000 of her very limited capital.

Queen Anne's War

The next war with France, the War of the Spanish Succession, started in April 1702, a month after King William died and Queen Anne came to the throne. This time it was decided not to seek any compulsory recruitment for the English Navy in Scotland, perhaps because relations with England were deteriorating, perhaps because it had been so unsuccessful in the past. However, men were demanded to crew the three Scottish warships and a levy was put on seaport towns in June 1703. When an English man-of-war arrived in Leith Roads with a convoy in March 1706, her captain was given permission to recruit volunteers and £2 sterling was offered to each man in the traditional manner.[57]

The two smaller ships of the Scottish Navy, the *Royal Mary* and *Dumbarton Castle*, were fitted out for sea soon after the war began and in September 1705 the *Royal William* was equipped and manned at the expense of the royal burghs after her return from the East Indies. In 1703 the *Royal Mary* was employed patrolling and escorting convoys between the Forth and Orkney, while English ships carried out the convoy work south of the Forth. The *Dumbarton Castle* patrolled between the Sound of Mull and Dublin. This time the ships saw slightly more action and captured a few French privateers. They were all quite small, such as the ship taken by the *Dumbarton Castle* off the Mull of Kintyre on 25 May 1705. She had 8 guns and sixty-two men and had already won ransom money for a Dublin packet-boat and a Greenock barque.[58]

Captain Thomas Gordon of Aberdeen took command of the *Royal Mary* in July 1703 and was allowed to charter her for a voyage to Italy during the following winter. He and the ship returned to naval service and in May 1704 he had a success in capturing two or three French privateers. He became commodore of the two ships on the east coast and in effect the head of the Scottish Navy, but he had secret Jacobite sympathies. When the Jacobite agent Colonel Hooke was ashore in Scotland, Gordon allegedly arranged secret signals to warn French frigates of his presence.[59]

Conflict and Union

Relations between Scotland and England worsened after a Scottish ship was impounded off Kent in 1704. Soon afterwards the English East Indiaman *Worcester* put into Leith, having sailed round the north of Scotland to avoid French privateers. The crew, under Captain Green, were convicted of piracy against a missing Darien Company ship, the inaptly named *Speedy Return*, which in fact had sunk in the Indian Ocean. Watched by a crowd of 80,000 Scots, Green and two of his crew were hanged on Leith Sands, dying 'with invincible patience, like innocent men'.

Relations were now so bad that complete severance between Scotland and England seemed possible: but the Scots were offered full free trade with the English empire. As the issue was debated in the Scottish Parliament in 1706, Lord Belhaven made a series of gloomy predictions about the effects of Union, including those on Scottish trade. 'I think I see our Mariners delivering up their Ships to their Dutch Partners; and what through presses and necessity, earning their Bread as Underlings in the Royal English Navy'.[60] But his views did not prevail and a treaty was agreed. Scotland was to preserve her church, currency and laws but no one was interested in keeping the Scottish Navy, which had won no great glory and barely earned its keep. On

1 May 1707 the two parliaments and governments were united. It has been described as 'a political necessity for England, a commercial necessity for Scotland'.[61] The three Scottish ships were merged into the English fleet and the last Scottish Navy became extinct.

Chapter 2

Sea Power and the Jacobites

The Jacobites remained an important political force for most of the first half of the eighteenth century. They enjoyed some support in Britain and from many exiles abroad, and from whatever foreign government was opposed to Britain at the time. Their natural supporters were Conservatives who believed that hereditary right was sacred, and those disaffected with the religious settlements after 1688, including Roman Catholics and Scottish Episcopalians, mainly in the Highlands. In Scotland there was potential support from the many people opposed to the Union of 1707, and again from Highlanders resisting the centralising tendencies of the government in London.

Sea power affected the Jacobite rebellions in several different ways. At the grand strategic level, the Royal Navy's blockade of the major French and Spanish ports attempted to prevent a major fleet from putting to sea. This was not immediately relevant to Scotland, as such a fleet, could it gain control of the English Channel, was more likely to attempt an invasion of southern England than Scotland. However, the Royal Navy's blockade was an important part of the general pattern of 'command of the sea', in which Britain's enemies could only move in small and fast ships.

At the next level a small fleet, perhaps of fast privateers, could take a small army to Scotland, as Forbin unsuccessfully attempted in 1708. Thirdly, and perhaps most important in practice, individual ships could maintain communication between Scotland and France or Spain, landing the Pretender or his son to launch or support a rebellion and delivering quantities of arms, troops and money to maintain the enterprise.

Finally, coastal naval power was important during the actual course of the rebellion, in ways which would have been familiar to Edward I and Cromwell. Ships could exert some control over the Western Isles, they could assist or prevent a crossing of the Firth of Forth and they could support an army in operations along the whole of the east coast, carrying guns, supplies and necessities such as coal to an army advancing in inhospitable country.

During the 1715 Rebellion, for example, the navy co-operated closely with government land forces in several ways. When part of a land bastion at Fort William collapsed the *Happy* sloop was used to cover the gap in the defences.[1] As government forces gathered strength, the main artillery train was sent by sea from the Thames to the Forth. The garrison at Inverness was reinforced by sea and guns were delivered to it. As the rebels marched towards Cromarty, Captain Steuart of the *Royal Anne Galley* placed his ship in front of the town and threatened to destroy it if the rebels entered.[2]

Over the years the Jacobite cause became increasingly associated with the Scottish Highlands and of course the two main rebellions, in 1715 and 1745, both originated there. But this concentration on the Highlands was never seen as inevitable at the time and the Jacobites were also strong in the north and west of England. The importance of the Highlands had much to do with the underlying effects of British sea power.

There was virtually no naval presence in Scotland in the first half of the eighteenth century, except when there was a specific threat from Jacobites, pirates or privateers. The West Country of England was very different. Many of the ships for the wars against France and Spain were based there, especially in the great dockyard at Plymouth. Moreover, the naval assets were defended by the army. Any rising in that part of the world would need strong support from the outside, not just from a few isolated ships such as those which reached Scotland in 1715, 1719 and 1745. Jacobite plans usually started with some scheme for the invasion of the west or south of England, for example in 1719 and 1745. In both these cases, by coincidence, the main enemy force was dispersed by storms, but there is little doubt that the Royal Navy would have beaten them had they been given the chance. Leaving aside the question of the level of support for Jacobites outside Scotland, it was simply much more difficult to organise and sustain a rebellion in western England.

The other strongly Jacobite area was in the north of England, where there was no substantial naval presence. The situation was slightly more complicated there. Rebel forces succeeded in reaching the area in 1715 and 1745, though they had little success in attracting recruits in the latter case. Again, sea power had an underlying effect. Because the British army relied on reinforcements from Holland, military forces were concentrated around Newcastle quite soon after the rebellion started, which in effect made the eastern route to London unavailable for the Jacobites. Instead they went down the west, being defeated at Preston in 1715 and going as far as Derby in 1745. In both cases they found themselves increasingly isolated from supplies from France. They had access to ports such as Preston and Lancaster, and perhaps could have taken Liverpool had they wanted, but the Irish Sea could be sealed off relatively easily by the Royal Navy; its entrances were only 50 miles wide in the south and 20 in the north. In 1745 the southern entrance, St George's Channel, was patrolled by four or five ships as soon as the rebellion started.[3] Having reached Manchester, the 1745 rebels had then to strike across country towards London, which further increased their sense of isolation. An advance down the east would have removed some of these problems. They could have kept in touch with ports such as Hull and Boston, and some supply ships, at least, would have got through.

Forbin's Attempt

By 1708 the war between Britain and France was six years old. In Scotland, most of the disadvantages of the Act of Union of the previous year were becoming apparent, but few of the advantages. Trade with America would certainly benefit Scotland in the long term, but in the meantime the Firth of Forth seemed an ideal target for a revolt. There was much discontent with more rigorous English customs duties and with the loss of business caused by the abolition of the Scottish government and parliament. Even strong Presbyterians were prepared to countenance a Stuart return, hoping that James's Catholicism would not last – 'God may convert him, or he may have Protestant children, but the Union can never be good.' Daniel Defoe, then an English spy in Edinburgh, wrote, 'I Never Saw a Nation So Universally Wild and so Readily Embracing Everything that may Exasperate them. They Are Ripe for Every Mischief.'[4]

One of the most famous Dunkirk privateer captains, the Chevalier de Forbin, was chosen to lead a squadron to take the Pretender and about 6,000 troops to Scotland. By the early spring he had gathered a force of thirty-three ships, including five with 50 guns or more. As usual, the British government had intelligence of Jacobite plans almost as soon as they were formed. Though most of the home fleet had been laid up for the winter, Vice-Admiral Sir George Byng was put in charge and by 27 February he had twenty-six ships off Dunkirk, including several of 70 guns, outgunning anything available to Forbin.[5]

Meanwhile preparations were made to resist an invasion on land. The bulk of the army was in Flanders under the great Duke of

Marlborough and ten battalions were put in ships at Ostend to be sent to the River Tyne, escorted by a force of warships. If the 'alarm from Dunkirk' did nothing else, it created a diversion of scarce resources. In Scotland, known or potential Jacobite leaders were put under arrest. Lord Belhaven, a leading opponent of the Union, complained that, though he had voluntarily surrendered on hearing of a warrant for his arrest and had never been involved in any disloyalty to the Crown, he was kept under house arrest.[6]

Despite Forbin's doubts and James's attack of measles, the Jacobite force was ready to sail by the end of February. On 1 March James issued a proclamation 'to his good people of his Ancient Kingdom of Scotland'. Old grievances were referred to. 'What they suffer'd under the tyranny of Cromwell, as also the usage they met with in the affaire of Darien, and the Massacre of Glenco under the usurpation of the Prince of Orange, and the present Union or rather subjection, demonstrate that usurpations have always been fatal and ruinous to the Liberty of Scotland.' The Protestant religion was declared safe and immunity was guaranteed to all except those who 'after Our landing in Scotland shall willingly, advisedly and maliciously, by land or sea, oppose us.'[7]

Blockade was never completely reliable in the age of sail, and on 2 March bad weather forced Byng to retreat across the Channel to the Downs, where he was joined by yet more ships. Forbin slipped out of harbour on the 6th but took refuge a few miles along the coast until the 9th, then headed north, keeping out of sight of the British coast to avoid detection, with the Pretender and many of his troops violently seasick but in good spirits. But their navigation was flawed, and on 12 March the force was visible from Stonehaven and Montrose, more than thirty miles north of the Forth where they hoped to land. Nathaniel Hooke, a Jacobite agent on board the flagship, suspected treachery by Forbin, who was not fully committed to the plan.[8] A French frigate went in close to Stonehaven and fired a gun, luring out a fishing boat with nine men who hoped to offer pilotage. Taking the fishermen on board and the boat in tow, the ships sailed south to the East Neuk of Fife.

A French frigate arrived off Pittenweem at 2 p.m. on the 12th and two men went on board from the shore. They saw 'five drums on her quarters and forty men in good habit walking on her quarterdeck.'[9] The wind was from the south-west so it was not possible to sail up the firth. That night the rest of Forbin's squadron anchored a few miles away in Skait Road, near Crail; a boat from that port went on board the French flagship and found that they intended to land somewhere in the Firth, though they were wary of an English squadron. The visitors were well treated and tipped with five shillings.

Byng was back off Dunkirk by 9 March, where he received a message from the British army in Ostend, that Forbin had already sailed. Byng called a council of war with his senior commanders and it was agreed that the French must have headed for Scotland, with the Firth of Forth as the most obvious objective. Byng's ships set sail and made up some distance on the run north, for they had no need to avoid the coast.

There was confusion along the east coast as Byng passed, especially at Berwick where the British fleet was identified as French. In Dunbar a Mr Hepburn, a known Jacobite who had been on the Bass Rock during the siege of 1691–4, was found trying to hire a fishing boat to take him to what he thought to be the French fleet. He was arrested and handed over to a party of dragoons to be locked up in Edinburgh Castle.[10] His defence, that he was simply trying to make contact with a ship smuggling some goods from England, did not impress his captors. According to the Earl of Leven he was an 'ingrained rogue'.[11]

Byng arrived in the Firth of Forth in the evening of the 12th and at eleven that night he anchored off the Isle of May, in poor visibility. He was reluctant to sail into the firth without certain information that the French were there, for fear that a change of wind might trap him.[12] As the sun dawned next morning his lookouts spotted the French about twelve miles away off the coast of Fife. Byng now had a powerful force of eighteen ships of the line of 60 to 70 guns, eight intermediate warships of 50 guns, twelve smaller ships and a fireship. Forbin's force was weaker; only five of his ships had 50 guns or more and none could expect to match a ship of the line in battle. Forbin, on sighting Byng, had no option but to raise his anchors and retreat.

There was some manoeuvring in the mouth of the firth as Forbin sailed south, towards the enemy, in order to get clear of Fife Ness and to bluff Byng into forming his fleet into line of battle, thus losing time. He claimed that he was successful in this, but in fact Byng was unclear about whether the French would head up the firth or to the north or south. His ships were merely manoeuvring for position in a wind which made it difficult for them to reach the French. In any case, Forbin turned his fleet about 8 a.m. and headed north, with Byng an hour or two behind.[13]

The British ships found it difficult to catch up with the French. It was said, for political reasons, that Byng's fleet had foul bottoms due, by implication, to corruption in the dockyards, but this does not bear examination.[14] French ships were just beginning to establish a reputation for speed in comparison with the British, though it would be dangerous to generalise from the circumstances of this chase. Forbin's ships, after all, were mostly privateers designed specifically for fast sailing. The core of Byng's fleet were the ships of the line, designed for strength and gunpower rather than speed.

The fastest ships of Byng's squadron, including the *Dover* of 50 guns, under Captain Thomas Mathews, pushed ahead and came up with the rear of the French off Montrose. The aftermost of Forbin's ships was the *Salisbury*, which had been built in England in 1698 and captured by the French five years later. She was in the rearguard, not because of her slowness, but because she had been built as a fighting ship and was the strongest in Forbin's force. Mathews pushed on past the *Salisbury*, trying to reach the French flagship which he knew must be carrying the Pretender, but he was blocked by another Frenchman, the *Auguste*, of 54 guns. The two ships fought until night fell on the evening of the 13th.

Meanwhile the *Salisbury* came under further attack from the *Ludlow Castle* of 42 guns, followed by three 50-gun ships – a new British *Salisbury*, the *Antelope* and the *Leopard*, commanded by Captain Thomas Gordon, formerly of the Scots Navy and harbouring some Jacobite sympathies himself. This fight too was broken off by nightfall but the French *Salisbury*, damaged in her rigging, was found again next morning and the fight continued all day. The two *Salisburys* drifted together, but late in the 14th it was a boat from Thomas Gordon's *Leopard* which got to the ship and claimed her as a prize. The *Salisbury* yielded a rich crop of prisoners, including two French marquesses, three Scots and English noblemen, fifteen émigré Irish officers of O'Brian's regiment and more than 200 soldiers.

Though the fleets had no further contact and no further captures were made, this was the nearest thing to a sea battle fought on Scottish waters in the age of sail. Edward Vernon, captain of the *Jersey* under Byng, claimed that 'had not the wind shifted in their favour, not a timber of that fleet could have escaped us.'[15] In an age before industrial and traffic noise the gunfire was heard a long way away. An observer in Inverbervie produced a fairly accurate description:

> Ther was a skirmish att sea yesterday, qch began of Bervie at 3 aclock, and he saw two destinck fleets, on consisting of about 26 sail the other about 30, and 4 ships at a distance from either. Affter some scattering single shots he saw 5 of the last fleet of great bigness and forse attack tuo of the first fleet about their own size, qch tuo mentainained a runing fight from betwixt 4 and 5 to eight, that they got out of his sight.[16]

In the meantime, Forbin's squadron had been dispersed. On 15 March he and James planned to land near Inverness, but unfavourable winds prevented them from entering the Moray Firth. Three of the French ships, including a frigate of 24 guns, arrived off the coast of Banff on the 16th. They made contact with three fishing boats and yet again they entertained the fishermen well, feeding them with biscuit and giving them French crowns. Speaking good English, they asked about the possibilities of buying provisions, and about making contact with the local Jacobite leaders, Lord Seaforth and the Duke of Gordon, who were in fact imprisoned in Edinburgh Castle. Some of the men went ashore at Buckie, staying in a local inn, bringing French wines, gambling amongst themselves and paying their bills in French money. The Countess of Seafield, wife of a member of the government then in London, sent a man to enquire what was happening, only to have him threatened with the stocks. The strange ships left after a few days.[17] Like the others of Forbin's force, they decided to head home round the north of Scotland and all of them eventually reached Dunkirk after an unpleasant voyage.

Byng saw no point in any further pursuit after losing sight of the main body of the French at nightfall on the 13th, with a dying wind and French ships which were clearly faster than his. His ships were seen passing Aberdeen on the 14th and the provost and baillies consulted local seamen who concluded 'that they are French ships by their build and sails.'[18] That evening Byng called another council of his senior officers which covered his decision to return to the Forth and anchor off Leith, 'which they looked upon as the place where the enemy's designs were chiefly bent, but thought it was for the security of the north part of Britain that that port should principally be guarded; and were of opinion that their appearing, would encourage the Queen's faithful subjects and dishearten such as should have any thoughts to rebel.'[19]

Byng's ships were misidentified yet again when they entered the Forth and Lord Leven alerted the troops under his command.[20] On the face of it Byng was welcome when he arrived at Leith on the 15th and the town council of Edinburgh elected him and his senior captains as burgesses and guild brethren.[21] But there was a strong undercurrent of support for the Jacobites in the city, which 'made a most melancholy impression' on Captain Edward Vernon of the *Jersey*.[22] Even government supporters felt that Byng had not returned in triumph. 'How he came to give over the chase and to return again to the ffirth is dissatisfying to many, for his ffleet is certainly of double strength to the ffrench, tho the ffrench be cleaner and sail better.'[23] The

Cabinet in London was of similar view and ordered him out again to seek out the enemy. Byng was sceptical and wrote, 'Surely had they landed on this side of the coast of Scotland, we should have heard of them, and think if we do not hear of them in four or five days more we may conclude they are gone back to Dunkirk.'[24] Due to the late arrival of his orders and unfavourable winds he stayed in the firth until 4 April, when he sailed to escort some of the British troops back to the Netherlands, as they were no longer needed urgently in Britain.

Could Forbin's expedition have succeeded even if it had not been harassed by sea? Vernon claimed that there was a good deal of passive support in Edinburgh, which had just lost its status as a national capital, and there was much discontent and plotting. Jacobite plans had suggested that on the fleet's arrival in the Forth, 'at the first signal, all the river would be covered with fishing vessels and others that would readily give their assistance in forwarding the disembarkation',[25] but in practice the fishermen of Stonehaven, Pittenweem and Banff seemed bemused by the intruders. Apart from Hepburn of Dunbar who was immediately arrested, the most significant action on shore came from a party of Stirlingshire lairds who heard a report that James would land north of the Tay and set out with their followers, taking a circuitous route through Perthshire. Even captains with Jacobite sympathies, such as Thomas Gordon (and even, as it later turned out, Byng himself), could perform well against the Jacobites in the heat of battle. It is difficult to know whether the troops from French ships would have been perceived as a foreign invasion force or whether they would have gained much sympathy on land.

Mar's Rebellion

During 1714 the political situation changed in several ways, not all in the Jacobites' favour. The war with France ended in June, removing the possibility of official support for a rebellion. Queen Anne died on 1 August and there were many, even among the English ruling classes, who felt that her half-brother, James Stuart, had a far better claim to the throne than the official Protestant heir. George of Hanover, now King George I, was a German who knew very little English, took very little interest in his new kingdom, had no personal charms and a rather tenuous claim to the joint throne. Several dignitaries, including the Duke of Ormonde, the Lord Lieutenant of Ireland, thought seriously about proclaiming King James in London. They were stopped in their tracks by Lord Bolingbroke, who said 'all our throats would be cut'. When George landed at Greenwich on 18 September, he was deeply suspicious of the Tories who had held power in the last years of Queen Anne, and snubbed the Earl of Mar, latterly Secretary of State for Scotland. Excluded from office and under threat of impeachment, several Tory leaders, including Bolingbroke and Ormonde, fled to France and began to plot a Jacobite revolt in Scotland, western England and Northumberland. In August 1715 Mar sailed from the Thames to Fife in a tiny collier and went on to his estates at Braemar.

Byng's Blockade

By 20 July the government in London was aware of a planned revolt and sent notice to Edinburgh and other towns to prepare their defences against a landing in the north. The Royal Navy had been reduced to a peacetime strength of 10,000 men instead of four times that number in wartime and it was heavily committed in the Baltic, where a squadron of twenty ships had been sent to guard British interests in the Great Northern War between Russia and Sweden. Most of the 240 ships in the fleet had been laid up 'in ordinary' in the dockyard ports and only 22 were in commission in home waters, including 4 storeships and 4 yachts.

There were only two naval ships in Scottish waters. The *Happy* sloop, under Captain Edward Gregory, was cruising between Carrickfergus in Ireland and the west coast of Scotland. The *Port Mahon* of 20 guns, commanded by Captain Haddock, had been ordered north in May to deal with a Swedish privateer which was reportedly harassing shipping in the Forth. There was no sign of the predator by the time Haddock arrived in June, but he was ordered to patrol between St Abb's Head and Buchan Ness, a distance of nearly one hundred miles, for 'owlers' smuggling wool to France.[26] On 21 July, the day after intelligence of the planned revolt was received in London, the Admiralty ordered Haddock to 'keep a diligent lookout in his station with an eye to the pretender'. Meanwhile the *Happy* was ordered to extend her patrol area in the west, 'somewhat further than the Capes of Galway and Kintyre'.[27]

Parliament voted extra money for the Navy, large loans were offered by the City of London and press warrants were issued to recruit men. As ships were brought forward, the first priority was to form a force for the English Channel, to prevent any large-scale French intervention. Byng took command again. Presumably his superiors did not know that at the beginning of the year he had been in contact with the Duke of Ormonde, suggesting that a scheme of invasion by 5,000

Swedish troops would land in the Forth while other forces invaded
Ireland and western England and the main force of 20,000 men
crossed the Straits of Dover to invade southern England.[28]

By the beginning of August Byng had twenty-six ships under his
command, ten already on station off the French coast.[29] The situation
changed drastically on 1 September, when King Louis XIV of France
died after a reign of seventy-two years. His grandson succeeded, but
was only five years old and power was in the hands of the Duc
d'Orléans, who was much less sympathetic to the Jacobites. In Le
Havre, four Jacobite ships were laden with arms and waited for
orders. The King's death prevented their sailing and the crew of
the *Speedwell,* realising the danger that the Jacobites might put them
in, deserted the ship. Byng blockaded the port, got detailed intelligence
from the deserters and eventually secured the support of the Duc
d'Orléans who banned any ships carrying ammunition from sailing.
Byng then moved the bulk of his forces to the ports of north-eastern
France, which the Jacobites were now more likely to use as bases.[30]

Despite the weakness of the Jacobite position, the revolt began on
6 September when the Earl of Mar raised the standard of King James
near his castle at Braemar. Two days later a plot to take Edinburgh
Castle by surprise was foiled, but on the 14th the Jacobites took Perth,
from where they could go south. But Mar was an indecisive and
incompetent leader and failed to move on. By early October, as the
clans began to come in to support him, he had perhaps 16,000 men
while government forces, near Stirling, under the Duke of Argyll,
consisted of around 3,000 men.

Meanwhile the plan for a rising in the west of England was a total
failure, for the government had adequate warning through the ambassador in Paris, Lord Stair. The army was mobilised, and many
Jacobite leaders were arrested. Ormonde tried twice to land in the
west, but failed.

The Navy in Scotland

To increase the naval forces in the east of Scotland, the *Royal Anne
Galley* of 42 guns, under the command of the inappropriately named
Captain James Steuart, was fitted out at Chatham and sent north with
the *Pearl*, of 42 guns, and the *Port Mahon* of 20. On 5 October, as
Mar gathered strength at Perth, they received orders to co-operate
with the Duke of Argyll, 'either in the transporting of troops, arms or
in aught else'.[31] By this time Steuart had six small ships under his
command, patrolling the coast as far north as Peterhead. But he was to

find his greatest test in preventing the Jacobites from crossing the Firth of Forth and attacking Edinburgh.

According to his orders, Steuart was to co-operate with the provosts of the respective burghs and follow their intelligence hunches about Jacobite landings, and they showed some annoyance when he did not.[32] Late in July, Customs vessels were armed as men-of-war from the Edinburgh City armoury.[33] When Captain Haddock went ashore at Aberdeen for intelligence at the end of September he was seized and the people voted whether to release him or not. It was agreed to let him go on his word of honour that he was not carrying any messages for any of the deposed magistrates.[34]

The *Tartar* of 28 guns was sent to the west of Scotland, and her captain, Christopher Parker, was in charge of a force of five ships by the beginning of September. Like their counterparts in the east, they had a dual role – to prevent men, arms, supplies and money from reaching the Jacobite army, and to stop rebel forces in the islands from crossing to join their colleagues on the mainland. In this, they claimed some success. In October, Captain Gregory took the *Happy* to Mull on hearing a report that 200 rebels were preparing to cross to the mainland. He landed a party of seventy militiamen who destroyed four large boats in the Sound of Mull, and at Duart Castle they took thirty head of cattle, threatening to kill the rest and burn the villages if the islanders showed any signs of rebellion. But even a royal naval ship was not free from the threat of revolt. Lieutenant George Weston of the *Happy* was overheard praying for King James III and court-martialled.[35]

Crossing the Forth

Fife was the key to any move south by the Jacobites after the Duke of Argyll had concentrated his forces round Stirling. On 19 September the magistrates of the ports were ordered to prevent their boatmen taking passengers to anywhere but Leith, where they could be under the eye of government forces. On 3 October the Lord Provost of Edinburgh reported that there were 'several Hundred Herrin boats about the coast touns in Fyfe which are capable to transport from thence to this syde above 3,000 men in a few hours time.' He suggested to the captains of two of the men-of-war that they should disable all boats between Burntisland and Montrose. Even in Leith itself, the water bailiff was instructed to seize the masts, sails and rudders of all ferry-boats now in the harbour and to take them upstream to safety.[36]

An ammunition ship was sent north from Leith with supplies for government forces in Inverness. On the way the captain anchored off Burntisland, his home port, allegedly to pass on a message to his wife, and was presumably delayed by contrary winds. A visiting Jacobite merchant heard about this and rode to Perth, where, at six in the morning of 2 October, he sought out John, Master of Sinclair, a family friend and one of the most efficient of the Jacobite officers. Mar, according to Sinclair, 'was at a loss how to behave in it.' A raid on Burntisland would involve passing within ten miles of government forces around Stirling. It was midnight before Sinclair persuaded him that the opportunity must be taken, as the wind and tide would soon allow the ship to sail. At five in the morning he rode south with eighty cavalry and on arrival at Burntisland they seized some boats and

> forced some toun's men to goe alonge with ours to bringe in the ship, which was seized with no difficultie; but the wind being contrary, it was hard enough to get the ship brought into the harbour . . . At last, those boats brought in the ship by maine force against the contrarie wind, and those aboard of ours, being seamen, did their dutie very well. I stood in the water to the middle of the leg and, with my own hands, receaved all the arms from the ship's side.

Sinclair was disappointed to find there were fewer than 300 guns rather than 3,000. Even so, the exploit 'gave some Reputation to the Earl of Mar', a much needed boost.[37]

Having discovered that Fife was virtually undefended by government forces, the Jacobites began to plan a crossing of the Forth. The original idea was to gather boats in small ports such as Pittenweem, Crail and Elie and send them to Burntisland, but it was pointed out that this involved a double movement. Government cruisers might well spot them sailing along the coast and be prepared for the crossing, so it was decided to send detachments from individual ports. A group led by Sinclair reached Crail on the night of 7 October and proclaimed James as King. They marched on to Kilrennie, Anstruther and Pittenweem.[38] At Anstruther, according to the loyal magistrates, 'Came to this Town Between 10 and 1500 foot and horse, hailed down out boats & Compelled all sorts of people to go in the boats.'[39] A Jacobite force of about 500 men marched towards Burntisland with great show, attracting much attention. This drew out the miscellaneous collection of small warships and customs smacks which Captain Steuart had assembled at Leith. But Steuart claimed in his ship's log that he had not been fooled by the rebels, 'being my opinion . . .

that the rebells only intended to make a feint at Burnt Island, when all the ships were in the Road, & would cross from some other parts of the lower end of the Frith.'[40]

He was quite right, for the force under Mackintosh of Borlum attempted the crossing from the East Fife ports. Mackintosh was convinced that the feint had worked. 'His Majesty's ships in the Firth, either espying them from their Top-Masts, or having Notice of their Design, weigh'd Anchor on the Top of the Flood, and set out to intercept them; but, the Wind not being fair, they were not able to come Time enough to prevent their Passage.'[41] Mackintosh had planned well, and the government vessels were too dispersed to be effective. Steuart's main problem was that he had only two major warships, the *Royal Anne* and *Pearl*, in the Forth, with the rest patrolling the whole length of the east coast. This was too few to guard an estuary 45 miles long and up to 15 miles wide. One Jacobite craft carrying 40 men was captured, and three boats carrying 300 men were driven onto the Isle of May to rejoin Mackintosh later, but about 1,600 succeeded in landing around North Berwick, Aberlady and Gullane. Mackintosh's forces then took Leith, but not Edinburgh, and marched south to join English Jacobites from Northumberland. They were defeated at Preston exactly a month after crossing the Forth.

James Stuart's Landing

On 10 November Mar at last left Perth with an army of about 16,000 men to deal with Argyll's force camped round Stirling, which had now grown to around 3,500. The latter marched north to meet him and there was an indecisive battle at Sheriffmuir, near Dunblane, on the 13th. The government forces now had the initiative as they began to receive reinforcements, while the rebels tired of Mar's vacillation and deserted.

James Stuart, or King James III to his supporters, had originally planned to sail from St Malo in western France, to land on the Clyde near Dumbarton. This was changed to a landing at Dunstaffnage Castle, north of Oban, where Mar's forces would meet him. His nautical advisers warned him against a passage from a western French port. Captain Cammock, 'in his blunt way', told him that passage outside Ireland in November was 'absolutely impracticable' while one between Ireland and England had 'insurmountable difficulties . . . The seas there are very narrow and rough, the season tempestuous, no harbour to retire to on either side, and even I may say needles to thread before I could get to Dunstaffange.'[42] James and his retinue travelled by land to Dunkirk, 'the king, as you may believe, and the rest of his company disguised as seamen'.[43] He joined a privateer of 200 tons and 8 guns and at last, on 17 December, he found favourable winds to take him north. He landed at Peterhead a few days later, after a good passage, but cut a sorry figure among the rebels. He went south to join Mar at Perth.

The main government artillery train had been ordered north by sea from the Thames on 14 November but was delayed by contrary winds at Harwich; it arrived at Stirling, via Leith, on 26 January. Argyll then advanced and Mar abandoned Perth on 31 January and was soon in Montrose, while Argyll's forces advanced up the coast, supplied as usual by sea. On 4 February they were only four miles away, with vastly superior forces. According to Mar's analysis, 'staying on would have been no use to his friends, but made their condition worse, happen almost what would, so at last he took the resolution of going that night in a ship that was by accident there.'[44] The *Maria Teresa* of about 90 tons, from St Malo, even smaller than the one in which he had arrived, had apparently been intended for a diplomatic mission from James to a foreign court. Mar went on board with James and they waited an hour and a half for two more of his leading supporters, Earl Marischal and Clephan, his adjutant-general, but they failed to arrive and the ship sailed. Again they made good passage and James landed at Gravelines, a few miles from Dunkirk, on 10 February. He attributed 'the visible protection of Heaven in the dangers from which I have so happily escaped.'[45]

Some rebel ships managed to evade Byng's blockade, but Jacobite hopes were dashed in the middle of January, when a ship carrying 100,000 ducats in gold was wrecked on the West Sands near St Andrews. The crew and passengers, including several noblemen, got safely into Dundee. There were hopes that some of the gold might be recovered at low spring tides, but Mar, cautious as always, refused to detach men from his forces.[46] At the end of the month Ormonde, now back in the Jacobite headquarters at St Germains, near Paris, proposed to send an ammunition ship, which would be obliged by the increasing rigour of the Royal Navy's blockade to go round Ireland. It was intended to land somewhere in the Western Isles and send the cargo on to Braemar.[47]

Though their cause was lost, the Jacobites in France continued to send ships in an attempt to rescue their leading supporters from capture and possible execution for treason. Early in March an ammunition ship was sent north, round Orkney, to supply some of the last remnants of the rebellion in the Western Isles. The Pretender had ordered two ships to Peterhead and Fraserburgh to 'bring off as many of the gentlemen as they could', but the Jacobites had now withdrawn westwards.[48] In the middle of the month, a Jacobite agent was trying to find a crew in Le Havre for a small barque to be sent round Ireland to Skye, loaded with wine, brandy, gunpowder and biscuit. But it was not easy, for the Royal Navy was beginning to instil fear in the seamen. 'Two different crews I had refused to sail from Havre, after they were paid and the ships just ready to go out, that is, whenever they guessed they were going for our Master's service, they immediately quitted.'[49] Meanwhile, Captain Tulloch of the *Speedwell*, the best of the Jacobite seamen, landed in Lewis. He found 200 Seaforth men and took them to Loch Ewe. They travelled overland to Inverness and Findhorn, but found that the Pretender had left. Tulloch returned to Loch Ewe where his ship was waiting for him. He left Lewis early in March and reached Dunkirk five days later, after a risky passage round the north.[50] More than a hundred of the Jacobite lords and officers, including the Earl Marischal and his brother James Keith, fled westwards and landed on Uist, where they were picked up by another privateer under Captain O'Sheridan and taken to Morlaix in Britanny.

The privateer *Vendome* was sent to Skye carrying arms, powder and bullets (listed in the cargo manifest as anchovies and apples). On 24 April HMS *Lively*, of 20 guns, met the *Vendome* off Stornaway and the latter gave in without a fight.[51] By that time another loophole had been closed and the Jacobite headquarters was aware that seven or eight British frigates were patrolling the Western Isles.[52] By 18 May it was recognised that it was useless to send any more ammunition to Scotland. Instead, Captain Tulloch was to go to Uist where the last four or five leaders were in hiding. They were back in France by early August. The campaign at sea was finally over.

The Rebellion of 1719

The rebellion of 1719 was dictated by international events rather than any movement within Scotland or the United Kingdom. The British government now had very good relations with France, so there was no question of the Jacobites getting any support from that quarter. Spain was now the unstable factor in Europe, and campaigned to regain her territories in southern Italy. In 1718 Sir George Byng had his finest hour when, as commander-in-chief in the Mediterranean, he destroyed a Spanish force off Cape Passaro in Sicily, capturing or burning twenty-two ships.

War with Spain began at the end of the year and the Spanish planned to retaliate by supporting two risings, one in the north of Scotland, and the more important one, led by the Duke of Ormonde, in the west of England. He would be provided with 5,000 troops carried in twenty-two transports and escorted by five warships. The British government, with its usual flair for intelligence of the Jacobites, mobilised a fleet under Admiral Sir John Norris to patrol the entrance to the English Channel, but it was a great storm which dispersed the Spanish force on 29–31 March. Equipment and even horses were jettisoned, the flagship was dismasted and the ships made their way back to Spanish ports.

This left only the tiny Scottish expedition. It was headed by the Marquis of Tullibardine and the brothers Earl Marischal and Lord Keith, survivors of the 1715 rebellion, but carried only 307 Spanish soldiers compared with 5,000. The main force, in two Spanish frigates, sailed from Santander in Spain on 25 February and arrived in Lewis in March, unaware of the failure of Ormonde's expedition.

Meanwhile Keith, a young man of twenty-two, had been sent to France to make discreet contact with James's supporters. On 8 March he sailed to join the expedition in a small French barque of 25 tons. They tried to go up the Channel and round the north of Scotland, but the winds were unfavourable, so they went to the west. Off Land's End on the night of 15 March they spotted a convoy escorted, they believed, by seven warships. This, they thought, was Ormonde's force on the way to start the rebellion in the west. They considered making contact, but the wind was fair and they pressed on, which was fortunate for them. What they had seen was a force of government troops on the way from Ireland to help defend the West Country against the threatened rebellion.

Keith arrived at Lewis on 24 March and spent two days looking for the main force, which he found at Stornoway. There was much discussion about seniority among the leaders, but eventually Tullibardine produced a commission as a lieutenant-general, which put him in command of the land forces. He was cautious and wanted to do nothing until he heard that Ormonde's rising in England had definitely taken place. This led to protests from the rest of the company and he was prevailed to sail to the mainland. They planned to land in Kintail, part of Seaforth's lands, but unfavourable winds took them to Gairloch, where letters were sent out to clan chiefs inviting their support. The force then sailed to Lochalsh, where they landed on 13 April. Again Marischal and Keith were impetuous and wanted to march straight to Inverness before government forces had time to rally. Tullibardine still wanted news of Ormonde. A camp was established at Glenshiel to await support from the clans and a magazine was set up in Eilean Donan Castle, close to the Kyles of Lochalsh. Marischal, in command of the ships but not the expedition, ordered the Spanish frigates to return home so that Tullibardine could not order a retreat.

The government decided to send a small naval force up the west coast. Five ships, under Captain Charles Boyle in the 50-gun *Worcester*, were detached from the force patrolling off Land's End on 28 April. By 2 May they were off Vatersay, and on the 9th, having picked up intelligence of the rebel positions, they reached Skye. Boyle detached two of his ships, the *Assistance* and the *Dartmouth*, to go north about the island, while he sailed south with the *Worcester*, the *Enterprise* and the *Flamborough*. At 8 a.m. on the morning of 10 May, the three ships anchored half a mile off Eilean Donan Castle ready to do battle. They sent a boat to the fort with a flag of truce, but this was fired on, so the three ships opened fire with their 18-, 9- and 6-pounder guns. There is no sign that the rebels had any artillery to reply and they inflicted no significant damages or casualties on the ships by musket fire. The only problem on board the *Worcester* was that William Bagnall, perhaps a relative of the first lieutenant, had to be confined for neglect of duty, possibly arising from Jacobite sympathies.

Over the next few hours the ships took it in turns to move closer to the castle, covered by the fire of the others. Early in the afternoon a Spanish deserter managed to contact them and told Captain Boyle of another store of powder in a house about three miles away, up Loch Duich. The *Flamborough* was detached to deal with it but the rebels set fire to it as the warship approached.

At 7.30 in the evening, after eleven hours of intense bombardment, the three ships ceased fire for half an hour. Then at eight, as night fell, they made a 'great discharge' of their cannon and two ships' boats, crammed with men under the command of the lieutenant of the *Worcester,* rowed for the shore. They entered the castle after a brief resistance and found it garrisoned by 'an Irishman, a Spanish lieutenant, a sergeant, one Scotch rebel and 39 soldiers'. They also found 343 barrels of musket shot and stores of corn.

Despite the great bombardment, the walls of the castle were not destroyed and Captain Boyle did not intend to risk its recapture by the rebels, who were camped two miles away. He sent sixteen barrels of powder ashore in the afternoon of the 11th and used them to blow up the westernmost part of the castle. The following day he used eleven more barrels to destroy the castle walls facing the sea. Eilean Donan was a picturesque ruin until restored in the 1930s.[53] Boyle, joined by his two other ships, remained on patrol in the Kyles of Lochalsh for the rest of the month, having occasional skirmishes with the rebels.[54]

On 10 June the main rebel force was defeated by government troops at the Battle of Glenshiel. It was decided that the Spanish should surrender as they would be well treated as prisoners of war. The Scottish rebels were more likely to face treason charges, so they dispersed and made their way to safety, either in their clan lands or in exile. Lord Keith was sick and had to hide in the mountains for several months. He was in Peterhead by early September and found a ship to take him to Holland in a four-day voyage. There he was reunited with his brother Marischal.[55] Both eventually went to Prussia, where they prospered. Marischal became ambassador to Spain and Keith a very distinguished field-marshal.

Chapter 3

The Navy and the 'Forty-Five'

Prince Charles's Landing

Comparatively little was heard of the Jacobites for a quarter of a century after the failure of the 1719 Rebellion, though the government had occasional scares. In 1723 there was a false report of a Jacobite landing in Ross-shire.[1] Two years later some Russian ships arrived at Lewis and the government was concerned that they might be supplying arms to rebels, though it was reported 'the people of Lewis are quaking for fear of foreign invasion, being wearied of rebellion.'[2] General Wade commented from his headquarters in Argyllshire 'that tract of islands are above a hundred miles in length, and so remote from the mainland that a voyage to Norway would be less dangerous and performed in a much shorter time.' He recommended that a warship be sent to patrol the Hebrides.[3] As a result, the 20-gun *Rose* was put under orders but not sent. Perhaps the threat had some effect, for in December 1726 Lord Advocate Forbes wrote 'the tranquillity is as great as I ever saw it', and three years later he commented 'there is not any project at present stirring in favour of the Pretender.'[4]

Jacobite hopes were raised in 1739 when the 'War of Jenkins' Ear' began with Spain. Meanwhile a more general European war was brewing and Britain eventually became involved in it after an indecisive naval battle off Toulon in 1744, against the French and Spanish. The French now began to activate their plans for an invasion of southern England. Small craft were prepared to cross the Straits of Dover, an army of nearly 100,000 men was assembled and the Brest Fleet moved up the Channel to cover it, but was dispersed by storms before the British fleet could intervene. The plans were abandoned.

The following year Prince Charles Edward Stuart, the 24-year-old eldest son of the Old Pretender, began a plan of his own, hastened by the belief that the French would soon make peace with Britain after a victory at the Battle of Fontenoy. He had virtually no support from the

French court or from the more experienced Jacobites such as Lord Marischal. Instead he relied on the zeal of his immediate followers and on money from French shipowners of Jacobite descent who had become wealthy through the slave trade in peacetime, and privateering against the British in war. The leader was Antoine Walsh, who provided the Prince with two ships. The largest was the *Elisabeth* of 64 guns, hired from the French Crown, a procedure which was not unusual in itself. She was to sail from the naval port of Brest carrying arms and sixty volunteers, while at Nantes Charles boarded a much smaller ship, the 20-gun *Du Teillay*. The two ships met off Belle Isle on 2 July and sailed north, intending to pass outside Ireland and land in the west of Scotland.

A week later the Prince had a taste of British sea power when HMS *Lyon*, of 60 guns, was sighted. As the British ship slowly gained on them, Captain Dau of the *Elisabeth* came over to the *Du Teillay* to warn the Prince that he would have to fight. A dramatic battle ensued in which the two larger ships, evenly matched, fought for hours until both were disabled and had to return home. The *Du Teillay*, as a small frigate, was not expected to take part in an action between two ships of the line and stood clear. But the volunteers, the arms and the prestige which went with the major ship had all been lost. About nine-tenths of the personnel and equipment of the expedition had to return to France.

The enterprise had seemed unlikely at the best of times and it now seemed desperate; but Charles was not deterred. The *Du Teillay* sailed on and reached the island of Eriskay in the Outer Hebrides on the 23rd. The expedition found little support and fled, because a supposed British man-of-war appeared at the anchorage. But the arm of British sea power was not quite as long as that. There was no warship in the area and the west coast of Scotland was unguarded.

On the 25th the *Du Teillay* reached the mainland of Scotland at Loch nan Uamh, where the Prince landed with his famous 'seven men of Moidart'. He and the ship remained there for several days sending out letters to the Jacobite clan leaders, and traditional Highland hospitality prevented them being betrayed to the garrison of Fort William, less than thirty miles away. The local minister, Lauchlan Campbell, was told that the ship was a smuggler but soon guessed what was happening from the mood of his congregation and sent a report to the Duke of Argyll's factor.[5] On 4 August the *Du Teillay* sailed away to carry out some privateering, leaving the Prince and his men to their own resources. In the Kyles of Lochalsh she found four small merchant ships carrying meal to Londonderry which were taking shelter in bad weather. She took possession of them and sent them to Charles. This was to prove crucial in the rebellion, for there was near-famine in the Highlands that year.

On 11 August the Prince and his forces began to move. His supporters from Clanranald marched along the shore while the Prince, with his artillery and baggage, moved by boat to Kinlochmoidart. After a short passage over the hills they reached Loch Shiel, where the equipment was loaded into boats again for a voyage to Glenfinnan at the head of the loch. Finally, on 19 August 1745, more than six weeks after leaving France, the Prince raised the standard of revolt at Glenfinnan. Two days later he began his march eastwards along Loch Eil towards the interior of Scotland. On the 24th he moved inland to avoid the government garrison at Fort William and lost touch with the sea for twelve days, until he arrived, with his forces considerably enlarged, at Perth on the other side of Scotland.

The Naval Blockade

News of Charles's landing reached General Cope in Edinburgh on 8 August, eleven days before the standard was raised. When the rebellion broke out there were three Royal Navy ships on the east coast of Scotland. The 20-gun *Fox* under Captain Edmund Beaver and the armed vessel *Happy Jennet* had gone north in a fruitless search for a French privateer and arrived in Leith Roads on 25 August, to receive new orders from the Admiralty.[6] The 10-gun sloop *Hazard* had been in Leith for some time to protect trade and came under Beaver's command.

Meanwhile there were moves to strengthen naval forces in Scotland. Admiral Edward Vernon was in command in the North Sea, with his base at the Downs, off the coast of Kent. He had become a popular hero at the beginning of the war when he captured the Spanish port of Portobello in the Caribbean, causing, among other things, the naming of a seaside resort near Edinburgh. Notoriously scruffy, he wore a cloak of grosgrain or 'grogram' and his issue of rum mixed with water in the West Indies led to the word 'grog'. Vernon soon became aware of the importance of the rising and sent Rear-Admiral John Byng with a small force of five ships to help deal with it. He was the son of the commander in 1708 and 1715, and was later to be executed for his failure to protect Minorca in 1755. Vernon told the Admiralty, 'We agreed it would be best for his Majesty's service that he should put to sea tomorrow morning . . . for his proceeding northwards in quest of the enemy, if from the intelligence he shall meet with after he has collected his ships together he thinks he has reason to believe they are moved that way; in which case I imagine these will push for the Firth of Forth, or Cromarty.'[7]

The Admiralty was not enthusiastic about Vernon's decision to detach Byng's force, for they felt that the most important task was to blockade the French in Dunkirk. Lord Vere Beauclerk wrote, of Byng, 'I am persuaded his presence is not absolutely wanted, yet it may give life to those who are in the King's interest . . . And to be sure by this time Sir John Cope is returned to Edinburgh with his forces, which will not only secure that city, but if our last accounts are true, will drive the rebels from that part and send them back to the Highlands from whence they came.'[8]

But the Jacobite army continued to advance from Perth. In view of the events of 1715, special efforts were made in mid-September to prevent the Jacobites crossing the Firth of Forth in strength. Walter Grosett, collector of Customs at Alloa and a Justice of the Peace, was commissioned to 'remove all ships, boats and vessels from the north side of the Forth to the harbours of Dunbar. Leith, Queensferry and Borrowstoneness on the south side', with the assistance of 'the constables and tide surveyors, King's boats and crews'.[9] He was successful but the rebels marched west. Stirling Castle held out for the government, giving control over the only effective crossing by bridge, but on 13 September the infantry crossed the river at the Fords of Frew a few miles above Stirling. This was an unsuitable route for the artillery and supplies which would be needed for a siege of a castle.

Moving Cope's Army

General Sir John Cope was in command of the government army in Scotland, with garrisons in forts such as Stirling and Edinburgh and in the Great Glen. He had a mobile force of fewer than 3,000 men and he was ordered to go north to seek out the rebels. Prince Charles outwitted him near Dalwhinnie and the rebels were now between Cope and the Scottish Lowlands. The General decided to march for Inverness, to rally government forces there and assert some control over the Highlands. Finding that support was small, and aware of the danger if the Jacobites captured Edinburgh, he now decided to go south. Travel by land was slow and difficult and would be done through hostile territory; moreover, the rebels were likely to control the Tay crossings, and perhaps the Forth, by the time he got there. Cope decided to leapfrog the rebels by moving to Edinburgh by sea.

On the last day of August Cope wrote somewhat incoherently to

General Guest in Edinburgh. Emphasising the need for secrecy, he ordered Guest to hire 2,000 tons of shipping in the Forth and send it to Aberdeen where Cope would meet him. The shipping had to be ready to sail within three days, but Cope wrote, 'I don't mean by this, that if they cannot be got in that time that they should not come at all but on the contrary they must be found at all events.' Even if there were not enough ships, Guest was to proceed. 'Though by our computation of two thousand tonnage for the transporting of these troops and artillery, yet so much tonnage cannot be got in a short time, you are to send what you can get and let the rest follow.' If warships were available they were to escort the transports.[10]

Captain Rogers of the army took the message south and arrived on 5 September. Lieutenant-General Guest was eighty-five years old and did not leap into action immediately. According to the Lord Advocate he was called at nine in the morning but 'Wee Delayed coming to any Resolution upon Sir John's Request until wee should have Lord Justice Clerk's Assistance, which we had not till half hour after one, when wee resolved to Set about provideing vessels According to his Desire And to Send them with all Expedition.'[11] With the assistance of Captain Beaver of the *Fox*, who happened to be in Leith at the time, about twenty merchant ships were quickly found to make up 2,000 tons. They sailed soon afterwards, escorted by the *Fox* and the *Hazard*.

Meanwhile Cope left Inverness on the 5th to march to Aberdeen. He used the coast road as much as possible, for his supplies of food were carried in a merchant ship, escorted by the *Happy Jennet*. At Banff on the 9th, he received the latest despatches from Edinburgh, dated the 4th, and was alarmed to hear that Rogers had not yet arrived.[12] Two days later he reached Aberdeen to find that the *Fox* had come in with the transport ships a few hours earlier and anchored offshore. They had to wait for high tide to get into the harbour, which took another day – the locals claimed that he could have saved that by using fishing boats from Footdee, Torry and Johnshaven to ferry the men out, but this would not have solved the problem of loading the army's artillery.[13] The men were ready to embark on Saturday the 13th, but went back to camp when the wind proved unfavourable. Finally, 'On Sunday, on one Tide he embarked the whole Army, even against the opinion of the Sea People, and got out of the Bay; but the Ebb Tide coming on, he could not proceed till seven that night.'[14] The winds were not particularly favourable next day but the small fleet reached the entrance to the Firth of Forth by nightfall.

The winds were light next morning, the 17th, and blowing out of the Firth, so Cope decided to land in the harbour at Dunbar. As the ships waited for the tide a boat came out with the staggering news that the Jacobite army was already in Edinburgh, which had surrendered without firing a shot. Cope landed his infantry that day and got most of his artillery out by nightfall. The rest was unloaded next morning. Because he was short of gunners, Cope took six from the *Fox* and the *Hazard*, but they showed the usual fecklessness of the seaman ashore; they were 'generally drunk upon the march' and disappeared with some of the priming for the guns.[15] The army marched east to meet the Jacobites on the field of Prestonpans, where they suffered a disastrous defeat. The survivors of Cope's army fled to Berwick, leaving the Jacobites in control of Scotland.

Reinforcements from Europe

On the news of the rebellion, ten British regiments in the war in Flanders were ordered to be withdrawn home. Under treaties of 1678 and 1716, the Netherlands government was expected to send troops to Britain in the event of an invasion. Seven battalions of 6,000 men were embarked at Heleveotsluis on board twenty-seven transports and sailed on 16 October. The ships were separated in a storm and Byng, at Newcastle on the 22nd, ordered one of his ships to go and look for the stragglers, for fear that they might be taken by privateers.[16] Some were on the way to the Forth, but Cope, after his defeat at Prestonpans, managed to get a message to its ships and divert them to Newcastle. They all arrived safely by 28 September. On 2 October, after the news of Prestonpans reached London, eight British regiments of infantry and three of cavalry were withdrawn from the war in Flanders.

Since the Dutch troops were technically on parole after their surrender at the sieges of Tournai and Dandermond, the French made a diplomatic protest and the Dutch were replaced by 6,000 mercenaries from the German state of Hesse, who landed at Leith on 8 February 1746. As it turned out, the Dutch and Hessians took no part in the fighting. However, their presence in the north-east of England had an indirect effect on the campaign, for their presence in the east coast ports compelled the Jacobites to use the westerly route to the south.

Byng on the East Coast

The defeat at Prestonpans created a new urgency for the Royal Navy's blockade. The Admiralty still wanted to tighten the patrol off

Dunkirk, but Vernon believed that it was useless to try to stop French forces from getting out. Dunkirk had three exits through the tortuous sandbanks and the winter nights were getting longer. It was, he said, 'little better than the labour of the wise men of Gotham for hedging in the cuckoo'.[17] Instead he favoured stationing forces off all the east coast ports where the enemy might land forces. For this his large ships of 90 guns were useless, unable to go into any ports in the east coast of Scotland except the Firths of Cromarty and Forth: they were simply a waste of scarce seamen.

In any case, Byng arrived back at the Downs on 13 October to replenish his ships, and soon received new orders, this time from the Admiralty, who now fully accepted the need for a force off Scotland. Byng was to head north with his three ships, to take command of eight others already in Scottish waters. He was to co-operate with Marshal Wade who was marching northwards, and to intercept any French or Jacobite forces which might be heading for the Forth or anywhere else in Scotland. He was to remove or disable any friendly merchant ships from ports threatened by the rebel advance.[18]

Byng arrived on the Tyne on 22 October in the 50-gun *Gloucester*, to find three sloops already at anchor.[19] He reached Leith on 25 October, joining the *Ludlow Castle* and the *Fox* which were already there. He received intelligence that 160 carts of ammunition were to cross the Forth at Higgin's Neuk, where Kincardine Bridge now stands. This indeed was a gap in the government defences. The firth below there could be protected by the Navy, while the river banks close to and above Stirling were too marshy to support heavy carts. At Higgins Neuk, according to a report of 1709, the river was 'no more than four, five or six ft deep when the tide is gone, about 18 or 19 at full sea'.[20] Byng's sloops, among the smallest ships in the Navy, needed about 12 feet of water to stay afloat and would be left high and dry every time the tide went out. As Byng pointed out, even musket shot from either side bank could reach a ship in the river. Byng ordered the *Happy Jennet*, commanded by Lieutenant Knight, to go upriver to prevent the crossing, but he was unsuccessful due to the lack of water in the river.

Meanwhile the blockade of the coast continued. Byng spent most of his time in the *Gloucester*, anchored off Leith, moving closer to the port on 5 November 1745, to within a mile and a half of the pier. He was punctilious in his observance of ceremonial, firing gun salutes on King George's birthday (30 November) and on the anniversary of the Gunpowder Plot to remind the Jacobites of his presence. Though Edinburgh and Leith were nominally in enemy hands, the Jacobites were too few in number to prevent Byng's communication with the shore. Regular supplies of meat were sent out to his ships, mainly in the yacht attached to the Customs House in Leith. A French officer was captured on shore, taken out to the *Gloucester* and then sent to Edinburgh Castle, suggesting that the Jacobite siege was not very effective. Byng fitted out a small sloop and used it to patrol the Forth, searching many merchant ships and usually allowing them to proceed on finding that they had no goods or passengers of value to the Jacobites.[21] The *Ludlow Castle* and the *Fox* were ordered to cruise between Montrose and Buchan Ness, but Byng had to admit that supplies could still get through.[22]

French Expeditions

There were three main things that the French could supply to the rebels – men, arms and money. There were several regiments of Scottish and Irish exiles in France and naturally all were keen to join a rebellion which opened up the prospect of victory for a cause to which they had devoted themselves, as well as a triumphant end to their exile. Arms, especially artillery, were necessary on the battlefield as an aid to the infantry, and more importantly in the siege of a castle such as Edinburgh, Carlisle or Stirling. As to money, the Jacobites levied the towns they captured, taking it from the public treasury rather than from private individuals in order to foster public support; but this was never enough and a large sum would boost the rebellion.

In the early stages, French support came from private sources. Four privateers carrying artillery succeeded in getting through to Montrose and Stonehaven during October 1745, before the British blockade was fully established. It would later be sent across the Forth at Higgins Neuk. Eight ships, the *Fine, Espérance, Renomée, Louis XV, Jeanneton, Sainte Thérèse, Paix* and *St Bernard*, slipped out of Dunkirk on 15 November 1745 during a storm. The first three were French naval frigates, for the government of Louis XV was warming to the Jacobite cause now that it showed some signs of success. The transports carried 800 men including Drummond's regiment of Scottish exiles in France and men from Irish regiments in French service.

The French ships were soon separated in the storm. The *Espérance* was taken by HMS *Sheerness* at Dogger Bank and twenty-two officers were captured. The *Fine* was chased by the *Milford* and ran aground at the entrance to Montrose Harbour on 26 November, breaking her back, and the *Louis XIV* was captured off the port two days later. The others arrived safely in Montrose, Stonehaven and Peterhead on or around 22 November, providing a boost to Jacobite forces in the area. However, even that had its disadvantages for the rebels. At Derby, on 5 December, as the leaders debated whether to go on or to turn back, the presence of Drummond's regiment was advanced as a reason for returning to Scotland.

The British too had their losses on the blockade. The *Fox* was wrecked at Dunbar on 14 November, in the same storm which had allowed the French to escape from Dunkirk, and the sloop *Tryall* was lost at Holy Island, while the *Ludlow Castle* was damaged. But there was one loss which was to prove particularly humiliating for the Royal Navy.

The Taking of the Hazard

On 15 November the sloop *Hazard* anchored in Montrose Harbour, with orders to unrig some merchant ships which might fall into rebel hands. Captain Thomas Hill found it difficult; he had more than a hundred men in his crew, but most were pressed men and fewer than a dozen could be trusted not to desert if sent ashore. However, the task had been completed by the 20th, and all the rigging put on board a merchant ship called the *Friends Goodwill*, ready to sail as soon as the winds were favourable.

On the morning of the 22nd Captain Hill sent a boat ashore with a midshipman and four seamen, unaware that three or four hundred Highlanders had captured the town during the night. The seamen attempted to flee back to the ship, but the rebels fired and one man was killed, one wounded and the others surrendered. Midshipman William Bruce was forced to write to Captain Hill that if the sloop fired on the town, 'he should see us hanging before his face in the morning'. There was little or no wind, so the *Hazard* could not escape, but she fired her guns at the rebels whenever an opportunity arose.

By the afternoon of the 23rd a wind had got up, but it was blowing into the harbour. At 3 o'clock a sail was seen in the distance, and identified as French. She was the privateer *Renommée* of 14 guns, carrying men from Drummond's regiment. They fired at long range, while the Highlanders did their best to signal the sloop's identity to the new arrival.

Guns were landed from the *Renommée* and on the morning of Sunday the 24th one opened fire from the south shore, right ahead of the *Hazard*. The sloop fired her bow guns and forced the abandonment of this gun, but another was soon set up higher up the hill, while one on the north shore kept up a continual fire for the rest of the day. Night fell and the men of the *Hazard* began to repair their rigging, in the hope of escaping at high tide in the morning, while the Jacobites set up two more batteries on the south shore and one more to the north. The ship found it difficult to reply in the dark, and the men had to retreat below decks. According to her lieutenant, 'At daylight wee found all our Rigging fore and aft cutt to pieces and several of our Guns Dismounted and our upper works torn very much.' A flag of truce was hoisted on the shore on the morning of the 24th and Lieutenant Burges went ashore to negotiate. The officers agreed that there was no possibility of escape and surrendered early in the after-noon. The captain planned to burn the ship, but this was not done.

The next day, another drama took place at the harbour entrance as HMS *Milford* arrived and spotted the French privateer *Fine*. Accord-ing to the log of the *Milford*:

> At 8 am, Red Head North North East two or three miles. At 9 saw a large ship at anchor off Montrose. 1030, French cut cable and made sail for harbour. Followed him in and anchored in three fathoms – fired – French went ashore in launches. *Milford* touched ground, used barge to set up hawser on shore, boat under heavy fire – hawser broke, but fire resumed.
>
> 2pm, floated off at high water, cut cable and sailed out, while shot cut *Fine*'s cable and she drove ashore on the north side of the harbour. Sent boats to fire on her but they were obliged to return – sailed away leaving the ship there.[23]

In fact the *Fine* had broken her back and was unusable, but stores were taken out of her for use by the captured *Hazard*.

Captain Hill and his crew were not handled well by their captors. David Ferrier, a merchant of Brechin, treated prisoners 'in so barbar-ous a manner that they must in all probability have perished had it not been for the assistance they received from the friends of the govern-ment in Montrose, Brechin and elsewhere.'[24] They were eventually released and tried by court martial for the loss of the ship. Hill and his lieutenant were found guilty and cashiered, the boatswain and gunner were reprimanded and the rest were acquitted.[25]

Meanwhile the Jacobites had secured possession of a good harbour on the east coast. They repaired the *Hazard* and fitted her for sea, using supplies and officers from the *Fine*. The first ship in the Jacobite navy, she was renamed the *Prince Charles*.

During the month of December the sea campaign was relatively quiet, but Admiral Vernon was not. He virtually resigned on 1 December due to his dissatisfaction with the administration and was succeeded by Vice-Admiral William Martin.

Meanwhile the Jacobite army moved south, crossing into England on 8 November. The towns of Carlisle, Lancaster and Preston were taken and it was decided to head for London. On 5 December they arrived at Derby, just over a hundred miles from the capital. Many of the leaders, though not the Prince himself, were becoming worried about the lack of real support and recruits from England and were feeling increasingly isolated. At a council of war it was decided to turn back and build up strength in Scotland, with a view to a later campaign in England. On 20 December, the Prince's twenty-fifth birthday, the army forded the River Esk near Carlisle and re-entered Scotland. The Hanoverian army was now under the command of the Duke of Cumberland, the King's third son, and it reached Carlisle as Charles crossed the Esk.

Protecting the Forth

As the Jacobites retreated they moved heavy artillery from Dunblane to Alloa, planning to ship it up the Forth to Stirling, in a final attempt to capture the castle. The government forces around Edinburgh received intelligence of this and on 5 January some of the crew of the *Happy Jennet*, anchored at Queensferry, went into a Kinghorn fishing boat and sailed up the river. They captured a small brigantine and brought it back to Queensferry next morning.

On the 7th the sloop *Vulture* arrived from Bo'ness and passed up river to Kincardine, accompanied by a Kinghorn fishing boat specially fitted with a deck, carrying fifty soldiers. Next evening the sloop and boat passed up to Airth, where the *Vulture* anchored. They found two small ships, a snow and a brig, one of which was the *William*, belonging to John Adams of Airth, who was serving as a pilot with the government forces. A boat was lowered from the *Vulture* and sent towards them, but they were fast aground and had to be burned, to the distress of John Adams.

By nine o'clock the next morning the rebels had moved cannon into position at Airth and began to fire on the warship, starting a fight which lasted an hour and three quarters, till the rebels withdrew. However, the *Vulture* dropped back a mile and a half to a safer anchorage off Kincardine. In the afternoon some small boats arrived carrying 300 more government soldiers. They were loaded into the Kinghorn fishing boat, while 50 sailors manned three ships' boats. It was hoped to get up to Alloa under cover of darkness, to capture or destroy any ships that the rebels might have there. They crept past a Jacobite battery of three or four guns at Elphinstone Tower (later

Dunmore House) on the south bank just above Airth. But the Kinghorn fishing boat ran aground close to Alloa and the crew made a
noise which alerted the Jacobite sentries. The cannon of Alloa opened
fire but she was refloated before any damage war done. It was
considered too dangerous to land the 300 troops, so the boats withdrew. In repassing Elphinstone, one sailor was wounded and another
killed by cannon fire.

On the afternoon of the 10th the *Vulture* herself, with a small vessel
called the *Ursula* and some armed transports, used a fair wind to sail
up the river, while the troops attempted to advance by land from
Kincardine. John Adams and another local man served as pilots in the
narrow, poorly charted waters. At one in the morning of the 11th, the
ships anchored a quarter of a mile from the Elphinstone battery and
began firing. Two of the Elphinstone guns were dismounted by the
Vulture's fire, but at four in the morning a shot from Elphinstone cut
the *Vulture*'s cable, causing her to drift in the ebbing tide. John Adams
and the other pilot each lost a leg from cannon fire and it was decided
to withdraw. Adams later died and two years later his wife was still
petitioning the government for compensation for the loss of her
husband and his ship. Though the government forces had no concrete
success, they claimed that they had prevented the ship at Alloa from
sailing.[26] But Lord Elcho, one of the Jacobite commanders, denied this
and claimed that the artillery was moved up immediately after the
Vulture was forced to withdraw.[27] In any case the Jacobite artillery
was far too light to have any serious effect on Stirling Castle.

The Siege of Fort William

No part of Scotland was more securely held against the Jacobites than
the Campbell fiefdom of Argyll. Even Glasgow, the most Hanoverian
town in Scotland, was held by the Jacobites for a time during their
retreat, but no rebel forces and very few fugitives penetrated the south-
west Highlands and the southern Hebrides.

Fort William, at the south end of the Great Glen, was almost an
extension of Campbell power in the territory of one of their greatest
rivals, Cameron of Locheil. It had a commanding position, at the
south-western end of the 'chain' which guarded the Great Glen. It was
also on the 'Road to the Isles' via Glenfinnan and Arisaig, and indeed
Charles had been forced to make a detour over the hills to get past the
fort in August 1745 when he began the revolt. Situated at the head of
Loch Linnhe where it turned into Loch Eil, Fort William could be
supplied by sea and this was a great advantage.

By February 1746 the Jacobites were concentrating on controlling the Highlands and they attacked the forts of the chain. Ruthven barracks was captured on 10 February. The rebel army arrived at Inverness on the 18th and Lord Loudon, who had rallied government forces in the area, withdrew by boat across the Kessock Ferry to the Black Isle. Inverness Castle fell two days later and Fort Augustus on 5 March after two days of siege.

As the threat to Fort William developed, government forces and supplies were sent in increasing quantities from February 1746. On the 15th the sloop *Serpent* commanded by Captain Thomas Noel, arrived from the Sound of Mull and anchored in Loch Linnhe. She was joined by the *Baltimore* under Captain Howe, later to become famous as the victor at the Glorious First of June in 1794. But the rebels tried to cut off the sea route at Corran Narrows, where Loch Linnhe is less than half a mile wide, and indeed the *Baltimore* had come under sporadic musket fire when passing through. On 1 March her boat, carrying letters, was captured off the Narrows. Three days later, government forces counter-attacked. A boat carrying dispatches to the fort met one carrying a party of militiamen as they anchored just below the Narrows to await the tide. Meanwhile an attack had been launched by the boats of the *Serpent* and the *Baltimore*. The men landed at Corran Ferry, destroyed any houses that might have given cover to the rebels and killed and wounded several of them 'as apear'd by the quantitys of blood left on the roads'. After that the passage was safe.

Meanwhile parties of rebels were gathering round Fort William and eventually numbered about 1,000, while Captain Caroline Scott took command of 300 defenders. The siege began on 5 March and the artillery arrived two days later. The Jacobites soon began to exploit the main weakness of the fort by mounting their guns on Cow Hill above it. The government forces maintained the supply links with Inveraray and Dumbarton by hiring wherries, small fast-sailing vessels of about 15 tons, carrying up to forty troops. The island fortress of Castle Stalker was still held by the government and served as a staging-post on the way. During the siege the two warships contributed with their gunfire, and their topmasts served as look-out posts; on 23 March they spotted a new rebel battery being set up. The defenders continued to raid the enemy by sea as well as land, using the wherries. On the 25th, for example, one took a party of men beyond Corran to raid rebel estates. But as Lord Elcho commented, 'as the *Serpent* and *Baltimore* Sloops of war were at that place they could never cutt off communication by sea.'[28] On 3 April the rebels bombarded the town heavily and then marched away, leaving some of their guns behind;

the men were needed more urgently at the other end of the Great Glen, where Cumberland's army was approaching.

Supporting the Army

The Duke of Cumberland and his army advanced towards Perth, which he reached on 6 February. He soon found himself short of supplies, especially bread and money. The march north was delayed until the 20th, when ships carrying food and £20,000 in money arrived from England. But after that he seems to have relied surprisingly little on sea transport, despite the incompetence of the government agents appointed to find his supplies locally.

Ships of the blockading force took positions on the east coast ahead of the army. On the 9th the *Gloucester* under Captain Gore arrived off Montrose. The captured *Hazard* had already sailed from there on 27 January and it was soon established that the rebel army had withdrawn towards Stonehaven and Aberdeen. The remaining Jacobites had loaded up four cannon in two boats, intending to install them on the Bridge of Dee at Aberdeen. One boat sailed on the night of 8 February, but the *Gloucester* arrived in time to prevent the other one, which had to beach its load. On the night of the 11th, the first lieutenant of the *Gloucester* landed with two boatloads of men and spiked up the guns, as well as two more at the town cross. Fearing a Jacobite return, Gore landed fifty marines to secure the town and the sloop *Saltash* was ordered to enter the harbour as soon as possible.[29]

HMS *Hound* entered Montrose Harbour on 17 February, ahead of Cumberland's advance. She was still there on the 22nd when the army arrived and she used her boats to help ferry some of the troops across the mouth.[30] Meanwhile Bligh's Regiment of the British Army was being sent north by sea. It met the rest of the army at Aberdeen, in time to fight with it in April.

The Blockade

After the arrival of the remnants of Drummond's regiment at Montrose and Peterhead during November, there were no further attempts to supply the rebels during the depths of winter. On 8 February the *Sophie,* the *Bourbon* and the *Charité* left Ostend with FitzJames Horse, a regiment of Irish exiles. The *Sophie,* the smallest of the ships, got away to reach Aberdeen, but the other two were forced to turn back in the face of the British blockade. They tried again two weeks later and were captured next day by four British warships.

In a letter of 16 February 1746, at a time when the Jacobites had retreated north of the Forth and the government army was soon to advance, the captain of the *Gloucester* describes the Royal Navy's dispositions. The flagship *Gloucester* and the 44-gun *Eltham* were cruising off Montrose, between Red Head near Arbroath and Todd Head south of Stonehaven. The 14-gun *Hound* was in the harbour, which had been vacated by the Jacobites but was not yet occupied by the government army. The *Winchilsea* was ordered to cruise between Stonehaven and Aberdeen; the *Bridgewater* between Aberdeen and Peterhead. The *Glasgow* was at Leith for a refit and then was to join the flagship. The *Shark* and the *Vulture* were in the Moray Firth between Peterhead and Findhorn, the *Saltash* had gone south to Holy Island and was to return to convoy trade between Leith and the Thames, while the *Happy Jennet* was guarding the Forth at Queensferry.

In the meantime two more French flotillas were preparing to sail. One at Ostend never left harbour but a force of six ships sailed from Dunkirk on 18 February carrying 650 troops. They evaded the blockaders in a fog and reached the coast of Scotland, only to find that the government army was advancing towards the ports where they wanted to land. They retreated to Dunkirk, except for the *Aventurier* which landed forty men in Peterhead on 25 February. Three British warships, led by Captain Charles Saunders in the *Gloucester,* spotted her coming out and she was driven ashore in Cruden Bay.[31]

The last ship to sail with any hope of supporting the Jacobite rebellion was the *Prince Charles*, formerly HMS *Hazard*, which left France on 14 March carrying 12,000 guineas (£12,600) in gold for the rebels. She arrived off Buchan Ness on the 24th, hoping to find a port which was still in Jacobite hands. Instead, the ship, commanded by Richard Talbot, was spotted by four of Commodore Smith's warships, led by the *Eltham* of 40 guns. The *Prince Charles* fled north, using oars in very light winds, and passed through the turbulent waters of the Pentland Firth, but could not evade pursuit by the *Sheerness*, captained by Lucius O'Brien. Taking advice from passing fishermen, Talbot headed into the Kyle of Tongue, hoping the waters were too shallow for the *Sheerness* to pursue him. He anchored with his broadside facing the entrance but O'Brien was not deterred. The *Prince Charles's* broadside of 36 pounds was soon overwhelmed by the *Sheerness's* of just over 100 pounds and the crew fled as the ship began to sink. The money was taken ashore by officers and soldiers, but they too were captured after disposing of most of it in loch and heather. The loss of the money was a serious blow to the rebels, now at Inverness, and they sent a strong force north to try to find it. Lord Elcho commented that 'this was a great loss to the Prince as he was in Great distress for want of money.'[32] The loss persuaded them to try their hand in battle against the Duke of Cumberland's advancing forces, and they went out to meet them on Culloden Moor on 16 April.

From the resumption of Byng's blockade on 26 October until the Battle of Culloden six months later, the French sent nineteen ships to support the rebels. Five of these were captured, two were wrecked and five more failed to accomplish their mission.[33] This gave the French a success rate of only 37 per cent and a loss rate also of 37 per cent, which would not be an acceptable level of losses in any conflict. In these terms, the Vernon/Martin blockade of Dunkirk and the Byng/Smith blockade of Scotland can be seen as a resounding success.

The Suppression of the Rebellion

Prince Charles was of course heavily defeated at Culloden and the whole affair was watched by HMS *Shark* off the coast of Inverness.

> About noon saw the engagement begin betwixt His Royal Highness and the rebels on Clydon Moor about three miles south-east from Inverness . . . At 1 pm weighed and made sail for Inverness, the convoy in company. At 2 ditto the firing on both sides ceased: anchored off Inverness . . . Saw a party of horse coming alongshore: sent the boat to enquire what news: at 3 spoke with the aforesaid party, who told us they had got a compleat victory over the rebels.'[34]

The Prince went into hiding. Meanwhile there was a severe repression of the rebels, both by land and by sea, and Cumberland earned his nickname of 'Butcher'. Prisoners from Culloden were removed to Inverness and put into merchant ships to be taken south for trial in London.

> They put so many aboard each ship that their own breath and heat made them swarm with vermine. You'd have laughed to have seen them lying 'twixt decks, like fish in a pond, and every one had a twig in his hand to defend himself from the atacks of his nighbour's lice . . . But at last, by hunger, bad usage, and lying upon the ballasts and 'twixt decks exposed to all weathers, they were ceased with a kind of plague which caryed them off be dozens, and a good many of those who woud have outlived their sickness was wantonly murdered by the sailors by diping of them in the sea in the crissis of their fevers. This was the sailor's diversion from Buchanness point till we came to the Nore.[35]

The story of Will Jack was similar. Only 49 out of 157 prisoners survived in the *Liberty and Property*. 'They wou'd have taken us from the hold in a rope, and hois'd us up to the yardarm and let us fall in the sea for ducking of us, and tying us to the mast and whipping us if we but made water in the hold. This was done to us when we was not able to stand.'[36]

Many of the prisoners were put on board warships as soon as possible. Sir James Stewart and three of his comrades were captured in Orkney and eventually sent to Captain Duff's sloop *Terror*.

> Within some hours after they came to this sloop, they were, by the great indulgence of their new captain, coop'd up in an ugly hole of about six feet long and somewhat less in breadth, where they suffer'd extremely for several weeks; nor could a Turkish bashaw have borne himself higher towards these prisoners than the young officer did towards them while under his command.[37]

Convicted prisoners who escaped execution were usually sentenced to transportation to the West Indian and American colonies as 'indentured servants' or virtual slaves. Altogether, 936 persons, about a third of the total captured, were treated in this way. Conditions aboard the vessels which carried them were as cruel as anything in the warships and a third died on some ships. In the New World some found relief, and help from Jacobite sympathisers.

The Prince in the Hebrides

There were four main parties in the drama of the Prince's flight from Hanoverian forces. The Prince himself, and his immediate retinue, were concerned with escape to France. This naturally involved finding a ship, either a French one sent to rescue them, or one which could be obtained locally. But the natives of western Scotland had few vessels of a suitable type. At this stage, their traditions of seafaring were confined to local voyages. There were very few seaports, which explains why Charles, in his first attempt at escape, went north into hostile Mackenzie territory at Stornoway. There he hoped to find a ship to take him to Orkney, where ships of various nations might be found.

The most immediate aim of the Prince was to escape from government forces, which were never far behind him. During the first three months of his flight, between his arrival on the coast at Borrodale on 20 April and 18 July when he began a move into the interior, he made a dozen separate voyages in small boats, through the choppy waters and disturbed currents of the Minches. He was never more than five miles from the sea during this period and often spent the night in an open boat. His attempt to go north to Orkney was a failure, and it was highly dangerous to go south of Ardnamurchan, where the Campbells held sway. Even Lewis, as it turned out, was difficult, for the Presbyterian Mackenzies were firmly opposed to the rising.

Charles's first voyage was the longest, and in many ways the most dangerous. Believing that he would be safer in the islands, he found an eight-oared boat piloted by Donald MacLeod. The crew included the pilot's fifteen-year-old son who had fought at Culloden, and Ned Burk, a 'common chairman' of Edinburgh – the carrier of a sedan chair, not the head of a company. The Prince was accompanied by four of his retinue. Donald MacLeod advised against sailing that night, 26 April, as he could see a storm brewing, but the Prince was anxious to be away. Out at sea 'a most violent tempest arose, greater than ever Donald MacLeod had been trysted with before, though all of his life a seafaring man, upon the coast of Scotland.' The Prince now changed his tune and demanded to be put ashore 'For I had rather face canons and muskets than be in such a storm as this.' MacLeod refused, pointing out that the boat would be broken to pieces on the rocky coast. The crew remained silent, in awe of the natural forces. The Prince slept occasionally with his head between the pilot's feet, waking up to drink from his flask. The boat made amazingly fast progress under sail that night, despite breaking its bowsprit off Arisaig, and at daybreak the coast of Benbecula could be seen. It had travelled 96 miles in eight hours. With great difficulty they landed among the rocks at Rossinish and the boat was hauled up on shore.[38] The same craft took him on to Lewis, where he hoped to find a ship in Stornoway.

The Prince's most famous voyage was of course the trip to Skye with Flora MacDonald. The Prince first met the lady on 21 June on South Uist, when government forces under Captain Caroline Scott, the defender of Fort William, were only a mile away. The fugitives made their way along the islands by sea and land, and the legendary voyage began from near Lochmaddy on 28 June. The Prince, at Miss MacDonald's suggestion, was disguised as Betty Burke, an Irish servant, despite his 'awkward way in managing the petticoats, and what long strides he took in walking along'.[39] The boat was navigated by John MacDonald and crewed by four MacDonald oarsmen. They sailed at 8 p.m. on the 28th, but the breeze was light and they made little progress. At one the next afternoon they were enveloped by a thick fog which caused them to stop rowing, for fear that they might hit the rocks of Skye. A light breeze dispersed the fog and they found themselves off a headland which turned out to be Waternish, in MacLeod territory. As the wind increased they came close inshore for shelter but came under fire from a party of about fifty troops on shore and in boats. As they retreated they were careful not to pull their oars too hard, for fear of arousing even more suspicion. Eventually they got away from 'the tedious point of Watternish' and headed across Loch Snizort, landing north of Uig on the afternoon of 29 June.[40]

The second party in the affair, the common people of the Hebrides and the west coast, reacted in different ways to the fugitive Prince, though no one was to betray him, even for the reward offered for his capture. Not all were active Jacobite supporters and indeed some, such as the Mackenzies of Skye, had opposed the rebellion. The boatmen were among the bravest. Like Donald MacLeod, they had to brave the Hebridean weather as well as the threat of reprisals.

Support from France

The third party was the Prince's supporters in France. Realising that the rebellion had failed, they made no fewer than six attempts to rescue him by ship. In March 1746, even before Culloden, Antoine Walsh sent two large privateers, the *Mars* and the *Bellone*, to help the Prince. Their first objective was to bring money and arms to promote the rebellion; but if it was already defeated when they arrived, as turned out to be the case, they were to rescue Charles. They arrived at Loch nan Uamh on 3 May (a week after Charles had sailed on to Stornoway) and landed 40,000 louis in gold, which was taken to Loch Arkaig. The ships were found at their anchorage by Captain Noel of the Royal Navy and the *Greyhound*, *Baltimore* and *Terror*. The French had superiority of gunpower; their ships had 36 guns each, mostly 9-pounders, while Noel had ships of 24 and 14 guns, mainly armed with 6-pounders. The French decided to fight at anchor in the narrow waters of the loch. The British ships used their manoeuvrability to attack the French bows and sterns, while the French fired at their opponents' rigging. After six hours of fighting, including a daring attack by Captain Howe in the *Baltimore*, the British withdrew to repair their damage in the Sound of Mull. The French sailed as soon as they could, knowing that British reinforcements would be on the way.

The would-be rescuers faced several serious problems: navigation in intricate and uncharted waters, avoiding British warships, and, most difficult of all, actually finding the Prince among the lochs and islands. The second attempt began late in May, when a small four-gun privateer, the *Levrier Volant*, left France. Off the west coast of Scotland on 9 June she stopped a small merchant ship, the *Agnes and Mary* of Irvine, and tried to use her captain as a pilot. But he knew little of the area and was soon put ashore. The privateer went to Loch Broom and Loch Ewe but failed to find the Prince, who was on Uist and Benbecula at the time.

The next ship was the *Hardi Mendiant*, formerly the English privateer *Sturdy Beggar*, which had been captured by Dunkirkers. She had first sailed on 3 May with Scottish and Irish volunteers to support the rebellion, found the Cromarty Firth occupied by the enemy and went north-about to Loch Broom. On hearing of the defeat at Culloden she returned to Nantes. She left again on 8 June, this time on a mission to find the Prince and rescue him. At Benbecula on 5 July (by which time the Prince had moved to the mainland near Mallaig) she found a party of leading rebels including John O'Sullivan, the Adjutant-General of Charles's army. The *Hardi Mendiant* sailed north and arrived at Bergen in Norway. O'Sullivan got back to Paris, where he helped to persuade the King to devote more effort to the rescue of Prince Charles.

Bien Trouvé, a brigantine of 80 tons, sailed from Dunkirk on 30 May carrying some of the officers who had been obliged to turn back with the *Elisabeth* last July. After a slow passage she rounded Cape Wrath on 17 June and a small party went ashore in Sutherland. They sailed on to Loch Broom and found Jacobite supporters, but no intelligence on the Prince. In Loch Ewe they were offered a chance to contact Murray of Broughton, the Prince's secretary, but sailed on to look for the Prince himself. After lingering on Priest's Island among the Summer Isles, they sailed north again and had several near encounters with British warships, who had received intelligence of their presence. On 22 July they were spotted by HMS *Glasgow*, of 24 guns, and chased into Loch Broom. The sloop *Tryall* went inside to get them, while the frigate waited outside. When the *Bien Trouvé* tried to escape the frigate placed herself across her bows and forced her to surrender.

Two more privateers, the *Comte de Lowendahl* and *Comte de Maurepas*, sailed on 19 June from Dunkirk with the *Hardi Mendiant* on another voyage, but the first two never got to the west coast because of contrary winds, while the *Hardi Mendiant* sprang a leak and was forced to return. Two large St Malo privateers, the *Heureux*, of 36 guns and 275 men, and the *Prince de Conti*, of 30 guns and 275 men, sailed on 20 August with Colonel Richard Warren, who had taken part in the rebellion and knew the Prince well. They sent parties ashore at Lochboisdale on South Uist on 6 September and put out word among the Prince's supporters that rescue was at hand. Rory MacDonald, who had been with the Prince on his long voyage to Benbecula in April, was taken on board as pilot. The two ships sailed over to Loch nan Uamh, now knowing that the people there had a better idea of where the Prince was hiding. They anchored in the loch and waited for thirteen days while the word was passed. British army headquarters at Fort Augustus did not hear of their presence until the 17th.

Charles was now hiding in 'Cluny's cage' above Loch Ericht, 25 miles east of Fort William. The news reached him on the 13th and he headed for the coast, passing among the mountains and along the south side of Loch Arkaig. He reached Loch nan Uamh on the 19th, to find that the two ships were still there and undisturbed by the pursuers. Colonel Warren was fetched from his dinner table on board the *Conti*, put on his best clothes and set out for the shore in a boat. Charles and a substantial retinue came on board. Both ships weighed anchor at three next morning and headed for France. They passed Barra Head and headed out round the west of Ireland, without meeting any British cruisers. After an eight-day voyage they arrived at Morlaix on the coast of Brittany, where Charles was rowed ashore to a 21–gun salute. He was safe after an absence of fifteen months, the last six in almost constant danger and discomfort.[41]

The Royal Navy in the Islands

The fourth party comprised the servants of the British government. During the first half of the pursuit, while the Prince was among the islands, the Royal Navy was the most important partner. It was an area of islands and sea-lochs, with many mountains and no modern roads, so sea power was essential. Now that the east coast was secure, more naval effort could be devoted to the west, though the great majority of ships were required for the war against France and Spain. By mid-May, a month after Culloden, there were nine warships in the west. The *Greyhound*, the *Baltimore* and the *Terror* had repaired their damage after the Battle of Loch nan Uamh and were ready for service. The 14-gun *Raven* arrived on 4 May and the *Scarborough* and *Glasgow* of 24 guns, with the *Trial* and *Happy Jennet* of 14 and 20 guns on the 13th. Captain John Fergusson arrived with the 14-gun *Furnace* on the 17th. By the rules of seniority, the force was now commanded by Captain Robert Jefferys of the *Scarborough*, who had been promoted six months before Captain Noel of the *Greyhound*.

The navy had other aims besides finding the Prince. One was to round up his active supporters.

Much of the search was based on intelligence and supposition, which was often spectacularly wrong, as when an expedition was sent to St Kilda in the belief that the Prince would head for the most remote part of the kingdom. The natives hid when General Campbell appeared on their shores and were amazed at the questioning they were subjected to, for they knew nothing of affairs on the mainland.[42]

Other attempts were more successful. Charles was back at Loch nan Uamh on the 10th, but government intelligence clearly knew something of his movements. Reconnaissance showed that no fewer than six men-of-war had anchored in Loch Nevis and 'they visibly saw the whole coast surrounded by ships of war and tenders, as also the country by other military forces'.[43] It was decided to head for the interior, despite a line of military camps between Loch Eil and Loch Hourn. This ended the island phase of Charles's escape, as he fled inland three months after Culloden.

The navy's third task was to suppress present and future rebellions, and that would be long remembered in the Hebrides. It was still feared that the revolt might be reignited in that region and efforts were made to prevent this. Captain John Fergusson of the *Furnace* was by far the most notorious of the naval officers who took part in the campaign. He came from a strongly anti-Jacobite family. One of his great-uncles had supported Monmouth's Rebellion in 1685; another had served in the Scots Brigade in Holland, came over with William of Orange in 1688 and became a major-general in the British army. His cousin, Elizabeth Fergusson of Kinmundy, rallied resistance against the rebels in Aberdeenshire in 1745 and had her house plundered.[44] The islanders had no doubt about their hatred for him. To Hugh MacDonald of North Uist he was 'most bent of any I had heard to take the Prince'. To John Walkingshaw he was 'this barbarous man'. To Nanie MacDonald of Skye he was 'a very cruel, hard-hearted man' and 'a man remarkably rigid and severe in his way'.[45] When two of the Prince's rowers were captured on 7 July, Fergusson led the interrogation. 'One of these, John MacGinnis, he caused to be stripped naked, tied to a tree, and whipped with the cat and nine tails till the blood gushed out at both his sides, threatening John McKinnon with the same usage and with irons, if he did not discover where the Prince was.'[46]

Fergusson obeyed the orders to suppress rebellion with some relish. His campaign had begun even before Culloden, for his men slaughtered sixty cattle on the tiny island of Canna in April, while other ships were harassing the Sound of Mull. At Raasay on 15 May, Fergusson ordered one Lieutenant Dalrymple ashore to execute his vengeance against the island, who burnt Rasay's good house to ashes, and also the whole houses upon the island excepting two small villages that escaped their sight, with all the poor people's furniture. The number of houses burnt, according to a strict account taken of them, exceeded three hundred.[47]

The next day Fergusson sailed to Loch nan Uamh and came under the command of Captain Duff from Banff, in the *Terror*. Crews disembarked from the two ships on 17 May and were attacked with explosives landed from the French ships two weeks before. In retaliation they burned the village and went on to Lochailort. They were rounding up the cattle when they were fired upon and again the village was destroyed.[48] Duff and Fergusson arrived at Eigg a few weeks later. The islanders had already delivered up their arms as required by law, but more were found by Fergusson's search parties. They searched one Captain Macdonald and found 'a devilish paper' with a list of all the men who had supported the Prince. Thirty-eight were taken and eventually sentenced to transportation; only sixteen arrived in the West Indies.[49]

Fergusson's zeal and competence made him particularly dangerous to the Jacobites. He was often hot on the heels of the Prince. On 10 May Charles passed the end of Harris in a four-oared barge which he had hired near Stornoway. Off Finsbay he passed close to the *Furnace*, which was under full sail. The barge too had all her sails set, but used her oars to increase her speed in light winds. After an exhausting chase of nine miles, the barge passed close to the shore at Rodel on the southern tip of the island and escaped among the rocks as the tide fell.[50] On 4 July, five days after the event, Fergusson was searching the house where the Prince and Flora MacDonald had hidden after the voyage to Skye.[51] His greatest triumph came early in June with the capture of Lord Lovat. Receiving information about his lordship's whereabouts, he landed on an island in Loch Morar, but missed his quarry. A few days later he found him (though not dressed as a woman as mythology suggested) and brought him back to the *Furnace*. The 78-year-old lord, who had changed sides several times in his career, was one of the most sought-after fugitives and his capture caused rejoicing in London. The following year he was executed at Tower Hill in front of vast crowds. When the grandstand collapsed he remarked, 'The mair mischief, the mair sport.'

The Aftermath

Charles's flight was not the end of the matter. Some Jacobites continued to shelter hopes of revival, while the government continued to see plots for several years. In January 1748 Lieutenant-General Bland reported that the Highlands were still quiet, and that reports of French ships at Mull were probably false. Intelligence was also received of French ships at Skye.[52] Later in the year he heard reports of men being recruited for French service on the island of Eigg, but Captain Edwards of HMS *Kingfisher* reassured him that they were probably groundless. The war with France had in fact ended a few weeks earlier, but the peace was an uneasy one at best. By December Bland reported unusual calm in the Highlands, but in 1750 Lord Justice Clerk Aerskine noted that the Jacobites 'absurdly entertain hopes of an invasion from Sweden, assisted by France and of an insurrection in England.'[53] Despite all this, Jacobite hopes and government fears were never realised and there was never another rebellion.

The Royal Navy tended to place operations in Scotland against the Jacobites a long way down its priorities, well behind the defence of southern England against invasion, the protection of trade against privateers, guarding British colonies and attacking enemy ones. It was no less essential, for it guarded an Achilles heel in the Hanoverian dynasty's relative success. At the time many Scots, probably the majority, saw the navy as a protector against Catholicism, absolute monarchy and the wild Highland hordes. Yet over the years the Jacobites took on a rosy glow of nostalgia in Scottish history and won the battle for the Scottish heart and mind in retrospect, if not at the time. In this context the Royal Navy's achievements seem less than noble. In the end they failed in their task of finding the Prince, and posterity has not always recognised the difficulties they faced and overcame. The repression by Captain Fergusson became part of folklore in the west. Mackintosh of Borlum crossing the Forth and the taking of the *Hazard* at Montrose seem heroic, while Flora MacDonald's concealment of the fugitive Prince is legendary. In retrospect, the Royal Navy is seen almost entirely as an oppressive force.

Chapter 4

Scottish Officers

Integration with the Royal Navy

It would not be surprising if the Scottish captains and lieutenants found themselves overwhelmed when their three ships were merged into the English Navy in 1707. The Royal Navy was just beginning its years of glory. It was already the biggest and most powerful in the world, having passed through its traumas of the seventeenth century to outbuild the Dutch and outfight the French. The Scots had three ships, the English had nearly 300, mostly much larger. There were six great dockyards in the south of England, forming the largest industrial organisation in the world. The Royal Navy was already beginning to develop a professional ethos, with examinations for the commissioned rank of lieutenant and a regular, or perhaps ossified, rank structure for captains and admirals. After the War of the Spanish Succession ended in 1714, all commissioned officers would be entitled to half pay when not employed at sea, creating a permanent career for the officer corps, though not for the seamen.

Into this, the Scottish officers found that their reception was lukewarm at best. Captain Gordon had great difficulty in having his seniority recognised in the new navy; he wanted it backdated to November 1705 when he had been appointed to the Scots Navy, but the Admiralty offered it only from when the Union came into effect on 1 May 1707. The seamen at Leith mutinied for fear that they might be sent to the West Indies, where disease was rife.

Because the English already had much larger ships with similar names, the *Royal William* and *Royal Mary* were renamed *Edinburgh* and *Glasgow* and put on the list of the Royal Navy as a fifth-rate and a sixth-rate respectively – the rating signifying the size of the ship rather than the quality. They were put under the orders of an English admiral but continued as convoy escorts for the trade to Leith. The *Edinburgh* did not last long; like her predecessor the *Pelican*, she was sunk as a breakwater in the English dockyard at Harwich in 1709. The *Dum-barton Castle* kept her name, was registered as a sixth-rate and remained on patrol in the Western Isles and off Ireland, where she was taken by a large French privateer in 1708. None of the three Scottish captains fared well under the English. After the capture of the *Dumbarton Castle* and his release by exchange of prisoners, Captain Campbell was acquitted by a court martial but not employed again. Captain Hamilton, now in command of the *Lark*, of 42 guns, died in the West Indies in 1708, perhaps justifying the fears of the mutinous seamen at Leith. When the *Edinburgh* went out of service Captain Gordon transferred to the *Leopard*, of 54 guns, and distinguished himself against the Forbin expedition of 1708. In 1716 he declined to take the oath of allegiance to George I and took service under Peter the Great in Russia. Neither the ships nor the officers of the old Scots Navy had any significant effect on the new British Navy.[1]

The First Scottish Officers

A few Scots, mostly of aristocratic descent, served as officers in the English Navy before the Union of 1707. One of the first, however, was of a much humbler background. David Mitchell of Leith served an apprenticeship in a merchant ship and became a mate in the Baltic trade. He was pressed into the Royal Navy during the Third Dutch War (1672–4) and rose to commissioned rank in 1678. He was a captain by 1683, but with his patron, Admiral Russell, he was out of the naval service during the reign of James II (1685–8). His Protestant sympathies made him a leading supporter of William of Orange, and ultimately a confidant of the King. He commanded a ship during the Anglo-Dutch defeat at the Battle of Beachy Head in 1690 and was flag captain to Russell in 1692 when he defeated the French decisively at Barfleur and La Hogue. He became a rear-admiral the following year, attended Peter the Great of Russia during his visit to England in 1698, served as a member of the Board of Admiralty and of the Advisory Council of Queen Anne's husband, Prince George, when he was Lord High Admiral. He died in 1710 as a vice-admiral and Gentleman Usher of the Black Rod in Parliament.

Lord Archibald Hamilton was the seventh son of the Duke of Hamilton. His naval career was presumably aided by the fact that his father was active in English as well as Scottish politics, serving on the English Privy Council and presiding over the convention which proclaimed King William in Scotland in 1689. Lord Archibald was commissioned as a lieutenant in 1690. In 1693 he served as first lieutenant of the *Duke* when she was David Mitchell's flagship and was soon promoted to captain. In 1704 he distinguished himself at the capture of Gibraltar and the Battle of Malaga which followed. In 1707 he became commander-in-chief at Portsmouth and then Governor of Jamaica. In 1729, as MP for Lanarkshire, he became a member of the Board of Admiralty, serving until 1738 and again from 1742–6. By the end of the period he was the senior Naval Lord and potentially had great influence. In practice he served during one of the lowest points in the Royal Navy's history, when its lack of imagination was legendary. He made almost no mark on the office, but in his last years the junior Naval Lord was George Anson, who was to carry out much-needed reforms.

Hamilton clearly played a role in encouraging Scottish officers to enter the navy and in developing their careers. In a different context it was said that he needed 'a Scotch colony about him'.[2] Certainly he visited Sir James Lockhart of Carstairs and encouraged his fifth son, known to history as John Lockhart Ross, to join his first ship in 1735.[3] It is probably due to Hamilton's influence that increasing numbers of Scots received their commissions in the navy in the 1730s, with the result that names like Dalziel, Geddes, Douglas, Crawford, Drummond, Murray, Duff and Fergusson appear on the Captains' lists in the 1740s. By 1748, at the end of nine years of war against France and Spain, at least twenty Scots had reached the rank of captain. This was a crucial stage in an officer's career; not only did it guarantee eventual promotion to admiral, but it allowed him to fill his ship with midshipmen and 'servants' from among his friends and family. The Scottish influence in the Royal Navy had reached its take-off point.

The Attractions of a Naval Career

The ancient Scottish aristocracy was in transition, with its political and economic power being slowly reduced. Noble families tended to have numerous children who were now less likely to die from diseases such as smallpox and therefore had to be found suitable marriages, or supported in careers. The landowners themselves sought a higher standard of living, for contact with Europe and England led to much greater expectations, so they improved their lands by making farming more efficient and invested in commerce and industry. At the same time they had less political power than their English equivalents, for they elected sixteen of their number to attend the House of Lords, rather than having seats as of right. Thomas Cochrane, Earl of Dundonald, wrote, 'Of our once extensive ancestral domains, I never inherited a foot. In the course of a century, and before the title descended to our branch, nearly the whole of the family estates had been alienated by losses incurred in support of one generation of the Stuarts, rebellion against another, and mortgages.'[4] It was from this class that most of the successful Scottish naval officers came.

The army was almost always the most obvious choice of career for a young Scots nobleman, especially an eldest son. The profession of arms was the epitome of aristocratic honour, without any taint of trade or commerce. It required much less technical skill than a naval career, and could be picked up or set down rather more easily, as estate and family demanded. Against this, it was much less attractive economically. It required some outlay for the purchase of a uniform and a commission, and for each step in rank up to colonel. An annuity was often needed to maintain an officer in style. The army had little prospect of wealth through prize money.

The established church offered some employment for sons of the aristocracy, but it was intrinsically less suitable than its English counterpart, which had a hierarchy of bishops and archbishops. The law was quite attractive, with hopes of honour as a judge or wealth as an advocate, but it needed a good deal of expensive training and financial support to get a young man started. In contrast, a boy's training in the Royal Navy was largely paid for. When George Elphinstone's family considered whether to put him in the navy a cousin, Charles Gascoigne of the Carron Iron Company, pointed out that 'he will acquire his education and business without expense'.

Commerce was far more attractive in the area round the Clyde ports, with their flourishing trade with the American colonies, than in the slightly decaying ports of the Firth of Forth. This explains why 35 per cent of Scottish officers in the wars of 1793–1815 came from counties round the Forth, compared with only 15 per cent from the Clyde.[5]

The East India Company offered a promising career in either the marine or the land services, and could be helped by the fact that the most powerful Scottish politician of the late eighteenth century, Henry Dundas, was on its Board of Control and keen to advance the interests of his supporters' relations. Some families, such as the Elphinstones, the Duncans, the Murrays of Atholl and the Woods of Largo, had members in both the East India Company and the Royal Navy at the same time.[6] This was possibly a kind of insurance, as one group would prosper in peace, the other in war. After he returned from a voyage in his brother's East Indiaman, George Elphinstone considered whether to return to the Navy or stay in the service of the East India Company.

Earl Marischal, his great-uncle, had no doubt that the royal service offered more honour, if the Company seemed more lucrative; but there would be family debates about it:

> ... my lady will be of opinion to continue in the service of the Company as least dangerous; your father will say that in time of peace there is less danger in the navy as well as more honour – that you will mostly be at home; and that in time of war you will be exposed to fight in the service of the Company, and the ship not fitted for fighting.[7]

Charles Gascoigne compared the two careers and their effect on family interest:

> He will, by the time he could be ready to go a second voyage to the E Indies, have served his 3 years on board a man of war, he will be as well received into that service as if he had been his first voyage in it, and he will be qualified for a lieutenant if ever there should be another naval war, for there [is] no probability of his advancement in this; ... he won't clash interest with Willie [already in the East India Company service], if he inclines to stay on board a man of war.[8]

John Balfour MP was more pessimistic when advising his nephew in 1794. 'I am at a loss to decide between the Navy and the India Company's Sea Service – but am rather inclined to give the preference to the former. Neither can in general be reckoned as better than daily bread.'[9]

A boy's entry to the Navy cost a certain amount of money. In 1758, George Murray's outfit cost £64 3s 9d (£64.19), including a sea chest with padlocks, a sword, books and stationery, clothing and £5 5s 0d (£5.25) for pocket money and travel.[10] This last sum matches the future Lord Keith's statement that he left home with £5 in his pocket in 1761. Thomas Cochrane needed £100 for his whole outfit in 1793, furnished by the Earl of Hopetoun who also had relatives in the navy.[11]

While the Navy gave the prospect of wealth and independence to the sons of the declining aristocracy, it also offered respectability and military glory to families which were rising from the middle class into the nobility. Adam Duncan's great-grandfather had purchased the estate and barony of Lundie in 1675 and their interests were expanding when Adam, a second son, entered the navy in 1746 under the patronage of a relative, Captain Haldane.[12]

Apart for the advantages to the family, the son's inclinations towards the sea life were also important, at a time when the Royal Navy was far more successful than the army, when it offered an

unrivalled chance to travel and was the country's main defence.
Thomas Cochrane entered against the wishes of his father, who
had once served as a naval lieutenant but wanted his son to enter
the army. Basil Hall wrote,

> The holidays, also, which released me from the irksome confinement of
> the High School of Edinburgh, were passed in the country, on a part of
> the rugged sea-coast of Scotland, peculiarly calculated to foster nautical
> propensities. During the weary months which preceded and followed
> these six delicious weeks of liberty, my thoughts, instead of being
> devoted to the comprehension of the abstract rules of grammar . . .
> invariably strayed back to the picturesque and iron-bound shore . . .[13]

George Duff was 'passionately fond of the sea, and was always to be
found among the boats in Banff harbour, near his father's house. At
the age of nine he managed to conceal himself on board a small
merchant ship, and actually sailed to a neighbouring port.' His son
Norwich Duff 'had always shown a strong predilection for the sea.'[14]

Sometimes the entry could be arranged quite quickly. James Gordon
of Aberdeen was surprised when his aunt arrived by coach and 'told us
she came to take me away, as I was to be sent to sea to fight the
French.' He was to leave next morning and was delighted to escape
from his tutor. In bed with his brother, 'We did not sleep much, as you
may suppose; we were building castles in the air till near daylight.' He
was sent to Chatham to join the *Arrogant* of 74 guns under Captain
Whitshed.[15]

Within certain limits, the Royal Navy allowed men of humble origin
to rise to high rank. Perhaps the most notable of the eighteenth century
was John Campbell, the son of a minister from Kirkcudbrightshire
who was in a Scottish collier when it was boarded by a press gang. As
an apprentice he was exempt from impressment, but he was affected
by the tears of the mate of the ship, who had a wife and family.
Campbell volunteered and was accepted in the mate's place, the press
officer saying, 'Aye my lad . . . I would much rather have a boy of
spirit than a blubbering man; come along.' In his previous station, he
might eventually have become master of a collier. In the Royal Navy,
he soon reached the quarterdeck as a master's mate. He took part in
George Anson's great circumnavigation of 1740–4, where he gained
the patronage of Anson himself, and of the future Admiral Augustus
Keppel. He became a captain in 1747 and was flag captain under Sir
Edward Hawke when he defeated the French fleet at Quiberon Bay in
1759. He eventually reached the rank of vice-admiral and served as
governor of Newfoundland.[16]

As in the days of David Mitchell, Scots pressed into the navy occasionally became officers. James Clephan had already served as a mate in a merchant ship before pressing. He eventually became a captain.[17] William Dumbreck had rather a different career. He ran away from home in Edinburgh in 1803 at the age of 14 and joined the *Glatton*, flagship of the Leith station. He moved from one ship to another until fate, and perhaps family influence, took a hand. On reaching the *Ruby*, flagship of Admiral Thornborough, he became a trainee seaman on the mizzen top, then a trainee officer on the quarterdeck. He was transferred to the *Defence* under fellow Scot George Hope, fought at Trafalgar and followed Hope from ship to ship until he was commissioned in 1810.[18]

A Naval Career

A naval career was 'open to the talents' as much as anything else in the eighteenth century. Ability counted for much in the navy and incompetence could not be concealed on the quarterdeck of a ship, where the crew would observe and criticise the seamanship of every officer. But that was far from being the whole story. Family connections were essential for all but a few of exceptional ability. They were needed to start a career which might lead to a commission, to get various steps in rank and to secure the appointments which might lead to fame, rank and fortune.

If the regulations were obeyed, a young man had to spend three years at sea before being rated as a midshipman. This usually meant being borne on the books of a ship as an able seaman or captain's servant, beginning at the age of about thirteen. The latter term was perhaps used more in the sense of an apprentice than a domestic, and in theory a captain was allowed a large number of servants – 4 for every 100 men of the complement, giving 34 in a first-rate of 100 guns with a crew of 850. From 1794 the captain's servant was replaced by the volunteer first class, but the essentials were unchanged. The great majority of these were sons and nephews of the captain's friends and relations, or perhaps the captain's own sons, like Norwich Duff in the *Mars* in 1805. In peacetime in 1787, Admiral Duff tried to get active employment for a young kinsman:

> I applied to two of my Naval Acquaintances who were here but command Guard Ships at Portsmouth for their assistance to get Andrew Duff into a coursing [i.e. cruising] ship, which I am persuaded they will do, and acquaint me when they have success. I did not ask

them to receive him on board one of the ships they command as he could not improve in his profession there. Yesterday I wrote to Mr Andrew Duff setting forth the difficulty of getting preferment in the Navy and earnestly recommending it to him to make choice of some other profession.[19]

The regulations were rarely if ever observed. Thomas Cochrane wrote, 'My uncle, the Hon. Captain, afterwards Admiral Sir Alexander Cochrane . . . had entered my name on the books of various vessels under his command; so that, nominally, I had formed part of the complement of the *Vesuvius, Caroline, La Sophie*, and *Hind*.'[20]

The next step was to become a midshipman, taking a certain amount of responsibility in running the ship, acting as deputy to a watch officer in charge of one of the ship's boats and as a divisional officer responsible for the welfare of a group of seamen. Again a suitable appointment depended on influence as well as ability, especially in peacetime when seagoing ships were in short supply. George Elphinstone served in three successive ships in peacetime between 1763 and 1766, under his kinsmen, Captains George Falconer, Keith Stewart and Charles Douglas.

The naval career was a hard one and some did not take to it. William Balfour, a lad of 'thoughtful cast . . . great naivety' and a temper which rendered him 'very easy of control', found the boredom of blockade service, combined with bullying by his superiors, too much to take. His father wrote back:

> . . . A stout lad of fifteen to talk of quitting his profession for want of activity! You forget that you are just at the age when habits of activity are to be acquired . . . You may trust me that, in every line of life, the man who does not exert himself must continue to be a drudge for others . . . You have now got over the worst of the business you have undertaken. It would be folly therefore as well as meanness to abandon it now. If you go on with spirit and alacrity, in a short time you will find it easy, and I trust honourable as well as profitable . . . When you consider the glory of the British Navy and the still higher pitch to which it is likely to arrive, you must be unwilling to abandon your share of it.

William soon found action at the Battle of St Vincent in 1797, but remained unsuited to a naval career, and in 1799 his father told him, 'You must get on with your profession, or be idle and useless for life. There is no possibility of changing it now; nor, if there were, of your succeeding better in a new one.' With the support of his influential uncle he was commissioned lieutenant in 1801 and became a commander five years later but never made the vital promotion to captain.[21]

After completion of six years at sea and attaining the age of twenty, a young man was entitled to offer himself for examination for the rank of lieutenant. There were many who did not reach this far. Some found one voyage as a captain's servant was enough and wanted no more of the sea. Some succumbed to ill health, such as Andrew Duff of Hatton, who lost his reason after an attack of fever in the West Indies and was unable to manage his own affairs. Thomas Gordon Duff entered the navy in his cousin's ship the *Mars* in 1803 but saw his brother killed at Trafalgar two years later and left soon afterwards, to join the army.[22] Some found it difficult to get a first commission as lieutenant and Alexander Fordyce's friends complained, 'In December 1825, after upwards of twelve years in uninterrupted service afloat, in which he uniformly obtained the highest testimonials from the distinguished officers under whose eye he served, our officer was appointed acting lieutenant.'[23]

Again the regulations could be broken and George Duff was commissioned in 1779 at the age of sixteen instead of twenty.[24] The examination was conducted by three captains. It too might be rigged with the use of influence, though not if the candidate came before Charles Middleton, who would ask, among other questions:

> You are sent in a ship ordered to be fitted out, the Captain not having appeared; the lower masts and bowsprit are in but not rigged: What part of the rigging goes first over the mast heads?
>
> Upon receiving orders to sail from Spithead with a south-east wind, at what time of tide will you begin to unmoor that you may have the advantage of it in plying down to St Helens?
>
> Your sails are still all set; the wind begins to freshen: what sails will you take in first?[25]

On passing, the candidate had to wait for a suitable appointment to an actual ship, and again friends in high places could help. Lord Keith, second in command of the Mediterranean Fleet at the time, was reluctant to promote Midshipman Adam Ross because 'he has no intellect and does not improve one bit'. Political pressure from home was brought to bear, and there was a shortage of officers to command prize ships in the area. Eventually, against his better judgement, Keith put him before a promotion board, which he passed, and Ross became third lieutenant of *El Teresa*, recently taken from the Spanish.[26]

A lieutenant was a commissioned officer by the authority of the King and the Board of Admiralty, so his appointment was much less under the control of an individual captain. It is significant that ships with Scottish captains, such as the *Defence* under Captain George Johnstone Hope at Trafalgar, had a much higher proportion of Scottish midshipmen and volunteers than lieutenants.[27] A lieutenant's appointment and further promotion were controlled by the Admiralty Board in London, unless he was on a foreign station such as the Mediterranean or West Indies, where the local commander-in-chief was all-powerful. In either case he had to attract the attention of authority. From the 1750s, one route was to serve as first lieutenant of a ship which distinguished herself in battle. James Walker of Fife was in the frigate *Niger* at the battle of the Glorious First of June in 1794 and was immediately promoted to commander. This, however, was slow and uncertain, for it took time to establish enough seniority to become first lieutenant, and even then there was no guarantee of action. A much quicker route was to serve on the flagship of an overseas commander-in-chief, where one would be under the eye of the admiral. Thus George Elphinstone joined in the *Trident*, flagship of Admiral Peter Dennis in the Mediterranean in 1771, and was promoted commander in 1772.[28] As such he was eligible to command a small warship of less than 20 guns.

Again, there were many officers who stuck at lieutenant. James Ogilvie Dalgleish from Fife served under seven captains, six of whom were Scots including Charles Hope, but got no promotion. He was a distant cousin of Captain James Dalgleish but, he complained, 'he has no other relatives of his own in the service.'[29] Many died, like Henry Clerk, son of Sir John Clerk of Penicuik, who succumbed to a 'lingring distemper' in the East Indies at the age of twenty-seven in 1745, to the great grief of his family.

Beyond commander, the next stage, and in many ways the most important one for an ambitious officer, was the rank of captain, which was achieved rather like the promotion to commander, by attracting the attention of the authorities by distinguished service or patronage. The rest of an officer's career was dominated by the date on which he took up his first command as a full or 'post' captain. His seniority in relation to other captains and his promotion through the various grades of admiral would be according to that date, and the order of seniority was immutable unless an officer died or was retired as a 'yellow' admiral. A captain had patronage of his own – he had almost absolute power over his ship and could fill the midshipmen's and servants' berths with the sons of his own friends and relations.

After fifteen or twenty years a captain could expect to be promoted to the lowest grade of flag rank, rear-admiral of the blue. He was likely to command a squadron under a commander-in-chief in wartime, but he had comparatively little patronage at this stage. The Earl of Northesk was third-in-command at Trafalgar, and second-in-command under Collingwood after Nelson's death, but he is almost unknown to history. It is significant that there was much less Scottish influence aboard his flagship, the 100-gun *Britannia,* than in the ships with Scottish captains, the *Defence, Mars* and *Swiftsure.*[30]

An admiral rose through the ranks of rear-admiral of the white and red, to become a vice-admiral of the blue, then went through the same process until he became a full admiral and, if he lived long enough, he became the highest-ranking officer in the navy as Admiral of the Fleet. At some stage, perhaps as a vice-admiral, an officer would become senior enough to be appointed a commander-in-chief, when his large-scale patronage would begin. Again, his appointment itself could be helped by influence. Admiral Robert Duff describes an interview with Lord Sandwich, the First Lord of the Admiralty, in 1777:

> On my arrival here, his Lordship told me I might have the command at Plymouth, or change with Admiral Graves for the Mediterranean Command, and added if I changed Commands with Admiral Graves, he would appoint Mr Leslie my First Lieutenant and soon give me an opportunity to make him a captain. The Mediterranean being a more honourable command than and on many accounts more eligible than Plymouth, joined to the prospect of making my friend Leslie a Captain, made me, with a good grace, agree to his Lordship's proposal.[31]

Duff is vague about what made the Mediterranean Command 'more eligible', but there can be little doubt that he was thinking of prize money. As an officer rose in rank, his entitlement to prize money rose too. When an enemy merchantman or warship was captured, it and its cargo were sold by auction and the value was divided, very unequally, among the officers and crews of every ship involved in the capture, as well as the admirals in ultimate command of the ships. According to the rules, the crew of each ship, below the rank of petty officer, had one-quarter of the value between them. Midshipmen, petty officers and sergeants of marines had an eighth. Warrant officers such as boatswains and carpenters had an eighth and lieutenants shared another eighth. The real money began with the captains – each had a full quarter share to himself, while the admiral commanding the station had an eighth for each ship captured, whether he was present or not. It was prize money, above all, that made the naval career unique. It allowed an officer to make large sums of money from a small initial outlay by his family, while at the same time faithfully serving king and country.

When Earl Marischal weighed up the relative advantages of the Royal Navy and the East India Company in 1769, he was perhaps a little pessimistic about the money to be made in a successful naval career. He could not be expected to foresee the great expansion in the Royal Navy over future decades, from 360 ships in 1771 to more than 1,000 in 1812. Nor could he predict that in the forty years after 1775, Britain would be at war for twenty-eight. The wars brought death and injury to many, from enemy action, accident and most often from disease. For the survivors there were plenty of opportunities for promotion, glory and prize money. Scottish officers, as it turned out, were well placed to take advantage of this. It was no coincidence that Marischal's great-nephew, George Elphinstone, Lord Keith, became one of the richest men in the navy, making between £100,000 and £200,000 in prize money. He built a new family seat at Tulliallan, while Admiral Robert Duff used his prize money to buy Fetteresso, the former seat of the Earls Marischal.

The End of Jacobitism

To a certain extent the Scottish influx into the Royal Navy represented a reconciliation between the Jacobites and the rest of the community. In the early stages the issue had caused much division in the landed families who provided officers for the navy. One of the pre-Union Scottish officers, Kenneth Sutherland, Lord Duffus, was an eldest son who, unusually, joined the navy; his 'genius . . . leading him to a seafaring life, he soon acquired such great knowledge and skill in maritime affairs.' In 1715 he took part in the Jacobite rebellion, fled, was captured in Hamburg and then released, eventually taking service under the Czar of Russia, where he prospered.[32]

The family of the Duke of Hamilton was split. The seventh son, Lord Archibald, served in the navy and as Governor of Jamaica during the 1708 and 1715 rebellions, while his eldest brother, who succeeded as Duke in 1694, was an active Jacobite who was imprisoned in 1708. The Atholls of Tullibardine also had their divisions. Lord George Murray fought for the rebels in 1715, 1719 and 1745 while his father, the first Duke, was strongly suspected of Jacobite sympathies. But Lord Frederick Murray, another son, entered the Royal Navy about 1728 and George Murray, son of the second Duke, joined in 1758 and eventually became a vice-admiral. In the Wemyss family, the Honourable James was commissioned as a lieutenant in 1745, the same year as his cousin Lord Elcho took part in the rebellion as commander of Prince Charles's life-guards.

For the Elphinstones, the Royal Navy offered a chance to regenerate the family fortunes. They were closely related to Lords Marischal and Keith who had led the 1715 and 1719 rebellions and had been in exile ever since. But Marischal, the most intelligent of the Jacobite leaders, realised that the cause was lost and made his peace with the British government. George Keith Elphinstone was able to make a distinguished career with Marischal's active encouragement.

Of course many Scots had no sympathy with the Jacobites, and some of the first Scottish officers were strongly anti-Jacobite to begin with. Sir John Clerk of Penicuik, who had helped negotiate the Treaty of 1707, fathered two naval officers as well as the naval tactician John Clerk of Eldin. Captains Fergusson from Aberdeenshire and Duff from Banff first made their reputations in the hunt for Prince Charles in 1746, where both gained a reputation for cruel treatment of the Highlanders.

There is no sign that Highlanders flocked to become naval officers even after the defeat of Jacobitism, though they joined the Highland regiments of the army in great numbers. It seems that even the natives of the Western Isles had not enough tradition of long-distance seamanship to want to sail across the oceans.

Nautical Education

One risk in a naval career was that a boy's formal education might end around the age of thirteen when he joined his first ship, for naval schoolmasters were few, and mostly ill-qualified. This was of concern to Scottish parents. It could be partly remedied by sending the boy to the Royal Naval College at Portsmouth for two years, like young George Murray in 1756; but most parents were aware that these years delayed the boy's entry to the real navy, and the beginning of his seniority.

Another remedy, if the family was rich enough, was to employ private tutors on board ship or to supplement the wages of a naval instructor to attract a better candidate. Vice-Admiral George Murray tried to persuade his brother, the Duke of Atholl, to send his son to join him in 1795, pointing out that there would never be a better opportunity for advancement. The admiral, as commander-in-chief in Halifax, had the power to promote his subordinates up to captain. Furthermore, the flagship offered educational facilities for a young man. 'Every care should be taken of him, & every attention shown him, and I have a schoolmaster on board (Moncur), who was both in Fintry's and Lintrose's families, where he gave intire satisfaction, who I would employ intirely about him, I therefor beg (if you still intend he should follow the sea) that you will send him to me by the first ship of war that is sent to me.'[33] But it was not to be, and the young man never joined the navy.

Young James Gordon was sent to school ashore at Rochester while his ship, the *Arrogant*, was fitting out at Chatham and later, on transfer to the *Goliath* in 1797, he benefited from the services of a schoolmaster named Strachan.[34] George Duff took good care of the education of his son Norwich in the *Mars* in 1805. He employed a Mr Dalrymple as purser and instructor and the latter wrote to the boy's mother,

> Norwich and all the young gentlemen are making proficiency. We have got an excellent globe which we shall study occasionally; every morning . . . a certain number of words. Learn English grammar once a week, and in the evening read geography, history, etc, after having pored over their navigation, French, arithmetic, etc, the greater part of the day.[35]

The Elphinstone family was much more frugal and refused to fund a short course in navigation for young George Keith before he went to sea in 1761: 'T'would be monstrous to throw away 5 guineas for his learning navigation for 14 days.' During 1764 he asked his father for money to pay the schoolmaster of the *Lively* 'for completing me in some parts of navigation, which I could not do the service without.'[36] A ship on active service might work its midshipmen too hard to leave time for education. As George Murray wrote in 1759, 'I have not so much time to spair as you immagin, for the midshipmen on board this ship are at watch & watch, consequently we must be 12 hours out of the 24 on deck, & we must necessarily have 8 hours sleep, & we have but 4 hours left for our malles & other necessary things.'[37]

Very few English officers ever attended university, but some Scots did; for Scottish students tended to be much younger than their English counterparts and W. G. Rutherford, who was later to command the *Swiftsure* at Trafalgar, attended both Edinburgh and St Andrews Universities before entering the navy as a boy in 1764.[38] Rather later in life, Thomas Cochrane was a 27-year-old commander, rich from prize money, when he attended Edinburgh University during the Peace of Amiens from 1802 to 1803.

A naval career allowed officers to travel and to pursue scientific interests, whether on their own behalf or for their families. In 1769

Captain George Murray sent a parcel to his brother, the Duke of Atholl, containing 'two buffulow skins, (the sort of cattle they have on the banks of the Missisippy,) one bear skin from the same place, a Tiger's skin, & a belt and garters the Indians in that part of the world wear.' To the Duchess he sent 'a red Virginian nightingale, 3 Blue birds, 3 Nonparrells, & a rice bird. Some of them sing very well.'[39]

Leaving aside problems with spelling, not all officers were well educated. Lieutenant Andrew Barclay, commissioned just after Trafalgar, wrote in the 1840s, 'When I write my best I am only a poor scribe.'[40]

The Influence of Dundas

Though he was a civilian who rarely went to sea, Henry Dundas had more influence on the Scottish entry to the Royal Navy than anyone else. Trained as a lawyer in Edinburgh, he first entered Parliament in 1774 and within a few years he had built up an unparalleled power base in Scotland. Manipulating an electoral system which was even more archaic and ramshackle than that of England, he controlled elections in most of the Scottish burghs, with thirty-six out of forty-five members under his influence at his peak in 1796. William Pitt the Younger became Prime Minister in 1783 and Dundas was his right hand man over the next quarter-century. But he was more than a political boss; he was Secretary of State for War during the wars with Revolutionary France which began in 1793 and sometimes showed strategic vision. In 1798, for example, while Nelson was searching the Mediterranean for Napoleon's expeditionary force, Dundas was the first in Britain to guess that they were going to Egypt, though it was too late to get a message to Nelson. But mostly Dundas's strategic efforts were highly criticised for dispersing British forces in irrelevant expeditions to the West Indies.

Dundas's control of the Scottish electorate was sustained by his ability to deliver jobs for the sons and nephews of the voters. One field for this was the East India Company, in which he became a member of the Board of Control in 1784, and Chairman from 1793 to 1801. As the Revd Sydney Smith put it, 'As long as he is in office the Scotch may beget younger sons with the most perfect impunity. He sends them by loads to the East Indies, and all over the world.'[41] For all that, he had many enemies in Scotland, for he led the repression of the radicals, such as Thomas Muir, in the aftermath of the French Revolution. His influence in naval affairs began in 1782 when he became Treasurer of the Navy. Though this was not a post which carried a great deal of patronage in itself, he was generally believed to be keen to advance young Scotsmen – a reputation which he tried to live down. When John Barrow was appointed Second Secretary of the Admiralty in 1804, Dundas said to him, 'By the way, I hope you are not a Scotchman?' When Barrow replied that he was from Northumberland, Dundas said, 'Mr Pitt and I have been so much taunted for giving away all the good things to Scotchmen that I am very glad, on the present occasion, to have selected an Englishman.'[42] Dundas was related to several of the leading Scots in the navy – a cousin of Charles Middleton of the Navy Board and Admiralty, the uncle of Adam Duncan's wife and himself married to the cousin of Captain George Johnstone Hope. The name of Dundas was well known in the navy, but this caused confusion – Captain Hon. George Heneage Lawrence Dundas came from a different branch of the family which often found itself in opposition to the 'Dundas despotism' in Parliament.

In 1804 Pitt returned to power after a three-year break and Dundas, now Viscount Melville, was appointed First Lord of the Admiralty and took control of the navy. But opposition to him within the party was growing and his past began to catch up with him. In a move which was largely political, he became the last person in British history to be impeached, for alleged maladministration while Treasurer of the Navy. His fellow Scot, Admiral Keith, was an ally of the Prince of Wales's opposition and wrote:

> The Prince thinks I am disinclined to vote against Lord Melville. I have no such feeling. Myself and my family have met with nothing in that quarter but opposition. He opposed me in Dunbartonshire and Stirlingshire. My nephew's last election cost £3000 against Lord M's son-in-law . . . I do not pretend to say I should not have had an unpleasant sensation in giving a vote so personal against one whom I had spent pleasant days in youth and had many a hard bout with, but there was no shadow for defence in my mind.[43]

Melville was forced from office in May 1805 after less than a year, to be succeeded by his cousin Charles Middleton, now Lord Barham, an administrator of a very different stamp.

Dundas's fall certainly did not signal the end of his family influence in naval affairs. On the contrary, his son Robert, now the second Viscount Melville, became First Lord of the Admiralty in 1812 and remained in the post, with a short gap, until 1830. Soon the Admiralty Board itself began to take on a Scottish complexion. Apart from the First Lord himself, the eight members included his cousin William Dundas, Rear-Admiral George Johnstone Hope of the Hopetoun family into which Henry Dundas had married in 1793, and Sir George Warrender of Haddington. Yet the second Viscount had much less dynamism and skill than his father and remained 'a mere respectable head of department', who did less than might have been expected to advance the interests of the 'Scotch legion' in the navy, the East India Company and in politics.[44] Indeed influence at the Admiralty could even be a disadvantage to an officer on a foreign station, where the commander-in-chief was all-important. Patrick Deuchar was sent to the West Indies in 1812, just as Melville was appointed, but the admiral had 'a great dislike to promote Admiralty mids till they died, of which there were several instances'. He spent six months at the head of the list of passed midshipmen but had to be transferred home to get his commission in 1813.[45]

Scottish Ships

Only three ships were built in Scotland in the days of the sailing navy, all very small, but some ships found a Scottish identity in a different way. When George Duff was appointed to the frigate *Glenmore* in 1795, she became perhaps the most Scottish ship ever in the Royal Navy. Its name apart, the ship was actually built from fir timber from the Great Glen, for shortage of English and Baltic oak had forced the navy to accept materials that it believed, with some justice, to be inferior. The Scottish captain had many countrymen appointed to his ship. An English lieutenant, William Dillon, commented, 'the officers appeared a nice set of gentlemen, but, the captain being a Scot, they were all, nearly, from the same country, so I found myself a sort of lonely person among them.' The Scots soon lived up to their reputation for meanness. 'We were invited to dine in rotation with our captain, at whose table the strictest frugality prevailed . . . The instant the quantity allowed was expended we rose, and the party broke up . . . my messmates lived on the ship's provisions. Salt pork and beef would not renovate me after all my fatigues.' When he bought some mutton privately, 'My messmates at first declined partaking of any. But soon it became evident that they were ashamed of not keeping a better table. They then agreed to purchase stock, helped themselves to my mutton, and offered to take the others off my hands.'[46] Eventually Dillon had himself transferred to a more congenial ship.

Another Englishman, Thomas Huskisson, had a very different experience in 1803 as a midshipman on board the *Revenge*, of 74 guns. He was pleased to serve under Captain George Johnstone Hope at the Battle of Trafalgar in 1805. 'No captain ever left his ship more esteemed by

both the officers and men than our excellent captain. In addition to the
best qualifications as a seaman, navigator and officer, he had a pecu-
liarly gentlemanly manner of attaching everyone to him.'[47] About half
the masters' mates and midshipmen were Scottish, with names such as
Buchanan, Grieve, Hope-Watson and Napier,[48] but Huskisson did not
mind: 'My messmates were most of them from Scotland – good-
humoured, pleasant young men amongst who I scarcely recollect anything like discord. We had at first starting one black sheep amongst us, a
native of Sheerness . . . but we got rid of him at the end of our third
cruise.' Not all Scots earned Huskisson's approval. When the captain of
the sloop *Beagle* cheated the *Defence* out of some prize money, he
commented, 'He outwitted our captain, who was a Scotsman too, but
there was a wide difference between the two. Our captain would not for
a thousand times the amount of prize money have resorted to the
quibbles to defraud a brother officer of his rightful share, but his
countryman had no such conscientious scruples.'[49]

The Scottish Identity in the Navy

There was never any prospect of a permanent Scottish part of the
Royal Navy, in the sense that the Scottish regiments form a very
distinct portion of the British Army. A regiment is a body of men and
simple administrative action can ensure that they stay together and are
succeeded by men of similar background. But a navy is centred round
its ships, and these have no permanent existence. Each will need long-
term repairs during its career, or it will be laid up in peacetime, when
its officers and crew will be dispersed. Eventually it will sink or be
scrapped and its men will be paid off or transferred to other ships. A
captain was allowed to take a certain number of followers (eighty for a
first-rate, ten for a sixth-rate) on his transfer from one ship to another
but that was not enough to ensure continuity over more than a few
years. Despite the activities of captains like George Duff, the Scots
were eventually merged into the mainstream of the Royal Navy. The
only thing which might have changed this would have been the
creation of a major Scottish naval base, which would have recruited
local people and encouraged others to settle their families nearby. This
did not happen until the twentieth century, when the process was
incomplete and too late.

The naval service creates mobility by its very nature, and it is not
surprising to find that many families which began as Scottish eventually moved to areas near the Royal Dockyards in the south of
England. Charles Middleton was the son of a merchant captain from

Leith, but spent most of his later career in London, in the offices of the Navy Board and the Admiralty. As he became wealthier he bought an estate at Barham in Kent and when he was ennobled he took his title from it. Later, naval officers were born to Scottish families in the dockyard areas. Sir Richard Strachan was from a family in the north of Scotland, but was born in Devonshire. John Dick, 'representative of an ancient family of that name, long settled in Braid, in Mid-Lothian', was born near Chatham.[50]

Others tried harder to maintain their Scottish roots. The aristocrats felt a natural pull back to their homeland. Even if they did not inherit the family estates themselves, they bought land in Scotland when they became rich from prize money, as did George Elphinstone and Robert Duff. At the other end of the social scale, some maintained their Scottish identity by their accents. John Campbell, a man of humble origin, was suggested as the model for a stage character of the time, Sir Archy McSarcasm. When offered a knighthood by Lord Anson he replied, 'Troth, my lord, I ken nae use that will be to me.' When Anson suggested his wife might like it, Campbell remarked, 'Weel then, His Majesty may knight her if he pleases.'[51] At the Battle of Camperdown in 1797, Captain John Inglis of the *Belliqueux* became confused by Admiral Duncan's signals and shouted to his helmsman, 'Damn! Up wi' the hel-lem and gang into the middle o' it.'

Though the Scottish representation was strong by the end of the eighteenth century, it was not numerically overwhelming. It is suggested that Scotland provided around 1,400 commissioned officers during this period out of a total of about 10,500 from Britain and the empire. It provided an estimated 1.22 officers per 10,000 of population during the wars of 1793–1815, which is very close to the English figure of 1.20 and much higher than Wales's 0.60. Scotland provided about a fifth the number of officers supplied by England, very much in keeping with her population as measured by the census of 1801. Fife was the most prolific county and contributed 3.09 officers per 10,000 of population, considerably higher than any English county except the dockyard areas of Devonshire, Cornwall, Kent and Hampshire. Since Scotland did not have the natural recruiting advantage that these dockyards offered, it can be argued that the country was well represented in the officer corps.[52]

The Duffs: a Scottish Naval Dynasty

Robert Duff was one of the numerous relatives of the Earl of Fife. In later years he claimed that his entry to the navy was due to the benevolence of the Earl of Bute, and in 1761 he sent his lordship a present of a pipe of Madeira, two turtles and a box of sweetmeats from the West Indies.[53] He was commissioned as a lieutenant in 1739 and promoted to commander in 1744, taking charge of the bomb-vessel *Terror,* in which he helped suppress the 1745 rebellion on both the east and west coasts. Despite the allegations of cruelty in his campaign against the Jacobites Robert Duff showed his humanity when he visited the new naval hospital at Haslar in 1755 and accused the contractors of disregarding the complaints of the seamen.[54]

In 1762 Robert Duff had a dispute with Admiral Rodney, who wanted to take over his ship as his flagship, and put in his own flag captain. Duff, typically, felt he had a property right over the ship in which he had invested money and influence. The *Foudroyant* was one of the finest ships in the fleet and he had gone to a good deal of trouble in fitting and manning her. The transfer would

> injure his majesty's service by putting a stop to the emulation there is amongst the captains to get their ships well manned and disciplined, and by creating a reluctance in officers to go from under the eye or immediate power of the Admiralty into distant services, when they find themselves thus liable to be turned from an eligible ship, which at considerable expense to themselves and at great pains and troubles they have got well manned and disciplined, into such ships as the commanding officer abroad may think proper to order them.[55]

Rodney got the ship and Duff was sent home. He became a rear-admiral in 1775 and commander-in-chief in the Mediterranean two years later, co-operating with the army when the Spanish besieged Gibraltar. He retired in 1780 and died in 1787.

George Duff took up the family's naval mantle at the age of thirteen when he joined his great-uncle Robert in the *Panther* off Gibraltar in 1777. The American War of Independence was at its height and young George was in action thirteen times in the next six years, culminating in the Battle of the Saintes in the West Indies in 1782. He was already a lieutenant, having been commissioned at sixteen, with less than three years' service, against all the regulations. With the patronage of Henry Dundas as well as the Earl of Fife, he was promoted commander in peacetime in 1790. He sought further advancement in order to marry his childhood sweetheart, Sophie Dirom. His father wrote to the Earl, 'Miss Dirom's friends are most desirous to get George forward, with this view they have solicite the Duke and Duchess of Gordon who have wrote favourably of him, the Duke to Lord Chatham [First Lord of the Admiralty], the Duchess to Mr Dundas, the consequences will in time appear, but Im not sanguine, the young ladys friends are.'[56] The marriage took place in 1791 and George was promoted in 1793. The only son, Norwich, was born in 1792.

In 1805 the boy, just short of his thirteenth birthday, sailed from Portsmouth to join his father's ship, the 74-gun *Mars,* in Lord Nelson's fleet off Cadiz. A few weeks later the ship went into action at Trafalgar, with Captain Duff on the quarterdeck as his duty demanded, while his son had been found slightly safer duties below deck. In the middle of the mêlée, the ship was surrounded and the action is described by Midshipman Robinson from Banff:

> Captain Duff walked about with steady fortitude and said, 'My God, what shall we do, here is a Spanish three-decker raking us ahead, a French one under the stern.' In a few minutes our poop was totaly cleared, the quarter-deck and forcastle nearly the same and myself and three men left alive. It was then the gallant Captain fell. I saw him fall. His head and neck were taken entirely off his body, when the men heard it, they held his body up and gave three cheers to show they were not discouraged by it, and they returned to their guns.

Young Norwich Duff had the task of writing to break the news to his mother, perhaps with the help of Captain Blackwood who took his welfare in hand:

> My Dear Mama,
>
>   You cannot possibly imagine how unwilling I am to begin this melancholy letter. However as you must unavoidably hear of the fate of dear Papa, I write these few lines to request you to bear it as patiently as you can. He died like a hero, having gallantly led his ship into action.[57]

Despite this trauma, Norwich went on to become a vice-admiral. The family naval connection remained into the twentieth century; one member was captain of a cruiser in the First World War and another commanded a division of battleships at Jutland.

The Four Leading Scots

Scotland produced four of the leading figures in the Royal Navy during the Napoleonic Wars, each very different in his style and achievements. Adam Duncan was a battle commander. Charles Middleton, Lord Barham, was a naval reformer who made the strategic dispositions which led to Nelson's victory at Trafalgar. George Elphinstone, Lord Keith, was an expert in amphibious warfare and a fleet administrator, and Thomas Cochrane, Earl of Dundonald, fought the greatest frigate action ever and became the model for more than one of the heroes of modern naval fiction.

Adam Duncan was born in Dundee in 1731 and entered the navy in 1746, serving under Robert Duff in the hunt for Prince Charles. He was taken up by the future admiral Augustus Keppel and distinguished himself at the capture of Havana in 1762. After that his career was much interrupted, with long periods of half-pay and bouts of sickness. In 1795, as a vice-admiral, he took charge of the North Sea Fleet and in May 1797, while a great mutiny was in progress at the Nore, he was obliged to confront the rebels in his own ship, the *Adamant*:

> My lads, I am not in the smallest degree apprehensive of any violent measure you may have in contemplation; though I assure you I would much rather acquire your love than incur your fear, I will with my own hand put to death the first man who shall display the slightest sign of rebellious conduct.

He asked if any man was prepared to dispute this. One came forward and Duncan, six feet four inches in height and of 'manly and athletic form', grabbed him by the collar, held him over the side of the ship and said to the crew, 'My lads, look at this fellow, he who dares to deprive me of the command of the fleet!' The mutiny on the *Adamant* was soon settled, though it was several weeks before the rest of the fleet at the Nore returned to duty.[58]

In October of that year, Duncan was at Yarmouth with his fleet when he received news that the Dutch fleet from the Texel was out. By the 11th he was off the Dutch coast with sixteen small and obsolescent ships of the line and supporting frigates – very much the 'second team' of the navy, which had heavy commitments elsewhere. An equal number of Dutch ships were sighted close inshore near the village of Kamperduin or 'Camperdown' and Duncan, ignoring the navigational dangers of the shallow waters and the conventional naval tactics of past decades, ordered his fleet into a headlong attack in two divisions. A bloody battle ensued, in which eleven Dutch ships of the line were captured. It was an immense boost to British morale when the war was going badly elsewhere. It was the most decisive naval victory of the age so far and a step towards the principle, usually attributed to Nelson, of annihilating the enemy. There was national rejoicing, Duncan was made a viscount, was showered with gifts from corporations and guilds, and Parliament voted him a pension of £2,000. He bought the estate of Camperdown near Dundee and died in 1804.

In his attack at Camperdown, Duncan may or may not have been influenced by another Scot, John Clerk of Eldin. Clerk claimed that he had been forbidden to join the navy as a youth, because the family had already suffered too many losses by land and sea. Instead he became a wealthy merchant and dilettante. During the American War he was struck by the fact that British ships were universally successful in single-ship actions, but that fleets almost invariably failed to bring the enemy to action. He published the first edition of his *Essay on Naval Tactics* in 1782, based on careful study and communication with naval officers among his friends and family. He described a dozen encounters in recent wars which had proved indecisive, and advocated a new principle of attack from windward and breaking the enemy line. He and his supporters were elated when Admiral Rodney won the Battle of the Saintes soon afterwards, apparently using Clerk's principles. This began a long controversy, in which the more extreme claims of Clerk's friends were refuted, but there is no doubt that Clerk's work had much influence on the navy, for decisive battle became the norm in the next war, from 1793 to 1802. Of his effect on Camperdown, the *Edinburgh Evening Courant* reported,

> It is a most remarkable instance in the history of Admiral Duncan that he lived himself to illustrate the truth of the doctrine of his early friend, Mr Clerk, whose system of naval tactics he was the first to patronise, and to recommend to the British Navy.[59]

Of his influence on Nelson, Captain Hardy wrote,

> Our departed friend, Lord Nelson, read Mr Clerk's works with great attention and frequently expressed his approbation of them in the fullest manner; he also recommended all the captains to read them with attention, and said that many good hints might be taken from them. He most approved of the attack from to-windward, and considered breaking through the enemy's line absolutely necessary to obtain a great victory.[60]

Charles Middleton, Lord Barham, had a very different career from Adam Duncan. His sea service was undistinguished but he made his name during a long period of service in the central administration of the navy. In 1778, at the age of fifty-one, he was appointed Controller of the Navy on the death of Maurice Suckling, Nelson's uncle and patron. As such he was a member of the Navy Board which managed the Royal Dockyards, placed contracts for shipbuilding and naval stores and was in charge of the administrative and technical aspects of the navy. During the next few years Middleton worked hard to maintain the fleet and send more and more ships to sea, as France, Spain and the Netherlands joined the war against Britain in support of the American colonists.

In the navy's most difficult period of the century, he was largely responsible for two innovations which helped to swing the balance of the war. He campaigned for the bottoms of all the ships in the fleet to be covered with copper sheathing, to protect them from weed and ship-worm and allow them to spend far more time at sea between dry-docking. He was also instrumental in having the carronade adopted by the navy. This was a powerful, short-range gun developed at the Carron Iron Works near Falkirk, which was able to add great power to the fleet's broadsides if used properly. After the war ended in 1783 Middleton devoted his attentions to reform in the dockyards, rooting out corruption and improving efficiency. He was always a difficult subordinate, bombarding his superiors with unwanted advice, and in 1790 he resigned, claiming that the government was not supporting his reforms. In 1794 he joined the Board of Admiralty but resigned again the following year after a dispute with the First Lord, Earl Spencer.

In May 1805, after the impeachment of his cousin Lord Melville, he was chosen by William Pitt to be First Lord of the Admiralty and head of the navy during another hour of danger, and was created Lord Barham. As such he made the dispositions when the French fleet, pursued by Nelson, left the Mediterranean on a diversionary cruise to the West Indies. It was stopped by Sir Robert Calder in an indecisive action off Brest in July and utterly defeated by Nelson off Cape Trafalgar in October. When the news finally reached London in the early hours of 6 November, the 79-year-old was wakened from his bed and immediately had it sent on to the King, the Prime Minister and the newspapers. He retired three months later on the death of Pitt and died himself in 1812.

George Keith Elphinstone first attracted notice as a 34-year-old captain in 1780 at the siege of Charleston, South Carolina, when he led a force of seamen and marines over difficult terrain. This helped establish his future career, for his unique eye for land and sea topography made him the navy's greatest expert in amphibious warfare. In 1795, as a vice-admiral, he captured the Cape of Good Hope from the Dutch and first showed his remarkable ability to make money. By a quirk in the prize system he also benefited from the capture of Dutch possessions in the Far East, because the ships which did it were technically under his command, though he was several thousand miles away. He was created a peer and was henceforward

known as Lord Keith. In 1799 he went to the Mediterranean under St
Vincent, but failed to bring the French and Spanish force under
Admiral Bruix to battle, partly due to interference from St Vincent
and lack of co-operation by his subordinate, Lord Nelson. He
succeeded to the Mediterranean command in 1800, over the head
of Nelson, who was deeply embroiled in Neapolitan affairs and
involved with Lady Hamilton. In October he joined with the Scottish
general Sir Ralph Abercrombie for an attack on Cadiz, which was
never executed due to Keith's lack of faith in the project. The partner-
ship was far more successful in Egypt in 1801, when a force landed
against strong French opposition and eventually took the country. But
all the gains of the war were soon handed back when the Peace of
Amiens was signed.

With the renewal of war in 1803, Keith took command of the North
Sea Fleet, with responsibility for defending the British coast from
halfway up the English Channel to the north of Scotland, including all
the most likely sites for a French invasion. Forces under his command
blockaded the invasion ports of Boulogne and Vlissingen and experimented with futuristic forms of warfare such as submarines, rockets
and aerial bombardment by balloon. Though the invasion was never
launched, Keith's forces would almost certainly have defeated the
French barges had they ventured out. In 1812, after five years on half-
pay, he accepted command of the Channel Fleet, with responsibilities
reaching as far as the north coast of Spain, where his forces carried out
a brilliant campaign supported by guerrillas.

In a navy and an epoch which is rich with heroes, Thomas
Cochrane, Earl of Dundonald, has a claim to be the most dashing
of all. In 1800 he was promoted commander by Lord Keith, but
complained that the influence of the admiral's secretary prevented him
getting a crack ship. Instead he was given the tiny *Speedy*, an aged brig
of 14 guns. He launched a brilliant campaign against enemy shipping
in the Mediterranean, taking the Spanish frigate *Gamo*, a ship with
four times the gun power and crew of his own, in April 1801. He was
captured himself by a French fleet under Admiral Linois three months
later, but released.

He continued to agitate for promotion to post-captain, which he
believed the capture of the *Gamo* entitled him to, but was blocked by
the First Lord of the Admiralty, Lord St Vincent. On the resumption of
war in 1803 he was sent on fishery-protection duties off Orkney in the
collier *Arab*, which he claimed sailed like a haystack. When Melville
came to the Admiralty he was given command of a fine frigate, the
Pallas, in which he cruised off the Azores and captured £132,000

worth of Spanish treasure. He continued his success in the *Impérieuse* of 38 guns, raiding French forces in the north-east of Spain. With his legendary success in winning prize money, Cochrane rarely needed press gangs to man his ships. One of his recruiting posters for the *Pallas* promised treasure from Spanish galleons and claimed, 'None need apply, but SEAMEN, or stout hands, able to rouse about the Field Pieces, and carry a hundred weight of PEWTER without stopping, at least three miles.'[61]

Meanwhile Cochrane had become disgusted with the corruption he found in the navy, especially in the prize-courts. He was elected Radical MP for Honiton in 1806 and for Westminster the following year. In 1808 he put forward plans for attacking the French fleet in Basque Roads using rockets invented by William Congreve. The attack failed and Cochrane claimed that he had not been fully supported by his superior, Lord Gambier. In 1814 he was convicted, probably unjustly, of a stock exchange fraud by spreading false rumours of peace with France. He was expelled from the navy, though re-elected by the voters of Westminster. In 1817, as Chile struggled for independence from Spain, Cochrane took command of their infant navy. He served the Brazilians for a few years and in 1827 he led the Greek Navy in the country's war of independence, using the first steam warship, the *Karteria*, against the Turks. In 1832 he cleared his name and was reinstated in the navy with the rank of rear-admiral. He commanded the North American station in 1848 and proposed new methods to attack the Russians during the Crimean War of 1854–6. He died in 1860 at the age of eighty-five.

The Nelson Legend

Horatio Nelson's rise to fame began in 1797, when he anticipated orders and left the line in the Battle of St Vincent, to win the battle. His reputation was boosted with the Battle of the Nile in 1798 and the attack at Copenhagen in 1801 when he famously put his telescope to his blind eye. His career ended with his victory and heroic death at Trafalgar in 1805.

To a modern Scot, Nelson has certain flaws as a national hero. It is not just that he displaced Adam Duncan as the most successful commander of the age, less than a year after Camperdown. Nelson never set foot in Scotland during a career which took in most of the seas of the world. His most famous signal was 'England expects that every man will do his duty', though that was not his first idea. He wanted to send 'Nelson confides . . .' and it was his signal officer, a

Cornishman, who suggested the changes in order to use fewer flags.

At the time however, his victories were celebrated in Scotland as much as elsewhere, and his death at Trafalgar in 1805 was commemorated. The news first reached Glasgow on Saturday, 9 November, nearly three weeks after the battle. The volunteers and militia fired a *feu de joie* on Glasgow Green, though all were aware of the ambiguous nature of the celebrations. The City Council sent an address to the King, concluding that 'To this part of your Majesty's empire in particular, the annihilation of that proud fleet which so recently threatened the devastation of our colonial possessions in the West Indies is an event singularly interesting . . .'[62] The town was illuminated and most citizens put lights in their windows. Some went further and displayed 'transparencies', like Cleland and Jack's upholstery warehouse and Mr Denholm's Academy in Argyle Street:

> In the east window was an urn, encircled with a wreath of laurel leaves referring to the death of the Hero. From the top of the urn arose a flame illustrative of his immortal fame with the words 'sacred to Nelson'. In another window were two figures of the crown and anchor, the nation's best hope; and in a third the letters GR surrounded with laurel.

On Nelson's death the *Glasgow Herald* commented, 'The loss of such a man at such a time may well be considered a national catastrophe. His memory however will be cherished for ages by his affectionate and grateful nation.'[63]

The first Nelson monument to be started anywhere was at Taynuilt on Loch Awe, a simple 12-foot granite pillar. According to tradition, a ship put in to the loch with early news of the battle. Another one, 70 feet high, was completed at Forres in 1806, but the best known are in the great cities of Glasgow and Edinburgh. The memorial on Glasgow Green is 144 feet high and was erected by public subscription in 1806. A crowd of 80,000 attended the laying of the foundation stone, at a time when the population of Glasgow was less than 100,000. The Edinburgh memorial, in the shape of an upturned telescope with a castellated top, is better known because of its position on Calton Hill. It was begun on 21 October 1807, the second anniversary of Nelson's death at Trafalgar, but took eight years to complete.[64] The more famous monument in Trafalgar Square, London, was not finished until 1843.

Surgeons

The 'commissioned sea officers', eligible to command ships and fleets, were by far the most glamorous officers of the navy, and apart from the marines they were the only ones who bore the King's commission. Below them, but no less essential in the running of the fleet, were several groups of specialist officers who had warrants rather than commissions. In general they are far less well documented than the commissioned officers, but Scottish influence is clear in some branches, especially among the medical officers of the fleet, the physicians and surgeons.

Surgeons were far more common than physicians in the navy. Every ship with a crew of more than about sixty was allowed one surgeon and most had one, two or three mates according to the size of the ship. Surgeons were of rather lower status than physicians; in Edinburgh it was only in 1718 that the final split between the barbers and surgeons took place, an association which is still commemorated in the traditional barber's pole. Surgeons generally learned the trade by apprenticeship rather than a medical degree, though in the university towns of Scotland they were often encouraged to attend lectures on anatomy and related subjects. Their status increased in 1778 when the Royal College was set up in Edinburgh. In Glasgow the rise of the surgeon began earlier, and in 1612 two branches of the medical profession were united in the Faculty of Physicians and Surgeons.[65] Surgeons were skilled at amputation and bleeding and had a general medical knowledge, but any kind of delicate operation was almost impossible in the days before anaesthetics.

Scotland, with its strong educational traditions, produced a large number of surgeons during the eighteenth century and many went south to make their fortunes in London and elsewhere. Some only joined the navy when other opportunities failed to materialise. Tobias Smollett travelled by wagon and foot in November 1739, 'My whole fortune consisting of one suit of clothes, a half-dozen ruffled shirts, as many plain, two pairs of worsted, and a number of thread stockings, a case of pocket instruments, a small edition of Horace, Wiseman's surgery and ten guineas in cash.'[66] He failed to sell his play *The Regicide*, but the 'War of Jenkins' Ear' had broken out with Spain and in October 1740 he joined the 80-gun ship *Cumberland* as surgeon's mate.

Robert Spotswood travelled by sea from Leith in February and arrived at Wapping on the Thames. After a brief encounter with the press gang, he fell out with his patron over the loss of a chest of books. He engaged as a surgeon of a whale-ship, but after one voyage he concluded that the navy was less dangerous in wartime.[67] Others joined the navy because they wanted to travel. Peter Cullen, a well-connected surgeon with a good position in Doune, chose the navy because of 'that ambition of seeing and knowing the world, carrying with it the dark and mysterious hope of honour, wealth, fame and distinction to be acquired everywhere but at home.'[68]

Since the qualifications of surgeons varied somewhat throughout the country, the navy insisted that its prospective medical officers should submit to an oral examination at Surgeons' Hall in London. Smollett provides a farcical account of the process in his novel *Roderick Random* with questions like 'If during an engagement at sea, a man was brought to you with his head shot off, how would you behave?'[69] A more accurate description is provided by Robert Spotswood of Edinburgh. Having been told that there were no vacancies, he met an apothecary he knew. 'Says he, go to Mr Carteret the Clerk, give him two or three guineas, he will get you appointed. Showed Carteret one guinea, ordered me to write Mr Stephens, one of the Commissioners. Having shown it to him, being transcribed, gave it to him, the board sitting, which was immediately returned with my name on the corner, second Mate of the *Anglesea*.'[70]

The actual examination is described by Peter Cullen in his usual pompous manner:

> One of the examiners arose, and taking Mr Cullen to the side of the room, enquired his age, his apprenticeship, studies and practice in his profession. To all these Mr Cullen having returned a satisfactory reply, the examiner proceeded to question him on anatomy, physiology and surgery, then states some of the more important surgical cases or diseases, and how he would treat them. This gentleman was quite satisfied with Mr Cullen's proficiency, and taking him up to the centre of the table, where the president was sitting, said, 'I find this young gentleman fully qualified as an Assistant Surgeon for His Majesty's Navy.'

Friends were useful in getting an appointment to a ship. Peter Cullen's employer in Doune recommended him to his nephew, the surgeon of the 24-gun *Squirrel*, and the young man was appointed to the ship.[71]

Surgeons' wages were enough to attract hungry young Scots in the 1740s, but by the end of the century they had fallen well behind conditions in civilian life, and in Scotland the standard of living for the middle classes had increased dramatically. As a result, the fleet at Camperdown found itself desperately short of medical officers. The surgeon of the *Ardent*, for example, had none of the three mates allowed by regulations. Alone he had to deal with 107 wounded men. When reform came it was Melville, as First Lord of the Admiralty, who instigated it. By an order-in-council of January 1805, a full surgeon's pay was to be raised from 2s 6d (12.5p) to a minimum of 11s (55p) per day. They were to have parity with naval lieutenants, with their own uniform and a guaranteed place in the wardroom with the lieutenants and marine officers. Mates were now to be called assistant surgeons and paid 8s 6d (42.5p) per day, though they still messed with the master's mates and midshipmen in the cockpit. This seems to have had some effect and recruitment improved.

Physicians in the Navy

Physicians were far rarer than surgeons – there were only four on the Navy List in the 1790s, compared with 550 full surgeons. They served as 'Physician of the Fleet' to each of the main naval commands, advising the commander-in-chief and supervising hospitals afloat and ashore. Physicians were better qualified, usually with a medical degree, though some were promoted after a few years as a surgeon. Again, most of them were Scots, or at least had degrees from Scottish universities. Leonard Gillespie was a native of Dublin and served for some years as a naval surgeon, partly on the east coast of Scotland, but he received a proxy degree from St Andrews in 1795, allowing him to become Physician of the Mediterranean Fleet in the year before Trafalgar.

James Lind was born in Edinburgh in 1716 and served an apprenticeship to a surgeon there. He became a surgeon's mate in the navy in 1739 and graduated MD at Edinburgh University in 1748. Nine years later he published *An Essay in the most Effectual Means of Preserving the Health of Seamen in the Royal Navy*, which included the first practical advice on how to deal with the most devastating of sea diseases, scurvy.

The disease had come increasingly to public attention in the war of 1739–48. George Anson's voyage round the world in 1740–4 had been almost wrecked by the deaths of three-quarters of his crews, though he had triumphed in the end and captured a Spanish treasure galleon. His chaplain describes the horrors of the disease:

> These common appearances are large coloured spots dispersed over the whole surface of the body, swelled legs, putrid gums, and above all, an extraordinary lassitude of the whole body, especially after any exercise, however inconsiderable; and this lassitude at last degenerates into a proneness to swoon on the least exertion of strength, or even on the least motion. This disease is likewise usually attended with a strange dejection of the spirits, with shiverings, tremblings, and a disposition to be seized with the most dreadful terrors on the slightest accident.[72]

Anson became First Lord of the Admiralty in 1751 and supported preventative treatment. One Scottish surgeon, Ramsay Karr of the *Invincible*, put forward the theory that woodsmoke would provide a cure.[73] But in his book of 1757, Lind reported on his experiments of ten years earlier on board HMS *Salisbury*. He was perfectly clear that it was caused by a deficiency of fresh vegetables in the seaman's diet. He advocated the use of lime and lemons in a Mediterranean climate where they were easily obtainable, and he was largely responsible for the issue of sauerkraut and 'portable soup' which drastically reduced the death rates on Captain James Cook's three great voyages, from 1768 to 1779. Though the officials of the navy lost sight of this lesson in the early stages of the American War which began in 1775, Lind earned the title of 'the father of nautical medicine'.

Sir Gilbert Blane was born in Ayrshire in 1749 and graduated from Glasgow University in 1778. He moved to London where he became private physician to Admiral Rodney, rich from prize money but plagued by gout. When Rodney became commander-in-chief in the West Indies in 1780, he took Blane with him as Physician of the Fleet. Blane soon saw that Lind's reforms, though proved off Brest and in Cook's voyages, were no longer being implemented. On his return from the West Indies he published his *Observations on the Diseases Incident to Seamen* in 1785 and ten years later the navy adopted them permanently, so that scurvy was virtually eliminated. He was responsible for several other reforms which made ships more healthy, such as the issue of soap, improved ventilation and better supplies of medicines.

Thomas Trotter was born in Roxburghshire in 1760 and graduated MD at Edinburgh in 1788. He started as a surgeon's mate in 1779 and became Physician to the Channel Fleet in 1794. He was not credited with any reforms as dramatic as those of Lind and Blane, and his campaigns for naval uniform and vaccination of seamen were unsuccessful in his lifetime. His *Medica Nautica*, published in three volumes from 1791 to 1803, provided an important textbook, with many shrewd comments on the character of the seamen and the naval service.

It is possible to believe that the Royal Navy would still have won its battles without the participation of Scottish officers like Duncan and Cochrane: it is not likely that it could have succeeded without the help of Scottish surgeons and physicians, especially Lind and Blane, the conquerors of scurvy. It was this achievement which made possible the navy's most enduring successes, from Cook's voyages of exploration to the continuous blockade of French ports such as Brest and Toulon.

Other Officers

Pursers were the supply officers of ships. They were paid less than other officers of similar status, but expected to make a profit, legal or not, on some of their transactions, such as the sale of clothing and tobacco. Though other forms of business were more convenient and profitable, a career as a purser attracted a significant number of Scots, with their taste for commerce. One of the first was John Steuart, son of a baillie of Inverness who desperately hoped for his return from Anson's circumnavigation of 1741–4, so that his prize money would save the family fortune. At the same time he advised him not to take up a new appointment until 'some impending clouds' – the 1745 rebellion – had disappeared.[74] Andrew Burn's father was a Dundee merchant who only became a purser after his business failed.

> Having met with many losses and disappointments in trade, particularly by the foundering of a ship that was not insured, found it impracticable any longer to maintain his family in that line of business in which he had been engaged; and having no other prospect of soon entering any other, he obtained, with some difficulty, a purser's warrant to a sloop of war.[75]

Another is described by William Mangin in the *Gloucester* in 1812. 'Mr Wilson, the Purser, was a Scot; taciturn, cautious, calm, and economical. He appeared to be – like Shakespeare's Cassius – "a great discerner" and "to look quite through the deeds of men" – he was, moreover, not a fat man, nor "one who sleeps o' nights", but tall, lean and anxious; he was always very complaisant and obliging to me.'[76]

Unlike a sea officer or a surgeon, there was little chance of fame and glory for a purser, unless he moved into another field. One Scot who did so was Archibald Campbell, the purser of several men-of-war in the middle of the eighteenth century, who published poems such as *Lexiphanes* which satirised Samuel Johnson.

William Falconer, born to an extremely poor family in Edinburgh about 1730, began an apprenticeship in the merchant navy but became servant to Archibald Campbell. By 1751 he was writing and publishing poetry of his own and in 1757 he reached the quarterdeck as an adult midshipman, in which rank he survived the wreck of the *Ramillies* in 1760. He returned to the merchant service and was shipwrecked again, leading to his most famous poem, *The Shipwreck*, of 1762, regarded as a considerable work of art at the time, as well as a primer of navigation and seamanship. 'Many experienced officers have declared, that the rules and maxims delivered in this poem, for the conduct of a ship in the most perilous emergency, form the best, indeed the only, opinions which a skilled mariner should adopt.'[77] He attracted the attention of the Duke of York and was made purser of the frigate *Glory* in 1763. He began work on his most enduring monument, his *Universal Dictionary of the Marine,* while the ship was laid up at Chatham. On the orders of the dockyard commissioner, 'The captain's cabin was ordered to be fitted up with a stove, and with every addition of comfort that could be procured; in order that Falconer might thus be enabled to enjoy his favourite propensity, without either molestation or expense.'[78] The book came out in 1769 and went through many editions. It served its purpose in training generations of naval officers and today it is an invaluable source for the technology and society of the eighteenth-century navy. Falconer was lost in the frigate *Aurora* a few months after the first edition came out.

Another literary Scottish officer was John McArthur, born in 1755. He joined HMS *Eagle* as a clerk in 1778. A year later he was promoted to be purser of a cutter, for his gallantry on boarding a French privateer. He acted as judge-advocate of the fleet and this led him to publish a treatise on naval courts martial. He also took an interest in signalling and in 1791, when he became secretary to Admiral Lord Hood, the two worked to devise new systems. In 1803 he declined a post as Nelson's secretary, perhaps because his literary interests were becoming more prominent. In 1809 he collaborated with James Stanier Clarke, publisher of the *Naval Chronicle* magazine, on a famous *Life of Nelson.*[79]

The marines (who became Royal in 1802) seem to have been quite attractive to Scots and anecdotal evidence suggests that they provided a high proportion of officers, often from the Highlands. A marine officer did not have to start his career in his early teens, like a naval officer (though some were commissioned incredibly early, such as the son of Lieutenant-Colonel William Adair, at the age of six). Unlike the army, his family did not have to pay for his commission. It was issued by the Admiralty, either to sons of officers or those with suitable references. Andrew Burn, the son of a Dundee merchant and purser, faced extreme poverty until he was commissioned in 1761 on the recommendation of the family patron, Sir Harry Erskine MP. He rose to become a major-general in a 53-year career.

The lack of financial outlay made a career attractive to the younger sons of the minor Scottish gentry, slightly lower on the social scale than those who became naval officers. Promotion was by seniority and was very slow, but marine officers at sea shared prize money with the naval lieutenants. Only three peers served in the corps during the eighteenth century, all Scots such as James Francis Leslie, 7th Baron Lindores. Family influence was strong. Major-General Maurice Wemyss served as Colonel Commandant at Portsmouth from 1794–8 and three of his sons were commissioned in the corps, along with two nephews.[80]

An early Scottish entrant was J. MacIntire, who published *A Military Treatise on the Discipline of the Marine Forces when at Sea* at the end of the Seven Years War in 1763. One Highland officer was Lieutenant Donald Campbell, who served in the sloop *Racehorse* in the late 1780s and was described by his mess-mate, the surgeon Leonard Gillespie:

> Has all the frankness, openness and liberality of a soldier and a gentleman. Free from all disposition to envy, and perfectly good natured, he is universally liked. A keen sportsman and a staunch bottle companion, the confinement of a ship gave him an overproportion of general disease, melancholy and his not having any taste for letters prevented him from using one of the most efficacious remedies on board a ship for *ennui*. He has therefore gone to his brothers at Ardtaraig, Cowal in Argyllshire, where he employs himself in sportsmanship, farming, gardening and in social visits to the hospitable neighbourhood.[81]

The other officers of a ship included the master, who was in charge of navigation, and the standing officers – the carpenter, boatswain and gunner – so-called because they stayed with the ship even when she was laid up at one of the dockyard ports, as most ships were in peacetime. They were invariably promoted from the lower deck and there is no sign that Scots were common among them. Carpenters, in particular, were usually recruited from men who had served apprenticeships in the Royal Dockyards in the south of England, so a Scottish presence is unlikely.

The Last Act

In June 1815 the Duke of Wellington won the Battle of Waterloo and brought the long wars with France to an end. Napoleon fled, and on 14 July he surrendered to HMS *Bellerophon*, the leading ship in a squadron blockading Rochefort. Her captain was Frederick Lewis Maitland, a native of Rankeilour in Fife and a grandson of the Earl of Lauderdale. The defeated emperor and the captain talked about the customs of the Scottish aristocracy:

He conversed a great deal, and showed no depression of spirits: among other things, he asked me where I was born. I told him, in Scotland. 'Have you any property there?' said he. 'No, I am a younger son, and they do not bestow much on people of that description in Scotland.'[82]

Maitland took Bonaparte back to Plymouth Sound, where he reported to another Scot, Lord Keith, now in command of the Channel Fleet. He had to break the news to the former emperor that he was to be exiled to the lonely outpost of St Helena. Above Keith was the Admiralty Board itself, headed by the second Lord Melville, with three more Scots among the junior lords. This was very different from Lord Belhaven's prediction more than a century before, on the eve of Union. No one could say that the Scots were 'earning their Bread as Underlings in the Royal English Navy'.

Chapter 5

Naval Operations in Scotland

Proposals for a Base in the Forth

In 1708, soon after the Union, the Admiralty in London received proposals from several town councils. Edinburgh suggested that a dry dock could be built at Leith, while the shipmasters of Prestongrange and the Earl of Mar, the Secretary of State, were keen to promote their own areas as a site for a new naval base. Trinity House was ordered to send three or four of its elder brethren and two or three dockyard officials to survey the Firth of Forth, 'as well with regard to the conveniences which are already in the said Frith, or which may be made for the careening, cleaning and refitting of Her Majesty's ships that may be employed on the said coast of North Britain'. John Naish and John Ward were employed to make 'a strict and careful survey of all the places in the said Frith' and a report was produced in July 1709.[1] It began with a general description of the firth, which

> lies nearly ENE and WSW in length from Fife Ness to Queensferry forty miles (each mile containing one thousand paces), in breadth between Fife Ness and St Abbs Head, 32 miles; it narrows gradually towards Queensferry, where the breadth is one mile. The several heads, bays, harbours, rocks and depths of water in the said Frith is more particularly set down in a map thereof. From the ferry westwards as far as Burrowstowness, 'tis called the waters of Forth, in length about ten miles, in breadth near two miles, and is an excellent anchorage, from three to eight and twelve fathoms at low water; well land-locked from violent winds and seas, and may be defended from being attacked or entered with an enemy's fleet by four forts that may be built at Queensferry, one on the rocky island of Garvie about 400 paces from the peninsula on the north side; another on the point of the peninsula; another on the rock Bimar (which is a little above the other two) and fronts the passage twixt the Garvie and the peninsula, which passage is

very deep and the most ordinary for ships. The other fort is to be built on the south side of the ferry, on a rock below the halls, only to be seen at low water and is no greater distance from the Garvie than the point of the peninsula on the north side, by which four forts the entry of this large harbour is thought sufficiently guarded.

Above Bo'ness,

> the water grows shallow to two fathoms nine feet and so to four, five and six feet as far as Alloa. The whole Frith hath good anchorage, excepting where the rocks are set down in the map, but especially the Road of Leith, which is defended by the Island of Keith from the easterly winds which blow right into the Frith and makes the greatest seas. The depth is from three a half to five fathom at low water, shallowing by degrees towards the south shore, but near the north shore there's a channel of 18, 20 and 22 fathoms water.

All the harbours in the firth were dry at low water, which tended to reduce their value as naval ports. Those which dried out least were Leith, Burntisland and Queensferry. They were 'the best qualified for cleaning, careening and refitting Her Majesty's ships'. The area was well supplied with 'all sorts of naval stores from the east country [i.e. the Baltic], such as deals, hemp, pitch and tar, iron' but 'for oak timber we saw none that was the growth of Great Britain; all we found there was brought from Lubeck, Danzig etc. 'Twas generally fit for hoys and small vessels . . .'

Leith, it was reported,

> Hath a beacon or seamark set up about 530 fathom without the piers, unto which it ebbs dry at low spring tides, save only a rivulet that runs through the harbour. About 88 fathom without the piers is a bar or bank of sand where, on ordinary spring tides, there is 14 and on neap about nine ft water. We observed that the sea, especially to the westward of the town, gains very much on the land, which being a sandy soil helps to increase the bar and flats, as well as fill the harbour. It is a considerable place of trade (the only port of Edinburgh). 'Tis capable of being secured from the insults of the enemy's ships by a small fort, that may be built on the rock whereon the beacon now stands, and the town (formerly a garrison, the ruins of the bastion and curtains still remaining) may be fortified to any degree shall be thought fit.

The surveyors agreed that 'the erecting a wet dock and putting this port in better condition than it now is . . . will be proper.' They recommended 'a dam of ten or twelve ft high be made above the bridge . . . to pen up the tide and river till low water, with a shore in the middle to be then set open. The rapidity of the current will scour away the mud and sand that gathers in the harbour.' The eastern and western piers were to be extended 200 yards out to sea and a wet dock was to be made on hard ground, 'wherein a ship being put and the gates shut, she may be kept continually afloat to unballast, unload, repair her upper works or careen.' A dry dock was to lead out of this 'for more substantial repairs to her bottom'. The total cost was estimated at £30,768.

At Burntisland the surveyors found the harbour 'is as deep at full sea as any harbour in the Frith wherein, for ordinary spring tides there's about 16 or 17 ft water on the west side. The ground is clean and a hard clay, where a fourth rate may lie on shore to grave, but a southerly wind blows right in, and there being rocks without the pier heads on each side, 'tis difficult to get out.' At Queensferry 'there are three bays, the East, West and North, all smooth, hard ground, as much water as at Burntisland. A fourth rate may safely lie on shore and clean at one or other of them any wind. All of them may be secured from enemy's ships by fortifying the Garvie and the peninsula as is before set forth.' Alloa was quite suitable for building a dry dock, but was too far up river. 'The inconveniency that attends this place is its remoteness from the Frith, it being for three or four miles a river of no more than four, five and six ft deep when the tide is gone, about 18 or 19 at full sea.'

Inverkeithing was 'a very large harbour or basin . . . and fit for small vessels.' Morrison's Haven, near Prestonpans, was an ancient harbour of little use in its present state. 'Mr John Adair, Mr James Smith, Captain Brown, several of the inhabitants and some of then petitioners that live thereabouts, showed us where the old harbour and mouth of it had been and the place proposed to make the new, which is full of rocks and loose stones, five or six ton weight, a narrow part only trenched to carry away water from a mill.' It would be useless to open up the old harbour because an easterly wind would soon fill it up with rocks and sand. It might be possible to build a new one just to the east, but it would cost £12,000 and the surveyors showed no enthusiasm for this.

The other harbours in the open part of the firth, the surveyors reported,

> are liable to the same inconveniences by the swell of the sea, from which
> Dunbar is by the situation of a rock that serves for a double pier the best
> secured. This place lies well for trade, especially the fishery, and is

capable of being improved by the piers being carried 80 yards further out to some rocks that lie there, splitting up the rotten ones at the bottom.

Edinburgh was keen to have naval docks built at Leith, in view of the business and employment they would create, and the utility of dry docks to the merchant shipping community. They were contemptuous of the claims of Morrison's Haven, when a bill for the repair of the harbour came before Parliament in 1709 – it was 'a mean and obscure village which contributes not six pence to the support of government'. The following year the Lord Provost of Edinburgh, Sir Patrick Johnson, spent some months in London pursuing the plan for Leith. He met opposition from the Navy Board and from a Captain Mudie, another Scot, who alleged that the want of deep water made Leith unsuitable. In August the Provost reported that he had gained the support of the Admiralty and the Privy Council, but the project soon began to falter, for the threat to Scotland seemed much less after British victories in Europe.[2]

Pirates and Smugglers

During the first half of the eighteenth century the Royal Navy rarely operated in Scottish waters unless there was a specific threat from Jacobites, smugglers or pirates. By this time Scotland was not a great centre of piracy, which enjoyed a kind of golden age in the Caribbean for a decade or so after the peace in 1714. There were occasional threats in more isolated parts of Scotland, to which the navy did not always react. In 1725, for example, there were reports of a pirate ship in Orkney whose crew, led by John Gow from Orkney, had mutinied and taken over the ship during a Mediterranean voyage. The information was passed to the nearest warship, the sloop *Weasel*, and the Admiralty issued instructions to all seafarers to 'take, sink, burn or otherwise destroy' it, but it was the local customs officers who acted and took control of the ship. It was a similar story with a ship called the *John and Marion* at Stranraer, which was also taken by the Customs.[3]

During the war which began in 1739, the Scottish merchants of the east coast began to feel aggrieved at the lack of naval protection. In June 1744 the Earl of Morton complained to the Secretary of State, 'Your Grace will see the necessity there will be of sending a ship of some force to clear these seas, for in all probability there are no less than four privateers and a French man of war now cruising there; and they will soon take rich booty considering the great numbers of ships which pass that way.'[4] But the Admiralty was quite used to lobbying of this nature from different towns and districts, and little was done before August 1745, when the Jacobite Rebellion made the situation very different.

After his searches and raids in the Hebrides, John Fergusson was promoted to full captain and appointed to the new 24-gun ship *Nightingale,* on the express recommendation of the Duke of Cumberland. He distinguished himself by capturing the *Dauphin Royal,* a French ship of superior force. By 1750 he was back in Scotland, in command of the sloop *Porcupine,* to patrol in the Clyde and the Western Isles. Since the war was now over, he devoted most of his attention to local smugglers. Showing his usual determination, he made almost as many enemies as he had done against the Jacobites. In August, for example, he found a ship off Arran, newly arrived from Jamaica. Her crew were unloading cargo into boats when the naval ship approached. Immediately the sailors began to throw bags over the side, until the water was thick with tea and coffee. He confiscated the goods and sent them to the Custom House at Port Glasgow. The owners of the ship resorted to law and sued Fergusson for £5,000. The area, Fergusson said, was 'nothing but a nest of smugglers' and he had 'but too good ground to believe that they are supported by some of the gentlemen of the country, and some of them justices of the peace.'

Fergusson laid the *Porcupine* up in the Gareloch each winter, regarding it as a safe anchorage which was convenient for Greenock. He also found it useful to be within half a mile of Loch Long, 'a noted place for smuggling wherries to unload their cargoes which are carried thence by land to Stirling and the Highlands.' In November 1751, with the *Porcupine* laid up, he used a wherry to stop a boat smuggling salt from Ireland, and to drive ashore a ship bringing brandy from the Isle of Man. The local people arrived in great numbers and a small battle ensued when customs men and soldiers came to seize the cargo.[5]

Despite his own rectitude, Fergusson often had to defend his officers against suspicion of incompetence or corruption. In 1751, during one of Fergusson's numerous absences in court, 'the poor lad, my purser' accepted some slop clothing on behalf of another ship, without the consent of either captain. The goods turned to be unsuitable and Fergusson had some of them returned but had to apologise to the Admiralty for the rest. Meanwhile his lieutenant was accused of taking four barrels of spirits from a smuggler for the use of the *Porcupine*'s crew. Fergusson argued that the goods had been embezzled first by the customs officer concerned, then given to the crew. By 1754 he was back in the Hebrides again, moving parties of troops, where his presence must have stirred memories of events eight years before. He was still able to sniff out conspiracies.

> Some days before I got to the Highlands there had been several mutinies of the principal people of the Jacobites from Arisaig, Knoydart and Moidart (headed by Lady Margaret MacDonald and her factor Mac-Donald of Kingsburgh) particularly at Portree on the Isle of Skye and on the Isle of Raasay, and afterwards Lady Margaret went on with some of them to North Uist, where she is at present.[6]

In 1754 Fergusson took the *Porcupine* back to the naval base at Plymouth to be paid off, accusing two of his crew of 'the detestable sin of sodomy'. There must have been relief in the west when he was appointed to his new job as head of the press gangs in Edinburgh.

The Thurot Scares

In 1756 a new conflict, eventually known to history as the Seven Years War, broke out between Britain and France. For Britain's main ally, Frederick the Great of Prussia, it was largely a war of conquest against his enemy, Austria. For the British it was a colonial war in which the French would be driven from India after Clive's great victory at Plassey, and from North America after Wolfe captured Quebec. Scotland was a long way from the centres of action and saw no fighting, but Edinburgh, Glasgow and even the tiny port of Irvine figured in the calculations of French strategists.

The French seaman who menaced Scottish waters in this war was Captain François Thurot, whose career oscillated between the *Marine Royale* and privateering, with spells as a smuggler and an ill-qualified surgeon. He left the privateer port of St Malo in July 1757 in his flagship, the 36-gun *Maréchal de Belle-Isle*, accompanied by three other ships. He knew that the waters round Scotland, Ireland and the north of England were thinly guarded by the Royal Navy and on 5 October, after many adventures and several near encounters with the Royal Navy, he anchored with his two remaining ships near Banff in the Moray Firth, causing consternation. The burgh court was convened under the Provost, who suggested evacuation of the town. One of the bailies wanted to buy the attackers off with a ransom, to which the Provost objected that this would require hostages while the money was raised. The assembly suggested the Provost himself, while he nominated the bailie who had made the suggestion.[7] Fortunately the weather intervened before a decision was reached. During the night the anchor cables of one ship, the *Chauvelin*, broke and she drifted off to sea. The *Belle-Isle* went off to look for her and Banff, Cullen and Findhorn were safe.

The *Belle-Isle* never found the *Chauvelin* but continued north-wards, and two days later she arrived off Shetland and anchored in Symbister Voe on Whalsay. Captain Thurot, who spoke fluent if inaccurate English, made contact with the laird, John Bruce Stewart: 'I have occasion for some beeves, sheep, bread, meal and other trifles which I shall be obliged to you and your people to supply me with. If you do it friendly, I shall pay the price you expect, but if you refuse, you can't take it that I furnish myself according to the Rules of Warr.' The laird was indeed friendly and supplied him with wine, bread and flour, as well as four sheep and some poultry. Thurot carried out some repairs to his ship and sailed on to Bergen in Norway.[8] In August he sailed round the north of Scotland, narrowly missing four British warships off Shetland. By the beginning of September he was in the North Channel between Scotland and Ireland, where he captured several ships including the *Henry* of 18 guns, carrying sugar from the West Indies to Glasgow. Having attracted attention to his activities, he retreated to the Faroes and then back to Dunkirk via Bergen and Ostend.

During the campaign of 1759, Thurot was cast as a minor player on a much larger stage. Many plans for the invasion of Britain were produced in France, some by Jacobite exiles who remained optimistic about a rising in Scotland. The most serious plan, however, was produced by the Maréchal de Belle-Isle, Thurot's patron and the Minister for War. The French Navy was smaller than the British (125 ships of the line against 57) but the British were dispersed around the world and it was hoped that a sudden concentration would give the French naval superiority in northern Europe. The main thrust of the invasion would take place at Maldon in Essex, where the French army would be less than 40 miles from London.

A secondary invasion would be launched from Brest and other ports of Brittany. A powerful force of 35 to 40 ships of the line would be collected by merging the Atlantic and Mediterranean fleets. It would sail with transport ships carrying 20,000 troops under the Duc d'Aigullon and pass round the west coast of Ireland and through the North Channel into the Firth of Clyde. The troops would land near Irvine and march to Glasgow and then Edinburgh. Meanwhile the ships would sail on round the north of Scotland to Dunkirk, where they would support the invasion of England.[9]

Thurot's task was to act as a decoy for this operation. His

instructions, soon leaked to the British, were to attack the important but weakly defended English ports of Bristol or Newcastle, or failing that, another port in England or Ireland. The French King, influenced by exiles, still believed that the Scots might prove friendly and he was not to attack there. He left Dunkirk in September 1759 with six ships led by the *Maréchal de Belle-Isle*. He carried around 1,300 troops in addition to the crews of the ships. He sailed north and called at Gothenburg in Sweden and at the Faroe Islands for repairs and replenishment.[10]

As part of the response to this threat, Commodore William Boys was sent north in his flagship, the new 50-gun ship *Preston*, with seven other ships, and he arrived in Leith Roads on 26 October. On a sweep north he received intelligence from local provosts and collectors of customs at Peterhead, Aberdeen and other towns, but since there was no regular naval presence in Scotland, he found the supply situation rather difficult. As a result one Walter Scott was appointed naval officer, that is, a civilian supply officer, at Leith. By this time Boys had heard a report that Thurot had gone back to Dunkirk, which he regarded with justifiable scepticism. On 21 December, having news of Thurot being in Bergen and no orders from London, he held a council of war among his captains and it was decided to stay on the Scottish coast, which was otherwise completely unguarded against enemy attack. One of his ships, the *Surprise,* sailed south with a convoy on the 27th, but Boys remained at Leith until March 1760.

In the meantime Thurot sailed south from the Faroes, passing St Kilda, and arrived at Lough Foyle in Northern Ireland. In mid February he sailed into Claggain Bay on the south coast of Islay, again looking for supplies, as his men were reduced to four ounces of bread per day. If he hoped for Jacobite support it was unlikely in such solid Campbell country.

By this time the French Mediterranean Fleet had attempted to sail to Brest, and was defeated off Lagos in Portugal by Admiral Boscawen. At Islay, Thurot heard the news of a much more decisive defeat, when the Atlantic Fleet under Admiral Conflans sailed from Brest and was chased into Quiberon Bay by the British admiral, Edward Hawke. In a dramatic action fought in a full gale, the French lost five ships, while seven more were forced to retreat up the River Vilaine, where they were effectively stranded for months. There was no prospect of launching Belle-Isle's invasion and the shores of Ayrshire would never see the French fleet.

Disappointed at the news, Thurot decided to carry on with his mission. He landed several hundred troops on Islay to take supplies, though he insisted on paying for them in accordance with his orders not to treat the Scots as enemies, and even punished an officer who stole money from a local gentleman. He captured a ship called the *Ingram*, carrying salt and oranges from Lisbon to Glasgow. He went on to Carrickfergus in Northern Ireland and then towards the Isle of Man. Off County Down his remaining three ships met a British squadron and were defeated. Thurot was killed.[11]

Though it had no tactical effects of any significance, Thurot's campaign showed up the weakness of the Scottish defences and this would remain an issue in politics for the next sixty years. Moreover, it came at a time when Edinburgh intellectuals, led by such figures as Adam Smith, David Hume and Joseph Black, were turning their attention to constitutional and military affairs. In such circles a part-time militia which would be mobilised only in wartime for home defence seemed an ideal military force, cheaper than a standing army, less likely to threaten civil liberties and under the influence of the county gentry rather than the central government. The militia had been re-established in England by Act of Parliament in 1757. Why not in Scotland? Despite the massive intellectual weight behind it and the support of many town councils, the campaign was not a success in this war or the next, if only because it was opposed by those who might be liable to service by selective conscription, or would have to find expensive ways of evading it.[12]

The Charting of Scotland

Though Ptolemy had produced the material for a rather misleading map of Scotland in classical times, and the country featured on the extreme fringes of most medieval *mappamundi*, the seas of Scotland were still not fully charted. Early mariners relied on their own memory and local knowledge, or employed pilots to help them. The earliest written information on Scottish waters took the form of sailing direction or 'Portalans' including one produced by Alexander Lindsay in 1540 on the orders of James V. In the years after that, it was often Britain's enemies of the moment who produced the best charts – the Dutch in the seventeenth century and the French in the early eighteenth.

The first official survey of the British seas was conducted by Captain Greenville Collins in the Royal yacht *Merlin*. He started in 1681 on the orders of Charles II, 'who was a great Lover of the Noble Art of NAVIGATION,' and found 'that there were no Sea-Charts or Maps of these Kingdoms but what were Dutch, and Copies from them, and those very erroneous.' Collins published an atlas called *Great Britain's Coasting Pilot* in 1693. He produced charts of Orkney and Shetland. His atlas also included a chart of the Forth or 'Edinburgh Firth', a detailed one of Leith, harbour plans of the Firth of Tay, Aberdeen and Montrose, and 'The Firth of Murry'. But Collins never got to the north or west coast of Scotland. In 1731 John Adair published a detailed chart of the Clyde, probably surveyed some years earlier, and of great assistance to the growing trade of the area. During the campaign of 1745–6, the French used a chart from the *Neptune Français* by their great cartographer Bellin, but this merely gave approximate locations for various lochs and islands, and it is no surprise that they sought local pilots whenever they had the chance.

Murdoch Mackenzie was a grandson of a Bishop of Orkney. During 1745–9 he surveyed Orkney waters, which were becoming increasingly important for whalers and for ships which wanted to make the voyage round the north of Scotland to avoid enemy privateers in the English Channel. He had very limited assistance from the Navy Board, by the loan of some instruments. Instead of taking compass bearings from ships as nautical chart-makers usually did, Mackenzie used triangulation of prominent points on land, which had been common among land surveyors for two centuries. He described his method:

> Having previously acquired a competent knowledge of the Islands, and planned the future Procedure in my Mind, I caused *Beacons* or *Landmarks,* to be built on the Summits of all the remarkable Hills and Eminencies; and, catching the Opportunity of a very hard frost, I picked the north-most Branch of the *Loch* of *Stenhouse* . . . as the properest Plain to be measured for the Basis of the following operation . . . When a complete map of an Island was made out in this Manner, I then went around the Coast in a Boat, sounded the depth of water all along, and round every Rock and Shoal, and through every Channel, marking out on the corresponding Part of the map the several Depths and Quality of the Bottom: taking notes of the landmarks for avoiding Rocks, sailing through Channels etc., also of the Setting and Irregularities of the Tides, and measuring their velocities when an Opportunity offered; which was done by letting a boat go, in a Calm, along with the Stream, a known distance without Impulse of Sails or Oars, and estimating the time by a Watch.[13]

He published his survey of Orkney in 1750. He also surveyed Lewis and was the first to correct the Dutch geographer Blaeu's error of 1654, which show the island with a flat rather than a pointed northern end. His work seems to have impressed the Admiralty. In 1751 they commissioned him to do a massive survey of the west coasts of Scotland and England and the whole of Ireland, in which he was perhaps aided by the groundwork done for William Roy's map of the Highlands and Islands which was completed in 1755, though not published till much later. Mackenzie completed a grand triangulation of the Hebrides, from Mull to Shiant Island, north of Skye, in 1751. His surveys of Scotland were essentially complete by 1757 and he went on to the coasts of England and Ireland. His charts were eventually published in 1776, the first real maritime survey of the Hebrides.

As well as accurate charts, Mackenzie produced interesting comments on the value of the harbours in the area. Of the Clyde he wrote, 'no River whatever can be safer, or is better provided with spacious well-sheltered arms of the sea, than the *Clyde* is. In approaching it, there are neither rocks nor shoals, nor rappid tides to be feared . . . This river is provided by nature with every conveniency for navigation, excepting a sufficient rise of the tide for wet and dry docks for great ships.' However he was aware that 'only lighters, or very small vessels, have water up to the kay at Glasgow.' Loch nan Uamh, the scene of so much activity during the 1745 rebellion, was 'all good ground [for anchoring] and the depth fit for the largest ship; but being open to the west, it is not safe in the winter-time, except to small vessels.'[14]

Mackenzie's son, Murdoch the younger, continued to be employed on Admiralty surveys, but his best work was done in the south of England. Alexander Dalrymple from New Hailes near Edinburgh was another Scottish surveyor, who became the first Hydrographer of the Navy in 1795. However he had left home at the age of fifteen to work in the East Indies. The Hydrographic Branch of the Navy continued to be responsible for the surveying of Scottish waters. A grand survey of British waters went on through most of the nineteenth century and Commander C. Robinson, for example, charted much of the west coast between 1835 and 1851.[15]

John Paul Jones

The next seaman to threaten Scotland was himself a Scot. John Paul, or John Paul Jones as he called himself in later life, was born in Kirkcudbrightshire in 1747. He was apprenticed in a merchant ship from Whitehaven, not far across the English border, served briefly in the Royal Navy and in slave ships. He found himself in America in 1775 as the revolt against British rule broke out and entered the

Continental Navy, the forerunner of the United States Navy, as a lieutenant. In 1777 he took charge of the 18-gun sloop *Ranger*, based in France, which was soon to enter the war against Britain. He had an independent command, with orders to make war against the British in any way he could legitimately find.

Glasgow and the Clyde ports had been doing very well in the tobacco trade with Virginia up to this point, and now found their supplies cut off, causing depression of trade. As Lord Frederick Campbell, brother of the Duke of Argyll put it, 'The inhabitants upon these coast are mostly sailors, one half of them idle from the stop put to the American trade . . .' Furthermore, the Glasgow merchants had been avaricious in their dealings with Virginia planters, many of whom were seriously in debt to them. A naval frigate was urgently needed in the Clyde because

> the trade of this part of the world having been almost entirely carried on with America only, the merchants had reason to believe this coast would be the first object of the resentment of their privateers – the more so as the Americans knew well that the inhabitants upon these coasts were without forts or arms to protect them, and that their warehouses were full of tobacco, become of late very valuable and all they had to make up for their losses sustained by the American rebellion.[16]

Jones set sail from Brest in April 1778 in the *Ranger* for his first cruise in British waters. After aborting a raid on his original home port of Whitehaven, he crossed the Solway Firth and landed with a party of twelve men on St Mary's Isle to raid the home of the Earl of Selkirk, who perhaps had seemed a great man during Jones's childhood in the area. Jones had a grandiose plan to use him as a hostage for the better treatment of American prisoners of the British. Finding that the Earl was not at home, he was ready to abandon his mission when some of his officers and men demanded the right to plunder the house, pointing out that 'in America no delicacy was shown by the English, who took away all sorts of moveable property, setting fire not only to towns and to the houses of the rich, without distinction, but not even sparing the wretched milch cows of the poor and helpless at the approach of inclement weather.'[17] Jones gave in to this against his better judgement and the depredations of the Americans were to be wildly exaggerated by popular report. Jones and his men sailed away after about half an hour on shore, leaving behind a legend which would create panic along many miles of sea coast. Sir James Oughton, the military commander, reported that he had 'thrown the whole western coast into consternation' and that people were complaining that Scotland had sent 12,000 men for national defence but their own shores were left exposed. The *Ranger* went on to capture HMS *Drake*, of 14 guns, off Belfast Lough and returned to Brest.

In August 1779, Jones set sail from France on another cruise in the 42–gun *Bonnehomme-Richard* with seven other ships under his command. They became separated in storms off Ireland and Jones proceeded round the north of Scotland in search of his missing ships. On 1 September off Cape Wrath, he captured a British privateer bound to Quebec from London, but on the 13th, when he sighted the Pentland Hills behind Edinburgh, he had only three of the original ships with him, plus two prizes.

Detailed plans were prepared for an attack on Leith, which Jones knew to be very weakly defended, with only a 20-gun ship and two or three cutters. Some of his men feared the guns of Edinburgh Castle, which they believed to be of great power, but since they were 2 miles away from Leith, they barely had the range to reach the sea, far less to hit ships with force and accuracy. Each ship was to provide a certain number of men for the landing party under Captaine Paul de Chamillard. When the town was captured, a letter would be sent to the Lord Provost of Edinburgh offering terms. The captors, it said, had the power to burn the town to ashes, 'did not the plea of humanity stay the hand of just retaliation'. Instead an indemnity of £100,000 would be demanded, half now and half later, to be secured by six hostages. The magistrates would be obliged to sign a guarantee that there would be no molestation of the Americans in the firth.[18]

The three ships tacked up the firth in contrary winds as far as Inchkeith by 4.30 in the afternoon of the 17th. Boats were got out and 140 marines were prepared for a landing. On the way in, the ships had captured a small Scottish merchant ship and a boy escaped from it in a boat belonging to the revenue cutter from Leith. The boy's message alerted the army in Edinburgh Castle and Captain Napier, in charge of the press gang at Leith. The navy had allocated three small ships to the Leith station. One was in the Netherlands with a convoy, while HMS *Leith* was derigged and had had her guns taken out ready to go into dry dock. Her captain, Peter Rothe, ordered the crew to drag the guns along the shore and set up two 10-gun batteries between Leith and Newhaven. Meanwhile the *Three Sisters*, of 20 guns, under Captain Wyborn, the only naval ship afloat in the firth, moved into position off the harbour mouth in an attempt to prevent an American landing by boat. At about ten in the morning a squall struck Jones's small fleet and the boats were hoisted in, while Jones became aware of the British ship watching his movements. His ships were driven from the firth by contrary winds, never to return.[19] But as with Thurot's raids in the last war, and with Jones's last incursion on the Scottish coast, the mere presence of an enemy was enough to cause panic on shore. Lawyers considered the possibility of arming the people for their own defence, but this was illegal under the acts passed against the Jacobites, and there was no part-time militia in Scotland.[20]

The War with the Dutch

In November 1780 Britain declared war on the Netherlands to prevent her from joining a League of Armed Neutrality of countries annoyed by the high-handed behaviour of the Royal Navy in stopping neutral ships. This was a new strategic situation in the North Sea. The Netherlands had been an ally during all the major wars between 1689 and 1748. They were neutral in the Seven Years War (1756–63). Their hostility had the potential to open up a new front in the naval war. They had a fleet of twenty-five ships of the line and forty frigates which, added to the fleets of France and Spain and the American privateers, might have been enough to tip the balance against the Royal Navy – though in fact only half were fit for service and there was a shortage of men and supplies. The Dutch were still dominant in the strategically important whaling trade in the seas around Greenland, which brought them close to Scottish waters and created peace-time business with Shetland. Britain's own whaling trade was of increasing importance during this period. Even more important was British trade with the Baltic which produced many of the stores which kept the navy afloat – oak, elm and tar made the area as important as the Persian Gulf is in modern strategic calculations. War with the Dutch meant that convoys to southern England were under threat, while others were routed further north, and eventually this brought Leith into prominence as a base.

Early in 1781 Keith Stewart, captain of HMS *Berwick* and a son of the Earl of Galloway, was in contact with the Earl of Sandwich, the First Lord of the Admiralty. Stewart wanted a command in the North Sea and Sandwich was sympathetic but had to defer him. 'The thing does not press, as we have no ships disposable for that station, and it is impossible to say as yet when we shall.'[21] Eventually Stewart, now promoted to commodore, was given charge of a small squadron for the northern part of the sea, while Vice-Admiral Hyde Parker took charge of a larger force in the south. Stewart arrived in the Firth of Forth in April 1781 with the 74-gun *Berwick* and four frigates, three ships of 22 to 28 guns and two cutters. He was aware that much of his task was to operate to the northwards. 'The British Greenland [i.e. whaling] trade will probably be mostly rendezvoused at Bressay Sound [Shetland] by the middle of June. So soon as they are all collected, a very large part of the squadron must convoy them till they are out of danger, and then return to the station, unless some unforeseen circumstance should render such a measure unnecessary.'[22] During the summer campaign he proposed to patrol off Shetland with seven of his ships for the purpose of 'protection of the fisheries and annoyance of the enemy'. He took a party of men northwards with him and landed some at Lerwick, where they began to rebuild the old fort which had been burned by the Dutch in 1673. On completion it was named Fort Charlotte in honour of the Queen. In addition he was ordered to protect a large and very valuable convoy from the West Indies which had been routed round the north of Scotland to avoid the French and Spanish. He found the convoy near Fair Isle in the middle of June. Its men were near starvation, so he had to transfer food to some of the merchant ships.[23] He stayed off Shetland for some time and stopped several ships, none of which turned out to be enemies.

Stewart was very keen to develop Leith as a base for operations in the northern North Sea because the English east-coast ports were unsuitable: Yarmouth had dangerous sandbanks, the Humber was difficult to get in and out in unfavourable winds and the others were too small to assemble a fleet or a large convoy. As he put it, 'I have mentioned the whole force employed in the North Sea to the northward of Yarmouth Roads being under my command because it appears to me that the ships destined for that service can and will be victualled etc at Leith than by going to the southwards.'[24] But in the meantime he was ordered to blockade the Dutch in their base at the Texel and came under the command of Hyde Parker. As such he was part of the squadron escorting a convoy of 120 ships back from the Baltic in July. Meanwhile part of the Dutch Fleet was escorting their own convoy of 70 ships out towards the Baltic and the Atlantic. The two forces met at the Dogger Bank on 5 July. A battle ensued, in which the Dutch lost one ship. The Dutch convoy was forced back while the British one reached home so, like Jutland 135 years later, the British were left in command of the North Sea but disappointed of a crushing victory.

For his winter dispositions, Stewart still favoured Leith as a base. He was convinced that the Dutch and French would launch a strong privateer campaign during the winter of 1781–2, perhaps using isolated Norwegian fjords as bases.

It appears to me, my Lord [the Earl of Sandwich], that all the coast from the Humber northwards to the Firth of Forth, there being no roadstead [i.e. large anchorage] between them, will be with more facility and certainty protected by the Leith Squadron than from Yarmouth Roads, on account of the very dangerous navigation between those places. If your Lordship would be of the same opinion, I would propose that a frigate, man-of-war sloop, and a cutter should be constantly stationed there to put to sea at all times when the weather would permit, and to be victualled and refitted at Leith, and whilst absent for that purpose to be relieved by some other upon the station. I would also recommend a frigate and cutter be stationed in the same way at Cromarty, under similar orders, to protect the coast of Scotland and to regulate themselves by the information they might receive. And lastly, for the general protection of the commerce in those seas, annoying the enemy, convoys, etc in Leith Roads, at least three frigates and two cutters, which I am confident will be as few as can possibly perform the service that will fall to be executed on this station.[25]

But in fact the Dutch threat never materialised. They were more concerned to protect their own trade than attack the British. Unlike the French they had no tradition of privateering, and their main fleet was in poor condition. Keith's force was never really tested before it was sent south to the English Channel. The war ended early in 1783.

The French Revolutionary War

The next war with France began in 1793, after the revolutionaries had executed their king, Louis XVI. It started as a great coalition of conservative forces against the Revolution, but one by one the European armies were defeated by the French. When the Netherlands was occupied by France, the North Sea came into prominence again as a potential theatre of war. Charles Middleton wrote to the First Lord of the Admiralty in 1794 suggesting, among many other things, 'a fourth squadron of small ships for the Baltic and Archangel trade, to be stationed at Yarmouth Roads and Leith'.

The admiral in charge of the North Sea Fleet, Adam Duncan, was a Scot from Dundee, but he had to concentrate his forces on blockading the main Dutch fleet in its ports from his bases in the Thames and at Yarmouth, and much of his energy on preventing mutiny in his own fleet. There were constant complaints from Scotland about the lack of protection to their trade. In early 1797, privateers were reported off Buchan Ness; the Provost of Aberdeen reported a French ship off the town and Lord Gordon heard of strange ships off the coast. The annual meeting of the Convention of Royal Burghs complained that trade was 'much annoyed by French privateers, particularly those from the numerous harbours on the coast of Norway' and that information was sent via the Lord Provost of Edinburgh to the Admiralty, but little was done about it, and the main fleet was far away at Yarmouth, allowing the privateers to escape. A few gunboats were stationed at Leith for convoy escort, but were too slow to chase privateers. They proposed 'a permanent officer at Leith under whose authority convoys can be appointed and ships of war (upon information being received of privateers being on the coast) could be instantly dispatched to intercept them.'[26] But there were no seagoing naval ships in Scottish waters in May that year, except the frigate *Dart*, detailed to protect the Clyde.[27]

In October that year Duncan defeated the Dutch at Camperdown, but his command gained no more ships because of danger in the Mediterranean early in 1798. That was removed by Nelson's victory at the Nile in August, but now the government found a new role for the North Sea Fleet. In August an invasion of the Netherlands was launched. It failed and the troops were withdrawn in October, but the remnants of the Dutch navy were captured.

Some resources were now becoming available to set up a convoy system based on Leith. In March 1798 the shipmasters of Leith applied for a vessel to take their trade to the Baltic and were allocated the 14-gun ship *Good Design*. But at the same time, when the Board of Ordnance wanted an ammunition ship escorted from Leith to Berwick, Duncan replied that he had 'no vessel of any kind under my directions to send on that service'. A month later the first patrol started, with the cutter *King George* operating between Leith and Red Head near Montrose. By August a regular system had been set up between Leith and the Baltic, with a convoy leaving every three weeks, with a less regular system from Orkney to the Baltic, leaving occasionally 'as trade collects'. Even so, the escorts were few and not always in good condition. After the *Lord Hood* arrived back from Helsingor in Denmark, she was found to be 'so weak from old age that it will be necessary for her to undergo a thorough repair if she is to continue in this Service'.[28] It became possible to extend the convoy system in Scotland over the next few years. By 1801, shortly before the war ended in a stalemate, there were occasional coastal convoys from the Thames to the Firth of Forth and the Moray Firth, from there to Shetland for the Greenland whaling fleet, from Dunbar to Shetland and from Aberdeen to Yarmouth, as well as the Baltic convoys leaving from Orkney and Leith. There were also occasional convoys from Leith to Hamburg.[29]

Leith Station in the Napoleonic Wars

When a new war with France broke out in 1803, William Pitt and his friend Henry Dundas were out of office, but this did not stop the defence of Scotland becoming more politically sensitive than ever. The Dutch were still under French occupation, and therefore hostile, but it took some time to set up a force at Leith, as part of the North Sea Fleet. In July 1803 Lord Keith, in overall command of that fleet from his base in Kent, wrote to St Vincent, the First Lord of the Admiralty,

> I understand the merchants of Leith and on the neighbouring coast begin to be clamorous at their not having naval force for the protection of their shipping. Therefore until we can get a ship ready to be stationary in Leith Roads, which is represented as absolutely necessary to prevent the Enemy's Privateers from cutting out the shipping waiting for convoy, something should be sent thither.[30]

In October St Vincent ruled that the admiral at Leith 'must not be a man connected with the country' and ruled out Rear-Admiral Charles Hamilton, a relative of the Marquis of Abercorn who 'would be readily drawn in to approve any suggestion from the party, which I have long observed to be influenced more by politics than the defence of the capital of Scotland.'[31] Keith was a highly independent political spirit who never fell under the influence of Dundas though the two had been brought up together and shared 'many a hard bout'.[32] He agreed with St Vincent that the agitation for a Scottish command was largely political: 'I see a riot stirring up at Edinburgh by the judges &c, about the defenceless state of the coast; the fact is all the law is in the interest of Lord Melville, and, of course, not well inclined to the interest of the present government.'hough he could see the value of the base as a defence against privateers, Keith was sceptical about the chance of an invasion in the area: 'Where is the expedition to come from?' The Dutch ports were careful blockaded and in any case they would soon be frozen up for the winter.[33] However, he agreed that all angles had to be covered. As he wrote in December 1803,

> As it is possible that an enemy's embarkation may sail from some of the Dutch or French ports in the North Sea unperceived, and attempt to land in Scotland or pass round that country and make for some of the

northern ports of Ireland, it becomes our duty, however slight their prospect of success may be, to guard against the attempt, and as much as possible to quiet the apprehension that may exist in the minds of his Majesty's subjects on that occasion.[34]

Admiral Richard Rodney Bligh (no relation to the unfortunate captain of the *Bounty*) was an admiral of some seniority and distinction, and was a Cornishman, so he fitted in with St Vincent's parameters in one respect. However, St Vincent still had doubts about his age of sixty-six and wrote, 'I remember the time when I should have considered Admiral Bligh well qualified for the employment.' Bligh was nevertheless appointed commander at Leith on 26 October.[35] He arrived on 5 November to find his first ship, the old 44-gun *Roebuck,* anchored at Leith as a static guardship; she had arrived there a few weeks earlier.[36] The following month, after seven months of war, there were still only four other ships on the Leith station, none larger than a frigate. The *Chiffone,* captured from the French in 1801, was a 36-gun frigate and was patrolling off the coast of Norway 'To look out for the scattered Trade from the Baltic, and afterwards to proceed to Cromarty.' The *Diligence* sloop was between the Forth and Tyne 'For the protection of the coast and trade, and the annoyance of the enemy', while the 38-gun *Amethyst* performed a similar function off the coast of Norway. The *Prince of Wales*, a cutter normally used by the Customs, was convoying the brig *Breadalbane* to Trondheim and was then to return to Leith. For the moment the old *Roebuck* was the only warship in the firth.

Bligh's new flagship, the *Glatton*, arrived on the last day of 1803 and Bligh transferred his flag the following day, taking 107 men from the *Roebuck*. The *Glatton* had begun construction as an East Indiaman and had been taken over for naval use in 1795. She was rated at 56 guns.

Almost from the start, Bligh looked for a better anchorage than the Leith Roads, which was too far up the firth to protect against raids and invasion. The Admiralty was concerned that an easterly wind, which might blow an invading force into the firth, would also trap Bligh's force at Leith. As his adviser he used Commander Joseph Brodie of the Sea Fencibles, an otherwise obscure officer 'whose general knowledge on the subject in question, and of the neighbouring coast, has been acquired, not only by his having taken a very accurate survey of the whole of the Firth, but by remarks made at various times, having sailed out of Leith ever since he was nine years of age.'[37] The anchorage at the Isle of May was well positioned but 'With a strong southerly wind, a ship would be obliged to slip and put to sea; and as she would consequently be driven to the northward, it would probably be a considerable time before she could regain her station.'

A few months later, Largo Bay on the north side of the firth was suggested but Captain McKinley of the *Roebuck* reported that

> the coasters which have got embayed in this bay by southerly winds have been many hours in clearing it, an indraught (though not strong) setting in and around the bay making it tedious to get out. In gales of wind from the south-east I should conceive a very great sea would roll in, and I think admits of a great doubt whether a ship even better fitted than the *Roebuck* would ride it out with safety.[38]

The only alternative anchorage in the firth was Aberlady Bay, where there were 'eight fathoms water and good holding ground', where a ship could 'ride and get under way with any wind.'[39] The *Roebuck* moved there in January, to be followed by the *Glatton* and other ships. But Admiral Lord Keith was never happy about the bay and wrote in the same month, 'I doubt Aberlady Bay to be safe in NE winds during winter. The ground is fine sand.' Keith had a very fine eye for maritime topography, so his judgement must be respected, though it was not entirely unbiased; he wanted to promote Longannet Point further up the firth, which happened to be his own property. It was surveyed at the end of February and Mr Whidbey of Woolwich Dockyard reported that it had 'every advantage possible in making a small naval arsenal, excepting its being so far removed from the sea.'[40] In the circumstances, this was fatal to the plan. In any case, the guardship eventually moved back to Leith as the threat of invasion receded, for it was a more convenient base to administer the squadron.

Bligh also took an interest in the defence of Cromarty after receiving a letter from the acting Lord Lieutenant of Inverness. 'You will know that in the whole extent of the east coast of Great Britain from Duncansby Head to the South Foreland, there is no harbour of equal capacity, of equal safety, or better protected than Cromarty Bay.'[41]

The force of the Leith command continued to increase throughout most of 1805, though it remained a miscellaneous collection of base ships, convoy escorts and small craft. In October 1805, on the same day that Nelson fought the Battle of Trafalgar, there were eighteen ships in the Leith command, of which four were actually present in the Roads. Three were escorting convoys directly to the Baltic, while two more were with convoys from Longhope to the Baltic. Two were on patrol, off Bergen and the Naze of Norway. Two more were out impressing men off Fife Ness and at Shetland, while another was carrying troops to Gravesend on the Thames.[42] By February 1806 the number of ships had fallen to eleven, though it rose again to thirteen in May as preparations were made for the summer campaign.

Bligh struck his flag in April 1804 on his promotion to full admiral and was succeeded by Rear-Admiral James Vashon, from Ludlow in Shropshire and another St Vincent protégé. The new commander was mostly concerned with impressment, especially after 1805, and with Baltic convoys. These began in mid-April every year and continued until October. According to Sir James Saumarez in 1809, 'The convoys for the Baltic will sail once a fortnight from the Nore [on the Thames], calling off Yarmouth as they did last season, and also once a fortnight from the Humber and Leith; and convoys will sail from Longhope Sound whenever a sufficient number of vessels are collected there as they did last year.'[43] In 1807 the importance of northern waters increased yet again. Napoleon was attempting to set up his Continental System, by which the ports of Europe were closed to Britain. This made previously neutral ports such as Hamburg a potential source of conflict. Meanwhile the British attacked Copenhagen in September, capturing the Danish fleet but enduring the hostility of that country and her satellite, Norway. Almost the whole east coast of the North Sea was hostile, though Sweden still assisted with the British trade in the Baltic. Vashon retired in 1808 and the merchants of Leith, satisfied with his work in trade protection, held a banquet for him and he was given the Freedom of the City of Edinburgh.[44]

There were many incidents on convoy. In July 1810 the brig *Forward*, escorting a convoy from the Baltic to Leith and Longhope Sound, was chased away by five enemy warships and all forty-two merchant ships were captured.[45] Sometimes large numbers of ships accumulated in Wingo Sound in Sweden, which was used as a base. In June 1812 there were 172 merchant ships there, including 46 bound for Longhope and 10 for Leith.[46] The voyage back was often difficult and in June 1804 captains of escort ships were complaining of 'the increased difficulty they experience when in charge of the homeward bound ships, which always return valuably loaded and consequently require a greater protection.'[47] Ships on convoy were often ill disciplined and in 1814 the Captain of HMS *Nightingale* reported in his log,

> PM 2.20 made the signal Ships to Windward to bear down and ships on either quarter to close – with a gun – hove to – 2.40, fired a shot towards the *Alexis* of Greenock, she disregarding signal to close – fired a gun to enforce signal to close and ships to windward to bear down, the *Alexis, George* and several others disregarding it.[48]

Vashon and his successors found it equally difficult to provide enough convoy escorts and patrols to satisfy Scottish merchants and town councils. In 1808 the Lord Lieutenant of Aberdeen and the Chief Magistrate of Fraserburgh complained about the unprotected coast. The admiral replied,

> All the ships and vessels under my command are constantly employed on the convoy service, or cruising for the protection of the coast, within the limits of my station, as their lordships may observe by the account I last transmitted of the disposition of the ships and vessels employed under my direction; and I beg leave to state that I really do not think Mr Kelman is strictly justified in his assertion that the coast is unprotected. There have been some merchant vessels carried off but the privateers that made the captures have been taken – two of them of small force by the excise vessels and two others by the *Ariadne* and *Ringdove*, within the last two months.[49]

In 1810 the citizens of Dundee demanded more warship protection. 'It is extremely probable that the inhabitants of Norway, for want of employment and provisions, will more readily induce them to privateering and predatory excursions, as they will have no other alternative but to starve or go to sea.' But the navy suggested that there was 'not the slightest foundation for the apprehension'.[50]

In 1814 Admiral Hope complained about excessive pressure from the Admiralty, which had stated:

> It is requisite such vessel should be at Bressay Sound on or before 15th June. I beg you will be pleased to acquaint their lordships that I have no vessel unappropriated from the regular succession of convoys, and the blockade of Norway; and request they will inform me if it is their pleasure that I should withdraw any one from these important services. I beg leave to add that the herring and deep sea fishery requires a vessel exclusively for above nine months of the year.[51]

Convoys continued in the North Sea, as elsewhere, even after the first abdication of Napoleon Bonaparte and peace with France in 1814, because of a new war with America. They finally stopped after the second defeat of Napoleon in June 1815 and peace with America.

The Sea Fencibles

The Sea Fencibles were a corps of maritime volunteers for local defence, rather like a coastal Home Guard – 'Fencibles', a corruption of 'defensible men', were originally part-time soldiers. After a few experiments by individual officers in the early stages of the war with France, the Sea Fencibles were set up on a regular basis in 1798, mainly for the coast of England. After the resumption of war in 1803, they were extended to south-east Scotland. They were commanded by regular navy captains and lieutenants, with locally appointed petty officers, one for every twenty-five men. They were recruited from rather a narrow band – men who habitually used the sea, but were not ocean-going sailors who would be away from home for long periods, nor men who were liable for impressment into the navy. In practice this meant fishermen, ferrymen and men from coastal craft on government service. The Admiralty was particularly sensitive that seamen would use the Fencibles as a way to evade impressment, and the Fencible captains frequently had to remove men from the lists. In November 1805, for example, the Admiralty ordered the dismissal of all 'who do not fall within the strict letter of the act'. Twenty-seven men, mostly shipwrights and ropemakers, were removed from the lists in Leith, fourteen in Dunbar and twenty-two in Fife. Nevertheless the corps peaked at 23,000 in Scotland and England in 1809.

The Firth of Forth claimed 839 men in December 1803, but that was largely aspirational. It had 653 men in August 1804. Numbers fluctuated over the years, approaching 700 at some periods. The Fencibles were to exercise one day a week with cannons, muskets and pikes, and be paid a shilling per exercise. They were

> expected not only to serve, against an Enemy attempting to land upon the Coast, but also to watch the Beaches, whenever the Wind and Weather shall be favourable for the Enemy to attempt a landing; to perform any services which may accelerate the progress of our Army, or retard that of the Enemy, if he should effect a landing; but also to embark on board and Gun Boat, or other Armed Vessel, for the protection of Merchant Vessels when any Armed Vessel of the Enemy shall be in sight.[52]

Captain John Clements was the first commander of the Sea Fencibles in Scotland, taking office in mid-1803. Captain David Milne, son of an Edinburgh merchant, was appointed under him. He was quite a distinguished officer for such a post, but was under a cloud since he had lost the frigate *Seine* the year before. A court martial acquitted him of all blame and St Vincent promised him a seagoing appointment, but fell from office before he could implement it. On arrival at Leith, Milne suggested that many of the fishing boats on the coast could be fitted with 12- or even 18-pounder carronades. This was opposed by Clements, who believed they would not bear the weight. Two were fitted out at the expense of the Duke of Buccleuch and were a great success. News of this reached Henry Dundas at the Admiralty and in August 1804 Milne was given overall command in place of Clements.[53] He had control of the other groups in the Firth, east of Edinburgh and in Fife, but under his immediate command he had lieutenants in Grangemouth, Kincardine, Limekilns and South Queensferry and believed that a total of 349 men could be recruited in these areas. At Queensferry, however, all the eligible men were already enrolled as artillery volunteers for the defence of the islands in the Forth.

In August 1804 the corps in the Forth had two armed ships which employed 132 men, with nine Kinghorn fishing boats armed with 18-pounder carronades employing 133 men. Three sloops from Leith, also armed with 18-pounder carronades and using 54 men, were to be employed to carry stores in wartime. There were 21 herring boats at Fisherrow and Prestonpans with 12-pounders and 173 men. They were 23 feet long, 9 feet broad and drew 23 inches of water when loaded. Each carried an arms chest with 46 rounds per gun. In the event of an invasion all boats were to rendezvous at Aberlady Bay, and the men from Dunbar who were not allocated to boats would go on board the guardship there. Fifty-two more boats could be found if necessary, to transport troops across the Forth.[54]

Because the Fencibles were a volunteer force, it was often difficult to maintain discipline. In October 1804 one William Thompson of Kirckaldy behaved 'in an improper manner' to his lieutenant. Captain Cardin suggested impressing him into the fleet, but Milne pointed out that this was illogical. If he was liable to impressment, he should not be in the Fencibles; if he was not, then it could not be done legally. Dismissal from the corps was no real threat and he might take some of his friends with him; Milne could only suggest a public apology to his lieutenant. Sometimes the officers, not always the cream of the naval profession, were negligent. Milne found out that Lieutenant James Campbell, stationed at Dunbar, did not bother to exercise the men at North Berwick and Cockburnspath in person, as these places were eleven and eight miles from his base. He left it to the petty officers, who were 'only fishermen'.[55]

One practical service performed by the Sea Fencibles was in fetching the Danish ships which had been captured at Copenhagen in 1807, after the British bombarded the city. Volunteers were sought among the Fencibles in September 1807 and offered payment of £1 8s during their absence.[56] A total of 861 men, either Sea Fencibles or protected men from the Greenland trade, were shipped out in nine transports and warships, leaving at the end of September and beginning of October.[57] In another case, they were used to man the flagship *Texel* to seek out some French privateers which intended to prey on the Greenland trade.[58]

Captain Milne took a keen interest in the defences of the Forth, which his men would have to help man in the event of invasion. In January 1805, as the new idea of the Martello tower took hold in the south of England, he recommended a survey of 'the different bays where an enemy might effect a landing, and proper places pitched on to erect the towers'. Later that year he found that the citizens of Edinburgh were raising money to build a memorial to Lord Nelson and wrote to the Lord Provost suggesting that it should be 'as conspicuous and ornamental to the neighbourhood as possible. The Roads [i.e. anchorage] of Leith and indeed the harbour are both entirely unprotected except when the King's ships are in the Roads, for the battery at Newhaven would not hinder an enterprising enemy from taking every ship in the Roads and burning those in the harbour.' He suggested building a Martello tower armed with 24- and 32-pounder guns and dedicated to the memory of Nelson on Beacon Rocks off the harbour mouth.[59] But the citizens preferred a more conventional memorial which was completed on Calton Hill in 1813.

Apart from both sides of the Forth, the only the part of Scotland to have Sea Fencibles was the Tay. Captain John Russell was put in charge there in mid-1804 The other areas were even more remote from the possibility of invasion. By 1806, with Trafalgar won and invasion a far more remote possibility, the Fencibles came under fierce criticism from William Cobbett the radical, who suggested that 'an immense saving' would be made by abolishing them – rather unfair to a force which cost very little.[60] In any case they were eventually disbanded in February 1810. Milne completed his accounts and left. He was apparently rehabilitated, for he was offered the command of a ship of the line and went on to distinguish himself.

Signal Stations

The coastal signal stations were another way in which the Royal Navy was involved with the local community, in south-east Scotland at least. They were set up on prominent headlands and hills round the coast in order to watch out for enemy movements, whether raiding privateers or a full invasion fleet. They should not be confused with another Admiralty system, the shutter telegraphs and semaphore stations which formed a chain between the Admiralty in London and the main naval bases in southern and eastern England. Each coastal station was commanded by a naval lieutenant, who recruited a petty officer as second in command and two signallers. Where possible an existing building as taken over and converted, but in most cases a wooden hut was built, with a canvas roof. Each had a mast and gaff on which to hoist a combination of balls and flags which would give warning of enemy movements to all concerned – warships and merchantmen at sea, and the local army and Sea Fencible units in case of an invasion. Of course this never came, but there were occasional false alarms, as in October 1805 when the admiral received a signal that a fleet of men of war had appeared at the mouth of the firth, but could not be identified because of bad weather. Two cutters were sent to investigate.[61]

Captain Milne took the signal stations under his wing as well as the Sea Fencibles, and this fitted in with his worries over communication in the district. As he wrote in July 1805, 'The communication with the different places where the Sea Fencibles and armed boats are stationed at is very difficult, and takes up much time in sending orders etc by post and the roads not passable by the shore on the north side in winter.'[62]

Eventually eight stations were set up in Scotland, all south of the Forth. As well as Calton Hill and Mill Stairs in Edinburgh, they were at Garristone Hills in East Lothian, North Berwick Law, Dunbar Pier, Blackheath Hill near Dunbar, Downlaw near Berwick and St Abbs Head.[63] According to a report of June 1805, the station at Calton Hill was 'so obscured by the smoke of Edinburgh passing down the valley between the Hill and Arthur's Seat that *for days* it is not to be seen from the next station at Mill Stairs.' This was a serious problem as it communicated directly with the admiral in his flagship, so it was recommended to remove it to Arthur's Seat. But an estimate showed that this would be too expensive, so Calton Hill remained.[64]

The End of the Leith Station

The Leith Station continued to be maintained even after the end of the wars with France in 1815, though it had to find a new role to justify its existence. It was now under the command of Rear-Admiral

W. Johnstone Hope, a son-in-law of the Earl of Hopetoun, and his main job was to supervise the revenue cutters on behalf of the Boards of Customs and Excise, though from 1816 he had an old ship of the line, the *Ramillies*, as guardship at Leith. On the east coast the main role was the prevention of smuggling, though actual catches were rare. In the quarter ending 30 June 1816 only one of the five ships reported any seizures, of malt and a whisky still on the island of Stroma near Orkney, and 108 gallons of illegal liquor at Portsoy in Banff. The west coast cruisers were much more active and only one in eight submitted a nil return, for the Highlanders had never accepted their favourite drink should be subjected to government control. Seizures of whisky and stills were reported in Islay, Cumbrae, Bute, Kintyre, Cowal and even Greenock. The biggest haul was by the *Royal George* which took 207 gallons on Bute on 6 April.[65] These activities did nothing to make the navy popular in Scotland.

In May 1824, following a reorganisation, it was decided to place the revenue cutters under the control of the Board of Customs in London. This left the naval command with only four ships. The veteran *Clio* was the only one in the east, while the *Cherokee*, the *Nimrod* and the *Martial* were in the west, the last-named devoted to fishery protection duties. This was clearly not enough to support the dignity of a rear-admiral and the Leith command was abolished in August 1824. The ship on the east coast was allocated to the admiral at Chatham, those in the west to the Cork command.[66]

Chapter 6

Naval Recruitment in Scotland

The right of the English Crown to impress seamen into the Navy was as old as the monarchy itself, and derived from its power to call on all men to defend the realm in time of danger. As the navy began to take on an increasing share of the country's military activity, the burden fell very heavily on a small group, the merchant seamen, who, despite popular myth, were the only people liable to impressment. There was no specific law which justified impressment, though it was mentioned in passing by many statutes.

Soon after the Union of 1707, Captain James Hamilton, formerly of the Scottish Navy, advised his new masters 'that the method of impressing may not be used [in Scotland] except in cases of absolute necessity.' Instead he undertook to find 200 seamen himself in western Scotland by offering cash bounties.[1] The government apparently took his advice about impressment and the British Navy showed little interest in recruitment in Scotland after that. In 1714, 1718 and 1739, embargoes were placed on English shipping in preparation for a general impressment of seamen, but there were no orders for Scotland. In the 1720s the Secretary to the Admiralty wrote, 'The Kings of England never used pressing in Scotland before the Union, and however the law may be altered in that point by a consequence since, it should be gone about with greater caution than in places where it has long taken place.'[2] In 1734, when the navy was mobilised on a passing threat of war with Spain, Admiral Sir John Norris complained: 'We have no number of tenders with lieutenants and press gangs, neither to the northwards, Scotland, westward nor St Georges Channel.'[3]

On a higher intellectual plane, the Edinburgh philosopher David Hume identified the press gang as a glaring gap in the English concept of liberty. 'It is a maxim in politics . . . that a power, however great, when granted to law by an eminent magistrate, is not so dangerous to liberty, as an authority, however inconsiderable, which he acquires from violence and usurpation . . . there is, however, one occasion, where the parliament has departed from this maxim; and that is, in the *pressing of seamen*. The exercise of an irregular power is here tacitly permitted in the crown.'[4]

The word 'prest' or imprest' was once quite innocuous and referred to a small advance of wages given to a man on his recruitment, but over the years it became confused with the verb to 'press' and took on a much more sinister meaning. Originally the task of getting seamen for the navy had been delegated to local government, which was too much influenced by local factors and did not perform well. By the seventeenth century, the navy was beginning to play an even greater role in national defence, placing a much greater burden on the relatively small seafaring community. Under the English republic from 1649 to 1660 the fleet expanded threefold and it is no coincidence that relations between seamen and press gangs reached a new level of violence. From Ipswich in 1659 it was reported: 'When our people began to press, and had taken a man or two, the town's people fell on our men, and rescued them, by which means there was likely to have been blood spilt had not our men been civil.'[5] After the restoration of the monarchy in 1660 most of the King's medieval prerogatives were abolished and there was doubt whether impressment was still legal. When the fleet was mobilised for the Second Dutch War in 1664, Samuel Pepys wrote from his position as an official of the navy, 'of necessity there is a power to press, without which we cannot really raise men for the fleet of 12 sail. Besides that it will assert the King's power of pressing, which at present is somewhat doubted.'[6]

The scale of naval operations increased yet again during King William's War, from 1689 to 1697. The navy grew from 20,000 to 40,000 men in wartime, while fleets now fought over much longer ranges. Ships no longer paid off after the summer fighting season was over and men might be 'turned over' from one ship to another, so that they were retained in the navy for years at a time. At the same time there was an attempt to reform the system by setting up a register of seamen, but it was not a success.

Not long after the outbreak of the War of Jenkins' Ear in 1739, no less a person than Sir Robert Walpole, the Prime Minister, told Parliament, 'the hardships of an impress have been long dwelt upon and displayed with all the power of eloquence. Nor can it be affirmed that this method of raising seamen is either eligible or legal.'[7] But in 1743 Mr Justice Foster reaffirmed its legality in England:

On one hand, a very useful body of men seem to be put under hardships inconsistent with the temper and genius of a free government. On the other, the necessity of the case seemeth to intitle the public to the service of this body of men, whenever the safety of the whole calleth for it . . . the right of impressing mariners for the public service is a prerogative inherent in the crown, and recognized by many acts of Parliament.'[8]

No one liked the system of impressment, even those who had to implement it, but no satisfactory alternative was found during the age of sail. The English were used to impressment, though it was barely tolerated and the seaman did everything in his power to resist it, often with the support of his local community. Captain Penhallow Cumming was sent to Fowey in Cornwall in 1756 to persuade men to volunteer, in order to qualify for the bounty. But when he tried to enlist the help of the local magistrates to press a man who was obviously eligible, the Mayor made him stand at the door, 'outside in the street with a great number of people of all ranks, who many of them, some pleading in favour of the man, which I hope their Lordships are sensible is always the case on such occasions.'[9]

Early Attempts at Recruitment

When war broke out in 1739, Lieutenant William Campbell was sent north in the first attempt at organised recruitment in Scotland since the Union. He did not carry a press warrant, which would have given him power to press seamen, but instead relied on the use of a cash bounty to attract men, as his poster, put up in Edinburgh and Leith, showed. He also toured the west, finding thirty volunteers at Irvine, six at Saltcoats, ten at Greenock, four in Glasgow and two more on the Clyde. In all he found 222 recruits for the navy.[10]

Robert Spotswood, a young surgeon from Edinburgh, went to London as a sea passenger in 1744 and landed at Wapping. He

was soon gripped by the fist by a gentile fellow, who commanded me to go along with him. I refused. He insisted with hideous oaths. An altercation took place, in the struggle tore a new coat and stumbled down in the dirty street, kept his grip with one hand, rose with a folded fist, threatened and swore he would drive my teeth down my throat . . . The good people in the streets and shops gazed but gave no assistance. I conjectured they might see innocence in my face and guilt in his as a blackguard and a robber . . .

Having never heard of impressing seamen on shore for the Navy, was convinced . . . I was to be robbed and perhaps murdered . . . At this point another stout fellow, not in a sailor's habit, joined him. Unable to resist two, they dragged me along each by an arm, I imagined to utter destruction and soon landed me in a public house, where I saw the sailor impressed from our ship the same day. This unfolded to me their design and became perfectly composed. An old lieutenant [asked] 'How long at sea?' 'Nine days.' Questioned and cross questioned me, the same answer. 'Let me see your hands.' He endeavoured to persuade me they had been pulling or hauling ropes for years, however he evidently saw it was not the case, asked profession. 'A surgeon.' 'What evidence?' Pulled out a lancet case and was set at liberty and never afterwards challenged.[11]

This gives a good example of the methods of the press gang in England. It confirms two essential points: that they were looking for experienced seamen, not landsmen as popular mythology would have it, and that these methods were not known in Scotland, despite thirty-seven years of union with England and five years of war with Spain.

The point about experienced seamen is important, for such men needed much skill and, more important, the right attitudes. A Scottish naval physician, Dr Thomas Trotter, drew attention to 'the unparalleled hardships to which seamen are exposed from the nature of their employment. Toil and danger are their constant attendants. They suffer privations to which all other men are strangers.' They had 'unfailing fortitude and matchless patience'. They could only be trained by years of service at sea:

> Nautical astronomy and all its auxiliary branches may be learned on shore. Even the manual duties of seamanship may be acquired in a short time, but there may still be wanting that soul of enterprise, that hardihood of frame that can mock danger and surmount difficulties in every hideous form; that can submit to sickness, privation and famine without repining at their fate and can view even death itself in all its most horrid aspects, of a sinking ship, a lee shore or wounds in battle. Such are the requisites necessary to form the true-bred British seaman.

They could not be learned easily and he wrote:

> No person will have the hardihood to contend that a seaman's duty can be learned in less than seven years, or after 21 years of age. He must be accustomed to it from boyhood, for no adult can ever be brought to endure privation, dangers and hardships which are inseparable from a sea life.[12]

This is largely confirmed by the captain of the *Peggy and Nelly* of Kincardine in a court case of 1807. He was asked, 'If a man was 24 or 25 years before he took to a seafaring life, could he even so acquire a knowledge of his profession as to become a seaman in the proper sense of the word?' The shipmaster replied, 'A person of these years can never become so perfect or be considered so able a seaman as one bred to it from his youth, though he may be a sensible man . . . if he followed it constantly for seven years he would call him a sailor, but before the seven years expired he would call him a lumper or land louper.' [13]

Why did skilled seamen hate the navy so much? The naval service was not necessarily worse than the merchant marine in treating its men, and indeed William Spavens wrote, 'I would just observe, that His Majesty's service is in many respects preferable to any other; first as when a ship in the merchant navy is cast away, the men and officers lose their pay . . . secondly, the provisions are better in kind and generally more plentiful.'[14] However, there were two main factors which made the seaman go to great lengths to avoid naval service. One was the question of pay. In peacetime there was little disparity between the two services, but in wartime many thousands of men were forced into the Royal Navy, creating a great demand for seamen, whose wages increased threefold or fourfold. Impressment into the fleet would prevent a man from sharing in this bonanza.

Secondly, a merchant seaman always had the option to leave his ship at the end of a voyage. The naval man too was only recruited, in theory, for a particular ship and a particular voyage. In practice he was 'turned over' from one ship to another, often until the war ended, without any guaranteed chance to set foot on shore. As the Secretary to the Admiralty wrote in the 1720s:

> This custom is very disagreeable to the seamen and has begot that aversion we have seen in them to the service; It takes from them the freedom of serving where they like, and many times the small [i.e. petty] officers are turned before the mast [i.e. lose their status]. It abridges them from the pleasure of seeing their families.[15]

John Nicol of Edinburgh was pressed into the navy in 1794 and later expressed his feelings: 'I found myself in a situation I could not leave, a bondage that had been imposed upon me against my will, and with no hopes of relief until the end of the war.' He left the navy in 1802, determined not to return, and during the next war he was forced to leave Leith and live inland. This blighted his life, for he had to undertake work which damaged his health. Yet he took perverse pride in his value to the state. When his friends mocked him he replied,

> 'Necessity had no law.' Could the government make perfect seamen as easily as they could soldiers, there would be no such thing as the pressing of seamen, and I was happy to be of more value than all of them put together, for they would not impress any of them, they were of so little value compared with me. [16]

Setting up the Impress Service

In 1755, as war with France was threatened again, a regular impress service was set up throughout Scotland and England for the first time, with an officer known as the 'regulating captain' at each major port. Each had several lieutenants under him, in charge of a press gang of about ten men. Captain John Fergusson, already notorious in parts of Scotland for his ruthlessness in suppressing the Jacobites and smugglers in the Firth of Clyde, was appointed regulating captain at Leith.

At four in the morning of 26 February 1755, with the co-operation of the army, Fergusson began the first attempt at organised impressment in Scotland. A hundred troops from the garrison of Edinburgh Castle moved into position, blocking the exits from the town of Leith, while the men of Fergusson's gang raided seamen's homes and taverns. The results were disappointing. Only 200 seamen were found and 175 of these had to be released, because they were whale fishermen from the Greenland trade, and so protected by law from impressment.[17]

Another press gang under Lieutenant Hay was sent to Bo'ness, which Fergusson believed had 'the greatest number and best seamen of any port in the Firth'. Because of shoal waters, they had to land some miles from the town, which gave the natives ample warning and no seamen could be found there. The gang went on board a snow from Glasgow and pressed two men, the only result. Hay was more successful at Montrose, where he found twenty-two men, but troubles at Bo'ness continued: Fergusson claimed that it was 'the only town in Scotland who by force opposed and prevented the impressing of men'. In fact the town, like at least twenty others, offered a bounty for men who enlisted in the Royal Navy, but it took this to mean that it was now exempt from the attentions of the press gang.

A second raid on the town was made in April, but a force escorted by soldiers failed to find any seamen. Early in May there was a further setback for the press gangs. They found some whaling ships anchored off the port, but by law they were not allowed to touch them. Instead the Greenland men allowed all the local sailors to come on board, and stood on deck in a threatening manner, armed with the harpoons and lances of their trade. Even worse, when the press gang took two men out of a trading ship coming into the port, the whalers got into their boats and surrounded the pressing tender. 'To show their contempt, beat drums, hurraed, put brooms on their topmast heads, declaring they would sweep us out of the Forth, and bonfires, all in the sight and hearing of my men.'[18]

Meanwhile, Captain Robert Grant volunteered to raise men in the Clyde, though Fergusson warned the Admiralty that he was 'well acquainted with the troublesome disposition of the people of the West of Scotland'.[19] But Grant was 'a cool man' well known in the area. He was in Greenock by the end of February, but found difficulty in organising his gangs. He had no boats and only three men were willing to join the gang. Despite support from the officers of the Custom House, he got nowhere and many seamen fled into the woods. Men from ships arriving at Greenock soon developed ways of evading the press gangs ashore.

Regulating Officers

Despite the obvious horrors of the impress, and the lack of any chance to gain either glory or prize money, many officers wrote to the Admiralty soliciting appointment. Thus Captain Patrick Drummond of Edinburgh wrote in 1776, 'Immediately on hearing the accounts of the present armament [i.e. mobilisation] I took the liberty to write to you that I should be happy to be employed on the impress service here or at any other place Lord Sandwich thought proper to appoint me.'[20] He was given the post at Leith.

Most of the officers of the impress service had undistinguished careers. Lieutenant William Campbell, the officer sent north in 1739, was promoted captain the following year but was dismissed after a court martial in 1741. Robert Grant, the first to set up the impress service in Greenock, commanded several ships of the line but saw little action. Patrick Drummond had served in the West Indies but saw no sea service after 1773.

On the other hand, John Fergusson, who set up the first impress service at Leith in 1755, had served with some success against the Jacobites in 1746 (at least in the eyes of his masters in London), and was to command a ship of the line at the taking of Louisbourg in 1758. At the outbreak of war against Revolutionary France in 1793, Captain

Jahleel Brenton arrived in Greenock as regulating captain. He was unusual in such a post because he had no connection with the area, having been born in America – perhaps the Admiralty thought that he would be less under the influence of local shipowners and merchants. He later reached the rank of vice-admiral and reared two sons who became senior officers.

The Composition of the Press Gang

In 1795 two press gangs were in operation at Greenock, and two at Leith. Each nominally consisted of a lieutenant, one or two midshipmen and about eight men. They rented a local inn and called it a 'rendezvous' for the recruitment of seamen, whether voluntary or not. Only professional seamen could be pressed into the navy. The idea that the press gang had the right to take any citizen going about his business was a popular myth and in practice the navy was often reluctant to take non-seamen at all, even as volunteers.

Brenton, like most officers, found difficulties with his press gangs ashore. James Lewis Wydown was a habitual drunk who once attempted to strike his lieutenant with a bottle. At one stage he went into the Merchant's Coffee Room where a book of ships' arrivals was kept. In it he wrote, 'the *Perseverance* from France, Tom Paine commander'. When finally put in jail he declared himself 'very happy in having Tom Paine's works by him'.[21] The government campaign against sedition, leading to the persecution of the Scottish Martyrs, was already under way by this time. A few months later, a member of the gang was suspected of the murder of a former comrade but released without charge.

At Leith some of the greatest difficulties were caused by the crew of the tender *Good Intent*. Given shore leave by their captain, they caused a disturbance in the street. When the regulating captain tried to discipline them they tried to burn down the rendezvous in Fisherrow. There were difficulties in recruiting enough men for the gang itself. In January 1798 Lt Grierson's gang, which should have included about ten men, had only a midshipman and four able seamen.[22]

Pressing Tenders

A regulating captain usually hired a number of small ships to use as 'pressing tenders' to serve in effect as a jail for impressed seamen, as a raiding vessel and as a transport to and from the main naval ports. One of the first was the *Adventure,* which was passing Berwick on the way from Leith to the Medway on 17 September 1758, when she was pursued by a much larger and faster ship, the French privateer *L'Infernal*, of 14 guns. Lieutenant James Orrock tried to defend his ship for over an hour with his own six guns and lost two men killed and seventeen wounded, but the *Adventure* was overwhelmed. Orrock was eventually promoted to commander for his bravery.[23]

The pressing tender's function as a jail was highlighted by the regulating captain's problems in Dundee in 1806. David Laird complained that he had no tender to keep the seamen, and was 'often obliged to keep them in the lockup house for days, and sometimes for a week or two'. There were two escapes when the lockup house was broken open. Laird applied to the magistrates for the use of the town jail, but was refused.[24]

Brenton's first task on arriving at Greenock in 1793 had been to hire two small ships, the brig *Polly* of 120 tons and the *Peggy*, later supplemented by the *Sprightly* cutter. We have no picture of these ships, but a drawing of a pressing tender of roughly the same period shows the layout. Even volunteers could be expected to desert after they had claimed their bounty, so they had to be kept in a secure place below decks. The idea was that at least one boat would be on station to hold men, for no building on shore was safe from the Greenock mob and the magistrates could not be trusted to protect it. Another tender, when full of men, would be on passage to Plymouth with men for the fleet. Thus the *Polly* and the *Peggy* made four or five trips south every year. But Brenton soon found that the westerly winds in the firth often delayed the tenders from sailing for weeks at a time. In 1795 Captain Thomas Pringle suggested a novel solution. A vessel of seventy or eighty tons should be procured and towed to Edinburgh through the new Forth and Clyde Canal, where the men would be delivered to the admiral in the Forth.[25] There is no sign that this was taken up, perhaps because the passage through the canal would give plenty of opportunities for men to escape.

Even the tenders offshore were not completely secure. On 4 June 1793 a party of eleven recruits on board the *Polly* tender hoisted a boat out and rowed ashore. Lieutenant Stevenson, captain of the tender, complained that his crew refused to help him prevent the escape. There had been a much more serious incident off Greenock in 1779 on board the tender *Trelandven*. To make the conditions for pressed men slightly more bearable as they waited to be sent south, they were allowed up on deck in small groups to take the air. At nine on a Sunday morning, one of the crew, guarding the pressed men with a cutlass, was seized from behind. A rope ladder was dropped into the hold to allow more men to escape, while the naval lieutenant and the captain of the ship were barricaded in the great cabin by a hogshead of vinegar. Seventeen men got on deck before a midshipman was able to cut the rope ladder, while the captain fired a pistol blindly out of his cabin, fatally wounding one man. But the escaping men in the boat found that it was chained to a carronade aboard the ship. Meanwhile the crew of the other tender in the harbour noticed the disturbance and sent their boat over and order was restored.[26]

Resistance

Greenock was the leading port in Scotland in the late eighteenth century, and furthermore it served as a base to recruit men from ships arriving in the Clyde from the West Indies and for forays to the other Clyde ports, including Glasgow. Brenton's returns to the Admiralty show that he was quite successful in getting both seamen and landsmen into the navy. By the end of the first week he had 54 volunteers, 148 by the end of January and after a year 1,183 men had entered the navy though his operation. Yet very few of these came from the press gang. It was May before the first three men were pressed and the figure rose to eight by the middle of October. Even after a year, only twenty-two men, less than 2 per cent of the total, had been 'prest' into the navy. The rest, in theory at least, were volunteers.[27]

Meanwhile, the local population gave notice of their intention to resist. The riggers, caulkers, carpenters and seamen of Greenock had a meeting and 'it was resolved by the whole body to stand by and support each other in case an impress should take place.' In June 'the lower class of people in Greenock became very riotous and proceeded to burn everything that came in their way and about 12 o'clock they hauled one of the boats belonging to the rendezvous on the square and put her into the fire.' It was recovered, much damaged, as the authorities began to restore order, while one of the press gang lieutenants wounded a rioter with his sword.[28]

However, Brenton sent his tenders and gangs out on a 'press from projections', in which, by Admiralty order, the exemptions which were issued to seamen in certain trades were revoked. At two in the morning of 16 June his boats set out to raid ships in the river between Dumbarton and Largs. They found plenty of seamen, but most turned out to be too old for the navy, or to be young apprentices who were still exempt.[29]

Evasion Afloat and Ashore

On the Clyde, seamen and ships' masters soon found various ways of evading the press gang. A classic method was for homecoming ships to land their men on remote parts of the coast. In 1795 it was found that the American merchant ship *Missouri* had dropped off several British members of its crew in the village of Dunoon, anchoring in the Holy Loch to do so.[30] Similar methods were adopted in Dundee, where there was no regular pressing tender. As a result, men were dropped off at the mouth of the river and the ships were navigated into port by mates and apprentices, who were exempt from impressment.[31]

In 1796 Captain Brenton transferred from the Clyde to the Forth and took over the rendezvous at Leith. Conforming to the modern stereo-type, he found that the people of Edinburgh tended to be less violent but more legalistic than those of the Clyde. As early as 1777, Captain Napier had complained that ships' masters often gave their seamen indentures for three years, to prevent them being impressed.[32] In 1804 a case before the Court of Session established the law on recruiting vagrants to the fleet.[33] In the same year Duncan Robertson, a gingerbread maker of Edinburgh, had a dispute with a gentleman in the precincts of Edin-burgh Castle. The man, 'dressed in coloured clothes, not regimentals', turned out to be the colonel of the Royal Irish Regiment and had Robertson pressed into the navy, being 'hurried on board of a tender in Leith Roads' and thus 'torn from his family and condemned to en-counter all the perils and hardships of a sailor's life.' He sued Captain Nash of the impress service for his release.[34]

Another case of 1807 dealt with three men who were impressed from Perth jail after Admiral Vashon at Leith heard they were sailors. They were sentenced to be whipped in the streets and then they were taken on board a warship 'before even their wounds were dressed, or their comfort in the least attended to'. One of them, by the name of Wylie, sued for his release on the grounds that he was a shoemaker, not a seaman. He did admit to making a voyage as a passenger from Kincardine to Perth and Dundee in the *Peggy and Nelly* of 60 tons. In any case, the court decreed that Wylie had to stay in the navy.[35]

A common legal trick was for the friend of a pressed man to raise an action against him for debt, so that he was transferred to the jurisdiction of a civil court, from which he could escape when the action was dropped. To prevent this, in 1777 Captain Napier at Leith issued orders to the lieutenant of the pressing tender 'not to allow any boat whatsoever to come alongside her without my order, or any civil officer to come on board'.[36]

Criminals and Smugglers

The popular view of naval recruiting has been coloured by Edward
Thompson's remark that the crew of a ship was made up of 'the
pressed refuse of jails and the scum of the streets'. In fact this was
greatly exaggerated, for naval officers had no wish to fill their ships
with such men. Some recruits were listed as being 'sent by civil officers'
or local magistrates – perhaps vagabonds or criminals, but the number
was never large. There were 20 such men recruited at Leith from 1776
to 1779 out of a total of 3,584, and 10 at Greenock from February to
March 1794, out of 1,183.[37]

It is often suggested that press officers were quite happy to recruit
from prisons, but in general they were looking for experienced seamen
on relatively minor charges. Lieutenant Carnegie heard of a group of
men imprisoned in Glasgow for 'rioting in the streets at a late hour and
no other crime alleged against them'. He found eight suitable men and
enlisted them for the fleet.[38]

Smugglers were the most acceptable form of offender. They were
good seamen and their crimes were not regarded as antisocial, like
robbery or murder. In 1777 Napier, the regulating captain at Leith,
reported that the naval sloop *Hazard* had captured a smuggling lugger
manned by 'twelve stout fellows' and that 'the man who pretends to be
the master of her' was 'a daring and resolute fellow'. Despite legal
protests, the men were pressed.[39]

Even the existence of the press gang created a certain amount of
anarchy which could be exploited by criminal elements. In September
1779 a small merchant ship anchored in Loch Don was approached by
'a black clinker-built cutter' armed with 16 guns. The merchant ship,
believing this to be a press tender, allowed herself to be boarded and
searched, but suspicions were aroused when the raiders took from the
captain 'my pocket book with a seventy pound bill and several other
bills and notes of great value and a watch and searched for money'.
The pirates made off when a real naval cutter was sighted. The black
cutter, it transpired, had been stolen at Dublin a few weeks earlier.[40]

There was no legal challenge to the principle of impressment itself
until 1812 when the magistrates of Glasgow disputed whether Scots
law allowed impressment and released some seamen who had been
pressed. The First Lord of the Admiralty, the Second Viscount Melville, wrote, 'I am yet to learn that the authority of the Lord High
Admiral to require the services of all seafaring men . . . does not
extend to the Clyde and to Scotland as well as to other parts of His
Majesty's dominions, or that the law in that respect is different or

ought to be differently administered in Scotland and in England.'[41] The case never came to court.

Expanding the Scope

In 1795 Captain Thomas Pringle was sent to inspect the rendezvous in Scotland and the North of England. Of Greenock he reported,

> This station and the contiguous country does by no means furnish to the navy the number of men it ought, owing to the little or no protection and countenance given by the civil power to the impress service, the magistrates refusing to back the warrants. Consequently when the gangs have attempted landing on different parts of the shore, they have been driven off by the people, and rescues have taken place more than once even upon the quays of Greenock. On this account the operations of the gangs are nearly confined to afloat, and therefore Captain Brenton very properly keeps one of them cruising in a small vessel off the mouth of the port.

Pressing in the Forth seems to have been more successful than in the Clyde, if limited in range. Pringle commented,

> The operations of the impress service here being limited to within 10 miles of Edinburgh, the effect of it is confined to a very small compass, and the more distant parts of the Firth of Forth, as well as the whole of the north east coast of Scotland, may be considered as nearly exempted from contributing to the navy, excepting by the few who come voluntarily from thence.[42]

New rendezvous were soon set up at Dundee and Inverkeithing, though not at Aberdeen as Pringle had suggested. Even so, a report of 1801 suggested that raids outside the main ports were not likely to be successful:

> All the small towns and villages along the coast to the northward are said to be full of seafaring men; but as most of the leading men in these places set their faces against the impress, it is doubtful if any attempt to impress men to the northward would succeed . . . Should their lordships determine to depend on the impress for men from the coast of Scotland, I presume that a number of armed ships will be necessary.[43]

This was confirmed by experience in 1803–6. When the Navy was mobilised for the restart of war in 1803, there was a night of 'general impress' on 10 March. The press gangs in the Forth raised seventeen able seamen, eleven ordinary seamen and one landsman who was presumably a volunteer – a total of twenty-nine. This compares with a dockyard town like Portsmouth, where marines from the barracks were formed into press gangs and raised 600 men.

When the gang attempted to impress some fishermen of Dunbar who had been caught smuggling, troops had to be sent to restore order. Raids were carried out on Aberdeen, Peterhead and Banff with limited success. There were considerable difficulties in Dundee, where Captain David Laird complained in February 1806 that the local government was preventing him from shipping pressed men out by bringing process of law against him in each individual case. The local officials did their best to delay the process.

> I was always ready to discuss the merits of the cause, without a lawyer being employed on either side, which might have been done in half an hour, but in place of that, I have been constantly served with papers, and obliged to answer them through the means of an agent, which has occasioned the delay of days and weeks, besides incurring a very considerable expense, and in many instances the magistrates have discharged men who have been impressed, without my being in the knowledge of their having done so.[44]

The Dundee rendezvous was wound up soon afterwards and Admiral Vashon at Leith expected that the town 'will become a hiding place for deserters and other seafaring men who wish to keep out of the way of the impress.'[45]

Other Means of Recruitment

The American War of 1775–83 was unpopular in many quarters, which made pressing even more difficult than usual. In Scotland as elsewhere, sums of money were offered to encourage seamen to enlist. The Earl of Hopetoun offered £500 while Orkney offered to find 100 men on condition that they would not be bothered by press gangs.[46] But meanwhile Captain Hon. Frederick Maitland used an almost feudal method to recruit men for his ship, the 74-gun *Elizabeth*. He raised 200 men 'from his interest in his own country' and sent them south, up to a hundred at a time, by tender.[47]

The supply of seamen became an even more acute problem in 1795, when Britain was opposed by Revolutionary France as well as by Spain and the Netherlands. Two Quota Acts were passed by Parliament, by which each seaport and local authority was to find a given number of men for the navy. These assessments give some idea of the importance of different seaports, though it is not clear how the figures were drawn up.

Parliament appointed four men to the task, including Admiral Lord Hood from the naval side and Henry Dundas from Scotland. The whole of the Clyde was assessed at 683 men, while Rothesay alone had to find 162. Even for a centre of the herring fishery, this seems strangely disproportionate and caused the Duke of Atholl to complain to Henry Dundas: 'The Isle of Bute is assessed to the number of 162 men. I did not know that the island was to be brought within the act, nor do I know on what grounds such an assessment was made.'[48]

In any case Leith had raised its 206 men by 20 April, which the Admiralty agreed was a 'very laudable and successful exertion', but it refused to take the embargo off the individual port until all the others had raised their men.[49] Meanwhile Glasgow was ordered to find 57 men, but had only recruited 15 by the middle of June. A special levy was put on the city by the Council, to raise money for a bounty.[50]

Even when men were lured into the navy by means of the bounty, there was always the possibility that they would take the money and disappear. Sixty-six of Brenton's 1,183 recruits were lost in this way. There were false alarms, caused by the well-known fecklessness of the seaman ashore. In January 1793 three men went missing from the *Polly* but were found to have gone to Glasgow where they spent their bounty drinking His Majesty's health, according to the report. Then they went back to the rendezvous in Greenock, penniless.

A few young men volunteered for naval service without such inducements. David Hay of Renfrewshire joined the navy at Greenock in 1803 at the age of fourteen because the weaving trade was 'exceedingly depressed'. On board the press tender anchored a mile off shore, he was regaled with 'an account of the moving accidents by battle and storm that had befallen some of the old seamen', when he was summoned on deck. 'In a press room, no ladder is allowed and the only means of ascent is by a rope with knots in it at short distances apart . . . If you can ascend this rope good and well, but if not you must remain below.'[51] The tender took him to the naval base at Plymouth. He was soon disillusioned with the navy, and deserted in 1811, to be pressed again a few months later.

Many more Scots entered the navy far from their native land, being pressed from merchant ships around the world. John Nicol, born near Edinburgh in 1755, was returning from China in 1794 when the ship reached the Downs, off the coast of Kent:

> I had allowed my beard to grow long, and myself to be very dirty, to be as unlikely as possible, when the men-of-war boats came on board to press the crew. As we expected, they came. I was in the hold, sorting

among the water casks, and escaped. They took every hand that would answer. I rejoiced in my escape, but my joy was of short duration. One of the men they had taken had a sore leg, the boat brought him back and I had the bad luck to be taken, and he was left. Thus were all my schemes blown into the air.[52]

The Definition of a Seaman

Since the press gang could only take professional seamen, the definition of such men assumed some importance, for example, in the case of those who worked part-time as fishermen. In 1771, Lord Kinoul wrote, 'The case of the salmon fishers in the River Tay is very particular. They hire the fishings from those who take them from the proprietors, they are neither seamen nor watermen; they occupy houses and lands on shore, they follow agriculture or other labour on shore out of the fishing season.'[53] In 1806 a fairly generous attitude was taken by the regulating captain at Greenock. He referred

> to those who, during the season, follow the herring, salmon or other temporary fishings, or to farmers, mechanics and others on this coast who, being generally employed on shore and subjected to the ballot [i.e. selective conscription] for the militia, are not considered as liable to be impressed from their occasional occupation as fishermen during the herring season, or fishing on the coast near their dwellings for the supply of their families.[54]

Of course this issue was particularly sensitive in the Northern Isles. Naval officers sent to Orkney and Shetland were well aware of the great reservoirs of men to be found there. In most of Britain, the seaman was almost a separate species from the rest of society, with his own skills, speech, manners and vocabulary. Shetland had been asked to find only six men under the Quota Acts, but this was a gross underestimate, for every man was a seaman:

> No sooner is a boy able to wield an oar than he is occupied in the fishing business, so that the whole male inhabitants of the lower class are inured to the sea from their infancy. To detail the dangers that they brave in occupying the fishing in their small open boats would be needless. Let it suffice to say that a more handy and resolute set of men cannot be anywhere found.[55]

But getting them into the navy was more difficult. The Greenland fishery was attractive to the young and about 600 or 700 men went every summer, despite the opposition of landowners who preferred them to work in the local fisheries. Nevertheless it was claimed that 7,000 or 8,000 men, out of a total population of 23,000, volunteered for the navy in the war of 1793–1801.[56] In the following war which began in 1803, however, only two or three hundred had been recruited in the first two years and Admiral Vashon found 'many of them objectionable, and some of them returned from the Nore as unfit for service'. Unfortunately Lieutenant Scott, in charge of the rendezvous in Shetland, did not make any 'great figure by his services'. It was hoped that reports of good prize money would eventually attract others. Even when men were signed up and had accepted the bounty it was difficult to keep them. When a transport ship arrived in the islands in 1805 offering wages of £3 or £3 10s per month, nine naval volunteers deserted. A hint that men might be impressed from the Greenland fleet led to the seamen assembling ashore 'in array', 'threatening murder to all who might attempt to take them.'[57] Lieutenant Scott found that the press gang conflicted with local fears:

> One day, when he was going out of the town of Lerwick, he saw a number of people running after him. He stopt, and spoke to a man whom he met coming from the country, and who said he was going to Lerwick to enter for the navy. In the meantime, the men who were running away from the town came up, and said the press had broke out in it, and they were flying away, to avoid being impressed. On this, the man who only a minute before was walking to the town to enter, turned about and scampered off with the rest.[58]

A more general problem was highlighted by the ambiguous orders issued to the press gang officers during the American War. They were to press 'seafaring men and persons whose occupations and callings are to work on vessels and boats upon rivers'. Did this include ships' carpenters who repaired ships afloat but never went to sea themselves? Did it include men like Thomas Law, 'A man whose usual employment was to work as a jobber on board of ships at Port Glasgow'? It was eventually ruled that he was liable, which must have disrupted work in the port.[59]

The reports of press gang officers give many insights into Scottish maritime history, for example, the fishing industry. A report of 1806 gives much detail on the fishermen of Argyll, arranged by parish and enumerating those who were mates of vessels.[60] Another report of the same year gives some idea of fishing activity on the Clyde:

> The fishermen who frequent this port [Greenock] are not numerous, two wherries and a decked smack belonging to Campbeltown

employing sixteen men, and two Torbay smacks with five men each, are all that come here regularly. Along the coast for about 20 miles, there are employed in small boats about 40 (from what information I can at present attain, as these do not come up the river, but send the fish by the carts.) There are also several fishing boats between Ayr and Stranraer, which do not trade this way, but I am not acquainted with their numbers.[61]

The case of Wyllie in the *Peggy and Nelly*, of 60 tons, like many of the press gang papers, gives some incidental material for the history of merchant shipping. It was stated that a round voyage from Kincardine to Dundee and Perth might take five and a half days at best, or up to three weeks if the winds were unfavourable.

The Final Years

In 1814–15, as the Great Wars with France finally came to an end, the problems of the Greenock gangs (or 'parties' as they now called themselves) got worse. In January 1815 they pressed three seamen on the Gourock Road. They passed the house of one George Robertson, who came out with two sons and several servants and released them. Later that evening, one of the released men spotted Lieutenant Ecker in the town square and called out, 'That is one of them.' He was severely beaten by a mob chanting 'murder him, murder him', and escaped into the White Hart Inn where he fell senseless. It was his third beating and he asked the Admiralty to relieve him, claiming 'the populace of this town has repeatedly threatened to murder me.'[62]

In June, Lieutenant Forbes wanted to be replaced 'in consequence of the repeated insults I meet with in the streets of Greenock, and the mob having proceeded even up the stairs to the door of my lodgings . . . It is hard to say what so ferocious a people might do.'[63] Ordinary gang members, mostly natives of the area, fared even worse. Four of them left for Ireland, 'fearing the resentment of those men now about to be laid off from the ships of war, many of whom were impressed at this port.'[64]

Scotland's Contribution to the War

According to the census of 1801, Scotland had 1.6 million people, or 15 per cent of the British population. The Scottish merchant fleet was similar in proportion to that of England and Wales, employing 13 per cent of the total number in 1792 and 12 per cent in 1800. There are no overall figures for the Royal Navy and it would take a major research project among 250,000 muster books to find the real proportion of Scots in the navy. In the meantime we can look at the position aboard three individual ships. Excluding foreigners, Scots made up 9 per cent of the seamen of the *San Domingo* around 1812 and 16 per cent of the marines.[65] They were only 7 per cent of the crew of the *Implacable* in 1808.[66] They were 9 per cent of the crew of the inaptly named *Caledonia* in 1810, and only 2 out of 158 marines were Scottish.[67] All this suggests that Scotland was under-represented on the lower decks of the Royal Navy and that the press gang never really worked as a means of recruiting there. At worst, it contributed to a feeling that the Royal Navy was a predatory English institution, which the twentieth-century navy had to work hard to eradicate.

Chapter 7

Nineteenth-century Neglect

The Years of Peace

As the long wars came to an end in 1814–15, and were finished off by the Battle of Waterloo in 1815, the greatest fleet in the world was largely paid off. From 1,009 ships in 1813, the navy had only 179 in 1826 and only a few of these were in commission. From a peak of 145,000 men in 1810–13, Parliament voted for 23,000 in 1826. Since there was no real system of reserves, most of the officers who had begun their careers in the boom years found themselves on almost permanent half-pay, with little prospect of employment and even less of wealth from prize money. The Keiths and the Hopes had already made large fortunes and had reached high rank. They were powerful enough to ensure that their sons and nephews would continue to make good in the much less lucrative peacetime navy. But there were many officers of humbler rank and background who spent decades on half-pay, or tried to find alternative careers. Lieutenant Thomas Chrystie of Fife was aware that 'there would be no chance of promotion for an officer who had little or no interest'. He took service in the merchant navy, complaining that 'the system of favouritism, particularly on account of corrupt Parliamentary reasons, may not continue to blot on the honourable government of this noble country.'[1] Alexander Maconochie, a commander of 1815 and a relative of the Cochranes, turned his attention to penal reform.[2] Commander John Finlayson had been Nelson's signal officer at Copenhagen in 1801, when he turned his blind eye to the admiral's signal. In the 1840s he complained, 'I joined the steam service under the idea of having a preference for a command in my own service, but found interest was wanting and merit or service had no chance, and now like many others growing grey with youngsters stepping over my head.' At the same time Lieutenant John Fullarton of Ayrshire wrote of his past career, 'Nothing but the common occurrences of services. Health broken from climate and hurts received, like a thousand others upon the active list. As Jack says, "not worth a single damn".[3]

Between 1814 and 1849 the Scottish intake to the officer corps seems to have remained proportional to that of England, with 264 known recruits from north of the border and 1,354 from the south, so the Scottish percentage remained as strong as during the wars. Things were already beginning to change. By the 1830s, as the Royal Navy began to move into a new age in which steam and iron would eventually wipe out sail and wood, the old world of the eighteenth-century navy was also dying. After fifteen years of peace, there was no longer any hope of great wealth by prize money. The natural right of the aristocracy to rule was no longer unchallenged, while Parliament was reformed, at least partly, in 1832, so that borough interest was no longer regarded as a fair way of getting naval promotion. The Scots were more aware of this than most and the Scottish intake to the officer corps seems to have declined, apart from well-established families such as the Duffs and the Hopes.

A superficial glance at the lists of office holders might suggest that the Royal Navy continued to be dominated by Scots throughout most of the nineteenth century. Certainly Lord Melville, First Lord of the Admiralty from 1812 until 1827 and again from 1828 to 1830, was as Scottish as his father had been. But Sir James Graham, First Lord from 1830 to 1833 and 1853 to 1854, was actually a borderer, from Cumberland. The Earl of Minto, who held the office from 1835 to 1841, was educated at Edinburgh University but was born in France and represented an English constituency for part of his parliamentary career. His successor, the Earl of Haddington (1841–5), was indeed Scottish, related to the Earl of Hopetoun and educated in Edinburgh, though he too mostly represented English constituencies before he inherited his father's title. But on the whole the Scottish interest was not so strong at the Admiralty after Melville finally left in 1830.

This was the age when Scottish maritime endeavour reached its peak. Her engineers led the world in the development of steam power and iron-and-steel construction, and in 1870, 70 per cent of British registered iron tonnage was built on Clydeside. At its peak in 1890, the Scottish fisheries employed 90,000 men and women and created a vast export market for herring. In 1912, six of the world's fifty largest shipping lines were Scottish. The Clyde steamers enjoyed a golden age, with thousands of people taking passage for leisure or work every year.

By the beginning of the twentieth century, the Royal Navy was enjoying a few of the fruits of this, through the building of warships on the Clyde and by means of the part-time naval men of the Royal Naval Reserve, but on the whole it concentrated on plans for a war against the traditional enemy, France, and on operations in the British Empire. It was the era when the Royal Navy had the least interest in Scotland. The indifference was mutual. In 1852 the clerks of the Accountant-General of the Navy worked late for two months to produce a detailed report on the birthplaces of seamen in the Royal Navy. They showed that 796 men out of 18,874, or about 4 per cent, were from Scotland. There was little prospect of improvement, for only 28 of 3,559 boys, or 0.7 per cent, were Scottish. Mr Crawford, the shipping-master of Glasgow, reported that he did not know any seamen who wanted to join the Royal Navy, that they had very little information on it and that perhaps 'the appearance of a well-ordered ship-of-war' would help with recruitment. But in the end his opinion was 'that few seamen in this district would enter for service in the Navy'. In Montrose there was 'a dislike to the Royal Navy among the seamen in this quarter; they are afraid of a man of war.' From Aberdeen it was reported 'that the fishing and pilot men are not inclined to have anything to do with the Navy. One man said "You don't pay the men well," and another said, "You don't allow smoking, and no spirits, so we will have nothing to do with you."' A far-reaching report of 1853 concluded that 'little is comparatively known of the Royal Naval Service in Scotland, from whence we believe that a much larger number of excellent seamen might be obtained than at present.' It suggested the re-establishment of the 'Scotch naval station', with a training-brig attached to it.[4] This was not done, but the whole system of naval recruitment was reformed. In the past the navy had taken on experienced merchant seamen; now it would recruit inexperienced boys, train them in naval ways and, for the first time, put its men into uniform and offer them a permanent career.

This had no effect on Scottish apathy about the navy. Even Queen Victoria was aware of it and in 1855 she wrote to the First Lord of the Admiralty that the setting up of a naval establishment at Leith would 'be very popular in Scotland, and by making the Queen's Navy known there, which it hardly is at present, would open a new field for recruiting our marine.'[5] In 1872 it was found that 90 out of 2,888 boys in the training ships were Scots, or little more than 3 per cent.[6] In HMS *Swallow* in the 1870s, with a complement of ninety men, Sam Noble of Dundee found 'I was the only *known* Scotchman in the ship. Certainly there were two more, but they weren't much good to me, and I didn't get hold of that fact till the ship had been over two years in commission. They were old hands, and knowing that they were very much in the minority, had the sense to keep their mouths shut.'[7]

In the 1880s, Captain W. S. Kennedy was mistaken for a railway guard at Inverness and for a Salvation Army officer in another Scottish town. But his greatest setback came in 1883 when he took HMS *Lord Warden* to Shetland in hopes of finding recruits among the excellent seamen there. Memories were long, and nearly seventy years after the last press gang, 'no sooner had the *Lord Warden* anchored at Lerwick than the natives fled to the mountains, fearing the press gang.' Captain Kennedy held a meeting at Lerwick to explain the modern navy, but got no recruits.[8] He wrote to the Admiralty, 'Absurd as it may seem, the terrors of the press gang are still remembered by the older inhabitants and related to the younger, so that the arrival of HM ship, with the avowed intention of seeking recruits, was a signal for all likely youngsters to hide themselves . . .'[9]

A booklet of 1891 suggested part of the reason for the lack of Scottish interest.

> The boys are mostly of the class of skilled mechanics, a large proportion being the sons of warrant officers, and petty officers who have been through the work and know what the service is like from experience. Sailoring runs in families, even more than soldiering; and in Portsmouth, Chatham and Devonport there are families who have sent five or six generations to the lower deck. The boys come from all parts of the Kingdom, the majority from the south coast.[10]

Early in the twentieth century it was said that only 3 per cent of sailors came from Scotland, because recruits were 'deterred from joining by the great distance that separates their homes from the existing naval Ports'. [11] J. Morrison, a future lieutenant, describes his journey. He 'arrived at Plymouth railway station, very tired and somewhat bewildered one hot day in July 1885. He had travelled by coasting steamer and rail from Stornoway, Isle of Lewis, and the journey had taken from Monday until Thursday.'[12]

Furthermore, the Admiralty did not pay rail fares for men to return to their homes on leave. An able seaman had a basic pay of 1s 7d (8p) per day or 11s 1d (55p) per week in the second half of the nineteenth century. A third-class rail fare from London to Glasgow cost 33s 8d (£1.68) in 1863,[13] and a return trip from Portsmouth to Edinburgh, at about 940 miles, would cost nearly £4, or more than seven weeks' wages. But there were also important cultural factors which did not attract the Scots to the navy.

Religion

During the eighteenth and early nineteenth centuries the Navy was governed by the *Articles of War* and by the *Admiralty Regulations and Instructions*. The *Articles of War* had first been passed by Parliament after the Civil War, readopted in slightly different form in 1661 and amended in 1749. They merely adopted the practices of the English Navy; in particular the first clause demanded that divine service be conducted every Sunday, according to Anglican ritual. Naval chaplains were exclusively from the Church of England and according to the Admiralty *Regulations*, divine service was to be performed 'twice a day on board, according to the liturgy of the Church of England, and a sermon preached on Sundays, unless bad weather or other extraordinary accidents prevent it.' This was rarely observed in the eighteenth century. Captain Charles Middleton, himself a strong supporter of the Evangelical movement, commented

> I was sixteen years in the sea service before I became a captain, and never, during that time heard prayers or divine service performed aboard of any ship . . . As soon as I became a captain I began reading prayers myself to the ship's company of a Sunday, and also a sermon . . . I did not indeed venture to further than Sundays . . . and I should only have acquired the name of methodist or enthusiast if I attempted it.[14]

Few ships actually carried chaplains, and if they did they had little effect. Edward Mangin of the *Gloucester* wrote, 'nothing can possibly be more unsuitably or more awkwardly placed than a clergyman in a ship of war; every object around him is at variance with the sensibilities of a rational and enlightened mind.'[15]

This began to change in Victorian times when both officers and seamen took religion more seriously. H. Y. Moffat was one of fourteen boys serving in HMS *Pembroke* in 1857, mostly recruited while the ship was in Leith Roads. None, according to his account, 'had been in the service long enough to have been converted to the Anglican form of worship'. A new chaplain was determined to enforce regulations but the boys refused to kneel during the service. 'We all agreed that bowing and scraping belonged to the Roman Church, and we gave our word that, happen what might, we would never bow.' Various punishments were used on the boys, including caning. Finally, each boy was seated next to a ship's corporal during a service and a cane was brought down on his neck at the vital point in the service, forcing him to bow. According to Moffat, 'the sky-pilot left the deck with a smile on his face.'[16]

Religion was to remain a difficulty for more than a century and perhaps it was exacerbated by the lack of Scots in the navy. There were too few for an effective protest, while the authorities could always argue that it would be impossible to provide Presbyterian chaplains for ships when they would minister to such a low proportion of each crew. During the Crimean War in 1855 a Scottish chaplain actually conducted services in a naval hospital, using the Church of England liturgy, as any other would have been illegal. Even so, some Anglican patients shunned the services and one protested to the admiral.[17]

The religious debate began to polarise in the middle of the nineteenth century, as the Free Church split from the Church of Scotland and the Oxford Movement brought more ritual to the Anglican Church. Naval regulations did little to help. In 1862, more than thirty years after Catholic Emancipation in the nation at large, a new edition of the *Queen's Regulations and Admiralty Instructions* allowed Roman Catholics 'full liberty to absent themselves' from Church of England services in the navy. This was the beginning of the well-known order 'Fall out the Roman Catholics', but there was no mention of other denominations.

In 1860 a new Naval Discipline Act replaced the old *Articles of War*, but its first clause still demanded Church of England worship. In 1879 the *Queen's Regulations* made a tiny concession when abstention from Anglican worship was allowed to 'Roman Catholics and others'. Officers and men who were 'not members of the Church of England' were allowed to go ashore for services when in port.[18] These concessions were indexed under the heading 'Dissenters not to attend', though of course members of the Church of Scotland were not dissenters. By a further regulation of 1893, Presbyterians were specifically mentioned, along with Roman Catholics and 'Wesleyans and others who entertain religious scruples to joining the services of the Church of England'.[19]

When the new Royal Naval Volunteer Reserve divisions were formed in 1903, two honorary Church of Scotland chaplains were attached to the Clyde Division, and during the First World War chaplains of various religions were given temporary commissions. They were attached to shore bases rather than ships, because the numbers of non-Anglicans were relatively few, and in 1943 a parliamentary question suggested that there was a ban on Church of Scotland chaplains going to sea. This was denied, but a month later an order-in-council regularised the position of chaplains from 'religious bodies not in conformity with the Church of England'. They were granted permanent commissions for the first time.[20]

In 1957, when a new Naval Discipline Bill was under consideration, it was initially intended to leave out the clause about religious worship. The Judge Advocate of the Fleet, himself a Jew, defended the Anglican service. He remembered his time under training as an officer at the beginning of the Second World War. 'I did not depart with "Fall out the Roman Catholics" . . . I was perfectly prepared to accept that, as the Church of England were the great majority, if we were to pray together it would be the Church of England service.'[21] It was the House of Commons which insisted on a modified clause, without reference to the Church of England. This produced a heated debate. Emrys Hughes, a Welshman representing South Ayrshire, made an essentially pacifist point about the hypocrisy of religion in the armed forces and members generally were concerned that attendance should not be compulsory except perhaps for boys, but there was no specifically Scottish comment.[22] By 1969, in a more ecumenical age, a joint church was built in the base at Faslane. It was not consecrated but there was a joint service of dedication presided over by the three head chaplains of the navy, representing Anglicans, Roman Catholics and the Church of Scotland and Free Churches. But this trend was later reversed by the Anglican Chaplain of the Fleet, who appointed a base chaplain of much less liberal views.[23] By this time religion was playing a smaller part in most people's lives than in the previous century and the issue aroused much less passion.

The White Ensign

The second issue was the flag. By the 1630s the English Royal Navy was divided into three squadrons: red, white and blue, each flying a different ensign. The red, white and blue ensigns were simply flags of that colour with the St George's cross in the 'upper canton', the top quarter nearest the staff. The admirals in charge of each squadron flew a flag of the appropriate colour without the cross in the upper canton, a full admiral from the mainmast, vice-admiral from the foremast and rear-admiral from the mizzen.

At the Union of the Crowns in 1603 the new Union Flag was flown from a jackstaff in the bows of a naval ship in port, hence the popular name, the Union Jack. In 1707 it was incorporated in the three ensigns which were normally flown from the stern. The St George's cross became established as a major part of the white ensign during the first half of the century, possibly to avoid confusion in battle with the white flag of the French. It was also used as the flag of admirals of the white, without the union flag in the upper canton.

In 1864 there was another change. The division into three squadrons, obsolete since the seventeenth century, was abolished. It was decided that the merchant marine, as the most senior service, would fly the red ensign as it had always done. The Royal Navy would use only the white ensign, while other ships in government service or commanded by reserve officers would fly the blue ensign. Thus a flag which was dominated by the St George's cross became the main flag of the Royal Navy. The admiral's flag was also changed, partly because the latest steam warships did not always have three masts and so the old system became meaningless. Now a full admiral flew the plain St George's cross while a vice-admiral used it with a ball in the upper canton and a rear-admiral had two balls, one in the upper and one in the lower canton. This meant that the fleet flagship, usually commanded by a full admiral, was dominated by the English flag. True, the admiral of the fleet flew the Union flag at the mainmast, but such exalted officers rarely went to sea. The flag was purely symbolic, but it did much to establish the Royal Navy's identity as an English rather than a British institution.

There was little protest about this at the time, though it did not pass unnoticed. By the early 1900s, prototype nationalist journals such as *Fiery Cross* and *The Thistle* complained regularly about the flag issue.[24] In 1916, at the height of British patriotism during the First World War, the Revd William McMillan wrote that the use of the white ensign in this form was a breach of

> the express declaration of the Treaty of Union between the two kingdoms which states as definitely as anything can be stated 'that the ensigns armorial of the United Kingdom [shall] be such as Her Majesty shall appoint, and the crosses of St Andrew and St George [shall] be conjoined in such manner as Her Majesty shall think fit and used in all banners, standards, ensigns, both at sea and land.' Unfortunately, however, those in power in the larger kingdom appear to have regarded this treaty as a 'scrap of paper', only binding on them so long as it suited them; and it so happens that the British Navy, paid for by the British ratepayer, and manned by British seamen, has for its flag the pre-Union flag of England, with a small and relatively insignificant Union in the upper canton.[25]

The Scottish Engineer

Steam engines were introduced to the Royal Dockyards in the 1790s for pumping out the docks rather than powering ships, and Marc Isambard

Brunel, the father of the great Victorian engineer, used them to power his innovative block-making machinery in Portsmouth Dockyard. The *Comet* sailed successfully on the Clyde in 1812, but steam engines were only fit for short, inshore voyages and in 1815 the navy introduced paddle-tugs for hauling ships in and out of harbour in light or contrary winds. Their engineers were recruited from the workers on the dockyard steam engines, and this was to remain a main source over the years. Other engineers came from the firms which supplied the engines, mostly Boulton and Watt of Birmingham and Maudslay of London. The navy's engineering work took place in the dockyards, especially in the 'steam factory' at Woolwich near London.

Scottish sea officers were enthusiastic protagonists of the use of steam at sea. At the Admiralty, Lord Melville is often falsely accused of stating, 'their Lordships feel it is their bounden duty to discourage to the utmost of their ability the employment of steam vessels, as they consider the introduction of Steam is calculated to strike a fatal blow at the supremacy of the Empire.'[26] In fact he did much to encourage steam power and wrote in 1823, 'There is every reason to believe from the purposes to which Steam Vessels are now applied that they would be found very useful in the protection of our trade in the Channel . . . It will be proper *now* to provide Steam Engines for at least six vessels . . . and I therefore desire that you will take the necessary steps for that purpose.'[27] Admiral Sir Charles Napier of Merchistoun Hall near Falkirk was a long-standing critic of the conservatism of the naval administration and captained the first iron steamship, *Aaron Manby*, on a voyage from London to Paris in 1822. However, this was not a happy experience and turned him against iron ships, though not steam. The Earl of Dundonald, now expelled from the Royal Navy, was the first to use a steam warship in action, with the Greeks during their war of independence against the Turks in 1825–8. The first steam manual was produced in 1828 by Captain John Ross of Wigton.

Meanwhile the engineer struggled for recognition as a full member of the navy, rather than an intruder on the decks of a warship. Eventually three main classes emerged. The engineer officers were granted warrants in 1837 and ten years later the leading members of the profession were commissioned. The Engine Room Artificers, created as a class in 1868, were skilled craftsmen who were rated as chief petty officers. The stokers did the manual work in the boiler rooms, and keeping a good fire going was far more skilled than most people realised.

It was the development of the screw propeller in the 1830s and 1840s which gave the first boost to naval steam, for the old paddle wheels had interrupted the ships' broadsides too much. By the Crimean War (1854–6) it was clear that a warship without steam power had no practical use, though steam was still regarded as an auxiliary to sail. In 1859, with the need to expand the steam fleet, the Admiralty became aware of the neglected resources to the north. It turned to George Murdoch of Glasgow, one of its few Scottish engineers, and sent him on a recruiting tour of Scotland and the north of England. He returned with 103 men, Murdoch's Hundred. One of them was Matthew McIntyre, who had just completed his apprenticeship in Glasgow. He served for thirty years in many parts of the world, retiring in 1889 with the rank of inspector of machinery. In 1875 however, Captain Sir Astley Cooper Key chaired a committee which observed that engineering students came almost entirely from families which were resident near the Royal Dockyards. It recommended that living accommodation be provided for others, and that civil service examinations should be held in centres outside London. This had some effect, but in general Scottish engineers were more attracted to the merchant service, where there was less class distinction. By this time the navy was building mastless capital ships, using the vastly more efficient compound and triple expansion engines developed on Clydeside. But when it set up colleges to train naval engineers, they were at Greenwich in the first instance, and then at Manadon near Plymouth. The Scottish marine engineer, inasmuch as he existed at all outside the pages of fiction, was a feature of merchant shipping rather than the Royal Navy.

The Annual Cruises

Scotland only saw the navy during its annual cruise round the British Isles, held from the 1860s onwards, when it called at ports such as Lamlash and Brodick on Arran, Scapa Flow, the Cromarty Firth and St Margaret's Hope in the Forth. Such visits, which might last a fortnight in each anchorage, were the subject of much celebration and often had a profound effect on local communities such as Invergordon. Cromarty Firth saw something of the operational fleet as early as 1854. Four steam frigates from the Baltic Fleet, under Sir Charles Napier, arrived to spend the winter there. They had been employed against the Russians in the Baltic, as part of the campaigns against them in the Crimean War. The sailors found the lack of eating-houses and pubs very inconvenient during their runs ashore, but made the journey to Inverness in coaches decked with ribbons.[28]

The first cruise round the British Isles was held in 1863 and it would not have been possible to withdraw so many ships from the English Channel in an earlier period, for fear that a new political crisis might develop before they could be got back, perhaps against contrary winds. But now the electric telegraph allowed an instant recall while the ships were in port, and steam power allowed them to return in almost any weather conditions, except severe storms which would keep an enemy in port as well.

The Channel Fleet had five brand-new ironclad battleships and frigates including the famous *Warrior* of 1861. The flagship, however, was one of the last wooden two-deckers, the *Edgar*, which had been fitted with engines and a screw propeller before her launch in 1858. The squadron also included two steam-powered wooden frigates and a screw gunboat for use as a despatch vessel. Before departure Captain Cochrane of the *Warrior* addressed the crew. 'To show the people of Britain our new navy the squadron have been given a special duty. Over the next three months we shall be visiting ports on the east and west coasts of England and Scotland, culminating in Dublin. Visitors will be allowed aboard and where possible leave will be given. I need hardly warn you that leave breaking and misconduct will be treated severely.'[29] Geoffrey Phipps Hornby, flag captain of the *Edgar*, was more sceptical about the purposes of the cruise and wrote, 'We are doing popularity to a great extent. Ostensibly we are to show the ships, and what happy fellows the British mariners are in a man-of-war – nothing but porter and skittles! Really I suspect we are doing a little electioneering.'[30]

The squadron left Spithead near Portsmouth on 11 July and on 4 August it sailed into the Firth of Forth to make its first Scottish call, anchoring off Inchkeith for a six-day visit to Leith. The hospitality proved too much for some of the crew, who had to be rounded up from shore leave. Though all the ships had some form of steam power, orders made clear that sails were to be used as much as possible. This, and the primitive boilers of some of the ships, proved a great strain to the officers and Captain Hornby had a severe liver attack. The duties in port were no less arduous and he devised 'A plan for enabling the squadron to show some special civilities to people whose acquaintance they make. It is, to set apart one ship every day, where only people will be received who are brought by officers of the squadron; and that there shall be a band playing for dancing, and a little tea, and so on.'[31]

The squadron visited the Cromarty Firth for four days in August, creating a small boom among the local shopkeepers and innkeepers.[32] Hornby recovered his health during a stay of six days in Orkney, but a further three days stormbound north of Hoy Sound cannot have been helpful. Eventually, on Tuesday, 1 September, the ships arrived in the Clyde where they anchored abreast of Greenock. On Wednesday they began a demanding social programme when the officers were entertained by the Provost of Greenock. Next day the officers had a tour of the Clyde and the Kyles of Bute in a steamer provided by the shipowners Burns of Glasgow. On Friday they were taken to Glasgow to look at the shipyards, which had very little experience of construction for the British Navy but were building ships for the Turks and (secretly) for the American Confederates. Hornby was impressed. 'I am delighted with the energy and skill of these Glasgow men, and the more I see of them the more Radical I grow with regard to our dockyard system and Somerset House. When these men sit down to plan a warship propelled by steam, they make a steamship of her, and don't go puddling on drawing large sailing-ships to put engines into.'[33] The day finished with a great banquet in the Corporation Galleries. With the officers in full-dress uniform and the Lord Provost and baillies in court dress the assemblage had, as *The Times* reported, 'an exceedingly brilliant appearance'.[34]

But for all this, the visit to the Clyde was overshadowed by the squadron's reception in Liverpool, which took the navy to its heart. Forty shipowners contributed £10 each to entertain 800 sailors and 200 marines, and more than 57,000 people visited the *Warrior* alone.

In 1868 the fleet spent a few days in the Clyde and the idea of entertaining carefully selected men seems to have taken hold.

> A dinner was given yesterday by the people of Greenock, to the men of the fleet, which went off capitally. The men (500) marched up, headed by our band, and were all seated by two o'clock, very comfortably. Then there was a delay, and till half past three they sat talking and listening to the band. No end of porter and beer and cigars were placed before every one, but though the dinner was a long time in coming no one touched either bottle or meat till a clergyman was called on to say grace, and they fell to with a good will.[35]

The fleet visited one part of Scotland or another in most years over the next half century. Early in the twentieth century, Campbeltown was often used as a base by destroyers and torpedo boats exercising in the Clyde. In the summer of 1908 A. B. Cunningham was in command of *Torpedo Boat 14* as part of a force of about two dozen destroyers with the depot ship *Hecla*. They found that the harbour had its deficiencies for such craft. 'We anchored close to the steamer pier. We had light anchors and the holding ground was poor. It came on to blow hard two nights later and both torpedo-boats started to drag. I managed to raise steam and get away; but *T. B. 13* started her career of misfortune by dragging ashore and being left more or less high and dry. Luckily she did not damage herself.'[36]

The Coastguard

Between the intermittent visits of fleets and squadrons, Royal Naval presence in Scotland was maintained by several institutions which had a local base but were organised nationally. The oldest of these was the Coastguard, which had grown out of the old Coast Blockade, formed by the Board of Customs for use against smugglers in 1817. In 1854 it was mobilised for the Crimean War and the results were ambiguous. It provided a vital core of experienced seamen for the navy, but most were too old to work aloft. In 1857 it was taken over by the Admiralty and from that point only men who had served at least nine years with the fleet were recruited. Housing was provided and the Admiralty went to some lengths to supply education for Coastguardmen's children on remote stations, so it was a desirable option for a seaman who wanted to settle down and have a family. Men wore uniforms and had ranks equivalent to those of the navy – a boatman was equal to an able seaman, a commissioned boatman to a leading seaman, petty officers and chiefs were similar to naval ranks. Naval lieutenants and commanders were the inspecting officers of divisions, based for example at Aberdeen and Montrose, while naval captains commanded districts. Scotland had two districts, Leith and Clyde, one for each coast, until 1903, when they were merged. From 1875 the whole force came under the Admiral Commanding Coastguard and Reserves. Old warships were stationed at the main ports as headquarters and drill ships. At Leith the first was the 60-gun *Pembroke*, built as a 74 in 1812 and converted to steam in 1855. At Greenock was the old 74-gun ship *Wellington* of 1816, with no power plant. The *Lord Warden* at Leith was an unusual vessel, the largest wooden ship ever built for the navy, though she was also clad in iron. Captain E. R. Fremantle, appointed to the command of the Leith district in 1877, found her difficult to run efficiently. There was a high turnover of officers, who moved on to better appointments as soon as they could. She had a permanent crew of only about 180, which was filled up with coastguard men, half of whom had to go on an annual cruise every year. In 1877 Fremantle took the ship south and found she was 'a great coal-eater'. Despite instructions he was obliged to go far faster than her economic speed of 3.8 knots, because the tides on many parts of the east coast were faster than that.[37] When not cruising or inspecting the stations under his command, the captain lived ashore in a house at Queensferry where the ship was moored.

By 1905 the Coastguard had thirty-three stated aims, besides its primary one of forming 'the first and mostly highly trained Reserve force for the Navy in case of war'.[38] These included watching the enemy coast for shipwrecks and dangers, smugglers and possible enemy action, and signalling reports to the authorities by Morse or semaphore. Its life-saving duties made the coastguard very popular and it was not difficult to get the support of local volunteers. In 1889 Boatman William Murray of Portpatrick used seventy locals to help rescue the crew of the barque *Roseneath* of Glasgow by rocket apparatus and was awarded a silver medal.[39] The Coastguard worked closely with the lifeboats run by the Royal National Lifeboat Institution, formed in 1824 as a charity. There had been some quite early lifeboats in Scotland, including one at Dunbar in 1809, and the provost asked the navy for protections from impressment for the seamen who operated it.[40] But the main expansion in the Scottish lifeboat service came in the middle of the century, when many new stations were set up.

The Coastguard's customs duties were much less popular. At the remotest station, Tongue on the north coast, in 1879, Commissioned Boatman Condon was left on his own while his assistant went to train with the fleet. With the half-hearted assistance of some reservists he captured a French smuggling lugger despite being threatened by the captain with a blunderbuss.[41] The preventative duties of the Coastguard tended to decline over the years. Successive governments were committed to free trade, and the reduction in tariffs made smuggling less profitable.

Protection of wrecked ships was another duty. In 1893 four men from the station at Stornoway were sent to guard the steamer *Inflexible* at the Island of Moriach more than seventy miles from their base. They found that the locals were already looting it and chased them away. They were awarded £20, but there was an outcry when it was found that this reward had to be divided like prize money, with the lion's share going to the chief officer who was not even there.[42] The regulations of 1911 restricted the Coastguard's power in dealing with such incidents. Though they were trained and regularly exercised in the use of firearms and naval cutlasses, they were 'only to be used when absolutely necessary . . . Firing over the heads of parties plundering wreck, for the purpose of terrifying or warning them, is on no occasion to be permitted.'[43]

In the early stages the Coastguard was strong on the east coast of

Scotland as far north as the Moray Firth, with nearly all the coast within sight of a coastguard station (in good weather). There was no coverage at all in the Hebrides. In 1886 the Admiral commanding Coastguard and Reserves made a tour round the west of Scotland in HMS *Hawk* and 'was much impressed by the want of any organised means of keeping watch and telegraphy from headlands and prominent parts of the coast to approach or movement of vessels in the neighbourhood, a want of which in time might be a cause of disaster.' In the previous year there had been tension with Russia and a warship of that nation had apparently lingered off the coast, avoiding the main ports. As a result twelve new stations were proposed in such places as Portree, Oban, Port Charlotte on Islay and the Ross of Mull. The one at the Mull of Kintyre was the most important in terms of coverage, but ready-made accommodation was scarce in that area for there were few habitations closer than Campbeltown. At other places the local police were asked to find lodgings, but were generally pessimistic. 'I beg to inform you that I have made every possible enquiry but failed to procure anything like the accommodation required. Arisaig is but a very small village and all the houses are occupied. There is a widow in the village who could open her living room and two rooms furnished.'[44]

Access to the remote stations was often difficult. Captain Fremantle found that 'landing from a gunboat could not be depended upon' and he travelled by rail as far as possible, then by horse-drawn carriage over inadequate Highland roads. Captain W. S. Kennedy, who took charge at Queensferry in 1882, found that Tongue and Cape Wrath in the north-east were the most difficult. The former was 40 miles from the nearest railway and the trip from there to Cape Wrath was another 47 miles of driving.[45] Fremantle was keen that proper uniforms should be worn and he had to wear a rather flimsy, but correct, frock coat in all weathers, as greatcoats were not authorised. His 'great object', as he put it, 'was to see that each coastguard station had its boat, boathouse and flagstaff.'[46]

The Coastguard also served as the public relations wing of the navy and its main recruiting service – coastguard men were awarded ten shillings (50p) for every boy they recruited. It had unusual difficulties in Scotland, for many of the stations were on remote headlands, well away from the main centres of population. This is perhaps another reason why few from Scotland joined the navy during the nineteenth century.

The Royal Naval Reserve

One effect of the Crimean War (1854–6) was to show that impressment, though still legal, was no longer a realistic option for naval
recruitment, even in wartime. As recently as 1852 Admiral Sir Byam
Martin had asserted that 'the power of impressment must unques-
tionably be maintained, and I fear must be resorted to in any sudden
armament',[47] but this proved impossible two years later. The navy
managed to find enough men to fight a war which never became total,
but new options were needed for expansion in any future crisis.

The Royal Naval Reserve was founded in 1859 to fill this gap. It
was made up of professional seamen of the merchant and fishing
fleets, who would carry out naval drills as stations reasonably near to
their homes, and spend periods of up to three months with the fleet to
learn naval ways, for a retainer of £6 per year. At first they had no
uniforms and were eligible for only the lowest naval ranks, but officers
of the merchant marine were able to take Reserve commissions after
1864.

The RNR was highly successful in Scotland. In 1875–6, a total of
5,096 men trained in the country, with disproportionately high figures
at some of the smaller ports – 1,249 at Dundee, 1,135 at Aberdeen,
726 at Stornoway and 1,073 at Lerwick, compared with 244 on the
Forth and 412 at Greenock. Figures for 1902 show that the country
produced a total of 7,175 men, compared with 13,725 for England
and 3,400 from Ireland. It was particularly successful in the outer
islands, especially Lewis and Shetland, where £6 was a real addition to
a crofter-fisherman's income. When the Registrar of the Reserve at
Stornoway was asked whether there was any way of advertising the
force better, he replied that it was 'Quite unnecessary in Stornoway'.
When the registrar at Lerwick was asked if a small fee should be paid
to men who recruited friends, he answered, 'No need at Shetland for
any stimulus.'[48] The authorities made special efforts to allow men
from remote parts of the islands to attend training. For drills at
Stornoway in 1911 they were paid subsistence of 5 shillings (25p)
for walking 9 to 24 miles, or up to 15 shillings (75p) for a journey of
49 to 72 miles, in addition to a penny for each mile actually travelled.
Men from the mainland of Shetland were also allowed the 'footage' of
one penny per mile, while those from Whalsay were given 2s. 6d.
(12½p) subsistence and a steamer fare.[49] Inspecting the district in
1877–8, Captain Fremantle found that the whalers and sealers did
their naval drills in the winter, for they were at sea all summer.

Thus at the Shetlands, for instance, there were 250 to 300 fine seamen on drill in mid-winter and the battery was closed in summer. I had a splendid chief officer of coastguard in charge of the drill battery at Lerwick, a Mr Johnson, who drilled capitally, and it was a pleasure to make the trip to *Ultima Thule* to support him. These men were of good Norse breed, though they spoke little English, and were supposed to think more of their retainer and drill pay, which was a boon to them during the winter months, than the possibilities of war service. One difficulty was that in December – and one had to inspect in December or January – there were only two or three hours of daylight, so that an inspection began and ended in the dark.[50]

In 1905 the system was fully developed, with training ships or batteries at or near the most important ports. HMS *Briton* at Inverness had two 64-pounder guns on loan from the Highland Volunteer Artillery. At Dundee, HMS *Unicorn* was the drill ship but the men exercised with two 64-pounder guns at Buddon Ranges ten miles away. At Aberdeen, the men trained on board HMS *Clyde* by firing 4-pound charges in old 32-pounder guns. *Durham* at Leith had more modern 7-pounder guns and a quick-firing 4-inch gun. New batteries were recommended at several places such as Banff, Fraserburgh, Castlebay and Portree. These would 'tap a very large field of recruiting for the Royal Naval Reserve amongst the Fishing population.'[51] But the obsolete guns were not much help. As early as the 1880s, Captain Kennedy had noted 'they were drilled with the same class of guns as were used at the Battle of Trafalgar!'[52] The Marquis of Graham commented a few years later, 'In the forty-eight drill ships and batteries training the R.N.R. in the United Kingdom, there were 233 guns, and of these 104 were muzzle loaders, which had been completely obsolete in the Navy for many years.'[53] It was decided to train RNR men during short periods with the fleet, rather than with obsolete weapons in docks and ranges.

The Royal Fleet Reserve, originally the Seamen Pensioners Reserve, was made up of former Royal Navy men who could be recalled in an emergency. In view of the small numbers of men from Scotland who joined the Royal Navy in the first place, it is not surprising to find that the Fleet Reserve was very weak there. In 1875–6 there were only 8 men in Scotland out of a total force of 511. In 1905 there were only 53 men in the Leith district and 13 in the Clyde district, out of a total force of 6,027, and it was noted that the Clyde force was the only one in the kingdom that had not increased in the last year.[54]

Fishery Protection

Since the Scottish fisheries became strategically important during the eighteenth century, the navy always had some concern with their protection. In wartime the whale fishery off Greenland was the most important and ships were devoted to guard it. In peacetime it was largely a question of keeping foreign fishermen out of territorial waters and enforcing regulations. By far the most controversial of these was the question of trawling. The earliest problem, however, was disputes among fishermen themselves.

For centuries the fishermen of Loch Fyne had used drift nets to catch herring for the expanding Glasgow and Clydeside market. In the 1830s the men of Tarbert began to use a new method, misleadingly known as 'trawling', though more correctly called 'ring netting'. They started by surrounding a shoal of herring with a drift net and then hauling it in, and soon began to design nets specifically for the new method. It required a smaller boat and less capital investment than drift-netting, but it soon inspired the wrath of other fishermen, especially in Inveraray. In 1851 an Act was passed to ban all nets other than drift nets in the herring fishery. The Fishery Board's ship *Princess Royal* was sent to Loch Fyne to enforce the new rules, along with HMS *Porcupine*, a paddle gunboat on loan from the Admiralty. A few nets were seized but prosecutions proved difficult. Early in the 1853 season the *Porcupine* was involved in a violent incident. One of her boats searched the Tarbert skiff *Annan* and found nothing. Then the helmsman of the skiff, Colin McKeich, hailed another boat to warn them of the naval presence and was shot and wounded from another of the *Porcupine*'s boats. Philip Turner, gunner of the *Porcupine*, and Peter Rennie, a marine from Hawick, were accused of the shooting and tried at Inveraray. They were sentenced to three months' imprisonment but petitions were organised in their favour and they were soon granted royal pardons. The *Porcupine* remained active in Loch Fyne with little success until 1854, when the Crimean War forced her withdrawal.[55]

By 1860 a new and stricter law was in place and HMS *Jackal*, another paddle gunboat, was in Loch Fyne to enforce it. But still the fishermen had to be caught in the act, not just in possession of ring nets. When the *Jackal* seized thirteen skiffs and their nets in September and towed them to Greenock, they could not be prosecuted for trawling, though they were all confiscated for a month because they were improperly named. Morale and health were already poor in the *Jackal* and got worse in November when the ship seized a net and was surrounded by eight or ten other boats, whose crews hooted and yelled at them. At the same time the opponents of trawl fishing criticised the lack of activity. 'Two of Her Majesty's war steamers are said to be continually at Lochfyne and the lochs, but we seldom hear of these vessels being far from Rothesay. At that place the evening enjoyments seem to be more attractive on land than hunting trawlers out at sea.'[56]

Things got even worse in 1861. Men from the ring-netters *Weatherside* and *Star* were fired on by the gunner and a marine from the *Jackal* while hauling their nets and Peter McDougall of the *Weatherside* was killed. Robert Hawton and William Parker of the *Jackal* were tried for culpable homicide in Edinburgh but claimed that they had fired blanks, first as a warning, and had then fired a live shot due to a misunderstanding. They were acquitted to loud applause in court. Meanwhile new legislation came into force, making prosecutions much easier, not just of fishermen but of anyone handling the catch. But the *Jackal*'s war continued and in 1865 the fishermen of Tarbert co-operated in reporting her movements to one another. In 1866 it was reported,

> The fishery constables and the *Jackal*'s crew were repeatedly threatened with violence and assaults by the trawlers and those who bought and trawled herrings, and in several cases carried out their purpose to the serious danger of human life . . . Firearms have been resorted to but most fortunately no accident occurred . . . I am informed that many of the trawlers and all the [buyers] carry guns to sea with them.[57]

In 1867 a new bill made ring-netting legal and the presence of the *Jackal* was no longer necessary. It had been one of the navy's least happy experiences in Scottish waters.

The true sailing trawler had originated in England in the second quarter of the nineteenth century. It spread west along the English Channel and up into the North Sea, but never reached Scottish waters in great numbers. The Scots were deeply suspicious of trawlers, believing they would damage fish stocks irreparably, so when steam trawlers began to appear in their waters in the 1880s they demanded action. The government banned trawling in several stages, in the Firths of Forth and Tay in 1885–7, in some east-coast bays in 1888 and in all the main bays and firths, including the whole of the Moray Firth, by 1892.[58] Two naval vessels were permanently allocated to the Fishery Board for Scotland to enforce these regulations, and others were drafted in as required during the season.

By 1905 another HMS *Jackal*, which had recently replaced the *Harrier* on the station, was permanently allocated to fishery protection in the Moray Firth, while the *Daring* cutter was in the other problem area of Loch Fyne. Other vessels were used as appropriate during the season. Two gunboats and a sailing cruiser were needed on the east coast in July to August for the herring fishery, with another gunboat for Orkney and Shetland. A fourth gunboat was needed for the Hebrides during the season but the admiral complained that 'invariably within a few weeks of the withdrawal of a vessel from these waters, complaints of illegal trawling are referred to me . . . As a rule the complaints are not substantiated.' The navy resented being under the control of the Scottish Fisheries Board in this matter, even if the captain of the *Jackal* was paid a bonus of £100 per annum by the Fisheries Board. 'The Scotch Fishery Board is very persistent in making applications for vessels to enforce their fishery bye-laws and, apparently the more their requests are complied with, the more they ask.' A meeting was held between the Treasury and the Admiralty and it was agreed that the Navy would no longer be responsible for enforcement within territorial waters – a force of small craft would be recruited locally by the Fisheries Board.[59]

The Crofters' Wars

The sea performed an important role in shaping the Highland agricultural landscape as we know it today. Before about 1800, tenant farmers usually held pieces of estate in common, using the strip-farming system of runrig. The landowners realised that they could make much more money by forcing tenants to work at finding and treating kelp, seaweed which could be made into fertiliser. The owners allocated the tenants fixed pieces of land, or crofts, next to the sea, using the inland areas for sheep. The kelp industry declined rapidly after the peace of 1815 opened up new sources of fertiliser, while southern industrialists and farmers campaigned successfully to have duties reduced on imported fertilisers such as barilla. There was terrible poverty in the West Highlands in the 1820s, but the pattern of landholding had been shaped. The role of the Royal Navy was quite positive at this stage. In 1846 frigates were sent to Tobermory and Portree with relief supplies during a famine: but it was the age of *laissez-faire* and they were not allowed to give the food away, but only to sell it at the economic rate.[60]

The crofters still retained a certain amount of loyalty to their traditional landlords, despite many betrayals, and were far slower to revolt than their counterparts in Ireland. They regained a measure of prosperity by keeping sheep on their land and by fishing the seas.

The latter activity brought increased contact with the outside world, including Ireland, where they learned something about resistance. When wool prices began to fall in the early 1880s, famine threatened again. In April 1882 at Braes, south of Portree on Skye, the tenants went on rent strike until old grazing rights were restored. Attempts at eviction led to resistance, and extra policemen were drafted in from Glasgow and Inverness. The revolt, led by the Highland Land Law Reform Association, spread through the island. In November 1884 the gunboat *Forester* was sent to Skye from the Clyde carrying forty-two men, including some transferred from HMS *Shannon*. Meanwhile the troopship *Assistance* at Portsmouth was ordered to collect 300 marines from the barracks there and take them north. But the MacBraynes steamer *Locheil,* intended to serve as a depot, was more difficult. The revolt was so intense that the captain and crew resigned. The marines landed on Skye and put on 'an imposing military spectacle to overawe the natives', who in turn were 'amazed rather than intimidated by the display'. But the marines were very restricted in their powers. The Gladstone Government, already committed to more repression in Ireland than it wanted, would not allow them to assist the police and bailiffs in carrying out evictions. Relations between the marines and the tenants were remarkably cordial, partly because many of the tenants were fishermen who had served with the Royal Naval Reserve. The police, on the other hand, were despised.[61] The tenants were quite successful in their aims, causing the government to set up the Napier Commission which led to the Crofters' Holdings Act of 1886, giving them security of tenure for the first time.

Meanwhile in 1886, before the Act came into force, revolt flared on the small island of Tiree. This time the Gladstone government refused to allow the use of the navy, but a new Conservative government came into power in July and sent a force of 40 police, 120 sailors and 250 marines in the turret battleship *Ajax*, the troopship *Assistance* and the hired steamer *Nigel*. Several men were arrested and given severe sentences.[62] Another force of 40 policemen and 75 marines landed in the north of Skye in October. Over the next few months they restored law and order to the island, but at the price of much bitterness.

Though the small landholders were placated when the Act came into force, the landless people of the islands were not. They began to occupy farms on Lewis and in January 1888 troops and marines confronted them. It was suggested that the fine discipline of many of the rebels on the island came from their training in the Royal Naval Reserve.[63] Peace was restored by the autumn of 1888.

That was not the last time the civil authorities asked for naval help in the Hebrides. In 1902 there was a dispute in Ness, at the northern end of Lewis, about 'which section of the Community shall have possession of the Church' and the county council asked for a naval ship to take seventy or eighty constables from Kyle of Lochalsh, for it was too difficult to take them thirty miles by road from Stornoway. None of the naval or coastguard vessels in Scotland were available, so the old cruiser *Bellona* was sent on a special trip from Portland on the south coast of England. She duly picked up the policemen and landed them, but had instructions not to land her own men or get involved in civil affairs except in an emergency. But the trouble blew over and the constables were not needed.[64]

The Training Ship *Caledonia*

By the middle of the nineteenth century, the idea of training boys for the sea in static harbour ships was beginning to take hold. It had originated at least a century earlier, when the Marine Society had set up the *Warspite* in the River Thames to train boys from impoverished backgrounds. By the 1860s, several factors seemed to converge to make the idea practical. Charles Dickens and others had made the public aware that there were thousands of destitute boys in the city streets, ready to turn to crime unless something was done. The repeal of the Navigation Acts in 1849 removed the legal requirement on British shipowners to train a certain number of apprentices, so there was now a shortage of skilled men for the merchant service. The navy still had a large supply of old 'wooden walls', demasted and slowly decaying in the dockyard ports, which could be let out to charitable trusts or local government. Aboard them, boys would be away from the pressures of their old environment and would learn how to live together aboard ship. They would be moored in a bay or estuary, where boys could learn the skills of sailing and rowing in small boats. An Act of 1866 encouraged the setting up of 'Industrial School Ships'.

Two training ships were set up in Scotland in 1869–70, to offer three-year training courses for boys between twelve and sixteen. The *Mars*, a former 80-gun wooden, screw-propelled ship of the line, was moored in the Tay two miles above Dundee. Though she was not intended as a 'reformatory ship' like some of the English vessels, she was partly funded by the local prison boards, but mostly by the national government. She had about 300 boys at any time, with a staff of 14 officers. The *Cumberland*, formerly a 70-gun two-decker, was anchored at Rhu Bay (then spelt Row) near the entrance to the

Gareloch. She was licensed to hold up to 360 boys with 15 staff and was run by the Clyde Industrial Training Ship Association with financial help from the Home Office and Glasgow ratepayers. The ship's purpose, according to an account of 1883, was 'not so much with a view to make good the deficiency in the supply of well-trained seamen for the merchant service, as to obtain the means whereby a number of the lads, in a state of destitution, and exposed to grievous temptation to crime, might be provided with an honest employment.'[65] The *Cumberland* was destroyed by fire in 1889 and replaced by the *Empress*.

The whole concept of such training was severely criticised during the 1880s. The shipowners did not want to employ boys from dubious backgrounds. Training in a static ship did not prepare a boy for life on the high seas. Few were motivated and many did not enter the merchant service, or had very short careers. The recruitment of half-starved adolescents was compared unfavourably with Royal Naval policy.

> The boys on board the training ships of the Royal Navy have immense advantages in the essential point of physical development. It would, indeed, be unfair to expect that a philanthropic institution should recruit from the same sources, or offer the same advantages as the Royal Navy. The training-ships maintained by the grants of Government and by philanthropic institutions, draw their recruits from a pauper class; and it is an inevitable consequence that boys, who have passed their infancy under the most favourable [sic] conditions, should be inferior in size and strength to the lads more carefully recruited, more abundantly fed, more perfectly trained, in the Navy.[66]

At this time the Navy had five training ships for boys on the south coast of England, in Portsmouth, Portland, Devonport and Falmouth. After the Naval Defence Act 1889 increased the size of the fleet, there was concern about recruiting more boys. The First Sea Lord, Lord George Hamilton, was a son of the Duke of Abercorn, though he had been born and educated in England and represented an English constituency. In the Naval Estimates of 1891–2 he announced,

> The increase to the number of boys in training will require an additional training ship. At present all the ships engaged in this work are located in the south of England. A training ship is a recruiting attraction, and the districts in which they are placed consequently contribute more than other parts of the country to the manning of the fleet. A large proportion of the hereditary seafaring class is now to be found in the northern districts of the country, and, with a view of obtaining recruits

from this natural source of supply, the new training ship will be placed in the Firth of Forth at Queensferry.[67]

The ship which was provided was not entirely new. The old 98-gun ship *Impregnable* had been launched in 1810 and served as flagship during the bombardment of Algiers in 1816. She was reduced to harbour service in 1862 as a training ship at Plymouth and in 1891 she was towed north and renamed *Caledonia*. Another ship was renamed *Impregnable* to replace the old one at Devonport.

Percy Lowe joined the *Caledonia* in 1901 and described the routine.

> We'd have to be up by 5.30. You'd have cocoa and then fall in. If it wasn't raining you would let fall the sails, square the main yard, scrub the decks and flake down all the ropes. By that time it was breakfast time . . . You did all sorts of sail drill such as shifting topmast and reefing the sail, and the Able Seamen who were on the yards with you, if you didn't do your job properly, they used to walk along the yards and pinch your backside with their toes as you were leaning over the yard. One man fell off the lower yard while I was there.[68]

The log of the *Caledonia* gives some idea of the training programme. On 27 May 1903 the port watch went off to practise rowing boats while the starboard watch did physical drill. A swimming class was landed by boat, while the rest of the boys attended divisions and divine service. At midday there were races between the boats' crews of the different divisions and a battalion and a gymnastic party were landed for drill ashore. At four in the afternoon the boys scrubbed and washed their clothes and at six o'clock they had more physical drill. Much attention was also paid to fire drill and time was spent in ordinary schooling and in painting the ship.[69]

By this time the training policy was also coming under criticism. Life in training ships built up to a hundred years ago had little to do with that in a modern warship, and the running costs were high. By the time he came into office as First Sea Lord in October 1904, Admiral 'Jacky' Fisher had made a list of dozens of obsolete ships he wanted to dispose of. The *Caledonia*, like the other training ships, escaped from category D: 'Absolutely obsolete ships, not being depots or special service vessels', which were to be broken up immediately. Instead she was listed among the 'Utterly useless ships for fighting purposes – Depot Ships' with the comment, 'Requires most careful consideration, quite beyond these notes.' He soon came to the conclusion that the *Caledonia* and others of her kind were to be disposed of 'as soon as barracks are available'.[70] The first shore training station for boys,

HMS *Ganges* on the Shotley peninsula near Harwich in eastern England, was opened the following year and boy training was now concentrated there and at Plymouth, where the old wooden ships continued despite Fisher's intentions.[71] The *Caledonia*, which had been described in Parliament as being in 'a parlous condition',[72] was sold for breaking up, for ships of her age had not yet gained any archaeological status, and boy training in Scotland came to an end after just fourteen years.

Naval Manoeuvres

On 6 August 1888 the *Glasgow Herald* carried the startling headline 'A Raid on the Clyde – Greenock Bombarded – The Town "in Ruins" – Booty Captured in Rothesay Bay'. A gunboat had entered the river, bombarded Greenock, forced the town of Rothesay to pay a subsidy and destroyed 32,000 tons of shipping in the lower Clyde. It went on to capture Oban.

In fact it was a report on the Royal Navy's Annual Manoeuvres, in which the gunboat *Spider* had evaded blockading forces at Lough Swilly in Ireland and gone on to 'raid' Scotland. It arrived off Campbeltown at 6 a.m. on the morning of 5 August and 'destroyed' over 5,000 tons of shipping. After that she went on to Rothesay and 'sank' five steamers in half an hour. Off Greenock that afternoon she spent an hour 'destroying in detail all the shipping in the Clyde'. She retired unmolested through the Kyles of Bute and went up Loch Fyne and on round the Mull of Kintyre to reach the Sound of Islay by the 7th. 'Large destruction was claimed' at the places visited.[73]

The gunfire heard at Greenock was blanks, but one Scottish MP, Sir Henry Campbell-Bannerman, complained that the Navy was 'causing needless disturbance and inconvenience to the inhabitants of the places visited, without any advantage to the naval service of the country'. The official report on the manoeuvres was less passionate:

> While it may be considered extremely doubtful whether any cruiser . . . could have done anything like the amount of damage claimed in the time, even if she met with no resistance, yet her movements show no great obstacle lies in the way of an enemy's cruiser entering any of the ports, including the Clyde, which were visited by the *Spider* for a hostile purpose, and this fact points to the necessity of the proposed military defences of the latter place being taken in hand as soon as possible.

There was a public meeting of 'various public bodies interested in the defences of the river and estuary of the Clyde against naval attack'.

The only existing defence was Fort Matilda at Greenock, with submarine mines laid by Volunteer Submarine Miners, under the supervision of the Royal Engineers. A report was commissioned and produced in September. It recommended a new fort at Kilcreggan, and another one above Greenock. Dumbarton Castle was no use in a modern defence – it was too far upriver, and the tortuous and narrow channel of the river was sufficient protection in itself. The first line of defence, it was suggested, should be at Little Cumbrae.

But the *Spider*'s expedition was a very rare event. Annual manoeuvres were usually held between the Mediterranean Fleet and the Channel Fleet, in the English Channel, south of Ireland and on the coasts of Portugal, and very rarely strayed any further north.

In the early years of the twentieth century, as Germany began to emerge as the main naval opponent, more manoeuvres were held in the North Sea. In 1908 the 'Red' Fleet, based in the Firth of Forth, 'patrolled the North Sea during the day, returning to base at night, while the destroyers took up patrol duties outside. Meanwhile the Blue Fleet patrolled around the Faroe Islands, between the Orkneys and Shetlands and down to Wick.' But the fleets never met, mainly due to communications failures, and no tactical lessons were learned. There was an important strategic lesson, that the North Sea is big enough for two fleets to operate for some time without meeting, but this was not learned for some years.[74]

The Volunteer Reserve

The navy tried various forms of local non-seaman reserves in succession to the Sea Fencibles of the Napoleonic Wars. The Naval Coast Volunteers of 1853 reached a maximum strength of 6,859 men but was allowed to die out in 1873. It was replaced by the Royal Naval Coast Volunteers, 'composed of men who have not, as a rule, practical acquaintance with the sea, but are attracted to the profession of sailors by sympathy and aspiration'. Their service was confined to 'the defence of the coasts of the United Kingdom, the Channel Islands, and the Isle of Man and the seas adjacent; but outside these limits only with the consent of the volunteers.' The Clyde Division was quite successful but professional naval officers could see little use for a force which they felt could not 'afford even part of the crew of a torpedo-boat'. It was disbanded in 1892 and the members given the option to transfer to the control of the army.[75]

When the Royal Naval Volunteer Reserve was formed in August 1903, it had a stronger Scottish conection than the other naval reserves. It was a personal triumph for James, Marquis of Graham, later Duke of Montrose. He was a great enthusiast for the sea, but could not enter as a naval officer because, as the eldest son of a nobleman, he was expected to look after the family estates. He had planned to enter the army until a shooting incident in the cadet corps at Eton left him partially deaf. Instead he devoted his youth to sea travel of different kinds. His father used his influence with Captain Lord Charles Beresford to allow him to serve as a volunteer among the midshipmen on several naval ships. He worked on a sailing merchant-man for a time and served as an army volunteer in the South African War. He also sailed on some of the great yachts of the day, including Lord Brassey's *Sunbeam*. His lordship, an enthusiast for naval volunteering in an earlier generation, passed the baton on to Graham. 'Lord Brassey was getting on in years, and he did not know of anyone willing to follow where he had blazed the trail. In reflection, I came to the conclusion that, though my deafness might prevent active service in the Navy or Army, it need not slam the door to my taking part in some part in the Reserve forces, or in public life . . .'[76]

The tradition of part-time, local volunteer service for the army had been strong in Scotland for several generations. It was his service as a sergeant in the Lanarkshire Rifle Volunteers that inspired William Smith to found the Boys' Brigade in 1883. More recently, volunteer units had formed a large proportion of the armed forces in the Boer War (1899–1902) and they had dispelled the myth that they were no use for overseas service. The naval profession was still sceptical about letting amateurs, however enthusiastic, on the decks of its ships. Its planning did not suggest a vast increase in the number of ships in wartime. But Graham and his associates led a strong campaign, which struck a chord in places like the Clyde, which still felt that its defence was neglected by the navy. On Trafalgar Day 1899 a meeting was held under the chairmanship of the Provost of Glasgow. The hall was filled and at least 200 men promised to serve in a naval reserve when it was formed. This led to a national campaign, which was boosted in 1903 when Erskine Childers published his novel *The Riddle of the Sands*, suggesting that the potential enemy was now Germany rather than France, and that yachtsmen who knew the coast had a vital role to play in the defence of the country.

An Act was passed and the Royal Naval Volunteer Reserve came into existence in 1903. Graham was its most senior officer, holding the relatively junior rank of lieutenant commander – actually meaning lieutenant in command, as the full rank of lieutenant commander did not come into being until 1914. Graham was in charge of the Clyde

Division, one of six in the United Kingdom, and the only one in Scotland for the moment. The headquarters were in Glasgow and money was raised to build a fine drill-hall with gun batteries. One of the subordinate companies was at Greenock and the sailing ship *City of Adelaide,* built in Sunderland in 1864, was purchased, gutted and fitted with gun batteries. She was renamed *Carrick* and has remained on the Clyde to this day, latterly as the RNVR club in Glasgow and finally at the Scottish Maritime Museum in Irvine. For the Leith Company, an old monitor was acquired and renamed *Claverhouse* after 'Bonnie Dundee', the famous Jacobite leader and member of the Graham family. The Admiralty protested that he had a reputation as a 'bloody butcher', but were too late to change it. In Dundee the old *Unicorn* was taken over from the RNR, which had adopted a new system of training.

Graham was determined to have a sea-going ship in his fleet and found the coastguard yawl *Rose* of 131 tons, built in 1880, was available at Chatham. He was not allowed to put the Admiralty to any expense, so he found a crew of volunteers to take her to the Clyde, and the affair showed how little the members of the new force knew about seamanship. When it was necessary to go aloft to repair the topmast, Graham was the only one who was able to do it. But when the ship reached Gourock after a passage of twenty-seven days all the crew, according to Graham 'had learnt to reef, steer and box the compass'.[77] The Clyde Division had 33 officers and 721 men by 1905, though still short of its establishment of 1,000.[78] By 1908, including companies at Greenock and Dundee, it had risen to 963 officers and men and formed more than a quarter of the national strength.[79]

In 1914, as the world entered into its most destructive war so far, Scotland was about to see far more of the Royal Navy than ever before, and for a longer period than almost anyone predicted. The war was to develop very differently from what most people had expected, both by land and by sea. Among the first to be disappointed by the role allotted to them were the officers and men of the Royal Naval Volunteer Reserve.

Chapter 8

The First Scottish Bases

The Old Naval Bases

The advent of steam and steel made the Royal Navy more dependent on fixed bases than ever. It was not just that the new ships needed coal. Steel hulls needed sophisticated facilities which could not be improvised. Modern guns were much larger and could only be hoisted by crane, not by ropes rigged from the ship's yardarms. Ships were also much longer, and some of the dockyards could not be adapted. In 1869 the navy closed its two oldest, at Deptford and Woolwich on the Thames, for they were too far up a narrow, winding river. Pembroke Dockyard in Wales remained quite small, as did Haulbowline in the south of Ireland, while Sheerness was a satellite of Chatham, ten miles up the River Medway. This left three yards, Chatham, Portsmouth and Devonport (Plymouth) as the 'first class' bases for the fleet. All were greatly expanded during the last forty years of the nineteenth century.

Each of these began to develop as a division of the navy for administrative, training, maintenance and manning purposes. This practice was regularised in 1894 when the First Lord told Parliament,

> During the year preparations have been made for definitely appropriating petty officers and men of all ratings to the three home ports, in order that each port may be self-supporting and capable of manning and providing for the care and maintenance of all ships attached to it. A complete establishment for each port has been drawn up, and the numbers voted have been divided between them in proportion to their requirements. New entries from the shore, and boys on completion of their training, will be appropriated to a port, according to the numbers required to complete the respective port establishment. It is hoped that the establishment of these port divisions will eventually provide for the actual needs of each port, facilitate mobilisation, and enable recruiting to be placed on a continuous and satisfactory system.[1]

As well as the dockyard with its ship repair facilities, each would have an armaments depot, victualling stores, training ships of various types, Royal Marine barracks and depot ships for stores and men. Every ship in the navy, home and overseas, was attached to one of these 'home ports' and would be manned and maintained from it. Ships might be transferred from one port to another but ratings would probably spend their whole career with the same one. When their ship paid off they would go to the depot ship at their home port until sent on training or to another ship from the same division. Their families would settle in the area and the men would probably retire there, perhaps sending their sons into the navy in due course, while remaining on the lists themselves as pensioners. It was parallel to the army's regimental system, but on a grander scale. Like the regimental system, the home ports created a certain amount of social cohesion in a force which had many disparate elements. Precisely because of the scale, it created even more inertia than the army's system: regiments could be merged or disbanded against strong pressure, but to change the home port system of the navy required much greater force if the whole navy was not to become unbalanced.

The Naval Works Act of 1895 allowed the Admiralty to borrow up to £10 million to construct and enhance naval facilities. Most of this was to be spent abroad, especially at Gibraltar, or in building a great breakwater at Dover. At home, its main effect was to allow the navy to 'come ashore' for the first time. New barracks were built at Devonport, Portsmouth and Chatham to replace some of the old 'wooden walls' where the men had lived between appointments to seagoing ships. The barracks, however, retained ship names, reinforcing the tradition that every seaman belonged to an 'HMS' of one kind or another.

None of the Naval Works Act money was spent in Scotland. When the Act was debated in the House of Commons there were some protests from Irish MPs who wanted more money spent on Haulbowline, but nothing from the Scots. Perhaps they felt that the navy was already spending enough in their constituencies, in the form of shipbuilding. After the Naval Defence Act of 1889 the Clyde yards began to enter the warship market on a large scale, and in 1895 their output peaked with the launch of sixteen ships totalling 42,000 tons.[2]

The buildings associated with the Naval Works Act were well advanced in 1900, when public and political opinion in Britain began to turn against Germany. During the Boer War (1899–1901) the British were shocked by the German support for their enemies. German efficiency and engineering skills seemed a much greater threat than the traditional enemy France, which was showing signs of faltering as a naval power. The fruits of Admiral Tirpitz's Navy Laws of 1898 and 1900 were already beginning to appear and a fleet of thirty-eight battleships was planned. There is no real evidence that this was part of a war plan against the British, but it seemed so at the time.

The Choice of Rosyth

The British fleet had already expanded considerably over the last few years, from thirty-eight battleships in 1883 to sixty-two in 1897.[3] British naval bases were now becoming overcrowded and were sited in the south of England to face France and the Netherlands, so a committee was set up to report on the facilities which were available to handle these ships. In January 1902 Admiral Wharton, the Hydrographer of the Navy, produced a detailed report which strongly advocated a site above the Forth Bridge as a place for a new dockyard, going far beyond a mere hydrographical survey with comments on strategy and naval recruitment.

1. The access to it is easy, and can be navigated by ships of all draughts, at all periods of the tide.
2. The anchorage is very good, and of great extent, and no place on the East Coast of Great Britain can compete with it in this respect.
3. It lies well up the estuary of the Forth, behind defences already constructed, and in such a position as to make attack difficult.
4. The position is strategically of value in war with the Northern Powers, as it provides a repairing base for ships watching the route North of Scotland and the Shetlands, 350 miles nearer than the Thames.
5. The railway communication is good, and coal and iron are found at no great distance.
6. A depot of seamen in a populous part of Scotland would tend to aid recruiting by providing a naval port whence Scottish seamen could more easily reach their homes than from the present naval centres.
7. The establishment of a naval port in Scotland would probably be very popular in that division of the Kingdom.

He went on to give reasons for choosing a site on the north bank of the Forth above the Bridge, at the anchorage known 'from time immemorial' as St Margaret's Hope:

1. It is on the more sheltered side of the river, and the anchorage is also best on this side.
2. As, from the great extent of shallow water on either side of the river, a dockyard must be mainly on reclaimed ground, the nature of the

land on the north side lends itself more readily to quarrying and levelling for the purpose of obtaining the necessary material. On this point it may be mentioned that there are no harbours otherwise suitable where a dockyard with a basin and wharf with deep water can be constructed without such reclamation.

3. Large quarries exist whence first-rate stone for building is procured.
4. The shape of the existing coast line permits a dockyard to be formed which will on two sides join the existing land, whereas on the south side it would only touch on one.
5. A reclamation on the north side could, as far as can be seen, be accomplished without in any way accelerating silting at North Queensferry or its piers, whereas on the south side South Queensferry would certainly be injuriously affected, entailing expense in compensation. &c.
6. So far as can be ascertained, there will be much less difficulty and expense connected with the acquisition of the necessary land on the North side than on the South. On the South side the dockyard would in any case border Hopetoun Park, and it is possible that closer investigation would show the necessity of encroaching on the latter, while any future extension of the yard would certainly require such encroachment. Dalmeny Park would come close up to the other end of the dockyard and the dockyard town that would arise between them would enormously depreciate the value of both these estates. On the North side are only three of four small residential properties that would be injuriously affected. Two would have to be purchased for the dockyard, and the others could be sold at greatly enhanced prices for building land in the dockyard town.
7. On the South side it would be difficult to get enough land without disturbing public roads, while on the North it does not appear that this is necessary.
8. Any extension of the dockyard on the North side can be carried out without interfering with any residential property or road.

The Hydrographer had to admit that there were certain doubtful points; in particular, 'Until borings are made it is impossible to say how far below the surface of the mud rock will be met with on either side of the river, and consequently how much expense will be entailed in excavating a basin . . .'[4]

The Admiralty was convinced and on 14 February 1903, at the end of his annual statement on the Naval Estimates, Lord Selborne, First Lord of the Admiralty, announced,

... in January 1902, the Board came to the conclusion that the time
had arrived for the creation of a fourth naval base and depot in the
United Kingdom. After an examination of all the available sites and a
thorough consideration of the question in all its industrial and strategical aspects, necessarily extending over a good many months, the
Board selected the Firth of Forth as fulfilling all the requirements of the
Navy. Provisional negotiations have been proceeding for some weeks
past, and proposals will be submitted to Parliament in the course of this
session for the acquisition of the land necessary to establish there a
fourth home port.

Colonel Exham, the Superintending Engineer at Portsmouth, was
ordered to inspect the area from a civil engineering point of view.
He posed as an inquisitive tourist and he too favoured the site. He was
appointed Superintending Engineer at Rosyth and the Admiralty
purchased 1,184 acres of land and 286 of foreshore around the
fifteenth-century Rosyth Castle, which stood on a small peninsula
on the shore. It cost of £140,000, which raised some comment in
Parliament.[5]

By 1903 the Admiralty was planning a highly ambitious project, a full
'first class' naval base, equal to Portsmouth, Chatham or Devonport,
with accommodation for a quarter of the Royal Navy. Exham visited
the German works at Wilhelmshaven and Kiel and in November 1904
he produced a plan for the full scheme, estimated to cost £10 million. It
was centred round a basin or wet dock which enclosed 52.5 acres of
water, with dry docks leading off it. This was a reflection of the
Admiralty's experience over the last forty years or so, in building the
St Mary's complex of docks at Chatham, the northern extension to
Portsmouth Dockyard and the Steam Yard at Keyham in Devonport,
for all of these were centred on large wet docks. When asked why a basin
was so necessary, the Director of Engineering and Architectural Works
replied, 'They do not like docking a valuable battleship in the [tidal]
stream.' The Assistant Director of Works at the Admiralty gave a
further reason. 'It forms a quiet sheltered spot for the ships to lie while
undergoing repairs which do not necessitate going into a [dry] dock.'[6]

The Rosyth basin was to be rectangular, enclosing the maximum
area of water so that ships could be moored in the centre if necessary.
In this respect it was different from a merchant wet dock, which
tended to be longer and narrower, to give the maximum length of
berths alongside the quays. The Rosyth basin could be entered and left
by a lock at any state of the tide, or through an 'emergency exit' in the
south wall of the rectangle at high tide only.

Delays

But the navy was already heavily committed to works in the south and overseas. The Naval Estimates peaked at £36 million in 1904–5, or £41 million including paying off debts incurred under the Naval Works Act. Exactly three months after announcing the Rosyth project, Lord Selborne wrote,

> The case of Rosyth is different. I have always regarded this more as a wise provision for certain future needs than as a provision for immediate needs. I should not, therefore, be sorry if no immediate progress were made with this work, and that ample time should be taken with our preparations and plans. It was wisely decided that the site should be plotted out so as to include in its proper order and in its proper place everything that is contained in a naval base of the first magnitude, but it does not by any means follow that all need be provided at once.

Selborne ruled out any prospect of shipbuilding at Rosyth, as happened at the other major yards, because 'In the first place, the development of the Government employment of civil labour is in itself a great political evil, and, in the second place, so much capital has been recently embarked by private firms such as Vickers', Laird's, Armstrongs, &c., . . . that I do not think a necessity really exists for an additional Government establishment in peace.'[7]

In addition to the dockyard, land was purchased at Crombie for a Royal Naval Ordnance Depot, not operational until 1914. Across the firth at Queensferry a naval sick quarters was set up, with two general wards, an operating theatre, an infectious block, staff quarters, with a small mortuary and a drug store beside the river. The first medical officers, a staff surgeon and a surgeon, were appointed in March 1908.

On 21 October, Trafalgar Day, 1904, Admiral Sir John or 'Jacky' Fisher took up office as First Sea Lord, the professional head of the navy, committed to cutting naval expenditure through radical technological and organisational reform. On taking office he urged Selborne in characteristic style, *'Don't spend another penny on "Rosyth"!'* Already the scheme was being trimmed down and in March 1905 Exham produced three proposals. The simplest and cheapest was to go ahead with the basin, to serve mainly as shelter for a floating dock, for the Forth was often too rough to allow such a machine to operate in the open water. There would be no lock and ships would enter and leave by the single gate of the 'emergency exit'

at high tide. The second idea was to build the basin and a single dry
dock leading from it. The third was to use the entrance lock as the dry
dock. This was regarded as the cheapest, at a cost of something more
than £1 million. The Admiralty decided to adopt the second scheme as
it had 'the advantage of being a small self-contained repairing base
and in no way prejudiced the larger scheme for a complete first-class
naval base'. It was known as Scheme III.[8]

The Dreadnoughts

In January 1906 the Liberal Party came to power, committed to a
programme of social reform and the reduction of military and naval
spending. But meanwhile Fisher had begun a strategic, social and
technological revolution in the navy which would have a profound
and complex effect on the Rosyth scheme. He reduced the size of the
fleet by scrapping dozens of obsolete ships which were to be replaced
by flotillas of small torpedo-armed craft that would dominate the
narrow seas. In the short term this seemed to make increased dockyard
accommodation less necessary. He supported the 'Selborne Scheme'
by which the engineer officers of the navy were to be merged much
more closely with the 'executive' officers, the only ones eligible for the
highest commands. Most important of all, he began designs for a new
type of capital ship.

Torpedo development was forcing ships to fight at longer ranges
and the Russo-Japanese War of 1904–5 demonstrated the potentially
decisive effect of large-calibre guns. The problem was to develop a
technique to allow these relatively slow-firing weapons to score
sufficient hits at ranges of four miles or more. Current battleships
relied on the sheer weight of fire from batteries of numerous rapid-
firing guns, individually directed by their crews. The new concept was
to fire big guns in salvos, with spotters to record the fall of shot and
take corrective action. When some fell on one side of the target and
some on the other it was being 'straddled' and the aim was correct.
The best way of doing this was to provide the ship with a uniform
armament and Fisher's new *Dreadnought* had a battery of ten 12-inch
guns. She had turbine engines giving a speed of up to 22 knots, 3 knots
faster than the older ships, and armour plating up to 11 inches thick,
though Fisher did not regard that as a priority. She was begun in
October 1905, launched in February the next year and began her trials
just a year after she was started, less than half the time it usually took
to build a battleship. When Fisher set his mind to it, no one was better
at getting things done.

The dramatic entry of the *Dreadnought* to the world stage ensured her place in history. Ships built to the same concept, however loosely, were to be known as 'Dreadnoughts' to distinguish them from older ships, the 'pre-Dreadnoughts', which could neither fight nor run away when faced with the new ship.

But Fisher felt that the Dreadnought type was forced on him by faint-hearted colleagues. What he really wanted was an all-big-gun armoured cruiser that could deal with enemy fleets and with commerce raiders in the open ocean. He proposed a ship which would carry an armament similar to the *Dreadnought*, but have about half the thickness of armour plating. The ships would be much faster, at 26 knots, and have a longer range. The first of them, the *Invincible*, was not launched until 1908, for few ships could be given the priority of the *Dreadnought*. They were soon known as battlecruisers, and became the fastest and most glamorous part of the battlefleet itself.

In the meantime the building of the *Dreadnought* had two main consequences. It made all existing battleships obsolete and gave Britain an unassailable lead in the naval race, though Fisher encouraged naval scares to keep the shipyards in business. By 1909 fears had been cultivated that the Germans were catching up rapidly in battleship construction, and crowds demonstrated in the streets under the slogan 'We want eight and we won't wait', orchestrated by the Navy League. They were successful and forced the government to double the capital ship programme for the year. The government was forced into a tax increase that led to a constitutional crisis.

Secondly, the new ships made new docks all the more necessary. Chatham had no docks at all able to handle a Dreadnought, Portsmouth and Devonport had to lengthen existing docks quite considerably to make them suitable. The only suitable commercial dock on the east coast was at Hebburn on the Tyne. Furthermore, the *Dreadnought* was far from the end of the story. The *Dreadnought* herself was of 17,900 tons and had 12-inch guns. The *Orion* class of 'super-Dreadnoughts', ordered in 1909, were of 22,000 tons and had 13.5-inch guns. And the *Queen Elizabeth* class, begun in 1912, were of 33,000 tons and had 15-inch guns. In all, forty Dreadnoughts and battlecruisers had been built or were under order for the Royal Navy by August 1914.

Delays

Fisher's opposition to Rosyth continued. He was not overly concerned about the German menace and he did not see that his large ships would be mainly concerned with the North Sea. He believed that the growing threat from submarines, on which he placed great emphasis as part of his concept of flotilla defence, would make the Forth indefensible. His colleague and supporter, Rear-Admiral Sir John Jellicoe, disagreed. 'My fear is that this submarine question may be made an excuse to avoid spending – what appears to me to be essential money – on dock accommodation on the East Coast.'[9] If Fisher's enormous energy and administrative skills had been applied to the task, Rosyth would no doubt have been completed much more quickly, but even if he had been wholeheartedly in favour, he was already committed to building Dreadnoughts and battlecruisers and to reform of the officer corps. Dockyards were not high on his list of priorities. Furthermore, the new Hydrographer of the Navy, Admiral Field, had objections to his predecessor's ideas. He felt that a bank just south of the proposed basin would pose a danger to navigation and was of hard material that could not be dredged easily. Borings were taken and it was found that the bank was gravel rather than rock. Meanwhile the Controller of the Navy, Admiral Sir Henry Jackson, visited the site and proposed another idea (Scheme IV) in which the basin would run from north to south and would therefore have its lock in the southern face of the wall, rather than the eastern face. In March 1907 another scheme was put before the Admiralty, basically the plan of two years earlier for 'a small self-contained repairing base', with one of the corners cut off the basin to avoid a very deep bed of sand and thus save expense. This was Scheme V and it was accepted by the Board on 16 July. It still had to run the gauntlet of various Admiralty departments who considered many of the details, and the revised plan was submitted on 29 October.

The delays attracted a good deal of criticism from the Conservative Party, now in opposition, and from the Imperial Maritime League, an extreme anti-Fisher breakaway from the Navy League. Admiral Sir Charles Beresford, Fisher's leading critic within the navy (until he retired in 1911 to resume his career as an MP), accused the government of procrastination.[10] The question was often mentioned in Parliament, though never fully debated. In May 1907 Lord Tweedmouth, the new First Lord of the Admiralty, told the House of Lords 'he believed it to be absolutely necessary that we should have on the East Coast a dock capable of taking our biggest ships'. Yet he had to admit 'He was not prepared to say offhand which was the best place for it.'[11] By the end of 1907, after Scheme V had been fully considered, Tweedmouth's public speeches suggested that the project would now go ahead. He said so at Duns in Berwickshire on 2 December and repeated the message the next day at Chelmsford, Essex, to a meeting disrupted by Suffragettes. According to *The Times*,

> Along the whole east coast of Scotland and England, he said, we had not a dock capable of accommodating our great fighting ships, and the government had decided to establish a new naval establishment at a place called Rosyth. This, they had come to the conclusion, would be the most suitable place, and one most useful to the navy. They proposed to construct, in the first place, a graving dock capable of taking our biggest ships, then a big basin and quays which would accommodate 22 warships alongside them. [A woman questioned 'Will the new dock have room for votes for women?' She was removed.]

Despite many more interruptions and evictions, Tweedmouth sat down to loud cheers.[12]

But the official announcement had to wait three more months. On 2 March 1908 the Parliamentary Secretary to the Admiralty addressed the House of Commons.

> Mr Edmund Robertson: . . . The Government has finally decided to proceed with the Rosyth works. [Some cries of 'Oh!' on the Ministerial side] The Government has finally decided to proceed with Rosyth. It has not been an easy matter to settle at all. It has been before the House for many years.
>
> Mr Wyndham: Five years.
>
> Mr Edmund Robertson: I think about eight years. With the exception of some minority protests, on the whole I venture to say that it has been accepted as sound policy that there ought to be a base on the east coast somewhere, and the selection of Rosyth has been a case of the survival of the fittest. We took plenty of time to examine all the alternative sites, and we came to the conclusion that Rosyth on the whole offered the greatest advantages . . .

Tweedmouth provided more detail in the Navy Estimates the following day. The time, he implied, had not been wasted, for the superintending engineer in charge of Rosyth had 'made an extensive survey of all the great naval establishments and buildings yards at home and of some abroad, in order that plans might be drawn for the laying out of Rosyth as a first-class Naval Base in such a way that any particular portion might be carried out without interference with the general scheme.' The intention, he said, was 'to avoid the repetition of the haphazard growth of a naval dockyard port, which the history of the old establishments at Portsmouth, Devonport and Chatham, has proved to be so expensive in the past.' He then described the overall plan.

> . . . to take in hand the construction of a graving dock, closed basin, and an entrance lock, capable of accommodating the largest modern warships, with a depot for submarines and destroyers, and provision for oil fuel storage. The basin is to be 52½ acres in area, with accommodation for 11 of the largest ships along the quays, or 22 when double banked.

It was to cost a total of £3 million, with £250,000 for machinery. It would take about ten years to complete, so would be ready in 1918.[13] The stonework would largely be in Norwegian granite, which caused some comment from the MPs for Aberdeen, Cork, Devonport and Shropshire who piped up about the qualities of their own local stone.[14] A model of the scheme was placed in the Members' Tea Room, but according to the member for Chatham, 'There was no foreman in any private yard in the country who would submit to his manager a model of such description.'[15]

Greenock and Loch Long

On 2 March 1908, at the same time as he announced the intention to develop Rosyth, Edmund Robertson told the House of Commons of plans for the Firth of Clyde:

> A torpedo is a horrible instrument, I loath the look of it; but it is as delicate as a watch and needs most careful adjustment and attention. Like everything else in naval warfare the torpedo has developed, and the range of 3,000 yards, which was the length of the range hitherto, is no longer sufficient. We want a range of 7,000 yards, and the requirements of proper water area are not easy to fulfil. A great many different sites and schemes were examined and Loch Long, again became a case of the survival of the fittest, and the range will be established there.'[16]

Again the First Sea Lord elaborated the next day. Land had been purchased for a torpedo factory at Greenock nearby, at a cost of £27,225. The range would replace the ones at Weymouth and Portsmouth in the south of England, which were too short. 'Visitors to that part of Scotland', he went on, 'need be under no apprehension that the beauties of the scenery or the convenience of access will be interfered with.'[17] The Civil Lord of the Admiralty explained some of the reasoning. In the past torpedoes had been manufactured at Woolwich and transported 120 miles to Weymouth, and many were damaged in transit, so it was necessary to have the factory and the range close together. The range should be 'in sheltered position and as free as possible from tidal influence, and that there should be as little interference as possible with ordinary shipping.'[18] It seems that the position of the factory was dictated by the position of the range.

The local people did not agree and suggested an alternative.

Loch Striven at the entrance to the Kyles of Bute in the near vicinity of the anchorage of the laid-up warships. The distance from Fort Matilda is practically identical with that of the range area in Loch Long, it is within easy reach of the important county town of Rothesay. Loch Striven is little frequented by the public and by yachts while the population on its shores is sparse.[19]

The Admiralty took no interest, probably because Loch Striven was not long enough for their requirements.

There were complaints from the steamship operators – Caledonian Steam Packet, North British Steam Packet and Glasgow and South Western Steam Packet Company – that the firing of torpedoes would disrupt their services in the loch. The Admiralty was conciliatory.

. . . the Officer in Charge of the Range will be instructed to exercise every precaution in carrying out his duties, and the fact that he will know the times when certain of the steamers are due will be of great assistance in enabling him to avoid causing delay and inconvenience to the traffic.[20]

The group most affected were the local fishermen, who would be driven out of business. The Admiralty had already made enquiries and found that the main fisherman of the area was sixty-year-old Finlay McNab of Portincaple, who had about £250 worth of fishing gear and employed two other McNabs, aged seventeen and twenty-one, as well as three other men aged seventeen, sixty and forty. There were five other boats in the area plus one operated by James Calder, a fish merchant of Uddingston in Lanarkshire who fished about two months every year and employed a man to help him. But the fishing of Loch Long was much less extensive than the famous herring fishery of Loch Fyne on the other side of the Cowal peninsula. About 75 tons were caught at Portincaple every year, and about 10 tons at Arrochar. The Admiralty agreed to pay compensation, up to a total of £250.[21]

The Building of Rosyth

After the usual tendering process, the Admiralty chose Easton Gibb and Son as the main contractors for Rosyth Dockyard. Sir Alexander Gibb, the 'son' in the title, had been born at Broughty Ferry in 1872, so he knew the area. He was a fourth-generation civil engineer, who had worked on the Caledonian Railway and Barry Docks in Wales. The main contract for the dockyard was signed on 1 March 1909.

When building the entrance lock, the designers tried to avoid a rock called Dhu Craig, which was close to where the eastern wall of the basin would be built. Borings showed that there was little else to form the foundations of the lock. Therefore the position of the lock was changed so that it now passed through the centre of the rock. The builders also tried to site the basin walls on bedrock as far as possible

Dredging work in the channels into the basin began in June 1911. A suction dredger, the *St Lawrence*, built by Simons of Renfrew, was used on some of the early work and the engineers were pleasantly surprised to find that the material was quite soft. Eight and a half million cubic yards of spoil would be produced and two million were deposited in three areas around Rosyth Castle, so that it would no longer be on a peninsula. When that was done a further area to the east would be filled up, starting at its western end.

Initially the plans only demanded a single dry dock, in the centre of the north side of the basin, the only one which faced the land. Since the creation of dry docks was the main object of the exercise, it was clearly uneconomic to spend a great deal of money building the basin for the sake of a single dry dock, even if up to four more could be fitted into the space later. By September 1912 a second dock had been agreed and Churchill at the Admiralty made plans for a third. Since the basin would be flooded quite soon, it was better to construct the entrance to the third dock and fit it with a caisson, or floating gate. Then the rest of the dock could be dug out when required, without the need to construct a dam. The area for the third dock was to be marked out on the land, and nothing else was to be allowed to encroach on it or its surroundings.[22]

Criticism of Rosyth

Fisher's opposition to Rosyth did not moderate after his retirement in 1910. He wrote, 'As you know, I have always been "dead-on" for Cromarty and hated Rosyth, which is an unsafe anchorage – the whole fleet in jeopardy the other day; and there's that beastly bridge which if blown up makes egress very risky.'[23] Commander D. J. Munro was appointed the first harbourmaster to the port in July 1911. He was a Highlander who had learned his trade under sail with the Paddy Henderson Line of Glasgow and joined the Royal Naval Reserve. He was one of the 'hungry hundred' of RNR officers recruited to the navy proper in 1895 as 'supplementary lieutenants' to help cope with the rapid expansion of the fleet. He was to prove a forthright and energetic man, though his main contribution was not to be at Rosyth. He was not impressed on his first visit:

> A very hasty 'fly-round' soon convinced me that for war purposes the Firth of Forth was a hopeless position. A start had been made with building Rosyth dockyard, but that was about all. It was easily seen that it would take years to construct at the leisurely rate of progress. As the dry dock ran in from the main basin it could not be brought into use until the basin had been completed. The defences of the Firth were practically nil, consisting of three 9.2 guns, two on Inchkeith and one at Kinghorn on the northern shore.[24]

Others were not opposed to the project in principle, but saw many faults in the details. In 1913 Mr L. Tweedie Stoddart, who had served briefly as a civil servant in the Works Loans Department, had several letters published in the press, including the *Times Engineering Supplement*. He suggested that there was not enough depth in the main basin to handle modern warships. His superiors replied that 'All the dimensions of docks, basins, etc., were very carefully considered by the Departments concerned and by Board when the scheme was being prepared, and some have been increased during the progress of the work, owing to the increasing size of modern ships.'[25]

Stoddart was not alone in his doubts and in April a committee was set up, chaired by Sir Maurice Fitzmaurice, recently retired as the chief engineer to London County Council, who had worked on the Forth Bridge twenty-five years before. The committee questioned various Admiralty officials including the Director of Engineering and Architectural Works, and several important concerns were identified. The depth of water in the basin was to be increased from 34 to 36 ft, to allow a damaged Dreadnought to enter, even if filled with water and listing. The emergency entrance came in for a good deal of criticism. Situated on the southern side of the basin, it could operate only at high tide, in which case there was likely to be a strong current which would make a ship very difficult to manoeuvre. It was claimed that it had been designed only for the entrance of ships, not the exit. But the committee feared torpedo or even air attack might disable the main lock, trapping a part of the fleet inside. It demanded that the gate be moved round to the east side, where it was out of the tidal stream and largely protected by the structure round the entrance lock. The committee was strongly of the opinion that the entrance lock should never be used as a dry dock, and one member also suggested that the emergency entrance should be turned into a complete lock by adding an extra gate. This was not agreed by the Admiralty, but the other suggestions were adopted at a projected extra cost of £350,000.[26]

Steps had already been taken to increase the width of all gates from 110 to 125 ft, to allow room for the largest ships. Mr Sims, the Director of Engineering and Architectural Works, was asked if that was enough, or were ships likely to get bigger in the future? He confessed himself baffled. 'Who can say? Ever since I have been in the Service I have been told that they have reached their limits in dimensions, but they have always been growing.'[27] But in fact he need not have worried. The *Queen Elizabeth* class battleships, already under construction, were 90 ft wide and they were to be the largest for some time. When they were fitted with anti-torpedo bulges after 1916, that would be increased to 104 ft, but no battleship would be more than 107 ft wide. The *King George V* class of the Second World War were deliberately restricted in beam so that they would be able to dock at Portsmouth and Rosyth. Only the last of all the battleships, the *Vanguard* of 1946, was too wide for Rosyth.[28] Among aircraft carriers only the *Ark Royal* and *Eagle*, completed after the Second World War, were bigger than that, at 112 ft. The dock complex at Rosyth was fortunate in that it was designed just as warship size was reaching a plateau.

In the same year, another Admiralty committee looked at Rosyth from a different perspective. Admiral Jellicoe, now Second Sea Lord, chaired a group which was ordered by the First Lord, Winston Churchill, to report on 'The Question of Docking Accommodation on the East Coast'. The Committee was strongly in favour of the old home port system and felt that Rosyth would disrupt it.

> It is almost a general axiom that to give facilities for rapid mobilisation and at the same time to deal fairly with all the personnel, it is essential that each manning port should have a proportion of *all* ratings based upon it, more especially the higher non-substantive [i.e. specialised] ratings. If this is not the case, men based on a port where a fair proportion of the higher ratings is not borne, will have a very natural grievance in regard to pay and prospects, and difficulty immediately arises in obtaining volunteers for such a depot.

This was a particular problem at Chatham, whose dry docks were too small to handle the new Dreadnoughts. 'The adoption of any policy which reduced Chatham to a manning base solely or principally for small craft would have the effect indicated, for in such an event either Chatham men would be deprived of anything approaching their fair proportion of higher non-substantive ratings, or on mobilisation a large transfer of these ratings to other ports must immediately take place.' They were sceptical of any idea of building up Rosyth as a manning base, as Scotland provided only 3 per cent of naval ratings at the time, implying that it would take decades to establish the naval culture of a place like Chatham. If Chatham was to be abandoned as a manning centre,

> it will be necessary to develop Rosyth on a full scale. This will involve the erection at Rosyth by 1918 of the whole of the usual fleet establishments, viz., naval barracks, marine barracks, gunnery and torpedo schools, naval hospital, victualling yard, &c., incidental to a first-class naval base, together with arrangements, both social and domestic, for inducing 40,000 men to make Rosyth their manning port, an obviously impracticable idea in so short a time.

Nor would it be desirable for the men to be based at Chatham, while the ships were being repaired at Rosyth.

> There is one very obvious objection which would cause widespread discontent amongst the men unless overcome, viz., when a ship comes under repair the men would not be near their homes. In such circumstances it would be necessary, in fairness to the men, to send the ship to her manning port *before* and *after* her refit for the special purpose of giving leave.

The navy, unlike the army, did not provide married quarters, which in this case seems to have made it more difficult to change a base. Nor did it allow travel expenses between the men's homes and their ships or stations. The committee, then, recommended that bigger dry docks should be built at Chatham, and that the narrow, winding channel up to the yard should be dredged.[29] None of this was ever done and the problem remained.

Rosyth and the Community

From the beginning the Admiralty was aware that the new naval dockyard would greatly expand the demand for labour in and around the nearest town, Dunfermline. The first problem was housing the workers who would build the yard. This was included in the main contract with Easton Gibb. In the first instance they hoped to attract enough men from the area by the provision of special workers' trains, but by 1911 this policy was beginning to fail. Following a strike in the autumn of 1912 it was decided to erect a village of temporary corrugated iron huts which had been used during the building of Immingham Docks on the River Humber. The village, 'bungalow city', was begun in February 1913 and virtually complete by June. Fifty or 60 huts could accommodate one family each, with 8 to 26 lodgers. A common lodging house for 150 single men was also built. By October 1914, 2,000 adults and 650 children were living in the village.[30] By this time more special trains were being provided. Twenty-four arrived daily from Edinburgh, Dunfermline and Kirkcaldy and the housing problem was largely solved.[31]

A longer-term problem was to provide enough housing for the yard workers and their families, without putting too much pressure on the local housing stock, and without the Admiralty, in the age of *laissez-faire*, getting too involved in the housing market. Dockyard workers required permanent accommodation to a higher standard than the navvies and contractors who built the yard. The issue had been mentioned in Parliament right at the start of the project, in 1903, and the latest type of 'garden city' had been suggested. This was based on the ideas of Ebenezer Howard, who had published his *Tomorrow: a Peaceful Path to Social Reform* in 1898. The first fruits of this had been seen in the town of Letchworth, north of London, that very year. In 1903 the Garden City Association published a pamphlet by Thomas Adams entitled *The New Naval Base. A Great Social Opportunity*, arguing the case for a town at Rosyth.[32] The following year the Civil Lord of the Admiralty confirmed that,

> . . . the Admiralty was sympathetically inclined to the proposal to have a model city in the neighbourhood of Rosyth, but they were not themselves prepared to build a garden city for the accommodation of the workpeople in the dockyard. All they would do was to see whether any land was available for workmen's dwellings after meeting all the requirements of the dockyard, and, if there was, they would encourage the erection of buildings there with due regard to hygienic considerations, space and so forth.[33]

This idea was revived in 1909, and the provisions of a new Town Planning Act of that year were taken into account. In 1912 Dunfermline Town Council was authorised to prepare a planning scheme and negotiations became very complex, involving the Admiralty, the Town Council, the Scottish National Housing Association, which was to carry out the building programme, the architects and Lord Elgin, who owned some of the land. Though the war interrupted the scheme, it eventually caused the Admiralty to accelerate it and 1,602 houses had been built by 1920.

Transport was essential if workers were to be attracted from the broader area, but the local tramway company was unenthusiastic about the Admiralty plans, considering in December 1913 that 'the Dockyard traffic in the near future will not be worth catering for.'[34] Eventually it was agreed that a tramway would follow the most direct route between Dunfermline High Street to the yard. With the start of the war this was designated a work of national importance, for it was needed by naval men on leave.

Though public opinion in the neighbourhood was generally in favour of the development at Rosyth and the work it would create, there was concern over the loss of access along the shore. Mr James Munro, a 68-year-old local resident, waxed lyrical about the foot-paths in the area.

> I have a vivid recollection of . . . the footpath leading from Rosyth Churchyard to the main road from the West to Inverkeithing and Queensferry – the uninterrupted use of it by young and old, and occasionally the improved facilities provided for the more easily getting over the walls, & c . . . We boys spent our Saturdays and holidays almost entirely, roaming about these fields, camping, gathering wild flowers which grew in great profusion, bird-nesting, and all the pastimes boys are given to. Later on I took part in picnicing, sea-fowl and wild duck and seal shooting, and all the time people would be seen walking along the footpath, and no-one dreamt of the word trespassing or thought of being interrupted . . . To go still further back, I have a distinct remembrance of being told by my mother of the numbers of people who went to Inverkeithing to hear the preaching of the cele-brated divine, Mr Ebenezer Brown, whose eloquence amazed Broug-ham and Jeffrey and I now have notes in my handwriting of the sermons she heard preached there in 1825. She distinctly told me these people went by the sea-braes path and the pathway under discussion.

Against evidence of this kind, the Admiralty solicitor advised caution:

> The Admiralty would probably lose if the case went to Court, and as the cost of this path cannot be anything but small, the balance of advantage would seem to lie in the direction of conceding gracefully what would probably be forced on us eventually, after incurring law costs and local odium. Further, I do not like the idea of fighting the local people on the question of a right of way enjoyed by the public for many years, though it is clear there cannot be a path through the Dockyard.[35]

Cromarty

Cromarty Firth was well known to the navy, for fleets had visited it many times during the annual cruises over the last fifty years and the people of the small port of Invergordon, just inside the entrance to the firth, had welcomed the navy many times, always with an eye to the profits to be made. Commander Munro, despite his formal role as harbourmaster at Rosyth, did not hesitate to put forward the advantages of the northern port. He listed the qualities to be looked for to the First Lord, Winston Churchill.

> Adequate space and good holding ground. Vision obscured from seaward [to make reconnaissance and attack more difficult]. Effective positions for the mounting of guns. Ease and safety of approach in all weathers and tide.

Compared with the alternatives on the east coast, the Medway, the Forth and Scapa Flow,

> The harbour which possesses most of the requirements enumerated in the foregoing is Cromarty. It will be observed that this harbour is easy of approach; in fact a ship making the harbour in thick weather has only the mainland to contend with, as there are no outlying dangers.
>
> Owing to the high land between the harbour and the open sea, vessels inside are almost entirely screened from view from the outside.
>
> The entrance is deep, and when in the harbour there are no rock, bank or other obstructions to contend with.

There was only one entrance, unlike the Forth and Scapa. The hills on either side, the Sutors, provided ideal positions for defensive guns. The entrance was quite narrow, so a boom could be constructed easily against attack by destroyer or submarine. Furthermore, the base was considerably further from Germany than Rosyth, so less vulnerable to attack.[36]

Munro was an enthusiast for the floating dock. These had been used by the navy for several decades, most notably a huge one which had been constructed for Bermuda in 1869. A floating dock was constructed in steel and launched like a ship. The tanks under it could be flooded to lower it in the water, and the ship to be repaired went in. The tanks were then pumped out and the ship was raised out of the water. Floating docks usually had high sides, partly to protect the ship from weather, partly to house workshops.

The navy's civil engineers were far more familiar with the fixed structures which formed the core of the Royal Dockyards, and opposed Munro's views. They argued that a floating dock could be sunk by torpedo or bombing. Munro countered that the floating dock was highly mobile. If the strategic situation changed and the east coast of Britain was no longer a potential scene of conflict, the dock could be towed wherever British interests seemed to be threatened. He enlisted the support of Jellicoe, then Controller of the Navy, who 'told me he was out for floating docks, but that it would be necessary to educate naval officers on the subject.' Munro gave a series of lectures in the newly constituted War College at Greenwich. He also attracted the attention of Churchill and was summoned to the Admiralty. Coming off the train from Scotland, he found the First Lord working late and they 'finished up with a long talk on Fleet requirements, docks, harbours etc.' Not long afterwards two floating docks were ordered, though only 32,000 tons each instead of the 40,000 tons Munro wanted.[37]

Munro went on to prepare a plan for a fully mobile naval base at Cromarty. His essential requirements were a large and small floating dock, a floating crane and a floating factory or workshop. In addition he would prefer to have a water-tank ship, a large and a small tug, three dockyard launches and two large lighters. He was sure that the waters in Cromarty Firth were sheltered enough for a dock to operate.

> Mooring the proposed establishment, it is considered, presents no difficulties; as the holding ground is excellent, tidal currents weak (chart shows 1 ½ knots midstream), and they run true, rising during the springs 14 ft, and 8 ft at neaps.
>
> It is considered that the difficulties to be met from winds are no greater, and in fact less, than in many places occupied by floating docks; as the winds more or less blow and down the harbor, or about east and west.[38]

The Hydrographer of the Navy was cautious. Fisher was supportive in his retirement, though his conception of the use of the base was rather eccentric. 'I still hate Rosyth and fortifications and East Coast Docks and said so the other day! But what we desire for Cromarty is for another purpose – to fend off German cruisers, possibly by an accident or fog or stupidity, getting loose in our small craft taking their ease or refueling at Cromarty.'[39]

Churchill was convinced, though money was short. The army had not enough to provide for the defences of the harbour, so it was agreed that the Royal Marines would supply and operate the guns on the Sutors. Finally on 18 March 1912, Churchill, following advice from the Imperial Defence Committee, announced to Parliament that a 'floating second-class naval base and war anchorage' would be created at Cromarty. Always ready to find reasons to visit ships and dock-yards, he went to Cromarty six months later in the Admiralty yacht *Enchantress*. He talked with Munro, who produced very grandiose plans for a completely mobile, self-propelled floating dock which was never built. Meanwhile a committee chaired by Fisher recommended that the fleet should be converted to oil-fired instead of coal-fired steam engines, and in 1913 it was decided to construct tanks at Invergordon. The defences at the Sutors were ready by the beginning of 1914 and a small air station was set up.[40] When a floating dock arrived in the firth soon after the outbreak of war, Cromarty was in many respects the best prepared of the east-coast bases.

Rosyth in Wartime

A few days before Britain entered the First World War on 4 August 1914, Rosyth Dockyard did its first repair for the Royal Navy, on the lighting circuits in the engine room of the battlecruiser *Indomitable*. But the work was mostly done by the ship's own artificers and the repair facilities at Rosyth remained very small, with only a small extemporised machine shop. There was a handful of managers and foremen, but no workmen under them. The engine fitting shop was operational, but fully committed to repairing the torpedo boats and destroyers of the port defence flotilla. It was agreed that 'repairs of a ship of a seagoing Squadron at this Port should be kept in the hands of the Admiral of that Squadron in exactly the same manner as it would be dealt with were the ship at Scapa Flow or any other Port where no Dockyard existed.'[41]

The Admiral was, however, ready to propose the staffing arrange-ments for Rosyth when it did become a fully fledged dockyard. One department would be headed by the King's harbourmaster and captain of the dockyard, who was responsible for the movements, berthing and rigging of ships. Captain W. F. Slayter had already been appointed to the post, in succession to Munro who had moved on to Cromarty. He would eventually have an assistant and three naval officers under him, and 132 workmen. The second department was headed by the chief constructor, a civil servant on a salary of £700 to £850, with a house or an allowance of £75 in lieu. He was responsible for the maintenance and repair of the ships themselves. Under him were to be a constructor, two foremen of the yard, a boatswain of the yard, three inspectors of shipwrights, an inspector of ship fitters, an inspector of painters and one for the smiths. This would be the largest department, with 636 workmen. The engineering department was headed by an engineer captain, with an assistant, a foreman and four inspectors for the engine fitters and the boilermakers. There would be 570 workmen. The electrical department was headed by an electrical engineer of the higher grade, on £450 to £650 per annum. He would have an assistant, two inspectors of electrical fitters, a senior station supervisor and 166 workmen. It was accepted that all these departments might expand, and that higher-grade officers might be brought in to head them.[42]

When the war started there was serious debate about whether to continue with Rosyth. Hundreds of Easton Gibb's men had joined the army in the great wave of patriotism which followed the declaration. More important, most people (apart from Lord Kitchener) believed that the war would be short, that it would 'all be over by Christmas'. Was there any point in continuing works which would not be ready for two years at the best estimate? The first two dry docks were now complete and the third had been authorised and started, but the basin itself still needed much work, so there was no access to the dry docks. The tidal basin, intended as a submarine base, was ready soon after the start of the war. The dam around it was breached on 25 August and the depot ship *Aquarius* was berthed there in the following week. Various improvisations were carried out to make this basin serviceable. The boathouse was converted to an emergency repair shop, the electricity substation became a torpedo store and temporary buildings were put up as offices.[43]

At the beginning of 1915, when a short war seemed less likely, two alternatives were identified:

1. To close down the works at Rosyth and divert the labour employed to other works. The advocates of this policy claimed this would give a more immediate return and shorten the duration of the war.
2. To recognise the abnormal conditions prevailing and co-operate with the contractor with a view to accelerating the works to the utmost possible extent and so bring them into use for some period of the war.[44]

The second was chosen and Easton Gibb signed two 'acceleration agreements', promising to complete the basin, entrance lock and two dry docks by the end of September 1915, in return for considerably increased payments. Many items were to be left unfinished. The lock, for example, was to be cut out of the rock at Dhu Craig but not lined with stone as originally intended. Instead, wooden floating fenders would be erected to protect ships from the bare rock.[45]

Work still continued slowly, because all the contractors had difficulty in finding and retaining men. At the end of 1914 Barrowfield Ironworks, constructing the oil tanks, explained that delays were due to exceptional circumstances – the difficulty in finding steel and the bad weather, and above all in finding men. In February 1915 it was 'principally due to the shortage of labour, owing to a large number of our men having joined the colours, and to our inability to replace them.'[46] Things were no better early in 1916, when the government was about to introduce conscription. Easton Gibb, the main contractor, pointed out some of the factors which had affected the issue since the Acceleration Agreement was signed:

1. Lord Derby's recruiting campaign.
2. A further absorption of men by the Ministry of Munitions.
3. The Conscription Act.
4. Certain works at the lock entrance had to be strengthened at the last moment and orders were received that this was to have precedence over all other work in the contract.
5. Orders were given for the Emergency Entrance to be pushed on at the same time as the lock, instead of after completion.
6. The exigencies of war have compelled you to order the various parts of the work to be carried out in a manner which have prevented our carrying out the work in a normal manner or anything like the sequence or at a cost which was expected and presumed at the time of the Agreement.

    The effect of items 1 and 2 has been to deplete the labour market of practically all the best men, so that those left for us to recruit are of a very inferior quality and totally unaccustomed to work the nature of ours.[47]

By the end of that year Easton Gibb found further difficulties. Through various national agencies 1,200 men had been recruited, but more than 700 were Irish, who were not liable to conscription in their homeland. When the government passed an Act requiring them to register for conscription, most of them went home to evade it.[48]

There were problems with the supply of materials. The iron work had already been made and it was fortunate that the Norwegian granite had mostly been delivered before the war started, for the sea route to Norway was soon to be disrupted. But cement largely came from works in the south of England and was transported by sea. Private shipowners were reluctant to carry it when the North Sea and the Forth became dangerous due to submarines. The Admiralty allocated some of its own store carriers, and provided enemy merchant ships which had been caught in port at the outbreak of war and interned. Before the war sand had been brought from the beaches at nearby Kinghorn and Burntisland and transported by sea, but navigation restrictions in the Forth at the outbreak of war made this extremely difficult. Sand was now obtained from land sources, and was more expensive.[49]

The excavation of the main basin was finished by 16 September 1915 and the entrance lock, due to be completed at the end of the month according to the second acceleration agreement, was ready for testing. The dam was removed and the lock was filled with water. There was some trouble when attempts were made to empty it again, and large pieces of timber were found jammed in the sluices. Divers had to be sent down to remove them. At 10 a.m. on 10 October the foreman of the works inspected the lock and found all in order. He came back again an hour and a half later to find that a great blister, 180 ft long, 35 ft wide and 8 inches high, was forming in the floor of the lock and water was leaking through a 1½-inch hole in the middle of it. The water had to be pumped out and the dam rebuilt to allow repairs to proceed. On 17 March 1916, in a flat calm and a high tide, the cruiser HMS *Crescent* was the first ship to enter the basin, through the emergency entrance. Ten days later the lock was ready. The pre-Dreadnought battleship HMS *Zealandia* passed through and went into one of the new docks.[50]

Construction of the dock buildings began in October 1914. All were built in the latest style, steel-framed with external brickwork and glazed roofs for lighting. Three dockside sheds, 510 ft long and 31 ft broad, one for each dry-dock, were finished during 1916. The first workshop was the smithery, 420 ft by 180 ft, completed in December that year. The doundry, with a 6-foot-deep sand floor for casting, opened in January 1917, with the engineering and boiler shops in April. The zincing shop, 100 ft long, was not completed until May 1918.[51]

In the afternoon of 31 May 1916, Rosyth received a long-awaited signal from the Grand Fleet, 'Fleet action imminent', warning the dockyards and naval hospitals to be ready for casualties in ships and men. Rosyth Dockyard was about to come to life to deal with the wreckage of battle. The final cost of its construction, including an allowance for wartime inflation and extras such as the submarine base, was £11,335,207.[52]

Chapter 9

The Grand Fleet and its Bases

The Outbreak of War

When Britain declared war on Germany on 4 August 1914, the British fleet was ready in men and materials. By good fortune the older ships of the Third Fleet, manned by the Royal Naval Reserve, the Coastguard and the pensioners of the Royal Fleet Reserve, had already been mobilised for a review by the King, and the ships were simply kept in commission as the crisis developed. The public and most of the navy expected a relatively short war. When Lord Kitchener suggested it might last as long as two years, Admiral Beatty was shocked. 'This I cannot think possible for a moment. The money in the world will run short before then, or they will have to construct some new form of barter & exchange.'[1] At least one great sea battle was expected, in which the upstart German fleet would be crushed in true Nelsonic style.

In such a battle there was no room for amateurs, such as the officers and men of the Royal Naval Volunteer Reserve. The members of the Clyde Division reported to their headquarters in Glasgow, where they found that all the regular naval staff had been mobilised themselves. They lived in a drill hall for three weeks until they were ordered to report to Dover. There they met men from the other RNVR divisions and were inspected by the First Lord of the Admiralty, Winston Churchill, who told them of his plans. They were to be mixed with marines and ex-army men to become part of an eight-battalion force, the Royal Naval Division, which was to join the land-fighting in Flanders. This caused very bad feeling and the Marquis of Graham received a deputation:

> They said they had been cheated and made the only 'conscripts' in all the British Forces. They demanded to be sent to sea at once, or sent home with authority to join up with their home regiments and friends.

They went so far as to threaten downing arms on parade, or making a wholesale desertion if their wishes were not met in a sympathetic way.[2]

Graham managed to talk them out of mutiny, and went to see Churchill, who promised to make sure that the men who had joined the RNVR before mobilisation would be given sea posts as soon as possible. But this was never fully implemented, as the Royal Naval Division became part of the defence of the Western Front, still keeping its naval ranks and talking about 'going ashore' and saluting the 'quarterdeck'. Thus Able Seaman Roland Caldwell of Stranraer and the Clyde RNVR Division went missing at the Battle of Beaucourt in November 1916 and was presumed dead; Able Seaman Clark of Bathgate was killed in April 1916 and Able Seaman McLachlan died of pneumonia in France in the same year.[3] In the meantime the Admiralty discovered that it needed such seamen after all, to man hundreds of small craft in a new and unexpected kind of war.

While the RNVR waited for the call, many thousands of Scots immediately volunteered for service with the army. But the land war always seemed a long way from Scotland. People on the south coast of England claimed to hear the great artillery bombardments of the Western Front, but Scotland only saw the departing troop trains, and occasionally those returning with the wounded. Only those who served at the front had any understanding of the terrible conditions there. The naval war was much closer to home. The great anchorage at Scapa Flow was visited by few Scots even in peacetime, and much less so when wartime travel restrictions were in force in the area. But the most glamorous part of the navy, the Battle Cruiser Fleet, was based in the Forth for nearly all the war, visible from the Forth Bridge and many points on shore. Fishermen from the numerous ports on the east coast joined the naval service as their vessels were taken up, or braved the dangers of the U-boat if they continued in their normal business – indeed, no communities in Britain were so affected by the war as the fishing ports, which also saw their normal export trade destroyed. Merchant seamen from Leith, Glasgow, Greenock, Aberdeen and Dundee also had their lives changed and worked under the threat of the U-boat.

In 1913 the Admiralty had introduced a new scheme for officer entry to meet the increasing demands for the new battleships. Instead of starting in the college at Osborne on the Isle of Wight at the age of 13, selected boys, mainly from the public schools, were to be recruited at the age of 18 and would undergo a much shorter course, becoming midshipmen after 18 months of training and being commissioned as sub-lieutenants after a further 20 months. The scheme continued during the war and by 1919, 611 young men had entered in this way. Of these, 35 came from Scottish schools, including 7 from Fettes College and 5 from George Watson's in Edinburgh, five from Loretto School in East Lothian and 1 from Kirckaldy High School, perhaps because of the new dockyard at Rosyth nearby. Since less than 6 per cent of the numbers were from Scottish schools, this does not suggest any great enthusiasm for a naval career; though of course there were certainly some Scots educated in English schools among the recruits.[4]

The Choice of Scapa

In one important respect the fleet was very ill prepared indeed in 1914. Because of shortage of funds and indecision over whether a 'Grand' fleet was needed at all, nothing had been done to prepare a suitable anchorage for a major force on the east coast. Rosyth was far from ready, and in any case the Firth of Forth was too open for the fleet to be protected from raiding torpedo boats and submarines. Even when the need for a base was developed, there was indecision about which base to develop, and for what purpose. The Forth and Cromarty both had their advocates and the battle between them helped to paralyse decision-making.

Fisher later claimed that he had 'discovered' the great naval anchorage at Scapa Flow in Orkney, by looking at a chart in 1905, and that he sent a ship up there to survey it at once. 'No-one, however talented, except myself, could explain how, playing with a pair of compasses, I took the German Fleet and swept the chart with the other leg to find a place for our fleet beyond the practicability of surprise by the Germans.'[5] This was greeted with considerable scepticism by those on the ground there. 'It was a great pity that when he did "discover" it that he did not take in hand its construction into a defended naval harbour . . .' wrote Captain Munro.[6] One person with a better claim, nearly a century earlier, was the naval surveyor Graeme Spence, who wrote in 1812,

> In capacity it far exceeds any Roadstead in Britain except Spithead, its area being upwards of 30 square miles . . . Nature seems to have given every degree of shelter to Scapa Flow that could possibly be expected in a Roadstead of such extent; and therefore it wants no artificial Shelter, a circumstance greatly in its favour . . . As there are three principal channels and some smaller ones leading into Scapa Flow, a vessel will have no great difficulty in getting into it through one or other of

them . . . And, lastly, the Stream of Tide is scarce sensible in Scapa Flow . . .[7]

The fleet made regular visits to Scapa during its annual cruises and manoeuvres, starting in 1863. In 1909, eighty-two warships arrived, led by the *Dreadnought* herself, still almost unique among the world's capital ships. The were reports of a plan to make a golf course for the officers, but no other preparations were mentioned. In 1910 an even larger fleet arrived, including the brand new battlecruisers, and 25,000 tons of coal were taken on board at Scapa Pier.[8]

In 1913 Commander Vyvian, the Assistant to the Chief of War Staff, reported to the cabinet that Scapa was the best of the three large anchorages on the North Sea coast of Scotland. It was 'ample for all requirements'. There would be no difficulty in keeping the movements of ships secret, compared with the much more populous area around the Forth or even Cromarty. The only real disadvantage was that 'owing to the wide expanse of water and rough winds, a sea rapidly gets up, and may sometimes entail colliers and supply ships laying off from warships during short periods.'

Rosyth, in contrast, was 'admirably situated as a repairing base when the dockyard is completed, but it is not considered suitable as a war anchorage' because 'the anchorage below the Forth Bridge cannot be made secure against torpedo attack, except at prohibitive cost.' It would be difficult to take a large fleet into the anchorage in daylight on a flood tide, and the approaches could be mined easily. Cromarty, he said, was open to the same objections to a lesser extent. Vyvian, however, assumed that fixed defences would be erected to protect the anchorage at Scapa before it was used.[9]

Vyvian's views were not unchallenged. In the same year Sir George Callaghan, in command of the Home Fleet, preferred the Forth out of all the possible options. Scapa Flow was 'the best natural harbour', but its distance from the area of operations was a fatal flaw, and it was unfortified. Cromarty was now being fortified and was an excellent harbour, but was also too far from the action. The Humber, in the east of England, was also unfortified, but too close to Germany and therefore liable to attack. The Forth, however, above the islands of Incholm and Oxcars three miles below the Forth Bridge,

> will hold any number of ships, and is protected by the heavy guns of the outer defences. The strategic position of the Firth is a very good one. The anchorage below [i.e. downstream from] the Bridge is, however, not safe from attack by torpedo craft, while the berthing space at Rosyth is limited in extent . . . The need, however, for increasing the

available safe anchorage in the Forth is already very great, and will before long become imperative, and it is therefore strongly urged that steps should be taken to render the anchorage below the bridge safe for use by the fleet.[10]

Strong arguments were advanced for the Forth and Cromarty on the outbreak of war, but Scapa Flow had two cardinal advantages. Firstly, it was well situated to block the northern exit from the North Sea. Since the naval strategists had now realised that any kind of close blockade was suicidal in the days of mines, torpedoes and submarines, a much longer range blockade had to be applied and the best way to do this was by preventing supplies for Germany and her allies from entering the North Sea. The 10th Cruiser Squadron would actually patrol the area and search the ships for enemy goods, but the Grand Fleet backed them up, in case the Germans should send a raiding battlecruiser amongst them, or even send their battlefleet out into the Atlantic to destroy British communications.

Secondly, Scapa Flow offered a much greater area of water than either the Forth or Cromarty. The last two bases had enough room to anchor the fleets themselves, but it was realised that much more space was needed to give room to practise gunnery, maneouvring and tactics. The usable area at Scapa was about seven miles by eight: the Forth offered a space about seven miles long and on average about two miles wide above the islands, which for the moment was the only area which could be protected from attack. Cromarty offered a similar area, with a single narrow entrance.

The fleet was ordered to Scapa Flow at the end of July and sailed up the east coast with some trepidation, for the Pentland Firth had a fearsome reputation, mostly from pilot books written in the days of sail. But the battleships steamed through it on the 31st in daylight and slack water without any difficulty.[11] The destroyers and colliers were already there. The battleships anchored in Scapa Bay, to the north of the Flow and close to the town of Kirkwall. In the expectation of imminent battle, all wooden items were cast aside, including many ships' boats, wardroom furniture and even pianos. Some were thrown over the side; others were dumped on beaches.

To a well-informed observer on the Orkney shore in August 1914, the Grand Fleet was an impressive and a daunting sight. The twenty Dreadnought battleships had low, lean and clean hulls and well-proportioned superstructures, contrasting with the obsolescent pre-Dreadnoughts (for the fleet had to make do with a squadron of eight of the latter until April 1915 when more ships became available). The great guns of the battleships were apparent enough, projecting 30 feet from their massive steel turrets. The older ships, including the *Dreadnought* herself, had ten 12-inch guns, the newer ones, the super-Dreadnoughts, had 13.5-inch guns and were instantly recognisable by their 'superimposed' turrets, with B turret just aft of A turret and raised enough to fire over it. The super-Dreadnoughts could fire all turrets at once on the broadside, sending a salvo of 6,250 pounds of explosive shell towards the enemy, at a range of up to 12 miles. Their modern turbine engines could send the ships through the water at up to 22 knots, but for the moment they were slowed down by the pre-Dreadnoughts, whose triple-expansion engines could make only 18 or 19 knots. The Dreadnoughts had armour 10 to 12 inches thick in their main belts and turrets. These ships formed the main striking force of the greatest fleet the world had ever known, in theory irresistible on the high seas except by another fleet of similar ships.

With them, for the moment, were four battlecruisers under the command of Acting Vice-Admiral Sir David Beatty. These were already the most glamorous ships in the fleet, and their leader's publicity skills would enhance them further in that respect. They had even longer and leaner hulls than the Dreadnoughts, and were just as well armed. They could reach 25 or even 32 knots, but had rather lighter armour – 6 or 7 inches on the older ships. They were the heavy scouting force of the fleet, ready to seek out the enemy and engage him until the main force arrived on the scene.

There were 21 cruisers with the fleet. They were its eyes and ears, intended to patrol ahead and to the sides of the main body, to find the enemy and report back his position and strength, while defending themselves against the enemy vessels of similar purpose. Since the battlecruiser had taken over the role as the core of the scouting force, the design of conventional cruisers had languished somewhat. The force at Scapa included eight armoured cruisers of the First and Second Cruiser Squadrons, all older than the battlecruisers, with mixtures of 9.2-, 7.5- and 6-inch guns, 6-inch armour plate and old-fashioned triple-expansion engines. Four more, of the First Light Cruiser Squadron, had 3-inch armour, 6-inch guns and modern turbine engines. The other cruisers were used as leaders of the destroyer flotillas, or were attached to the flagships of the battle squadrons. They were mostly of the very light 'Scout' classes, with 4-inch guns and armour that was no more than 2 inches thick.

There were forty-two destroyers, organised into two flotillas. Descended from the torpedo boats of the end of the previous century, they were technically 'torpedo boat destroyers'. Their role was to protect the fleet from torpedo attacks, and to launch attacks of their own. They were unarmoured but relied on speed and manoeuvrability for their protection. They usually had three 4-inch guns and two torpedo tubes.

Time alone would show the weaknesses of the Grand Fleet, in gunnery, in the quality of its shells and in its armour plating. Leaving that aside, there were already other rivals for the command of the sea. The submarine and the mine would show themselves to be effective naval weapons in the next few weeks, almost impossible to defeat until new methods were developed, and soon the Grand Fleet would have to retreat in the face of them. The aeroplane was less advanced, but it too might eventually threaten the dominance of the battle fleet. There was a strategic problem which was to prove even greater for the officers and men of the Grand Fleet. What could they do if the enemy chose to avoid battle? A navy, unlike an army, could withdraw from the scene of conflict by simply staying in port, or only leave on its own terms.

Admiral Sir John Jellicoe arrived at Scapa in the afternoon of 2 August as the second-in-command of the main British naval force, now known as the Grand Fleet, having just given up the post of Second Sea Lord. At four o'clock in the morning of 4 August he received instructions to open a secret envelope he had been carrying with him. It ordered him to take command of the fleet in succession to Admiral Sir George Callaghan, who was considered too old at sixty-two. The fleet was ordered to sea, as war was imminent, so Callaghan left by 8.30 that morning.[12] Jellicoe hoisted his flag on board the *Iron Duke*, one of the newest Dreadnoughts, and war between Britain and Germany started formally at midnight.

The Retreat from Scapa

Aware that nothing had been done to create a safe anchorage, Jellicoe wrote, 'I was always far more concerned with the safety of the Fleet when it was at anchor in Scapa Flow during the exceedingly brief periods which were spent there for coaling in the early days of the war, than I was when the Fleet was at sea, and this anxiety was reflected in the very short time the Fleet was kept in harbour.'[13] For the first few days of the war the Germans actually had little idea where the British fleet was, and tended to misunderstand their strategy, but on the seventh day of war intelligence sources suggested that the Germans knew about the Flow. On 7 August the whole fleet coaled at Scapa in just over twelve hours, despite delays. On the 9th the fleet was cruising between the north of Scotland and Norway when the cruiser *Birming-*

ham sighted a submarine. She turned quickly and rammed it, then sank it by gunfire. The destruction of *U-15* was the first success of the anti-submarine war, but it confirmed beyond any doubt that the U-boats had the range to reach Scapa. The fleet went to coal at Loch Ewe on the west coast of Scotland, further from the submarine menace. But on 12 August it was ordered back to the North Sea, because of fears of an invasion of England. At the end of the month it returned to Scapa to refuel.

On 1 September Jellicoe's worst fears about Scapa seemed to be realised. At 6.30 in the evening a lookout in the cruiser *Falmouth*, anchored west of Holm Sound, reported a periscope about fifty yards away, and the ship's guns opened fire. The battleship *Vanguard* opened up too, believing she had sighted a submarine, and the whole fleet was ordered to raise steam to be ready to go to sea. The great flotilla of attendant drifters and yachts got under way and were ordered to cruise about, creating as much confusion as possible, while the destroyers of the Second Flotilla hunted for the submarine. The cruiser *Drake* reported another sighting at 7 p.m., and the *Falmouth* fired again. It took several hours to raise steam in a battleship and there were navigational difficulties in the growing darkness and mist. It was 11 p.m. before all the ships had left harbour, except for the Second Flotilla which was still searching. Thus ended the 'First Battle of Scapa'. But there was no German submarine in the area. The *Falmouth*'s lookout had probably seen an old target pole caught in the wash of a passing destroyer.[14]

The fleet went back to Loch Ewe. Two wires were laid across the entrance, one 3 inches in circumference and 40 ft deep, the other 2 inches in circumference and 2ft below the surface, supported by three floating practice targets in the middle of the channel, with an entrance between two of them. The channel between Ulva and Glasgill Island was blocked by two wires. Destroyers patrolled the entrance and all ships were darkened at night and had their own, rather ineffectual, net defences laid out.[15]

The Grand Fleet returned to the North Sea early in October, on reports that the Germans might sortie into the Atlantic to attack a convoy of Canadian troops which was crossing, and spent several days at Scapa again. Meanwhile Loch Ewe became more questionable when a base ship in the harbour reported a submarine. There was another spurious 'Battle of Scapa' on the 16th, and the fleet went to Lough Swilly in the north of Ireland, with some squadrons in Loch na Keal in Mull.

On 17 October Beatty was despondent and wrote to the First Lord of the Admiralty. 'The menace of mines and submarines is proving larger every day, and adequate means to meet or combat them are not forthcoming, and we are gradually being pushed out of the North Sea, and off our own particular perch.' He described the position to Churchill.

> . . . we have no place to lay our heads. We are at Loch na Keal, Isle of Mull. My picket boats are at the entrance, the nets are run out, and the men are at the guns waiting for coal which has run low, but ready to move at a moment's notice. Other squadrons are in the same plight. We have been running now hard since the 28th July; small defects are creeping up which we haven't time to take in hand. 48 hours is our spell in harbour with steam ready to move at 4 hours' notice, coaling on an average 1,400 tons a time, night defence stations. The men can stand it, but the machines can't, and we must have a place where we can stop for four or five days now and then to give the engineers a chance. Such a place does not exist, so the question arises, how long can we go on, for I fear very much not for long, as the need for small repairs is becoming insistent.[16]

The Anti-submarine Defences

A week after Beatty's letter, Winston Churchill wrote an order in a style that was to become familiar to millions in a later war.

> Every nerve must be strained to reconcile the Fleet to Scapa. Successive lines of submarine defences should be prepared, reinforced by contact mines as proposed by the Commander-in-Chief. Nothing should stand in the way of the equipment of this anchorage with every possible means of security. The First Lord and the First Sea Lord will receive a report of progress every third day until the work is completed . . .[17]

It was probably Beatty who first spotted the potential of Commander Donald Munro, having seen some of his work at Cromarty, and he told Churchill that he was 'a man who grapples with things as they are'.[18] Munro was summoned to the Admiralty in London, and feared that he would be called to account for exceeding his authority in erecting the boom. Instead he was promoted to captain and sent to organise the defences at Scapa. He wrote,

> It was with deep regret that I surrendered my charge of Cromarty. Motoring along the high ridge dividing the harbour from the Moray Firth I beheld this noble port bathed in moonlight with a mighty fleet lying peacefully at anchor and more dimly the floating dock where a

glare told of the docking work in progress. On the twin headlands behind me the flashing of numerous searchlights proclaimed the ceaseless vigil over the open sea.[19]

Scapa Flow had nine entrance routes, three of which were considered navigable by the largest ships, one by smaller vessels and five which were not normally considered navigable. However, a daring U-boat commander might brave the navigational difficulties (as one did in 1939), so four channels in the west and one in the east (Burra Sound) were to be blocked by sinking old merchant ships in them. But first ships had to be found, and that took some time. Even placing a blockship was not as simple as it sounds. According to Munro,

> Sinking a ship so that she will remain upright is not an easy operation, as during sinking there is a point in which she has no stability and the least bit to one side and the water runs to that side and over she goes. We got over that difficulty by cutting plates abreast each hatchway of a definite size, filling those holes with wood and placing a small charge of gun-cotton at each corner. These holes were below the water line. During spring tides the tide runs at over eight knots and slack water lasts only a few minutes. Moorings were laid, the vessels placed in position, charges exploded and down they went perfectly upright where they remained to the end of the war . . .[20]

The first blockship, the *Garthmore*, was sunk in East Weddel Sound on 14 September and that channel was largely blocked two days later. Most of the work was done during November, but extra ships were added in February 1915 to fill gaps.

In channels where it was necessary to allow access, Munro developed a form of boom defence. There were two main elements, a wire rope or hawser 3 inches in circumference to stop surface craft, and nets of 1-inch wire rope underneath, to stop submarines. Both were attached to floats made up of 20 railway sleepers, 48 ft apart. Every 600 ft along the line was an anchored fishing boat, manned and with a winch which could be used to haul the rope and nets tight against the current. Some of the boats had guns to help defend the barrier.

Munro had to go to great lengths to get materials for his barriers. Wire rope and chain cable for anchors were in short supply and even shipwrecks had to be searched for them. Since the fishermen were at sea, the young women of Inverness and Aberdeen were trained in the difficult art of wire-rope splicing to make the nets. Sections of boom were constructed at Rosyth and Inverness and taken by rail and steamer to St Margaret's Hope in Orkney, the headquarters of the boom defence organisation.[21]

Booms were erected in late 1914 in Hoxa Sound to the south, the main entrance for the battleships; in Switha Sound, just to the west of that, to protect the base ships which anchored in Longhope Sound; in Hoy Sound to the west; and across Holm Sound, inside the barrier created by the sunken ships. Each boom had a main gate about 1½ cables (300 yards) wide. One boat acted as the pivot, another used her winch to open the gate and a third was needed to close it; the whole operation took five minutes. Side gates were also fitted near the end of each boom to allow smaller craft to pass. One end of the hawser was attached to a buoy near the shore and the other to the nearest fishing boat. It was lowered to allow a vessel to pass.[22]

On 25 January 1915 there was a great storm which wrecked much of the boom defences. There was a shortage of trawlers, so less seaworthy drifters had to be used in many places. Since virtually all the suitable vessels had already been taken up by the navy, more trawlers had to be drafted in from other bases.[23] The barrier across Holm Sound, duplicating the effect of the blockships, was not re-placed. The Hoxa Sound barrier was rebuilt a mile further in, using the tiny island of Nevi Skerry as a centre, and the whole system was completed by the middle of 1915. Churchill and Fisher left office at the Admiralty in May 1915 after the failure of the expedition to the Dardenelles, but the construction of 'successive lines of submarine defences' continued. During that year the Switha and Hoy Sound barriers were doubled up as an extra insurance against a submarine trying to follow a ship through. There were now 14 miles of net defences.[24]

The first minefield in the base was laid off Croo Taing, off South Ronaldsay, at the end of 1914, and it was intended to help close Water Sound to the east, in conjunction with the sunken ships to seaward. It was made up of five rows comprising 156 electro-contact or EC mines. These were detonated by a ship striking the mine, but could be made safe by electrical means, from a watch-hut on shore. The Cantick Field was laid in the following month, across the passage between Hoy and the island of Switha. It had four rows, each of 18 EC mines. Both these fields proved very difficult to maintain, because of strong tides. The electric cables to the mines were constantly chafed as they went slack in falling tides, while on one occasion more than half the Croo Taing Field was accidentally detonated by strong currents. A third EC minefield was laid at Roan Head in September 1916, at the northern end of the main entrance to the harbour.

The Houton Head Field was laid in the middle of 1915, across the eastern entrance to the Flow. It too was electrically controlled, but on a different principle. A hydrophone was used to detect submarines by the noise of their propellers and engines. An observer on shore would then press a button to detonate a group of the mines. It had nine lines arranged in two rows. Each line had six mines and could be detonated separately. A third row was laid at Houton in February 1916. The second 'Observation' minefield of this type was laid in December 1915, across Hoxa Sound, the main entrance for the battleships and cruisers. It was the most complex of the fields, with three sections entitled X, Y and Z, each with three rows which could be fired separately. Each row consisted of eight or nine lines of six mines, making a total of 156. It was the only one to see any action during the war. At midnight on 12–13 April 1917 the hydrophone station at Stanger Head reported a submarine, which was also heard at 2.30 a.m. from Hoxa. At 9.20 next morning it was reported that the intruder was passing through the barrier and the six mines of Y2 line were detonated; but no wreckage was ever found and no submarine was lost by the Germans.

At 10.21 in the evening of 28 October 1918 the Stanger Head hydrophones had another contact. Hydrophones suffered from the difficulty of being non-directional, so that the operator could not tell exactly where the submarine was; but in this case six operators in different stations worked as a team, comparing the intensity of sound that they heard. At 11.32 line X1 was fired and afterwards the wreck of *UB-116* was found. This was the only concrete success by any British-controlled minefield during the war, though there is no doubt that they acted as a deterrent to the enemy and gave reassurance to the ships anchored behind them.[25]

Another type of barrier, consisting of steel hurdles, was developed in 1916 and tested across Burray Sound, by ramming them with a wooden drifter. Between April 1917 and March 1918 108 of these hurdles were laid across Hoy Sound from Clestron on Mainland to the island of Graemsay, in depths of up to 75 ft. Since this was one of the main entrances, a 406 ft gap was left in the Clestron side.[26]

As well as the fixed defences, the entrances to Scapa Flow were patrolled by fishing boats inshore, and destroyers further out. In the early stages, each ship of the Grand Fleet had to find an officer, a petty officer and one or two gunners for every patrolling drifter while the ship was at anchor. Sub-Lieutenant Angus Cunningham-Graham of HMS *Agincourt* found it very hard work:

The weather at the boom always seemed to be foul and a seven knot
tide . . . kicked up the nastiest sort of sea. The drifter was lighted by
acetylene gas, and if I smell carbide, even now, my mind goes straight
back to that patrol. In short, it provided the best emetic I can remember.
I used to spend practically all these patrols cooped up in the drifter's
glassed-in bridge . . . The crews of these drifters were a splendid lot and
usually made up of a family. The son was skipper and the mate and
engineer were other sons or cousins; the old father was sort of odd job
man and had to do what he was told.[27]

By June 1915, five destroyers patrolled regularly outside Scapa, one
off Hoy, one off Switha and three in the Pentland Firth. These three
left from Pentland Skerries every evening at nine, to sweep eastwards
on slightly diverging courses at speeds of 17 and 20 knots. At midnight
each turned through 180 degrees and they met again off the Skerries,
to resume a patrol there. In the much longer nights of winter, an armed
boarding steamer patrol would take over the duties in the outer area.
By day the Hoy destroyer was to 'patrol outside the entrance to Hoy
Channel steering irregular courses and varying her speed but not to
keep too far out.' By night she was to be at anchor, but ready to raise
steam at five minutes' notice.[28]

The Protection of the Base

At the outbreak of war the landward defences of Orkney were manned
by the local territorial regiment, the Orkney Royal Garrison Artillery,
but they were barely enough to guard strategic points in the communications chain against sabotage. Marines began to arrive over the
next few weeks and gun batteries were set at strategic points near the
entrances. The biggest was at Stanger Head overlooking the Hoxa
Sound entrance, with 192 men and seven guns. The next biggest was
at Hoxa on the other side of the entrance with 183 men and the same
number of guns. In all there were eight 6-inch guns around the islands,
with 33 of a smaller calibre, manned by 31 officers and 942 men.[29]

To prevent enemy landings on an isolated stretch of coast, a lookout
and patrol system was set up. Men from the ORGA were issued
with signal flags and sent to some of the more remote islands. By
February 1915 a telephone system had been set up and lookouts were
stationed in thirty-six posts on fourteen islands. The average post
consisted of an NCO and four men and they had orders to report
movements of enemy submarines, surface ships, aircraft or anything
suspicious.

One of the great advantages of Scapa, as Captain Vyvian had noted before the war, was that is was possible to protect it from prying eyes. To ensure this, an elaborate system of permits was set up for those wishing to enter or leave the islands. Those to be granted permits included people who lived or had family there, those who intended to live there (after their stories had been carefully examined) and those with business which could not be done by correspondence. Dealers were allowed to attend the lamb sales in the autumn. Tourists, commercial travellers, hunters and anglers were banned and so, subsequently, were 'theatrical and music hall artists'.[30]

Yet no system of security could protect against tragedy. The battleship *Vanguard* of 1907 was lying peacefully at anchor off Flotta on the night of 9 July 1917, when a tremendous explosion lit the night and was heard all over the islands. A local man describes the scene. 'There was a V-shaped column of flames between sea and sky, then a frightful detonation, then the spreading over the harbour of innumerable blazing fragments of everything combustible, then the smoke and glare arising from our own hill of Golta off which the doomed ship had been lying, and the heather which had been set on fire.'[31] Twenty-four officers and seventy-one ratings were ashore at the time, but only two of the thousand men on board survived the blast. Beatty was stunned and wrote to his wife about the 'terrible calamity'. 'It is an overwhelming blow and fairly stuns one to think about. One expects these things to happen when in the heat of battle, but when lying peacefully at anchor it is very much more terrible.'[32] There was suspicion of sabotage or a U-boat attack, but it seems that it was caused by an accident.

Moorings and Anchorages

In the early stages the battleships of the Grand Fleet moored to the north of the Flow in Scapa Bay. During the first winter this was found to be too exposed to gales, and the battleships and cruisers moved to an area between the islands of Cava and Flotta, where they were well protected from the west and the south. A fixed mooring buoy was laid for the fleet flagship, with telephone and telegraph lines so that the commander-in-chief could communicate instantly with his superiors when he returned from a patrol; another was laid for the second-in-command's ship. The other ships used their own anchors.

Destroyers were less seaworthy in bad weather and they were given an anchorage in Gutter Sound, half a mile wide, between Hoy and Fara, protected by the hills of Hoy from the worst of westerly gales.

They too had fixed moorings in order to save space. Some were single buoys, but trots were also laid, a row of seven buoys, each of which could take two destroyers. Trawlers and drifters used the traditional anchorage of Longhope Sound where shelter was good and the water was shallower. This area was also used for base ships but the floating dock, when it arrived in February 1917, was moored in Gutter Sound to be close to the destroyers it was intended to service. It had the most elaborate mooring of all, with a 131-cwt anchor in the direction of the tidal stream, a 90-cwt one in the opposite direction and two 90 cwt anchors laid out on each side. There were other anchorages for fleet auxiliaries and hospital ships and for merchant ships under examination, though most of these were brought into Kirkwall outside the Flow.[33]

Fuel Supply

At the beginning of the war the only fuel supply in Scapa Flow was a small coal hulk used for local trawlers. Since there was no pier where coal stocks could be landed, it was all stored in ships afloat throughout the fleet's stay there. Thirty colliers were used to start with, and they were anchored in Scapa Bay inside the battlefleet. In November 1914 they were moved to a more sheltered position between Cava and Hoy. One collier was allocated to each large ship, or occasionally one collier to two ships. When it was empty, the collier was sent to Cardiff to reload, for Welsh coal was the best for steaming, with good thermal efficiency and relatively little smoke.

Ships normally coaled up as soon as they came back from an operation, when the men were already tired. It was a filthy, laborious business:

> The ship had barely dropped anchor when the collier *Mercedes* came alongside and was made fast. Again the bosun's pipe – 'Hands to supper and clean into coaling rig. Coal ship in half an hour's time.' Away we hurried to eat and change into that most hateful rig.
>
> The bugler sounded 'The General Assembly, at the double' . . . As soon as the watches were reported present the Commander gave his orders. 'The country is now at war. We have to take in 2,500 tons of coal at utmost speed. The squadron gets under weigh at dawn. Hands coal ship! Carry on!'
>
> Away we doubled to the sound of 'The Charge' on the bugle. The competitive spirit to try and get the first hoist inboard made us work like slaves. Each hoist consisted of ten bags, each containing two

hundredweight. The hold gangs began shovelling furiously to get the bags filled. Soon the winches began to work and up went the first hoist . . . Throughout the night the shovels were working and the winches rattling away, whilst the inboard gangs were clearing the dumps at the double to have the coal tipped into the bunkers. Those poor devils in the bowels of the ship were trimming the bunkers as the coal shot into them. The stokers were enshrouded with an indescribable cloud of dust, which got right into the lungs, and they had only a Davy safety lamp to guide them . . .

At length the 'Cease Fire' sounded on the bugle and a tired and dusty ship's company downed tools and had a breather. Nor for long, however. Soon came the pipe 'Clear Collier', followed by 'Stand by to cast off collier'. Shovels and coal bags were hoisted across, the collier's holds covered and a tired crew climbed inboard.[34]

In some ships the Royal Marine band played to get the men into a rhythm, but not in the cruiser *Good Hope*, where the commander said, 'Put that tin gear away and get hold of some bloody shovels. You'll be more good than making that bloody noise.' Even officers had to take part and Stephen King-Hall claims that he did it more than 200 times in three years in the cruiser *Southampton*. In all, more than 1.6 million tons of Welsh coal were loaded at Scapa during the war, plus 680,000 tons of other coal.[35]

Already at the beginning of the war, some ships were using oil rather than coal to fire their boilers. This had been started by Fisher earlier in the century, and was accelerated during the war, so that new ships were oil-fired to start with, and many older ones were converted. Oil offered many advantages, including greater fuel efficiency, the reduction of large numbers of stokers from the crews and better control of smoke. But its most important effect on the lives of the seamen was that coaling ship was no longer necessary. William Saban commented, 'The Seamen were free as soon as they had secured the Oiler alongside and then it was up to the stokers – they passed the hoses and all the filling up. Then unbutton the hoses and all they had to do was cast off. That was, I think, the biggest step forward in the Service ever.'[36]

At that time oil came from America. There was a steady stream in the early years, interrupted by the unrestricted U-boat campaign in 1917–18. There were storage tanks ashore at Rosyth and Cromarty, but none at Scapa. In order that the transatlantic ships should not be held in Scapa waiting to unload, each discharged into base oilers as soon as it arrived. At Scapa 1.9 million tons of oil were used, transported by 320 ships.[37]

The Logistics of Scapa Flow

Besides 100 or so regular warships of the Grand Fleet, and the vessels of the Auxiliary Patrol looking for U-boats outside, Scapa was home to nearly 300 auxiliary vessels. There were 120 trawlers in the boom defences, 74 uncommissioned drifters used as tenders to the major warships, and other vessels used as target tugs, mail carriers and on various duties. There was also a 'floating city' of base and repair ships anchored in Longhope Sound. The first to arrive was HMS *Cyclops*, a former merchantman of 11,300 tons which reached the Flow in August. She was no stranger there, having serviced the fleet on previous visits. She was followed by the *Assistance*, of 9,600 tons. In September two old training ships, *Fisgard I* and *II*, formerly the battleships *Audacious* and *Invincible* built by Robert Napier on the Clyde in 1869, were converted to depot ships and sent to Scapa; but *Fisgard II* foundered off Portland in the English Channel. *Fisgard I* was renamed *Impérieuse* and finally reached Scapa on 1 October.

As the war progressed and began to look like lasting a long time, the Admiralty continued to send more repair ships to Scapa, though the bad luck continued. SS *Caribbean* was fitted with dockyard machinery in Belfast, but was lost on passage in September 1915. Meanwhile shore accommodation for civilian dockyard workers was proving difficult and an old battleship, HMS *Victorious*, was sent north in March 1916 as an accommodation ship. Seven hundred dockyard workmen were now employed, under forty salaried staff. The workmen were offered a 56-hour week on a four-month contract, with home leave if the contract was renewed.

The Admiralty had always been sceptical about using a floating dock in the exposed northern waters of Scapa, preferring to send ships to Cromarty or the southern dockyards for major hull repairs or cleaning. In July 1916 they relented and a suitable one was eventually found at Ellesmere Port on the Mersey. It arrived in February 1917. It was too small for the battleships and cruisers, but during the remainder of the war it docked 137 destroyers, submarines and auxiliaries.[38]

The shells for the fleet's guns were of course the most volatile of all cargoes, and indeed half a dozen major warships were lost due to the explosion of their own ammunition. In the early days ammunition was sent as part of a general cargo in supply ships for the individual squadrons, eight large passenger-cargo ships, originally used for the run to India by companies like P&O. By the end of 1914, colliers were converted as specialist armament carriers, two to each squadron of battleships. By August 1915 ammunition was transported to Inverness by rail, then shipped to Scapa. By the end of the war it was stored ashore in a new base at Lyness on Hoy, in a store which could hold 8,000 heavy projectiles. Torpedoes, unlike shells, needed a good deal of maintenance, and this was done by an engineer officer and thirty-seven men on the depot ship *Sokoto* of 1,969 tons.[39]

A population of about 150,000 sailors, fishermen and civilian workers had to be fed and supplied. The naval victualling organisation was based on the store-ship *Ruthenia*, of 6,000 tons, with four refrigerated ships to store frozen meat: 320 tons of meat were needed per month, along with 800 tons of potatoes and 20,000 lb of bread supplied every week. One thing that could be obtained locally was fresh water, for the men to drink and wash and for the boilers of the ships. However supplies were limited: Stromness could supply up to 200 tons a day and St Mary's Holm 150 to 200 tons. As always, the answer was to keep stocks in ships, and eleven water craft were employed in the course of the war, with room for up to 650 tons. Eventually the navy decided to build its own reservoir at Mill Burn near Lyness on Hoy, but it was not begun until March 1918 and was completed after the war ended.

The base ship *Cyclops* was the fleet's main link with the outside world in the early stages of the war. Anchored in Scapa Bay and then in Longhope Sound, she had telegraph links through Kirkwall Post Office by which the movements of the greatest fleet in the world were controlled. Increasingly sophisticated systems were set up during 1915, including a direct link between the moorings of the fleet flagship and the main national system. Telegrams were now available for private purposes and the numbers sent soared, from 4,000 a month in the early days to more than 20,000 by the end of 1917. *Cyclops* was also given a small telephone exchange and links with the outside world, while temporary lines were set up between the various elements in the defence of the islands. Submarine cables were laid in the course of the war, but there was one serious breakdown, caused by a snowstorm in February 1918. Mail services started from the Fleet Post Office in HMS *Impérieuse* in November 1914 and nearly 130 million items were transmitted during the war.[40]

Many of the seamen in the Grand Fleet had their homes and families at almost the opposite end of the United Kingdom, in the Plymouth area. Few were Scots, for the Grand Fleet was mainly manned by regulars rather than from the RNR and RNVR, so Jellicoe's figure of 3 per cent of Scots in the navy in 1913 had not changed much. When leave did become available, most of the men had a long way to travel. The first stage, unless the ship was at Cromarty, was the rough passage across the Pentland Firth. The train from Thurso to London Euston was known as the 'Jellicoe Special', or just the 'Jellicoe'. It was often grossly overcrowded and its doors were locked for security reasons; it took twenty-four hours or more to complete its journey.

Life at Scapa

The rhythm of the Grand Fleet's work began to change soon after the base at Scapa was made safe during 1915. It spent longer periods at anchor, sometimes a month at a time, and tended to go to sea for specific purposes, in reaction to German raids or intelligence reports that the High Seas Fleet was out. Boredom and lassitude, rather than fatigue, were now the main enemies.

Wherever it was based, the Grand Fleet was always at a disadvantage in gunnery practice compared with the Germans, for they had the Kiel Canal to transfer ships quickly to and from the relatively protected waters of the Baltic. From Scapa, the British had to do the best they could. They started off by using peacetime floating targets, but these soon became invisible in a rough sea. Rocks were also fired on at this stage, but they were few in number, and might offer chances for submarine attack. Jellicoe was shocked when 'an idiot in the *Gloucester*' sent a photo of a rock used for target practice to the newspapers.[41] By the end of 1915, squadrons were sent south to the Moray Firth where a protected area was created.

Meanwhile the facilities at Scapa were developed. Once it was protected from submarines the Flow was a secure area in which guns up to 6-inch calibre could be fired. Night manoeuvres could be practised, and occasionally a division of battleships would exercise in company without lights, to train the officers of the watch.[42] A torpedo range was set up along the north shore of the Flow. For longer-range firing of guns, a ship in Scapa Bay could fire south towards a target moored off Switha, about ten miles away. According to Munro, 'Steaming up Hoxa Sound on a still day it was awe-inspiring to hear a salvo of great shell go roaring overhead to fall about a target in the dim distance.'[43]

Angus Cunningham-Graham records, 'From joining the fleet to November 1914 we spent 44 days at sea to 41 in harbour. Sometimes 10 or 11 days at sea with the fleet. During this period we coaled ship 12 times. But if we battleships had our share of seagoing, it was nothing to what the destroyers and light-cruisers . . . had to cope with.' He describes the routine when the fleet left harbour:

The cruisers and heavy ships left by the Hoxa Gate and the destroyers left by the Sw+itha Gate, making a rendezvous with the units they had to screen in the Pentland Firth.

For us in the *Agincourt* the receipt of this signal meant that a lot of things had to be done quickly. If the signal was made in the daytime:

Officers and men were recalled from the Hoxa Patrol.

Men ashore on duty or recreation recalled.

Stewards and canteen manager collected from Kirkwall or Lyness.

Any civilian workmen on board had to be landed.

It was a fine sight to see the Grand Fleet leaving harbour . . . The cruisers who were to be the outer screen left first, then the battle-cruisers (if any, they were mostly at Rosyth), then divisions of battle-ships in sequence and the fleet flagship, the *Iron Duke* . . . bringing up the rear.

Once clear of Hoxa, units met their destroyer screens, which formed up according to one of the diagrams laid down in the battle instructions considered to suit the occasion. When in the open water to the eastward of the Pentland Firth the C-in-C made the signal for the fleet to take up its cruising order.[44]

Stephen King-Hall claims that 'Scapa Flow has some magnificent scenery but of those who spent some time in that part of the world it has been said that they passed through three stages. First, they talked to themselves; then they talked to the sheep; and lastly they thought the sheep talked to them.'[45]

According to Cunningham-Graham,

For the officers, at any rate those who were country-bred, there was more to do. There were two or three trout lochs within reach: the distance we could go was limited by the notice for steam that we were at, normally four hours, never more. It was also possible to catch sea trout at the mouths of the burns: I was never clever enough to get even one . . .

The refrigerated ship *Borodino* was 'equipped with a high-class stage with elaborate lighting and equipment. She used to go alongside a ship giving a play or a concert, and could accommodate a large number in the audience . . . Besides frozen meat the *Borodino* was equipped as a dry canteen with a sort of Fortnum and Mason attachment for the officers, where we could buy all sorts of luxuries.'[46]

Football was always the first love of the lower deck, and in December 1914 the Marquis of Zetland gave his uncultivated land on Flotta for the use of the fleet. But he could do nothing about the weather and all too often the pitches were waterlogged. Rowing regattas between the ships and squadrons of the fleet provided a more reliable form of entertainment. Other shore facilities were developed by the YMCA and the Church Army for ratings during their very limited periods ashore.

Air Bases

Early in the war it was considered necessary to use seaplanes from Scapa to patrol for submarines and to accompany the fleet as a reconnaissance force, though there was no need for fighter defence so far from the German bases. The first air station was in Scapa Bay, but seaplanes could not be operated when the tide was low. Houton Bay was chosen as a site for a larger station, with instant access to deeper water. It took some time to construct the base, mainly due to transport difficulties in the area, and it was not ready until 1917. Another seaplane station was set up in the inland waters of Steness Loch five miles to the north, and in September 1917 it was hoped that more sheltered conditions would make it possible to operate three squadrons, of the 'large America' type flying boats, thirty-six aircraft, but difficult cross winds spoiled that plan.[47] A third station was set up at Smoogroo a few miles east of Houton in 1917, to deal with the landplanes now being operated from the battleships and cruisers of the fleet. Kite balloons were towed behind ships and carried an observer. Half of Houton station was used to maintain them. An airship station was established at Caldale with two SS-type 'blimps', but these were lost and not replaced, so Caldale became a kite balloon station.[48] In April 1918 all these stations, plus their personnel and aircraft, became part of a new service, the Royal Air Force, which was formed by the merger of the RNAS and the army's Royal Flying Corps.

The Cromarty Base in Wartime

Being more sheltered from strong winds than any of the anchorages at Scapa, Cromarty was chosen as the site for a floating dock, which meant that large ships visited there from time to time. By early 1915 it was established policy to send squadrons there in rotation, to give the men a break from the monotony of Scapa as much as for maintenance purposes.

For the crews, Cromarty was much preferable to Scapa. To Angus Cunningham-Graham in the *Agincourt*, a brief visit was 'heaven' for the officers. There was even contact with women for a fortunate few.

Stephen King-Hall started a flirtation with a farmer's daughter who lived next to the football field. 'She gave me flowers for my cabin, and I presented her with a knitted scarf.' The ratings had fewer opportunities but still benefited. In 1917, Rear Admiral Halsey wrote, 'I am quite certain that when the Squadrons began to visit Invergordon in turn it made a very great difference to the general morale of the Fleet.'[49]

The Blockade of Germany

One of the main reasons for choosing Scapa as a base was the control it offered over the northern exit from the North Sea. The Straits of Dover to the south were quite easy to block to surface ships, but the gap between Scotland and Greenland is much wider, and has much worse weather conditions. If Germany was to maintain any regular contact with the outside world, it would have to be through that gap.

The job of the Tenth Cruiser Squadron was to counter this. It was formed on the outbreak of war and consisted of eight old cruisers of the *Edgar* class, built in the 1890s, plus four armed merchant cruisers, under the command of Rear Admiral Dudley de Chair. The winter of 1914 soon exposed the weakness of these ships and in November the work was done entirely by the armed merchantmen, including armed trawlers operating off the Icelandic and Norwegian coasts. The armed merchant cruisers still carried merchant crews, but with a naval officer in command, RNR officers, a detachment of marines to act as a boarding party and a party of seamen from the Newfoundland RNR, expert at handling small boats in such conditions. In 1915 they operated four patrol lines: Iceland to the Faroes, due north from Shetland, Hebrides to the Faroes, and north-west from St Kilda. Later the patrol between Iceland and St Kilda was divided into two parts, B and C Patrols. B Patrol, closest to Iceland, was by far the busiest and had six ships in 1917. The ships were placed 30 miles apart and routes were arranged so that any ship heading for the North Sea would have to pass through one of the four lines in daylight. Two types of patrol were used. With the 'in and out' patrol the ships steamed back and forward in parallel lines along the shipping routes. This was used in the central areas, where most ships were encountered. With the 'cross patrol' the ships steamed in succession across the shipping tracks and this was used in the outer areas, where ships could easily be placed further apart to cover a wider area.

Any suspect ship would be stopped and a boarding party of an officer and six to eight men would be rowed over by the

Newfoundland men. The ship's papers would be examined to see if she belonged to an enemy country and her hold would be searched to see if she was carrying 'contraband' goods – items of strategic importance to the enemy. If the ship did not pass the examination, the armed guard stayed on board and it was taken into Kirkwall. Sixteen ships were sunk by submarine while being detained in this way.

At the end of the war Sir Eric Geddes, the First Lord of the Admiralty, paid tribute to the Tenth Cruiser Squadron.

> The blockade is what crushed the life out of the Central Empires. That blockade was exercised by a little-advertised power – the 10th Cruiser Squadron. That Squadron, from 1914 to 1917, held the 800 mile stretch of grey sea from Orkney to Iceland. In those waters they intercepted thousands of ships taking succour to our enemies, and they did that under Arctic conditions, and mainly in the teeth of storm and blizzard, and out of that 10,000 they missed just four per cent, a most remarkable achievement under the conditions. In every individual case where an armistice was signed by our enemies, and in one or not two cases before, the one cry that went up was 'Release the blockade'.
>
> If anything more strikingly demonstrated the value sea-power can be given, then I don't know it.[50]

It was a war in which there was remarkably little operational contact between the army and the navy, but it might be argued that, though they never met, the Tenth Cruiser Squadron was a continuation of the army's line on the Western Front, completing the work of encircling the Central Powers. Though it was directed mainly against commercial shipping and commerce raiders rather than the enemy battle fleet, it is tempting to compare it with the blockaders of Brest in the Napoleonic Wars, described by Captain Mahan in a famous phrase as 'Those far-distant, storm-beaten ships, upon which the Grand Army never looked, stood between it and the domination of the world.'[51]

The Battlecruisers in the Forth

In November and December 1914 the German First Scouting Force, the equivalent of Beatty's Battle Cruiser Squadron, bombarded the English east coast towns of Yarmouth, Lowestoft, Whitby, Scarborough and Hartlepool. Though the raids did no significant material damage, Jellicoe came under strong pressure either to move the Grand Fleet south or to split it. He resisted equally strongly, but on

20 December Beatty's ships were moved to Rosyth from where they were more likely to intercept a German raid. They were partially successful on 24 January 1915, when Beatty's five battlecruisers met the First Scouting Force near the Dogger Bank in the centre of the North Sea. One German ship, the ineffective hybrid *Blucher*, was sunk, but four battlecruisers escaped, mainly due to poor gunnery and signalling in Beatty's force. Nevertheless his legend was reinforced. He was seen by the public as the dashing front-line commander, compared with Jellicoe in his base 400 miles from the action.

The move to the Forth suited Beatty very well. It increased his independence of Jellicoe and his force was renamed the Battle Cruiser *Fleet* in February 1915, incorrectly suggesting a separate formation. The facilities of the Forth were more attractive, and his wife, an American heiress, was already set up in Aberdour House, a seventeenth- and eighteenth-century mansion in Fife. But training facilities in the Forth were considerably less than those at Scapa and the gunnery of the Battle Cruiser Fleet could only deteriorate, a point which worried both Jellicoe and Beatty.

Lieutenant-Commander Arthur Longmore was also happy with the situation in the Forth.

> After I joined the ship it was not long before my wife found it possible to park our two children at her father's home and come up to South Queensferry, where she stayed at the Hawes Inn and later got some lodgings close to the landing pier. On the days when I got ashore for the stipulated four hours, she would join me in some expedition. As we had our car with us there was much that we could do in the time; even a late lunch was possible in the Caledonian Hotel, or with some friends in Edinburgh. There were at least three good golf links within reach and we had the use of tennis courts at Hopetoun House, the Linlithgow home, and of one or two squash courts.[52]

Lieutenant Stephen King-Hall was one of a group of officers who hired a cottage at Limekilns, 1½ miles from Rosyth, and set up a social club under the motto 'Abandon rank all ye who enter here', though it is not clear if this applied to the lower deck. Ratings were allowed only an hour or two ashore, often confined to the limits of Lord Elgin's park. At one stage his lordship found a seaman in a compromising situation with one of his housemaids and remonstrated with him. 'The naval Don Juan in reply to his protests told him to go to hell and get a girl for himself.'[53]

The Effect of Jutland

At midnight on 31 May 1916 ninety-eight ships of the Grand Fleet left Scapa Flow on hearing an intelligence report that the Germans were about to sail. The Second Battle Squadron had already left Cromarty to rendezvous with the main force, while Beatty's battlecruisers sailed at almost the same time as the Grand Fleet, with orders to meet them off the Danish coast where the Germans were expected. Beatty had an unusually powerful force, for it included the Fifth Battle Squadron, the *Queen Elizabeth* class, the only ships on either side with 15-inch guns. Though a knot or two slower than the battlecruisers, they had been sent to Rosyth for fear that Beatty might encounter the might of the High Seas Fleet before Jellicoe could arrive.

The Germans were indeed at sea, and at 3.48 that afternoon the Battle Cruiser Fleet was in action with its German opposite numbers. The powerful Fifth Battle Squadron was late to engage because of its slower speed, another signalling error on Beatty's part, and the lack of initiative of Rear Admiral Evan Thomas, in command of the squadron. But more serious than that, Beatty's gunnery was still poor, the British shells proved to be ineffective and dangerous ammunition-handling arrangements in most of Beatty's ships were invitations to disaster. Just after four the *Indefatigable* blew up, with 1,017 men, followed by the *Queen Mary* about twenty minutes later with 1,266. Beatty turned to his flag captain, Chatfield, and remarked calmly, 'There seems to be something wrong with our bloody ships today.' Then his battlecruisers sighted the main force of the High Seas Fleet and he retreated north to draw them on to Jellicoe's forces.

The Battle Cruiser Fleet's system of reporting enemy movements had many flaws and Jellicoe had only the most basic information on the enemy's course and speed. Nevertheless he managed to compete a deployment in a masterly fashion, even though it was later criticised as over-cautious by Churchill and others. At 6.17 the first British battle-ships of the main force opened fire. They were about to 'cross the T' of the Germans, concentrating the full force of their broadsides on the enemy's van, which could only make a weak reply. The German gunfire was still accurate and a third battlecruiser, the *Invincible*, blew up. The Germans now escaped by a highly skilled 'battle turn-away', in which all the capital ships turned simultaneously and retreated southward. But the Germans returned to the attack an hour later, perhaps because Jellicoe was now between them and their bases, only to find their T being crossed again. This time they launched a torpedo boat attack under smoke screens and turned away again. Jellicoe, in his most criticised action of the battle, followed a prearranged plan and turned away from the torpedo boats, allowing the Germans to escape. During the night there were several actions between the destroyers and torpedo boats of the fleets and the pre-Dreadnought *Pommern* was sunk. The battlecruiser *Lutzow*, which had taken tremendous punishment from the Fifth Battle Squadron and in the crossings of the Ts, finally succumbed during the night and sank, the biggest British success of the battle. It proved a terrible disappointment to a fleet and a public which had wanted Nelsonian victory of annihilation, against a fleet which was only about two-thirds of the British in numerical strength. British losses were approximately twice those of the Germans, who considered they had done very well. After their damaged ships had been repaired they came out again in August to try to inflict more attrition. Only the loss of his submarines to the war against trade eventually forced Scheer to give up his risky sorties into the North Sea.

The scientists at Hawkcraig in Fife had listened many times to Beatty's ships as they moved in and out of the Forth and watched the return of the survivors in silence.[54] The officers' wives had heard news of battle and assembled in North and South Queensferry, not knowing which ships had been sunk, as Lieutenant-Commander Arthur Long-more of the *Tiger* reports. 'My wife easily identified the *Tiger* by her three evenly spaced large funnels but there was the *Indefatigable* missing and one of the other three big ones. It might have been the *Lion, Princess Royal* or *Queen Mary*.' HMS *Tiger* reached Rosyth at 10 a.m. on 2 June and 'anchored with a single anchor, as our starboard cable was cut and the cable-holder out of action. Then the work of getting the wounded ashore commenced, ammunition cases were unloaded and a general clearing up of the debris went on. About 3 p.m. the tugs came alongside and we went into Rosyth basin, alongside the *Princess Royal*, who had also suffered some damage . . . The *Warspite* was already in dock and after dinner I went and had a look at her. Inside, she was an extraordinary sight.'[55]

In the *Southampton*, there was pathos when a man was buried at sea off the Isle of May, having died of shock. Then hospital boats came to take the wounded ashore. Spirits improved in the afternoon. 'At 5 p.m. a definite order to go into the basin of Rosyth dockyard relieved the strain, and, with a job in hand, everyone became cheery again. As we slowly wharped through the lock-gates, large crowds assembled to greet us, chiefly composed of dockyard men, and men from the *Warspite*, and survivors of the *Warrior*, which had sunk some eighty mile from the action.'[56]

Though Beatty's forces had shown far more flaws in gunnery and signalling, Jellicoe got little credit from the press and the public for his Jutland performance. In December he was made First Sea Lord, technically a promotion, though it took him away from the real action. Beatty, more of a popular hero than ever, became commander-in-chief of the Grand Fleet in Scapa Flow.

The Birth of the Aircraft Carrier

The Royal Naval Air Service was formed in 1912, as a branch of a semi-unified Royal Flying Corps. Encouraged by Churchill, it soon broke away from the RFC and in some senses from the navy as a whole. It was to prove a remarkable service, combining the skills of the regular naval officer with the innovative spirit of the many who joined it directly from civil life. It did not confine itself to matters naval, or for that matter aeronautical, and mainstream officers joked that the initials stood for 'Really not a sailor'. In its six years of existence it was to give birth to several of the weapons systems that would dominate the next war – the armoured fighting vehicle, the anti-submarine air patrol and the strategic bomber. It would also develop the true aircraft carrier, through a series of experiments and failures.

The idea of flying an aircraft off the deck of a ship was not new. The US Navy had done it in 1910 and the British two years later, in the Medway. The problem was to land it back on again. In the early stages seaplanes were used, and several fast ferries were converted to carry them, including the *Engadine* and *Riviera*, built by Denny of Dumbarton in 1911 for the English Channel. They made valiant attempts to raid German airship sheds in 1914 and to support the fleet at Jutland in 1916, but with little success. A seaplane was almost impossible to operate in the open sea except in a period of settled calm, and navigation difficulties made reconnaissance very ineffective.

Admirals like Jellicoe and Beatty were far from being the blinkered Luddites that some air historians have implied, and they could see many uses for air power at sea – in finding the enemy, directing the guns of the fleet onto him, launching a torpedo attack and in protecting the fleet from air reconnaissance or attack. In the case of reconnaissance and air defence, it was possible to ignore the problem of landing on, either allowing the aircraft to find its way to a land base, which was just possible in most operations in the North Sea; or to ditch in the sea and rescue the pilot, who was more valuable than the 'stick and string' aeroplane he flew. In normal conditions the aeroplane could also be recovered.

Aircraft became part of the normal equipment of the ships of the fleet. In November 1917 the cruiser HMAS *Sydney* was fitted for aircraft in Chatham Dockyard. A platform was built above the gun turrets, so as not to restrict them. *Sydney* sailed north and early in December at Scapa she flew off a Sopwith Pup biplane. During the first trial in the North Sea in January 1918, the Pup landed at the naval air station at Donibristle in Fife. When the captain requested a Sopwith Camel to replace the obsolescent Pup he received the immortal reply from Smoogroo Air Station, 'Does the Camel refer to part of equipment or to a particular type of aeroplane?'[57]

The fixed platform was suitable for a cruiser, but a battleship could not afford to leave the line and turn into wind every time it launched an aircraft. The answer to this had already been developed, by fitting a platform on top of a main gun turret, so that it could be turned into the apparent wind as the ship steamed along. The first trial was made in October 1917 four miles east of Inchkeith, with a Sopwith Pup from B Turret of HMS *Repulse*. Her captain reported 'the pilot did not seem to have any difficulty in flying off, and immediately rose into the air with about six feet of the platform untouched.' Soon all capital ships were ordered to be fitted in this way, usually to carry a single-seat fighter such as a Pup or Camel, and a two-seat reconnaissance plane such as a Sopwith 1½ Strutter, known somewhat obscurely in its naval version as a 'Ship Strutter'. Forty-four battleships and battle-cruisers were ordered to be fitted, and the fleet would have been able to launch a substantial, if expandable, air strike. But it seems that only thirty-six ships were actually fitted, and ten of these never embarked aeroplanes before the war ended.[58]

The battlecruiser *Furious* was one of Fisher's wilder fancies during his second term at First Sea Lord in 1914–15. She was to be armed with two 18-inch guns, but was commissioned with only one, her forward section being fitted with a large flying-off deck and aircraft hangar. As such she operated with the Grand Fleet from Scapa Flow. On 5 August 1917 she sailed across the Flow at high speed and Squadron-Commander Edwin Dunning flew his Sopwith Pup round the superstructure and at his stalling speed, which was equal to the airflow over the ship, he was pulled down by carrying handles fitted to his wings. The following day he tried again and was killed and the experiment was deemed a failure. In March 1918, her 18-inch gun proving impossible to use on such a lightly built ship, the *Furious* was fitted with a flat deck aft for flying on, with tracks around the superstructure so that aircraft could be moved fore and aft. Trials commenced but nine aircraft crashed and it was recognised that the currents from the central superstructure made the concept impossible.

Beardmore's, the Clydeside engineers, shipbuilders and aircraft manufacturers, had produced an experimental design for an aircraft carrier before the war. However it was probably just coincidence that the Italian liner *Conte Rosso*, whose construction in Beardmore's yard at Dalmuir had been suspended, was taken over for completion as HMS *Argus*. She was to be the world's first true aircraft carrier, with a completely flush deck and no superstructure at all.[59] She was completed in September 1918 and went to the Forth where deck-landing trials were carried out using two Sopwith 1½-Strutters based at Turnhouse. There were many issues to be resolved, especially finding the best point on the deck for the pilot to bring the plane down:

> . . . we agreed that the Argus, her deck not yet filled [*sic* – fitted?] with the ramps and wires, should go down the Forth next day to a point near the mouth and then turn into the westerly wind. She would then be manoeuvred to give a relative wind of about 20 knots along the deck. A 'negative' flag being displayed would be replaced by an 'affirmative' as soon as H H was satisfied. Cocky and I, each in a 1½-Strutter, would meet the ship, and take it in turns to make six landings. We would not attempt to stop but would touch down, taxi forward, and fly off again. Two sailors equipped with a paint pot and brush were to be stationed in the nettings aft. After each landing they were to emerge and put a blob of paint on the deck where the machine touched down. We executed the operation as planned . . . We went on all morning, by the end of which we were confident that we could touch down well aft.[60]

The captain of the *Furious*, who knew the problems, wrote on 6 October that these experiments were 'by far the most satisfactory that have yet been carried out'.[61] At Rosyth, *Argus* was fitted with a dummy island superstructure to the starboard side of the flight deck to test that concept in the Forth, and with arrester wires.[62] All the characteristics of the next generation of aircraft carriers were in place by the end of the trials.

By October 1917 Beatty was advocating a 'sustained air offensive' using up to six aircraft carriers to attack the High Seas Fleet in its bases, thus breaking the deadlock in the North Sea. In July 1918 he regarded the torpedo-carrying aeroplane as 'a weapon of great potential'.[63] But the war had not long to run and Beatty's great attack, which might have anticipated the events of Taranto and Pearl Harbor by more than twenty years, never took place.

The Defence of the Forth

Construction of anti-submarine defences on the Forth began on the outbreak of war, when nets were hung under the Forth Bridge. The second layer of defences was begun in November 1914 to run from the Fife shore near Dalgety Bay and then between the islands of Inchcolm, Oxcars and Inchmickery. It had a single gate south of Inchcolm, mostly for the passage of warships and auxiliaries. In July 1915 it was decided to block the channel between Cramond and Inchmickery, which was only 9 ft deep at low water but had up to 20 ft at high tide. Booms 60 ft apart were erected, with wire hawsers between them.[64] A further line of defences, consisting of dolphins with hawsers and torpedo nets between them, was constructed parallel to the shipping lanes between Inchmickery and Hound Point, 1 ¼ miles east of the bridge. There were batteries of guns on the islands of Inchgarvie, Inchcolm and Inch-mickery, and on the mainland at Carlingnose near North Queensferry and at Dalmeny on the south shore. There was room to anchor eight Dreadnoughts in relative safety below the bridge, plus more above it. To help protect commercial shipping at anchor, another boom ran between the island of Inchkeith and Leith Harbour.

In May 1916 Jellicoe looked very carefully at the advantages of moving the Grand Fleet to the Forth. The most obvious was the shorter distance between him and the enemy fleet. He considered that there were two possible areas where a battle might take place. One was off the Danish coast, which would only be 30 miles closer after a move to the Forth-330 miles compared with 360. The other was off the Dutch coast, in the event of an interception of a raid on the English east coast. This was 130 miles closer to the Forth. Another advantage was that, in better weather and over shorter distances, there was an increased chance that the escorting destroyers would be able to stay with the fleet. Thirdly, anti-submarine craft such as destroyers and trawlers could concentrate on the defences on one port. Against this were the old problems – the dangers of mining in, foggier weather and the possibility of spying by neutral ships. Furthermore the removal from Scapa would end the support given to the 10th Cruiser Squadron off Iceland, but Jellicoe did not consider that significant. Experience now suggested that the enemy would not risk his battlecruisers in such an attack to the north. The commander-in-chief concluded: 'There is no doubt that strategically Rosyth has the greater advantages. I have constantly recognised this point in communication with the Admiralty.' But a meeting on the 12th of the month was less confident. 'The strategic advisability of moving the fleet bases south was discussed; no definite conclusion was come to.' It was agreed to enhance the defences of the firth by building a new outer defence line, from Elie in Fife to Fidra Island near North Berwick, across a relatively narrow neck, thirteen miles wide. A gap of two miles was to be left in the centre of it, for neutral shipping could not be expected to negotiate the gates left in a more conventional net, and presumably there would be a threat to security if the gate had to be opened for them. Convoy was not in use at this time, so such shipping was only lightly controlled. Instead, the gap was to be heavily patrolled on the surface and partially closed by lines of deep indicator nets to stop submarines.[65]

The possibility of using the dockyard basin to house a large part of the fleet was looked at several times. In theory there was room for twenty-two Dreadnoughts, but the difficulty was getting them in and out. The emergency entrance could only be used for two hours every tide, which would allow one large ship to pass out this way and two by lock. At other states of the tide, one large ship could pass out through the entrance lock every two hours. It was 'not practicable', the meeting on 12 May concluded. However the destroyers could be treated differently. It was felt that they could not lie safely at anchorage below the bridge in winter. Leith Docks was suggested as a haven for them, and the dockyard basin at Rosyth was again considered. It might be possible to keep them in the basin when they were not at notice for steam and they could lock out nine at a time. But another possibility suggested itself. The small harbour at Port Edgar was little used because it had silted up with mud. If dredged and fitted with mooring pontoons, it could hold a considerable number of destroyers. It was also decided to raise its eastern wall as a protection against gales.[66]

Further refinements were ordered in the next few months. Burntisland was taken over for the use for vessels erecting the booms, and was closed to neutral traffic in July 1917. The boom between Inchcolm and Inchmickery, in the second row of defences, was to be moved half a mile backwards, missing the island of Oxcars, and a second gate was to be opened in it. Another completely new line of defences was started, a mile and a half down from the main line at Inchcolm, Inchmickery and Granton. It would run from Black Rock, west of Burntisland, to a point in the centre of the firth, then to Granton Harbour. It was to consist of heavy anti-submarine nets supported by trawlers, as at Scapa Flow, and was to have three gates for shipping. The Black Rock Boom was in an advanced state by the end of March 1917.[67] It considerably increased the anchorage and practice area above Leith, though the area was still not big enough for fleet exercises. That would have to await the completion of the Elie–Fidra boom, which was far advanced by October 1916. The southern arm from Fidra was finished, and nearly half the northern arm leading south from Elie.

New Facilities in the Forth

Meanwhile, work went on to increase the other facilities of the Forth. A destroyer base at Port Edgar was now regarded as the key to the scheme and regular reports were made to the admiral superintendent at Rosyth. In August 1917 the superintending civil engineer reported 'Drilling, blasting and removing by dredger small quantity of rock still left in shore berth' at Port Edgar. The rock-breaker *Viking* was working with satisfactory results: about 50 holes per day being made.' The first penstructure had been completed for the first three berths and the completion of the fourth was in abeyance until the removal of rock was completed. The building of workshops had been completed and internal fittings were being installed in the torpedo store.

Further work was going on in and around the dockyard. The first shed of a new seaplane station was almost complete. The foundations for a torpedo depot were being laid, after piling. The opening under the entrance pier was being closed, though materials were short. The Crombie Ordnance Depot was being extended to the east, new machinery stores were being built and a gun-storage ground was being excavated. The offices were being extended and the police station had been gutted with a view to rebuilding it with more partitions and extra accommodation.[68]

Though the sick quarters at South Queensferry were quite small, this did not create any difficulty because the Grand Fleet would bring its own hospital ships with it. One problem was the supply of fuel. At the beginning of the war Welsh colliers had supplied Scapa Flow, but now the problem was rather different, for most of the fleet had been converted to oil, which mostly came from the USA. To avoid a voyage through the U-boat-infested waters of the North Sea, it was decided to land the oil on the Clyde and build a pipeline from there to the Forth. The line of the Forth and Clyde Canal was chosen, because it was reasonably level and the towpath could be used. The western terminal was set up on Glasgow Corporation land at Old Kilpatrick, where the canal passes very close to the Clyde. A berth was dredged to thirty feet and sixteen tanks were constructed. The pipeline itself, eight inches in diameter, was built by the United States' Navy, which had experience in such things. The heavy work was done by a party of the Royal

Marine Engineers, who lived in converted barges. The pipeline consisted of three sections between pumping stations at Hungryside and Castlecary. At the eastern end of the line, in Grangemouth, the canal was drained and a trench dug to cross it. It was intended to pump the oil into tankers and carry it down the Forth to Rosyth, where the fleet would be refuelled; but unfortunately the pipeline was not completed until 9 November 1918, two days before the war ended.[69]

The Grand Fleet in the Forth

By April 1918 the facilities in the Forth were judged sufficient, and at six o'clock in the evening of 11 April the Grand Fleet began to raise steam for the last time at Scapa. At 8.15 the first group of ships headed out of the harbour, and at 9.30 the flagship *Queen Elizabeth* slipped the cable which held her to the mooring buoy. The fleet headed south and at 4.08 in the afternoon of the 12th the *Queen Elizabeth* passed the Black Rock gate into the main protected part of the Firth of Forth. By 4.50 the flagship was secured to buoy B14, off Rosyth, with the fleet anchored round her.[70]

Sir David Beatty found the move south had some advantages for his social life. For more than a year he had been conducting a long-distance courtship with Eugenie Godfrey-Faussett, the wife of a naval officer, largely in the form of erotic letters, with brief meetings during the occasional visit to London on business. In July 1918 he contrived a liaison in the North British Hotel in Edinburgh, usually the setting for less romantic meetings on Baltic convoys or the defences of the Forth. Elaborate arrangements were made to keep it secret, for Beatty was as famous as any film star. Afterwards he wrote, 'What a dream it has been, but just a dream, come and gone . . . And interlaced with some golden moments and one hour that will remain for ever a dream of perfect happiness . . . I thank you from deep down for bringing into my dry and burdensome existence a glimpse of perfect bliss.'[71]

The only thing that would have given Beatty total satisfaction was a successful battle against the High Seas Fleet, but that too would remain a dream, and from that point of view his stay in the Forth was as frustrating as Scapa. In November 1918 he would at last see the German Fleet again, though not in the circumstances he had hoped for.

Chapter 10

The First Submarine War

The Rise of the Submarine

The submarine was a new weapon in 1914, untested in war. Various attempts had been made to develop one in the late eighteenth century. An invention by the American Robert Fulton had been shown to Lord Keith, as commander of the North Sea Fleet, in 1804, but it was the Irish-American John P. Holland who produced the first practical boat in 1897. Britain adopted the Holland boat in 1901 and Germany completed her first *Unterseeboot*, or U-boat, in 1905. Submarines had internal combustion engines, usually diesel, as motive power on the surface and to charge their batteries. Since these consumed too much oxygen to be used underwater, electric motors were used below the surface.

When the war began there was virtually no means of detecting a fully submerged submarine, except visually from an aircraft in clear waters, which were not common round the British Isles. However, submarines had to show their periscopes during an attack, and they had to spend a considerable amount of time each day on the surface to recharge their batteries. Boats of this period were really submersibles, which went under water when occasion demanded, rather than true submarines which spend most of their time underwater. At the start of the war the submarine was just beginning to move beyond its original function as a coast-defence vessel. The most recent boats had a range of 1,000 miles or more. But Germany had not planned for a submarine war and Admiral Tirpitz, the founder of the new navy, had been opposed to it. Germany had only seventeen U-boats in 1914, at various stages of construction, and not all of these were capable of long-distance operations.

Most of the east coast of Scotland was within 400 miles of the German bases, so it was only to be expected that it would come under some kind of submarine attack. But there were several additional factors which made submarine warfare highly likely in Scottish waters. Firstly, and most obviously, the main British fleet was based there for practically the whole of the war. Since the Germans were inferior in the number of battleships, their best hope was for their submarines to pick them off by penetrating the harbours such as Scapa Flow, or by attacks on ships at sea. Secondly, the route round the north of Scotland offered the best way to reach the west coast and the Atlantic. The Straits of Dover are little more than twenty miles wide and relatively easy to block, even to submarines (though the Dover Patrol was disappointing in this role until near the end of the war). To the north, the passages are much wider and deeper.

Thirdly, the Firth of Forth offered an unusually tempting target, even before it was filled with warships. It is wider than any other estuary on the east coast of Britain, except for the Thames which is dotted with dangerous sandbanks. It had a good deal of commercial traffic from the factories and coalfields, and on 24 September 1914, *U-22* noted 100 ship movements in a single day.[1] Fourthly, eastern Scotland provided bases for the trade to Scandinavia. Iron ore and timber were vital to the war effort, while Norway, in particular, depended on British coal for survival through the Arctic winters.

Attacks on the Forth

The first submarine alarm in the Firth of Forth came on 2 September 1914, less than a month after the start of the war, when the great battlecruisers *Invincible* and *New Zealand* offered tempting targets. At 10.30 that morning, the battery at Carlingnose in North Queensferry opened fire on a suspected submarine. The firth had no aircraft patrols or net defences at this time, so caution was perhaps justified, but higher authority believed, rightly, as it turned out, that there was no submarine in the area.

Unknown to them, two U-boats left Germany that very day to attack the Forth. *U-22* broke down on the way, but *U-21* was off Dunbar early in the morning of 4 September. Off the Isle of May at 10.30 she sighted the destroyers of the Forth patrol and was forced to go out to sea and surface to charge her batteries. There she met *U-20*, which had been sent to replace *U-22*. *U-20* made several attempts to penetrate the firth during the nights of the 4th and 5th, but by the time she had evaded the British patrols her batteries were low and she had to retreat. At 3.20 on the morning of the 5th, *U-21* began her attempt to enter the firth. Four hours later she surfaced off May and saw the British cruiser *Pathfinder*, of 1904, the leader of the 8th Destroyer

Flotilla, which had the duty of patrolling the Forth. The cruiser soon disappeared but was back off May by three in the afternoon. At 3.45 *U-21* fired a torpedo at a range of 1,500 yards and hit the *Pathfinder*, in the area of her magazine. The cruiser sank in four minutes with the loss of most of her crew, the first British warship to be sunk by a U-boat. *U-21* escaped back to Germany.[2] Seventeen days later the old cruisers *Aboukir*, *Cressy* and *Hogue* were sunk by *U-9* off the German coast, with the loss of more than 2,000 men. The U-boat threat was already apparent, though for the moment it seemed a danger to warships rather than merchantmen.

On 23 September, the day after the sinking of the cruisers, *U-19* and *U-22* arrived off the Isle of May and were spotted by the naval trawler *Defender*. Destroyers were sent out to look for them and *U-22* spent the night lying on the bottom of Largo Bay. Next day she headed up the firth as far as Inchkeith but found no large ships which offered a worthwhile target. She went back to Largo Bay for the night. *U-19* had a similar experience and retreated out to sea. Meanwhile, the British destroyers and patrol craft were searching the firth. Just before noon on the 25th, *Torpedo Boat 33* was hit by a torpedo from *U-19* off the Bass Rock, but it failed to explode. In the afternoon the destroyer *Vigilant* was off May with three others, when a torpedo missed her and surfaced when its power ran out. Fifteen minutes later the destroyer *Stag* was fired on by two torpedoes at long range but evaded them easily. Further reports followed and a thorough search was instituted on the night of the 25–26th. Sightings of torpedoes and submarines continued to be made for several days, but the U-boats had left the Forth on the night of the 25th, after the torpedo was fired at the *Vigilant*.[3] Neither side had achieved anything, because of the novelty of submarine warfare. They were still quite amateurish, compared with what they became over the next three years, and *a fortiori* over the next thirty years.

By this time there was paranoia on shore and at sea. It was a particular problem in the Firth of Forth, which has heavily populated communities on both banks, with good views over the sea. One officer based at Granton commented, 'We had very little rest, day or night, in those days; everybody was seeing submarines. Ladies saw them from trains, children from the coast, and farmers from their farms.' A colleague wrote,

Oh, those memories of early days, when a certain captain in one of the premier line regiments *always* saw a submarine every Sunday afternoon, and the resultant stunts to bag her, until it was discovered by a logical coastguard that the Hun was always in the same spot, and that the periscope was really a fishing stake with the tide feathering past it.

Or the famous day when an enthusiastic patriot reported that she had seen (from a train) a large grey submarine cruising on the surface on the Firth, as a result of which one of HM yachts chased her for twenty-four hours, ably assisted by 'all available trawlers and drifters'.[4]

In the last two days of January 1915, a submarine was reported inside Oxcars and therefore near Rosyth, and all shipping movements were stopped. More submarines were seen in Stronsay Firth in Orkney, two off Stornoway and two more off Loch Ewe. In the weeks that followed there was a report of a submarine six miles east of the Isle of May, another in Nairn Bay in the Moray Firth and five more were seen in the Minches. But none of these reports were true: there were no British or German submarines in any of these areas at the times concerned.[5]

In the middle of March there was a small but completely spurious campaign in the firth. The armed merchant ship *Calyx* first sighted the wash of a periscope at 7.10 on the 15th off Methil, and fired on it. Two and a half hours later a destroyer reported a periscope two miles off Elie, so destroyers, torpedo boats and drifters were sent out in search of it. At 6.30 in the afternoon the listening station at Oxcars reported hearing the machinery of the submarine and a sighting was reported by a trawler a mile to the east just after 8 o'clock. There were several sightings the next day and it was concluded that two U-boats were in the area. On the 17th a trawler hit a submerged object and oil was seen in the water, suggesting that one of the submarines had been damaged. Five destroyers and a fleet of trawlers continued the search, until a blizzard on the night of the 17th made their work impossible. It was concluded that the submarines had gone, but on the morning of the 18th Oxcars reported another contact. Finally, in the morning of the 20th, a periscope was reported five miles east of Kirkcaldy. But nothing definite was found at the time and the Admiralty censured the officers on the spot for 'want of resource, brains and energy'. Admiral Lowry at Rosyth defended his officers and pointed out the great difficulties under which they were operating: but the last word went to the authors of the staff history of the war in home waters, who had access to captured enemy documents after the war and commented tartly,

The real cause of the failure of the hunting forces in the Firth of Forth to destroy a submarine on this occasion was neither the want of resource, brains or energy imputed to the officers concerned in the Admiralty

Top. The Dutch Fleet hove to off Buchan Ness for a council of war, August 1665. From a drawing by William Van de Velde the Elder, National Maritime Museum

Bottom. Argyll's campaign, 1685

Top. The Bass Rock, from Slezer's *Theatrum Scotiae* of 1693. The crane features prominently in the centre of the rock. National Library of Scotland

Bottom. Eilan Donan Castle as a ruin in the 1880s. From *The Castellated and Domestic Architecture of Scotland*, 1889, by William Daniell

Top. Captain Lord George Graham in his cabin, painted by William Hogarth. Fourth son of the Duke of Montrose, Graham became a captain in 1740 and died seven years later, just before uniform for naval officers was introduced. The picture shows the captain smoking a pipe at the centre of a group of followers; his cook, secretary, chaplain, a black servant and two dogs, one wearing a wig. National Maritime Museum, BHC2720

Bottom. A young man (on the ladder on the right) is introduced to the midshipmen's berth, where anarchy prevails. Royal Naval Museum

Above. Napoleon is rowed aboard the
Bellerophon after Waterloo in 1815, by
the French artist Baugean. National
Maritime Museum

Right. Captain Francois Thurot.
National Maritime Museum
PAD2800

Monsieur Thurot
Capitaine de haut Bord

Gravé par Petit Se vend a Paris chez la Vᵉ de F. Chereau rue Sᵗ Jacques aux 2 Piliers d'or.

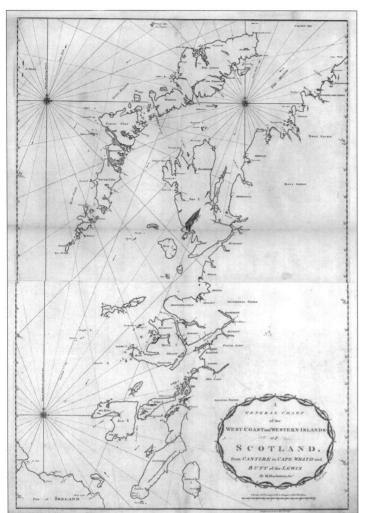

Murdoch Mackenzie's survey of the West Coast. National Library of Scotland

Seamen in 1807

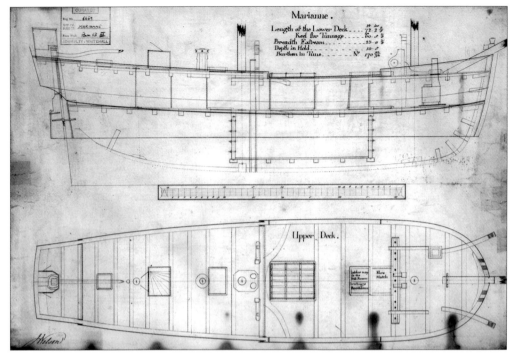

Marianne.

Length of the Lower Deck . . . . . 72. 2 ⅔
Keel for Tunnage . . . . . 60. 0 ⅔
Breadth Extream . . . . . 25. 0 ½
Depth in Hold 10. 8
Burthen in Tuns . . . . . Nº 170 ¾⁄₉

Upper Deck.

Above. Plans of a typical press tender of around 1800. Note the strong bulkheads round the 'press room.' National Maritime Museum, 6650-60

Below. A print of Greenock in 1768. Scottish artists had evidently not yet learned to draw ships accurately.

The Forth Bridge and HMS *Caledonia*. Scottish US Museum

HMS *Unicorn* at Dundee. Author

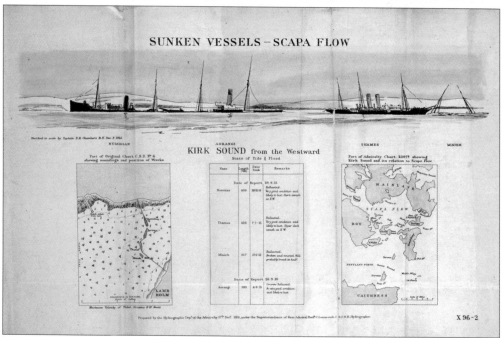

Top. The Home Fleet at Scapa Flow, Orkney

Bottom. Sunken ships blocking Kirk Sound. From a drawing of December 1915 in the Public Record Office

Top. This claims to be the first landing on the decks of the *Argus,* but it conflicts with reports that the ramps and wires had not yet been fitted. The wires were not arrester wires in the later sense, but were intended to stop the aircraft being blown over the side when it stopped. Imperial War Museum A70885

Bottom. A U-boat of the type active in the Forth on 1914-6

Top. Hawcraig from the air. From *Technical History and Index,* TH7, *The Anti-Submarine Division of the Naval Staff*

Right. A boom defence vessel of the type developed early in WWII. From *Britain's Glorious Navy,* edited Bacon, 1942

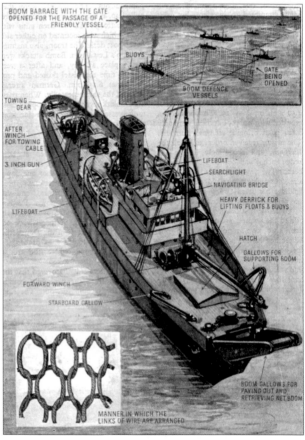

BOOM BARRAGE WITH THE GATE OPENED FOR THE PASSAGE OF A FRIENDLY VESSEL

BUOYS

GATE BEING OPENED

BOOM DEFENCE VESSELS

TOWING GEAR

AFTER WINCH FOR TOWING CABLE

3 INCH GUN

LIFEBOAT

LIFEBOAT

SEARCHLIGHT

NAVIGATING BRIDGE

HEAVY DERRICK FOR LIFTING FLOATS & BUOYS

HATCH

GALLOWS FOR SUPPORTING BOOM

FORWARD WINCH

STARBOARD GALLOW

BOOM GALLOWS FOR PAYING OUT AND RETRIEVING NET BOOM

MANNER IN WHICH THE LINKS OF WIRE ARE ARRANGED

The German battleship *Derflinger* sinking. OPL

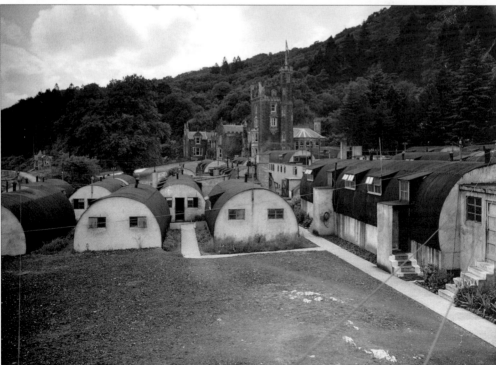

Top. The captured U-boat *Graph* (ex *U-570*) off the depot ship in the Holy Loch. IWM

Bottom. HMS *James Cook*, the training school for naval beach parties near Tignabruach, showing a typical layout with a castle surrounded by Nissen huts. Imperial War Museum A29904

A wartime view of the Clyde over Gourock Bay, with the *Aquitania* at anchor in the centre.
Imperial War Museum A29941

HMS *Diomede* damaged in a collision in the Cod War in 1976.
Imperial War Museum FL10866

telegram, nor the difficulties detailed by Admiral Lowry, but the simple fact that, in spite of all appearances, which at the time seemed quite conclusive, there was no submarine in the neighbourhood.[6]

The real attack on the Forth resumed in May 1915, when the German *Admiralstab* sent a succession of boats to the firth. *U-14* arrived there at the end of the month but found the patrols too dangerous, so her orders were changed to attack commerce and fishing further north. She found the fishing fleet off Aberdeen but did not realise she was falling into a well-laid trap, for disguised trawlers of the Auxiliary Patrol were mixed among the fishing boats. *U-14* torpedoed one trawler, the Swedish *Lappland*, without warning. Later she surfaced and opened fire on the *Oceanic II*, one of the armed trawlers, which replied in conjunction with the *Hawk*, another Auxiliary Patrol vessel. The submarine was damaged and unable to dive and was rammed by the *Hawk*. Twenty-seven of her crew were rescued but the captain decided to go down with the ship.[7]

After this loss, four more boats were dispatched between 8 and 18 June. *U-17* arrived first, on the 10th, and stopped a neutral Danish merchant schooner. Her cargo of timber was regarded as contraband of war and the submarine would have been entitled to sink her, but two vessels from the Granton Auxiliary Patrol chased her away. She searched another Dane but let her go. She headed north, up the coast, and on the morning of the 12th, fifteen miles east of Tod Head, she found the *Desabla*, a tanker carrying oil for the British Fleet. Even ships of such strategic importance were not escorted north of the Forth, and the captain of the *Desabla* was following his orders to avoid all headlands, so was well away from the protection of patrols and shore guns. *U-17* sank her, creating an enormous oil slick.[8] She sank another Dane, and then, on 18 June, she sank the steamer *Ailsa* off the Bell Rock. On the way home she was chased by two trawlers from Peterhead but escaped.

U-6 arrived off the Forth on 16 June and sailed through the *Desabla*'s oil slick She had to dive seven times during the next twenty-four hours to avoid Auxiliary Patrol vessels and her batteries were close to exhaustion when she found *U-17* on her way home. But *U-6* failed to penetrate the Forth or find any acceptable targets, except for the armed yacht *Salvator* of the Granton Patrol off St Abbs Head. Her torpedo missed and she was rammed and damaged by the *Salvator*.[9] The defences of the Forth, though they had destroyed no submarines, were effective enough to make the firth reasonably safe.

The Auxiliary Patrol

The activity in the Forth and elsewhere in the autumn of 1914 caused
the Admiralty to augment the Auxiliary Patrol, a force of small craft,
mainly manned by RNR officers and ratings. Fifteen large yachts were
already in use, and the force was soon increased to about 300 trawlers
and drifters and 100 motor boats. The main anti-submarine weapon
was the 'modified sweep', described by an officer at Granton as 'nine
charges of TNT encased in wood floats. They are fitted to an electric
wire; the charges are placed 100 ft apart, and extended to about
1,000 ft astern of the vessel towing. The charges are kept below the
surface by means of a kite similar to that used for mine-sweeping.'[10]
The Granton Patrol had seven yachts in 1916, of 58 to 265 tons. The
largest was the *Mingary*, built in 1899 by Ailsa of Troon for Charles
D. Rudd of Glasgow. She was 187 ft long, 27 ft broad and carried two
6-pounder guns in wartime.[11]

Area I of the Auxiliary Patrol, which included the west coast of
Scotland north of the Mull of Kintyre and all the Hebrides, was based
on the depot ship *Iolaire* moored at Stornoway. In February 1917 it
had five large yachts for use by the leaders of the flotillas. There were
thirty-one trawlers and drifters, including five for the defence of the
boom at Stornoway harbour; and four whalers. There were twelve
motor launches, built in Canada during 1915, 75 to 88 ft long, armed
with one light gun each and carrying a crew of eight to ten men. Area
II was the region around the Shetland Islands and had a total of forty-
two craft. Area III, Orkney, was one of the most important, in view of
the need to defend the Grand Fleet. Early in 1917 it had six yachts and
twelve motor launches, but its main strength was in nearly 300
trawlers and drifters. Some of these were not commissioned as warships, but served as tenders to the individual ships of the fleet. Others
were confined to the defence of the booms across the entrances to the
Flow, while the rest supported the Northern Patrol. Area IV, Cromarty, occupied the whole of the firth and was based in the depot ship
Thalia in Dunskaith Naval Base. It had seventy-six vessels in early
1917. The Peterhead Area, No. V, stretched from Kinnaird Head to
Tod Head, north of Montrose, and had forty-eight vessels.

In view of the importance of the Firth of Forth, Granton harbour
grew into one of the biggest stations for the Auxiliary Patrol, for
minesweepers and for decoy vessels as well as anti-submarine patrols.
It began on a small scale in 1914, with six officers and thirty men in
trawlers. The Customs House was used as an office and two adjoining
offices and a hut at the end of the pier were taken over on 11 August, a

week after the start of the war. By this time there were three yachts and twenty-nine trawlers.

On 15 March 1915, in a gale with heavy snow, Sir James Startin arrived to take command. He was a vice admiral who had dropped in rank to join the RNR as a lieutenant-commander. In the early stages of the war he commanded the yacht *Shemara* in the defence of Lerwick, until he was promoted to captain on the direct orders of Lord Fisher. The base was now named HMS *Gunner* after the largest trawler in its flotilla. Startin became something of a legend in the war.

There was a great deal of concern for the welfare of the men and women of HMS *Gunner*. A church was consecrated and a 'mine-sweeper's rest hut' was opened by the Prime Minister's wife in 1916, with an extension opened by the Duke of Connaught. It was run by a voluntary staff and included a billiard table, bagatelle board, piano, organ and gramophones. The first members of the Women's Royal Naval Service, the WRNS, arrived during 1918. After the war Sir James Startin paid them a tribute which would be regarded rather ambivalently today. 'The bevy of Beauty for Duty, second to none of all the Bases; as efficient as hard-working.'[12]

The command at Granton in the Forth was divided into two parts, Area VI, north of the Forth, and Area VII, stretching south as far as St Abbs Head. The northern area had a large complement of 24 motor launches and a force of 18 paddle minesweepers, as well as 30 boom defence vessels, among its flotilla of 103 craft. The southern area was much smaller, with a total of 47 yachts and fishing boats. In the west of Scotland, the Clyde formed part of the command based at Larne in northern Ireland, with 1 yacht, 6 trawlers, and 14 net drifters and boom defence vessels. The Larne Command, which included Islay, had a total force of 94 net drifters for the defence of the North Channel which formed the entrance to the Clyde and other main port areas, as well as 18 motor launches, 3 yachts and 17 trawlers and drifters.[13] Fifty-nine vessels of the Auxiliary Patrol were lost in Scottish waters during the war, including 44 trawlers.

The War on Commerce

A new era in naval warfare began on 20 October 1914. The steamer *Glitra* of Leith left Grangemouth a few days earlier carrying coke, oil, coal and general goods to neutral Norway. As she neared her destination of Stavanger, the submarine *U-17* surfaced close to her and gave the crew ten minutes to take to the boats. Lieutenant Feldkichner, in command of the U-boat, then sank the *Glitra* by shots from his 2-inch gun. In past wars, it had always been regarded as much more desirable to capture rather than sink merchantmen, for their assets would be added to the captor's strength and the officers and crew of the capturing ship would gain prize money, while the officers of a ship sinking another could be held liable for any non-contraband goods belonging to neutrals in the ship. But German regulations allowed the destruction of any enemy merchant ship 'if it seems unsafe or inexpedient to bring her in'. *U-17*, with a crew of twenty-eight, was not likely to have spare men for a prize crew, so sinking was clearly the only option. But U-boat warfare was still highly civilised. After allowing the crew of the *Glitra* to take to the boats, the submarine towed them some distance towards the Norwegian shore until they were picked up by a pilot vessel.[14]

On the western side of Scotland, U-boats tended to operate singly, with one replacing another on station off the Hebrides. Their main prize, however, was to penetrate the eleven miles of the North Channel between the Mull of Kintyre and northern Ireland, and menace the trade of the Clyde, Liverpool and Belfast. When a U-boat was reported in this area it was normal to stop all traffic from these ports for a few days, as in February 1915 when a periscope was sighted off Liverpool. One long-term answer was to close the North Channel to U-boats. This was proposed in February 1915 and was accepted by the Admiralty, despite the fear that a minefield in the North Channel could be equally dangerous to friendly ships. The North Channel is ten miles narrower than the Straits of Dover, but is more than twice as deep and has strong currents of six knots or more. A quadrilateral area of sea between Rathlin Island and Kintyre was forbidden to all merchant ships, which were now ordered to pass between Rathlin and the mainland of Ireland. A slightly smaller quadrilateral within the large one was to be filled with drift nets, 800 yards long, which were replaced every two or three days by a force of eighty drifters and eighteen trawlers. The nets would force a U-boat to dive deep and arrive exhausted on the other side of the nets, where it would be dealt with by strong patrols.[15] On 20 February, the day on which the net barrage was ordered, a steamer from Liverpool was torpedoed off the Welsh coast and this gave added urgency to the system.[16] By March 1916 the North Channel Patrol had expanded to 120 drifters, 18 armed trawlers, 2 armed yachts and 5 motor boats, but it was not totally effective, and none of the ships could stay at sea in bad weather. Several ships were attacked off Galloway in March 1916.[17] Furthermore, a submarine outside the barrage could disrupt trade. When a U-boat was reported off Skerryvore in March 1916, this was enough to hold up vessels from leaving the Clyde, Liverpool and Belfast.[18]

On 23 February 1915 the trawler *Alexander Hastie* was 100 miles off the Tay when the conning tower of a submarine was sighted. The U-boat fouled the wires of the trawler's nets and then appeared on the surface, either upside down or on her beam ends, for no sign of the conning tower could be seen. After about 20 minutes it appeared to sink and large quantities of oil were seen. The crew of the *Alexander Hastie* were given a reward of £100, but in fact the submarine in question, *U-34*, reached Germany safely.[19]

Q-Ships and Decoys

Many ingenious schemes were tested in an attempt to defeat the U-boats. Among the first to be effective were two means of decoying them. Admiral Beatty's secretary, Paymaster F. T. Spickernell, suggested that a trawler should act as bait, towing a submerged submarine with a telephone link between the two vessels. When a U-boat surfaced to attack by gunfire, the British submarine would slip the tow and get into position to launch a torpedo. The trawler *Taranaki* was converted and on 24 May 1915 she left Aberdeen. She patrolled between there and Peterhead for fifteen days with HM Submarine *C-27* astern, until at last, on 8 June, *U-19* appeared half a mile away. But when *C-27* reached what seemed like a good firing position she found the German heading straight for her on the surface and had to dive. The U-boat disappeared.

Taranaki sailed from Aberdeen again on 23 June with *C-24* in tow. This time there was not long to wait, for at 9.30 that morning *U-40* surfaced 2,500 yards ahead. It took some time to get the telephone working and then *C-24* could not slip the tow. The crew of the *Taranaki* simulated panic to play for time, and at the same time they slipped the tow from their end. *C-24* had some difficulty with her trim with 100 fathoms of steel towline still hanging from her bow, but at 9.55 she was able to fire a torpedo at *U-40* at a range of 500 yards and hit her below the conning tower. She sank instantly and three out of her complement of thirty-two were rescued.[20] This was judged a great success and eight more submarines were allocated to this task, two from Scapa Flow and the rest in eastern English waters. On 20 July *C-27*, towed by *Princess Marie Jose* from Scapa, sank *U-23* which was making her way through the Fair Isle passage to the west coast.[21] The scheme was abandoned in November 1915, when new U-boat tactics made it irrelevant.

The other scheme was the more famous 'Q-ship', known officially as the 'Armed Decoy'. On the orders of Admiral Colville, in charge of the defences of Orkney, the collier *Prince Charles*, of 373 tons, was given a concealed armament of two 6-pounder and two 3-pounder guns, more than a match for the typical U-boat's single 3.4- or 4.1-inch gun. She kept her original merchant-ship crew as well as a party of naval ratings. She sailed from Scapa on 21 July and was ordered to cruise round Orkney and Shetland towards Stornoway, keeping about sixty miles from land and following a typical merchant-ship route. If a periscope was seen, the *Prince Charles* was not to react. The majority of her crew were to keep below at all times, in order not to arouse suspicion, and a 'panic party' was to be ready to cause delays in abandoning ship. Three days later, near North Rona, north of the Butt of Lewis, she saw a merchant ship stopped with a submarine on the surface close to her. Lieutenant Mark-Wardlaw of the *Prince Charles* described what happened:

> Shortly after this the submarine was observed to start her oil engine and proceed towards us at full speed. I then hoisted my ensign. At about 7.5 pm, submarine being about 3 miles distant, 5 points on the port bow, she fired a shot which pitched about 1,000 yards over.
>
> I then stopped my engines, put ship's head to swell from NNW, blew three blasts, and boats' crews were ordered to get boats out.
>
> All this time the submarine was coming very fast towards us (20 knots) and at 7.10 she fired a second shot which went between funnel and foremast and landed 50 yards over.
>
> The submarine then turned so as to bring her broadside to us at about 600 yards, and as the submarine continued to fire and seeing that the range could not close any more, I opened fire with both port guns.
>
> Directly I opened fire the gun's crew of the submarine deserted their gun and entered the conning tower and she apparently attempted to dive.

But she had already been damaged and her crew abandoned ship. Fourteen were saved and eighteen killed or drowned, while the *Prince Charles* had no casualties.[22]

Small sailing coasters were also used and the base at Granton fitted out the first, the *Ready*, in the summer of 1916, but she went though a year of 'long monotony of unadventurous days' before she met her first enemy in the English Channel. The *Merops*, an iron brigantine fitted out at Granton in April 1917, was regarded as 'the best equipped Q-ship of her class. She mounted a 4-inch gun and two 12-pounders and sank a U-boat off Cape Wrath.[23]

The Q-ship had one fatal flaw. If the Germans were to obey

international law as interpreted by the British, they could not sink a merchant ship without first warning the crew and allowing them time to take to the boats, perhaps even assisting them on the way, as quite often happened. In March 1915, even after the commencement of unrestricted warfare, *U-27* sank the *Hartdale* in the North Channel but invited some of the crew on board the submarine and gave them a bottle of brandy.[24] But if the seemingly innocent merchant ship might be a disguised warship, then the U-boat had no alternative but to torpedo her without warning. This, at least, was one of the arguments used by the Germans when, in February 1915, they instigated a new phase of submarine warfare. They declared that all ships in British waters were liable to attack by gun or torpedo. This was the beginning of the first campaign of 'Unrestricted Warfare'. It was to be carried out by a fleet of thirty-seven U-boats, of which only about twenty-five were available for operations.[25]

The great danger was in upsetting neutrals, especially the United States, which happened when the great liner *Lusitania* was sunk off the coast of Ireland in May, with the loss of 128 American citizens. Increased and often contradictory restrictions were put on the U-boats' activities and the unrestricted campaign was abandoned in September, after doing considerable damage to British and allied shipping. It was to resume in greater force in January 1917. The Germans now had a fleet of 148 U-boats, but they took a calculated risk on American intervention. In April the United States declared war on Germany.

By this time the British were developing the depth charge, which would become the most effective anti-submarine weapon of this war and the next. It was simply a charge of explosive which could be dropped over the stern of a destroyer or trawler and set to explode at a particular depth. Initially 40 ft and 140 ft were the only depths available, but later it could be set to any depth up to 140 ft. But there were teething troubles. In January 1916 the cruiser *Blonde* was searching for a submarine east of Scapa when a charge exploded accidentally on her deck, damaging the ship and killing two men. All depth charges of this type were withdrawn from ships of the Grand Fleet to await the arrival of a new model, Type D, in March.[26] This version was to remain standard until the Second World War.

German Minefields

The submarine mine had been used by the Russians during the Crimean War, and in the American Civil War (1861–5) when it was known as a 'torpedo'. It had developed considerably in recent years. It floated under the surface at the end of a line attached to a block on the sea bottom. At the beginning of the war all were 'contact' mines, detonated by a ship striking a horn projecting from the body of the mine. In the early stages of the war they used a 'fixed reel'. A length of wire appropriate to the depth of water was set by the crew of the minelayer. Later in the war they used a pressure gauge to set the depth automatically.

The German Navy was very active in its use of minefields right from the beginning of the war: indeed the minelayer *Koenigen Louise* was already on her way across the North Sea when war was declared. The first success, however, was on the west coast. The armed merchant cruiser *Berlin* left Wilhelmshaven on 9 August, apparently intending to mine in the Firth of Clyde. If she had been successful she would have confirmed the *Glasgow Herald*'s fears of 1888, but in fact she laid her mines off Tory Island, north of Ireland. The Dreadnought battleship *Audacious* of 1912 was sunk by one of them on 27 October, the most serious British loss of the early stages of the war.

In August 1915 the Germans decided to lay extensive minefields in the Moray Firth, aware that the area was used by ships of the Grand Fleet. To carry out the operation they chose a ship of British appearance. The *Meteor*, formerly the *Vienna* of the Leith, Hull and Hamburg Line, was built by Ramage and Ferguson of Leith in 1905 and seized at Hamburg on the outbreak of war. She left on the 6th carrying 374 mines, and meanwhile *U-17* was carrying out a reconnaissance, following one already done by *U-25* as far inshore as the line of nets between Findhorn and Tarbet Ness, but the airship SL-3 had to return due to unfavorable weather. The British decoded signals about the *Meteor*'s passage and discerned that she was minelaying, but did not know where. Cruisers were sent out to look for her.

The *Meteor*, under Commander von Knorr, rendezvoused with *U-17* forty miles north of Kinnaird Head in the evening of 7 August. The *Meteor* then headed south-west to lay her first line of mines across the steamer track into the firth, seeing two trawlers and a destroyer which failed to challenge her, and turned away, being at the end of her patrol line. The *Meteor* had now penetrated the first patrol line and laid her second field, just north of Banff. Reaching the coast, she turned north-east to begin the next line, when the armed yacht *Agatha* arrived and demanded the secret recognition signal. Of course this was not given, but the captain of the yacht took her for a British destroyer and did not report the incident. But von Knorr did not know this and assumed that the alarm would soon be raised. He carried on dropping his mines, but set some of them to shallower depths to hinder pursuing forces. They were therefore dropped in the right area, but closer together than had been planned. Just after midnight he lost sight of the *Agatha*. He went back through the outer patrol line, passing very close to a destroyer which paid very little attention to him. Abandoning the prearranged plan, he dropped the rest of his mines on the steamer track between Peterhead and the Pentland Firth. At 2.15 he met *U-17* again, and attributed his miraculous escape to the fact that it was Saturday night. 'No other explanation seems possible that the crews of the English [*sic*] patrol boats were either too drunk or too stupid to be able to recognize as hostile a vessel coming from inside the patrol lines, although the challenge had not been answered.'

But von Knorr's luck was running out. On the way home he made a long radio signal which allowed the British cruisers to intercept him and forced the crew to scuttle the ship. Meanwhile on 8 August, *U-17* attacked and sank two merchant steamers in the firth and was pursued by the destroyer *Christopher* and the Peterhead Auxiliary Patrol. There was particular concern because, unknown to the Germans, the Prime Minister and the Chancellor of the Exchequer were lunching with Admiral Jellicoe on board the *Iron Duke* in Cromarty Harbour. Then there was a further crisis when a minesweeper spotted two of *Meteor*'s mines 12 miles north of Banff. More reports followed and the hunt for *U-17* was called off. As well as local craft, six converted Clyde steamers which had been working on *Berlin*'s field off Tory Island were sent round to help. By 10 September two channels, 10 miles wide, had been swept along each shore, though the middle portion of the firth was left uncleared.

Once the events of the night of 7–8 August began to emerge, there was an enquiry into the spectacular failure of the patrols. There was no mention of Saturday-night drunkenness, but the crews of the destroyers were accused of keeping a bad lookout. It was found that two of the three destroyers on the outer patrol had been operating on obsolete orders and had left the patrol station too soon, leaving a gap in the line. Their navigation was inadequate and in future the lights of Kinnaird Head and Noss Head were to be switched on at specified times to allow them to take better fixes. The neglect of the *Agatha* was not discovered until October, when her captain was dismissed from the ship. [27]

Britain was developing minesweeping techniques, using a wire sweep fitted with wire-cutters which would cut the cable of the mine and allow it to float to the surface, where it would be destroyed by rifle fire. Initially it was towed between two trawlers, but this was highly dangerous. In 1916 a small float known as the paravane was invented and took one end of the sweep and helped protect the bows of the ship carrying it.

As well as trawlers for the bulk of minesweeping, and converted warships for work with the main fleet, the paddle steamer was found to be suitable for work in offshore fields, because its shallow draught made it relatively safe. More than twenty Clyde steamers were taken up for this work, including the pride of the Caledonian Steam Packet Company, the *Duchess of Hamilton* of 1890, which was sunk by a mine off Harwich in September 1915. The requisitioning of these steamers had a serious effect on the holiday trade in the Firth of Clyde. Unlike resorts in other parts of Britain, towns like Dunoon and Rothesay had no other means of communication.

In the last days of 1915 another German minelayer left on a mission in Scottish waters. The steamer *Pungo* was taken over, fitted as a minesweeper and renamed *Moewe*. She was fitted with four 5.9-inch guns, which made her a powerful armed merchant cruiser, as well as torpedo tubes and as many as 500 mines. Her captain, Count Zu Dohna-Schlodien, was ordered to lay some of his mines at the western entrance to the Pentland Firth, blocking one of the routes used by the Grand Fleet. He was then to lay the rest of his mines elsewhere at his discretion and proceed to the Atlantic as a commerce raider.

The *Moewe* was off the Faroes by 2 January 1916 and she proceeded to a point 9 miles south-west of Sule Skerry Light, where she began to lay her mines at 6 p.m. She was helped in her navigation by the lights on Cape Wrath and Sule Skerry, which had to be left on to aid the British fleet. In the teeth of a westerly gale she spent 8 hours laying 252 mines in eleven lines, and then rounded Cape Wrath with great difficulty in the gale. She went on to lay the rest in French waters.

The weather was still bad on 6 January when the pre-Dreadnought *King Edward VII* left Scapa Flow for a refit in Belfast. Destroyers could not operate in the gale, so she was alone. At 10.47 a.m., after she had travelled 30 miles, there was a violent explosion in her engine room. At first it was believed to be a torpedo and destroyers were sent out from the Grand Fleet despite the gale. They found her with both engine rooms flooded and listing 8 degrees. She was towed part of the way to Scapa but the line broke. With the weather getting worse, it was decided to disembark her crew into four destroyers and she sank nine hours after the explosion.

This meant that the whole area north of Cape Wrath and the Sutherland coast was considered dangerous, and indeed a Norwegian merchant ship was mined on 8 January. The Whiten Bank Minefield, as the British called it, took a good deal of time to clear, for the bad weather continued. By 8 March a safe channel had been swept through it.[28]

The greatest success of German minelaying came by accident. *U-75* was one of three boats detailed to lay mines off the Scottish coast in May 1916, as part of a general plan which led to the Battle of Jutland. *U-72* turned back, *U-74* was sunk by the Peterhead Auxiliary Patrol, but *U-75* reached Orkney on 29 May after making a wide loop to avoid the Shetland patrols. She laid twenty-two mines off Marwick Head which was believed to be a main channel for warships. This was the first time a U-boat had laid mines north of the Forth.

Lord Kitchener, Britain's greatest military hero of the age and star of the famous poster 'Your Country Needs You', arrived at Thurso on 5 June, to be picked up by a destroyer which took him to lunch with Admiral Jellicoe in Scapa Flow. He then went on board the cruiser *Hampshire* which was intended to take him on a mission to Russia. She sailed immediately in a heavy storm, against Jellicoe's advice. The Whiten Bank minefield, laid by the *Moewe* in January, was well known and it was decided to bypass it by sailing close to the west shore of the Orkney mainland, rather than make a long detour round it. At 7.40 that evening, in heavy seas off the 200 ft cliff of Marwick Head, a great explosion shook the ship. The helm jammed, electricity failed and brown smoke poured from what had been the stokers' mess in the centre of the ship. To cries of 'Make way for Lord Kitchener', the most important passenger was brought on deck, but was never seen again. Due to the power failure it was impossible to launch the ship's large boats and only three life rafts got away. One started with six men but only two survived to reach Skaill Bay. A much larger one had forty or fifty men but only four of them survived when the raft was washed ashore in the storm to the north of the Bay, containing forty-two bodies. The third raft started with about forty men and picked up twenty or thirty more but most fell asleep and died from exposure. Early next morning six survivors were found among the rocks, north of Skaill Bay, numbed and exhausted and with their fingernails torn away from the scramble to safety among the rocks. In all there were 12 survivors from a crew of nearly 700. Kitchener's body was never found, giving rise to several hoaxes and conspiracy theories.[29]

British Minefields

The Royal Navy had taken comparatively little interest in mines before the war, except for purely defensive purposes in certain harbours. It had only 4,000 in stock, all of one type which was to prove defective in service. Nevertheless a controlled field of eighteen mines, which could be made live by an operator on shore, was laid across the relatively narrow entrance to the Tay at Broughty Ferry. It was done in too much of a hurry and they had to be raised in March 1915, and twenty-four larger mines were laid in their place, in five lines.[30] The minelaying policy had now been extended and orders were placed for new and much larger mines. Much of the work on the east coast was 'independent' minefields, intended initially to forestall the activities of German minelaying submarines.[31] Later on, they were intended against all kinds of U-boat activity.

The first such field in Scottish waters was off Tod Head, one of several headlands where U-boats were known to linger in search of prey. The mines were laid in June 1915 at a depth of 48 ft to prevent interference with surface shipping, and they were 150 ft apart. Two months later a deep minefield was laid off the Firth of Forth and in October fields were laid near South Carr off Fife Ness and in St Andrews Bay to the north. Plans for further fields off Fife Ness and the Isle of May were vetoed by Admiral Jellicoe, who feared they might interfere with the movements of his ships in the Forth.[32] But after the *Moewe*'s expedition to the Moray Firth, Jellicoe had three deep minefields laid in 1916, at great trouble, in Lybster Bay, Tarbet Ness and Stotfield Head off Lossiemouth. A field was laid across three-quarters of the North Channel between Scotland and Ireland in May 1918, using American cruisers and Clyde puffers based at Lamlash on Arran.[33] However, the long minefield off the east coast of England, the East Coast Barrage, intended to keep U-boats away from the coastal convoy routes, did not extend as far as Scottish waters.

Minelayers came from several sources. At the beginning of the war seven old cruisers had been converted, but they were too slow to reach the desired area under cover of darkness, lay the mines and escape without detection. Other minelayers were converted from fast merchant ships, mostly built by Denny of Dumbarton who had specialised in ferries for many years. The most successful were the *Princess Irene* and *Princess Margaret*, intended to run from Vancouver to Seattle but taken over when almost complete on the outbreak of war. They were oil-fuelled, which was a great advantage in smoke control, had a speed of 20 to 21 knots and could carry up to 500 mines. The *Princess Irene* blew up at Sheerness in 1915.

The *Biarritz* and *Paris* were smaller ships intended as ferries from Dover to Calais. They too were taken over in Denny's before completion but were slightly less successful. They were coal-fired, had too small a radius of action and had to carry the mines on the upper deck, creating stability problems. The *Biarritz* was of 2,700 tons, had a wartime crew of 197 officers and men and a speed of 20–21 knots. She could carry 180 of the older *Elia*-type mine, or 125 of the later H2 type. The *Biarritz* was particularly prolific in Scottish waters, for she helped lay the Firth of Forth and South Carr minefields in 1915–16 and three deep fields in the Moray Firth in 1916.[34]

The Scottish minefields were 'defensive', intended to protect fleet and merchant-shipping movements in local waters. The British also laid 'offensive' minefields close to German waters. Most of the vessels which laid these fields were based in the ports of eastern England, but during 1916–17 the *Abdiel*, formerly a destroyer flotilla leader, was based at Grangemouth in the Forth to lay mines in the Heligoland Bight off the German coast.

The success of the independent minefields was rather limited: only three U-boats were sunk by them in the whole of the war; none in Scottish waters. Their effect, if any, was as a deterrent and a diversion.

The Development of the Hydrophone

Commander C. P. Ryan had an undistinguished early career in the Royal Navy, scraping through various exams and then specialising in wireless telegraphy. He left in 1911 to work for the Marconi Company but returned at the beginning of the war to command the defences at Inchkeith in the Firth of Forth. Unofficially he began experiments by laying microphones on the river bed near the anti-submarine boom, in 5–21 fathoms of water. He was able to detect Beatty's battle cruisers 10 or 12 miles away, and it became clear that his methods might be used to detect submerged submarines.

In February 1915, perhaps at the instigation of Beatty, Ryan was moved to Granton where he used a small hut at the end of the pier and had the drifter *Tarlair* as a guinea-pig. Within a month the first 'hydrophone' station had been set up on Oxcars Island in the firth, to detect enemy submarines. It moved to Inchcolm two months later and further listening stations were set up at Elieness and Cromarty. In July the experimental station transferred to a peninsula at Hawkcraig near Aberdour in Fife. It was close to the waters of Mortimer Deep, which were sealed off at one end by the anti-submarine boom and therefore closed to normal traffic. There were depths of 5 to 21 fathoms and tides of up to 4.5 knots. From the first hut, which overlooked the firth, a small wooden settlement grew up. Ryan enjoyed the enthusiastic support of Beatty over the years and was invited to stay at Aberdour House by Lady Beatty, causing a certain amount of strain in the marriage.[35] Ryan was given a staff of RNVR officers from various backgrounds, including several musicians (one of whom would later conduct the Hallé Orchestra), and civilian scientists from the Board of Inventions and Research. But he needed technicians.

> What holds us all back (at Hawkcraig) is the lack of instrument fitters and workshops. It is a great pity that such men are allowed to enlist. I have to scrape together a staff. We have borrowed one man from Liverpool University, one from Leeds University . . . It is quite exasperating that so much should turn on getting hold of the instrument makers and when they are got it is necessary to fight to keep them.[36]

Hydrophone training moved from Granton to Hawkcraig early in 1916. By the following year, six- to eight-week courses were offered to officers and ratings, generally men who were new to the naval service. The first part of the course was devoted to lectures on the theory of sound. The second stage involved listening to gramophone records through telephones, identifying differences in intensity, pitch and time. For the third stage, trainees listened to real ships and submarines in the nearby waters of Mortimer Deep, learning to distinguish them from fish and currents. Finally, trainees went afloat in a converted drifter, the *Couronne*. In the former fish-hold they put on headphones and listened to the various noises in the water. In all, 2,731 officers and ratings were trained at HMS *Tarlair* at Hawkcraig, by parties visiting the naval bases and by another school along the Fife coast at Elie.[37] More than 10,000 hydrophones were manufactured for shipboard use during the war, mostly by the Auxiliary Patrol, but ultimately the hydrophone afloat was not a success. For it to work, it was not only necessary for one's own ship to stop its engines: all other ships around, perhaps in a convoy, would have to stop as well, and this was not a happy prospect in submarine-infested waters.[38]

Hydrophones were slightly more successful as part of fixed defences at the entrance to a port or estuary. They were laid out in a chain of four to sixteen from a listening station over a distance of up to eighteen miles. Each had a range of three miles in good conditions, half a mile in bad. The operator listened to each station in turn, but it was exhausting and he did only two-hour watches before relief. By the middle of 1918, twenty-one hydrophone stations had been set up, including seven in the Forth and three in the rest of Scotland, at the strategic points of Stanger Head in Scapa Flow, Cromarty and the Mull of Kintyre. They were mainly used to operate controlled minefields, which could be turned on electrically if a U-boat was in the area. Only two submarines were certainly destroyed by such means, including *UB-116* off Stanger Head in October 1916. Two more were probably sunk and another two damaged. Nor could they be regarded as a true deterrent, for the Germans never knew that they were not conventional minefields.[39] However they did give increased confidence to the defenders, and allowed the Forth to be developed as a fully fledged naval base.

The Development of Asdic

In December 1916 it was suggested that sea-lions might be trained to detect submarines. A.B. Wood was sent from Aberdour to Glasgow to meet 'Captain' J. G. Woodward and his 'performing seals and jugging sea-lions'. Wood had a ringside seat at Hengler's Circus on 6 January 1917 and saw 'the wonderful balancing feats of his sea-lions'. Next day it was arranged to do some experiments. The survival of the British Empire might depend on finding ways of detecting U-boats, but at Hengler's Circus the show had to go on. Woodward refused to miss his afternoon performance, so his two sea-lions were to be trained in the mornings at Glasgow Corporation Swimming Baths, in a pool 56 ft long. He was not prepared to risk them in the Alexandra Park open-air pool, 144 ft long, for fear that 'they might play about with me and not come out of the pond just when wanted'. However, the larger pool could be used on Sundays, when there was no performance. The sea-lions were muzzled and live trout put into the pool. The animals were trained to ignore the fish and react to a bell, for which they were rewarded with dead fish. 'Subsequently, realising the futility of chasing the trout, it became more attentive to the bell signals.' Later experiments were conducted off the coast of Wales with a real submarine, but were not a success. It was concluded that the sea-lions were perfectly capable of finding submarines, but much preferred to chase fish. The experiment was abandoned and the animals were allowed to 'return to their legitimate business'.[40]

Meanwhile, more productive work was being done elsewhere on the Clyde. A new system of sending out a signal and listening for its echo had been developed by scientists in France and by the Lancashire Anti-Submarine Committee in the Mersey and the Menai Straits. However, conditions in these areas were not ideal and in 1918 they transferred to the Clyde, initially at Ardrossan, where deeper water was available. In the meantime, the Clyde Anti-Submarine Committee had been set up using scientists from Glasgow University. It took over the Shandon

Hydropathic Hotel on the shores of the Gareloch, originally built in 1852 by Robert Napier, the 'father of Clyde shipbuilding', to house his collection of books, works of art and exotic plants. The Hydropathic allowed instant access to the deep, sheltered and little-used waters of the loch, and some of the Aberdour scientists were transferred there, finding it 'palatial in comparison with the somewhat primitive wooden huts of Hawkcraig and Parkeston Quay'. According to A. B. Wood,

> The establishment was well provided with facilities for recreation. Beside the golf course it had hard tennis courts and two indoor swimming pools, not to mention yachting possibilities on the Gareloch and walking and rock climbing around Arrochar. It might be assumed that all this was not conducive to hard work, but the bracing climate neutralised any tendency to an easy life! In the main building was a splendid dance hall (with sprung floor), a large dining room, a lovely drawing room (which appropriately became the drawing office), and many bedrooms which housed a large proportion of the unmarried members of staff.[41]

The echo-sounder, soon to be known as Asdic for reasons which are not quite certain, made great progress in the area, which became the main anti-submarine research station. A few small ships were fitted out at Parkeston Quay in eastern England in the middle of 1918, but they were too late to have any effect on the war. The Admiralty, however, was now confident that it had solved the problem of detecting submarines.

The K-Boats

In 1917 the Gareloch witnessed a submarine disaster. The boats of the K class were powered by steam engines on the surface, to allow them to keep up with the battlefleet at sea, so that they could act as a submersible attacking force when the enemy was met. *K-13*, the first to be built on the Clyde, was launched in the Fairfield yard at Govan and on 29 January she went down the river for trials. She had a near collision in the narrow channel on the way, and was briefly aground. She completed her speed trials successfully at the Tail of the Bank off Greenock and by mid-afternoon she was ready for her third and final diving trial in the Gareloch. As well as her crew, she carried twenty civilians from Fairfield and elsewhere, including Percy Hillhouse, a professor of naval architecture. As *K-13* reached 20 ft, one of the massive design flaws of the class became apparent. Steam engines were not suitable for submarines, they needed 'too many damned holes' for the condensers and funnels. The boiler room flooded and the boat plunged another 25 ft to the bottom of the loch. Two men managed to escape as she went down and were spotted in the water by a house-maid from Shandon Hydro. She ran indoors to report it, but no one believed her. The two were swept away to their deaths and it was more than an hour before the naval observers in submarine *E-50* on the surface realised that anything was wrong. By that time it was too dark for salvage work. Professor Hillhouse described the situation on board:

> As the air in our submerged prison became more impregnated with carbonic acid, so did our breathing become more and more difficult, and we had to inhale and exhale with painful rapidity. For some the process was only carried out under great pain and difficulty. Many found standing the easiest posture, while our good pilot, Captain Duncan, during almost the whole course of our imprisonment, walked to and fro in the control room as though still in command on the bridge of a surface craft. The great majority, however, were rendered more or less inert and apathetic, and lay down anywhere and everywhere, half asleep, half awake, and breathing stertorously. There were a few berths, and each of these usually had two or three occupants . . .[42]

Petty Officer Moth was less scientific. 'What a bloody rotten way to die,' he said.[43]

During the night salvage vessels and divers arrived at the loch and contact was established with the survivors by Morse code. The captain and a visitor, captain of *K-14,* escaped from the conning tower of the submarine, but the latter was drowned on the way out. More than 24 hours after the sinking divers managed to connect an air line to the submarine, as the men were on the verge of suffocation. Eventually the bows were floated off the bottom and forty-six men got out after two and a half days underwater. Thirty-three men died. The submarine was salvaged and renamed *K-22.*

Among the recommendations of the court of inquiry was that no more submarines were to be numbered 13. But the fortunes of the K class did not improve, perhaps because one the flotillas was numbered 13 instead. Exactly a year after the *K-13* disaster, nine K-boats exercised off the Isle of May in the Firth of Forth, forming a line with the ships of the Second Battlecruiser Squadron and the Fifth Battle Squadron. During a fleet turn, *K-14* had to avoid some trawler minesweepers which were not part of the exercise, and then her helm jammed. She collided with *K-22* (the salvaged *K-13*). In the mist the battlecruiser *Inflexible* hit *K-22* again, but still she did not sink. Meanwhile the cruiser *Ithuriel*, leading the 13th Submarine Flotilla, turned back with three K-boats to assist. One of them, *K-12*, was narrowly missed by the battlecruiser *Australia* but another, *K-17*, was hit by the cruiser *Fearless*, leader of the 12th Submarine Flotilla, and sank with the loss of all but eight of her crew. In the confusion *K-4* collided with *K-6* and the former sank with all hands. The K-boats, in addition to their other faults, were unmanoeuvrable on the surface and their low silhouette could not be seen from a surface ship in poor visibility. They continued to be accident-prone until the last of them was scrapped in 1932.[44]

Air Patrols

From early in 1915 it was realised that patrols by aircraft, seaplanes and airships could do much to reduce the U-boat menace. It was relatively easy to spot the wake of a submarine periscope from the air, especially in calm water. The aircraft could then attack with bombs or machine guns, or radio to patrol vessels to attack. More importantly, the presence of aircraft acted as a deterrent to U-boat commanders, who rarely attacked when aircraft of any kind were present.

In the case of convoy escort, the main type of aircraft was the airship, which had a much longer endurance than an aeroplane of the time. The British failed to keep up with German developments in rigid airships before and during the war, but instead they produced much simpler and slower non-rigid types, known as 'blimps'. The speed of less than 60 mph was not necessarily a disadvantage when keeping in touch with a convoy, though it was rarely able to attack a U-boat before it submerged. The SS or Sea Scout airships used at the beginning of the war could stay in the air for up to 24 hours at low speed, though this posed a great strain on the crew of two, sitting in open cockpits. The final anti-submarine airships of the war, the NS or North Sea Class, were designed for a normal endurance of 24 hours, but one later set the world record by staying in the air for more than 100 hours.[45] They had a crew of ten, comprising two pilots, helmsmen, engineers, radio operators and gunners, with half on watch at any given moment. They had facilities for cooking and sleeping. Twelve were built and they entered service in July 1917. Most were based at East Fortune in East Lothian.

That station, founded in August 1916, was the largest in Scotland, and one of its three hangars was a double one which could hold two airships side by side, one of only three in Britain. East Fortune mounted patrols out to sea and along the coast as far south as Middlesbrough, where the airship often sighted the patrols from stations on the River Humber. The other station on the east coast of Scotland was Longside in Aberdeenshire. It too had three hangars, and sent patrols far to the north, and to the south to meet those from East Fortune. On the west coast the main station was at Luce Bay near Stranraer, founded in July 1915, with a single hangar, patrolling the North Channel and the Hebrides. Inchinnan, on the south bank of the Clyde near the modern Glasgow Airport, was mainly used for rigid airships copied from the German Zeppelins. Beardmores, the Scottish shipbuilding and engineering giant of the day, built the *R-34* there. It was not completed until after the war, when it left East Fortune to fly direct to New York and then back to Britain, making the first double crossing of the Atlantic by air.

The navy also used seaplanes on anti-submarine patrols, though these were less common in Scotland because of the greater distances involved. The only full seaplane station in Scotland, apart from those directly connected with the naval bases, was the one at Dundee Stannergate, founded in 1912.

Though German Zeppelins raided Edinburgh and Leith on 2 April 1917, airships saw much less action in Scotland than in the south, where many enemy ships were shot down during raids and several British ones were lost in action or by accident. The airships from Longside and East Fortune seem to have been effective in preventing attacks on the East Coast Convoys. According to the *Technical History*,

> Airships were in company with convoys during dark as well as daylight hours, and were undoubtedly very valuable scouts. During the summer months of 1918 continuous air patrols of airships and seaplanes were (weather permitting) maintained throughout the whole passage of the convoys. The presence of aircraft has not always prevented successful attacks being made by enemy submarines, but, the attack being made, the submarine's subsequent movements have been followed and direct action taken by the aircraft, which afterwards directed the surface craft in their depth-charge offensive.[46]

Interestingly enough, the simple kite balloon was also favoured by some officers. This was towed behind a ship and carried an observer. According to some reports they were just as effective as airships in scaring away U-boats, and even unmanned ones could act as a deterrent. Kite balloon stations were set up at Houton Bay in Orkney and at North Queensferry in the Forth.

The Scandinavian Convoys

In the spring of 1917, opinion at the Admiralty was still against convoy as a means of defence of shipping, though in fact it had been instituted for the coal trade from the south of England to France in February. Meanwhile the Scandinavian trade posed special problems. It was carried out with neutral countries and largely with neutral ships. There was a risk that the most important participants, the Norwegians, would refuse to let their ships sail unless adequate naval protection was visibly provided. At first Britain tried to force their hand by detaining Scandinavian ships in port until others were sent out with suitable cargoes. Later in 1917 a tonnage agreement with Norway allowed the British government to requisition 1.25 million tons of Norwegian shipping and to have full facilities for transit of goods to Russia. This also allowed the British to continue to import iron ore, sulphur, pyrites, ball bearings and timber from Norway and tended to deny these goods to the Germans. In return the Norwegians were to be guaranteed a fixed amount of British coal. In the circumstances, some kind of naval protection was necessary.[47]

In November 1916 a system of 'protected sailings' was instituted for the Norwegian trade. Ships would be escorted part of the way, but would use the cover of darkness as far as possible. On 30 March 1917 a conference of senior naval officers was held at Longhope Sound, Orkney, attended by the new Naval Vice-consul at Bergen, Captain Arthur Halsey. It was agreed that a system of convoy should be set up with not more than six merchant ships escorted by two trawlers and two whalers. Less than a week later another conference decided that further convoys should protect the trade from Lerwick as far south as the English port of Blyth which were bound for Scandinavia. The system was in place by the end of April.

Lerwick became the centre for such convoys. The harbour was protected by booms to the north and south, but large fleets of ships soon began to assemble to await escorts and it was sometimes necessary to moor them in Brei Wick, outside the booms. At the other end, shipping was collected at several appointed rendezvous off the Norwegian coast, under the direction of Captain Halsey in Bergen.

As it happened, it was surface ships which did the greatest damage to the Norwegian convoys. On 17 October 1917 a convoy of twelve merchant ships, escorted by two destroyers and two trawlers, was about fifty-five miles out from Shetland and heading eastward. At four o'clock in the afternoon the destroyer *Strongbow* sighted two German cruisers, the *Brummer* and *Bremse*. They soon opened fire and did great damage to the destroyers. Lieutenant James of the *Strongbow* was one of the survivors:

> Captain then sent me down to throw the Confidential Books in the W/T [wireless telegraphy] office overboard. I found the operator killed and the W/T office smashed to pieces. Went back to bridge. Found Quarter-master killed and bridge and steering gear wrecked, and Captain badly wounded. Captain ordered me to go to his cabin and throw the steel chests overboard. I threw the small one overboard, and got the Gunner to assist me to throw the big one overboard. Going forward again, I noticed the after gun had fired all rounds but two, Sub-Lieutenant, trainer and gunlayer being the only three present, the Sub-Lieutenant loading. On my way forward, I found midship gun out of action. Gunner had just fired one torpedo with extreme angle on the tube and foremost tube was reported out of action, the LTO asked me if he should fire another torpedo, I told him to do so. He then fixed [fired?] second torpedo.[48]

The *Mary Rose* had already sunk with all hands The *Strongbow* stayed afloat until next morning and the trawlers picked up the survivors. Meanwhile the merchant ships dispersed, but nine of them were picked off by the cruisers' gunfire. The *Brummer* and *Bremse* returned victorious to Germany without interference from the British fleet, although Beatty had been warned by intelligence reports and eighty cruisers and destroyers had been spread out on patrol. There was severe criticism in the national press and the *Daily Mail*, campaigning against Jellicoe at the Admiralty, hysterically demanded an inquiry. The government considered prosecuting the newspaper under the Defence of the Realm Regulations but decided it would be too difficult to get a conviction.[49]

On 12 December another eastbound convoy was forty miles from the Norwegian coast when four German destroyers attacked. One of the escorting British destroyers was sunk, the other severely damaged and all six ships of the convoy were sunk. Again two British cruisers were in the area, but not close enough to have any effect. Jellicoe was already in dispute with the First Lord, Sir Eric Geddes, over his caution and his failure to delegate. On Christmas Eve he was dismissed and replaced by his deputy, Sir Rosslyn Wemyss of Wemyss Castle in Fife, a member of a family which had provided naval officers since 1745. The Board of Admiralty was now almost as Scottish as it had been at the end of the last great war in 1815. The First Lord himself had been born in India to Scottish parents and educated in Edinburgh. Admiral Sir Alexander Duff, Assistant Chief of Naval Staff and former Director of the Anti-Submarine Division, was another member of a famous Aberdeenshire naval family. Sir George Hope was a relative of the Hopetoun family.

Meanwhile the Scandinavian convoy system was proving unsatisfactory in other ways.

> On the East Coast, convoys were late in their arrival off Lerwick and, on account of darkness and other reasons, could not be taken over by new escorts without entering harbour; between Lerwick and the Norwegian coast arrangements were continually breaking down – slow convoys could not sail and escort forces arrived too late – and ships returned to Bergen for further instructions; westbound convoys were scattered after leaving the coast and straggled into Lerwick hours overdue, instead of proceeding own the east coast with a new escort; eastbound convoys were prevented from leaving Lerwick Harbour through either bad weather or mining activity.[50]

In January 1918 a conference was held at Rosyth and it was decided to set up a new system, in which convoys would assemble at the Fife coal port of Methil and bypass Lerwick on the way to Bergen. The Scandinavian convoy system was now just one part of a great chain stretching over the seas, for in April 1917, partly inspired by the success of these and other local convoys, the Admiralty had reluctantly taken steps to make convoy the standard means of defence against U-boats. A fairly sophisticated organisation was set up in Methil, headed by a naval captain with a staff of twenty officers, including four working on intelligence, and twenty-six ratings plus two girl messengers and three boy scouts. A convoy office was set up at the head of No. 1 Dock. Merchant ships anchored in an allotted area and a small fleet of drifters collected the masters before the convoy was due to leave, to take them to a conference ashore. Detailed instructions were issued on the route to be taken, the escort, the position of each ship in the convoy and any special signals. Convoys were now larger and better escorted than when the system began. OZ65, which left on 4 November 1918, had thirty-eight merchant ships with an escort of one armed boarding steamer, two destroyers and nine trawlers. At sea the merchant ships were to sail in eight columns of four or five ships each.[51]

Under the old system up to January 1918, 1,617 ships were convoyed to the east and 1,806 to the west. Forty were lost, a rate of 1.16 per cent, which compares very well with 7 per cent among ships in the south-western approaches in March to June 1917.[52] Under the new system more than 16,000 voyages were made between the Humber and Methil and only 35 ships were lost: a rate of 0.22 per cent. Between Methil and Norway 4,250 voyages were made under the new system and 15 ships were lost, a rate of 0.35 per cent.[53]

The Northern Barrage

Since August 1917 the Admiralty had been looking at ways to block the passage of U-boats to the outside world. The minefields in the Heligoland Bight and elsewhere took their toll, but they were not impassable. To be completely successful, a line of mines would have to end close to the shore, but it was too dangerous to lay them in such proximity to enemy territory, so a mine barrage would have to have each end in friendly or neutral coasts. The first idea was to lay one between the Dutch and Danish coasts, but both these countries were subject to much pressure from Germany and could not be guaranteed to protect their territorial waters. In any case, it would not prevent submarines escaping from the Baltic. A line from southern England to Norway was considered, but it would be difficult to lay and protect so close to enemy territory and would tend to restrict British shipping movements unless there were several gaps in it. Another proposal was to run from Aberdeen to the Norwegian port of Egersund. Norway, though neutral, was much more likely to support British rather than German interests, and at that time it was thought likely she might come into the war in protest at the U-boat campaign. The line was practically the shortest possible across the northern North Sea, it was far enough away from enemy territory to be protected, and would not restrict the movements of the Grand Fleet once it moved to Rosyth. But it would require a vast number of mines, and only the industrial resources of the United States, having recently entered the war against Germany, could provide them.

The initial plan was to have three areas. The central one, Area A, was the largest and was to have both deep and shallow mines, so it would be a danger to submarines as well as surface ships. It would be declared as a minefield. The western area, B, was close to the British coast and was would be about eighty miles wide. It would have only deep mines, for the British were confident in the new hydrophones which were under development and felt they could patrol the area against surfaced submarines. The eastern area, C, extended sixty miles from the Norwegian coast. It too had only deep mines and it was hoped that the Norwegians might co-operate in patrolling it. Neither B or C would be declared as a minefield, and A was planned to look like a self-contained field, leading the U-boats into a trap. The

Americans, sceptical about the hydrophone, would have preferred deep and shallow mines in all areas.[54]

In December the plan was changed. The line was now to run from just east of the Orkneys to approach the Norwegian coast between Bergen and Utsire. This was slightly shorter, 240 miles against 260, and further from the threat of enemy surface craft. It would allow the Grand Fleet to remain in Scapa Flow, rather than being forced to move to Rosyth prematurely. It would encroach less on the fishing areas and it would benefit from the long hours of northern daylight in the summer months. It would not interfere with the Scandinavian convoys, which were still routed from Lerwick to Bergen. This scheme would leave the Pentland Firth open, but the British authorities were convinced that its dangerous currents made it impassable to U-boats.[55]

The Americans developed a new mine specially for the barrage, with an antenna which would cause it to explode when a submarine passed anywhere along the length of its 140-ft cable. The British were critical of this, perhaps rightly, and suggested that a submarine would not be damaged by an explosion so far away. In January 1918 it was agreed that the Americans would mine the largest area, A, while the British would be responsible for B and C. There would be three rows of mines at each level, 150 ft apart horizontally. In Area A they would be from 8 to 200 feet below the surface, in the others they would be at least 65 ft deep. But in May 1918, the shipboard hydrophone having proved a disappointment, the idea of patrols at each end was abandoned and it was agreed to have shallow mines in Area C, off Norway, to be laid by the Americans.

Grangemouth, already in business as a minelaying base on a small scale, was adapted for the British part of the effort. Six large storehouses, each 300 ft long, were erected between the Eastern Channel and the banks of the River Carron and a railway line passed among them to deliver the mines. The entrance channel was dredged for 11 ft to 15 ft to allow the passage of large minelayers such as the *Princess Margaret*. The American mines were to be delivered to the west coast and then transported to the east. A depot was set up at Corpach at the western end of the Caledonian Canal. The mines were loaded into motor lighters manned by British naval ratings and taken through the canal. Up to then it had only operated by day, but thirty-two navigation lights were installed and extra staff were taken on to allow night-time operation. At the other end, a mine depot was set up in the Glen-Albyn distillery near Inverness, and 3,000 gallons of whisky were removed. The third base was another distillery at

Dalmore, in the Cromarty Firth, three miles above Invergordon. Mines were landed at Kyle of Lochalsh and transported by means of the Highland Railway. This base, Corpach, Dalmore and Glen-Albyn were all manned by American sailors. The American depots were finished by May 1918, and Grangemouth was in use by then, though not completed until September.[56]

The British minelayers, including the veterans *Paris* and *Princess Margaret*, began work in March, laying the first mine in the south-eastern end of Area B, ten miles off the mainland of Orkney. But soon there was trouble when the sloop *Gaillardia* blew up, probably the result of a German mine, as no British ones had been laid there. The whole area had to be swept before work could recommence, and the sinkers of the British mines were tested in Loch Ness in case they had been responsible. It was decided to proceed with Area C, the furthest from British waters. The American Minelaying Squadron, consisting of two old cruisers and eight converted merchant ships, arrived at the end of May, to begin Area A. They intended to use buoys to mark out the limits of the field and to help with the accuracy of their laying, but these proved unsatisfactory. There was trouble with the antennae of the mines, which had to be shortened to be effective. But by July it was clear that the U-boats were avoiding the area of the declared minefield after two of them had been damaged in it, proving that it was not a bluff. There was evidence that they were now increasingly using Norwegian territorial waters, so further pressure was put on that country to protect her neutrality. Meanwhile work at last started again on Area B, off Orkney, during September. On 26 October the Americans laid 3,760 mines in Area A, 300 ft apart and 60 ft below the surface. Six lines were laid for 19 miles and two lines for a further 35 miles. Then they had to stop due to bad weather.[57]

As it turned out, that was the last minelaying operation, for the war ended soon afterwards. In all the Americans had laid 56,033 mines and the British 13,733.[58] It was a highly creditable effort, making full use of American resources and ingenuity, but its effects remained controversial. Though it claimed the destruction of six U-boats, it is doubtful if the barrage really sealed off the North Sea as intended.[59]

The End of the War

In November 1918, as the German army and navy began to collapse under pressure of the economic blockade and her allies withdrew from the war one by one, Admiral Sir Rosslyn Wemyss was sent to France on behalf of the British government to negotiate an armistice with the

Germans. He took his old friend, Admiral Sir George Hope, the Assistant Chief of Naval Staff. At a famous meeting in a railway carriage in the Forest of Compiègne, they haggled with the German delegation as well as with Maréchal Foch of France, who was 'very ignorant about all matters Naval',[60] but Wemyss insisted that no cease-fire could be agreed unless the bulk of the German Navy was handed over.

Under the terms of the Armistice which ended the war on 11 November, the German High Seas Fleet was obliged to surrender all its submarines. Seventy-four surface ships, including the ten best battleships and all six battlecruisers, were to be interned with German crews on board. Ten days later they rendezvoused fifty miles east of the Isle of May to steam into the Forth. The German guns were de-ammunitioned, the breech blocks were removed and they were trained rigidly fore and aft. Formed in a single line with the battlecruisers leading, they steamed into the Forth behind the British light cruiser *Cardiff*. They were met by a total of 370 allied warships, including representatives of the French and American navies, in two lines. It was the greatest concentration of sea power the world had yet seen, and in terms of gun-power alone it was the largest ever. The allied guns were not loaded but the ammunition was ready and the ships' directors were constantly trained on the former enemy. The Germans anchored outside Inchkeith and Admiral Beatty addressed his men: 'They are now going to be taken away, and placed under the guardianship of the Grand Fleet at Scapa; there they will enjoy (laughter) as we have enjoyed, the pleasures of Scapa. (laughter)'. Then he made the signal which in effect ended the naval war. 'The German flag will be hauled down at sunset today, Thursday, and will not be hoisted again without permission.'[61]

Chapter 11

Lean Years

The High Seas Fleet at Scapa

On their arrival in the Firth of Forth on 21 November 1918, the Germans of the High Seas Fleet soon became aware of the many indignities they were going to have to suffer. Their ships, already disarmed, were searched by parties of British officers and ratings, who even turned over the coal in the bunkers to make sure there was no ammunition hidden there. According to German accounts, the British could not help admiring the workmanship of the German equipment.[1] The fleet attracted comparatively little attention from the shore, perhaps because there was thick fog in the firth for most of their short stay; but occasionally steamers went out to look at it and at least one woman shook her fist at the Germans.

The High Seas Fleet had expected to be interned in a neutral port, but they were informed that none was available and that they were to go to Scapa – evidence suggests that the British government had done very little to find a neutral haven. The torpedo boats went north on 22 November, the battlecruisers two days later and the battleships on the following days. The Fourth Squadron, which sailed at noon on the 25th, was escorted by the *Emperor of India* sailing ahead, with two more British battleships on each side. At Scapa a British pilot came on board each ship and the larger ones were anchored in a semicircle round the tiny island of Cava, with the destroyers in Fara Sound. Because communication between ships was severely restricted by the British, the destroyers had little contact with the main fleet.

Admiral von Reuter, in command of the 'Internment Formation' for most of its stay in Orkney, records his impressions of Scapa Flow:

> The islands are mountainous and rocky. The lower parts of the land showed signs of rude cultivation, trees and shrubs were nowhere to be seen; most if it was covered with heather, out of which stuck the naked

rock. Several fishing villages were just in sight on land in the far distance – apart from which here and there on the rocky coast stood unfriendly-looking farm-houses built of the grey local stone. Several military works, such as barracks, aeroplane sheds or balloon hangars, relieved the monotonous sameness; in ugliness they would beat even ours at a bet.[2]

Yet the beauty of the area did not escape his notice.

And yet this forgotten corner of the earth had its attractions. Its beauty – not by day during glaring sunlight or when the rain-clouds painted everything grey on grey, but in the evening or by night. Then it was that the Northern Lights would cast their rays like searchlights over the clouds and light them to a yellow hue, then again pour themselves over the whole firmament in a single sea of fire.[3]

The German experience of Scapa was worse than the British. They suffered the gloom of imprisonment, without feeling that they had been really defeated. The officers found their authority undermined by the Sailors' Councils which operated on most ships. Communication between ships was forbidden, and the German vessels were designed for short passages, not for extended periods of living on board. The men were effectively imprisoned in conditions which were none too liberal. There was no dentist in the fleet and men who suffered from tooth decay were sent home. They were not allowed ashore in any circumstances, even for the funeral of a comrade. Food had to be sent out from Germany, which was still starving, as the blockade had not been lifted.

Life slowly settled down to some kind of routine as the officers and men learned to endure a long stay. In the torpedo boats and destroyers things tended to be less formal and there was more trust between officers and men. In the largest ships the authority of the Soldiers' Councils was supreme at the start of the internment, mitigated by the fact that only the officers had the technical skill to run and navigate the ship, and only they were recognised in negotiations with the British, who had good reasons to isolate their own crews from revolutionary influences. Reuter's flagship, the *Freidrich der Grosse*, was the most revolutionary ship of all, described by the admiral as 'a madhouse'. The Germans followed the news from home, usually several days late, and officers and men reacted differently to revolution and counter-revolution. When the extreme-left Spartacist Revolt was crushed in January with the execution of its leaders, the Soldiers' Councils organised a wake at which great quantities of liquor were consumed, and some of the officers had to hide. But the sailors of the destroyers soon voted overwhelmingly to support the new, moderate Social-Democrat government, providing some kind of structure of authority. On 24 March von Reuter at last escaped from the revolutionaries of the *Freidrich der Grosse* and transferred his flag to the cruiser *Emden*, where the atmosphere was very different.

The German crews were gradually reduced in numbers over the months. They started their internment with 200 men on a battlecruiser (out of a normal complement of up to 1,200) down to 20 on a destroyer. In April 1919 it was agreed to reduce the battlecruisers by 75 men, and the destroyers to a level to be decided by the commanders of the flotillas. By mid-June they were reduced to 75 in a battlecruiser, 60 in a battleship and 30 in a light cruiser. The destroyers, semi-independent under Commander Herman Cordes, had about 400 men between 50 ships. On 17 June, three days before midsummer, 2,700 men left Scapa Flow for Germany in the transports *Badenia* and *Schleswig*.

Clearing the Minefields

Meanwhile the allies began clearing the minefields left by the war, both friendly and enemy. The observation fields were no problem, for they could be detonated by pushing a button and the lines of mines at Houton Head, Hoxa, Mortimer Deep and Inchmickery were detonated for experimental purposes during February 1919, though two mines at Inchmickery failed to explode. The Cromarty field was blown up in April and all gear was removed by the middle of May.[4] The EC fields were lifted; the mines were made safe and then removed one by one. Meanwhile the Germans were given responsibility for clearing their own minefields, and their detailed positions were published so that they could be avoided until this was done. No. 595 in the Firth of Clyde, for example, was identified by its position at 55 degrees 44.6' north, 4 degrees 58.7' west, between Cumbrae and Bute, with mines running at 17 degrees, 50 degrees, 57 degrees, 315 degrees and 324 degrees from that point.[5]

The Northern Barrage was a far bigger problem, and that was left to the US Navy, operating mainly from Scapa Flow and Inverness. They chartered two wooden sailing ships in December 1918, but found that when mines exploded nearby their planks tended to spring. Steel vessels were then acquired, but were difficult to navigate with sufficient accuracy due to deviation of the compass. Eventually the force was built up and by March 1919 there were twelve minesweepers.

Since the Americans had no need to stay on board in case of a sudden wartime emergency, they spent considerable time ashore between sweeps and got to know the people of Orkney quite well. They built huts ashore near Kirkwall, held many dances and several charitable organisations became involved with their welfare.

The US Navy developed many new techniques, often more applicable to peacetime sweeping of one's own mines in known positions. For example, they worked faster by going along the length of a line of mines rather than across it. But sweeping remained a dangerous activity, especially from 'counter-mining', or the explosion of another mine close to the one which was being swept. The worst casualty was the trawler *Richard Buckley*, which sank with the loss of her captain and six crew members. In all, thirteen Americans were killed in accidents ashore and afloat. The last mine was swept on 30 September 1919 and the American ships headed for home the next day.[6]

The End of the High Seas Fleet

Ever since the first suggestion of internment, Admiral von Reuter had been considering the possibilities of scuttling the fleet to save the honour of the German Navy. This was the force which, on the eve of national defeat, had considered the possibility of a 'death ride' into battle against a superior enemy, and was only stopped by a mutiny among the crews, who did not share the officers' sense of honour. Reuter always claimed that he had no orders from Germany to scuttle the fleet, and no real evidence has ever been found to the contrary.

On 17 June Reuter issued his secret orders in preparation for scuttling:

> The following preparatory measures are to be adopted: all internal doors and hatches, such as gangway doors, bunker doors, doors of fore-and-aft and transverse bulkheads, hatch companionways, ventilators, portholes etc, to be kept open permanently; according to the judgement of the captains, the following steps can be taken: necessary measures to ensure the swift opening of torpedo tubes, the opening of a condenser, the opening of vents and sluices for flooding (except the latter) etc.

A boat was to be ready to take the crew off and a secret signal – 'Paragraph 11. Confirm' – was to be sent if the Admiral decided that scuttling was necessary. This would be done if it was feared that the British were likely to seize the ships.[7]

The Armistice of 11 November 1918 expired formally on 21 June and no one seems to have told Reuter that it had been extended for another two days. As far as he knew, the war was about to be resumed and his duty was to prevent his ships from falling into the hands of the enemy.

On the morning of the 21st the ships of the British First Battle Squadron, under Vice-Admiral Sir Sydney Fremantle, left the Flow for exercises, leaving behind two destroyers as guardships, along with depot ships and the numerous drifters and trawlers which were always on hand when the fleet was using the Flow as a base. Reuter knew that his chance had come. He put on his full dress uniform and went onto the bridge of the *Emden* to see a fine midsummer morning. After ten he signalled for all his ships to look out for further signals. At 10.30 he hoisted 'Paragraph 11. Confirm'.

In most ships this was the first the crews had heard of the plans to scuttle, though in at least two ships they had guessed that something was afoot. The order was received with jubilation: the first real unity in the German Navy since the outbreak of mutiny in the previous November. Lieutenant Freidrich Ruge describes the scene in the destroyers:

> The strange feeling that the great moment had come did not last long because there was a lot to do. The flotilla commander briefly communicated the order to scuttle the boats to the officers and crew near him. Then we all went to our stations and what followed went according to plan.
>
> The technical personnel opened the valves and the covers of the condensers and smashed the pipes which had been previously earmarked. The sailors hoisted the ensign, the commanding officer's pennant and pennant 'Z'. Then they opened the hold-covers, the cabin doors and portholes, immobilised the anchor capstan and threw all the equipment overboard which might serve to free the boat from the buoy. Apart from the cutter, they launched life rafts for all emergencies. Those who had finished their work packed their things and got ready to disembark.
>
> In the meantime, crews came over from the unmanned boats. They had lowered their cutters, which were not otherwise used, because it was too difficult to haul them in again without steam. There, too, everything seemed to be going according to plan.[8]

The *Hindenburg* went down on an even keel because her captain wanted to make sure that her crew could disembark safely. Reuter's former flagship, a great battleship of 24,000 tons, 564 ft long, behaved differently.

Shortly after 12 o'clock the *Frederick the Great* took up more and more of a list while steadily sinking deeper, her boats were already lowered and lay off aft – now the loud and vigorous tones of single strokes of the ship's bell sounded across the water, the signal for 'Abandon Ship'. We saw the crew man the boats and shove off. *Frederick the Great* heeled more over on her side, torrents of water poured into her through her opened ports – then, in a few minutes, she capsizes and sinks into the depths, the air expelled through the funnels throwing up two spouts of water – then all is quiet, small fragments of wreckage float in the empty berth. The time is sixteen minutes past twelve.[9]

Ironically Reuter's flagship, the *Emden*, was not sunk. Two British drifters and a water-boat were alongside when the scuttling started and their crews managed to keep her afloat until a destroyer arrived to tow her into shallow water.

A party of local schoolchildren, on a day trip round the harbour, watched in amazement. One of the adults described the scene:

Some went down with their sterns almost vertical above the water, others listed to port or starboard with vast clouds of steam and rivers of oil pouring out of their vents and bubbling to the surface after the ships had reached the bottom, and there was the roaring of escaping steam and the shouts of thousands of sailors as they made off in the boats.

From the shore, many Orcadians noticed that something was happening and came out to watch. The guard destroyers radioed to Fremantle's squadron at 13,00 and they suspended the exercises and hurried back to the Flow. Some of the crews of the drifters showed signs of panic and opened fire on the unarmed Germans in the boats. 'A drifter was towing two or three lifeboats full of German sailors. One of them got up with a knife in his hand and tried to cut his boat free of the towrope. A Royal Marine raised his rifle and shot him.'[10] Nine men were killed in this way and buried on Orkney. Since the war was technically not over until the Treaty of Versailles was signed on the 24th, these were the last of the eight and a half million military casualties of the Great War.

Thus the High Seas Fleet sank in silence, except for small arms fire, not amidst the noise of gunfire of a great fleet battle as its enemies had hoped and predicted. It was a marvellous creation of naval architecture, engineering, seamanship and administration, but in the end its purpose was never fulfilled, either as a deterrent or as a fighting force.

It contributed to the causes of the First World War, but was not strong enough to win it.

Twenty-two of the German ships failed to scuttle themselves, or were rescued and beached by British forces; but the pride of the German Navy had sunk to the bottom. Von Reuter was taken on board Fremantle's flagship, the *Revenge*, and harangued on the quarterdeck in front of an armed guard. 'Admiral von Reuter, I cannot permit you and your officers to leave naval custody without expressing to you my sense of the manner in which you have violated common honour and the honourable traditions of seamen of all nations.'[11] But von Reuter's mind was at peace and he felt that his duty was done. The officers and men were taken south by train and von Reuter enjoyed the view of trees and hills on the way to Perth. He was held at Donington Hall in Derbyshire until January 1920 and was one of the last German prisoners of war to be released. He went home to a hero's welcome.

Perhaps it was not such a disaster for the former allies, who were already beginning to quarrel over the allocation of the surrendered ships. Arrangements were soon made to salvage them, as scrap iron rather than as fighting ships. In 1924 the firm of Cox and Danks bought twenty-eight of them. They were raised one by one and towed south to the Forth, to be broken up in the former naval dockyard at Rosyth. The largest, the 28,000-ton battlecruiser *Hindenburg*, proved the greatest challenge. It was at the third attempt, in 1930, that she was finally raised. The last ship, the *Derfflinger*, sister to the *Hindenburg*, was not raised until 1939 and lay upside down for the whole of the Second World War. Eleven ships, including three battleships, remain on the bottom of the Flow. The presence of the scuttled fleet, combined with the under-used naval facilities at Rosyth and elsewhere, gave a great boost to the Scottish shipbreaking industry, which was to remain important until the 1970s.

The Closure of Bases

On 6 November 1918, less than a week before the end of the war, an Admiralty committee reported on what was to be done about the numerous naval bases which had been opened or extended during the war. It did not look at the dockyards like Rosyth and Portsmouth, but at the lesser facilities. Scapa Flow, it agreed, 'occupies a position of considerable strategic importance. It possesses important natural defences against attack by Submarines or Torpedo Craft, and the strong tides outside the Islands make it most difficult to mine the approaches. The anchorage space is practically unlimited, and the high land surrounding it renders direct bombardment impossible.' Permanent breakwaters in the sounds were recommended as 'the only certain means of defence'.

There were twenty-nine other bases in Scotland, all hurriedly commissioned during the war. Invergordon (as the Cromarty Firth base was now commonly known) was to be retained while urgent repairs were completed. Granton was to be used for the demobilisation of the Auxiliary Patrol, then to 'revert to its pre-war status'. Grangemouth, however, was to be retained, as a base for minelaying. Hawkcraig was to remain in service until it was decided what to do about hydrophone training. The former distillery at Dalmore was to be acquired permanently as another minelaying base. Work had started on dredging channels into Inverkeithing as a new submarine base, and that work was to continue for now. A small refuelling facility had been created at Ardrossan and that was to be retained. Port Edgar on the Forth was to be kept on as a port in which 'the Admiralty have many interests . . . chief of which is its use for the Destroyer base . . . Torpedo and paravane storage is also provided for.'

Eleven other bases were to be kept on until their work was completed. Stornoway, Lerwick, Kirkwall, Cromarty (town), Peterhead, Troon and Oban were to be used for minesweeping operations. Inverness, Corpach and Lochalsh were to remain with the US Navy while they cleared the Northern Barrage. Aberdeen was to be used for the demobilisation of fishing craft of the Auxiliary Patrol. Nine bases – Swarback Minns in Shetland, Stromness on Orkney, Wick, Dundee, Kirkcaldy, North Queensferry, Burntisland, Loch Ewe and Lamlash – were to be decommissioned right away. These recommendations were accepted by the Admiralty a month after the Armistice.[12]

By July 1920 the future role of Scapa Flow had become clearer. It was decided to close it as a war anchorage, but maintain it as a fleet exercising area. Defences such as guns, hydrophones and searchlights were to be removed. Boom defence gear went into store. Oil tanks had been constructed at Lyness and these were to be kept for storage, but not for the supply of the fleet in peacetime. Canteens and lookout huts were placed under caretakers and Scapa was to revert largely to its pre-war existence, visited only occasionally by the Grand Fleet, though rather more often than in the past.[13] This left the thorny question of what to do about the sounds which were protected by blockships. Far from getting resources to block them permanently, the navy was obliged by local pressure to open some of them up to shipping again.

Running Down Rosyth

Four days after the Armistice in 1918, the Admiralty returned to an issue which had been first raised fifteen years before – should Rosyth become a manning port? The Director of Dockyards commented that 'If it is to become a manning port, I think it should have its own Depot and its own Gunnery, Torpedo and Signal Schools, and a training school for Engine-room ratings.' It would 'probably be particularly attractive to Scotchmen, and would encourage Scotch recruiting.' The naval staff commented, '. . . the accommodation at the three home ports will suffice for the immediate future.' The First Sea Lord, Wemyss, had divided loyalties with his castle on the Fife coast. 'This proposition can only be justified on the ground of *General*, as opposed to Naval policy, i.e., There can be no doubt that the Navy, at any rate at present, can do without it. Against this, there is the question of desirability from recruiting and Scotch point of view, as the Home port for Scotsmen now has to be Chatham or Portsmouth.' Sir Eric Geddes, the First Lord, settled the matter with a terse note: 'No case for additional manning port and consequently expense.'[14]

The post-war navy was in a very different environment from the days of Fisher and the Dreadnought programme. In the past, the public had demonstrated in the streets demanding more battleships; now, the Admiralty had to fight hard to justify their very existence, after they had seemingly failed to bring decisive victory, and were threatened by aircraft and submarines. There was no clear enemy in western Europe, so the North Sea was no longer a potential battle-ground. Instead, the navy looked at the possibility of a war with America, though it would be unpopular and could not be sustained for long. Japan now began to emerge as a threat in the Far East, and naval strategists hoped and expected that it would only become real when there was no danger in Europe. It was decided to construct a great naval base at Singapore in answer to this. There was no alliance with France, so the Mediterranean, the vital trade route to India and empire, had to be protected. A large fleet was based in Malta and it enjoyed something of a golden age, with regular visits to ports like Cannes, Nice and Monaco, or 'Hands, knees and boomps-a-daisy' as the lower deck called them. It was a return to the pre-1905 navy, with many ships on overseas stations.

There was a real threat of an arms race with the United States in 1920. At the Washington Conference in 1922 all the major naval powers – Britain, the US, France, Japan and Italy – agreed to limit capital ship construction. Britain was to have parity with the United

States in capital ships at 525,000 tons. Older ships were scrapped, so by 1922 the Royal Navy had only twenty-eight post-Dreadnought battleships and battlecruisers, compared with forty-eight in 1918. Apart from the *Rodney* and *Nelson*, which were completed in 1927 as the largest battleships in the navy so far, new construction concentrated on cruisers and smaller ships. The pressure for large dry docks was less intense than in 1914.

Much of the intellectual effort of the navy was devoted to refighting the Battle of Jutland and debating endlessly whether Beatty would have been more successful than Jellicoe. Beatty spent eight years as First Sea Lord after 1919, during which time he suppressed the Harper Report on the battle, which was highly critical of his own conduct. The heat has been taken out of the argument by the decline of the battleship, but it is significant that the debate still continues in a different form. A major work with something new to say on the battle still appears approximately every ten years.[15]

Above all there was pressure for economy in defence spending. After the horrors of the war, there was a strong pacifist strain in Britain. This was particularly so in Scotland, which had suffered grievous losses among its young men, and where a radical tradition was developing around 'Red Clydeside'. A new service, the Royal Air Force, was a rival for defence funds and undermined the navy's claim to be the sole defender of Britain against invasion. When introducing the Naval Estimates every year, successive First Lords now prided themselves on how much expenditure had been cut; a return to the early Fisher era, before the great Dreadnought race had got up to speed. In 1920 the 'ten-year rule' was imposed. This implied, not unreasonably as it turned out, that no major war was to be expected in the next decade. Unfortunately the rule soon became 'rolling', so that it was extended indefinitely into the future.

The officers of the Royal Navy suffered from this. They had nearly all joined as boys, and had been encouraged to expect a full career for life in an institution which often became their real home, the focus of all their professional and social life. They had joined a pre-war navy which was already inflated by the threat of war, or a wartime fleet which was even larger. They had not realised that under normal peacetime standards, with no clear prospect of war, many of them would have to go. When the cuts came in 1922, naval officers saw it as a great betrayal. It was all the worse because the 'axe' was wielded by Sir Eric Geddes, a former First Lord of the Admiralty, who had once, uniquely, been commissioned as an honorary vice-admiral, and had worn the uniform. Geddes had never been popular at the Admiralty, but the uniform made naval officers regard him as 'one of them' and this seemed like treason. Captain Edward Kennedy, nephew of the man who had found that the natives of Orkney were still in fear of the press gang in 1884, describes his reaction to his own redundancy. 'Arrived in office after lunch to find a large envelope addressed personally. I fear the worst as I find another inside marked Confidential. My service career is finished. All ambitions, all hopes, are in one moment dashed to the ground. I did not truthfully expect it, but as other good people are similarly dealt with, why should I go free? Feel just crushed to pulp.'[16]

In these circumstances, the role of Rosyth came under further scrutiny. It had been designed to handle big ships, but these were much fewer in the new navy. It was on the North Sea, facing only the defeated Germans. In 1921 a committee considered 'the reduction of the establishment of Rosyth Dockyard which may be possible, consistent with carrying out the work of docking such ships as cannot be dealt with in the Southern Yards.' It acknowledged that 'Rosyth is not a popular Yard with Staff and employees from the South.' But the yard was still necessary, especially for docking the 'bulged ships', the five battleships which had been fitted retrospectively with anti-torpedo bulges.[17]

In April 1925 Britain returned to the Gold Standard, guaranteeing that paper currency would be backed by gold. This restricted government spending and further cuts were inevitable. Since the fleet at sea had already been reduced and the temporary wartime bases closed, the permanent dockyards were next. It was clear that at least two of the home dockyards would have to go. In July the Director of Dockyards reported very unfavourably on Rosyth. Its labour costs were double those at Malta, 1.9 times those at Devonport, and one and a half times those at the smaller yard at Sheerness. It had 'no naval roots – the Yard could be closed and the men moved without any great social dislocation'. The Director was much more concerned about which of the other yards to close, for the small yards at Sheerness and Pembroke had towns which were 'off springs [*sic*] of the Yards and would close down with them'. £111,500 would be saved every year by putting Rosyth on a care-and-maintenance basis. There was only one major job in hand there: the conversion of the battlecruiser *Glorious* to an aircraft carrier, and that could be transferred to Devonport when the ship was afloat.[18]

It did not take long for the Admiralty to reach a decision. On 2 September the commanding officer, Coast of Scotland, was warned by telegram that 1,200 men would be discharged, 700 at Rosyth and the rest at Pembroke. The press was told the next day, and there was uproar in Scotland. Dunfermline and Edinburgh Town Councils led the protests and sent deputations to London, while the Trades Union Congress passed a resolution against the closure. The economic effects on the new town of Rosyth were of course severe. It was later reported that the local co-operative society, which had spent £25,000 on a new store at Rosyth, had its annual turnover reduced from £64,000 to £33,000 because of the closure.[19]

There was considerable criticism of the decision at government level and the Admiralty had to defend it. Firstly, it emphasised that 'the Admiralty decision is not to scrap these Dockyards, but to reduce them to a care and maintenance basis, keeping them fully efficient and ready to open at short notice.' The dockyard was irrelevant to any war in the Far East. It was claimed confidently that 'the German Navy is so restricted by the Treaty of Versailles, which prevents her becoming a first-class Naval Power for some years after the outbreak of War, and it is not necessary to consider her in this connection.' War with France, though unlikely, had to be considered. It was expected to take place mainly in the Mediterranean, in the first instance at least.

This was severely criticised at the October meeting of the Committee of Imperial Defence. The Air Minister, Sir Samuel Hoare, commented that other services were trying to move facilities out of range of air attack, but this seemed to be a reversal of that policy. He was backed up by the Chief of Air Staff, Sir Hugh Trenchard, who agreed that French aircraft might reach Rosyth, but only with a light load of bombs and after running the gauntlet of British defences. Beatty pointed out that 'we could turn Rosyth into a Chatham at enormous cost, but at present there was no question of choosing which to keep.' Leopold Amery, a former First Lord of the Admiralty, suggested a long-term policy. Portsmouth, Plymouth and Chatham, it seemed, were 'our great naval centres, and it was impossible to shift them . . . Could we not close down the building and repair work of Chatham and Sheerness with a view to gradually developing Pembroke and Rosyth?' Winston Churchill, now Chancellor of the Exchequer, was sceptical about this.

> The cost of shifting the mechanism and population of a Southern Dockyard (say Chatham) to Rosyth would be enormous, and he would rather spend the money on aircraft for the defence of Chatham . . . He was opposed to upsetting the domestic economy of the Navy by which certain ships were affiliated to certain Southern Ports where the men

had their homes and attachments and which had developed on the lines which were peculiar to and necessary for great Naval Dockyard Ports. This consideration did not apply to Rosyth.

Lord Balfour, a former Prime Minister, had doubts about the Admiralty decision, though he wrote, 'Personally I do not believe there will be any first-class war in the lifetime of the youngest member of the Cabinet.' He dissented from the committee's support for the Admiralty, along with Hoare, Trenchard and Amery.[20]

In December the issue came before Parliament, when the MP for West Fife, William Adamson, raised a motion

> That, in the opinion of this House, the decision to close His Majesty's Dockyards at Rosyth and Pembroke was taken without due regard to the Government's responsibilities to Parliament, to the Municipalities concerned, and to the workmen affected.[21]

Adamson was anxious to placate the pacifist wing of his own party:

> If the Admiralty and the Government think that we have reached the time when we can do without a Navy and without dockyards, I am certain that no part of the United Kingdom will more readily agree than Scotland. We will welcome the time when we can afford to do without navies and without Royal dockyards, but so long as these are essential to the well-being of the United Kingdom then, as we pay our share of the money required for running them, we insist and are entitled to insist on getting our fair share of the money that is spent in running these national departments.

He raised the point, not for the last time in debates about Rosyth, that the closure would 'strengthen the rapidly growing demand for Scottish Home Rule' and suggested that 'It will increase the feeling of injustice as far as Scotland is concerned.' There was a heated debate but the House divided on party lines. The Conservative government had a huge majority and the motion was defeated by 237 votes to 65.[22]

The Admiralty had already begun to consider exactly how much to reduce Rosyth. Repair work on ships was to be transferred to other yards as soon as present jobs were finished. The supply of naval stores to visiting ships and to other depots in Scotland was mostly to go to the southern yards, with only a small transit depot at Rosyth. The torpedo depot was to close. On the other hand, the boom defence depot was to stay, and Rosyth would remain the base for maintenance work for the other Scottish bases and the various fuel depots. Staff would be reduced from 3,164 to 579, including 110 officials and workers who would carry out the actual care and maintenance. The rest would be 'discharged or otherwise disposed of'.[23]

Port Edgar, originally a satellite of Rosyth, was now the main base in the Forth. HMS *Columbine* was home for two reserve destroyer flotillas. A. B. Cunningham, a future First Sea Lord, served there twice in the 1920s. During 1922, he commanded of the Sixth Flotilla, manned with only two-fifths of the full complement. He combined with the captain of the other flotilla at Port Edgar and occasionally they were able to leave half the ships in port with only two or three men each, and take the rest, almost fully manned, on exercises with the Atlantic Fleet at Invergordon. In 1924 he returned to Port Edgar as base commander and lived in the corrugated-iron house reserved for the captain in charge. He had two reception rooms and four bedrooms and lived 'in great comfort' as a bachelor. Already the establishment had been reduced, with only one reserve flotilla and about 400 men. There were occasional visits from the destroyer flotillas of the Atlantic Fleet, but these too became less frequent as there were now only three flotillas – twenty-seven ships – in full commission and most of the maintenance was done in the southern yards. As Cunningham says, 'When the Atlantic Fleet flotillas were away there was little to do.'

Two new battleships, the *Nelson* and *Rodney*, were allowed to be built under the Washington Treaty. At 33,500 tons and carrying nine 16-inch guns, they were the largest so far, and as it turned out, were to be the most heavily armed ships that the Royal Navy ever had. Five new cruisers were also ordered and the seven ships were approaching completion by 1926. They needed 3,200 men between them and that was enough to strain the resources of the navy, which now had fewer than 100,000 men in its reduced circumstances. It was necessary to cut down the peace complements of many ships and to recruit 1,400 extra boys. Since the old training establishments had been reduced since the war, 500 of them were sent to Port Edgar after their initial training, and Cunningham arranged for them to spend as much time as possible at sea with the destroyers.[24] The Port Edgar base lasted until 1929, when naval recruiting was drastically reduced because of an economic crisis.

The Navy and Invergordon

After all the closures, Invergordon became the main Scottish naval base. Most years in the 1920s the Atlantic Fleet (the much reduced successor to the Grand Fleet) made two extended visits, in the spring and in the autumn. Instructor Lieutenant-Commander C. R. Benstead of the *Rodney* waxed lyrical (and went on too long) about its beauties:

And always the hills and the woods were calling to us, offering that escape from routine which serves routine so well. Invergordon in autumn is usually warm and comfortable, as mellow as the heather that spills itself like claret on the hills, but in the spring and early summer, when the young leaves are burgeoning, it is green and crisp and upright, like the bracken that snaps underfoot as you climb . . . Choose, then, a day when the afternoon sun lies warm on the hills. Strike inland from Evanton and follow the valley beyond the Black Rock where, deep in a hundred-foot chasm, a moss-grown cleft so narrow that fallen trunks have bridged it, clear brown water from the Wyvis pours itself foaming white over the boulders and hurries away to sea . . .[25]

Invergordon was just the right size to interest the navy. Scapa Flow was far too remote and was still hated. The Forth, on the other hand, was too heavily populated, with too many interests of its own to take the navy to its heart. Invergordon was small enough to be flattered by the naval presence and its economy was well adapted to take advantage of its stay. The sailors themselves spent a certain amount of money ashore, but often preferred to travel to Inverness. More important were the officers' wives who stayed in hotels or rented houses for part of the year – for 75 per cent of officers were married in the modern navy.[26]

Visitors came from miles around to see the fleet. Ludovic Kennedy, son of a naval captain and later a wartime RNVR officer, describes his first introduction to the navy:

But I have left to the end the most thrilling event of the holiday, and one to which I always looked keenly forward. This was the Navy's annual visit to Invergordon. Early one morning someone in the household would shout out, 'They're here!' and we all ran on to the lawn to see for ourselves. There in line ahead, ten miles away across the Moray Firth, standing out sharply against the high ground of the northern shore, glinting in the morning sun, were the ships of the Home Fleet . . . There were so many that it took them all morning to pass in, and for most of that time, through binoculars and with the naked eye, and with my father at my elbow explaining the function of each type of ship, I watched transfixed.

One year my cup of happiness brimmed over . . . A picket boat from the *Nelson*, its crew holding aloft raised boathooks, and commanded by a young midshipman, came deftly alongside. We embarked, and with a surge of power which left one tingling all over, the boat weaved a path through the crowded waters to where, at the foot of *Nelson*'s gangway, two sailors were waiting to help us out . . . After tea, a sailor was detailed to take me round the ship: to the bridge, the charthouse, the wireless office, the engine room, and I thought I would faint with the beauty and strangeness of it all. I had tears in my eyes as the boat took us away; and as the midshipman saluted for the last time, I thought, 'I want to be you, I want to wear a uniform like yours, I want to command a boat like yours, to belong to a ship like yours, like you to be part and parcel of the Navy.'

But his father, a victim of the Geddes axe, poured cold water on this ambition.[27]

The officers of the navy were fond of their stays in the Cromarty Forth and Benstead wrote that 'Invergordon really belongs to the Navy.'[28] A. B. Cunningham, captain of HMS *Rodney* in 1930, wrote, 'Invergordon in May is always delightful, and on this occasion my wife came up and stayed in a local hotel. We had many a fishing expedition when my duties in the *Rodney* permitted.'[29] According to Admiral Chatfield, 'It was a pleasant enough life for the seamen, three months' strenuous work, fighting efficiency, the training of the new, young personnel, the practice of the others; the pulling regatta, and plenty of sport, fishing, shooting and golf on the Scottish links; and football for the men.'[30] As an engine room artificer, John Gurr represented the more intellectual end of the lower deck and he was sceptical about the facilities offered to the ratings at Invergordon:

> There was not a lot to do ashore except play football – ship versus ship and Department versus Department, the matches always keenly competitive and attracting large gatherings of supporters. Of course, the Canteen and Cinema also attracted the crowds and it was quite hectic at the jetty every night when the Canteen was closed and all the ships' drifters came to pick up their human cargo.[31]

As a junior officer, Anthony Hogg tended to agree. Apart from exercise, 'At Invergordon there were no other attractions.'[32]

As Chatfield implies, the journey to Invergordon involved a great deal of hard work for the crews. According to Benstead, the visits

> offer the Fleet invaluable opportunity, not only for handling ships in the mass, but also for working out those hundred and one problems that arise when opposing sides each have an aim in view which the other seeks to frustrate. And the fleet avails itself to the full. For nowadays fuel is precious. Economy demands that every ton of oil blown through the sprayers in the boiler-rooms shall represent a corresponding increment in the tactical efficiency and experience gained. Therefore, once

the fleet puts to sea, it is never idle; it is always exercising some part of its fighting organisation, if not the whole; and even though that same economy more often than not compels the Fleet to carry out its manoeuvres at the pace of a pedal cyclist, since fuel consumption soars with speed, the opportunity is still there.[33]

Usually the trip was part of large-scale fleet manoeuvres:

> Red and Blue are at war. Red, we learn, lives at Margate and owns Yorkshire, while Blue territory embraces the north of Scotland. A Blue Fleet with a sprained ankle (let us say) is endeavouring to reach the shelter of its base at Invergordon before an avenging Red one can stop it. But the only Red forces immediately available are, though sound on their legs, themselves handicapped with inferior reach and punching power. Two days must elapse before Red can be strong enough to destroy Blue in battle. Till then he must seek to delay him, to damage the other ankle. And Blue, on his side, must take care not to be delayed and to reach Invergordon before it is too late.
>
> It may be that a convoy is thrown in to complicate the scheme still further, and always there is an aircraft carrier that lurks with a sort of maidenly detachment in touch with, but not too compromisingly close to the Fleet during the day, until such time as she finds it necessary to dash in with quite unmaidenly bravado to pick up her homing pilots. But, whatever the scheme and its complications, we know that the one course we may not elect to steer is the one leading straight to Invergordon.[34]

The navy kept its main supply of targets at Invergordon, so that gunnery practice could be carried out in the relatively uncrowded waters of the Moray Firth.

After Invergordon and Scapa, the ships usually dispersed on courtesy visits to ports in Scotland, Northern Ireland or the north of England. In 1927 the *Empress of India* went to Oban where she received 'a great welcome . . . and attracted thousands on board on the two "open" afternoons, proving a godsend to the local boatmen who augmented their earnings considerably during our stay.' After that she went on to Lamlash to rejoin some of the other ships and take part in the fleet regatta.[35]

Yet the fleet still felt that Scotland was alien territory. After commenting on the different banknotes, Benstead remarks of the Scottish press 'They proffer Gorbals when we crave for news of Tooting, and Gorgie instead of Golders Green. In them, too, we daily read of Cowdenbeath, of Motherwell and Partick Thistle, and if we desire a word of the Arsenal we have to search diligently in obscure corners, where, incidentally we may – but only *may* – find a reference to Plymouth's gallant Argyle.'[36]

Discontent on the Lower Deck

The Royal Navy was no stranger to mutiny in the first third of the twentieth century, and several key ones had taken place in Scotland before and during the First World War. In pre-war society, which was racked by industrial strife, suffragette protest and potential army mutiny over the Irish situation, there was serious doubt about whether the armed forces would remain loyal in wartime. This was soon swept aside when the actual outbreak of war seemed to unite all classes. There were some minor mutinies in the Grand Fleet during the war, but the main outbreaks came soon after it ended. On 3 January 1919 the crews of minesweepers at Rosyth, mostly from the Auxiliary Patrol, refused to go to sea in protest at low pay and were awarded a £2 per week bonus.

The biggest single cause of discontent in 1919 was the campaign against the new Soviet regime in Russia. A few seamen had ideological sympathy with what seemed at the time to be a new and hopeful form of government on behalf of the common man. Many more saw the new campaign merely as something to delay their long-awaited demobilisation, or at least a return to peacetime routine. On 10 October the First Destroyer Flotilla was at Rosyth on the way to the Baltic. Ninety men from three ships left against orders and marched towards Edinburgh. Forty-four of them boarded a train at Aberlady and headed for London, where they were stopped by police at Kings Cross station. They went passively to the naval barracks at Chatham.[37]

In 1919 the lower deck was given a substantial pay rise from 1s 8d (8.3p) to 4 shillings (20p) a day for an able seaman, finally catching up with wartime inflation. But in 1925, with the return to the Gold Standard, it was decided that new entrants should be paid one shilling (5p) per day less than those on the 1919 rates throughout their service. Parliament, however, debated the cut and affirmed that the pay of existing men would not be affected; thus the 1919 men came to believe that they were safe for ever. Privately this was affirmed by the Admiralty as late as 1931, when they wrote that there was a 'contractual obligation' to the 1919 men, 'were it not for the Crown's privilege'.[38]

The world was already in a deep depression after the Wall Street Crash of 1929 when a new banking crisis began in May 1931. In order to maintain the value of the pound while remaining on the Gold Standard, the government had to find £120 million of savings in its expenditure and £96 million of that had to come from cuts in spending. All departments had to bear cuts, largely by paying lower wages. The men of the navy on the 1919 pay scale, overpaid compared with the rest of the fleet, seemed like an obvious target. Though the government as a whole decided on the scale of the cuts, it was the Admiralty which chose that particular method of reduction. The outlines of the cuts in all departments were announced in the Chancellor of the Exchequer's budget speech on 10 September and the details, in theory, had already been sent by telegram to the commanders-in-chief of the main fleets.

There were serious flaws in the chain of command. The new National Government had recently taken over from Labour and all the political members of the Admiralty had changed. The First Lord, Austen Chamberlain, had no Admiralty experience and had wanted the Foreign Office. The very experienced Secretary of the Admiralty, Sir Oswyn Murray, was on leave at the time. And the commander-in-chief of the Atlantic Fleet, Admiral Sir Michael Hodges, was ill, though crucial messages were still routed through his flagship *Nelson* rather than the *Hood* in which the second-in-command, Rear Admiral Wilfred Tompkinson, was based.

On 8 September the ships of the Atlantic Fleet left their home ports to sail north. On the way they carried out their usual exercises. *Rodney*, *Warspite* and *Malaya*, with cruisers and destroyers, had to protect a convoy against the attacks of the *Hood*, *Repulse* and *Valiant*. But already the seamen of the lower deck had heard rumours of the cuts and there were signs of discontent in individual ships. On 10 September, while the fleet was at sea, the Admiralty made the official announcement. In the most drastic part of all, the basic pay of an able seaman on the 1919 rates was to be cut from 4 shillings (20p) a day to 3 shillings (15p.). In fact it was rarely as stark as that. Most men in this position were paid a little extra money for good conduct or trade qualifications, and married men over twenty-five had an allowance. Probably the worst aspect of all was the apparent breach of contract, against men who did not have the option to leave the service. If the 1919 pay scales, confirmed in Parliament and defended by the Admiralty, could be thrown aside, what lower deck privilege was safe?

The fleet arrived at Invergordon on Friday, 11 September and the ten biggest ships anchored in two lines. On Sunday the men who went ashore were able to buy newspapers and confirm that their pay had indeed been cut, in what they considered a most unfair way. But the official signal announcing the cuts had not been received by Admiral Tomkinson, so no announcement was made.

The sailors now had three days in Invergordon to digest the news and consider what to do about it. On Saturday and Sunday one watch from each ship, or half the crew, was allowed ashore between 1 p.m. and 8.30 p.m. On Monday the other watch would be allowed ashore after 4.30. Order was kept in the town and the canteen by patrols under officers and petty officers, with each ship taking a turn to provide it: the *Warspite*, for example, on the 13th.

As men from different ships began to congregate in the canteen, discussion soon turned to the cuts and impromptu meetings developed. It was probably during Sunday, the second day after the cuts became common knowledge, that feelings became most intense. For centuries the navy had tried to encourage rivalry between ships' companies, but here it backfired, as men from one ship accused another of being too 'yellow' to do anything.[39] By seven in the evening men were climbing onto tables in different corners of the room and making speeches, suggesting a march on London or a naval strike. One of the leaders to emerge was Able Seaman Len Wincott of the cruiser *Norfolk*, who certainly played a significant part, even if he later tended to exaggerate his role. It was noted that the most passionate speakers were the 'three-badge men', seamen who had served at least thirteen years and were entitled to wear three good-conduct chevrons on their arms. Fearing rowdiness, the patrol officer from the *Warspite* signalled back to the ship for extra men. But on board, few men could be found when they were needed and the commander had to muster the whole crew and pick twelve sullen men at random.[40]

By the time the leave expired that evening there was some kind of consensus amongst the men that they would refuse to raise anchor when the ships were due to sail on Tuesday morning. There was much shouting in the drifters on the way back to the ships, but still most of the officers were reluctant to accept that anything was wrong. Back in their ships, the men held meetings on the mess decks. The petty officers, who messed separately, tended to keep out of the way and maintained a position of neutrality throughout the affair.

On Monday morning Tomkinson signalled the Admiralty.

> *Important.* There was a slight disturbance in the Royal Naval canteen at Invergordon yesterday Sunday evening caused by one or two ratings endeavouring to address those present on the subject of reduction in pay. I attach no importance to the incident from a general disciplinary

point of view but it is possible it may be reported in an exaggerated form by the press. Matter is still being investigated.[41]

That afternoon the men were allowed leave again and unusually large numbers went ashore, considering how little there was to do in Invergordon. In theory these were men from the alternate watches, different from those who had taken part in the Sunday meetings, though some may have changed with their opposite numbers in the other watch. According to a man from the *Valiant*:

> We decided to – well, more or less down tools, go on strike, that's what we called it. The spokesmen said that we ought to show our disapproval of what was going to happen and the only way to show that disapproval was to just stop work. They stood up . . . I think there was two or three men spoke. I can't say who they were because they were from other ships. There was nobody from our ship. People had removed their cap ribbons, so we're not supposed to know . . . There was so many of us we could hardly move. We had a show of hands, what we should do, and it was agreed we should down tools.
> Then we heard a banging at the door. Someone looked out of the window and said, 'It's the Officer of the Patrol.' We'd got the door on a latch so that he couldn't push it in if he wanted to.[42]

This was Lieutenant Robert Elkins of the *Valiant*, who had received a message that a meeting was starting in the canteen. He was admitted, and addressed the men:

> After a short while I was able to make my voice heard, and everybody in the canteen listened quietly while I told them that I would stay in the canteen until I was satisfied that what was being discussed was not to the prejudice of discipline. When I stopped speaking the cat-calls and shouts continued, although I was not jostled. I heard one man behind me say, 'That stops the meeting,' and I hoped it had.[43]

One hothead threw a glass at Elkins, who was pushed out of the door by a kind of rugby scrum. Patrols were reinforced again and officers noticed that in town the men were reluctant to salute them. As the men boarded the boats and drifters to return to their ships, some called from one boat to another, 'Don't forget. Six o'clock tomorrow.' There was now a deep sense of foreboding among some officers, but Tomkinson was still inactive, perhaps out of his depth, perhaps hoping that it would all blow over if he did not provoke the men.

At dawn in the morning of Tuesday, 15 September, all seemed quiet in Invergordon Harbour. The first ship due to sail was the battlecruiser *Repulse,* moored at the harbour entrance away from the other ships. Her crew had been together only two weeks and they had taken little part in the discussions ashore. Her men raised the anchor cable and she sailed at 6.30.

But the revolt had already started in the other ships. In the *Rodney* and *Valiant,* the petty officers failed to rouse the men from their hammocks and even the marines refused to get up in the latter ship until they were called individually by their captain. In *Nelson* the mutiny began with the stokers, who passed through the seamen's mess deck and took many with them to a gathering on the forecastle. In the *Hood* too, the men assembled on the forecastle. The crew of one ship shouted to another, '*Rodney*! Are you with us?' and was answered with a cheer. The *Valiant* was due to sail next, but there was no chance that the men would raise the anchor. By 9 a.m. Tomkinson at last realised the seriousness of the situation and telegraphed the Admiralty. He cancelled the exercises and recalled the *Malaya* and *Warspite* which were already out in the Moray Firth, as well as the loyal *Repulse.* Meanwhile the cruisers, including Len Wincott's *Norfolk,* joined the revolt, though they were not actually under orders to sail.

Many of the senior officers had survived the Geddes Axe, not because they were more competent or intelligent than the others, but because they had kept out of trouble. It was a culture in which conformity and caution were rewarded and imagination was penalised. Various schemes for commissions from the lower deck had failed to produce high-ranking officers, so most captains and admirals came from quite privileged backgrounds, and very few had ever experienced poverty. In a major ship the captain lived in a large cabin, remote from the crew. When addressing the men, some did very badly. Burges-Watson of the *Nelson* suggested that the men send their wives out to work and this was taken to mean prostitution by the crew, who responded by 'rumbling'. In the *Valiant,* a similar suggestion by Captain Scott led to a roar of protest. Captain Dibden of the *Adventure* burst into tears in the presence of his men. The circumlocutions and understatements of the civil service did not help. On Wednesday the 16th, when the men read in the papers the Admiralty statement that 'the reduced rates of pay have led to unrest among a proportion of the lower ratings', they were incensed.[44]

The commanders, the seconds-in-command who did the real administrative work and were much closer to the men, did far better. In the *Hood,* Commander McCrum said, 'Lads, I am afraid I can do nothing for you, any special case of hardship will be looked into. I will do my best for you.' He almost succeeded in returning a part of the crew to duty, till the others called out, 'Come back, if we do not strike now they will crush us.'[45] In the *Nelson* Commander 'Lou' Lake won the men over with a populist speech and good order was maintained:

'I don't blame you chaps for what you're doing.' These were his actual first words. Of course everybody cheered. Cheering died down. He said, 'But I'd ask you fellers to remember that there are officers in this fleet who have had their salary docked every year . . . Now those of you who are suffering as a result of this, I want you to write it down on a piece of paper, don't give it to anybody. I shall leave my cabin window open and just drop it through, so I don't know who it is. I want to collect all these together so I've got something to show how much you are suffering.'[46]

During Tuesday and Wednesday the crews behaved in different ways. In the *Norfolk* the atmosphere was close to revolutionary, with the officers losing all their authority to lower-deck committees. In the *Nelson* the men were well disciplined and normal business continued as far as possible in the circumstances. In her sister-ship the *Rodney* there was chaos as no one made any attempt at organisation. Many men treated it as a holiday, a well-earned rest after the efforts of the exercises on the way north, and a piano was hoisted out of the men's recreation room, no doubt using the seaman's legendary skills with ropes and pulleys. It helped create a party atmosphere and signalled to the other ships that the mutiny was still going on:

We spent the rest of the day till dinner time on the upper deck, joining in with the lads, cheering the ships in the Fleet. We came down to dinner, and then in the afternoon volunteers were called for; the baker needed flour and asked for volunteers to go to the stores, and the galley wanted meat, so volunteers were called for to bring up meat from the cold store. They were never short of volunteers.

They were playing the piano, a bit of a sing-song, they played the 'Red Flag' very often. Leaders stood up on the forecastle with some of the crew around, giving morale-boosting speeches. 'Stick together – we don't want this pay cut – if we all stick together they're bound to give in eventually.'[47]

A petition was produced by Wincott in the *Norfolk* and several copies made. It announced the men's general loyalty to the King, but indicated their refusal to serve while the pay cuts stood.

The Cabinet met at noon on Wednesday the 16th, more than a day after the mutiny started. The use of force had been considered, but rejected. Instead it was decided to promise to reconsider the pay issue and to order the ships back to their home ports. This was likely to be popular with some of the seamen at least. As Able Seaman Ackland of the *Adventure* put it, 'The people that lived in Devonport or Plymouth were all for it – they were going home. But the foreigners, like the Welshmen or the Irishmen, or the Scotsmen, who didn't care two hoots, they wasn't concerned.'[48] There was fierce debate in some ships about whether to obey the order. In the *Norfolk* there were fights between groups of men before it was agreed to sail. But in the *Repulse*, *York* and *Rodney* the order was seen as a positive victory. All the ships raised their anchors and sailed from Invergordon that evening. The admiral was determined to get to the home ports early on Saturday morning, to give the men a full weekend leave. To do this he had to exceed the 'economical speeds' of some ships on the run south, against standing orders. But nearly all the ships were in port in time.[49] The government feared even greater revolt in the future and was forced to make real concessions. The cuts were adjusted so that no man would lose more than 10 per cent. There were never any formal charges against any of the men, but twenty-four were dismissed from the navy, 'Services no longer required'. These included the pianist on the *Rodney* and Len Wincott, who was promptly taken up by the Communist Party.

The affair has become universally known as the Invergordon Mutiny, or just 'Invergordon', though it was not in any sense about that town. It was about cuts in pay, about the steady decline in the position of the men of the lower deck and perhaps about the failure of leadership by many officers.

That said, the circumstances at Invergordon made it much easier to organise a mutiny. If the ships had been dispersed on courtesy visits to various ports, as the Mediterranean Fleet was when the cuts were announced, then it would have been difficult to organise more than a single ship. If they had been in their home ports, then there would have been no general organisation and the mutiny might have remained a Chatham, Devonport or Portsmouth affair. Or it might not have taken place at all. The married men would have been at home. Would that have alerted them even more to the plight of their families? Or would it have caused them to be more cautious? The cool reception given to the ships when they arrived home on Saturday the 19th suggests the latter. Many of the single men would have visited their parents, and it is difficult to believe that would have made them more radical. The rest of the men would have dispersed round the seamen's rests, clubs and pubs of the port. There would have been no focus for revolt, even within the area.

At Invergordon on the other hand, the ships of the Atlantic Fleet were brought together from the three home ports. Family influence, though not far in the background, was not immediately active. The men went ashore in a town where there was notoriously little to do, especially on a Scottish Sunday, where they were likely to congregate on the football pitches and the canteen and meet men from other ships. It is difficult to see how the revolt could have been so effective in any other circumstances.

A minimalist view of the Invergordon Mutiny suggests that only four ships – the battleships *Valiant* and *Rodney*, the cruiser *Norfolk* and the minelayer *Adventure* – were in a full state of revolt for more than a few hours. In the others, it is claimed, the officers' authority was restored on Tuesday as soon as the exercise was cancelled. Even on the ships most affected, the mutiny lasted only thirty-five hours, from 6 a.m. on Tuesday to 5 p.m. on Wednesday, when they began the voyage to their home ports.[50] An opposite view might suggest that the mutiny had cancelled the sailing of the Atlantic Fleet, the British Empire's most powerful fighting force, the pride of the greatest navy in the world. Certainly that is how it was perceived at the time, however much the press might be accused of exaggerating it. The Atlantic Fleet included the navy's largest and most prestigious ships, the only capital ships designed with the Jutland experience in mind, the *Hood, Nelson* and *Rodney*. All these took part in the mutiny.

Furthermore, some ships were only kept under control by enormous concessions. The *Hood* and the *Nelson*, for example, were only restored to order after the exercise had been cancelled. The battleship *Malaya*, which arrived late at Invergordon on Tuesday, after the mutiny had started, was an interesting case. The commander addressed the crew, sympathised with their grievances and told them that he was not going to give them any orders on the running of the ship. In effect there was nothing to mutiny against, so the *Malaya* was technically loyal during the whole affair.[51]

The Effects of Invergordon

The officers of the Atlantic Fleet were far less keen than the lower deck to sail for their home ports on 16 September 1931. As C. R. Benstead puts it,

> In the ordinary course of events the fleet stays at Invergordon about six weeks in the Autumn, and officers who can afford to do so book lodgings and bring wife and car to the north for the period – by land of

course. But now, just as the nest has been established, and, incidentally, the people of Invergordon had stocked up sufficiently with oranges and tartan garters to supply the needs of 12,000 men for six weeks, the Fleet was hurrying south. Wives had to be comforted and fortified with ready cash to get them back to Devonport or thereabouts, 700 miles at least. Landladies and garage-keepers had to be paid off and placated. Officers who had brought cars round by sea (this is possible and allowed in some ships) or had availed themselves of permission to drive them up by land, had now to make immediate arrangements for sending them back by land, since the shortness of sailing prohibited embarkation.[52]

Initially the navy was nervous about returning to Invergordon after the mutiny – it was a 'chilly experience' according to Benstead. At first King George V was opposed to a return, and his wishes were respected.[53] But soon the fleet was back in force and in 1933 the largest squadron ever seen in the firth arrived with 20,000 men. Despite this, the port never regained its standing as a favourite among the officers.

One effect of the Invergordon Mutiny was to strengthen the manning port system. After all, it was the sending of the ships to their home ports that got the navy out of its worst ever peacetime crisis. A. B. Cunningham, as commodore of the barracks at Chatham, failed to reform it soon afterwards:

My Secretary . . . and myself worked for a time for a scheme of central drafting and removing once and for all the iron curtain which still exists between Portsmouth, Devonport and Chatham. Why, we thought, should a warship be manned entirely from one or other of these ports? Why should not the crew, most of whom were specialists, or highly-skilled technicians, be drawn from all three? A central system, we thought, would simplify drafting, and ensure fairer proportions of sea service and shore service, and service at home and abroad.

In the end however, we abandoned the idea. Nobody seemed to want it. The fact was that most of the married men made their homes in the neighbourhood of their depots at Portsmouth, Chatham and Devonport. If a Devonport man was serving in a ship which refitted at Chatham, for instance, it would mean a long and expensive railway journey to see his wife and family. The scheme we suggested all depended upon the railways granting free travelling facilities to naval ratings at all times, whether on duty or on leave, in return for an annual *per capita* contribution.[54]

Rearmament

Adolf Hitler took power in Germany in January 1933, pledged to reverse the effects of the Treaty of Versailles, rebuild the German armed forces and restore the country to her former greatness. Even so there was no immediate move to rearmament in Britain until 1936, when the expansionist German policy began to become obvious with the reoccupation of the Rhineland followed by intervention in the Spanish Civil War, and the annexation of Austria and parts of Czechoslovakia in 1938. Italy began its invasion of Abyssinia in 1935 and Japanese campaigns against China continued.

The need for an expanded peacetime fleet was now recognised. Capital ship construction resumed in 1937 after the London Treaty of 1930 expired and it was decided to take many boys for the future fleet. The old liner *Majestic*, built in 1914 in Germany as the *Bismarck*, was taken over and commissioned as a static training ship for 1,500 seamen boys and 500 artificer apprentices, who would become the technicians of the future navy. She was moored alongside the western wall of the basin at Rosyth and was commissioned as HMS *Caledonia* on 23 April 1937. Her first captain was Sir Atwell 'Lou' Lake, who had pacified the *Nelson* during the Invergordon Mutiny. The officers and men of the *Caledonia* seem to have tried quite hard to make links with the Scottish community. The boys carried out displays of drill in Ibrox Stadium, visited Edinburgh as tourists and competed in local sports and model-making competitions. The Church of Scotland Chaplaincy was strong and the base was visited by the Moderator of the General Assembly. But there is no sign that this did much to increase recruitment among Scots, for artificer apprentices at least. The regulations gave priority to the sons of seamen, especially 'boys whose fathers can show long and faithful service'. Seventy-five candidates passed the examination for training at Chatham in March 1939, and only two had addresses in Scotland. The Admiralty wrote to these two, and another from Northumberland, suggesting they might like to transfer to a Rosyth course. One boy, from Blantyre, wrote back to say that he would rather start right away at Chatham, instead of waiting until October to start at Rosyth. As a result only one Scot, whose home was in Rosyth, was among the sixty boys who joined the Artificers' Course at HMS *Caledonia* in October 1939.[55]

Recruitment of time-served men as artificers did not go well in Glasgow, partly because of the tradition of 'Red Clydeside'. The recruiting staff officer for the area, Commander H. T. Strawbridge, reported to the Admiralty,

> The political views and activities of the 'masses' in the Glasgow district
> is firmly believed to be the principal deterrent to Naval Recruiting in
> general. The great majority from whom recruits of all branches are
> taken are rabidly anti-service, so much so, that there have been cases
> where applicants have stated they dare not mention the fact that they
> were joining the navy to anyone in their neighborhood for fear of being
> 'roughed'.

The commander addressed a meeting of the Amalgamated Society of
Engineers and was heard politely, but was made to understand 'how
much the Services were hated and everything connected with them . . .'
Even the managers of the labour exchanges had 'Socialistic views' and
did not encourage recruiting, while MPs and local politicians were
'rapidly undermining the patriotic spirit which is so essential to the
youth of the Nation, if suitable and voluntary recruits are to be
obtained the future'.[56] General recruiting in Scotland was more
satisfactory. During 1938 1,200 Scots joined, out of a total of about
15,500; nearly 8 per cent, or more than twice the rate before the Great
War.[57]

By 1937 there were fears that the *Caledonia* would be vulnerable.
She would take up valuable space if Rosyth was to reopen as a
dockyard and all the east-coast ports were considered to be in danger
of bombing from Germany. *Caledonia* was large and unarmoured and
could easily be sunk at her moorings, where she would be very difficult
to remove. Artificer apprentices had to be kept near a working
dockyard to have access to modern machinery, so King's Road School
in Rosyth was requisitioned from Fife County Council. Boy seamen
could have continued their training afloat in *Caledonia* and a suitable
anchorage was sought on the west coast of Scotland. Loch Long was
considered seriously, and the only real problem was the disposal of
sewage; but eventually it was decided to remove the boys to shore
training on the Isle of Man. The *Caledonia* was planned to be beached
on a sandbank for the duration of the war. In fact she was accidentally
burned in September 1939 and her wreck was sold in 1940, but not
removed until 1943.

In April 1937 the Admiralty agreed that Rosyth would be reopened
in the event of war, and that bomb-proof shelters were needed as
protection against air attack. By June 1938 the Naval Staff 'had
expressed the view that Rosyth Dockyard should be put in such a
condition that it would be able to undertake the refits of one capital
ship and two cruisers at three months from any given rate.' [58] In July
1939 it was proposed to use the entrance lock at Rosyth as a dock,

which would have been capable of handling the largest ships in the navy. This would of course have restricted ship movements to the emergency exit at high tide – just possible, since Rosyth was no longer a fleet anchorage. But eventually the plan was laid aside, and a new site was sought on the western side of Britain. A floating dock was considered for the Holy Loch, but it was considered too vulnerable to bombing and a new dock was started at Belfast.[59]

Early in 1939, plans were made for a joint Navy–RAF maritime headquarters at Pitreavie Castle, near Rosyth. In peacetime the naval element was to have facilities for the admiral and 6 members of his staff, with 3 naval writers (clerks) and 3 Royal Marine orderlies. In wartime this would be increased by 17 men and 20 women officers, plus 38 male and 15 women ratings.[60]

But there was still much to be done to get British defences ready in September 1939, when the German invasion of Poland precipitated the next Great War.

Chapter 12

The Second World War in the North

The Home Fleet and the Phoney War

At 11.30 on 3 September 1939, as Neville Chamberlain ended his mournful broadcast in which he announced that 'this country is now at war with Germany', the air-raid sirens sounded across London. Citizens took to trenches and primitive air-raid shelters, but the 'all clear' soon signalled a false alarm. At almost the same moment the sirens sounded in parts of Scotland, but it was another false alarm and the 'all clear' sounded soon afterwards. For now, the Germans had decided not to attack British civilians and the air war was to be carried on against shipping, largely in Scottish ports.

The North Sea was no-man's-land again, but not in the same sense as in the previous war, for the Germans had no battle-fleet as such. Radar and improved aerial reconnaissance made it far easier to track the movements of surface ships in a relatively narrow sea. Invasion of Britain was far more likely than in the First World War, but could only have taken place in the south where the Luftwaffe could provide effective air cover. The British used the North Sea less for coastal convoys. The U-boats now had much greater range than in 1914, so from the start the main submarine war was largely fought in the Atlantic. As a result of all this, neither side put a great deal of effort into controlling the surface of the central North Sea, and it was abandoned rather than disputed.

The Home Fleet, the descendant of Jellicoe's Grand Fleet of 1914, was under the command of Admiral Sir Charles Forbes. It had five battleships at the start of the war and two aircraft carriers, one of which was used for training. The fleet's role was not to defeat the German fleet as such, but to prevent individual raiders getting into the Atlantic where they could devastate British supply lines. With this in mind, some of the ideas of 1914–18 were revived. A Northern Patrol began three days after the start of the war, using old cruisers in the first instance. From October they were gradually replaced by converted liners, known as Armed Merchant Cruisers (AMCs), based at Scapa and later on the Clyde. With an average of two ships south of the Faroes and three between the Faroes and Iceland, they sent more than 250 doubtful merchant ships to Kirkwall for examination. Only seventeen Germans were intercepted, but in effect their trade with the rest of the world was cut off.[1] This was done at a cost. After the *Rawalpindi* was sunk during a sortie by the battlecruisers *Scharnhorst* and *Gneisenau* in November, the AMCs were withdrawn for a time. Forty-six were available in February 1940.

John Charles Jones of the destroyer *Jupiter* describes his experiences:

> For a while we were based at Scapa Flow and on one occasion endured the miseries of the Northern Patrol. We were never very far from the Arctic Ice Barrier and torpedo tube mountings, depth charge traps and throwers were frozen solid . . . Our upper works carried such a weight of ice that to make an 180 degree turn in heavy sea was to run a serious risk of capsizing. We met neither friend nor foe.[2]

The Northern Patrol became less important after the German occupation of France in June 1940, for the passage round the north of Scotland was no longer the best route to the outside world, and the AMCs were finally withdrawn in July to be used as troopships. An examination service was still based at Kirkwall on Orkney and in August 1942 it employed thirty-six small vessels on examination duties.[3]

The main job of British submarines in the early stages of the war was to help the RAF patrol the North Sea, especially against a breakout by German surface raiders. Coastal Command Anson aircraft from Montrose combined with flying boats from Invergordon to keep a lookout, but their use was restricted in bad weather, and the Ansons did not have the range even to reach the Norwegian coast, much less maintain long patrols off it. Therefore the submarines of the Home Fleet were stationed in the gap at twelve-mile intervals, which proved to be an unsatisfactory arrangement. A week after the start of the war, HM Submarine *Triton* torpedoed and sank the British boat *Oxley* and a few days later the *Sturgeon* fired on the *Swordfish* but fortunately missed.[4]

The idea of a Northern Barrage was revived in November, when Winston Churchill, back in office as the First Lord of the Admiralty, prepared a plan. It would have cost nearly £20 million and used 181,000 mines. Furthermore, it would have raised issues about Norwegian neutrality and was shelved by the cabinet.[5]

Until 1938 it had been assumed that the Home Fleet would be based in Rosyth as at the end of the last war. The area had many amenities for the ships and their crews. Its air defence could be combined with that of Glasgow and Edinburgh, saving the resources of the hard-pressed RAF. But it was pointed out that it was badly placed for intercepting the enemy trying to break out, for it was 150 miles further than Scapa from the cutting-off position between the Shetlands and Norway. Its approaches were easy to mine, especially from the air, compared with the Pentland Firth, where strong currents would prevent this. It was decided, on the eve of war, that Scapa Flow would be revived as the main fleet base.

There was little time to prepare the defences, and in the early stages the political will was lacking. Even in the spring of 1939, the government was reluctant to take any measures which might alarm the British public or antagonise the Germans. When the navy wanted to buy an old merchant ship to use as a blockship, the owners demanded £12,000, but the Treasury had set a cash limit of £10,000, so it was not acquired, and the Senior Naval Officer was told that not another penny was to be spent.[6] A decision had been taken to build a naval base at Lyness on Hoy, including sixteen above-ground tanks for 100,000 tons of oil fuel, and more underground; but progress was slow. Without wartime powers, it was difficult to persuade workmen to stay in the north, even with double wages.[7]

Six battleships of the Home Fleet arrived at Scapa during August 1939, during the run-up to war. By that time booms had been completed across the three main entrances to the Flow, Hoxa, Switha and Hoy Sounds, made from 3-inch wire with an 8-inch mesh. Some blockships had been sunk in the eastern sounds, though not enough. Buoys had been laid out to moor the fleet and teleprinter communication had been established with Rosyth. The above-ground fuel tanks were complete, but Lyness was defended only by four anti-aircraft guns supplied by the army; on the day before war was declared, Royal Marines landed with machine guns to supplement them. There was no RAF presence, though the naval air station at Hatston had opened for business on May 1939. Jellicoe's old flagship the *Iron Duke*, disarmed in 1932 under the Treaty of London, arrived to serve as a depot ship and flagship. There was shore accommodation for eighty-five men. Though Admiral French estimated that 1,200 berths were needed, he was told to wait for a fall in the price of hutting.[8]

Four days after the start of the war Admiral Forbes received a report which greatly exaggerated the enemy air strength in north-west

Germany and decided to abandon Scapa until better air defences were prepared. He took the fleet to Loch Ewe, where anti-torpedo nets were laid out. The only major ship left behind was the *Royal Oak*. Launched in 1914, she was regarded as too slow to keep up with the fleet.

The *Royal Oak*

As war approached Admiral Karl Donitz, in charge of the German U-boat arm, was already considering an attack on Scapa Flow, despite the loss of *U-18* and *UB-116* in the last war. After war broke out he got aerial reconnaissance photographs from the Luftwaffe and came to the conclusion:

> In Holm Sound, there are only two steamers which seem to be sunk across Kirk Sound and another on the north side. To the south of the latter end and up to Lamb Holm there are: a first gap 17 m wide at low tide mark, where the depth reaches 7m; and a second smaller, to the north. On both sides the shore is almost uninhabited. I think it is possible to pass there during the night and on the surface at flood tide. The greatest difficulty remains the navigation.[9]

Donitz offered the job to Gunther Prien, captain of *U-47*, who 'possessed all the qualities of leadership and all the necessary nautical knowledge'. Prien took the charts and papers home and studied them before agreeing to go. The night of 13/14 October was chosen because slack water was in the middle of the night – the tides could be up to 12 knots and the maximum speed of a submerged U-boat was 7 knots. *U-47* sailed on 8 October and four days later she was submerged off Orkney with her officers taking fixes on the navigational lights and observing shipping movements. Early in the morning of the 13th the crew were crowded into the forward compartment and Prien told them what they were going to do. There was silence, but he observed, 'Their faces were quite calm and nothing was to be read in them, neither astonishment, nor fear.'[10] The crew rested until the afternoon and then were given a 'feast' of veal cutlets and green cabbage. They surfaced at 7.15 in the evening, German time (one hour ahead of British time), and prepared for action, getting the torpedoes ready for reloading and setting charges so that the boat could be blown up if it fell into enemy hands.

Prien headed into Holm Sound but was shocked that it was 'disgustingly light' due to the Aurora Borealis. At one stage he mistook

the blockship in Skerry Sound for the one in Kirk Sound and nearly
went the wrong way. But the navigator used dead reckoning to correct
the course. The submarine turned sharply to starboard and headed
north, then turned west into the ill-defended Kirk Sound. Prien was
well prepared for the passage and went through with 'unbelievable
speed', scraping against the cable of one of the blockships as the
submarine swung violently to and fro in the currents.

Inside the Flow, Prien headed west to look around for warships.
There was nothing south of Cava so he turned north to see what he
believed were two capital ships, one of the *Royal Oak* class and the
battlecruiser *Repulse*. In fact the second ship was the aircraft transport
Pegasus, formerly the *Ark Royal*, an early seaplane carrier of the First
World War. Prien fired one torpedo at the supposed *Repulse* and two
at the *Royal Oak*. Only one struck home.

Around midnight Commander Renshaw, the engineer officer of the
Royal Oak, was in his bunk when he was awakened by a violent
explosion below him in the after part of the ship:

> Turned out and pulled on a few clothes and hurried to the Admiral's
> lobby. Saw R. A. 2 [Rear-Admiral H. E. C. Balgrove, Second Battle
> Squadron]. He said 'That it came from directly below us. Locate what it
> is, Engineer Commander.' I said 'I agree Sir,' I then opened up W. T.
> [watertight] door to Tiller Flat. Ordered Mr Dunstons, Warrant
> Engineer who had arrived to open sliding door cautiously, fully
> expecting to find compartment flooded. I descended into Tiller Flat,
> searched, found all in order and came out of it again shutting sliding
> and W.T. door.[11]

Renshaw searched other parts of the ship on the captain's instructions
and found nothing. He was beginning to think it was an internal CO_2
explosion. But in the meantime *U-47* got ready for a second attack:

> Torpedo fired from stern; in the bow two tubes are loaded; three
> torpedoes from the bow. After three tense minutes comes the detona-
> tions on the nearer ship. There is a loud explosion, roar, and rumbling.
> Then come columns of water, followed by columns of fire and splinters
> fly through the air. The harbour springs to life. Destroyers are lit up,
> signalling starts on every side, and on land 200 metres away from me
> the cars roar along the roads. A battleship has been sunk, a second
> damaged, and three other torpedoes have gone to blazes. All the tubes
> are empty. I decide to withdraw.[12]

On board the *Royal Oak*, as Renshaw reported,

. . . A second terrific explosion shook ship which immediately began to list to starboard. At intervals of a few seconds, a 3rd and 4th explosion shook ship and list rapidly increased and lights failed. Heard Captain say he was going up to forecastle and followed him up Forward Hatch with a number of others. Made my way aft along Port side to Quarter Deck with list increasing the whole time. Someone, I think a Warrant Officer said to me 'What is to be done now' I said "Nothing can save her now.' R.A.2 emerged from darkness and said 'What caused those explosions do you think?' I said 'Torpedoes, Sir.' He said 'My God', turned away and walked forward. I did not see him again.[13]

Many seamen slept through the first explosion but could not ignore the others. Leading Seaman Green was on watch on the starboard side of the flag deck when he heard the second explosion and saw a column of water alongside the forecastle, followed by more alongside the bridge. On the marines' messdeck a big yellow flash came through the starboard door and all the hammocks caught fire. The man in the hammock next to Marine A. R. Jordan jumped out but went straight on down, for there was no deck for him to land on.[14] Other survivors had equally horrific experiences as the ship turned over:

As he went, half blown, half running, it was hard to keep upright. With all dark below, the ship had begun to heel slowly and remorselessly over to starboard. It was hard to find the doors, still harder to open them, because they were no longer vertical. Several times, Wilson found himself across the diagonal of a door before he had reached out to open it. The ship was really turning now, and he knew he had a long way to go. His goal was a ladder by the galley, leading to the upper deck. About forty men were struggling round it, milling, shouting, cursing, unable to see what they were doing . . .

Also in the scrum was Batterbury. The second explosion had sent him running from forward to his chums in the mess, which was near the ladder. He had only a hundred yards to go, but some of the watertight doors were closed for damage-control purposes and others were slamming to with the heel of the ship; it was impossible to go in a straight line.

A door slammed behind him, crushing the head of a man who was trying to get through it. Batterbury saw his eyes and tongue sticking out, then came the sound of the third explosion, and the lights failed. He ran on. The anti-flash curtains in the battery aft were aflame and people were pouring up from the stokers' messdeck below, 'hollering and howling about men being on fire down there'. This new scrum of men, many of them dazed with horror, scrambled for the ladder. It was, said Batterbury dryly, 'survival of the fittest'. The fear of being trapped inside the heeling ship was overwhelming. Batterbury himself was frantic to get a foot on the ladder.[15]

Meanwhile *U-47* was retreating through Kirk Sound.

It is now low tide, the current is against us. Engines at slow speed and dead slow, I attempt to get away . . . Course 058, slow. I make no progress. At high [speed] I pass the southern blockship with nothing to spare. The helmsman does magnificently. High speed ahead both, finally three-quarters speed and full ahead all out. Free of the block-ships – ahead a mole! Hard over and again about, and at 02.15 we are once more outside.[16]

The life-saving arrangements on the *Royal Oak* were inadequate, as her captain had recognised before the sinking. The boats and rafts were insufficient to accommodate the whole crew and could not be launched quickly in an emergency, while requests for life-jackets for all the men had been lost in the Admiralty machine.[17] The hero of the episode was Richard Gatt, skipper of the drifter *Daisy II* which was alongside the *Royal Oak* at the time. He backed his boat away from the sinking ship and then lit a gas lamp to alert the men in the water. About 250 were picked up. Boats from the *Pegasus*, anchored about half a mile away, were launched as soon as the alarm was raised, and went over to the scene, but the base at Lyness was too far away to send help in time. Most of the survivors were taken on board the *Pegasus*. In all, 833 officers and men were lost out of a total of 1,400.

A court of inquiry concluded that the *Royal Oak* had indeed been sunk by torpedoes fired by a submarine and there was no evidence of any other form of attack, though conspiracy theories involving sabotage have always surrounded the sinking. The inquiry noted that any of the seven entrances to the Flow was possible, though Switha Sound and Water Sound were extremely unlikely. For example, a U-boat might have entered by

Passing through the gap in the Flotta end of the Hoxa boom on the surface or trimmed down. This gap is [blank] wide with a least depth of water of 15 ft at High Water and considerably more over the greater part. There was no lookout on shore at the gap. One drifter was patrolling the whole entrance which is 1½ miles wide. Approaching this gap would take the submarine within 5 cables of the battery on Stanger Head.

Another possibility was 'Passing through the opening of Kirk Sound south of S.S. "Thames" on the surface: this opening is 400 feet wide with a depth of 4 to 4½ fathoms at Low Water. There is another opening about 200 feet wide with a depth of 15 feet or more at High Water.' It was conjectured that 'in many respects Kirk Sound would present the least difficulty.' The inquiry identified nine possible gaps in the defences and much needed to be done if Scapa Flow was ever to be safe again.[18]

The Start of the Air War

When the sirens sounded over the Forth on the afternoon of Monday 16 October, two days after the sinking of the *Royal Oak,* it was not a false alarm. Nine Junkers 88s of the Luftwaffe were under orders to attack the great battlecruiser HMS *Hood,* which they knew had travelled up the east coast to the firth. But the *Hood* had already gone into dock at Rosyth and the raiders were instructed not to attack targets ashore, for fear of civilian casualties. Instead they bombed two cruisers, the *Southampton* and *Edinburgh,* and the destroyer *Mohawk,* killing fifteen men in the *Edinburgh.* The local squadrons of the Royal Auxiliary Air Force, 602 and 603, were already on patrol and shot down two of the Junkers, after mistakenly firing on an RAF Anson. This was the first raid of the war on British territory, and the two Junkers were the first enemy aircraft to fall on British soil. The following day there were raids on Scapa Flow, though the fleet had moved to Loch Ewe by now. The *Iron Duke* was damaged by a near miss and beached. She was to remain in this state for the rest of the war, still serving as a depot ship.

The wide estuary of the Forth remained a tempting target for bombers, as it had been for U-boats in the previous war. In November, when the Germans first used their 'secret weapon', the magnetic mine, they were dropped by aircraft in the Forth and the Thames and the new cruiser HMS *Belfast* was blown up on the way out of the Forth on the 21st and spent more than two years under repair. It had been put in place by *U-31.* On 9 February 1940 the Luftwaffe lost two Heinkel 111s, the first in the sea off Peterhead and the second near North Berwick. On 16 March Scapa Flow was raided by fifteen aircraft and some bombs were dropped on land; Mr James Isbister of Bridge of Waithe ran out of his house to help a neighbour but was killed outright by a bomb – the first civilian casualty of an air raid in Britain in the war. A newspaper report of April 1940 suggested that 13 out of 25 bombing raids on Britain had been aimed at Scotland, and 28 out of 47 reconnaissance flights.[19]

If anyone thought this was the shape of things to come, they were

wrong. Eventually London *was* bombed, but the Forth saw very little
of the Luftwaffe after the spring of 1940. It was early in 1940 before
the first RAF fighters arrived at Scapa and by March three fighter
squadrons were operating from the air stations at Wick and Hatston,
and Fleet Air Arm squadrons, albeit with obsolete aircraft, were
allocated to the air defence. Subsequent German raids on Orkney
suffered quite heavy losses. The attack on the Flow intensified in April
because the Germans, preparing for a campaign in Norway, had
particular reasons to neutralise the Home Fleet. On 8 April a force of
sixty bombers arrived, but were driven off by more than 1,700 rounds
fired by anti-aircraft guns, while three bombers were shot down by
fighters. They attacked again on the 10th and six German aircraft
were lost, including one which crashed on landing at its base. There
was a half-hearted raid on the 25th but the attack was not pressed
home and the only casualty was one chicken.[20] Scapa was no longer
an easy target for the Luftwaffe, and by now their attention was
diverted fully to Norway.

The Return to Scapa

Early in 1940, the different Scottish fleet bases were assessed for their
vulnerability to aerial bombing and air-dropped magnetic mines. The
Forth was the most difficult, with a long and wide estuary, with
relatively shallow water and on the exposed eastern side of Britain.
The Clyde had much deeper water in its approaches. Only the area
abreast of Toward Point was shallow enough for mines, and a deep
water channel would be dredged through there soon. Scapa had three
different approaches and some effort would be needed to keep them
clear, but in general it was regarded as safer than the Forth.

Loch Ewe was considered as a base for the main fleet early in 1940,
when the new defences of Scapa were being repaired. Also known as
Aultbea from the name of the largest village in the area, or more
cryptically as 'Port A', it was relatively easy to keep clear of mines,
though for the moment the sweepers were not available. In other
respects it was considered inferior to Rosyth and the Clyde, for both
these estuaries were protected by the RAF's fighter cover. Loch Ewe
had few fixed anti-aircraft defences, and more could not be moved
there quickly. Enemy aircraft could approach the loch over the sea and
arrive without any warning, so the main fleet would be highly
vulnerable in the area.[21] Its vulnerability was confirmed on
4 December 1939 when the battleship *Nelson* was damaged by a
magnetic mine on entering the loch. It had been laid by a U-boat.

The strategical advantages of the different bases were considered. The Clyde, Loch Ewe and Rosyth were 'equally acceptable', though Loch Ewe was slightly nearer the probable area of operations. But Scapa was the best sited and it was agreed that it 'should have absolute priority in the Naval quota of A/A defence' and become the main base of the Home Fleet. Rosyth should be the base for light forces operating locally in the North Sea, and the Clyde for armed merchant cruisers. Loch Ewe should be 'developed as an alternative anchorage when material becomes available after the other three bases have been fully protected.'[22]

In contrast to 1914, the British planned for a long war and investment at Scapa now seemed worthwhile. The new base differed from the old in that it was under threat from heavy air attack, so more of the facilities were to be constructed ashore rather than on depot ships, offering slightly better amenities to the crews – though in practice the Luftwaffe switched its tactics after April 1940, then concentrated on British cities after September and never attacked Scapa in force again. The first priority, of course, was to make it safe from submarine attack. As a temporary measure more blockships were sunk, and one was placed in the gap in Kirk Sound very soon after the loss of the *Royal Oak*. The anti-submarine booms were also strengthened and a second line of nets had been laid across each entrance by May 1940.

The strengthened defences of Scapa Flow were first tested by using dummy battleships as decoys and the *Hood* and *Valiant* arrived there on 7 March. More ships arrived on the 9th. At a meeting on board the *Rodney,* Churchill made two important decisions. Firstly, it was decided to block off the eastern entrances to the Flow through Holm and Water Sounds, making them impenetrable to U-boats. This would take a long time to implement, but the other decision had a more immediate effect. The defences were far from perfect, but it was possible for the Home Fleet to return to Scapa. The Royal Navy had few strokes of luck in its early campaigns in northern waters, but this was one, for the six months of 'phoney war' were about to end in the waters to the east and north of Orkney.

Operations from Scapa

On 14 February 1940 HMS *Cossack,* one of sixteen glamorous 'super-destroyers' of the Tribal class, left Rosyth in the company of a cruiser and four other destroyers with orders to search off the Norwegian coast for the *Altmark*, the supply-ship of the German raider *Graf Spee,* scuttled off Montevideo in December. They found the ship in Jossingfjord and technically violated Norwegian neutrality in boarding her and releasing 299 merchant navy prisoners with the famous cry 'The Navy's here'. They were taken to Leith on board the *Cossack* to be met by ambulances on the dockside, for the authorities had received exaggerated reports of the *Altmark* as a 'hell-ship'.

Whether or not the *Altmark* affair had any direct effect, both sides were now turning their eye towards Norway and planning to violate the country's traditional neutrality. The British were conscious that the German war effort was heavily dependent on iron ore from Sweden, shipped by rail through the Norwegian port of Narvik and then by sea, through Norwegian territorial waters, to Germany. From the first month of the war Churchill had advocated mining Norwegian waters to force the traffic out to sea, but it was only at the beginning of April that he was allowed to proceed with the plan. As the first part of Operation Wilfred, three groups of destroyers were to sail from Scapa and lay two real and one simulated minefields off Norway. It was recognised that this might cause Norway to retaliate and troops were got ready to occupy the country's main ports if that happened. At Rosyth four cruisers embarked the men to attack Stavanger and Bergen, while a force of transports assembled in the Clyde ready to sail, escorted by a cruiser, to invade Trondheim and Narvik to the north. The operation was originally planned for 5 April but was postponed to the 8th, though the first ships had already sailed from Scapa on the 5th.

The Germans were already beginning to implement a plan which would violate Norwegian neutrality much more seriously. Ignoring the conventional view that amphibious operations demanded command of the sea, their major ships were already at large, carrying troops for landings at all of Norway's major ports, including the capital, Oslo. British intelligence suggested some movement, perhaps a breakout of German capital ships into the Atlantic, and the Home Fleet sailed north-east from Scapa on the evening of the 7th. The troops were disembarked from the cruisers at Rosyth and they too went to sea to seek out the enemy. There were two German groups in the area – the force of destroyers heading for Narvik covered by the battlecruisers *Gneisenau* and *Scharnhorst* and the Trondheim force escorted by the cruiser *Hipper*. The Home Fleet failed to make contact with them, but the destroyer *Glowworm*, having lost contact with the British fleet, rammed the *Hipper* and seriously damaged her. The German landings were almost completely successful, despite local Norwegian resistance which allowed the government and the royal family to escape. They now had to carry out what they regarded as the most dangerous part of the operation – the withdrawal of heavy naval forces in the face of the Royal Navy.

The Second Destroyer Flotilla under Captain Warburton-Lee had sailed from Scapa as part of the abortive Operation Wilfred. They were now ordered to attack the German warships and transports in Vestfjord on the approaches to Narvik, which they did with some success on 10 April. Three days later the battleship *Warspite* entered the fjord supported by nine destroyers and sank eight German destroyers and one U-boat.

This helped the British cabinet to decide to land troops in the northern ports before the Germans could consolidate their hold. On 11 April three liners left the Clyde carrying troops for landing at Narvik, to be joined by two more from Scapa Flow, while the military commander sailed from Scapa in the cruiser *Southampton*. On the 14th it was decided to detach two of the liners for an attack on Namsos, north of Trondheim, and a party of marines from the cruiser *Glasgow* had already landed that day. Meanwhile four sloops sailed from Rosyth with a hastily assembled force of 700 seamen and marines for Aalesund. But such ships were not suitable for northern waters and bad weather forced them into Invergordon, where they received orders to attack Aandalsnes instead. They were augmented with a force of 1,000 troops carried in four cruisers from Rosyth, which landed on the 18th. But Operation Hammer, a proposed attack on the crucial German position at Trondheim from Scapa Flow, was cancelled by the War Cabinet on the 19th. Meanwhile the forces at Aandalsnes and Namsos came under heavy attack and had to be withdrawn. The whole force, apart from two destroyers which had been lost, arrived back at Scapa Flow on 4 and 5 May.

On 15 April the troops of the Narvik expedition landed at the small port of Harstad and reinforcements were sent to bring the force to a total of 30,000 men, but the town itself could not be captured. Meanwhile the Germans began another advance through Holland, Belgium and France and naval support had to be withdrawn. Early in June the men were re-embarked in large troopships and some of the RAF's fighters were landed on the aircraft carrier *Glorious*, which sailed for Scapa. Commanded by an officer who had notoriously bad relations with his pilots and misunderstood the role of air power at sea, she encountered the *Scharnhorst* and *Gneisenau* and was sunk on the 8th. On the same day the troopships carrying the first group of

15,000 men met the battleship *Valiant* and were escorted back to the Clyde without loss, while another group of 10,000 also got home safely.[23]

From this point the role of Scapa Flow changed again. Norway stretches more than a thousand miles north-east of Shetland, with a deeply indented coastline more than 16,000 miles long. There were innumerable harbours in which the great German battleships *Bismark* and *Tirpitz* (as yet incomplete) could hide or replenish in preparation for a breakout. Slightly smaller ships, battlecruisers, pocket battleships and large cruisers, were almost dangerous.

The Home Fleet's greatest test began on 21 May 1941 when Coastal Command reported that the *Bismarck* and the cruiser *Prinz Eugen* were in a fjord south of Bergen. They finished refuelling and left the same day, to raid the Atlantic. HMS *Hood* was already operating from a base in Iceland, but three battleships were at Scapa. The brand new *Prince of Wales* was sent to join *Hood* in the Denmark Strait between Iceland and Greenland, where two cruisers sighted the German ships on the evening of the 23rd. In one of the navy's greatest disasters of all time, the *Hood* blew up in the morning of the 24th after an engagement with the *Bismarck* and the *Prince of Wales*, still not properly worked up, had to retreat.

Meanwhile the rest of the Home Fleet had sailed from Scapa late on the 22nd, to be joined by the battlecruiser *Repulse* from the Clyde. With them was the new aircraft carrier *Victorious,* carrying dismantled aircraft for Malta and only a small complement of Swordfish torpedo aircraft. Nevertheless she managed to hit the *Bismarck* with one torpedo at midnight on the 24th to 25th, doing no serious damage. It was aircraft from the *Ark Royal*, diverted from the Mediterranean, which scored a fatal hit on the ship on the 26th, damaging her steering so that she was caught and destroyed by the Home Fleet's battleships. They returned to Scapa a few days later having avenged the loss of the *Hood*.

After the invasion of Russia on 22 June 1941, the main task of the fleet at Scapa was to protect the convoys to Russia, which left from Iceland and Loch Ewe. Operating in waters far more unpleasant than those of Scapa, they engaged with submarines, surface ships and aircraft. On Boxing Day 1943 they triumphed when a force led by Admiral Sir Bruce Fraser in the battleship *Duke of York* engaged and sank the German battlecruiser *Scharnhorst,* in the Royal Navy's last great gun action.

The Development of Scapa

Scapa Flow was vastly improved in the five years after March 1940. In the 1930s the navy had developed several special classes of vessel for laying and maintaining net defences. The *Barricade* or Bar class of 1935 was recognisable by two large horns in the bows, to lift and lower equipment. They had a large hold to carry buoys and a rigger's workshop. Eleven of them were in Scapa Flow in August 1942, along with fifteen converted trawlers.[24] At the height of the war the boom defence of Scapa Flow employed 1,100 naval personnel and 130 civilians. In addition to the laying, opening and maintenance of boom defences, groups of trawlers and drifters were used as minesweepers and anti-submarine vessels around Scapa.

The idea of permanently closing Kirk Sound, Skerry Sound, East Weddel Sound and Water Sound seemed simple enough, but the enormous tides of the area made the project very difficult. Kirk Sound was up to 59 ft deep at low water, but the tide could rise up to 12 ft on top of that. Furthermore the movement of tides could cause currents of up to 12 knots and slack water between tides lasted for only 20 minutes. There was a fear that the gradual closing of the Sounds would constrict the flow, causing even greater currents. The area was not fully surveyed because of the tidal problems. Models were made in Manchester University to test methods of closing them. Eventually it was decided that the barriers should be founded on rubble continued within steel wire bolsters, with five-ton concrete blocks on the outside to make them more secure.

The labour problems were almost as intractable. An old passenger liner, the *Almanzora* of 16,000 tons, was taken on as an accommodation vessel and arrived in May 1940, but many of the men had to live in tents at first, and then on huts on shore. One labour force which was not available in peacetime was prisoners of war. Up to 1,200 Italians were employed at the peak, with an average of 920 Italians and 350 British workmen during most of the work. This too created some difficulties, for technically it was a breach of the Geneva Convention to employ prisoners on direct war work. It is commonly believed that the 'barriers' eventually became known as 'causeways', linking the islands, because the latter term implied more peaceful uses. An artist, Domenico Chiocchetti of Trento, created a beautifully decorated Roman Catholic chapel in Lamb Holm. However, the chapel was only completed in 1945 after the need for it had passed. It had its first sung mass in 1959.

One of the biggest problems of construction was to find a way of getting the materials, especially the concrete blocks, into position. Barge work was impossible in the strong tides, so overhead cableways were needed. Four were found in Iraq, where they had been used to construct a barrage across the Tigris, but it was 1941 before they could be shipped round the Cape of Good Hope to Scapa. The first one was erected across Weddel Sound in June. A fifth was found nearer home, having been used to bridge the River Dornie in Sutherland. The cableways had masts 172 to 190 ft high on shore and cables of $2\frac{3}{4}$ -inch diameter were slung between them. By the end of 1942 the barriers were effective in that there was enough above and below the water to prevent a submarine passing through. Early in the following year they were secure against surface craft. Roads were built across the tops of the barriers to link the islands, but these were not opened until just after the end of the war in Europe.[25]

Although air attack was never again the menace it seemed in early 1940, the defence of the Flow could not be neglected. Apart from fighter cover, it was estimated in 1940 that the defences would need 140 anti-aircraft guns, 108 searchlights, 17 coast-defence guns and the same number of lights.[26]

Initially there was scepticism about the use of barrage balloons in the Flow. The first 40 were installed in 1940, then all but one of them were immediately blown away in a gale. Furthermore, there would be a large gap over the water. Balloon trawlers were used to cover that, and in 1942 there were 17 in service, with a total of 81 balloons in the area at the peak in 1943. A naval anti-aircraft range was set up at a remote spot on the west of the island, where it would not interfere with flying operations. Crews from visiting ships went on short refresher courses and came to like the remoteness and the supply of fresh eggs and vegetables. One device that had not been available in the previous war was radar, for the detection of both surface ships and aircraft. The first station opened at Sumburgh Head on Shetland on Christmas Eve 1939, to be followed by more on Fair Isle, the northern Shetland island of Unst, South Ronaldsay in Orkney and on Dunnett Head in Caithness. All the stations were placed as high as possible, from 300 to 710 ft above sea level and the system was complete by the end of 1940.

There was also a threat of surface attack, especially a sudden raid by fast German E-boats. Surface guns were sited at the main entrances to prevent this, and two flotillas of motor launches were intended to fight them off. The most important function of Scapa was to harbour, refuel, replenish and repair the ships of the Home Fleet and any others which might use these waters. During the war 1,200 men were involved in ship repair.

By 1942 the islands were littered by the famous Nissen huts, invented in 1915 by a Canadian colonel. They were buildings of semicircular section made from corrugated iron, usually with brick ends. They came in three widths, of 16 ft, 24 ft and 30 ft, and could be any length, in multiples of 6 ft. Despite the accommodation ashore, depot ships were still needed. The *Iron Duke,* still aground, was the headquarters for the auxiliary patrol and motor launches and also had the fleet ophthalmic surgery, a court-martial room and cells for offenders from small ships. HMS *Exmouth* was a relic from an even earlier age. She had been launched in 1854, during the Crimean War, as a screw-propelled wooden ship of the line and became a reformatory training ship in the River Thames in 1905. In 1942 she replaced the former Orkney ferry *St Sunniva* as the headquarters ship for the Drifter Pool. The *Dunluce Castle* was a former liner on the South Africa run, used as an accommodation ship, and the *Prosperine* was the headquarters for boom defence, target tugs and rescue ships. The *William Archibald* arrived in July 1940 as a mission ship for the fishermen in the drifters and trawlers.[27]

As in the previous war, drifters continued to serve the warships in ferrying men and supplies. Ships now had larger complements and increased anti-aircraft armaments needing supplies of ammunition, so ships' boats could no longer cope. Drifters were allocated on the basis of one per ship and two per aircraft carrier, but were kept in a common pool, known as the 'marine menagerie' because of the great variety of craft. In August 1942 there were more than 150 vessels including trawlers, ferries and yachts as well as wood and steel drifters powered by steam or diesel.[28] In 1941–2 the navy decided to pay off the local crews and use men from the Royal Naval Patrol Service. Though there was a good strategic reason in that the boats might have to be transferred to another base such as Iceland, the decision was resented by the locals.

Administrative and domestic facilities were also needed for running the great base, with the naval headquarters in Kirkwall and the army in the only other town, Stromness. The Admiral Commanding lived in Melsetter House. Two shredding machines were set up for confidential documents, and a laundry at Lyness handled 170,000 blankets in three years.[29]

In the early stages Scapa remained as unpopular with the seamen as it had been twenty-five years earlier. Ludovic Kennedy, then a junior officer on a destroyer, wrote:

> The islands were treeless, just heather and grass, seabirds and sheep, and across the bare face of the Flow tempests blew, often for days on

end. There were no women, shops, restaurants, just a couple of
canteens that dispensed warm beer, a hall for film shows and the
occasional concert party, and football fields that too often displayed
the sign 'All grounds unfit for play'.[30]

The facilities were gradually improved over the years. D. A. Rayner of
the destroyer *Shikari* visited in August 1943 after a three-year gap and
found

> There had been fantastic changes. Where there had been miles of
> muddy roads and open fields there were now hard roads and serried
> ranks of good huts. There were canteens for the men and there was also
> a giant mess for the officers. A busy town had sprung up in the salty
> wilderness, and there were even Wrens about on roads where before
> only the male of the species had ever been seen.[31]

Even before the war ended, the main battle had moved well away
from Scottish waters and Scapa began to run down. With the sinking
of the *Scharnhorst* in December 1943 and the final bombing of the
Tirpitz by the RAF in November 1944, there were no major German
surface ships left, though the Russian convoys still needed protection
against aircraft and U-boats. As early as February 1944 three anti-
aircraft battalions were withdrawn from Orkney and the gradual run-
down began.

The Shetland Bus

After the German occupation of Norway in 1940, links between the
resistance and the allied war effort were maintained from a base in
Shetland, commanded by Major L. H. Mitchell. David Howarth, then
a sub-lieutenant in the RNVR, arrived in the spring of 1941 as the
second-in-command. After long reconnaissance Lunna Voe, a small
inlet twenty-seven miles from Lerwick, was chosen as offering a good
harbour and the right amount of isolation. Apart from the two officers
there were about forty civilian Norwegian seamen when the base was
set up, as well as three British army sergeants including the quartermaster, 'Q', Sergeant Almond. There was a civilian typist and three
domestics for the large house which the team occupied on the Voe.
Norwegian fishing boats formed the main means of communication
with Norway:

> To a casual observer they all look the same: two-masted wooden
> vessels, unusually high in the bow, with a very large wheelhouse aft.
> The bulwarks and upper works are white, and the hull is not painted

but treated with linseed oil . . . The most noticeable feature of these Norwegian craft is their engine, for with only a few exceptions it is a single-cylinder semi-diesel with a large reverberant exhaust pipe which comes out of the top of the wheelhouse and emits a slow, solemn, very loud tonk-tonk-tonk. This tonk can be heard for miles away in calm weather, and it is a very nostalgic sound to all who have happy memories of the Norwegian coast.[32]

Intelligence services were maintained and one Norwegian member claimed to know the Christian name of every German NCO on a watchpost in Norway. Boats were fitted out with numerous disguises, using the registration numbers of others which were known not to have defected to the allies and had bases which were close, but not too close to the areas of operations. Guns were disguised in oil drums and 'Chariots' (manned torpedoes) could be carried on deck. Agents and instructors were landed with their equipment, fugitives were taken off and the Norwegian resistance was supported to become a very effective organisation.

Submarine Operations

When the war began all the operational British submarines in home waters were sent to flotillas based at Blyth and Harwich on the east coast of England, and at Rosyth and Dundee. The last port was deemed unsafe from air attack and the depot ship there, HMS *Forth*, arrived at Rosyth on 14 October with four submarines. A few days later the depot ship at Blyth, HMS *Titania*, moved northwards to Rosyth to be further away from German bombers, but this concentration lasted only two weeks. Rosyth was found to be too crowded, with three flotillas operating from the basin and the third Submarine Flotilla, now based on HMS *Cyclops* rather than *Titania*, which was refitting at Rosyth, went back to Blyth.[33]

Able Seaman Sydney Hart describes his first patrol from HMS *Forth* in the early months of the war:

A narrow gang plank ran down to *Triad*'s slippery deck; we scrambled down it in single file, passed our kits through a small hatch, and so squeezed ourselves into our ship's interior. The atmosphere was warm and stuffy. The lights seemed dull and listless by contrast with the late autumn sunset outside. So we went through the engine-room into the small mess, cramped as it normally was, and now, with our steaming bags all over the place, looking like any London Tube at the rush hour. For us this state of affairs would be normal for three weeks duration or thereabouts.

Returning unblooded from the patrol, the men were glad to be back at the depot ship.

> Once we were secured to moorings there was a dash to the parent ship for baths – a treat we had missed for eighteen mortal days – and a blissful reality when available. Our beards needed clippers instead of razors. But to be back after well-nigh three weeks without the decent creature comforts of life . . . Best of all, to breathe fresh, pure air that had not been polluted by the conglomeration of scents bred in a submarine's interior – ah, this was bliss indeed.[34]

The headquarters of the Flag Officer Submarines was at Aberdour on the Forth until Sir Max Horton took over the command in December 1939. He was unhappy with the distance from London and wrote:

> The position of Flag Officer Submarines was in had been the subject of countless proposals. No decision having been reached, the Flag Officer Submarines, at the time being in command of all S/Ms in home waters under C-in-C Home Fleet, sought an HQ in the Firth of Forth with his operational staff, while the material side remained at Portsmouth – thus the majority of papers had to make a nice little trip of 450 miles each way to be minuted, and the personal touch between the two divisions of the staff was almost completely lost. Further, the Flag Officer Submarines, as personal adviser to the Admiralty on S/Ms, was quite out of touch, and his own operational supervision was not so good.
> I couldn't bear such an organisation, despite the golf course just outside the front door, and decided to move nearer the Admiralty where one would be in close personal touch with at least one of my masters.[35]

Plans for a submarine base at Dundee were approved in February 1940. It was to be self-contained, with no depot ship. The Dundee Orphans' Home was taken over for 18 officers, while the disused factory of Lindsay and Lowe was to be converted for the accommodation of 26 chiefs and petty officers, 81 junior ratings and 25 Wrens. Submarines were to be berthed in Camperdown Dock or at the western end of Eastern Wharf in fair weather, where they could berth at any state of the tide. The base was commissioned in April 1940 as HMS *Ambrose*, the headquarters of the Ninth Submarine Flotilla.[36] By this time Norway had fallen to the Germans and there was a need for submarines in the north to patrol the numerous ports where enemy ships could operate.

In May 1940, as France was invaded and the southern bases became increasingly unsafe, it was decided to concentrate on Rosyth again, and the third and tenth Flotillas moved there from Harwich and Blyth.

Dundee had been suggested for one of these flotillas, but it was felt that it was still relatively poorly defended from the air and that a depot ship would be vulnerable. The depot ships *Cyclops* and *Jules Verne* were in the Forth by the 18th, but again there was the problem of overcrowding. This was partly removed at the end of the month, when the *Jules Verne* and the Tenth Flotilla were ordered to the Mediterranean on the threat of a war with Italy. By 19 June a complete redistribution to the west was under consideration, for the fall of France was imminent and it was believed that the enemy might base his surface ships on the west coast of France, and that Spain might be induced to enter the war and provide even more harbours for the Germans. Two days later the *Cyclops* left Rosyth for the Firth of Clyde, to begin a naval presence that was to last for the rest of the century. The Vice-Admiral (Submarines) chose the Holy Loch as her anchorage in preference to the site in Rothesay Bay. She was to be the headquarters of the Seventh Flotilla, and to provide submarines for anti-submarine and combined operations training, which were being set up in the area. More submarines moved into the area over the next few weeks, along with the small depot ship *White Bear*, and at the end of July the War Diary recorded:

> In view of the possibility of operating additional submarines from the Clyde area shortly, FOIC Greenock was asked to examine the question of a possible berth for the *Forth* and the Second Flotilla. He replied that Holy Loch or Rothesay appeared to be the most suitable berths . . .

It took some time to reach a decision, but by the end of August the *Forth* was ordered to go to the Holy Loch, while the *Cyclops* would move to Rothesay. The submarine force in Scotland now consisted of the *Forth* and *White Bear* in the Holy Loch with the Second Flotilla, consisting of eight boats, mostly of the modern T class; the Seventh Flotilla at Rothesay with *Cyclops* and fifteen older boats, mostly used for training; and the Third Flotilla at Rosyth with the *Titania* and five modern boats, mostly of the S Class. But this was not to last, and on 19 October the Vice-Admiral (Submarines)

> pointed out that at least three submarines would be needed to maintain an efficient watch on Brest, and suggested moving *Titania* with three S class submarines to the Clyde in order to compete with the increased commitments on the west coast of France, and in order to have them readily available for the threatened invasion of Ireland.

This was confirmed on 1 November when the *Titania* was ordered to 'Proceed to the Holy Loch to assist *Forth* and *Cyclops* in the accommodation of the Second, Third and Seventh Flotillas.' She arrived at Greenock on the 22nd and the concentration of submarines in the Clyde was largely complete, with twenty-five boats based there. The submarine base at Harwich was closed on 5 November and only the Ninth Flotilla remained on the North Sea coast, operating from Dundee.[37]

Submarines from the Clyde ranged widely over the seas, from Norway to the Mediterranean. Their main task was to patrol the waters of the Bay of Biscay and attack enemy ships and submarines using the bases there:

> The ward-room of HMS *Forth* had been nicknamed the Globetrotters'
> Club. Submariners sprawled in the deep chairs and swapped yarns with
> officers from other boats with whom they had shared depth charges in
> the Mediterranean. Men back from the Bay of Biscay discussed tactics
> and experiences with friends down from the Arctic Circle or across
> from Norway. There was great talk about Norway.[38]

Some of the patrols read like episodes from a past age, and perhaps confirm the submariners' conception of themselves as modern bucca-neers. Off L'Orient the *Talisman* captured a French sailing ketch, put a prize crew on board and sent her to a port on the other side of the Channel.[39]

Clandestine Operations

On 30 November 1942, the submarine *Tuna* slipped her moorings alongside HMS *Forth* in the Holy Loch and began the journey to the west coast of France. She was carrying six canoes and twelve officers and men of the Royal Marines under Major 'Blondie' Hasler. They had already spent some time training in Loch Long with their canoes, and in the Holy Loch they had devised a method for lifting the canoes, using an extension to a submarine's gun barrel. They were launched off the River Gironde and paddled up to Bordeaux, where they fixed limpet mines on merchant ships in the harbour. Several ships were damaged but eight of the men never returned, being drowned, or captured and shot by the Germans.[40] This episode later became a book and a film, *Cockleshell Heroes*.

In April 1943 Lt-Cdr Ewen Montagu RNVR arrived at Greenock in a van containing a 400-lb canister for delivery to HMS *Forth*. He and his colleagues had just driven overnight from London, no mean feat in the blackout when only dipped headlights could be used. There was some confusion, as the naval authorities had expected several small packages and sent only one sailor to help load the cargo onto a launch. Montagu found a Wren officer he knew and arranged a larger party. The canister was taken across the Clyde to the depot ship and then loaded onto the submarine *Seraph*, commanded by Lieutenant N. A. Jewell. At this stage he was the only person in the submarine who knew that it contained a body, posing as 'Major Martin RM', planted with fake documents suggesting that the next Allied invasion was to take place in the Greek Islands rather than Sicily. *Seraph* sailed from the Holy Loch next day and the body was duly launched off the coast of Spain, where it played its part in fooling German intelligence. This too became a book and a film, *The Man who Never Was*.[41]

Chariots and X-Craft

The idea for the chariot or 'human torpedo' was inspired by Italian attacks on Alexandria Harbour early in 1942. On the orders of Churchill himself, development was started at Portsmouth and the design of the standard 21-inch torpedo was adapted to carry two men in diving suits sitting astride it. They had full control over its movements, including depth, and could carry limpet mines to attach to an enemy hull.

The new weapon was ready by the spring of 1942 and a naval party proceeded north to join the depot ship *Titania* in the Clyde. She sailed to a new base, code-named Port D, in Loch Erisort just south of Stornoway on Lewis. Training started with a wooden dummy torpedo known as 'Cassidy':

> The usual drill with 'Cassidy' was for the two divers to get into the water, discover if and where the suits were leaking, and if they did not feel too wet and miserable haul themselves astride. The towing motor-boat would then go ahead, and when the appropriate signal was passed the diver who was riding as Number One would open the main ballast-vent, release the air and cause the machine to dive. After fifteen or twenty minutes of being towed underwater, he would bring 'Cassidy' to the surface again.[42]

The first actual chariot, 'the Real One', arrived in June and a demonstration took place in front of the sceptical Admiral King of the US Navy. Various nets were laid in the loch for practice.

> The nets were of two varieties, the large-mesh, deep, anti-submarine specimen and the small-mesh, shallower anti-torpedo. Their depth was determined by the weight that their supporting line of buoys and their

jackstay could stand. One day Boom Defence produced one covered with interwoven barbed wire – just to make it a little more realistically difficult. In the end the whole chariot party won a bet of 'Gins all round' from the Boom Defence Officer by getting through his, according to him, impenetrable nets.[43]

After a time Loch Erisort became too easy and the *Titania* was moved to Loch Cairnbawn, Port HHZ, on the north-west mainland. The new battleship *Howe* anchored there and was used for an exercise in which seven chariots attacked by night. Although the defenders knew the day and approximate hour of the attack, four chariots succeeded in placing their charges on her hull, though one was spotted on the way out, and three failed to attack. In a second night of attacks, all four succeeded in placing mines, though two were detected on the way out. But on a third night, one officer went unconscious under the hull of the *Howe* and his number two brought the chariot to the surface, but the officer died. Another successful practice attack was carried out in October on the battleship *Rodney* in Loch Erisort.

There was one obvious target for such craft – the great German battleship *Tirpitz*, lying in Asenfjord near Trondheim where she could threaten a breakout into the Atlantic or an attack on the Russian convoys. Her destruction would immediately free some of the ships at Scapa Flow for other duties. On 26 October the Norwegian fishing boat *Arthur*, commanded by Leif Larsen of the Norwegian resistance, left Lunna Voe with two chariots slung under the hull. Their forged papers got them past the German patrols, but the chariots broke adrift and the operation had to be abandoned. The crews escaped to neutral Sweden and some were eventually flown back to Leuchars in Fife after an absence of a month.

Another type of small submersible craft was already under development. The X-craft was a small submarine which the crew would travel inside, rather than sitting on top. The design had been started by a retired commander, Cromwell Varley, and his company of Varley Marine. The first example, named *X-3* because *X-1* and *X-2* had been used for previous experimental designs, was launched in the spring of 1942. The interior of an X-craft is described by two of the men who operated them:

> There was much less room, for instance, than in the smallest types of domestic air-raid shelters. In a way, living in an X-craft was rather like being cooped up beneath the stairs. Under the periscope-dome a small man could stand upright, but elsewhere in the craft there was scarcely head-clearance from a sitting position. Progress from one part to

another was made bent double, and nowhere could one stretch one's arms apart without encountering either the external pressure-hull or internal equipment. The small hatchways were roughly two feet in diameter and presented quite a problem for anyone wearing lots of woollens and oilskins. When the three – and later four – members of the crew were at action stations the skipper, in the centre of the control-room, could touch each of the others without moving his feet and without undue stretching. Aft, in the engine-room, conditions were even worse. To work the engine or motor one had to lie flat on a foot-wide fuel-tank, with the pressure-hull rising only two or three inches clear of one's head and shoulders. And to operate the air-compressor it was necessary to pass one's arm through a six-inch gap between a red-hot exhaust trunking and a fly-wheel turning at anything up to two thousand revolutions a minute.[44]

A few months after her launch in southern England, *X-3* was set north by rail to the new port at Faslane and attached to HMS *Cyclops* at Rothesay for training. A new base was set up in the Port Bannatyne Hydropathic Hotel and named HMS *Varbel* – a combination of Varley, who had designed the craft, and Bell, the commander in charge of personnel and training. Loch Striven to the north, 'a long, narrow, fjord-like waterway'[45] out of sight of most forms of human activity, was cleared of all other vessels and dedicated to training. The shooting-lodge at Ardtaraig House was taken over as an advanced base and became *Varbel II*. In March 1943 the flotilla of X-craft, now known as the Twelfth Submarine Flotilla, proceeded to Loch Cairn-bawn with the depot ship *Bonadventure*, though three boats remained behind at Port Bannatyne to train new crews. By August there were six X-craft at Cairnbawn and *Titania* joined as depot ship for conven-tional submarines, for it had been decided that the best way to get the midget submarines to the scene of the action was to tow each behind a larger sister.

Again the target was the *Tirpitz,* now anchored in Kaafjord at almost the most northerly point in Europe, 1,200 miles away from Loch Cairnbawn. Also in the area were the *Scharnhorst* and *Lutzow.* The unsung heroes of the operation were the passage crews, who had to endure eight days of living in extremely cramped and uncomfort-able conditions during the tow. Two of the six X-craft dropped out during the passage. Off Altenfjord the attack crews took over and on the night of 20–21 September 1943 they began to enter the fjord. *X-10* was forced to turn back and *X-5* was never heard of again. *X-6* and *X-7* succeeded in laying charges under the Tirpitz and seriously damaged her engine mountings, putting her out of action for several months, but they did not sink her. Lieutenants Cameron and Place were eventually awarded the Victoria Cross. But in the meantime the surviving crews' arrival back at *Bonaventure* on board the submarine *Truculent* was less generous. As they went down to the wardroom, one officer complained about their dishevelled appearance.

The X-craft were to make one further attack in Norwegian waters, besides those they undertook in the Mediterranean and Far East using their training at Loch Striven and Loch Cairnbawn. In September 1944 they sank a large floating dock which was used by U-boats in Bergen Harbour.

The Role of Rosyth

Since Scapa Flow had revived as the main fleet base in home waters, Rosyth served mainly as a repairing and refitting yard for major ships. It was a vital but humdrum role, for Rosyth never again became a main fleet base after 1940, nor did it suffer great danger from the Luftwaffe; Plymouth was devastated, Portsmouth severely damaged and Chatham less so, but Rosyth was never hit at all. In all there were 117 air reconnaissances in the Forth and Clyde area and twelve actual raids but none hit Rosyth.

Rosyth's first major repair was of the cruiser *Belfast*, damaged by one of the first magnetic mines on 21 November 1939 at the mouth of the Forth. She was towed there by the tug *Krooman* and given a temporary repair over seven months and then sent to Devonport for a complete rebuild. The port's importance as a bomb-free yard was first stressed at the end of 1940 when the battleship *Queen Elizabeth*, partially refitted at Portsmouth, was transferred to Rosyth as soon as she was able to go to sea. All five of the new battleships built during the war, the *King George V* class, were sent to Rosyth for fitting out, as were most large aircraft carriers. During the winter of 1941–2 the *Nelson* was given a major repair and refit after mine damage and men were seconded from the southern yards because of the 'parlous situation in respect of battleships at this time'. Priorities were different for the cruiser *Liverpool*, which was taken in hand in July 1942 but not completed for three years because she was not needed urgently. The biggest repair was to the battleship *Warspite*, also mine damaged, in June 1944 on the way from the invasion beaches to change a gun barrel in Rosyth. She suffered from 'Complete fracture of the main turbine feet; destruction of the alignment of Port shafts, one of which was badly bent; destruction of a large amount of auxiliary machinery;

main engines and condensers lifted bodily; one 15-inch turret and ship's outer bottom badly damaged.' 'Unorthodox methods' were needed to repair the hull and six of the eight 15-inch guns were replaced. In all there were 14 battleship and three battlecruiser refits of more than a month during the war, with 5 on fleet aircraft carriers, 21 cruisers and depot ships, 29 destroyers and 80 smaller vessels.

Rosyth was still better equipped for large ships than small ones, though a floating dock was installed in the basin. As a result 2,000 repairs of smaller ships were done by contract in the private shipyards of the firth, under Rosyth's supervision. Robbs of Leith, Devlin of Granton and Menzies of Leith led the way, with several hundred repairs each. Emergency repair depots for destroyers and smaller craft were set up at Corpach near Fort William and Dunstaffnage near Oban, each with about 1,000 men and a floating dock.

At the beginning of the war Rosyth employed ten naval officers, 32 senior and 133 junior civil servants and 1,670 industrial workers, with a wage bill of £10,390 per week. Naturally there was need for vast expansion and 1,695 men were transferred from the southern yards with an extra allowance of 21 shillings (£1.05) per week. More men were brought in from the coalfields, factories, breweries and garages of the region. There were still difficulties, particularly in finding men for the yard tugs and lighters, and there was a perpetual shortage of experienced draughtsmen, as many had been promoted to management. Unlike the other yards, Rosyth did not have a pool of recent ex-apprentices to draw on.

There was one solitary woman among the industrial employees in 1939. Perhaps this was because there was no flag loft (which employed 'ladies' in the traditional yards) or ropery (which employed 'women'). Soon women began to take on many of the unskilled tasks, then in April 1941 they began training as machinists in Ramsey Technical College, Edinburgh, and Glasgow Technical College. By the end of the war there were 2,204 women workers in the yard along with 7,096 men. There were 21 naval officers, 101 senior civil servants and 409 junior.

The influx of workers put severe stress on accommodation in the area. Eight hundred small houses were built in the Rosyth area while the Pilmuir Hostel in Dunfermline was taken over and fitted with cubicles for 257 single men. This was not nearly enough and by 1942 about 3,000 workers were travelling by rail from Kirckaldy, Edinburgh and as far away as Falkirk – unusual with the long working hours of the pre-commuter age.

Many other tasks were undertaken by the dockyard, including the manufacture of beach signs for the D-Day landings and aircraft trolleys for the Fleet Air Arm. The yard set up eleven sites around Scotland to decoy enemy bombers. Rosyth itself had a twin at Valleyfield further up the firth, where the night-time appearance of the yard and the Crombie magazine were reproduced. The largest site in Scotland was in the Kyles of Bute, intended to draw the attack from Greenock and the Tail of the Bank anchorage. It was four miles long between Buttock Point and Rudabodach and had simulated ships' lights, railway signals, 'leaky' lighting which had apparently failed to live up to the standards of the blackout and electrically controlled fires.[46]

Chapter 13

The Clyde Convoy Base

The U-Boat War

As the Second World War approached, the Germans rebuilt their U-boat fleet. The Royal Navy had a good deal of faith in Asdic, but it was also aware that the bombing could close the southern and eastern English ports, such as London and Hull which accounted for more than 40 per cent of British trade in the 1930s. Already there were plans for the diversion of shipping to the western ports, including the Clyde. The U-boat campaign began within a few hours of the British declaration of war, when *U-30*, against orders, torpedoed the liner *Athenia* carrying more than 600 passengers. The people of Clydeside knew about this on 5 September when 500 survivors arrived at Glasgow and caused some strain on the welfare services. A convoy system was immediately set up. Methil resumed its role in the last war, as base for coal convoys to Norway.

The first two victories against the U-boat in this war took place off the Hebrides. On 14 September the *Ark Royal*, the navy's only modern aircraft carrier in service, was on anti-submarine patrol 150 miles west of the Hebrides when *U-39* fired two torpedoes at her. They exploded prematurely and the *Ark Royal*'s escorts damaged the U-boat with three depth-charge attacks. She broke surface and her crew abandoned her, allowing her to sink. Meanwhile there were reports that a U-boat was stopping fishing boats sixty miles west of the Hebrides and destroyers of the Home Fleet and naval aircraft went out to look for her. On 20 September *U-27* was sighted on the surface by the destroyers *Fortune* and *Forester*. Again the U-boat's torpedoes exploded prematurely and *U-27* dived. She too was damaged in a depth-charge attack, with one propeller shaft bent and water coming in through holes aft. She surfaced just as *Fortune* was launching another attack and the crew abandoned ship. Her captain got a coded message out from his prisoner-of-war camp and the Germans soon learned about the faults in their torpedoes and rectified them.[1] For the rest of the war, the U-boats' main armament became increasingly deadly.

A few months later the Firth of Clyde had a taste of anti-submarine action. *U-33* under Kapitanleutnant Hans von Dresky entered the firth to lay mines. On the night of 12 February she was spotted on the surface just south of Arran by HMS *Gleaner,* a converted survey vessel, and dived quickly. *Gleaner* dropped three patterns of depth charges and the U-boat was forced to the surface, where she was scuttled. Three rotors from her Enigma coding machine were recovered, a stage in the battle to decode German signals, which was eventually to give the Allies an advantage in the U-boat war.[2] But there were to be no more such battles in the Clyde itself. Most of the action in the first six months of war took place off Land's End, but in February HMS *Cornelia* attacked an Asdic contact off Stranraer, and a lorry driver on the Mull of Kintyre reported a sighting, which was investigated by HMS *Whirlwind.*[3]

France surrendered to the Germans on 22 June 1940. During July and August, as German air attacks increased, traffic in the English Channel was limited to coastal convoys which travelled short distances under cover of darkness. The Germans now had bases at Brest, L'Orient and St Nazaire on the west coast of France, from which the U-boats could reach far out into the Atlantic with little interference from British forces. From the Fall of France to the German invasion of the Soviet Union in the following year, the most intensive fighting in the U-boat war was in a funnel spreading about 600 miles west and north-west from the Mull of Kintyre, where the great majority of British merchant-ship losses occurred. It was the 'Happy Time' of the submarine commanders, in which they sank 217 ships for the loss of 2 of their own during the attacks. After that, increased air surveillance forced the U-boats further out into the Atlantic.[4] Since Eire was neutral, the RAF relied on bases in Scotland, Northern Ireland, South Wales, the south-west of England and in Iceland to give their planes the chance to patrol far out into the ocean. In those days most long-range aircraft were flying-boats and in March 1943 six British-designed Sunderlands operated from Bowmore, on Loch Indaal on Islay; nine flew from Oban Bay; and six American-built Catalinas were based at Sullom Voe on Shetland. New long-range landplanes were beginning to arrive from America and eighteen Flying Fortresses were based on Benbecula, the flattest of the Outer Hebrides.[5] Later the Scottish bases were used less and long-range aircraft mostly flew from Northern Ireland, south Wales and south-western England.

The Clyde was expected to be safer from aerial attack than other ports. This seemed to be disproved when Clydebank was raided on the night of 13 and 14 March 1941, when a third of the houses in the town were so badly damaged that they had to be demolished, and almost all were damaged in some way. About a thousand people were killed in the raid and the same number seriously injured, but shipbuilding and industrial production suffered little.[6] But the Clydeside Blitz was short-lived and lasted only from March to May 1941. Figures showed that Liverpool was raided twenty-four times between September 1940 and May 1941, London seventy-two times, the Clyde only four times.[7] In Liverpool 414,000 tons of shipping were put out of action during the great raid of 8 May 1941.[8] The transport facilities of the Clyde were never disrupted as seriously as those of other major ports.

The Docks and the Railways

David Lloyd George, Prime Minister during the second half of the First World War, wrote that 'the submarine was fought on land as well as sea'.[9] This was even more true for the second war, especially for the Clyde ports which had to make enormous adjustments to cope with very different conditions.

The Port of Glasgow was an artificial creation, built by constricting and dredging the River Clyde over nearly two centuries. It was twenty miles up the river from the firth at Greenock, along a narrow channel. Glasgow had a total of about twelve miles of quay, compared with thirty-eight miles on the Mersey. About two-fifths was in riverside berths on both banks from the centre of the city to Renfrew. The main artificial docks, Queen's Dock north of the river and Prince's Dock to the south, were not true wet docks in that they were open to the rise and fall of the tide. Queen's Dock, the largest, with 3,334 yards of berthing, dealt with ocean-going traffic, Prince's Dock with coasters and puffers. King George V Dock, two miles down the river at Shieldhall, was relatively new and offered a mile of quays for the largest ships. Its opening in 1931 had coincided with the Great Depression and it was still poorly equipped, for some of its cranes had not been installed.[10] Another two miles downriver at Clydebank was Rothesay Dock, which specialised in bulk cargoes such as coal, iron ore and limestone.

Greenock had four miles of quay, about a third of that of Glasgow, and much of that was taken up for naval use. The town was served by a single railway, which joined the main network at Glasgow. The East India Harbour, built in 1805–9, was far too small for modern seagoing vessels. The Victoria Harbour and Albert Harbour had only 14 ft of water at low tide. The Great Harbour was as large as its title implies, with 58 acres of water, but it was intended for shelter rather than cargo handling and had only two small cranes, and no warehouses. The James Watt Dock, the only true wet dock on the Clyde, was the best. It offered more than a mile of quay space with twelve cranes, including one capable of lifting a 150-ton load. Though limited, Greenock's facilities were useful because they were close to the anchorage at the Tail of the Bank.

Before the war the Clyde ports had been relatively small compared with London and Liverpool, accounting for less than 4 per cent of British trade. Glasgow had dealt mainly with liner traffic, with cargoes of 2,000 to 5,000 tons, whereas in wartime it had to handle ships carrying 10,000 tons each. It had mainly handled exports, whereas imports were now the priority. There were only 3,600 dockers in Glasgow, compared with 27,000 in Liverpool and 28,000 on the Thames, but 5,000 to 6,000 would be needed. They were less well organised than those in other ports and were fiercely opposed to registration until this was enforced by an Essential Work Order from the Ministry of Labour in 1940.[11] The road and rail links at Glasgow Docks were adequate for the pre-war local trade, but not for the new demands.

According to a report of March 1941,

> In peace-time, a large proportion of Glasgow's overseas import trade was received as part-cargoes of about 500 tons to 2,000 tons in liner vessels running to regular time schedules. The consignments were mainly for use or consumption in Glasgow or in other parts of Scotland within the economic distribution area of the port. The traffic flowed through the well-established channels. The transit shed accommodation was ample to accommodate the goods as they were discharged ashore: the vessels were discharged by stevedores employed at day-work rates and working generally during ordinary hours, with occasional overtime or week-end working: the goods were removed from the sheds by the importers in time for the berth to be clear for the next vessel, the date of arrival of which was known in advance: and the importers were often allowed by the Clyde Navigation Trust to spread the deliveries over a prolonged period unless the berth was required.[12]

In wartime all this was changed. Whole cargoes now had to be unloaded, and sent on for distribution to all parts of the country. Large numbers of ships would arrive at once in a convoy and had to be unloaded as quickly as possible. Dock facilities at Glasgow were limited compared with London and Liverpool, and even these were not all in good condition after the depression of the 1930s. The biggest problem was the onward movement of cargoes. According to an official report, 'The most severe case of delay to the ocean ships in war is always liable to be, and in fact was in the winter of 1940–1, congestion on the railways.'[13]

The handling of cargoes was a complex affair involving several organisations. According to the 1941 report,

Clyde Navigation Trust; provide the berth, quay and shed accommodation but do not themselves operate the berths, except at Meadowside Granary.

Shipowner; provides the ship, but does not himself perform the discharge.

Consignee; usually employs a carman or railway company to obtain the goods for the docks and frequently employs a forwarding agent to pass Customs Entries.

Master Stevedore; employed by the shipowner to discharge the vessel.

Master Porter; employed by the shipowner or consignee to receive the goods on the quay, sort and make them available for delivery.

Carman or Railway Company; employed by the consignee to load the goods from the shed and deliver out of the docks.[14]

A Port Emergency Committee was set up to speed the passage of goods through the docks, consisting of the harbourmaster as chairman, the assistant traffic superintendent, movement officers from the Ministry of Food and Ministry of Supply to decide priorities, a storage officer from the Ministry of Transport, a representative of the Ministry of Shipping and men from the two railway companies in the area and the Glasgow Dock Cartage Organisation.

The volume of goods handled by Greenock and Glasgow increased by 31 per cent in July, August and September 1940 compared with the three months before the Fall of France, and was still 23 per cent up in the spring of 1941. Liverpool's traffic actually decreased during the same period, partly due to difficulties caused by bombing. In April, May and June 1940, Liverpool handled 992,000 net tons, more than three times the Clyde's 321,300 tons. In January, February and March 1941 the two ports were much closer. The Clyde had 401,000 tons, nearly two-thirds of the Mersey's 628,300 tons. During the peak year of 1944, Glasgow alone handled over nine million tons of goods, compared with about 6.5 million in an average year before the war. This illustrates the achievement of many people, including managers and dockers brought in from the Port of London, in making the best of the facilities of the Clyde in very difficult conditions, with many other demands on resources and labour.[15]

The Clyde Anchorages

Another problem was that, in normal peacetime service at least, only six ships could leave the Glasgow Docks in a single tide.[16] This made the anchorages off Greenock very important for assembling a convoy over a period of several days, for incoming ships awaiting a berth at Glasgow or Greenock and for ships which unloaded directly into coasters and lighters.

The water beyond the Cloch Lighthouse was generally too deep to anchor in. The best known anchorage in the area was the Tail of the Bank, which was used by naval ships, though it was dangerous in gales. Unlike Liverpool, escorts did not go alongside the docks when in port. Fleets of drifters and naval auxiliaries ferried men ashore on leave, but it was less convenient than being in dock. Nicholas Monsarrat describes the experience.

> But *Campanula* was hardly ever alongside, in any case. The corvette and destroyer anchorage was about half a mile off-shore, at the Tail-of-the-Bank, and here we lay in isolation, swinging to our own anchor cable, served by supply and liberty boats which, being converted herring drifters built like wooden tanks and crewed by stalwart Scots fishermen who like to signal their arrival with a good solid thump, were a constant menace to paintwork and plating.[17]

There were fifty anchor berths for merchant ships off Kilcreggan Patch where the holding ground was only regarded as 'moderate' and this caused problems in bad weather. 'Much of the damage is caused by ships with light anchors breaking away. When it is known that a ship's ground tackle is inadequate, she is berthed at a buoy, if one is available, and will shortly be reduced by one on Admiralty instructions.'[18] The navy was as reluctant to use buoys for mooring as it had been at Scapa Flow more than twenty years earlier. Ships moored to buoys reacted differently to changes in wind and tide than those at anchor, and it was impossible to mix the two in the same area without danger of collision. There were forty more anchor berths in Loch Long, five in the Holy Loch and twenty-six in the Gareloch.

In Loch Long, the depth of the water caused problems in bad weather. According to Rear-Admiral Hill,

It must be realised that the average depth in Loch Long is between 30 and 36 fathoms, and that half the berths at the Main Anchorage are outside the 20-fathom line. The length of cable carried by merchant ships is regulated, and the average merchant ship would have no more, under present conditions, than 120 fathoms on the port anchor and 105 on the starboard. This is insufficient to allow the usual scope of five times the depth of water.[19]

Graeme Ogden describes his arrival in the river in the armed trawler *Lady Madeleine.*

In 1941 the Clyde was chock-a-block with shipping of all descriptions. When we had gone through the boom opposite Dunoon we could see two or three battleships anchored in the roads, towering above a host of merchantmen. After passing Gourock we saw the destroyers riding to their moorings at the Tail of the Bank. Such was the crush that the small fry such as trawlers had to tie up as best they could, whether at Princes Pier or alongside the outer wall of the Albert Harbour. We had been given a berth at Princes Pier at Greenock, but I had no idea how to find it. After several abortive attempts we found an empty space and tied up.[20]

The Defences of the Clyde

The main anti-submarine defence of the Clyde anchorages was the boom erected between Cloch Lighthouse and Dunoon, on the same principle as those which had protected Scapa in the last war. Specially designed boom defence vessels of the 'Bar' class, 150 ft long, were beginning to supersede the converted trawlers as used in the last war. The Cloch to Dunoon boom had three of these in the middle of 1942, as well as nine trawlers, supported by two tenders and two net-laying drifters.[21]

The situation of the boom left the Firth of Clyde relatively open, though by 1942 its waters were heavily patrolled by a force of five harbour defence patrol craft, four motor launches and eighteen naval auxiliary boats.[22] Early in 1940 there was concern that neutral trawlers, especially from Eire, could still enter the firth and spread gossip or hard intelligence about ship movements without any British control. The Scottish Fisheries Department had always wanted to close the firth to foreigners, but it was the Admiralty that had opposed them. Territorial waters extended three miles off the coast and it was not normal to close a bay or estuary more than six miles wide. The navy felt that to close the Clyde would be to set a precedent which might be used to exclude British warships from other areas, for example in Norway. Instead it was decided to declare a largely fictitious minefield between Kintyre and the south Ayrshire coast, outside of Ailsa Craig. Two prescribed channels would be laid out inside the firth for shipping movements and the rest of the area carefully patrolled.[23] For gun defences, the Clyde had two 4.7-inch guns at Toward Point south of Dunoon, two 6-inch guns and a 9.2 at Ardhallow on the same stretch of coast, with two 12-pounders in the hills above Gourock to cover the boom.[24]

U-boats made no serious attempts to penetrate the Clyde for five years after the early stages of the war, for Admiral Raeder, head of the German Navy, clashed with Hitler on the *U-33* raid and ruled that such operations were too reckless to be repeated. On the British side there was a fear that the defenders might become complacent. In May 1942 the flag officer at Greenock staged an exercise to test the attention of the harbour defence Asdic operators at Wemyss Bay. The Dutch submarine *09* tried to sail up the centre of the river after submerging off Toward Point, but for safety reasons she was accompanied on the surface by a motor launch and a large number of officers had to be informed about the exercise – almost everyone, it seems, except the actual Asdic operators. The submarine duly submerged at 9.30 on 19 May and was not detected by the fixed beam of station A at Wemyss. Station B, with a moveable beam, did pick up an echo from the submarine but thought it was from the motor launch. It did not classify the echo properly until it had passed Wemyss Bay and was more than 2,500 yards to the north, and even then the presence of an officer from the anti-submarine training station at HMS *Osprey* may have helped. The report on the exercise was lukewarm and recommended more training for static Asdic operators, for, unlike sea-going ones, they rarely had a chance to listen to the enemy.[25]

The Glasgow and Greenock Commands

Naval forces in the west of Scotland formed part of Western Approaches Command, based in Liverpool. One part was based at St Enoch's Hotel in Glasgow under Vice-Admiral Sir James Troup and was mainly concerned with administrative duties. Named HMS *Spartiate*, it was largely concerned with the crews of ships under construction in the Clyde – 1,549 warships and auxiliaries were built there during the war along with 354 merchant ships.[26] In addition the admiral had many ceremonial duties. In November 1942, for example, Mrs Eleanor Roosevelt, America's First Lady, cruised up the river in the Clyde steamer *Queen Mary II* and addressed the workers at John Brown's shipyard. Two months later King Haakon of Norway inspected an anti-submarine vessel belonging to his free forces and King George VI toured the shipyards in a naval motor launch, escorted by Flag Officer in Charge, Glasgow.[27]

Captain David Bone of the merchant navy wrote:

> At Naval Headquarters in Glasgow one had to learn the rules. Security was served by curt contacts and a caller had to be amply documented when the base was established in St Enoch's Hotel. The elderly P.O. in charge of the gangway on the fourth floor was a grim custodian then and to be feared at first acquaintance, but missed later as the very figurehead of *Spartiate* – as the base was named – when he was retired or demobilised.[28]

The admiral on the lower Clyde, the Flag Officer in Charge, Greenock, was closer to the scene of war. The first officer to hold the post was Vice-Admiral Bertram Watson, who, like Admiral Troup, had family connections in Broughty Ferry. He had previously served as Rear-Admiral (Submarines). In February 1942 he was replaced by Rear-Admiral Richard Hill, who was nearly sixty-two. He had retired as a vice-admiral in 1935 and became a convoy commodore, with RNR rank, at the outbreak of war. He had a wide-ranging command, including forces at Oban, Loch Ewe, Stranraer, Ardrossan, the research station at Fairlie and the famous training base, HMS *Western Isles*, at Tobermory. But his most immediate concern was the Clyde itself, its defence and the organisation and protection of the convoys which sailed from there. To do this he had an enormous force of small craft in the Clyde alone – 21 harbour defence motor launches, 19 boom defence vessels, a similar number of river patrol craft, more than 100 naval auxiliary boats, drifters, motor fishing vessels, colliers, tugs, water boats, minesweepers and accommodation ships.[29] Great ships of the Home Fleet often visited the Clyde but were not under the FOIC's command. Instead he had a constantly varying force of medium-sized warships as ocean-going and coastal convoy escorts.

The Clyde Escort Force

The escort forces based in the Clyde tended to be smaller than those in Liverpool and Londonderry. The former port was the headquarters of the whole Atlantic campaign and had up to sixty destroyers and corvettes early in 1942. Londonderry, with few dock facilities for merchant ships, was operated mainly as an escort base and had sixty-eight destroyers, sloops, corvettes and other ships at the beginning of 1942 when the Clyde had only thirty-seven.[30] The Clyde forces never became as famous as those from the other ports. Londonderry had Commander Peter Gretton's Seventh Escort Group which sank five U-boats in defence of Convoy ONS 5 in May 1943, while Liverpool had Captain Frederick Walker's even more famous Second Support Group which sank six boats in February 1944.

In September 1940, during the early stages of the Atlantic campaign, there were thirty anti-submarine ships based on the Clyde, consisting of one destroyer, three corvettes, a minesweeper, sixteen trawlers and nine yachts.[31] At this stage the ocean escorts were still based at Rosyth, Liverpool and Plymouth and the trawlers and the yachts were intended for short-range work. But already many of the Liverpool ships were spending a good deal of time operating from the Clyde and eight of the new Flower Class corvettes were there on 6 November.[32] These became the most common and famous escorts of the Battle of the Atlantic. They were 205 ft long overall and of 925 tons, half the size of a contemporary destroyer. They initially had a crew of eighty-five men with a single 4-inch gun, a light anti-aircraft armament and depth charges as the main anti-submarine weapon. Designed originally for coastal convoys on the east and south coast of England, they had to be pressed into service in the battle of the Atlantic after the Fall of France. Their tendency to roll and their short forecastles made them almost uninhabitable in typical Atlantic weather: 'Well it was like a corkscrew. About the third dip you get tons and tons of water come over the fo'c's'le, and if you happened to be in the waist, you see, you probably get washed astern sort of style.' Below decks was little better. The worst part, I suppose, was that, when you were at sea in rough weather, [the corvettes] were thrown about like corks, and water was usually slushing about, not only in the bunk space but in the mess decks as well, and because you were battened down the air was quite foul at the time.'[33]

By the middle of November three full escort groups had moved to the Clyde. The Third Escort Group, which was to remain formally attached to the river for the rest of the war, had three destroyers of the pre-war A class, two more operated by the Free Polish Navy and three Flowers. By the end of the year the Eleventh Escort Group had also transferred to the Clyde, with a small force of three ships. Officially the Clyde Escort Force reached a peak in the spring of 1941, as ships were diverted north due to the bombing of Liverpool. The Third Group (3EG) had twelve ships, though they were actually on detachment to the Home Fleet; 4EG had six destroyers and five corvettes, with another corvette under repair; 10EG had four destroyers including one repairing and the Fourteenth Group had a similar strength.[34] According to Peter Coy, in 1941 'this Force appeared to be a rather motley collection of elderly destroyers, untried corvettes and unallocated French and Polish vessels whose capacity may have seemed unclear to Their Lordships in those early days.'[35] On 24 February 1941 the Third Escort Group became B3 Ocean Escort Group, the 'B' distinguishing it from American and Canadian groups. As well as the British ships, one of the main parts of the Free French Navy was based on the Clyde. This consisted of six corvettes built in Britain in 1941 and manned by French officers and ratings.

HMS *Harvester* was no stranger to the Clyde in the first two and half years of the war, for she visited it many times although attached to the Liverpool force. She was one of six ships which were building for the Brazilian Navy but were taken over in 1939. With four 4- to 7-inch guns and eight torpedo tubes, a speed of 35 knots and a range of 5,300 miles as well as good seakeeping qualities, they proved to be excellent convoy escorts, though too expensive for mass production, and were generally used as group leaders. *Harvester* was torpedoed by *U-432* on 10 March 1943 while escorting convoy HX 229. The survivors were picked up by the Free French corvette *Aconit* and brought back to Greenock on 11 March, with survivors of both U-boats.[36]

The Clyde Escort Force peaked again early in 1942. There were five 'Special Escort Groups' consisting of sixteen destroyers of relatively short range. Their duty was to escort outward-bound convoys for Russia and the Middle East on the first stage of their voyage and to meet the monster liners as they approached land. B3 and B4 Groups had six destroyers and ten corvettes, charged with protecting Atlantic convoys to and from the Eastern Ocean Meeting Point in the middle of the Atlantic, where Canadian-based escorts took over. By August of that year there were only two groups based in the Clyde, the Greenock Special Escort Division with nine destroyers and four corvettes and B3 with three destroyers and six corvettes. By the beginning of 1943 many of the ships from the Clyde, even from the long-standing B3, were actually operating from Londonderry, taking them slightly closer to the battleground in the Atlantic and freeing space for merchant ships in the river.[37]

By the middle of 1942 a new class of escort, the frigate, was beginning to enter service. The ships of the River class were nearly 100 ft longer than the Flowers, had twice the engine power and four more knots of speed, and were equipped with the latest weapons and

sensors, such as hedgehog, radar and new types of Asdic. To the
seamen, the biggest advantage was that they were much more stable in
a heavy sea than the Flowers. The next group, the Lochs, were similar
in form, but specially designed for mass production, using techniques
of welding and prefabrication. Most of the design work was done by
Robbs of Leith and the prototype was built by John Browns at
Clydebank.[38]

Convoy Organisation

On the Clyde, convoy conferences were held in Marymount, 'a modest
villa set on an eminence above Gourock Pier', though for an important
convoy where security was vital the conference might be held on board
the flagship of the escort.[39] Graeme Ogden describes the procedure at
'these quiet, sinister gatherings':

> The Commodore sat at the high table, flanked by the Naval Shipping
> Control Officer and the C.O. of the Escort. The grim-faced merchant
> captains and the C.O.s of the escort vessels formed the audience. Sailing
> orders and routing instructions were handed out (marked 'most secret')
> by N.S.C.O. and the Escort CO. then told the room what had to be
> done in various emergencies. He adopted a rather cheerful note in his
> deliverance and intimated all would be well with convoy.[40]

According to Captain Bone,

> Conference followed the customary lines. We were to weigh and
> proceed at 2200 hours, passing the boom gateships in the order detailed
> in the sailing orders. Clyde pilots would be disembarked off Rothesay
> Bay. Thereafter the ships of the convoy would continue in single line
> ahead until instructed by the Commodore to take up 'Formation B'
> which would be maintained until daybreak – or until otherwise
> ordered. Ocean formation was laid down in diagrams 'A' and 'A1'.
> Would the masters please check up on their convoy pennants and agree
> that the matters are fully understood? A pause while spectacles were
> adjusted; papers rustled and eyes lifted from the mimeographed sheets
> to a blackboard facing the company and silence was accepted.[41]

Captain Joseph Wellings, Assistant US Naval Attaché in London,
was not impressed when he attended a conference in Marymount in
February 1941. It was 'not conducted with the efficiency and the
clarification of the doubtful sections of the instructions as was a
similar conference attended by the observer at Halifax.' However he
conceded the difficulties of holding the conferences in three different

places, for ships that would join from Liverpool, the Clyde and Milford Haven.[42]

The ships in the convoy were given precise times to raise anchor and then pass through the boom between the Cloch and Dunoon. Captain Bone suffered some anxiety as his ship attempted to catch up with a convoy which was already outside:

> It was only when we were held up at the Boom Defences off the Cloch in late afternoon that the consequences of delay occurred to me. For over half an hour we lay stopped awaiting the signal from the gateship to proceed; a straggling group of small coasters was coming in from the sea and they had the right of way. With growing impatience and concern, I though of the fleet of high-powered transports pressing on at speed towards the North Channel.[43]

The convoy would then assemble off Kintyre, joining contingents from other ports. When fully assembled and including ships from Milford Haven and Liverpool, convoy WS6, carrying troops round the Cape of Good Hope to the war in the Middle East, was 'formed in 10 columns, three ships to a column. Speed of convoy 9 knots. Distance between columns 1000 yards, distance between ships in column 600 yards. Station keeping between columns fair, between ships in columns, fair to poor.'[44]

Overside Discharge

Even before the Fall of France was a *fait accompli*, plans were being made for increasing the amount of traffic which the limited facilities of the Clyde could handle. As early as 22 May 1940, as the Germans advanced through northern France, the scenario which was envisaged was the temporary closure of one of the east-coast ports, perhaps by mines or bombing, and the diversion of large quantities of shipping to the Clyde. It was planned to begin a scheme for the 'overside discharge' of cargoes from newly arrived ocean-going ships into small coasters, which would then unload at the smaller Clyde ports or carry the cargoes onward. The Clyde, with its large and relatively sheltered anchorage at the Tail of the Bank, was the only west-coast port suitable for such an operation. The project was boosted by the capture of some Dutch coasters when their homeland fell to the Germans, but there were many difficulties.

In the first place, no one wanted to take responsibility for the Tail of the Bank, which belonged neither to Glasgow nor Greenock. Under pressure, Greenock agreed to take charge, but the operation was put

under the control of the assistant general manager of the Port of
London Authority. Secondly, the Clyde had no tradition of discharging into barges, so the London firm of Scruttons Ltd brought up 500
of its men from the Thames. There was difficulty in finding accommodation for them in Greenock, already crowded with shipyard
workers and sailors. Overside discharge could be quite expensive
in terms of labour and shipping time. The dockers would assemble at
Greenock pier at 8 in the morning, go out to the ship and start work by
9. They would be collected to go ashore for a dinner hour at 12 and
would be back at work by 2 in the afternoon. If they worked till 6.30
they would be back at the pier by 7, having worked 7 hours but being
paid 8 hours' normal time and 3 hours overtime.[45]

Then there was the problem of finding ports in the Clyde where the
barges could unload. Greenock was the most obvious and it was
originally hoped that four ocean-going ships could unload at a time
into ten barges, landing 5,200 tons of cargo. But there was not enough
railway siding accommodation to cope with this. Other ports were
considered:

> Wemyss Bay, Largs and Fairlie are all small passenger Piers outside the
> boom and there are obvious objections to ocean-going vessels anchor-
> ing outside the boom to discharge or to barges having to await the times
> of opening the Boom gates. Paisley comes under the Glasgow Port
> Emergency Committee but it must be remembered that it is over twenty
> miles from the nearest of the anchorages, which would make it more
> suitable for small coaster than barge traffic. Gourock is the most
> suitable of all the small Piers for barge traffic but this Pier is on the
> same railway line to Paisley (part of the Caledonian section of the LMS)
> as the main section of the Greenock Docks, and development of it
> would rob the railway outlet from Greenock while the part of Greenock
> Pier most suitable for barge traffic also is in daily use by passengers and
> at times in extensive use embarking and disembarking troops by tender
> – a very important matter since the closing of Princes Pier, Greenock,
> recently.[46]

But the passenger piers had no cranes and there was no real prospect
of getting any large ones. Helensburgh, on the other side of the Clyde,
had no direct rail access and could only be used for discharging into
road vehicles. Mr Halliday of Scruttons reported that

> Greenock's present facilities will be fully required to handle the tonnage
> that can be landed there on the quays ex ocean steamers discharging at
> the five available berths and that, in consequence, no barges should be

sent there for lading until it has been demonstrated that they can be handled. The facilities for off-loading barges with heavy and bulky packages would have to be used for this purpose, as at present there are no alternative facilities in the district.[47]

Overside discharge began in September 1940 and right from the start it was found that the distribution of an actual cargo was complex. When the *Scottish Star*, of 7,300 tons, arrived that month, 750 tons of railway sleepers were unloaded at Bowling and sent by rail to Stirling; 1,800 tons of plywood went round to Leith by coaster. Pigs of lead went to Glasgow Docks by coaster then on by rail. Other quantities of metal went by coaster to Liverpool, London and Cardiff and small quantities of woodpulp and sundry goods were unloaded at Greenock. A month later, the *Richmond Castle*, of 7,800 tons, unloaded copra, cotton and lead at Craigendoran, whence it went on by rail; maize was sent to London by coaster, groundnuts were taken by barge to Greenock Docks and another quantity of lead was sent by barge to Paisley Harbour and then on by road. As the official report commented, 'No-one, and particularly the importing ministries, would start to believe that the sort of operation involved in discharging ships within this sort of cargo was possible.'[48]

The operation began in a small way with the arrival of the first ship on 12 September and five were being worked at the end of the month, but it never expanded much beyond this. It was needed most in the winter of 1940–1 when the ports of the west coast of the United Kingdom almost, but not quite, reached saturation point. From the autumn of 1940 the ships discharged in the more sheltered waters of the Holy Loch, rather than the Tail of the Bank.[49] But the general shortage of coasters prevented the system coming fully into play. After that period there was less pressure and overside discharge was only used when there were no alternatives, for example, when the river was crowded with shipping. In 1941 709,000 tons of cargo were discharged, 515,000 tons in 1942 and 412,000 tons in 1943. It was also useful for dangerous cargoes such as explosives, but in fact it never reached the expectations of mid-1940; about 3 per cent of inward cargoes were handled this way during the war.[50]

The Military Ports

The other scheme was the building of two entirely new ports in western Scotland, designed specially for the embarkation of troops and their equipment for service overseas. Several established ports were looked at in Scotland and northern England, such as Barrow, Maryport, Troon, Ayr, Ardrossan and Oban, but it was soon found that there was a problem as to 'whether or not the existing ports can be extended to provide additional berths capable of taking vessels up to, say, 20–24 ft in draught'. One official commented 'Development of an existing port like Ardrossan seems to me preferable, and would be permanently useful.'[51] But instead it was decided to create two entirely new ports – No. 1 Military Port at Faslane on the Gareloch, and No. 2 at Loch Ryan near Stranraer. The Gareloch was largely undeveloped before the Second World War, apart from hotels such as Shandon Hydro and as an anchorage for shipping laid up in the depression. Para Handy's friend Hurricane Jack found himself 'An Ideal Job' as shipkeeper of 'a great big whupper o' a barquenteen caaled the *Jean and Mary*, wi' a cabin the size o' a Wee Free Church'. Captain Bone remembered the days of the Great Depression:

> I had known the loch in many aspects. In less exciting days, to be ordered there was almost a penal sentence for a ship, frequently but a prelude to sale abroad or to the indignity of the shipbreaker's yard. But its sheltered waters had often provided anchorage for many worthy vessels 'laid by in ordinary' to await better times during recurrent trade depressions.[52]

Before the war there were some doubts about the suitability of the Gareloch as a port, largely due to the difficulty in entering. A report of March 1939 considered using the loch as an extension to the anchorage at Tail of the Bank, but drew attention to

> the extreme narrowness of the channel between Limekiln Point and Rhu Point. There is a least depth of 22 ft with a rise of 10 ft, but the channel is narrowed on both sides by banks extending on the west side 150 ft into the channel from a line drawn between the two western marks and on the east side 200 ft, into the channel between a similar line between the eastern marks leaving an extremely difficult passage (of 270 ft) for anything but vessels considerably smaller than those envisaged . . . I was informed that no ships of the size contemplated have ever entered the Gareloch, RMS *Carmania*, 650 ft and drawing 26 ft, when laid up was berthed off Helensburgh.[53]

The Faslane site was chosen because 'it gave the depth of water required, had the prospects of good ground to construct upon, and was within easy access of the West Highland Line of the London & North Eastern Railway.' Hundreds of men of the Royal Engineers were drafted in to work 8–hour shifts for 24 hours a day and seven days a week. Jetties were built along the five-fathom line in Faslane Bay. The sea bottom was difficult to work with and special techniques had to be developed to sink piles. The land at Faslane had to be levelled to create railway sidings and vehicle parks. The entrance to the loch at Rhu Point had to be dredged to make it accessible to large troopships. The banks had to be built up to make room for railway sidings and parks for military equipment. Cranes were acquired from the ports in the south of England which had been rendered useless by the threat of bombing, including twenty-two from Southampton Docks, and two giant float-ing cranes were brought in. When finished, No. 1 Military Port had a deep-water wharf 3,000 ft long, with six berths for ships up to 33 ft draught; a 900 ft wharf for lighters to carry goods out to ships at anchor; a motor transport wharf from which vehicles could drive directly onto landing craft; and a heavy crane berth 400 ft long. It had thirty-eight dockside cranes plus two floating, five military camps for 4,000 men and six railway sidings. The lighterage wharves began operating in the middle of 1941 and the deep-water wharves loaded their first ship in May 1942. The port was complete by December.

No. 2 Military Port was built at Cairnryan on Loch Ryan, near Stranraer. There was some debate between that and another site in the loch, at the Wig, but at Cairnryan berths could be built on the five-fathom line with no need for dredging. The ground was very hard and some difficulties were encountered. When finished in July 1943, the new port had two deep-water wharves offering four berths, with two lighterage wharves. It had thirty-eight cranes plus a large 60-ton hammerhead one, eight camps for 4,000 men and a shunting yard for 2,000 wagons.[54]

Oban and Loch Ewe

The Royal Navy knew Oban quite well in the years between the wars, for it was one of the seaside towns visited by ships of the fleet. In February 1940 it was decided to use the anchorage in Kerrera Sound as an additional assembly point for convoys. Patrols across the entrance were carried out by trawlers and anti-submarine nets were laid between May and August. Its first outward convoy sailed in November and throughout the war it was to take some of the overflow from other bases.[55]

The return of the Home Fleet to Scapa Flow in early in 1940 left Loch Ewe free for development as a merchant-ship anchorage. In January 1941 it was decided to use the loch as a convoy-assembly anchorage to relieve the pressure on Oban. At Loch Ewe, ships from across the Atlantic bound for east coast ports linked up with the coastal convoy system. Army anti-aircraft gunners from the Marine Royal Artillery came on board to help defend them in the waters of the North Sea, where attacks by the Luftwaffe were far more likely. By March 1941 the ships were equipped to a common scale, with those over 500 tons carrying a 12-pounder oerlikon gun, two machine-guns and two rocket launchers.[56] Loch Ewe soon became the base for the British parts of the Russian convoys.

Drifters and a rescue ship were sent to Loch Ewe as soon as it became a convoy anchorage. There were limited refuelling facilities from colliers, but most ships which needed coal were diverted to Oban. An army detachment of one officer and forty to fifty other ranks were sent there in October 1941 to help with cargoes, especially explosives which could be transhipped away from heavily populated areas. Mail and passengers could also be landed at the loch, though it was thirty miles from the nearest railway station.

S. A. Kerslake, coxswain of the armed trawler *Northern Gem*, describes the departure of convoy JW 51B for Russia in December 1942:

> The time to weigh anchor and sail out through the boom came and we steamed out of the loch into the Minch on the first leg of our two thousand mile journey. Once outside the boom, I watched from the wheelhouse as the deeply laden vessels made their way out in two columns in order to move more comfortably up the narrow Minch, between the Outer Hebrides and the West Coast of Scotland. This was to be the only peaceful and calm part of the trip as far as the weather was concerned had we but known it.[57]

Atlantic Convoys

The transatlantic convoys to and from North America were the bread and butter of the Atlantic war. Before the war only 16 per cent of British trade, by weight, was with North America. This was greatly increased by the diversion of shipping from other routes, the growing need for American oil and the supply of American goods by 'lend-lease'. In the first eight months of war this rose to 36 per cent and by 1941, 54 per cent of imports came from North America. British survival in food, fuel and war materials depended totally on this lifeline, far more than on any other.[58]

The outward convoys from British ports to the assembly point at Halifax, Nova Scotia, were coded ONS if they were made up of slow ships and travelled at a standard speed of 7 knots. Faster convoys in the ON series made a speed of 10 knots. The return convoys, the ones which carried the vital goods, were coded HX if fast, SC if slow. Two slow and four fast convoys crossed each way in the average month of the war and 609 ran from 1943 to 1945, consisting of 30,330 ships. In September 1942 New York replaced Halifax as the eastern terminal, but Halifax was revived six months later because of congestion in the American port. A voyage across the Atlantic took from fifteen to seventeen days, and ships and men of the British merchant navy, as well as Americans and several allied merchant fleets, were exposed to the possibility of U-boat attack through all that, as well as ocean storms. A hundred and twenty-six were sunk in North Atlantic convoys in 1942 alone, plus thirty-nine stragglers.[59]

For the Royal Navy crews on board the escorts, the problem was rather different. The destroyers and corvettes in use in the early stages of the war did not have the range to cross the Atlantic and escorted the convoy out to a fixed position, then met an incoming one. Range was increased by refuelling in Iceland, by taking on oil from ships in the convoy and by the development of new types such as frigates. From the spring of 1943 it was possible to escort a convoy all the way to New York or Halifax, but this was only done in special cases. Otherwise, the ships from Britain linked up with Canadian- and American-based escorts in mid-Atlantic. U-boats rarely attacked escorts; the weather was their main enemy.

The size of convoys increased throughout the war, with an average of 36 ships in 1942, 50 in 1943 and 68 in 1944, and up to 167 in one case.[60] The large outward-bound convoys formed up off the Mull of Kintyre, meeting ships from other ports such as Milford Haven, Liverpool and Loch Ewe.[61] Graeme Ogden wrote, 'Assembling the convoy with its escorts was quite a business. It took hours to get everybody sorted out, and why the Germans never took more advantage of this I don't know, for the assembly points were common knowledge and presented a fine target for a U-boat – fortunately they were mostly operating much further out to sea .'[62]

Commander D. A. Rayner of the destroyer *Verbena* describes the procedure:

> We met them off the Mull of Kintyre. A long line of ships in two columns extending for nearly ten miles. Ahead of them was a 'V and W class' destroyer – *Velox*. Signal lamps flashed from her. We were being given our stationing signal. A corvette bucketing cheerfully over the seas and looking, to our eyes, quite indecently efficient gave us a resume

of all the signals made since leaving Liverpool on the previous afternoon, and particulars of *Velox*'s own group orders for use in event of
an attack on the convoy. By the time she had passed all the signals it
was getting dark. We were bound up the Minches, and until past the
Butt of Lewis the convoy would stay in two columns. The two columns
would then become eight, ten or even more, with four or five merchant
ships in each column. As this was a slow convoy, and probably made
not much more than six knots, it took a long time to form up the
following morning. Some of the ships could not make more than seven
knots, even if the leaders reduced to four, and it would be four hours
before the rearmost ones had covered the twelve miles necessary to take
up their stations.[63]

The reverse considerations applied when homeward-bound convoys
were formed in Halifax or New York:

Allocation would not be haphazard; 'portions' of convoy with a
common destination would be allocated places in the convoy appropriate to their direction of travel from the 'Split Position' on the further
side of the Atlantic Ocean. For example, an eastwards convoy might be
so arranged that ships due to split off after reaching 7 degrees or 10
degrees west would have ships for Loch Ewe in the port-wing columns,
ships for the Clyde on the port side of centre, ships for the Mersey on
the starboard side of centre and ships for Milford Haven in the
starboard-wing columns.[64]

In practice it was not quite so simple. Convoy HX 150 left Halifax on
16 September 1941 with forty-seven ships in nine columns. The first
column, to port, had four ships for Loch Ewe and ultimately for the
east coast ports of the Tyne and Immingham, carrying iron ore, sugar
and munitions. The second column had four ships for Loch Ewe and
two for the Clyde. The third had two for Loch Ewe, three for the Clyde
and one for the Mersey, and the fourth had three for the Clyde, one for
Loch Ewe and one for Liverpool. One ship, bound for Liverpool, was
destroyed by fire but the Clyde would soon receive cargoes of fuel oil,
steel, refrigerated food and munitions.[65]

Some ships were considered fast enough to cross the Atlantic
without convoy. One example was the SS *Politician* of T. and
J. Harrison, which left Liverpool on 3 February 1941, routed through
the Minches and among the Hebrides by Admiralty instruction, in
order to evade the U-boats. Two days later, Captain Beaconsfield
Worthington mistook the Sound of Eriskay for the Sound of Barra and
the ship ran aground. Fiction would suggest that the whole ship was

filled with whisky. In fact she carried a general cargo for export to the Caribbean, including manufactured goods, cigarettes, biscuits and £3 million of Jamaican banknotes. But hold No. 5 did contain 264,000 bottles of the finest quality whisky, being sent abroad for safekeeping during bombing raids. This was looted by the islanders, in an episode which became famous in the novel and film *Whisky Galore*. But again, reality departs from the light-hearted note of fiction. Nineteen men served terms in Inveraray Jail for offences connected with the looting.[66]

Arctic Convoys

On 22 June 1940 German troops crossed the Soviet border and began their invasion. Winston Churchill was a strong anti-Bolshevik who had organised the Baltic expedition of 1919 against the revolutionaries, but he had also inspired the Dardanelles expedition of 1915 and could see the value of supplying Russia's vast, well-disciplined but ill-equipped armed forces with modern western arms. The day after the invasion he broadcast promises of support on the BBC, saying that 'Russia's danger is our danger.' There was no question of supplying them through the Black Sea, as the Mediterranean was now heavily disputed, so the only possible route was the northern one, round Norway to the ports of Archangel and Murmansk. These were to prove the most dangerous and difficult convoys of the war. There was the danger of U-boats, as with all convoys. The weather was stormier and much colder than in the Atlantic. Furthermore, there was a much more serious danger of attack by aircraft, for convoys could not go too far from Norway because of the polar ice-pack. Finally, there was a constant threat from German battleships and cruisers hidden among the fjords.

Most of the early convoys sailed from Iceland apart from PQ2 (actually the third convoy, as the first, code-named Dervish, was not part of the numerical series), which assembled at Scapa and sailed with six merchantmen on 17 October 1941. However, they were served by convoys in the UR and RU series, which went between Loch Ewe and Iceland. In June to July 1942, convoy PQ17 from Iceland was ordered to scatter in the belief that the *Tirpitz* was about to attack it and twenty-three merchantmen out of thirty-six were lost to aircraft and U-boats. After that, convoys sailed directly from Loch Ewe. PQ 18, consisting of forty merchant ships, left there on 2 September 1942. It was escorted and covered by a small aircraft carrier, a battleship, five cruisers, more than two dozen destroyers as well as corvettes, minesweepers, trawlers and submarines, but fared little better. Thirteen merchant ships out of forty were sunk. After that the convoys were recoded in the JW series for security reasons, starting with JW51A, which left Loch Ewe in December and arrived in Russia without loss. Three more left Loch Ewe during the winter of 1942–3 and no ships were lost, though some turned back due to bad weather. But in the spring of 1943 the Battle of the Atlantic intensified and all available escorts were needed there, while the lengthening days increased fears of attack by surface ship. JW53, which left Loch Ewe in the middle of February, was to be the last outward-bound Russian convoy for some time. It reached Kola Inlet in northern Russia without loss but in the return voyage, code-named RA53, three ships were sunk by U-boat and one foundered.

By November 1943 the U-boat was largely defeated in the Atlantic and the allies had secured North Africa, so the Russian convoys could resume. Thirteen left Loch Ewe during the next fourteen months and only one, JW 65a, suffered serious casualties, three merchant ships lost to U-boats. Three British escorts were sunk on other convoys, but in return the German battle cruiser *Scharnhorst* was sunk by the covering force of convoy JW 55b on Boxing Day 1943. JW64, the first Russian convoy to assemble on the Clyde, sailed on 3 February 1945. Three more left the Clyde that year, including JW 67, which sailed just after the end of the war.[67]

Military Convoys

The first Clyde convoy, 'Glasgow Convoy' or GC 1, sailed on 5 September 1939, two days after the war started. Controlled from Plymouth, it consisted of eleven troopships carrying reinforcements to Egypt, Singapore and India. At this stage in the war, German surface raiders such as the pocket battleships *Graf Spee* and *Deutschland* seemed more dangerous than the U-boats, so the ocean escort consisted of the battleship *Ramillies*, aircraft carrier *Courageous* and four destroyers. The local escort, for anti-submarine purposes, consisted of ten destroyers, mostly of the V and W classes of the last war. The convoy assembled off Little Cumbrae at daylight on the 5th and formed into two divisions, of five and six transports each in line ahead, as that was thought to be the best protection against mines. All ships arrived safely.[68]

Over the next two years, many WS (Winston's specials) convoys left the Clyde with reinforcements for the armies in the East. In October 1941, two months before Pearl Harbor, the Director of Movements pointed out that 'The Clyde area is our principal base for preparing for any overseas operation, and also for normal overseas movement to or from Canada, the Middle East etc.: with the construction of the new military port at Faslane it is becoming a principal base for stores movement. If American personnel movement ever materialises it will be largely through the Clyde.'[69]

The first large-scale offensive amphibious operation of the war in the West was Operation Torch, the invasion of North Africa. The decision to invade the French colonies of Morocco and Algeria was taken in July 1942 and General Eisenhower was appointed commander-in-chief of British and American forces. Nearly all the convoys for the invasion of Oran and Algiers would assemble on the Clyde and Loch Ewe, while the invasion of Casablanca would be mounted directly from the United States. The new port at Faslane, not quite complete, came into use and nearly all the heavy equipment was loaded there. Clyde dockers had to learn the techniques of 'tactical loading', in which all the equipment was embarked in the reverse order to which it would be needed. Beginning on 2 October 1942, five advance convoys sailed from the Clyde to build up forces at Gibraltar, totalling 76 ships and 40 escorts. The first of the assault convoys, KMS(A)1 and KMS(O)1 (for Algiers and Oran respectively), left the Clyde and Loch Ewe on 22 October with 47 ships and 18 escorts. The next pair of convoys left four days later, including the headquarters ships *Bulolo* and *Largs*, which would control the landings. Two more sailed in the next few days and in the evening of 7 November the troops stormed ashore at Algiers and Oran. In one sector of the Oran landings alone, 29,000 men, 2,400 vehicles and 14,000 tons of stores were landed from thirty-four ships. The landings were largely un-opposed but much experience was gained.[70]

Many follow-up convoys had to be sent to sustain the campaign and the Clyde became more crowded than ever. In January 1943, bad weather and fog delayed many sailings and shipping collected off Greenock. On the 21st the War Diary noted a new record for the port – 134 merchant ships were in harbour, totalling 1,017,222 tons. This was considerably reduced by the afternoon, when fifty-eight ships of Convoy KMS8 sailed for Gibraltar and the North African ports. Two days later, the liner *Empress of Scotland* sailed, as did convoys WS26 and KMF8, for the Far East and North Africa respectively.[71]

Besides the movement of British troops out to the war overseas, there was a vast inward movement of more than a million Canadians and Americans to the war in Europe. The first Canadian troop convoy, 7,450 troops in five liners, arrived in the Clyde in December 1939, covered by the Home Fleet, and two more arrived in the next two months.[72] The movement intensified after the United States entered the war in December 1941 and President Roosevelt gave priority to winning the European war rather than defeating the Japanese. The great Atlantic liners, the 'monsters' (the *Queen Mary, Queen Elizabeth, Aquitania, Mauretania, Pasteur, Empress of Scotland* and *Andes*), had mostly been employed on WS convoys until 1942. Now they were used on the North American run. Initially the two Queens carried 6,000 men each, compared with about 2,000 peacetime passengers. On the shorter American run they could carry many more sleeping in shifts in four-berth cabins. The *Queen Elizabeth*, for example, arrived in the Clyde on 11 January 1943 carrying 10,500 men, and sailed again for New York eight days later with about 4,000 on board, largely government officials or trainee aircrew – the 'usual westward cargo of brass-hats and lesser officers, RAF and Fleet Air Arm trainees; commercial magnates, economic experts, politicians, mail and exports too rare to be entrusted to the slower way of convoy.'[73] But she could take considerably more, and in mid-1942 the Queens were converted, at American request, to take 15,000 men. There were considerable risks in this, for excess numbers caused stability problems. There were not enough lifeboats for all the men and a single torpedo could have caused a major disaster. Even a smaller liner like the *Aquitania* could take 8,000 men, and the *Empress of Scotland* arrived on 13 January 1943 with 4,191 service personnel and 14 civilians.[74] Most of the arriving troops were transferred into smaller ships to be taken straight to Northern Ireland for acclimatisation and field training.

Because of the great speed of more than 28 knots, compared with 17 of a U-boat on the surface, the liners tended to travel alone until met by a cruiser in the western approaches to Britain. Since speed was their only protection, it was hazardous to stop, and in October 1942, when the *Queen Mary* sliced through the cruiser *Curacoa* north of Ireland, she was unable to pick up survivors and 338 men were lost. Each liner voyage was considered as a convoy in its own right and had its own code letters and numbers in the AT series.

The very size of the liners created problems in the Clyde, for of course they were designed to run to Liverpool and Southampton where there were special facilities. There was no question of using any dock at Greenock, and laying at single anchor they would swing over a diameter of 4,000 feet. In the naval anchorage each would occupy four or five warship berths; in the merchant anchorage each would take up fifteen berths. There was also concern about whether they could stand a Scottish winter. 'In the bad weather which is frequently experienced in the Clyde, and the moderate holding ground which prevails throughout the anchorage, the possibility of these ships dragging is a definite danger.' It was suggested they might be laid up in Loch Long if they had to stay in the Clyde for a long period, but this was never found necessary.[75]

Another specialised type of military convoy was the transport of aircraft, especially short-range fighters, to the war overseas. The *Argus*, the oldest aircraft carrier in the world, was taken away several times from her duties in training pilots on the Clyde. In August 1940 she sailed from Greenock in 'Operation Hurry' carrying twelve Hurricanes which were launched in the Mediterranean to reinforce the hard-pressed island of Malta. But a second operation in November failed, and eight out of twelve planes ditched in the sea. After that the Mediterranean route was abandoned for a while. Carriers such as the *Argus* and *Furious* sailed several times from the Clyde to Takoradi in West Africa, where the planes landed to begin an overland flight to Egypt. On 12 May 1941 *Furious* took 42 Hurricanes from the Clyde to Gibraltar and transferred 23 to the *Ark Royal* on the way. In June 1941 the new carrier *Victorious* joined in the operations, loading 64 Hurricanes for Gibraltar at the Tail of the Bank. In April the following year, USS *Wasp* took on 47 Spitfires besides her own complement of 60 aircraft and flew them off for Malta. By August, Malta was well enough supplied with fighters to keep the German and Italian air forces at bay for a while.[76]

Coastal Convoys

Methil's role as the base for the coal convoys to Norway ended in the spring of 1940, but the port became one of the main assembly points for coastal convoys, which were still needed to carry bulk goods and relieve pressure on the railways. Coal was still by far the most important fuel for heating, rail transport and electricity generation. The railways carried about seven and a half times as much coal as ships during the war, but ships covered the longer distances and in ton-miles the ratio was more like three by rail to two by sea. Furthermore, some important sites were designed to be served by water, such as the power stations and gasworks on the River Thames, without which London would come to a standstill and would freeze in winter. Other cargoes carried by coastal convoys included seed potatoes, sugar beet and scrap iron.[77] In terms of ship movements,

Methil became the most used port in Britain during the war, though most of these were small ships making short trips.

Peter Gretton, then first lieutenant of the destroyer *Vega*, wrote:

> Coastal convoys were a very different affair from ocean convoys. They were smaller for one thing and were never more than two columns so that the ships could keep in the narrow swept channel. Their shape was long and thin, therefore, and station-keeping was even more difficult than in the open sea because of the tides and the bends in the narrow channels which twisted their way through the sand-banks of the east-coast route. We used to pick up a north-bound convoy off Southend and drop it off Methyl [*sic*] opposite Leith in the Firth of Forth, reversing the process shortly after arrival, and returning with a south-bound convoy.[78]

Sailors Ashore

Nicholas Monsarratt, then an officer in a corvette, was transferred from the Mersey to the Clyde in 1941 and he did not like the change.

> Our home port was now Greenock, a small, unlovely collection of brick and granite terraces, well-run docks, dirty streets, and shops with fly-blown cardboard advertisements designed, seemingly, to drive the customer elsewhere at the fastest clip he could imagine . . . Further down the coast was another town, Gourock, of the same mean, drab quality.

The Bay Hotel in Gourock was the main centre for officers' entertainment, though it was 'presided over by a lady whose universal nickname, Two-Ton Tessie, was never a subject of dispute'. 'Flash Alf' Turner, captain of HMS *Boadicea*, was however famed for his ability to deal with her.[79] The hotel's manageress had a more amenable personality, though she had seen tragic survivors from many of the ships lost, including those carrying children to 'safety' across the Atlantic.[80]

A trip to the city offered Monsarratt no consolation. 'To me Glasgow seemed uncouth, filthy, and complacent, all at the same time; and on Sundays it added a fourth element, a God-fearing pursed-mouth piety which closed the cinemas and pubs and spread an additional layer of gloom over the whole city.' Only the view from the ship relieved the gloom. 'The Firth of Clyde was and is one of the fairest sea-gateways in the world; from the moment we rounded the Mull of Kintyre, chugged past the strange gaunt cone of Ailsa Craig, and set course northward for Holy Island . . . we were on peaceful passage past a most marvellous coastline.' [81]

Visitors from the larger ships in the firth could have a lively time ashore. Midshipman P. G. La Niece of HMS *Hood* records

> It was a high-spirited gunroom and one evening we went ashore to Helensburgh, on the northern side of the Clyde, to see a film; on leaving the cinema we 'borrowed' a framed picture of the Film Star Loretta Young; this was borne back on board, signed by all concerned, and hung in the Gunroom as a trophy. Later on it was captured by a raiding Gunroom from another ship; in due course it was recaptured. It was then replaced by a Barber's Pole, also acquired from Helensburgh.[82]

Support Facilities

The Clyde, of course, had several dry docks for the repair of damaged ships. In September 1940 the cruiser *Sussex* was in Yorkhill Basin when a bomb landed on her during an air raid. It was decided to sink her rather than allow her ammunition to explode in the centre of the city, but she was later refloated. Floating Dock IV was sent up to supplement the Clyde facilities, and in the middle of October 1941 it was used for the monitor *Roberts*. At the end of the month it docked the battleship *Royal Sovereign*, though the dock was in need of some repair and there was difficulty in pumping the water out.[83]

Sherbrooke House in Pollokshields, Glasgow, was taken over in 1941 for use as a radar establishment for ships operating from the Clyde and soon acquired the usual crop of Nissen huts in its grounds. It was run by Commander Stuart Neill, RNVR, well known as a law unto himself. Technicians from there went out to fit new equipment in ships, while operators were trained in the house.[84] Captain Bone went on a one-day acquaintance course for non-radar operators and reported 'its mystery was explained to me and a group of the ship's officers. I thought it strange to be schooled and instructed by a cinema film there and marvelled at its interest and sufficiency.'[85]

In another example of the latest technology in warfare, degaussing ranges were set up off Helensburgh and in Loch Goil. These were designed to demagnetise ships so that they would be less vulnerable to the new magnetic mines.

The war put great strain on accommodation in the Clyde. Many houses were damaged by bombing, especially in Clydebank. The shipbuilding industry now had full employment and accommodation for workers was in short supply, while extra dockers had to be

brought in from London. There were always many thousands of
troops in the area training for amphibious warfare. The navy resorted
to its traditional policy of accommodating most of its men afloat,
either in their own ships at anchor, or in depot ships. Lord Graham's
old *Carrick* of RNVR fame was used as an accommodation ship at
Greenock, offering very basic conditions. There were depot ships for
boom defence vessels, for destroyers and for rescue tugs.

Rescue Ships

The Clyde was the main base for the rescue ships which accompanied
convoys on the North Atlantic and Arctic routes to pick up survivors
of torpedoed ships. Originally, despite the shortage of merchant
shipping, most of these were converted merchantmen from trades
which were no longer relevant in wartime. Among the first were the
sister ships *Zaarafan* and *Zamalek*, built for the Khedival Mail Lines
of Alexandria. *Zamalek*, under Captain O. C. Morris, had the most
distinguished record of all. She accompanied thirty-one convoys in the
Atlantic and Arctic, and rescued more than 600 survivors from
nineteen ships, including those from her sister-ship which was sunk
by bombing on PQ 17.

   Rescue ships were operated by merchant-navy crews. Each carried a
naval gun party and an RNVR doctor and was fitted with facilities for
treating the survivors. Later in the war, as the submarines began to
withdraw from the Atlantic, several Castle-class corvettes were converted to rescue ships.[86] Campbeltown was the base for naval rescue
tugs on the Atlantic route. These ships went far out into the ocean to
tow back severely damaged ships. The wardroom of the *Tenacity* had
twenty-four flags, representing the nationalities of the ships she
rescued during a single year.[87]

Research at Fairlie

In November 1940 the Asdic research establishment was transferred
from the very exposed base at Portland on the south coast of England,
to Fairlie on the Clyde, for the First World War site on the Gareloch
was already earmarked as a military port. The famous yacht-building
yard of William Fife was taken over. The site was close to Fairlie Pier,
with access to the deep water of the Clyde, and had a unique 'trajectory
range'. Six hydrophones were placed in 140 ft of water, three-quarters
of a mile from the shore, to measure the underwater paths of various
experimental depth charges and missiles. The laboratory ships *Dun-*

vegan and *Harbinger* were moored alongside for experiments with Asdic, the steamer *Icewhale* was a mobile laboratory and the corvette *Kingfisher* was available for deep-sea work. There were plenty of submarines based in the Clyde on which to test new Asdic sets.

By 1942, Fairlie had perfected the Type 144 Asdic, fitted with a bearing recorder to allow the operator to track the target more easily, and with an automatic training system so that the ship could be steered directly from the Asdic bearing. Its widespread use coincided with the turn in the tide of the Battle of the Atlantic in the spring of 1943. The Type 147 followed a year later. It was the first depth-determining set, and combined with the Type 144 it gave a very accurate indication of the target's position in the water, taking much of the guesswork out of an attack.

Fairlie also worked on the other problem of anti-submarine warfare. Depth charges were dropped when the ship was directly over the target, but the Asdic could not read immediately under the ship, so there was still an element of guesswork, and a ship had to drop a large 'pattern' of up to fourteen charges to have any chance of success. The answer was a weapon which would throw charges ahead of the attacking ship. Fairlie worked on an idea for an 'ahead-throwing weapon' known as the 'Fairlie mortar'. Developed by a team headed by B. S. Smith, it fired ten 20lb depth charges on each side of the ship's forecastle. The Admiralty felt that 20 lb was too light and ordered an increase to 30 lb, but in 1941 the Fairlie mortar was dropped in favour of a different weapon. This caused difficulties with Smith, the designer, and his eventual removal from Fairlie in 1942. The new weapon was the Hedgehog, which fired a circular pattern of twenty-four projectiles ahead of the ship. Unlike depth charges they exploded on contact with the target, so they were only 65 lb each compared with 290 lb of explosive. Designed by the Admiralty Miscellaneous Weapons Department in the west of England, Hedgehog was tested on Fairlie's range and put into service early in 1942. Initially it was a disappointment and was credited with only eight U-boats during 1943. Meanwhile the Admiralty returned to the principle of the Fairlie mortar and developed it somewhat further, to fire a pattern of three 60-lb depth charges ahead of the ship. This weapon, the Squid, could be controlled directly from the Asdic, including the depth settings. Theoretical studies were started early in 1942, it was tested in the trajectory range and had its sea trials off Portland in May 1943. It was in service by September of that year. Combined with Type 144 and Type 147 Asdics, it was a devastating weapon against the U-boats of the time. Ships fitted with double Squids had a 40 per cent success rate in each attack during 1945.[88]

Alarms and Accidents

During six years of war there were many accidents and near misses in the river. One of the most obvious causes was sheer overcrowding. According to Graeme Ogden of the trawler *Lady Madeleine*,

> The Clyde is tidal at Greenock, and above, and at spring tides the river runs as fast as seven knots. One must go alongside into the stream; coming home from the sea on a flood-tide produced the most harrowing experiences, it being necessary to turn the ship in this narrow, busy channel. Single-screw ships with slow-revving engines do not turn easily in a confined space by 'backing and filling', as when you go astern the thrust of the right-hand screw makes the ship sheer off to starboard. With a stiff off-shore breeze and the river full of traffic, which might include anything from a battleship coming down from John Brown's yard to hoppers, scoots, drifters and merchantmen, tying up alongside had its problems.[89]

Angus Cunningham Graham, in command of the cruiser *Kent* in 1941, records that 'Off the Clyde estuary our radar failed to reveal a large convoy with its ships darkened and almost invisible. We only sighted it just in time for me to reduce speed and avoid running into the middle of it at 22 knots.'[90] It was no safer for submarines under training. The *Torbay*, under Anthony Miers, one of the most famous, if controversial submarine commanders of the war, had a collision in Loch Long early in 1941:

> The southerly part of this loch was a convoy-assembly anchorage. As we found to our cost, if the anchorage was congested, ships were apt to spread over into the northern or exercise area. *Torbay* was proceeding submerged near the south limit when a merchant ship came up, turned to starboard and anchored right in our path. Miers went deep under her and resumed periscope depth between her and the next in the anchorage. This happened to be a small tanker. He ordered the motors be stopped, and to surface . . . the motors were stopped, but it did not follow that *Torbay* was.

The engines were put into full astern, but not soon enough to avoid a slight collision. The tanker had to be beached, which counted as a black mark against the submarine captain.[91]

One of the most mysterious accidents was the explosion in the Free French destroyer *Maille Breze* in April 1940 while she was anchored off Greenock, and shattered many windows in the town. There were many who attributed it to sabotage, though the official report suggested accident. Part of the ship remained visible for the rest of the war, disconcerting Nicholas Monsarrat:

> . . . a wreck-buoy, painted green, flashing green every five seconds – green for the colour of grisly death. It marked the grave of an ill-starred French destroyer, whose mast and funnel still showed above water, whose crew still lay imprisoned within. Her story had been one of the brief, early horrors of the war: an explosion on board had been followed by a fire, and the ship quickly became one vast incandescent torch, fled by a few leaping men, before the sea surged over and snuffed it out for ever.[92]

There were frequent collisions with the boom defences. In January 1943 the *Empress of Scotland* destroyed part of the boom but was herself undamaged. Two months later the submarine *Severn* fouled the boom at Campbeltown but was got clear without damage to herself or the boom.[93]

There were also collisions between ships, as the War Diary of 18 August 1944 reported:

> At 0520 signal was received from *Smiter* stating she was in collision with a steamer 160 degrees Toward Point 1 mile. The Merchant vessel was the SS *Delane* – British 6,054 tons. Both ships were able to return to harbour under their own steam. *Smiter's* bows were damaged and it was estimated that repairs would take 4–5 weeks, or 4–5 days for temporary repairs before sailing to a refitting port.[94]

Bad weather was always a problem, especially in winter. January 1943 brought more troubles. On the 3rd SS *Venus* was reported aground at Polanfhein Rock, off Islay, and was refloated with the assistance of two tugs from Oban. Two days later two American merchant ships, heading north to join a convoy, got into gales north of the Isle of Man. The rescue tug *Bustler* sailed from Campbeltown to tow the *William M. Stewart* to Belfast, while the *John Marshall* went aground south of Portpatrick, to be salvaged four days later by the *Bustler*. Ship movements were affected for much of the month and on the 31st the barometer recorded the lowest reading for thirty-five years.

Worse was to come, for between 2 o'clock and 6 o'clock in the morning of 5 February, when 126 merchant ships were at anchor, a gale struck from the west and south-west, gusting up to 70 miles per hour. In the Tail of the Bank anchorage thirty-three ships got into difficulties, of which nine went aground. Most were quickly refloated, but the *Chemong* and *Westmoor*, driven onto the rocks near Kilcreggan, were still there five days later, and *Westmoor* was holed below the waterline. Thirteen ships were unable to join convoy KMS9 for Gibraltar and North Africa when it sailed the next day. But gales could have their advantages as well. It was reported that many mines, both friendly and enemy, were washed ashore on the coasts, having broken loose in the gales.[95]

In October 1943 there was an alarm when part of a German submarine escape apparatus was found off Rosneath Point. It was feared that a midget submarine had penetrated the firth and all ship movements were stopped while their bottoms were inspected for limpet mines. But an inquiry found that it was a souvenir taken by the Free French ship *Aconit*, then thrown over the side. The Flag Officer in Charge drew attention to 'the repercussions of such thoughtless Actions'. [96]

The most traumatic and alarming accident came in the afternoon of 17 March 1943. The escort carrier HMS *Dasher* was between Arran and Ardrossan, heading back to Greenock after a day's deck-landing practice, with all but one of her nine planes struck down below in the hangar. An explosion shook the after part of the ship and she sank rapidly, killing 379 men. It was seen by hundreds, if not thousands of people on shore and many of the 149 survivors were brought back to Ardrossan for treatment, but the affair was kept secret until after the end of the war. The cause of the accident is still something of a mystery. There was certainly no enemy presence in the area and rumours of sabotage are far-fetched. It may have been caused by an explosion of petrol fumes which had been allowed to build up below decks, setting off the depth-charge magazine.[97]

The End of the War

As the Battle of the Atlantic approached a climax, the War Diary of the Flag Officer in Charge at Greenock recorded some statistics:

> During the last quarter of 1942, 1,227 Merchant Vessels of over 300 tons visited the port. 60,080 tons of cargo were discharged overside and 28,493 tons of coal were discharged. Only 7 ships missed convoy sailings. A total of 4,259 Merchant Navy survivors were landed.
>
> During the whole calendar year 1942, similar statistics show 3,960 merchant ships over 300 tons and 6,650 Coasters and Harbour Craft visited the port. Average turn round of merchant ships over 300 tons – 4.1 days. Total number of ships loaded or discharged – 589. 502,464 tons of cargo discharged overside. 104,991 tons of coal discharged. 69 ships programmed to sail did not carry out their programme. 6,450

Merchant Navy survivors were landed at the anchorages. Gross total since April, 1941 – 8,223.

As a result of the various efforts, the Clyde was able to handle about 20 per cent of British shipping needs during key periods of the war.

In the winter of 1944–5, as the Germans were pushed out of France and lost control of their Atlantic U-boat bases, more shipping could be routed southwards, and in that sense the Clyde declined in importance. Ironically this led to increased U-boat activity in Scottish waters. To reach the Atlantic they now had to pass round the north of Scotland and the Tenth Escort Group patrolled off Shetland to stop them. On 3 February the group attacked one contact off Muckle Flugga and a large quantity of oil floated to the surface; but no submarine was sunk. Eleven days later the group attacked another contact with squid and hedgehog and rescued two men from the water, one of whom was the captain of *U-989*, which had been destroyed. Three days later they attacked again and large quantities of oil came to the surface, with a rubber dinghy and a rubber ball covered in green canvas. This proved to be the remains of *U-1278*.

The Germans had now developed the snorkel, which allowed their boats to stay underwater for much longer periods. They could operate in the Irish Sea with much less fear of detection by aircraft and there were several reports in the North Channel, off the Mull of Kintyre, during the next few months, though none were sunk. Operations resumed in the Moray Firth, which had seen no U-boats for five years, and *U-309* was sunk there by the Canadian frigate *St John* on 16 February.[98] There was a new mining campaign, largely in the Firth of Clyde and its approaches. The minesweeping base at Ardrossan was fully employed in clearing them.

Admiral Donitz, who had commanded the U-boat arm from the beginning of the war until he became head of the German Navy in 1943, had a further promotion on 30 April 1945, when Hitler committed suicide and Donitz became Führer of what was left of Nazi Germany. On 4 May a short signal was issued to recall the U-boats at sea, for they now had few bases to operate from and the war was clearly lost. The German armies finally surrendered on the 7th and 8th and the U-boats still at sea were ordered to surface, report their position in plain language and follow prescribed routes to certain anchorages including Loch Eriboll in the north of Scotland. Five boats surfaced west of the Hebrides on the 9th and 10th, and another on the 13th. Five more surrendered in the waters around Shetland and entered the loch. On 16 May the Norwegian warship *Stord*, on her way to Narvik, met a convoy of fifteen U-boats, the German Admiralty yacht *Grille* and four support ships off Vestfjord. The surface ships were allowed to proceed but the submarines were sent to Loch Eriboll under the eyes of the Ninth Escort Group.[99] They were then taken to Kyle of Lochalsh under armed guard. The Battle of the Atlantic was over.

Chapter 14

Naval Training

During the Second World War, the West of Scotland became the most important area for naval training of several different kinds. The navy expanded nearly sixfold in the first five years of conflict. Men put to sea after a few weeks in shore training schools, compared with a minimum of nine months of training for seamen boys before the war. In peacetime officers had received more than six years of training before being commissioned, but now men could become sub-lieutenants in the Royal Naval Volunteer Reserve after three months on the lower deck followed by a three-month training course. Basic training in seamanship and naval discipline required relatively little equipment. It was mainly conducted near the traditional bases in the south of England, or in former holiday camps on the coast, including HMS *Scotia* at Ayr, built in co-operation with Butlin's so that it could become a holiday camp after the war. Technical training was still carried out in the traditional naval bases. Beyond that, the training of crews in the specialised tasks of modern warfare required real ships, submarines and aircraft and areas in which they could work relatively undisturbed.

After the Fall of France in June 1940, the west coast of Scotland was safer than other parts of the United Kingdom from bombing and submarine attack, not to mention the threat of invasion. It had waters which could be protected relatively easily, particularly the Firth of Clyde which had a good range of facilities of all kinds. Scotland offered deep waters where submarine crews could learn their trade and where anti-submarine escorts could practise detecting and des-troying U-boats. Beaches could be used for training in amphibious warfare and desolate stretches of coast could become bombing and artillery ranges. There were many isolated and under-used harbours with good access to deep water, where seamen could be kept away from most of the distractions of the shore and work could be carried out in relative secrecy.

Many country and small-town hotels were taken over as messes, offices and training bases. The Keil Hotel in Campbeltown was the Royal Naval Hospital. Most hotels taken over for naval use had their furnishings put into store, so that more utilitarian naval furniture and equipment could be fitted. One exception was HMS *Osprey* in a hotel near Dunoon. 'What struck me as unusual was that all decks and stairways were carpeted. Everywhere else carpets and rugs had been removed and stored, where the military had taken over private accommodation.'[1]

But the most common type of accommodation was the ubiquitous Nissen hut. The larger ones served as lecture rooms and messes, the smaller as sleeping accommodation, workshops, stores and toilets. There were other types of hastily built accommodation in training bases, some made of brick, but the Nissen was by far the most common and famous. The hastily built airfield at Machrihanish was known as 'Nissen city'.

Most sailors, even temporary wartime ones, dreamt of postings to the Mediterranean or warmer climes and training in Scotland came as something of a shock. Virtually all the published memoirs of the period dwell on the cold and the rain. As an American, A. H. Cherry was used to central heating and the cold became an obsession. On a single page, describing his arrival at Campbeltown, he manages seven references to the weather – 'howling winds', 'winds and storms', 'icy drizzle', 'penetrating wintry winds from two sides', 'the terrible coldness of room and bed', 'dreadfully cold in the room' and 'the room remained colder than an ice-box.'[2]

Operational training had several elements. Lectures were universal and specially made films were used whenever possible. Mechanical simulators were developed for various activities, especially in aviation and anti-submarine warfare. By 1945 the Scottish anti-submarine training bases, *Osprey* and *Nimrod,* had twenty-eight 'attack teachers' in which officers and ratings could learn to direct a ship onto a submarine using Asdic.[3] There was also a 'tactical table' at *Osprey* on which large-scale exercises were carried out, involving a number of officers. In the Royal Naval Air Station at Crail there was an ingenious 'torpedo attack trainer'. A 'link trainer', a machine normally used to train pilots in blind flying, was installed in a round building with a seascape painted on the walls:

> Some of it with a calm sea, a blue sky and a horizon and some rough
> and foggy. It was illuminated to simulate various times of day. Fitted
> under the link and connected to it by a computer was a projector which

through on to the seascape the white silhouette of a ship. As you flew towards it the ship got bigger at a rate linked to the speed of approach. The shape of the ship varied according to the bearing of the aircraft from it. Changes of speed of the ship and avoiding action could also be simulated. The movements of the silhouette gave a very realistic illusion as the pilot flying the link, without the hood of course, made his attack. He approached – dived – made his torpedo settings . . . When he had everything right he pressed the button. The computer did its sums, everything stopped and a light appeared below the ship where the torpedo had hit or in the sea ahead or astern if he had missed.[4]

Amphibious Warfare

The Royal Navy was unprepared for the kind of war it had to fight from 1940. The inter war navy had concentrated largely in keeping up its strength in battleships and cruisers. The Fleet Air Arm was not ready, because twenty years of debilitating dispute with the RAF had inhibited development, and priority had been given to strategic air defence. The anti-submarine branch was hard pressed and it had never been fashionable between the wars. Too much faith was placed in Asdic, and pre-war plans had not considered the effect of the Fall of France on a future Battle of the Atlantic.

But it was in the field of amphibious warfare that the Royal Navy, along with the other services, had to develop almost from nothing. Nearly all British wars of modern times have involved landing troops on foreign shores. Sometimes this was done in friendly territory, as with the British Expeditionary Forces in France in 1914 and 1939. In older wars, such as those against France up to 1815, there were many landings but few were strongly opposed on the beaches. The First World War offered few lessons in modern amphibious warfare. The only large-scale opposed landing, at Gallipoli in 1915, had been done mainly with ordinary ships' boats. The only ship specially adapted for landing troops was the converted collier *River Clyde*, which had large sally-ports cut in its sides for troops to disembark, across a hopper which formed a bridge to the shore. Casualties were heavy when this was tried in action. There was some theoretical study of amphibious warfare between the wars, but few practical experiments. The problems were now much greater, because armies needed large numbers of tanks and other vehicles, with fuel and equipment, to sustain a campaign ashore.

Yet there had been little progress; in an exercise in 1938, troops landed in open boats with muffled oars, as their ancestors had done for centuries. Later that year the army expressed interest in further development, but the Air Ministry 'did not think the landing of troops against opposition was a likely form of operation for British troops in the near future'. The Admiralty was no more helpful and 'could not visualise any particular combined operations taking place, and were not, therefore, prepared to devote any considerable sum of money to equipment for combined training.' The only body to study amphibious warfare, the Inter-Services Training and Development Centre, was disbanded on the outbreak of war in September 1939 but reformed a few months later. The Royal Navy had precisely two dozen landing craft of assorted types on order, and some would prove completely useless in practice.[5]

By the summer of 1940 it was clear that the British would have to fight their way back to the European continent against strong defences. Combined operations techniques had to be learned almost from scratch, in a very short space of time. Such operations might cover the full range from commando raids in which a dozen men would land for a few hours to damage key enemy installations, to full-scale invasions of a continent, in which the army, having landed in some strength, would be built up and supplied until ultimate victory.

On 17 July, eleven days after the Dunkirk evacuation was completed, Admiral of the Fleet Sir Roger Keyes was appointed to a new post as Director of Combined Operations. He was as experienced as anyone in amphibious warfare, having been at Gallipoli in 1915, and he was the hero of a famous raid on Zeebrugge in 1918, of which he never ceased to remind Churchill. He had his headquarters in Richmond Terrace in Whitehall, but he was a frequent visitor to the north, where he set up numerous training bases. 'I spend a good deal of time in Scotland. I spent ten nights in the train in the last three weeks, most of the intervening nights on the beaches since we must work by night,' he wrote in June 1941.[6]

Inveraray

Inveraray, on Loch Fyne, was surveyed by a naval and an army officer in July 1940 and it was reported: 'From the naval point of view there is a suitable site for the anchorage at Kames Bay on the west side of the loch above Otter Ferry; a military camp is possible in the area of Inveraray Castle and on the park and golf course belonging to the estate.'[7] It was therefore chosen as the home of the Combined Training Centre and commissioned as HMS *Quebec* in November 1940. According to Rear-Admiral L. E. H. Maund it was 'as far distant as possible from attack but yet within the umbrella of some fighter organisation . . . Here the rain might fall almost continuously, but it gave sheltered water and was, as it were, behind the defences of the Clyde.'[8] Vice-Admiral Theodore Hallet took command. The military camp was to hold 1,200 men and a naval camp, initially for 50 officers, 300 ratings and the support of 60 landing craft, was hastily erected to the south of the town. Buoys were laid off Inveraray for a fleet of troop transports.[9]

One of the first to be trained there was Ordinary Seaman Rowland Draper:

> The Majority of Inveraray's population of about 450 lived in stone houses gathered on each side of the one short main street. There was one shop, two hotels and a café. One house slightly larger than its neighbours sported a flagpole from which flew the white ensign; this was the admiral's house and naval headquarters. It was a peaceful scene with snow still hanging on the tops of the hills, but it was all due to change. Soon a naval camp was going to be built further down the loch, and camps to house troops which would be sent for training in combined operations.[10]

There were several useful beaches in the area. 'At the head of Loch Fyne there were sandy beaches with a rough hinterland of heath and heather; and there was an area some two miles long, near Strathlachlan, where two companies could storm ashore firing all their weapons live, to the considerable disturbance of the MacLachlans of MacLachlan in their ancestral home of Castle Lachlan.'[11] Seamen arrived there after two weeks' initial training at Northney near Portsmouth. They were divided into crews soon after arrival and efforts were made to keep the groups together, selecting good-quality men to take charge of small landing craft crewed by four men. Officers, who shared much of the training programme, would join to take charge of the medium-sized craft.[12]

As well as the training of individuals and crews, large-scale exercises took place with the army:

> There were, by February 1941, some twenty LCM [landing craft mechanised] and thirty-six LCA [landing craft assault] available and it was decided to carry out a forty-eight hour exercise in which the assaulting troops, followed by reinforcements, were to land from their LSI [landing ship infantry] near the head of Loch Fyne and certain positions inland were to be occupied against opposition. But more important still, guns and supplies were to be ferried in to support the

force by the craft, the shore near the Castle taking the place of the transports in the anchorage. It was a bitter cold day, with the wind whistling down from the north-east as the troops went ashore and I fear the cold may have blinded many to the lessons that were to be learnt during that exercise concerning problems of traffic control, dump location, beach roadways and road circuits, and the need for special vehicles. Still, here in February of 1941, a first realistic exercise had been put on at the CTC [Combined Training Centre], and the first real list of practical lessons for the advancement of technique had been learnt.[13]

As the war went on, lectures at Inveraray became increasingly sophisticated. Trainees were told about the differences between amphibious and land assaults – 'The number of ships and craft available may limit strength and composition of the military forces. Reconnaissance limited. The lack of flexibility once units have been embarked . . .' The stages of an assault were illustrated by diagrams. Different types of landing craft were illustrated with slides and their onboard accommodation was described. In a landing craft infantry (large) 'Troops are accommodated on troop decks, which are fitted with water fountains, latrines, racks for equipment, racks for rifles, limited cooking facilities, but plenty of hot water can be provided by the Royal Navy for making tea.' The vehicle deck of a Landing Ship Tank looked 'like a large garage'. The men were given lectures on how to relate to other services, particularly important for soldiers who might spend some time as guests of the Royal Navy. They were told about relative ranks in the navy, the 'Dos and Don'ts for personnel of the Army and RAF when they are embarked in a white ensign ship' and about 'ship sense – the art of finding one's way about a ship in any circumstances.' The instructors were enjoined to 'tell a few anecdotes if possible' and allow time for questions.[14]

Ayrshire

Largs, on the Firth of Clyde, was initially a centre for training the new commando groups of the army. Their organisation is described by the novelist Evelyn Waugh, who served as an officer with them.

Commandos were originally intended to supply raiding parties, primarily against the occupied coast of France; . . . they were to be commanded by youthful officers, to consist in all ranks of volunteers for hazardous service, and to have an abnormally high proportion of officers and NCOs to men. Administrative staff was to be reduced to a minimum; this was effected by paying a special allowance and leaving men to find their own accommodation in England [*sic*], an indulgence which made service particularly attractive.[15]

On his arrival in Largs in November 1940, Waugh was delighted to find that his fellow officers included many 'dandies' such as the Prime Minister's son Randolph Churchill, but he found it impossible to match their expenditure on gambling and on restaurants in Glasgow. He found the Marine Hotel 'expensive and avaricious', the food was 'beastly' and Waugh supported Churchill in a dispute with the landlady – 'These seem to me the kind of people who would try and cheat you,' he told the waiter. Waugh got drunk and cut his mouth in the blackout. The town, he felt, was 'A smug, substantial, modern pleasure resort – or rather pleasure as the Scots conceive it.'

Others were more charitable about seaside landladies.

> For training or on an operation everyone came under starter's orders; nobody had to be left in barracks to do the inevitable chores of the spud-bashing variety. The administrative tail therefore consisted of a body of some five hundred landladies, who, whether in Plymouth, Largs, Seaford, Weymouth, Worthing or wherever else our journeyings took us, proved a fine body of women with a fine *esprit de corps*! Some of the soldiers developed the system to such a fine art that they would get the people in their billets to clean their equipment, or would send them round to Troop Headquarters to read Orders![16]

By March 1941 it was agreed that the main assault force of the army would be based in the Firth of Clyde, where they could train and be ready for embarkation. Accommodation was needed for up to 20,000 men, including 8,000 of the assault force in the Inveraray district. Three thousand men could live on board ship, there was already shore accommodation in the area for 3,000, so more was needed for 2,000 men. The other 12,000 men of the 'first echelon' would live in Ayrshire. Many more camps had to be set up, using tents or requisitioned buildings.[17] The Hollywood Hotel in Largs was taken over in October 1941 as the Headquarters, Combined Training under Commodore G. L. Warren. The base was commissioned as HMS *Warren* a year later, taking the name of its commander.

Further training centres for specialised tasks were established on the Ayrshire coast during 1942. The army camp at Auchengate, near Troon, was commissioned as HM ships *Dundonald I* and *Dundonald II*. The former was responsible for the initial training of ratings for major landing craft. *Dundonald II* was the Combined Signal School. Also at Troon, HMS *Dinosaur* became the headquarters of the captain commanding tank landing craft after Castle Toward was found to be unsuitable due to lack of maintenance facilities.

The First Landing Ships

Several types of vessel were needed for amphibious operations. Landing ships were relatively large, able to make the journey across an ocean if necessary, carrying small landing craft which they would lower or launch to take the men, vehicles, armament and supplies onto the beaches. Some would carry infantry, others would transport landing craft, launching them by means of gantries or stern chutes, or using a floodable dock at the stern of the ship. Landing *craft* included medium-sized vessels able to make the journey across a sea such as the English Channel or the Mediterranean, as well as the smaller craft which were launched from ships. Within these three types there was a further subdivision, between those designed mainly to carry personnel, those carrying vehicles and their crews and support craft which would go close inshore carrying guns or rockets to support the invading forces against enemy aircraft or shore artillery, or carry out other tasks such as aircraft direction.

At the beginning of the war the Admiralty took over three new, fast cargo liners built in Scotland for the Glen Line, the *Glenearn*, *Glenroy* and *Glengyle*. They were originally intended to carry fuel and ammunition, but in June 1940 they were converted to landing ships by providing troop decks in the hold and fitting davits to launch landing craft. They could carry 87 army officers and 1,000 men, in addition to the ship's crew and landing craft crews. They became known as landing ships infantry (large) or LSI(L).

No. 8 Commando embarked on the *Glenroy* in December 1940, for training on the beaches of Arran, said to resemble the Mediterranean island of Pantelleria, which Keyes hoped to invade. Relations between the soldiers and sailors were appalling. The captain of the ship, a retired naval officer, was known as 'booby' and 'the old bugger on the roof'. The junior naval officers, mostly volunteer reservists, were regarded by Evelyn Waugh as 'jejune, dull, poor, self-conscious, sensitive of fancied insults, with the underdog's aptitude to harbour grievances'. The army officers believed they were first-class passengers with the navy as guard. There was much to be done to create a cohesive fighting force.[18]

The three *Glens* sailed for Egypt in February 1941, to begin outstanding service careers while remaining in contact with the Clyde. *Glengyle*, for example, took part on a raid on Bardia in North Africa, helped with the evacuation of Greece and Crete by Allied troops and assisted with the supply of Malta. She returned to the Clyde in 1942 for repairs and then took part in the disastrous raid on Dieppe in August 1942. After further repairs in her home river she took a leading part in Operation Torch, the invasion of North Africa and then the landing at Salerno in Italy. She missed D-Day in June 1944 because she was in transit from the Mediterranean after Salerno, but she went to the Far East in preparation for operations against Japan which never materialised.

Meanwhile more landing ships worked up in the Clyde. Two Belgian cross-channel ferries were converted to become LCI (Medium) with accommodation for 22 army officers and 350 men. Five more Belgian ships became LSI (Small) with 250 soldiers, while the *Royal Scotsman* and *Ulster Monarch* were taken from the Northern Irish ferry trade to carry 450 men for short-range operations. The *Karanja* and *Keren* were ships of the British India Steam Navigation Company and they had merchant navy crews during the early part of their service. In the *Karanja,* according to Waugh, the sergeants lived in relative luxury in second-class cabins, while the quarters for the rank and file were extremely cold.[19] In the same ship, Rowland Draper found that 'the food, which was cooked by Merchant Navy cooks, was appalling' because the Goanese stewards had no experience of cooking potatoes.[20]

The Firth of Clyde

Most of the training with landing ships took place in the Firth of Clyde and there was much to learn. According to Waugh in early 1941, 'The boat training consisted of packing into ALCs [assault landing craft] which the military seemed to consider an esoteric art requiring great practice, and letting the naval officers make a nonsense of the navigation.'[21] In May 1941, in the presence of Sir Roger Keyes, troops were landed on Arran from four of the Belgian ships. The transports anchored in line in Brodick Bay and the men were put into ordinary ships' boats. Most had no engines, so they were towed in strings by the powered boats and made the last part of the journey under oars. The whole process took hours.[22] The situation was much improved during 1941 as increasing numbers of specialised landing craft, with flat bottoms and bow ramps, came into use.

An important part of the technique was to let go the kedge (stern) anchor at the right moment, so that the craft could be hauled off the beach after the load was discharged. John Holden, an able seaman in LST 418, records:

We were constantly wet through with rain and sea spray, doing endless landings on the beach from early morning to late evening. The worst part was if we lost our kedge anchor wire by dropping the stern anchor too soon. Apart from the skipper losing face in front of the other LSTs, it was a cold, wet job for a boat to fish for the cable with grappling hooks. The practice paid off, however, as we never lost our kedge anchor during operations in the face of the enemy.[23]

With Inveraray becoming increasingly crowded, a new base was started in April 1941 at the southern tip of the Cowal peninsula. 'Castle Toward, opposite Rothesay, was requisitioned and an army of Nissen huts sprang up around the estate for the 6th Armoured Division to start their training.'[24] The new Combined Training Centre was commissioned as HMS *Ararat* (later renamed *Brontosaurus*). By October the base was offering a twelve-day course to armoured regiments, one arriving every week.

As part of the lend-lease agreement of March 1941, the United States Navy was allowed several bases in British waters, having failed to persuade the government of Eire to allow them to use Lough Swilly.[25] They chose Rosneath on the Gareloch, with the intention that it should be used for their destroyers and submarines if and when America entered the war. After Pearl Harbor in December 1941 most of the American destroyers and submarines were sent to the Pacific, so Rosneath was not needed in its original form. In the meantime it was available for use by British forces. It was commissioned in April 1942 as HMS *Louisbourg* after some time as an outpost of HMS *Warren* and became, according to Mountbatten, 'the centre of our combined training area and all our plans were based on the assumption that we should be able to use it continuously.' It had fine workshops and access to deep water. Officers' accommodation was in the Ferry Inn at Rosneath and the men lived in eighteen Nissen huts, twenty-two to a hut.[26] But in July 1942 the Americans asked for it as a base for the training of construction battalions which would operate enemy ports after capture, and as a reception area for landing craft arriving from the United States.

Preparations for Operation Torch, the invasion of North Africa, were in train at the time and Rosneath was vital – 'It was not unlike telling a ship's captain that his bridge and engine room were being requisitioned, but he was to get on with the job all the same.'[27] Mountbatten protested, going as high as General Eisenhower, the American Commander-in-Chief. But Rosneath had been lavishly equipped to American standards and alternative bases were not acceptable. British forces were allowed to return, using it as a base for mounting operations in the Mediterranean, though they were cautious about putting down roots there. A large American presence remained and in February 1944, 6,329 officers and men were stationed there.[28]

Other amphibious warfare bases in Scotland included the Tank Landing Craft Training Base at Bo'ness, HMS *Stopford*, commissioned in April 1942, which used LNER docks for its ships and the works of Bo'ness Hosiery for ratings' accommodation. At Acharacle on the Ardnamurchan peninsula, Special Forces were trained at HMS *Dorlin*, situated in Dorlin House.

The Lochailort System

In 1942 it was realised that many new officers would be needed to command medium-sized landing craft and to lead groups of smaller craft. The proportion of officers to ratings was much higher than in the navy as a whole; the most common types of tank landing craft, the LCTs, needed two officers and ten men each. The officers did not need all the skills of a fully fledged naval officer, for example in ocean navigation, so a special six-week course was set up to train them, compared with three months for a normal wartime officer and more than six years for a regular officer.

An army camp at Lochailort, between Fort William and Mallaig, was transferred to the navy, and thus began the 'Lochailort System', giving considerable prominence to a village which has been described as 'little more than a place-name with a telephone kiosk' – perhaps because it had been looted by Captains Duff and Fergusson and the crews of the *Terror* and *Furnace* in 1746.[29] The geography of the new camp was not very different from others in Scotland. At a 'respectful distance' from the house, 'Nissen huts were scattered around the parade ground with its white ensign flying. Larger huts housed the gymnasium, the main lecture and cinema hall and the mess.'[30] The camp was served by the West Highland Railway from Fort William, with its two trains a day – those who dropped out of the course were put on the 1.43 to return to their units.

Initially there was some confusion about the type of entrant wanted for the course. The commodore of the Royal Naval Patrol Service was horrified when seven out of ten of the men he recommended were sent back as failures. They were men who had already had one try at officer training, failing the more regular course at *King Alfred* at a time when the demand for officers was much lower, and since then had spent much time on the lower deck. They were, according to Commodore de

Paas, 'men of quality though not of great polish . . . experienced men of character and purpose'. They spent much of their time on the course helping out young men with no experience of the sea and were mortified to find that the young men passed while the older ones failed. The commodore suggested that this meant 'Practical seamen are not required. It was a question of education and accent.' In reply, Combined Operations Headquarters commented tartly that 'although candidates selected for Lochailort may be above average in the Patrol Service they do not compare favourably with candidates from other sources.' However, it was agreed to modify the standards on the course, that the priority was 'leadership and practical seamanship' and the Naval Assistant to the Second Sea Lord directed that 'no candidate shall be unnecessarily rejected.'[31]

At first sight the experience of the Patrol Service ratings might seem to conflict with the welcome Lieutenant Munford gave to a new course early in 1943. 'I will warn you of one thing – I don't like failures. My last Division passed one hundred per cent – Munford's Marvels they were called. Let's see that you do likewise!' It soon became apparent that failure had several meanings and many men were weeded out before the final examination. 'But among Munford's Marvels "red lights" would generally begin to glow early on. After a fortnight three or four disappointed men might be told to catch the 1.43 train, while another one or two, unable to stand up to the physical aspects of the course, would resign of their own free will. Lieutenant Munford would have thus weeded out his doubtful finishers and be determined to bring the rest through one hundred per cent.'[32]

Though Lochailort was considered less formal than the more conventional course at *King Alfred* near Brighton, officers could not neglect the social graces. 'There was a Wren petty officer in attendance to note every false move with the cutlery. Every knife filled with peas, every roll cut instead of broken, every spoonful of soup scooped from the wrong side of the plate, could count against them – or so they had been told.' Though motor boats were provided for training on the loch, the course had a strong emphasis on drill, on physical training including boxing, and on gruelling expeditions over glens and mountains. Much of this would not be very helpful of landing craft commanders. 'Most of their time at sea would be spent standing on the bridge of an LCT or an LCI or in some minor landing craft; and the strain would not be so much physical as mental – keeping awake and alert for very long periods of duty and being able to go for long periods without rest or sleep.'[33]

At the end of the course, successful candidates were summoned to the castle for tea and cakes with the staff and given first class rail warrants home, though they were still wearing ratings' uniform. Many of them would later undertake further training and become fully fledged officers.

Development of Techniques

If combined operations were to develop beyond mere raiding parites, certain specific problems had to be solved. The first was the overall command and control of the operation.

Signalling was an important issue in the control of landings, for the three services had developed their own systems over the years. Mountbatten, a wireless officer, took a special interest in this. A Combined Signal Board was set up at Inveraray in the autumn of 1940, with an officer from each of the three services. A signal school followed in November 1941, situated, like many another wartime organisation, in a collection of forty-five Nissen huts. It soon became apparent that further RAF input was needed, but there was no airfield near Inveraray. In April 1942 the school moved to Dundonald near Troon, close to the airfields at Ayr and Prestwick. It was commissioned as *Dundonald II*. The centrepiece was a mock-up of a headquarters ship, but personnel were also trained on landing craft in the firth.[34]

The second problem was to give adequate big-gun support to the troops as they landed. This took two forms. The big ships of the navy, the battleships and cruisers, could stand offshore and bombard enemy positions from a distance, at a range of up to twenty-five miles. In October 1941 the captain of the cruiser HMS *Cardiff*, based at Lamlash, identified a suitable gunnery range on the shores of the Kintyre peninsula and a gunnery school was opened at Inveraray soon afterwards.[35] But the actual landing required much closer support, from vessels which would go in with the landing craft and engage enemy guns directly. Landing craft were fitted with guns at Inveraray as soon as the CTC opened there, but experience showed that ever larger ones were needed and development continued over the years.

The third problem was the control of the beaches, where landings, forward movement of troops and vehicles and the need for defence against counter-attack all had to be co-ordinated. Training began at Inveraray late in 1940, and in April 1942 naval training began at Inverkip near Gourock on the Clyde. In November that year a special wing was set up at Dundonald for training inter-service beach groups, based on the experience of previous landings. The personnel of all three services were to live together to foster close co-operation.[36]

Until late 1943 Loch Fyne remained the centre of tactical training. 'This was the only spot in all the United Kingdom where landing with the use of live ammunition was possible; and the rocky features of Barr nam Damh and Barr an Longeart bore no relation to the fat, flat pasture-lands at the back of the Normandy beaches.'[37] Five new sites for live training were found, one in the south of England, one in South Wales and three in Scotland. Culbin Sands and Burghead Bay in the Moray Firth were relatively lightly populated, but many people had to be moved out from Tarbat in Easter Ross.

The Rattle Conference

Keyes's relations with Churchill became increasingly difficult after the Prime Minister eventually vetoed the Pallenteria operation. Keyes would not give in and was rebuked by the Prime Minister. 'It is not possible for me to argue out with you privately, either by letter or in conversation, every decision of the Defence Committee which affects your command. My burdens would become intolerable if I were to attempt such a thing. You and your Commandos will have to obey orders like other people.'[38]

In October 1941 another legendary naval figure took over as Chief of Combined Operations. Apart from his connections with the Royal family, Lord Louis Mountbatten was famous from his rather reckless adventures as captain of the destroyer *Kelly*, and these would appear in the Noël Coward film *In Which We Serve* within a year. He was rapidly promoted from captain to vice-admiral and given parity with the chiefs of staff of the three services.

As late as the spring of 1943 there was still doubt about where the invasion of Europe would take place. The Army and the RAF tended to favour the short crossing over the Straits of Dover, while the navy preferred the much longer distance to the beaches of Normandy. Mountbatten organised a conference at HMS *Warren* in Largs from 28 June to 2 July 1943, to present the case for Normandy. It was known as 'the Field of the Cloth of Gold' after Henry VIII's famous meeting with the King of France in 1520. 'There were twenty assorted generals, eleven air marshals and air commodores, eight admirals, and brigadiers galore. There were five Canadians; fifteen Americans, including two from COHQ; two officers from the Admiralty, three from the Air Ministry, nine each from the War Office, COSSAC and the embryo of 21 Army Group; thirteen from ETOUSA and seven from Fighter Command. There was one solitary Paymaster Lieutenant, Royal Navy.'[39]

It is entirely characteristic that the conference itself was treated as a military operation, with the code-name *Rattle*. It was stage-managed in typical Mountbatten style. 'The showmanship could not have been excelled. Domestic arrangements were perfect. On guard was a commando of such magnificent bearing as to disarm the most carping army critic. As there were suspected to be savage breasts among us, the pipe band of the local Home Guard appeared to rend the atmosphere with the indigenous substitute for music. Even the weather was apparently cajoled into giving us perfect days, and a perfect day on that Scottish coast is almost as perfect as a day can be.'[40] As Brigadier Sir Bernard Fergusson put it, it was a 'sort of psychological motor show'.[41]

For once no one complained about the cold. The conference was held under the tin roof of the former swimming pool of the hotel in July and August and the temperature was high; 'the faces of everyone present were soon as red as the gorgets of the many generals.'[42] But consensus was reached on many issues, including the site for the invasion of Europe.

Preparations for D-Day

There were always those who objected to the use of the Clyde as a base. In October 1941 the Director of Movements pointed out that an extra fifteen trains a week were needed to get troops up to Scotland for training and suggested that the Southampton area was more suitable. 'Exposure to air attack is perhaps an advantage rather than a drawback.'[43] The temporary loss of most of Rosneath to the Americans caused some movement south; half the naval trainees were now sent to Brightlingsea on the east coast of England, the rest to Inveraray, while engine-room ratings of landing craft were to be trained at Northney near Portsmouth.

By spring 1944 the Scottish bases had passed their peak and several training schools had been set up elsewhere. Even so, the dangers of the south coast were underlined in April when some German E-boats got among the ships of an American exercise and caused more than 600 casualties. The Clyde had launched operations against Madagascar, North Africa and Sicily when the greater distance from the objective, as compared with southern England, was insignificant. But the biggest combined operation of all time, the ultimate target of all the amphibious warfare training, was conducted at shorter range, across the English Channel. The ships for the invasion of Europe gathered in a wide range of ports, from East Anglia in the east to South Wales in the west. Force S, consisting of 28,000 soldiers and destined to form more than a fifth of the invasion force and capture Sword Beach, completed its training in Scottish waters and left for bases on the south coast of England in April 1944. The Bombarding Force, intended to cover the landings with heavy gunfire, included four British and three American battleships. HMS *Rodney* and the Cruiser Assault Forces E and K, intended to bombard Juno and Gold beaches, sailed from the Clyde on 3 June, before the invasion had been given the final go-ahead. Concrete-filled blockships, for the breakwaters of the Mulberry Harbours in Normandy, gathered at Oban before sailing south. Even in southern England the Scottish contribution was noted. Admiral Warren, who had been Senior Officer Assault Ships and Craft at Largs, was present. 'Familiar ship after familiar ship came into view; and Warren suddenly realised that there was scarcely one which had not passed through his hands in preparation for battle at some time or another.'[44]

Anti-Submarine Warfare

HMS *Nimrod* was commissioned at Campbeltown early in 1940 as the principal training school for officers and ratings who would operate the main anti-submarine detecting device, Asdic, which had partly been developed in the Gareloch in the last war. Among the officers to be posted there was an American volunteer, A. H. Cherry. He found *Nimrod* sited in single-storey buildings formerly part of the local school, with the officers' mess in the former Argyll Hotel.

> Anti-submarine devices are founded on electrics and sound waves, with which I was quite at home, and I followed the theoretical instruction with an easy understanding. In the afternoon we went on to the practical usage of the devices. This primarily consisted of training periodic sound transmissions through a compass arc, sweeping this arc for contact or target, which might be a U-boat. Immediately the sound-wave came in contact with a body, an echo would be set up, and it was this echo which was the basis of study. This echo could be a school of fish, a whale, tides, the wake of a passing ship, a submarine, or the track of a torpedo being shot at your ship.'[45]

There was a certain amount of sea training and at that stage the vessels attached to *Nimrod* comprised the converted yachts *Shemara*, *Tuscarora* and *Carina* and two former Antarctic whalers, *Bulldog* and *Spaniel*, as well as the submarine *Oberon* as a target. Cherry's first experience in sea exercises was not a fruitful one:

The submarine had submerged, but the waters were too rough for the yacht on the surface, and her submerged oscillator, from which the sound emissions emanated, was bobbing out of the water most of the time . . . resulting in loud quenching noises which sounded like someone gargling in the depths below. There were many echoes from tide ripples, reefs, fish and whatnot, but the submarine was perfectly safe. Not one officer who took a turn in the hunt could locate our quarry. By noon a couple of the students were spending their time between stretching out and leaning over the side; they weren't exactly happy.[46]

By November 1943 the Campbeltown Training Flotilla, serving both *Osprey* and *Nimrod*, had expanded to fourteen vessels, most of which were of no use for anything else. It included seven yachts (two built in the previous century), two French torpedo boats and five trawlers. The captain in charge of the base pointed out the inefficiency of using old and unsuitable vessels: most had no room for instruction; the French torpedo boats needed crews of sixty-nine officers and men each, which was wasteful of manpower; 30 per cent were unserviceable at any given moment; none could do more than 12 knots and the Asdic sets were usually out of date.[47] He was eventually given more modern corvettes and then frigates.

A report of 1943 throws some light on training methods for submarine detector ratings in HMS *Nimrod* at Campbeltown. A good Asdic operator was a key man on any ship fitted for anti-submarine duties and the training was of great importance. The standard of teaching was praised. All instructors were aware of the basic level of ignorance of most ratings, but only professional schoolmasters kept it constantly in mind and adjusted their teaching to it. Training in the operating procedure of Asdic was particularly good, though men with no sea-going experience needed further practical training aboard ship, to distinguish the many noises they would hear at sea, and Campbeltown had only limited facilities for real sea training. However, the introductory training film was not helpful. 'The film *Meeting the U-Boat Menace* is unsound both in conception and execution. The forced heartiness of its acting and its attempt to "boost" Campbeltown moved even the dullest rating in Class P to derisive laughter. The showing of it at HMS *Nimrod* and elsewhere should be discontinued forthwith.'[48]

Another anti-submarine school, HMS *Osprey,* was moved from Portland in the south of England to Dunoon in January 1941. It offered two levels of advanced courses for officers. Cherry commented, 'HMS *Osprey* was a veritable bee-hive. Here the theories upon which anti-submarine devices worked were expounded at great length, and officers appointed for the long course came out as specialists in the field. Instructors at *Osprey* were top flight men in anti-submarine warfare and Commander P. W. Burnett, probably one of the keenest minds, was to become well known later in Washington. Those of us on short courses rubbed shoulders with long-course officers and learnt much from the contact with evenings over a gin or beer in the friendly wardroom life.'[49]

The Terror of Tobermory

The most famous, or notorious, of Scottish training bases was HMS *Western Isles*, in Tobermory Bay, used for the working-up of destroyers and escort vessels. The officer in charge, Commodore Sir Gilbert Stephenson, became one of the legends of the war. Hundreds of new escort vessels were commissioned to fight the U-boats in the Battle of the Atlantic and often reached Tobermory with only a few key men who had been to sea before. Stephenson's job was to 'work up' the ships, making them ready for action after fourteen days of intensive and unconventional training.

Stephenson had retired in 1929 as a vice-admiral but was brought back at the beginning of the war as a commodore, the highest rank available in the Royal Naval Reserve. As such he served during the evacuation of Dunkirk. He was a man of great energy and character, known as 'Monkey', 'Puggy' or 'Electric Whiskers' to the crews under his command. His efforts were devoted to a very lively programme, by which half-trained officers and men were made fit for the rigours of the Battle of the Atlantic.

His headquarters were in the converted passenger ferry HMS *Western Isles*, built as a Liverpool to Isle of Man ferry and converted by Barclay Curle of Glasgow in 1940. She was anchored in Aros Bay at the eastern end of Tobermory Harbour and eventually employed a staff of 230 officers and men. Much of the training was done in the deep waters nearby, with friendly submarines acting as mock targets or 'clockwork mice'. But the most important resource was the energy, determination and imagination of Stephenson himself, who spared no efforts to make the officers and men aware of what they would have to face in the Atlantic.

Many stories were told about Stephenson. Richard Baker provides the 'authorised version' of a celebrated incident. The commodore came on board a corvette one winter's morning:

Without any preliminaries he flung his gold-braided cap on the deck and said abruptly to the Quartermaster – 'That is a small unexploded bomb dropped by an enemy plane. What are you going to do about it?' The sailor, who had evidently heard about these unconventional tests of initiative, promptly took a step forward and kicked the cap into the sea. Everyone waited for a great roar of protest from the Commodore. But not at all. He warmly commended the lad on his presence of mind, and then, pointing to the submerged cap, said, 'That's a man overboard. Jump in and save him!'[50]

Another account is given by Cyril Stephens, a seaman in HMS *Orchis*:

> Tobermory, oh my God, it was murder. We had this Commodore Stephenson, 'Monkey Brand', they nicknamed him. He used to have two little tufts on his face. And he was about seventy odd and [he and his training staff would] come aboard at any time of the night . . . It was him who used to sort us out in the working up trials and he had some quite funny tricks he used to do. He'd allocate a ship to raid another ship during the night and pinch anything they could find, like the log books or gun off the bridge or something like that, and woe betide the officer next morning . . . You'd come on board and you'd have exercises: 'abandon ship', 'collision at sea', 'fire in the galley', 'fire somewhere else', pipes and wires all over the place, but in the finish we knuckled down.[51]

Even officers appointed to his staff had to earn his respect. Lieutenant Donald Fry came from the minesweeping base at Port Edgar in the Forth.

> The job of going to Tobermory to work up the frigates fell to my unhappy lot. Quite understandably the base commander there, the formidable Commodore 'Monkey' Stephenson, resented bitterly the time that his valuable frigates, so urgently required for anti-submarine work, had to spend being worked up in minesweeping . . .
>
> He then swung round on his heel and said, 'Who are you?' When I told him I was the minesweeping officer from Port Edgar his whole bearing changed and with a sweet smile he said 'Oh yes, the expert from Port Edgar. Now I understand that you require fourteen days of glassy conditions to carry out the exercises with these valuable ships . . .' That's the way he started, but he turned out to be extremely helpful, if a bit of a tiger.[52]

Stephenson earned his nickname 'the Terror of Tobermory' but 1,132 ships were trained under his command.

The base at Stornoway was much less famous. An extension to Tobermory was first proposed early in 1943, with a satellite establishment at Loch na Lathaich on the Ross of Mull. This is much less sheltered than Tobermory and had far fewer shore facilities, so a new, independent command was set up at Stornoway for the new frigates and destroyers which were coming into service.[53]

Submarine Training

In the early stages of the war submarine training was carried out from Portmouth and Portland on the south coast of England, and in the Forth from Rosyth, where several flotillas were based. By the middle of June 1940 it was realised that the southern training was no longer possible. On the 18th it was ordered that torpedo trials should be moved entirely to the range at Loch Long and it was recognised that as Portsmouth was

> unsuitable as a base for sea training of the Commanding Officers' qualifying course, it was proposed that this should be carried out in the Campbeltown area, *Cyclops* being used as a depot ship for the submarines required in a suitable area north of Arran. She would also serve as a depot ship for the submarines for anti-submarine training at Campbeltown.

The Portland base in the south was even more exposed and submarine training there was ended early in July. Training in the Forth was abandoned early in August.[54]

The *Cyclops*, stationed in Rothesay Bay from mid-1940, was one of the oldest depot ships in the navy, having been built in 1905 as a merchant ship and purchased on the stocks. She had served throughout the First World War as a fleet repair ship. However she was quite large, at 11,300 tons, and this allowed room for training facilities such as an attack teacher. 'The purpose of the Seventh Submarine Flotilla was twofold: to give sea training to new submarine officers and ratings, and at the same time to provide live targets for destroyers and other escort craft. Many of the boats in this flotilla were dispersed at the various bases where anti-submarine forces had their training. So we spent the next few winter months up and down the rugged and beautiful coastline of Western Scotland, dividing our time between Rothesay, Campbeltown, Ardrishaig and Tobermory.'[55]

Potential submarine commanders set out from *Cyclops* on practical courses, which soon became known as 'Perishers'. One theory suggests that this was simply a corruption of the 'Periscope' Course, another that they were so called because failure would bar the candidate from any further appointments in the submarine service. Edward Young describes his experiences in 1943. After two weeks' shore training at Gosport near Portsmouth he was billeted in the Glenburn Hotel but had to catch a boat to the *Cyclops* every morning before breakfast. He describes his first mock attack:

> I swept [the periscope] rapidly across the green shores of Bute . . . swung past the entrances to Loch Fyne and Kilbrannan Sound, and continued along the steep shores of Arran, which rose nearly three thousand feet to the imposing summit of Goat Fell. The only ship in sight apart from the target was an outward-bound merchantman steaming down the main channel of the Firth of Clyde. Completing the circle I came back once more to the target, still going away to the eastward . . . Waiting for the *White Bear* to turn, I felt horribly uncertain of myself . . . In as calm a voice as I could muster, I gave the order, 'attack team close up'.

After three hard weeks he was sent to Scapa to practise with modern warships and conducted a mock attack on the battleship *King George V*. He passed, as did all but one of his course, and was appointed to command an old submarine operating as a 'clockwork mouse' from Rothesay.[56]

Submarine crews found some time for recreation ashore, and Stoker Arthur (Tancy) Lee describes his adventures:

> Doing the rounds . . . Deep dives in Loch Long, Scapa, Tobermory where we held out 'Uckers' [ludo] championship (under the clock) . . . Dunoon . . . Campbeltown . . . Where a churn of Ideal Milk was purloined, trying to get it back to the boat . . . Stoker Regan falling into the 'oggin' while eating his fish and chips in the blackout . . . Yes Campbeltown was always 'lively', what with Jan Pearce taking on half the crew of a destroyer, Billy Brown doing his 'noble art' turn, yes it was extremely lively at Campbeltown.
>
> Surviving an involuntary ramming which snapped off the periscopes we returned to Rothesay alongside *Cyclops*. The lads were quite thrilled to get a run ashore there, as the Ivy Benson ladies band was performing at the local. Being duty watch that night I was assisting the ERA . . . Later the boys returned from their shore leave all merry and bright and recounting their experiences ashore; apparently half the crew of submarines alongside had been 'tapping up' the Ivy Benson band, although not very successfuly. Anyway PO Jordan (what a helping SPO he was, couldn't do enough for the lads) brought me

fish and chips from ashore, so the evening finished off nice and quietly . . . All creeping off to their billets and kipping it off. [57]

The Fleet Air Arm

During the 1920s and '30s naval aviation, now known as the Fleet Air Arm, was formally under the control of the Royal Air Force but many naval officers trained as pilots and observers and much of this was done at Leuchars in Fife, founded by the Royal Naval Air Service in 1918 and used by the RAF ever since. The first pilot's course, consisting of forty-seven Royal Navy and Royal Marine officers, began at Netheravon in 1924 and then part of the course transferred to Leuchars. From No. 10 Naval Pilots' Course, which began in March 1928, all pilot training was done at Leuchars. One pupil was Caspar John, a future First Sea Lord, who was sent north after basic training to learn the naval aspects. He found Leuchars 'A most salubrious spot, the sea a matter of some three miles away and some of the finest Scotch scenery about forty or fifty miles inland.' He had his first air accident in 1926, a relatively mild matter in the days of low-powered biplanes. His engine seized up at 2,000 feet; he crash-landed in a field and the plane turned upside-down. He was helped to a farmhouse, unhurt.[58]

In was only in 1937 that it was decided that the Royal Navy would take full control of the Fleet Air Arm and the transfer took place two years later on the brink of war. There was much to do in training aircrew and servicing crews, as well as building a shore infrastructure. Land-based maritime aircraft operating patrols over the seas were part of the RAF's newly formed Coastal Command, while the Fleet Air Arm's aircraft operated from ships, whether in large numbers from aircraft carriers or in ones, twos and threes from the catapult flights of battleships and cruisers. When it was set up the Fleet Air Arm relied on the rest of the RAF for the shore bases it needed for training and maintenance. Now it needed its own. Aircraft carriers generally send the planes ashore when in port to allow aircrews to carry on with training and operations, and airfields were needed to receive the disembarked squadrons.

On the transfer in 1939 the FAA inherited only five airfields, including the former First World War station at Donibristle near Rosyth. It was given a ship name in the usual fashion, HMS *Merlin*. This was a small site with little room for development, hemmed in by Dalgety Bay on one side and the main line railway on the other, and with a hill at one end of the runway. Initially its single runway was only 800 yards long, whereas 1,000- and 1,100-yard runways were now regarded as necessary. By 1944 another had been built, 970 yards long, but at an angle of only ten degrees to the first. Donibristle was used relatively little for disembarked squadrons but developed as a communications unit and as a maintenance base or Royal Naval Aircraft Repair Yard.

The Fleet Air Arm quickly began to build its own airfields, the Royal Navy's biggest civil engineering programme during the war. A large proportion of them were to be sited in Scotland. This was partly because the RAF had already earmarked many of the sites in southern and eastern England, but also because it was important to site training bases away from possible enemy action. Indeed by 1940 the skies of Britain were crowded with aircraft, both friendly and hostile, and basic flying training was conducted across the Atlantic in Canada, the West Indies and the USA. Operational training required much closer integration with the work of the fleet and this is where the Scottish bases became important.

The new Royal Naval Air Stations (RNAS) differed from RAF bases in several respects. They usually had four runways instead of three, and indeed Arbroath was one of two airfields in the United Kingdom with five. One legend is that naval pilots could not deal with cross-winds as they were used to landing on carriers that turned into the wind. A more plausible explanation is that they were built in inhospitable sites where winds were strong and variable. The runways were made of tarmac rather than concrete as used by the RAF. The Navy was accused of waste in building them but it was able to argue that the tarmac lasted much longer. RNAS runways were mostly 30 yards wide instead of 50, because the Fleet Air Arm had no large aircraft. The standard RNAS control tower was three storeys high instead of two, with a glasshouse on top. The airfields had extensive training facilities but most of the buildings were the ubiquitous Nissen hut, for bricks were scarce in the remote areas where the new air stations were built.

Hatston, just north-west of Kirkwall, was the first new naval air station to open, as HMS *Sparrowhawk*, in October 1939. Its main purpose was to serve disembarked squadrons from the fleet in Scapa Flow, but it had many training functions as well; because carriers, like the Grand Fleet twenty-five years earlier, often spent considerable time at anchor in the Flow, while squadrons might spend several months ashore awaiting allocation to a carrier.

Airmen had different attitudes to Orkney. Most regarded it as the end of the earth, and shared some of the attitudes of the Grand Fleet in 1914–18 – 'a really bleak airfield, and nearer to Norway than to Newcastle'.[59] Some saw the beauty of the islands, their archaeology

and wildlife, and found 'a sort of stillness and peace that people who
live in cities can't even dream of', though this was marred by the
navy's dive-bombing practice.[60] They found the people welcoming,
the food relatively good and a wardroom of superior quality: 'the
best-stocked bar I experienced in the whole of my service.'[61]
H. J. C. Spencer found that 'Hatston was an exciting place in
1944, very much a front line airfield with many first line squadrons
passing through between operations.'[62] One diversion was to fly
between the Old Man of Hoy and the land. Training facilities were
good. 'We did dive-bombing practice on Sule Skerry, much to the
annoyance of the rock's hundreds of thousands of gulls, shags, skuas
and tern. We carried out dummy torpedo attacks on ships exercising
from Scapa Flow and dummy depth-charge attacks on towed targets
from the Woodwick Range. We practised air-to-air firing, navigation,
homing on ASV [air-to-surface vessel] contacts and beacons and aerial
photography.' After three months in the Flow, 835 Squadron had
achieved a high standard of flying, though it was frustrated at the lack
of real action.[63]

As well as providing planes for specialised aircraft carriers, the
Fleet Air Arm manned the aircraft which were allocated in small
flights to battleships and cruisers. In January 1940, 700 Squadron
was formed by merging several other units. It had eleven Seafoxes
and twelve Swordfish floatplanes, but its main strength was forty-
two Supermarine Walruses. These were designed to be catapulted
from the decks of ships, then to alight in the sea after the flight; the
Walrus was an amphibian and could land on a runway as well.
Naturally the aircraft of 700 Squadron found their way around the
world, but nearly all the crews had trained in Scotland. A ten-week
course was set up by 1942, consisting of three weeks at Donibristle
for aerodrome flying and water landing, wireless instruction and
practice, anti-submarine and dive-bombing attacks and air photography. At Dundee for the second three weeks, crews came together
for navigation exercises and night landings. After a week in the Irish
Sea learning to use ships' catapults, the crews returned to Donibristle
before going on to Orkney.[64]

RNAS Twatt had a name which provoked more mirth than any
other airfield in the United Kingdom. It was christened after the village
nearby, in the north-west corner of the Orkney mainland, served as a
satellite to Hatston and then became independent as HMS *Tern*. From
June 1942 it was the headquarters of 700 Squadron and its catapult
aircraft. The RAF stations at Skeabrae and Grimsetter were also used
by the Fleet Air Arm before they too were taken over fully by the Navy.

RNAS Arbroath was opened in June 1940 as HMS *Condor* and was mostly used as a training school for observers – officers (and occasionally petty officers) who navigated the aircraft and carried out numerous other tasks. The Admiralty's publication *Fleet Air Arm* of 1943 describes the progress of a fictitious trainee observer. Some of his colleagues were sent to Trinidad for training, but

> Oliver and the remainder went to a station on the east coast of Scotland known as HMS *Condor*, where his principal instruction was in reconnaissance and in navigation as a means to that end. Soon he went into the air on exercises on Swordfish and Walruses. He learnt to find his way about in the air without using landmarks, relying on his skill in plotting and air navigation. The early practices were over the land, but little by little he became accustomed to working over the sea, until he was familiar with its changing moods of wind and fog and cloud. He also had practical experience in ship recognition, and learnt to take air photographs, which were processed by specially trained Wrens.[65]

Trainee observers, still ratings, were flown on exercises by rather disgruntled, but commissioned, pilots.

> 'And where would we be going today?' 'If you don't mind, Sir, could we please depart over the Seaforth Hotel swimming pool on a course of 095 degrees.' It was always the swimming pool: an imaginary aircraft carrier would 'sail' from that point at a speed of 25 knots on a course of 030 degrees, this bringing it close to the little port of Stonehaven after an hour, by which time we would have completed a dog leg course over the sea and would attempt to arrive over, or 'intercept' the carrier at the appropriate time and place on the coast. These attempts brooked much sarcastic comment from our pilots. 'Lost again, are we? And where would you suggest we go now if we're not to miss lunch?'[66]

Some pilots posted to observer training tried to make up for the slight by daring flying, for example when a Swordfish used by the 61st Observer course at Arbroath crashed into the sea near the Bell Rock lighthouse, killing the pilot and two Dutch trainees.[67]

Meteorology was part of an observer's training and its importance soon became clear:

> The early weeks were spent more in the class-room than in the air. It had never occurred to me to wonder how one set off from an aircraft carrier, flew in all directions, blown by unforeseen winds, and arrived back to whatever spot in the ocean the carrier might have sailed to in the meantime.[68]

Arbroath was well liked as a posting. The weather was less extreme than in Orkney or Kintyre and the town was close and pleasant. Weekend leave could be spent in Edinburgh, a relatively short train journey away.

RNAS East Haven, near Dundee, was opened as HMS *Peewit* in May 1943 and was mainly used to train pilots in deck landing. A dummy deck was painted on one of the runways, as at Arbroath. East Haven also became the centre for the training of deck landing control officers or DLCOs, the famous 'batsmen' who signalled course corrections to pilots landing on carriers. Originally it was intended that all DLCOs should be volunteers, but Lieutenant Dunstan Hadley was drafted in against his will in 1943, and disciplined when he protested. It is not surprising that volunteers were short, for DLCOs missed the joys of flying, but still faced an element of danger. They often had to flee for their lives when pilots made bad landings.[69]

The airfield at Crail in the East Neuk of Fife, HMS *Jackdaw*, was commissioned in October 1940 and used mainly to train pilots in the specialised art of dropping torpedoes. After practice on the Torpedo Attack Trainer, the trainees flew over the Forth to drop dummies from Swordfish or Albacore aircraft. After some experience they used 'runners', real torpedoes without warheads, which could be recovered by drifters and used again. The paddle steamer *Glenavon* steamed at 9 knots off the Isle of May as a target. Sometimes real battleships and destroyers took part in the exercises, as when the *Nelson* and her escorts were attacked by Dunstan Hadley and his colleagues. 'Well chaps, out of nine aircraft we got one hit – on the stern, it's not good enough. Most of you dropped too far away. I warned you about its size.' Barr spoke up. 'The destroyers were in the way.' 'Of course they were, that's what they're there for, you have to get round them somehow.' However, they did better than the pilot who accidentally dropped his practice torpedo on Crail police station, fortunately without any casualties.[70] Crail had a satellite airfield, *Jackdaw II*, five miles away at Dunino near Kingsbarns. Transferred from the RAF in 1942, it was one of the most primitive in the Fleet Air Arm, with a single grass runway.

The Fleet Air Arm needed a base on the Firth of Clyde, where new aircraft carriers were sent to work up. At first the former civil airfield at Campbeltown was used though the facilities were extremely primitive. 'Ground-to-air signals were still in the stone age, and there was only one small hangar, supplemented by a Bessemer hangar with a tendency to fly off on its own. The control tower consisted of Mr McGeachy, a stove, ample supplies of tea, and a telephone.'[71]

In June 1941, the new station at Machrihanish, four miles away, was ready. This became, according to E. E. Barringer, 'probably the most-used naval airfield of the war'.[72] Hugh Popham called it the 'Crewe Junction of the Fleet Air Arm', though this was not a compliment – it was 'the uniquely desolate station you arrive at in the early hours of the morning, wait about at, and finally depart from, none the wiser . . . supremely it is the place of departure, from which one flies to deck-land within the shadow of Ailsa Craig; an uneasy, queasy staging-point, a bowl in the hills full of the filthiest weather in the British Isles.'[73] According to Norman Hanson, 'it would be a desirable posting in high summer', but 'in late Autumn or winter Machrihanish was a penance bordering upon a sentence. The weather could be and nearly always was foul. Our average evening's entertainment seemed to consist of putting extra lashings on all aircraft exposed to the fury of the gales, while we ourselves were being soaked by driving rain.'[74] Not everyone was so negative. According to Spencer, 'The squadron greatly enjoyed its stay at Machrihanish . . . we were to keep returning there and it was to become our home port, if there is such a thing for a squadron.'[75]

HMS *Argus*, the first true aircraft carrier in the world, was stationed in the Clyde for part of the war and used for deck-landing training off Ailsa Craig. The procedure is described by Norman Hanson:

> The drill was quite simple. *Argus* had six arrester wires strung across the after end of the deck. She had no 'island' in the accepted sense, only a rather comical structure somewhat reminiscent of a submarine's conning tower at the forward end of the deck, which could be raised or lowered at will. She had no crash barriers. Instead, standing near the island was a very brave young officer who waved a red flag if an aircraft failed to engage any of the wires with its arrester hook. The pilot was thus energetically exhorted to open the throttle and take off again, to make another circuit and another approach to the deck. We were each to do six landings, preceded by two dummy runs with the wires in the down position and with arrester hooks up.[76]

Pilots were apprehensive before their first landings, not without reason:

> In the last 200 yards to the deck, he drifted to port ever so slightly. The batsman slanted his bats to correct him, more and more energetically as Johnny failed to react. As the aircraft came in over the side of the deck and supported only by fresh air, the batsman dropped for his life – and we, standing in the nets, dropped with him. The port wheel went into

the nets and the Fulmar, at about 65 knots, slewed to port and fell into the sea. As she went, we could see Johnny making the greatest and last mistake of his life; he was casting off his harness and climbing out of the cockpit. He and the Fulmar were gone.[77]

When new escort carriers came into service from 1941 most of them were based on the Clyde, even those working with escorts from Liverpool and Londonderry, so Machrihanish became busier than ever. There were very few operational squadrons which did not make many visits to Machrihanish during the Second World War. It had the standard pattern of four runways, from 1,050 to 1,200 yards long. It had accommodation for six squadrons, or eighty-five aircraft. There was storage for 162,000 gallons of aviation fuel but only 66 tons of bombs.[78]

The air around Machrihanish was to become as crowded as the waters of the Firth of Clyde. According to Spencer,

> There were usually several squadrons at Machrihanish, due to its strategic position close to the carrier playground in the Firth of Clyde. So there was competition for the sky, particularly at night. Everyone behaved reasonably at first, each squadron having its night. The weather would take a hand. But programmes were not cancelled, just postponed. Come the first clear night everyone flew. It was an air traffic controller's nightmare, only there weren't any. No radar either. One squadron would be doing deck landing practice with its batsmen out on the runway batting in all comers. Others would be going off to the bombing ranges, or to play with HMS *Graph* [a captured U-boat used for training], or to do navigation exercises, or perhaps formation practice.[79]

In 1942, as Britain began to prepare for the naval war in the Pacific, a great demand for carrier pilots was predicted and several RAF stations were taken over. Fearn near Invergordon was commissioned in August 1942 as a satellite to Donibristle and became HMS *Owl* in its own right two months later, for the working-up of torpedo bomber squadrons. Evanton, further up the Cromarty Firth, had been used by the Fleet Air Arm since 1940 before it was taken over in 1944 as an aircraft maintenance yard. The airfield at Abbotsinch near Glasgow was built by the RAF and the Fleet Air Arm had lodger rights until August 1943, when it was transferred and commissioned as HMS *Sanderling*. It was used mainly as a maintenance base and for storage of aircraft. Ayr was another former RAF station commissioned as HMS *Wagtail* in October 1944. It supplemented Machrihanish as a base for disembarked squadrons in the Clyde, as well as carrying out miscellaneous duties such as communication, compass calibration and training in artillery bombardment spotting. RAF Dounreay was also transferred in 1944, to be used as a satellite of Twatt, but it was hardly used. The atom bomb ended the war in the Pacific before the new aircrew were needed.

The airfield at Drem near North Berwick was built by the RAF and the Fleet Air Arm had 'lodger' facilities there until it was transferred just before the end of the war in Europe in 1945. In 1943 it was used to train carrier pilots in the new skills of night flying, which it seems to have done with considerable success. 'Training continued, and very high quality material was sent to us to be trained. This was now a problem. We had more instructors, course followed course, but there was nothing for the aircrew to do once they had qualified.'[80]

A Fleet Air Arm pilot, observer or telegraphist air gunner had a nomadic life, even by naval standards. In training he would move from one base to another learning different skills. On operations his squadron would leave the carrier every time it entered port, and there was no guarantee that it would return to the same ship. Thus 817 Squadron, equipped with Albacore torpedo bombers, was allocated to HMS *Victorious* but landed ten times at Hatston, Twatt, Donibristle and Machrihanish between August 1941 and November 1942, staying ashore for one to three weeks on most occasions.[81] The servicing crews of the squadron had to come ashore too, with a stock of tools and spares, and this was a more complex logistical task. On average the crews consisted of about 100 ratings with a sprinkling of RAF personnel, and they were usually taken ashore by boat from an anchored carrier, then by road to the air station.

The Fleet Air Arm was to see an enormous expansion during the war, from 232 aircraft in 1939 to more than 11,000 in 1945. Pilots had to be trained for all of these, along with observers for the larger ones. There were very few who did not spend some time at the Scottish bases.

Coastal Forces

Coastal forces were another new arm of the Second World War. They had their origin in the Coastal Motor Boats of the previous conflict, but had been little developed in peacetime, so the thread was lost. They comprised the motor torpedo boats or MTBs, motor gun boats (MGBs), motor launches (MLs), harbour defence motor launches (HDMLs), motor minesweepers (MMs) and many other miscellaneous types. The MTBs were amongst the most glamorous and publicised types in the navy. In the middle years of the war they were constantly in contact with the enemy in the English Channel and North Sea, often fighting with the German equivalent, the S- or E-boats. HDMLs and MMs had much more mundane but often equally dangerous duties. More than any other part of the service, it was the preserve of the temporary wartime RNVR officer.

The main training base for these craft was set up at Fort William and commissioned as HMS *St Christopher* in October 1940. At its height it had a staff of thirty officers and used five hotels – the Highland was the administrative base, the Grand provided accommodation for senior officers, while Wrens lived in the Station, Palace and Waverley. This of course was not enough and most of the men lived in Nissen huts, or were billeted on local families.

The school had nineteen MLs, eight MTBs and nine MGBs at its peak. These were moored to trots on the other side of Loch Linnhe at Camus na Gaul, accessible by open boat from Fort William pier. The training boats had skeleton crews as instructors, with the other berths filled by trainees of the different branches and skills – officers, gunners, torpedo-men, mechanics, radio operators and so on. Boats usually went down the loch towards Oban for several days at a time, though it was felt by some that the enclosed waters of the Firth of Lorne did not give a full range of sea-going experience. About 50,000 men passed through *St Christopher* during the war.

Another school was set up at Ardrishaig on Loch Fyne in January 1941, as HMS *Seahawk*. Its role was to train coastal forces crews in anti-submarine warfare. It had three MLs, two botor anti-submarine boats and an HDML, but no MTBs, because they were not intended for anti-submarine work. It also had two midget submarines or X-craft as 'clockwork mice', plus the services of boats from the Seventh Submarine Flotilla when needed.[82]

Minesweeping

Port Edgar on the Firth of Forth was commissioned as HMS *Lochinvar* in November 1939. The only major sea-training establishment on the east coast of Scotland apart from Bo'ness, it used the relatively shallow waters of the firth to train the officers and crews of mine-sweepers. Part of the Hopetoun estate was taken over for living quarters and offices, while the lecture rooms and training equipment were down in the harbour. Officers were sent for a six-week course, combining practical sea experience with lectures in minesweeping, gunnery and seamanship. Twenty arrived every three weeks. Ratings were also trained at *Lochinvar*. At the height of the war, fifty arrived each week to begin a three-week course.

> Like the officers, they spend two days at sea and acquire practical experience in the manual working of the sweeps, in splicing the wire hawsers, in steering the trawler, and in those deck duties which the navy describes by the expressive term 'pulley-hauley'. Ashore, Petty Officers give them general instruction in trawler gunnery, rifle practice, deck work and general seamanship, so that they may take their places as efficient members of any minesweeping ship, whether she be trawler, drifter, dan-layer, or fleet sweeper.[83]

The other task at *Lochinvar* was the working-up of newly commissioned ships and their crews.

> The process of working-up consisted of taking a newly commissioned ship, usually fresh from the builder's yard and sea trials, and in 14 days turning it into a unit sufficiently efficient to work with the fleet at sea, or in the case of trawlers to go immediately into operations around our coast. So far as it was possible we would work up the Fleet sweepers together and the trawlers together, because the two did not work together very well.[84]

The mainstay of the trawler service at the beginning of the war were the skippers, RNR, former fishermen appointed warrant officers in the Royal Navy. 'The trawler skippers could be a problem. They were nearly all professional fishermen and great seamen, but they were not easily amenable to naval discipline, nor did they take kindly to too much flag signalling.'[85] The new German magnetic mines needed a different approach and the old-fashioned skipper RNR became redundant:

> There was little increase during the war in the number of minesweeping officers of the RNR Skipper class . . . The reason lay partly in the reluctance to deprive the food producing fishing industry of all the most knowledgeable trawler- and drifter-men, and partly in the realisation, born of war experience, that the average Skipper could not contend with the intricacies of influence sweeping. The necessity for meticulous station keeping, navigational accuracy and constant vigilance ran counter to his ingrained habits. The temporary reserve officer of the other classes, usually better educated, more amenable to training and bringing to the task a fresh, enthusiastic and unbiased mind, proved far more efficient and reliable.

RNR skippers had made up 43 per cent of minesweeping officers at the beginning of the war. By the end they were only 6 per cent while RNVR officers formed 63 per cent.[86]

The Aftermath

By late 1942, the Royal Navy had 112 bases throughout the world in which men were borne for accounting purposes. Twenty-nine, more than a quarter, were in Scotland. These included depot ships at Scapa, Loch Ewe and Greenock, and hotels commissioned as ships such as HMS *Spartiate* in Glasgow. At the end of the war, nearly all the Scottish training bases were closed down and the hotels returned to civilian use. Future guests would hardly ever be aware of their wartime role. As Admiral Sir Angus Cunningham Graham wrote a few years later

> In both wars the Royal Navy flooded into Scotland to make use of our deep water ports and sea lochs for large scale and safer anchorages. The navy also took the opportunity to recruit from Scotland's ample supply of first class technicians and her splendid seamen of the Highlands and Islands. After each war the Navy unimaginatively retreated 'en masse' to the channel.[87]

Chapter 15

Cold War and Cod Wars

After 1945, as at the end of previous wars, Scots seemed to dominate the navy at its highest levels. In 1954 Lord Mountbatten received the Freedom of the City of Edinburgh and an honorary degree from the University, and responded in typically flattering terms:

> I do not know what proportion of the Navy are Scots; but those we have certainly seem to come up to the top. Not only is the present First Sea Lord, Sir Rhoderick McGrigor, a Scotsman, but so were his three immediate predecessors. And for good measure we have yet another one, Sir John Lang, as Permanent Secretary of the Admiralty.[1]

Admiral Sir Angus Cunningham Graham pointed out that 'the unbroken succession of First Sea Lords from 1944 ran Cunningham, Cunningham, Fraser, McGrigor.'[2] But in fact most of the naval leaders were displaced Scots, whose connection with the country was rather tenuous.

Andrew Browne Cunningham, First Sea Lord at the end of the war, wrote on the first page of his autobiography, 'Though born in Ireland I am a Scot.'[3] His father was a professor at Trinity College, Dublin. He was educated at Edinburgh Academy before being taken away to a school in Hampshire which specialised in cramming boys for the navy. He was Commander-in-Chief in the Mediterranean for the first half of the Second World War and won the Battle of Matapan against the Italians. He led the naval side of the Torch landings in North Africa and became First Sea Lord on the death of Sir Dudley Pound in 1943. Many regard him as the greatest admiral since Nelson.

Sir John Cunningham was First Sea Lord from 1946–8. Despite the name, he had only slight connections with Scotland. He was born in British Guiana and educated near Portsmouth. Bruce Fraser, later Lord Fraser of North Cape, was born in London to a general in the Indian Army and was also educated in Hampshire. Sir Rhoderick McGrigor, who held the post from 1951 to 1955, was an adopted son of a colonel in the Grenadier Guards. He had connections with St Andrews University, served as Rector of Aberdeen University and retired in that area.

The navy had three main roles years after 1945. The first of these was to help in the various conflicts which followed the dissolution of the British Empire, in places like Cyprus, Malaya and Rhodesia. All of this took place a long way from Britain and had no particular impact on Scotland. The second task was to pursue the Cold War against the Soviet Union and her allies and satellites. This turned out to be very relevant to Scotland. Initially, as the Soviet submarine fleet grew, it revived prospects of older strategies, of barrages to stop their escape into the Atlantic and convoys sailing from the Clyde. Later, Scottish harbours were to provide the main bases for nuclear-armed submarines. The third role was the protection of British offshore interests, initially in the fisheries and later in the extraction of oil and gas. Both of these would involve Scottish ports very much.

Any idea of parity with the United States Navy had disappeared in the Pacific. When the British Pacific Fleet went to war in 1944–5 under the command of Sir Bruce Fraser, its officers were amazed with the scope, range and efficiency of the American effort. The lower deck, in a different vein, was impressed by the relative comfort in which the American seaman lived. From that moment Britain began to accept a role as the junior partner in a coalition. Excellent relations were forged between the senior officers of the two navies and there was a good deal of exchange of technical information as well as personal friendship. This was to have a profound effect on future development.

In the immediate aftermath of the war, there was much tidying up to do. No. 2 Military Port at Cairnryan began the post-war period as an assembly point for U-boats sent round from other ports like Loch Eriboll. Eighty-six were eventually sent there and moored on the west side of the loch. During the winter of 1945–6 most of them were towed out into the Irish Sea and scuttled; thirty-six of them sank prematurely in the severe weather. Others were torpedoed by the boats of the Third Submarine Flotilla from the Clyde, giving them a chance to test new weapons and techniques. Then Cairnryan took on a much more hazardous role. A hundred thousand tons of ammunition were loaded into landing craft during the first year of peace and taken out to the deep water of Beaufort's Dyke in the Irish Sea. Up to 1,500 soldiers were employed in the task and seven were killed by an explosion on a jetty in June 1946. Even more deadly were 71,000 German nerve-gas bombs. Between September 1945 and July 1956, they were loaded into ten old merchant ships which were taken out and scuttled in the Atlantic, from Land's End to the Hebrides.[4]

At the end of the war, ships under construction were largely abandoned. A few were left aside as shipyards concentrated on replacing the losses in the merchant fleet. Three cruisers, *Tiger*, *Lion* and *Blake*, lay uncompleted for fourteen to sixteen years after being launched in 1944–5 at Clydebank, Greenock and Govan. There were periodic defence reviews in which the navy had to cut its coat according to an increasingly smaller cloth. None sounded as pessimistic as the *Revised Restricted Fleet* of 1949, but the *Radical Review*, the *Outline of Future Policy*, the *Way Forward*, *Options for Change* and the *Strategic Defence Review* all, in practice, signalled reduced expenditure and a smaller fleet. Britain had to come to terms with her reduced economic circumstances, combined with rising costs. Labour was far more expensive than before the war, and more skilled men were needed in the new navy, which relied far less on conscription than the army or air force. The jet aeroplane, the guided missile and advanced electronics were all vastly more expensive than anything the navy had used in the past, but they were enormously greater in range and destructive power.

The Closure of Bases

Planning for the closure of the Scapa base began before the end of the war. 'As soon as Scapa is no longer used by any "worth-while" targets or as soon as all U-boats have been accounted for, whichever is the earlier, the work of reduction and removal of defences can commence.'[5] Items which could be put into store were to be maintained and reconditioned. Fixed items such as shore-control positions would stay, provided they did not interfere with peacetime use. A few towed targets were kept on, along with a tug to pull them. The floating dock was towed away. Scapa would be used only occasionally as a fleet base, as in pre-war years.

The smaller bases were also closed. Combined operations moved from Inveraray to Fremlington in Devon in 1946, but were given low priority for the next ten years. Anti-submarine work went mainly to Portland, but many of the naval air stations remained in commission for the moment. By about 1947, only the submarine depot ship remained in the Clyde and the future of Rosyth was under debate. On a slightly more positive note, HMS *Caledonia* was reopened at Rosyth in 1946 as a training school for artificers.

The Scottish training bases have a low profile in history, apart from

Western Isles at Tobermory. Basic training, with its transition from civilian life into a new and strange culture, made a great impression on the autobiographers of the war. The operational training in Scotland seemed less dramatic than that, and far less dramatic than action against the enemy. At the time the locations were little publicised, for obvious security reasons. The temporary nature of the bases made their physical removal quite easy and they disappeared quickly, leaving traces in the form of old Nissen huts. The naval establishment was keen to return to pre-war standards of discipline and organisation and preferred to efface the memory of the more casual aspects of the war years; one suspects that it was a little embarrassed about how easy it actually was to train sailors when really needed and it preferred to surround the trade with its old mystique.

The early 1950s saw a wave of war memoirs and novels, followed by films of the 'stiff upper lip' school, which largely neglected the role of the Scottish training bases. In the film of *The Man Who Never Was* the submarine is seen sailing from Portsmouth rather than the Holy Loch. In the film of *Cockleshell Heroes* the training takes place in the Portsmouth area and the marines are based in Eastney Barracks, rather than in the Holy Loch. The film of *The Cruel Sea* is more positive about the role of the Clyde than Monsarrat was in his memoirs, but strangely quiet about Tobermory. Instead of the forthright Commodore Stephenson, the corvette in the film is assessed by a sour-faced lieutenant-commander with very negative views. *Above Us the Waves*, about the Chariot and X-craft attacks on the Tirpitz, has a few Scottish references but was clearly filmed in and around Plymouth. Film-makers preferred southern locations, with better weather and nearer London.

The Survival of Rosyth

In November 1944 a delegation of councillors and MPs from both sides of the Forth, along with the Earl of Elgin, whose father had let the land for the original dockyard, went to the Admiralty in London to express their concerns about the future of Rosyth to the First Lord, A. V. Alexander. Provost Thomson Kennedy of Dunfermline was appointed spokesman and the First Lord expressed the hope that he would talk about the future rather than the past. The Provost replied, 'Yes, My Lord, mainly about the future. If I may, I will stick to a short memorandum which I have here, which will serve more clearly to put the points before you and avoid any undue repetition. In 1911 Dunfermline Town Council . . .', beginning a long historical account of the yard.

After this unpromising start, Provost Lawson of South Queensferry also got off on the wrong foot. 'So far as I am concerned, Drake can go West and he can stay there. I am more concerned about having a Cunningham up North . . . Give us the opportunity of training our Scottish seamen in a modern Scottish port, in the atmosphere not of Drake and Blake, but of Cunningham and Bruce Fraser . . .' This was too much for Alexander, a west-countryman himself.

> *First Lord:* . . . Nobody appreciates more than I do Scotland's great effort, but I object to Drake going west . . .
> *Provost Lawson:* He can stay there for me.
> *First Lord:* Do not let us get it into our minds that there are no modern admirals coming from other places. Speaking as a humble descendant, born in Somerset where Blake was born who saved the Navy perhaps in its greatest crisis in the old days, James Somerville is a modern admiral who has done us very good service and he was born and brought up in Somerset . . . It is only a matter of pride.

Despite everything, Alexander listened carefully to the delegation's other points, none of which were entirely new. The navy, Provost Lawson said, was still associated with the south of England,

> So much so that many people in Scotland look upon the Royal Navy as being an almost exclusively English institution. Now, I want to see that all altered. I want to see my countrymen getting an opportunity of becoming Navy-conscious. I want to see the youth of Scotland taking a more direct interest in the Navy. I want to see more of our Scottish boys looking to the Navy for a career. There are thousands of potential officers and shipwrights and artificers and seamen to be found in Scotland, but the Navy will never appeal to the youth of my country as it does to those of the South of England until there is established in Scotland a naval port on a scale similar to those on the Channel coast.

The old question of Rosyth as a manning port was revived. It had been suggested by the Commander-in-Chief as early as January 1943. After the war Admiral Cunningham was First Sea Lord and he had already attempted to reform the home port system in a relatively junior rank, but he was exhausted, unwell and far too involved in the problems of demobilisation to carry out a major reform. In 1946 the shop stewards of the dockyard pointed out that

> H. M. Dockyard, Rosyth is the only real link that the Scottish people have with the Royal Navy. It is not in the best interests of the Nation that this tie be severed, rather there is a need for strengthening such a tie.

Attention should be devoted to the utilisation of Rosyth as a
manning port – until Naval Barracks are built Rosyth cannot reach
full stature as a Naval Base. This development is long overdue and
would greatly assist in popularising Naval recruitment in both Scotland
and Northern England . . . The realisation of this project would fashion
a secure and insoluble bond.[6]

Sir Angus Cunningham Graham, superintendent of the yard from
1947 to 1951, privately agreed. Of the home port system he wrote,

The failure of this organisation, which the Navy has never put right to
this day, is that by not having a depot in Scotland or the North of
England the Navy has consistently lost many of the recruits that it most
needs, namely the fishermen from northern waters – superb seamen –
and many fine technicians and craftsmen from Scotland's central belt
and the northern part of England.[7]

In view of its chequered history, it is not surprising that the buildings
of the dockyard were in poor condition at the end of the war, with
many temporary structures. Cunningham Graham comments: 'My
office was erected as a temporary wooden building in the first decade of
the century when Rosyth yard was built. There was a story that a man
applying for a job at the office looked round and left saying, "No good
applying here; the whole place looks as if it is going bust."[8] The Shop
Stewards' pamphlet of 1946 showed a picture of a Nissen hut with the
caption 'Note temporary structures in 1st Class Dockyard'.[9]
The future of the dockyard was under serious consideration in 1947
when the First Lord told the Defence Committee of the Cabinet,

I consider we have now reached the position in which we must either
announce our intention of retaining Rosyth permanently as a main
Royal Dockyard . . . or reduce Rosyth to care and maintenance. I must
emphasise my considered view that the theoretical middle way of
continuing the present state of uncertainty is not an admissible solution.
The present position is politically most embarrassing; in addition to a
long series of Parliamentary questions, my Department is constantly
assailed by local authorities of every degree, who complain that their
planning work is hampered or prevented by our lack of policy . . . It is
unfair to the workpeople, who are denied many of the benefits of the
'good employer' policy which we should wish to adopt as soon as the
future of the Yard were on a firm basis. It is also financially uneco-
nomical, since the drift of men away from the Yard reduces numbers
and consequently productivity, without appreciably affecting continuing overheads.[10]

The yard also had to compete against claims from the other side of Scotland. In January a delegation arrived at Whitehall pointing out the vital role the Clyde had played in the recent war and suggesting a dry-dock at Greenock.[11] But the pressure from the Forth was even stronger. 'Corporations, local authorities, Chambers of Commerce, Trade Unions, and Co-operative Societies are all pressing for a decision. During the last month, at least seventy communications from such bodies have been received at the Admiralty, and further questions in the House may reasonably be anticipated.'[12]

The naval officers at the Admiralty found many good reasons for retaining Rosyth. Experience showed it would take two years to get a yard back into full production after being put into care and maintenance. Strategically, 'the concentration of all our Royal Dockyards so close to a foreign coastline which is vulnerable to occupation in war by a hostile power . . . would be most unsatisfactory and would involve a considerable risk of having practically all of our purely naval ship repair facilities immobilised.' The navy was back in a big-ship phase, with five battleships and fourteen aircraft carriers on the list, though few were in commission. Apart from three docks at Rosyth, there were only three more in the whole navy for the larger ships. 'Most of our aircraft carriers require modernisation, a lengthy process which without the use of Rosyth, would probably buy up two of our three large docks over a space of many years.' The enormous Reserve fleet left over from the war would need constant maintenance. Rosyth was the only yard with a modern layout, as the Director of Dockyards pointed out. It had the most modern machinery and had not been damaged in the war. It was the only Scottish yard, which would not only aid recruitment – there were still twenty smaller bases in the region, and these needed a larger one to maintain them.

For all that, the financial side had its doubts. 'We must be able to say, as we could not last time, that within our present forecast limits in service manpower and money, we shall permanently have enough work to keep Rosyth going and absorbing *productively* its own overheads. Is this so?' In the end caution prevailed and the First Lord decided in October 1947, 'We should not commit ourselves definitely to retaining Rosyth permanently but should say we are retaining it on an active basis.' If it came to closures in the future, it would have to be assessed by the same standards as the other yards.[13]

The manning port question was even more difficult. There was general agreement that it would be useful, but the Head of the Military Branch at the Admiralty summed up official feeling when he wrote:

It is clearly impossible to embark, at any rate for some considerable time to come, upon the major structural work which would be necessary to erect the barracks and other buildings which are associated with a large port. The reduction in numbers has weakened the case for a fourth manning port.[14]

Others pointed out that Rosyth would in fact be the fifth manning port, as Lee-on-Solent, near Portsmouth, had recently taken on that status for the Fleet Air Arm. The proposal was shelved indefinitely.

Rosyth in Operation

Admiral Cunningham Graham, superintendent of Rosyth Dockyard as well as Flag Officer Scotland, disliked the financial part of the work; he found the other aspects quite satisfying. 'The chief interest in the job was having people to look after, lots of them, about ten thousand as far as I can remember. There was further interest in learning about the making and repairing of the armament, machinery and equipment of the warships that came in for a refit.'[15]

As Flag Officer Scotland he co-operated with the army commander, based in Edinburgh, and the RAF commander at Pitreavie.

Scotland has many official lunches, dinners and other public occasions to which the Army Commander, the Air Vice-Marshal and I had to attend either singly or in a bunch. In London these could be shared by many members of the Board of Admiralty and of the Army and Air Councils. In Scotland there were only the three of us to cope with them all. We came to know ourselves as 'The Crazy Gang' – and our wives as 'The Swing Sisters'. Before my time all three of the men and sometimes the women as well would have to attend. I started the plan that, where possible, only one of us would go, in turn, to represent the fighting forces. The telephone would ring and from the Army Commander, Gordon MacMillan, would come, 'I say, Angus, it is your turn to dine with the Royal College of Surgeons next week, isn't it?' I would reply, 'No. It is yours.' Having successfully fixed it on him he would say, 'It is not a Swing Sister affair, is it?' to which I would agree. As for me and the airmen, we had a problem of getting home by the ferry across the Forth. We therefore looked with great disfavour on people who made long speeches, causing us to miss the last ferry and subjecting us to a long drive home via Stirling.[16]

Cunningham Graham did his best to keep up relations between the dockyard and the town.

'Our Chargeman of Blacksmiths, Mr Gellatly, level-headed and an excellent public speaker, was a Town Councillor who was elected Provost of Dunfermline. I told the electrical engineer manager to fit a telephone in the blacksmith's shop for his personal use. The reply I got was 'Who is going to pay for it?' which I ignored! He became an excellent Provost. From then on we and the town got on famously.'[17]

The Reserve Fleet and its Scrapping

Within a year of the end of the Second World War, Faslane saw two reminders of the First. Jellicoe's old flagship, the *Iron Duke*, had lain aground in Scapa Flow since the bombing raid of October 1939. In April 1946 she was refloated and in August she was towed to Faslane where Metal Industries now leased the Emergency Port from the Admiralty. The wharves and cranes proved very useful, though as yet there was no beach where the final stage of demolition could be completed, so the last part of the *Iron Duke* had to be towed across the Clyde to Port Glasgow. Her old rival, the German battlecruiser *Derfflinger*, had also lain at Scapa Flow throughout the war, afloat and upside down after being raised in 1939. With great difficulty she was loaded into a floating dock and towed to Faslane two weeks after the *Iron Duke*. Then it was the turn of the other British survivors of the First World War, then the two interwar battleships, *Rodney* and *Nelson,* which arrived at Inverkeithing for breaking up in 1948–9. By that time the navy had only five battleships, four survivors of the *King George V* class, launched in 1939 and 1940, and the *Vanguard*, completed by John Brown's of Clydebank in 1946. Of these, the *Anson* and *King George V* were laid up in the Gareloch soon after the war and the *Duke of York* arrived in 1950, to join the carriers *Illustrious* and *Indefatigable* and the cruiser *Swiftsure*. The other military port, at Cairnryan, was also used for ship-breaking. Two other veterans of the First World War, *Ramillies* and *Valiant*, were broken up there in 1948.[18]

Hundreds of other ships, mostly the destroyers and convoy escorts of 1939–45, were kept in reserve in preparation for any future war. The ships of the Reserve Fleet were divided into three categories. Some were ready to go to sea at short notice, others were on extended notice and the rest were on the sale list. Vital parts of ships were dehumidified, a process popularly known as 'mothballing' and officially as 'Kooncoting'.

The equipment to be Kooncoted is cleaned, refitted and greased. It is then covered with a fine net, and up to eight layers of plastic are sprayed on like paint to form a water- and air-tight casing. A hole is then cut in the casing, quantities of desiccating material called silica gel inserted, and the hole resealed. A gauge to register the humidity, which can be read through a small perspex window, is fitted inside. Once Kooncoted, a mounting should remain dry and preserved for years, and requires only a periodical inspection of the gauge to ensure that someone has not put his foot through the plastic and let the damp in.[19]

The Reserve Fleet needed 10,000 men to maintain it in peacetime, nearly a tenth of naval strength, but was not a popular posting for sailors. Younger men had joined the navy to go to sea; the older ones disliked the out-of-the way places where the ships were laid up. Both resented the kind of maintenance work which was normally done by the dockyards. As early as 1946 there were problems among the crews of landing craft at Inveraray and the Gareloch, where ships were moored to buoys in the middle of the loch, rather than alongside quays and jetties as in most ports. Flag Officer Scotland was drawn into the controversy and wrote that, though the scenery of the loch was beautiful and Helensburgh was 'a large flourishing residential area with every amenity in the way of Hotels, Picture Houses and Dance Halls', transport was very difficult; when buses were crowded with sailors the locals could not get a place, which caused hostility. At Inveraray the problem was rather different. The ships were moored quite close to the town, but it was small and had few amenities. It was agreed, against precedent, that beer bars could be set up on the depot ships at both ports.[20]

In 1953 the Flag Officer Commanding Reserve Fleet wrote that the ships under his command were 'the Royal Navy's biggest asset'. The fleet 'comprised some 300 ships at the present time and some 300 more craft to come. These ships were irreplaceable in an emergency.'[21] But this was not to last much longer. With the advent of the ballistic missile and the hydrogen bomb, a long maritime war seemed increasingly unlikely. In 1956 the First Lord told Parliament:

> The possibilities of thermo-nuclear warfare demand the maintenance of a Reserve Fleet more highly prepared for mobilisation than before. The maintenance of ships in such a high state of readiness is expensive in both naval manpower and money, and it is not possible to maintain all our ships in this way . . .
>
> It would be too expensive to bring the remaining ships in reserve up to the most modern standards and thereafter keep them up to date. The best of them have been, and will be, made available to friendly navies. The rest will be scrapped when they reach the end of their useful lives and their equipment has been removed.[22]

The first victims of this policy were the *King George V*s. Three were broken up at Faslane and only had to be towed a mile from their buoys in the Gareloch. *Howe* was demolished at Inverkeithing. The older aircraft carriers soon followed, for they could not operate modern aircraft without expensive modernisation. By 1960 there were fewer than a hundred ships in reserve, mostly undergoing refit. On 4 August that year the old navy ended when the last battleship, the *Vanguard*, was towed away from Portsmouth, where she had served as flagship of the Reserve Fleet for four years. There was embarrassment as she ran aground at the harbour mouth watched by thousands of people. Crowds were out too when she finally arrived in the Gareloch five days later and was gently pushed alongside the jetty at Faslane by five local tugs.[23] The new era began eleven weeks later at Barrow-in-Furness when Britain's first nuclear submarine, the *Dreadnought*, took to the water. It took three years to get her into service, but she too would see much of Faslane and end her active life in Scottish waters.

Defence Reviews

The next round of cuts to naval bases came in 1957–8, as part of the *Outline of Future Policy* defence review, though Mountbatten had won a good deal of naval control over the closure programme. Though more than 120 establishments were cut in total, Scotland escaped quite lightly. Recent history was remembered: 'The experience of closing Rosyth in the inter-war years strongly suggests that the unavoidable transfers and discharges of labour would affect the three surviving yards, and the men's fear of working themselves out of a job would probably be exacerbated.' It was reported, 'the closure of Rosyth instead of Chatham would raise similar unemployment and naval problems. It would present a numerically smaller but more intractable unemployment problem than in the case of Chatham, but in addition there would be the political difficulty of closing the only remaining naval dockyard in Scotland.'[24]

The naval air station at Donibristle had always been restricted in scope for development and now served as the maintenance yard for the Fairey Gannet anti-submarine aircraft. Since that type was now to be replaced by helicopters, the yard was closed. At Port Edgar, the minesweeping school at *Lochinvar* was finally shut down and the training scheme for upper yardsmen – young seamen chosen from the lower deck to train as officers – was transferred south to Dartmouth.[25] On the other side of Scotland, the torpedo factory at Greenock had been superseded by the one across the Clyde at Alexandria in 1955, but the Torpedo Experimental Establishment remained at Greenock. That too was now to be shut down and naval research was to be concentrated in southern England – at Portsdown for above-water systems and at Portland for underwater work. The Greenock establishment had long since lost the respect of naval officers and Captain John Coote called it an 'unproductive establishment . . . It had magnificent workshops, all kinds of laboratories staffed by enthusiasts, with superb test-firing facilities of all kinds on its doorstep. I was told that during its lifetime it had never actually produced a new torpedo that functioned as intended, although doubtless it laid the groundwork for several that were later produced by private enterprise.'[26] But there was much national and local protest about the decision. The Minister of Labour wrote, 'Greenock is one of the three areas in the country with the worst employment problem at the present time. The case on employment grounds against taking the Torpedo Establishment away is, therefore, extremely strong.' Greenock Town Council was 'extremely perturbed' by the closure. The Shop Stewards' Committee at the works professed to be mystified. There was no problem with housing the workers, the efficiency and craftsmanship of the workforce had been highly praised, and 'the adjacent waters here are unsurpassed for trial-running purposes'. The Official Secrets Act prevented a full inquiry from outside, but the shop stewards demanded an independent arbiter, to no avail.[27] The First Lord, the Earl of Selkirk, himself a Scot, was far more concerned to defend the extensive cuts in the Medway area, in which Sheerness Dockyard was closed and Chatham ceased to be a manning port.

The airfield at Hatston near Kirkwall had been transferred to the Ministry of Civil Aviation soon after the war but civil flying ceased there in 1952. Part of it was leased to an agricultural college in 1951 but the Admiralty retained some rights over it until 1960.[28] Crail in Fife continued to serve various purposes after the war, for St Andrews University Air Squadron and as a training school for coders and linguists. It was put on the market in 1962 and attracted interest from Caledonian Egg Producers Ltd, from a geriatric hospital and a bulk food storage company until it was sold to a local firm for £5,000.[29] Abbotsinch was the main aircraft storage yard for the Home Fleet, but by 1959 it was in competition with nearby Renfrew for airspace. It was in poor condition and would need a million pounds for modernisation, so in 1963 it was transferred to the Ministry of Aviation for development as Glasgow's main airport.[30] *Condor* at Arbroath remained a naval air station until 1971, training technicians in aircraft maintenance. It was then transferred to the Royal Marines as a training base.

NATO and Naval Exercises

The North Atlantic Treaty was signed in April 1949, to bring the NATO Alliance into being. The United States, Britain, France, Canada, Iceland and six other west European countries agreed to combine their military efforts to resist Soviet aggression. Over the next decades, fleets from many countries would exercise in Scottish waters. In April 1951, however, the pre-war pattern was still in evidence, as the ships of the British Home Fleet, including three aircraft carriers and the battleship *Vanguard,* exercised on the way north to Invergordon. In June RNVR units in several east-coast ports, including the Forth, were mobilised to form the 101st Minesweeping Flotilla. A destroyer laid practice mines in Kirkcaldy Bay and the RNVR swept them.[31] The following year saw a change to NATO operations with Exercise Mainbrace. Denmark and Norway were provided with air and sea support by the Blue forces during a mock invasion. A convoy was sent from Methil to Bergen, refuelled on the way, and then returned, under attack from the submarines of Orange forces. An amphibious task-force sailed from the Forth to support Denmark. Naval aircraft from Leuchars attacked an enemy raider in gales and poor visibility. The whole operation was controlled by Admiral Sir Patrick Brind from the air-maritime headquarters at Pitreavie in Fife and covered an area of 900,000 square miles.[32] After that there was a move south as the new naval headquarters opened at Northwood in the suburbs of London.

The 1953 exercises were the largest so far. Exercise Mariner lasted for nineteen days and involved 300 ships, 1,000 aircraft and half a million officers and men from nine different navies. One of the main purposes was to practise the naval control of shipping in war. The British Home Fleet sailed from ports on the east coast of Scotland to cover a convoy from Loch Ewe to Bergen. It was heavily attacked on the way by submarines and aircraft but the aircraft carrier *Victorious* was crucial in getting it through.[33]

Some of the Scottish exercises were secret and potentially more controversial. In September 1952 it was planned to release biological warfare agents from HMS *Ben Lomond* off the coast of Lewis, where they would drift onto a cage of animals 25 yards downwind. Unfortunately the trawler *Carolla* sailed into range at the wrong moment and ignored all signals to stop. The captain of *Ben Lomond* decided to release the chemicals anyway, since the trawler was two miles away. This was condemned by the First Sea Lord as a 'serious error of judgement' but no court of inquiry was held.[34] Less controversially in 1954, groups of Thames lighters were towed across a range between

Oxcars and Inchkeith in the Forth and monitored from Burntisland. The object was to find a system which would neutralise the new 'pressure' mines, activated by the change in pressure as a large ship passed over. Various groupings of barges were tried, but the problem remained intractable.[35]

Plans for the Clyde

In 1954 Flag Officer Scotland, Vice-Admiral Sir W. G. A. Robson, became concerned that the Clyde would be needed again as a base for a war in Europe, this time run by NATO. He set up a Joint Planning Staff to consider the role of the firth:

> The Clyde Area will be required in a future war to fulfil the following functions:
> (a) A Main Base for U.K. Naval Forces.
> (b) A Main Base for N.A.T.O. Naval Forces, including the Striking Fleet.
> (c) A Logistic Support Base for United States Naval Forces.
> (d) A Principal Port for the National Port Emergency Organisation
> (e) A Military Embarkation Port

The plan assumed a phase of conventional warfare, but 'the possibility of any type of nuclear war must be taken into account where feasible.' One member of the Advisory Group later asked whether the port facilities of Glasgow were to be considered and was given the chilling answer, 'If Glasgow was functioning at all the Navy would be making full use of it.'

The Clyde Navigation Trust representative was taken aback at the first meeting on 22 February 1954. 'Mr Wilson said he rather expected to get an alarming list of Naval requirements but it was larger than he had anticipated and he had not foreseen it would be anything like the size given.' The naval plan was indeed very grand and far-reaching. Some of the old wartime policies were revived, such as overside discharge. War transport would be concentrated in the Holy Loch, the northern end of the Gareloch and the Greenock and Gourock areas. The emergency port at Faslane was in considerable demand among the war planners. According to a naval representative, 'the Navy wanted the wharfs [sic] at Faslane, the Ministry of Transport also wanted the wharfs at Faslane but in fact the Army had got the wharf's and as far as Faslane was concerned *that is it*.' There would be moorings for convoy escorts, though 'the number in harbour at any one time will be limited: thus the need for the dispersal of these vessels can be overridden as a calculated risk . . .' More than 200 buoys were allocated to different types of ship, including large American aircraft carriers. The old anchorages at the Tail of the Bank and Loch Long would be available for troopships and merchant ships, besides new ones off Dunoon, Rothesay and Fairlie. Because much more was expected than in the last war, the defended area of the firth was to be extended. Instead of a boom running across the river at Dunoon, the new one would be between Great Cumbrae and Bute, with subsidiary ones between Cumbrae and Fairlie, and across the East Kyle of Bute near Colintraive. The main depot for boom defence would be at Fairlie. Accommodation for troops was to be arranged in many places, including 4,000 at Heads of Ayr, 2,500 in Irvine, Troon and Ardrossan and 3,700 at Greenock. The NATO ammunition store was to be at Glen Douglas, served by a deep water wharf in Loch Long.

The effects of the base extended over the rest of Scotland. At Lyness in Orkney, 126,000 tons of oil would be stored, 117,000 tons at Invergordon, 230,000 tons at Rosyth. Finnart in Loch Long could be used as a deep water tanker berth, though it was currently leased to the Grangemouth Refinery. Oil could be pumped from there to Grangemouth using a 12-inch pipeline following the old 1918 path along the Forth and Clyde Canal, while a newer line took a more northerly route through the Forth Valley. Airfields at Turnberry, Castle Kennedy and West Freugh in south-western Scotland would be used for carrier-based planes and for maritime reconnaissance, and planes shipped across the Atlantic would be unloaded in the Military Port at Cairnryan.

For all its grandiose conception, the Clyde Base Plan was never given enough resources to be workable. Captain Eaglesome, of the Clyde Navigation Trust, stated at the first meeting that it was becoming quite clear to him that the solution of the matter was beyond local thought and that a decision must be given from the top as to what requirements Greenock and the Clyde were to fulfil. Was it to be given top priority for Naval purposes or was it not? There was no clear answer.[36]

Some elements in the British defence establishment were beginning to question any possibility of long wars in the event of thermo-nuclear or even atomic warfare, in which transport and communications would be severely disrupted. In March 1955 it was reported,

> Under such conditions, the concept of the United Kingdom as a major support area appears quite impracticable. Exercise Thunder with a threat from atomic weapons alone virtually pointed to this conclusion.

The increased order of magnitude of the effect of Hydrogen warfare
throws it into even sharper relief.[37]

Some faith was still placed in 'broken-backed war' – the idea that the
navies would continue to fight on if the devastation of the homelands
was not total. In 1957 Flag Officer Scotland tried to get some air cover
for his 'large and vital NATO base' in the event of war. Though the
Soviets had not yet developed the ballistic missile submarine he was
worried about the operations of more conventional submarines to the
westwards, especially those which might launch non-ballistic missiles.
He suggested they would concentrate in the areas between the Outer
Hebrides, Tiree and Northern Ireland and that minelaying or torpedo-
carrying submarines would come up for a last breath of air before
their attack. He proposed a fleet of fast anti-submarine craft to look
for them, along with short-range aircraft and helicopters based at
Machrihanish and Islay. The Admiralty offered him no encouragement. It pointed out that Soviet land-based missiles with a range of
1,000 miles could hit anywhere in Britain, so the submarine-launched
missile was not the greatest threat to the Clyde:

> . . . it would be unrealistic to assume that forces could be made
> available on the scale which your proposals would require. Such
> defence as is possible would have to be provided by the general system
> of anti-submarine defence in the North Atlantic. If the GM [guided
> missile] submarine threat increased to the extent that the A/S [anti-
> submarine] defence of the North Atlantic became 'swamped', the
> possibility of using any part of the British Isles as a NATO base would
> be seriously threatened and re-assessment of NATO policy would be
> required.[38]

The GIUK Gap

Several NATO, American and British naval bases were set up in
Scotland in the late 1950s, besides the best-known one of all on the
Holy Loch. In 1959 the United States Navy asked for permission to
base six Radar Picket Destroyers at Rosyth. These were part of the
American early warning system against nuclear attack and were
equipped with the latest long-range radar systems. No families would
come with the ships, for they would return to the US in rotation. Six
would always be in UK waters, four in harbour and two at sea at any
given moment. By the end of 1960, the number of bases in Scotland
was already causing concern to the Conservative Government, which
was anxious to maintain public support. The Secretary of State for

Scotland listed thirteen NATO bases and eight for US use. The former included airfields at Machrihanish, Stornoway and Lossiemouth, oil storage at Rosneath, Loch Striven, Campbeltown and Loch Ewe, a boom defence depot at Fairlie, rocket facilities at South Uist and St Kilda, a command centre at Pitreavie and ammunition storage at Glen Douglas. The US facilities included a Transport Command station at Prestwick Airport, radio stations at Thurso and Edzell and a Distant Early Warning Station in the north-east. There was a far more controversial base on the way at the Holy Loch and the Secretary of State wrote, 'I do not want to over-emphasise the difficulty of carrying Scottish opinion with us in the provision of facilities for NATO and for US Forces: the Polaris agitation is the work of a minority. However, a considerable number of projects of this kind have come, or are coming, to Scotland.'[39]

During the Cold War, Scotland's northerly position was vital in patrolling and servicing the GIUK (Greenland, Iceland, United Kingdom) Gap. In an attempt to monitor or stop Soviet submarines entering the Atlantic, lines of underwater surveillance buoys and controlled mines were laid in the sea and patrolled by surface ships, submarines and aircraft. It is the third time this idea has occurred. The germ of the idea can be found in a report of 4 September 1958. The ballistic missile of the Polaris type, as adopted by the Soviets,

> ... is intended to be fired from submerged, and the submarine, if nuclear propelled, need never surface, except transiently for position fixing. The problems of defence become much more difficult, and the best solution would probably consist of interception in a Greenland/ Norway A/S barrier.

In such a project, 'the Americans would doubtless take a major lead.'[40]

The details of the defences are still shrouded in secrecy. One thoughtful and well-informed writer of 1983 failed to penetrate the veil:

> If we take, as an example, the defence of the Greenland–Iceland–United Kingdom Gap, we may assume that the naval staff, both in Whitehall and in Norfolk, Virginia, have done the necessary calculations. They will have figures, subject to all the inevitable margins of error, for the numbers of Soviet submarines attempting to penetrate the gap and the numbers of surface ships, submarines, aircraft and helicopters needed to ensure a high rate of detection. They will have estimated how many Soviet submarines, in various scenarios, can nevertheless be expected to

reach the Atlantic and what forces – and methods – will be required to deal with them there. Plans undoubtedly exist to cope with attack, by air or sea or both, on the detection systems, the airfields, the minefields, the harbours, the islands that make the gap a choke-point.[41]

In fact a little more is known from Soviet sources, if they can be assumed to be accurate. In 1976 they suggested three submarine patrol areas in the Denmark Strait between Iceland and Greenland, supported by the Caesar underwater surveillance system and 'captor' mines; three more submarine patrol areas in the much longer distance between Norway and Iceland, with two more behind them, between Shetland and Iceland, all backed up by the same surveillance system. Faslane on the Clyde was one of the main bases for these submarines. Maritime patrol aircraft would operate from St Maughan in Cornwall and Lossiemouth in northern Scotland. It seems that three British frigates patrolled in the gap, supported by two Royal Fleet Auxiliaries (RFAs) which could refuel and replenish them at sea.

The Clyde Submarine Bases

The Clyde bases were still important after the war. *Montclare* and later the *Adamant* were moored in Rothesay Bay, where they were seen from the Clyde steamers by thousands of day-trippers and holidaymakers every year. 'Sandy' Woodward, then captain of the submarine *Tireless*, records:

> The final approach to the depot ship moored in Rothesay Bay for Clyde Week is often littered with yachts nearing their finishing line, no doubt full of important local figures more concerned to chop up their opponents than make way for the working classes. In order to get alongside in good time, I had to barge my way through the infuriated Dragon Class helmsmen and, in the end, I had to 'tack' between the leaders and drive across the finishing line with them. I glanced round nervously to – see my Squadron Commander smiling quietly. A dedicated fisherman, he considered all yachtsmen a bloody nuisance, and coming third, in a submarine, in the Clyde Week Dragons Race had really made his day.[42]

Other captains experimented with the navigational possibilities of the area. One was relieved of his command for returning via the Kyles of Bute, but reinstated when another officer went sick on the eve of exercises.

The Perisher Course continued in Scottish waters. Captain John

Coote passed it in March 1948, 'honing our art in Inchmarnock Water, starting with straight targets at moderate speeds, then graduating to dealing with high-speed Fleet destroyers escorting a zig-zagging convoy, by day and night.'[43]

> No candidate is selected for the course unless his qualities of leadership and mental equilibrium have already been proven. The most common cause for failure was for Teacher to realise early on that a student lacked 3-D vision through a periscope, not being able to size up a given situation in full perspective. Or he may lack the mental agility to cope with a rapidly developing situation. Sadly for some very fine officers, the weakness of their periscope eye is not exposed until they get out there in the Perisher boat, after years of faultless service from Fourth Hand to First Lieutenant. So they are reverted to General Service without a stain on their record, or so they are blandly assured by Flag Officer Submarines. In practice, they might as well start reading the appointments column in the *Daily Telegraph* right away.[44]

Numerous exercises took place with the submarines of the Third Flotilla (renamed Squadron in 1952). One aim was to test the possibilities of using submarines against other submarines, important since the new snorkel, invented by the Germans towards the end of the last war, allowed them to stay under the surface much longer. In July 1950 HMS *Alcide* simulated a 'U-boat' operating from a base in the Sound of Sleat between Skye and the mainland. HMS *Truncheon* patrolled north-west of Canna and attempted to intercept her. The following February *Truncheon* tried to intercept her sister-ship *Tireless* off the north of Arran:

> Tireless was detected as soon as she commenced snorting at a range of 15,000 ft, but owing to the configuration of the land and the proximity of a fishing vessel, it was not until much later that the H.E. [hydrophone effect] was correctly classified. *Truncheon* altered course to put *Tireless* on the beam and shortly afterwards detected the snort. Under the misapprehension that *Tireless* would alter course through Bute Sound, the plot was incorrectly interpreted and *Truncheon* altered course to what was considered to be a parallel course to *Tireless*. The HE faded rapidly but it was not appreciated until too late that *Tireless* had not altered.[45]

As a result, no attack took place. Difficulties between submarines and fishing boats would become far more serious in the future.

In August 1951 *Truncheon*'s gun was removed and parts of her hull were faired to increase speed and reduce underwater noise. A silent

listening position was created for her sonar operators and it was
found, in Exercise Areas Able and Baker between Arran and the
Ayrshire coast, that she could move silently at about 3 knots, instead
of 2.4. Her listening capacity was increased and false contacts les-
sened. It was a step towards the streamlined, gunless submarine that
would become standard in the second half of the decade.

Ashore at Port Bannatyne, the Rothesay Attack Teacher continued
to be used for training:

> Life as Officer Commanding Rothesay Attack Teacher (OCRAT) had
> much to be said for it. One lived ashore, in my case in a squalid little
> terraced house within sight of the Attack Teacher. The depot ship HMS
> *Montclare* was out of sight at anchor off Rothesay Pier, but available
> for Sunday evening movies and other entertainments. Our little girls
> enjoyed Scottish primary education, unequalled anywhere. The locals
> were agreeable and friendly, from the gregarious Lord Bute through all
> the golfers on the precipitous 9–hole golf course, with its stunning
> views of The Cobbler one way and Arran to the South, to the farmer
> from Ettrick Bay.[46]

The Clyde was still seen as the most suitable submarine base in
wartime. Though the headquarters of the peacetime service was at
Fort Blockhouse, opposite Portsmouth, the Third Submarine Squadron was still in Rothesay Bay attached to the old depot ship *Montclare*. The two other squadrons in home waters, the Second at
Portland and the Fifth at Portsmouth, would move to the Clyde on
the outbreak of war, while the First Squadron would continue to
operate from Malta. It was agreed that 'there seem to be two places
where the location of some submarine activity can be classed as "near-
permanent" and at which shore-basing is possible: (a) Rothesay (b)
Malta.'

Naval planning suggested four levels of support for the submarine
service: for NATO operations, for British submarines in a non-NATO
war, for training and for administrative support. With 300 submarines in the Soviet fleet in 1953–4, a third Battle of the Atlantic seemed
quite possible. The anchorages in the Holy Loch and Gareloch were
reserved for convoy operation. The former was ruled out as a submarine base because it would 'already be overcrowded with moorings
laid by Port Emergency Planning staff'. Rosneath had been planned as
a base for both British and American submarines, but by 1953 it was
in poor condition. 'No maintenance had been carried out on the jetty
or the buildings in the base, and its condition is already such that it
cannot be used until it has been virtually rebuilt, which would take

many months. It would therefore be useless on the outbreak of war.' Furthermore it would be too concentrated a target if both American and British submarines were based there, and it was agreed that 'all reference to Rosneath as a base for any part of the British submarine force be deleted from Admiralty plans, and the area be left entirely clear for US use.'

Limited facilities might be built at Rothesay, but there was neither time nor money to construct a new base and Flag Officer Submarines preferred a depot ship in any case.

> Despite the many advantages which the building of a submarine shore base at Rothesay in peace would provide the submarine branch, Flag Officer, Submarines does not consider that such a project should be undertaken at the expense of a new construction submarine depot ship. Experience in the last war proved that if workshop machinery is available a submarine shore base can quickly be improvised in war by the use of temporary or requisitioned buildings and existing harbour facilities, whereas a depot ship takes many years to design and build. The use of depot ships permits an overall flexibility in the conduct of submarine operations which will be an even greater need in a future war than it has been in the past, and the loss of a depot ship while the total number available worldwide is only three might seriously impair our ability to wage a submarine war.

All three squadrons in the area were therefore to be based on depot ships, despite the shortage of such vessels. The old *Montclare* was about to be reduced to a hulk by the removal of her engines, though Flag Officer Submarines urged that she retain some auxiliary power to support her services. Apart from that there was only the *Adamant*, refitting to be ready to replace the *Montclare* at Rothesay, and the *Maidstone* at Portsmouth. To provide a third ship in the Clyde, it was suggested that *King George V*, one of the ageing battleships in the Reserve fleet in the Gareloch, might be converted as a temporary measure.

If Rosneath was not to be used, the question arose of where to base the other two British depot ships. Rothesay Bay was not big enough for three of them, and it would be dangerous to place them all too close together, especially since the recent Exercise Mariner had shown that the bay was not safe against attack in wartime. Two more anchorages were found in the East Kyle of Bute, one just north of Ardmaleish Point at the south end of the Kyle, the other south of Colintraive. The Ardmaleish position was difficult in certain weather conditions, but the depot ships were two miles apart for safety. This was probably not enough to accommodate all the NATO forces which might operate from the Clyde, and further bases in Scottish lochs were to be considered, as well as those in Northern Ireland. The Dundee base might be revived in certain circumstances.

It was agreed that the administrative base could not remain long at Fort Blockhouse in wartime and accommodation was already earmarked in Rothesay to move it within two months of the start of war. The area would eventually become the base for 1,100 officers and ratings who would be recalled from the reserve and allocated to submarines. If there was not enough shore accommodation in Rothesay, some sites in Ayrshire might be used.[47]

The Third Submarine Squadron at Faslane

By the late 1950s, a long war seemed increasingly unlikely. The reserve fleet was being cut and the emergency port at Faslane was less likely to be needed. In September 1957 the submarine depot ship *Adamant* left Rothesay on an exercise and a month later she arrived at Faslane to set up a new base, occupying the southern end of the Military Port wharves, while the other end was still used by Metal Industries for shipbreaking.

The port was not in good condition. The timber wharves, built hurriedly to meet a particular emergency, were nearing the end of their lives. Reconstruction was planned at a cost of £750,000, but to save money the wharf was allowed to taper towards its southern, naval end, where fewer railway tracks were needed. When the frigate *Exmouth* wanted to use the wharf it was found to be unsafe. Agreement was reached with British Petroleum for the use of their fuel depot to the north, but the navy was hardly made welcome. Use was restricted to weekends, and only when commercial traffic was not using the jetty; forty-eight hours' notice were needed, the telephone (Garelochead 46) was only to be used on official business and the ship's company were to leave the area without loitering.[48]

Another kind of fuel facility had been built at Faslane itself; tanks for an experimental submarine propellant called hydrogen peroxide, which offered much greater range and submerged speed. The Germans had begun trials during the war and one of their boats was captured and renamed *Meteorite* for service in the Royal Navy. Two British boats, *Explorer* and *Excalibur*, took years to develop and were not accepted into service until 1955. A shed-like building was erected at Faslane in 1954 to house the fuel and it remained the most imposing one in the complex for some years. But hydrogen peroxide was not a success. Its unpredictability caused the lower deck to name the submarines *Exploder* and *Excruciator*, and in any case the whole concept was already being overtaken by the Americans' development of the nuclear submarine.

Faslane was not the most desirable posting in the Royal Navy around 1960. Life on a depot ship in peacetime could be quite demoralising, especially for the younger unmarried ratings who actually slept on board:

> The Faslane facilities were *Maidstone* on its jetty, a floating dock, a facility for storing the High Test Peroxide for the experimental submarine, HMS *Explorer,* a fenced patch of cinders about a hundred yards square with a guard room, telephone exchange and some old WW2 military caravan bodies and various dumps of stores and empty crates.[49]

The submarines allocated to the squadron were not of the latest type. When one rating at Faslane saw a poster advertising 'Britain's Modern Navy' he asked how he could join it. Crime was high because of poor amenities, which caused boredom among the ship's crew, who, unlike the submarine crews, tended to be underemployed most of the time:

> The lack of recreational facilities didn't matter to those with families in the area. We were pleased we could go home to them most nights. It was a different matter for our testosterone-charged, unmarried young sailors. There was nothing for them nearer than Helensburgh, five miles away. That might seem a trivial distance but sailors rarely had cars, public transport was inadequate, and there was not much to do except drink when they got there.[50]

In an attempt to vary the routine, the *Maidstone* often sailed away on cruises:

> A new pattern of working was adopted. About once a month when the operational submarines departed for the week on Monday morning, *Maidstone* sailed and spent the week away from Faslane, giving the ship's company practice in their job of running a ship at sea, and visiting some other port before returning to Faslane on Friday in time for the return of the boats. The first expedition was to Liverpool, then best known for a club called The Cavern at which the Beatles had made their name. No prizes for guessing how much that raised morale.
>
> When *Maidstone* was away, specialist officers and ratings were left behind to support submarines which were left in harbour for maintenance. The old caravans in the compound were pressed into

service for all sorts of purposes. The arrangements were crude but we made them work and we lived as best we could in the primitive conditions. One caravan, for example, was the cabin for the Officer in Charge while the ship was away. I did my turn and enjoyed the novelty of cooking my own supper on a gas ring. Would it ever happen in the Guards?[51]

The Seaman Afloat and Ashore

Junior ratings were expected to wear uniform ashore until about 1960, so naval towns, a category which now included Helensburgh, had a particular atmosphere. Peter Cobbold, a National Service seaman in the destroyer *Savage* in 1956, was not attracted by the town of Rothesay, consisting of 'rows of grey granite houses and hotels which lined the front. A few of my shipmates had been there before and were discussing the few merits of the town. Apparently it was not exactly a good run ashore; ladies were in short supply and drink could only be had in the hotels, whose atmospheres left a lot to be desired.' He decided to visit his married sister in Glasgow and was the only man to apply for shore leave next morning. Taken to a Govan pub by his brother-in-law, his uniform soon attracted attention. 'Suddenly, the crowd around me claimed nautical antecedents far outstripping my poor experiences and as the night wore on, my ear was full of the exploits of my new acquaintances, most of whom appeared to have served at least a century in the engine room of some tramp steamer or battleship, and had been in service in the most obscure places ever heard of.'[52]

Heavy drinking was still common in the navy. As late as 1969, a crew member of a newly commissioned Polaris submarine could comment, 'I think she will be a happy boat – as long as the beer and cigarette ration doesn't run out!'[53] The following year the minesweeper *Iveston* visited Ullapool. Some of the crew were disgruntled with the captain, Lieutenant Stephen Johnston, complaining that he spent more time entertaining guests, including a 'gentleman of the road' than dealing with their problems. On the night of 5–6 July five men got very drunk indeed. Able Seaman Edward Kirkbride of Washington, County Durham, claimed to have consumed his tot of rum and three cans of beer on board ship, followed by 18 or 19 pints of beer and about 18 whiskies ashore; Able Seaman Joseph Bowers of Kelso was relatively moderate with his rum, two cans of beer and 13 pints on shore. Back on board, the five acted out a pirate scene, sang Irish rebels songs just outside the wardroom and one of them allegedly assaulted a chief petty officer. Four of them were escorted ashore by three members of the local Constabulary. Six weeks later their trial for mutiny opened at HMS *Cochrane*, Rosyth, and for a week the nation was entertained by farcical echoes of Invergordon. This turned sour when the men were sentenced to twelve to twenty-one months' detention, and dismissal with disgrace from the service.[54] This was not a good image for the new technological navy, and abolition of the 'tot', the daily issue of rum, had already been announced and took place the same month as the court martial.

Rosyth and Nuclear Refits

The nuclear-powered submarine was developed in the United States Navy in the mid- 1950s under the leadership of Admiral Hyman Rickover. Earl Mountbatten, First Sea Lord from 1955 to 1959, cultivated a special relationship with him to get access to American technology and persuaded the British government to invest in it. The nuclear submarine had the great advantage that it could stay underwater almost indefinitely, making it far more effective than the diesel electric boats of the past. The first British nuclear submarine, HMS *Dreadnought*, was launched at Barrow-in-Furness on Trafalgar Day 1960. The name and the date echoed the innovative battleship of 1905, but the Americans already had a fleet of seventeen nuclear submarines and plans for seventy-five.[55] Indeed the *Dreadnought* was fitted with an American reactor, as the British one was not ready. She was a 'hunter-killer' or attack submarine which did not carry nuclear missiles but was intended mainly to seek out and destroy enemy submarines. *Dreadnought* was not ready for service until 1963, when she joined the Third Submarine Squadron at Faslane. She was followed three years later by HMS *Valiant*. Eventually Britain would build seventeen nuclear attack submarines and most would be based at Faslane.

Though all the nuclear submarines were built in private shipyards, it was agreed in government circles that 'we cannot rely on these yards for refitting and refuelling, for which we must have dockyard facilities under our own control to ensure operational availability.' Figures showed that Rosyth was the safest place for nuclear refits, because the major population centres were outside the short range of a nuclear accident. For a release of 500 Curies of iodine over 24 hours, Rosyth had a danger factor of one, while Chatham came close at 1.5, though only because the naval population of the barracks did not count for statistical purposes. Everywhere else had much higher risks – 22 at

Portsmouth, 27 at Devonport and 32 in the private shipyards at
Barrow and Birkenhead. But there were possible problems in recruiting and training skilled workers at Rosyth:

> Most of the work in nuclear submarines demands better than average
> reliability and craftsmanship. It is necessary to provide ordinary work
> sufficient to occupy the less-able and less-experienced workmen, i.e.
> We need the cream for nuclear submarines and we need conventional
> work to employ the skimmed milk.

There was a 'need to provide additional non-nuclear work to balance
submarine load, which would mean a major expansion at great
expense and at the cost of creating under-employment and uneconomic working in southern yards.'

Rosyth was assessed against the old rival, Chatham, which until
then had been the lead yard for submarine work. It was agreed that
'Chatham could not be regarded as an alternative because of the
navigational hazards and operational difficulties created by its approaches.' Rosyth on the other hand 'already possesses dry docks with
sufficient depth to accommodate these relatively deep-draught vessels;
it has deep water access and suitable berths which could be used by
nuclear boats at all states of the tide.' In July 1962 the Admiralty
agreed that Rosyth should be the main yard for refitting nuclear
submarines, but for the moment the decision was to be kept quiet.
Some of the work could proceed but no official announcement was to
be made.[56] The board had two contradictory fears. Chatham, a
traditional dockyard town, would react badly to its work going
elsewhere. Fife, with less of a naval background, might resent a
facility which could be perceived as highly dangerous.

By the time the decision was announced in March 1963, there was
another factor. In December the government agreed to buy the
Polaris missile from the United States, so new submarines would
be built, not just with nuclear propulsion but also with missiles
carrying nuclear warheads. This disrupted the building of nuclear
attack submarines, and only two were completed by 1970; but
instead, four of the much longer Polaris boats were to be built.
These too would be refuelled and refitted at Rosyth. There was some
local protest when the decision was announced; the churches were
suspicious and Campaign for Nuclear Disarmament signs began to
appear round the dockyard, 'probably mainly the work of apprentices and youngsters' according to the Admiral Superintendent. The
Daily Express implied that Rosyth was to become a Polaris base but
the navy made it clear that the missiles would already have been

taken out before the submarines were refitted. 'The task of the yard would be little more than refitting Nuclear Propelled Merchantmen to which nobody could object any more than the installation of a Nuclear Power Station of the area.'[57]

There was much confusion about the schedule for the Rosyth nuclear submarine complex in its early stages of development. The 1963 announcement suggested it might be ready for emergency work by 1965, another document implied it would be needed by 1967 when *Dreadnought* would be ready for refit, and others suggested full operation by 1969. In fact *Dreadnought* was taken in hand in 1968 and in 1970 *Resolution* arrived for the first British Polaris refit, to be followed by *Repulse* a year later. In the 1970s, as more nuclear submarines came into service, Chatham became the second refitting yard.

The Naval Reserves

After the experience of the Second World War the navy began to take its reserves seriously, including even the Royal Naval Volunteer Reserve for a time. As in wartime, it was some way from the original idea implied in the third word of the title; it was used for conscripts who had completed their term with the active fleet, as well as more literal volunteers. In 1951 RNVR officers ceased to wear the wavy stripes which had become so common during the war, and now had the straight stripes of the RN with the letter R inside the curl. The reserves were important after the war because the Reserve Fleet would have to be manned in wartime. In 1954, as that organisation began to run down, the RNVR took on the role of minesweeping, for its men had good knowledge of local harbours and could be mobilised quickly in a crisis without moving too far from home. The RNVR would also form the main reserve for the Fleet Air Arm in wartime. The first squadron of the force, W 1830, was formed at Abbotsinch in 1947 and the airfield became the headquarters of the Scottish Air Division. But that role was not to last for long, for the RNVR Air Branch was disbanded ten years later. As partial recompense, the RNVR was to play a leading role in manning the wartime headquarters, such as Pitreavie in Fife and Inverkip on the Clyde. In the following year the amateur seamen of the RNVR were merged with the professional merchant seamen of the RNR to form a new Royal Naval Reserve. There was some new investment and Tay Division moved from HMS *Unicorn* of 1824 to a new shore headquarters, HMS *Camperdown*, in 1970.

At the beginning of the century the Admiralty objected to the use of the name *Claverhouse* on the grounds that he was a 'bloody butcher', but now it commemorated the Marquis of Graham by naming all the ships of the Scottish RNVR after his family. The Glasgow Division remained HMS *Graham*, Leith stayed as HMS *Claverhouse* and Dundee had HMS *Montrose* from 1946. For thirty years after the war each division had a succession of vessels as training ships, all minesweepers and all taking on the name associated with the division. The Dundee Division had a motor minesweeper or 'Mickey Mouse' until 1948, a slightly larger vessel, 'Big Mickey', for the next five years and then a succession of four Ton-class inshore minesweepers until 1975. After that ships were shared between the divisions on the east or west coast until 1982, when a much smaller *Tracker* class patrol craft was allocated. The division received a boost in 1985 with the new River class fleet minesweeper *Helmsdale* of 850 tons, twice the size of a Ton class ship. But the RNR was run down with the end of the Cold War, for mining in British waters no longer seemed likely and *Helmsdale* was withdrawn in 1990.[58] Today the role of the RNR is to provide personnel, mainly specialists, for small limited wars around the world, rather than to take part in local defence. The force was reorganised in 1994, leaving HMS *Dalriada* in Greenock and a satellite base in Glasgow; and HMS *Scotia* at Rosyth, for training the Forth and Tay units.[59] Other reserves, such as the Royal Naval Auxiliary Service for older, locally based men and women, were disbanded. In 1968 the first University Royal Naval Unit or URNU was set up at Aberdeen University, to train undergraduates. More were set up over the years, including one at Glasgow. Each has a small training ship attached. These have proved very useful as the modern officer corps mainly recruits graduates, and they also help to introduce 'society's future leaders and opinion formers' to the role of the navy.[60]

The Cod Wars

In 1958, when Iceland declared a twelve-mile limit to her territorial waters instead of the conventional three miles, it was mainly trawlers from Hull and Grimsby that were affected, though a few boats from Aberdeen and other Scottish ports sailed in the area. The Royal Navy was still keen to enforce its own version of the freedom of the seas and it attempted to protect the trawlers inside the new limit against harassment by Icelandic patrol boats (or 'gunboats' as the British press called them). This operation was based at Port Edgar, already the home of the Fishery Protection Squadron, under a captain who reported to the Flag Officer Scotland. The main force consisted of four second-rate frigates of the Captain Class including HMS *Duncan*, the flotilla leader. Ships from other areas called in at Rosyth for refuelling and a final briefing from the staff of the Fishery Protection Squadron, for example, the Fourth Destroyer Squadron in February 1959. They also took on an experienced trawler skipper as an adviser in the ways of fishermen. One such was Skipper C. Whiting of Hull. 'He is one of the most experienced men of his calling (forty-two years at sea) and one of Hull's most senior skippers. It was perfectly clear to me from the tone of respect and friendliness which was employed towards him by the skippers of all the trawlers off Iceland that he is a man of the highest standing in his profession.'[61]

The main enemy of the British ships in Icelandic waters in the early stages was the patrol boat *Thor*. Captain Sinclair of the Fourth Destroyer Squadron reported in 1959,

> I was impressed with the cleanliness and shipshape appearance of *Thor*, and by the alertness of her officers, all of whom speak English to a greater or lesser degree, except for the engineer officer. The ship is fitted out most comfortably and so arranged that she can carry Icelandic ministers on short journeys . . . Captain Kristofersson fitted well the description given of him by the commodore, Fishery Protection Squadron. He is 68 years old with 53 years' sea service . . . Although of course he supports the Icelandic case in the fishing dispute I am sure he dislikes his present task every bit as much as the Royal Navy dislike theirs.

By 1960 the Icelanders had three patrol boats and five converted trawlers in operation. Kristofersson had transferred to the new *Odinn* and his successor in the *Thor* was 'Co-operative but can be difficult'. Captains of the other boats were assessed as 'aggressive', 'reasonable' or 'nice friendly type'.[62] They attempted to board British boats and arrest their skippers, to ram them, to cut their nets and occasionally to stop them by firing blanks. The Royal Navy countered by guarding the trawlers within specified boxes and heading off the Icelanders as they approached. But the war began to wind down early in 1960 when the trawler owners began to withdraw their vessels pending negotiation, and a compromise was reached.

The Second Cod War began in September 1972 when the Icelanders extended the fishing limit to fifty miles. Seven British frigates took part in it over the next year, supported by three auxiliaries and four tugs, much more strongly constructed than modern frigates and able to cope with the ramming tactics of the Icelanders. One of the tugs was the *Lloydsman,* commanded by Norman Storey. In June 1973 he arrived at Rosyth:

> A small tug had been sent out to assist me berthing. I thought this amusing but did not use him. There must have been 30 men in the shore mooring party and when I enquired why so many? I was told the big 'L' was Britain's biggest tug and they were not sure what to expect. My chest went out another 6 inches that day. The biggest gangway I had ever seen landed on the forecastle head. I swear we laid over a degree or two towards the quay that night.

Storey had previous experience of the Cod Wars and was ordered to brief Admiral Lucey, the Flag Officer Scotland and Northern Ireland, who came on board with his staff.

> They were very interested in how the ICVs [Icelandic Coastguard Vessels] attacked the warps, what angle they cut on, how they did a loop cut, and how they laid with the cutter on the bottom and let the trawler tow over it. Also, what the trawlers and frigates could do to ward off these attacks, bearing in mind the no-collision rule, what could they do if the no-collision rule was lifted, would water cannon be effective, how best to use it. The discussion lasted about an hour. I noticed the aides taking notes.[63]

The *Lloydsman,* like other tugs, operated on two-month patrols and generally changed crews at Greenock. Again the British were unsuccessful and in October 1973 their ships were withdrawn.

The third and final Cod War began in November 1975 when the Icelandic claims were extended to 200 miles. A large number of British frigates took part in the next seven months, twenty-two according to Icelandic sources, with nine tugs, seven Royal Fleet Auxiliary supply vessels and three other auxiliaries. By June 1976, six frigates were on the station at any given moment, usually on three-week deployments. The frigates came from all the main dockyards and tended to return to them for repair or to pay off, for example the *Leopard* to Chatham in December 1975 and the *Brighton* to Plymouth. Both the main Scottish naval ports were involved. The *Leander* was damaged in a gale 200 miles north-west of Scotland in January 1976 and struggled to Faslane with the help of tugs and another frigate. In March the *Diomede* arrived at Rosyth with a 20 ft gash in her side, cause by a ramming incident with the Icelandic *Baldur,* which had hit her four times.[64]

Captain Storey was employed again with the *Lloydsman,* whose crew were delighted to find that they now had one month on and one off, instead of two months as in the last war. The *Lloydsman* too had her collisions and in December 1975 she arrived back at Greenock with a hole after an incident with the *Thor*. In all, according to Icelandic sources, there were thirty-five ramming incidents in the Third Cod War, compared with fourteen in the second.[65] Nimrod aircraft from RAF Lossiemouth carried out regular patrols over the disputed areas.

The war ended in June 1976, for the British withdrew yet again. With the discovery of oil and gas in the North Sea, it was clearly time to rethink the old attitude to territorial waters. The Royal Navy now had much less interest in keeping the seas open around the world. A new agreement emerged by 1982, with different national rights at different distances from the shore – 12 miles sovereign territory, fishing rights up to 200 miles and mineral rights on the continental shelf up to 200 miles from the shore.

The Offshore Tapestry

Barely noticed by the British public, North Sea oil had a profound effect on the economy, not just of Aberdeen and the north-east, but of the whole of the United Kingdom, allowing the country to survive several waves of recession and decline. It was discovered in 1965 and was first pumped ashore ten years later.

Though it was a British admiral who coined the term 'Offshore Tapestry' to describe the interests in the oilfields and fisheries, the protection of this important resource has tended to be low in the Royal Navy's priorities. Partly this is because of the nature of the problem. Static oil rigs would be much more difficult to defend against torpedoes and missiles in wartime and would probably have to be written off in a general war. But in a limited-war scenario a small power, perhaps under attack as part of a 'police' action, might use submarines or other weapons to do considerable economic damage in the North Sea. Beyond this is the much more prevalent terrorist threat.

The first response to the growth of the oil interest was to convert mine warfare vessels of the Ton class and to build a class of fast patrol boats based on the design of RAF air-sea rescue launches. In the search for a small, long-range vessel which could operate in all weathers in the uncomfortable conditions of the northern end of the North Sea, the navy came across the *Jura* of 778 tons, built by the Scottish Office to police the fisheries. She was taken over by the navy in 1975 and operated from Rosyth with the tug *Reward*. Her design was used as the basis for seven more vessels of the Island class, built by Hall Russell of Aberdeen in 1976–9. At 925 tons, with a crew of five officers and thirty ratings, they have good sea-keeping qualities but are criticised for their lack of helicopter facilities and speed – with only 17 knots maximum, they could not be expected to react quickly to a terrorist incident or a major accident. In answer to the first problem, *Dumbarton Castle* and *Leeds Castle* were built by Hall Russell in 1981–2. They are 31.4 metres longer than the Islands and can operate, but not service, a helicopter. They are a little faster at 20 knots, but an expected class of six never materialised. In an attempt to solve the problem of speed the navy bought an experimental hydrofoil, the *Speedy,* from Boeing, the aircraft manufacturers, in 1980. She could do 43 knots, but development did not continue along these lines, perhaps because helicopters can perform many of the tasks in the relatively narrow waters of the North Sea.

Offshore oilfield protection differs from the fisheries in that constant vigilance is not needed in the same way, for an oil rig could not encroach on territorial waters, for example, without being noticed. But the protection of the oilfields is not clearly separated from fishery protection in the navy's organisation. In 1982 there were five civilian-manned Island class offshore patrol vessels under the Captain, Fisheries Protection at Rosyth, and five more naval-manned ones. There were nine Ton class minesweepers, with ships of the Eighth Frigate Squadron available if needed. Naval and RAF helicopters could also help, but the variety of agencies was part of the problem. 'The Royal Air Force, Royal Navy, Department of Trade, Environment, Energy, Agriculture and Fisheries of Scotland, Customs and Excise, Commissioners of the Northern lights, Coastguard and Port authorities had all got police powers, some of them up to and including authorisation for the use of firearms.'[66] Commachio Company of the Royal Marines, based at HMS *Condor* near Arbroath, was used for the protection of the oil industry against terrorism. This work is now done by the Special Boat Squadron at Poole in Dorset, who keep extensive dossiers on Britain's 'maritime assets'. There has never been a terrorist incident on the North Sea platforms. Perhaps this is because of the lack of publicity, perhaps because terrorists tend to lack the right kind of technological sophistication. They do not move easily across the seas as they do across the land and, lethally, through the air.

Submarines and Fishermen

Relations between submariners and fishermen have often been bad. Until quite recently they were almost the only users of the underwater domain and their interests tended to conflict. The situation became more difficult from the 1960s onwards when the pelagic or mid-water trawl became increasingly common. Unlike earlier trawl nets they do not drag along the bottom making a noise which can be detected by sonar. Their lines have to be much stronger than those of an old drift net. If a submarine at speed fouls one, it not only damages the nets; it is quite likely to cause the fishing boat to founder or capsize. Yet submarine exercises still have to be carried out in inshore waters, including those frequented by fishermen. In 1979 the USS *Alexander Hamilton* fouled the nets of a boat off Jura and reportedly towed her backwards for forty-five minutes before the nets could be cut. In 1984 there was an incident involving the trawler *Huntress* in the Clyde and in 1988 HMS *Conqueror* collided with and sank the yacht *Dalriada* in the North Channel. The crew was rescued by a frigate. In January 1989 the USS *Will Rogers* surfaced under the fishing boat *New Dawn* in the Firth of Clyde, but there were no injuries.[67] There were fifteen reported incidents during the 1980s alone.

On 12 November 1990 the hunter-killer submarine *Trenchant* sailed from Faslane to begin a Perisher course. At Loch Ewe she picked up the commander of the course, the 'Teacher' and six students. After two days of exercises between Scotland and the Faroe Islands the course had been reduced to four students. On 17 November *Trenchant* returned to the Clyde to begin the inshore phase of the exercise. At 6 p.m. on the 21st one of the students took his turn as duty captain and laid a dummy minefield in the Hunterston Channel, opposed by the frigate *Charybdis*. That was completed by one o'clock the next morning. The watches of the submarine changed, but the same student continued as duty captain. He then undertook an hour or so of mock attacks on the *Charybdis*. At 2 a.m. the Teacher went into the wardroom with the captain of the *Trenchant* and ordered the duty captain to hand over to his successor. There was 'a general lowering of awareness among the watchkeepers in the control room with a certain amount of movement for cups of tea etc.' There was some confusion about who was in command of the vessel for the next twenty minutes. The duty captain and his relief were engaged in conversation and the watch officer was not sure of his responsibilities.

Meanwhile two fishing boats were working in Bute Sound, 'the back of Arran' as the fishermen called it. The *Antares* of Campbeltown and the *Heroine* of Troon were towing pelagic trawls, the *Antares* heading south-east and the *Heroine* in a north-westerly direction when they passed at about five past two in the morning. At the same time the Trenchant was turning through 180 degrees to head towards the Cock of Arran for another exercise. The *Antares*

reached the end of her run about 2.16 a.m. and also began to turn
through 180 degrees, to starboard. The *Trenchant* had completed her
turn and the sonar operator picked up a sounding from a bearing of
304 degrees. Since a passive sonar gives an indication of bearing but
not distance, he was not to know that there were two vessels, and the
Antares was much closer than the *Heroine*. *Trenchant* turned to port
to avoid the supposed signal from the *Hercules* but in fact that brought
her closer to the *Antares*. At 2.19 a.m. banging noises were heard
forward outside her pressure hull. She had snagged the trawl of the
Antares, which had her trawl running out abeam; the pull from the
Trenchant caused her to capsize and she sank very quickly with the
loss of her four-man crew.

In the control room of the *Trenchant*, the order was given to stop
engines. Within forty-five seconds the Teacher and the captain of the
Trenchant were in the room and assessing the situation. One of the
sonar operators heard a sound 'like a propeller winding up' which
lasted four or five seconds. The Teacher was unwilling to take the
ship up until he had established the position of other vessels in the
area, but by 2.39 a.m., twenty minutes after the accident, the
Trenchant was at periscope depth. Two fishing boats were sighted,
the same number that had been detected by sonar. Radio contact
was made with *Charybdis*, but nothing unusual had been heard.
Trenchant surfaced at 2.52 a.m. and tried to make radio contact
with the two boats, but there was no reply. The captain contacted
Faslane and advised that the exercise should continue. She submerged again at 5 a.m.

Later in the morning of the 22nd, the Secretary of the Clyde
Fishermen's Association heard of the incident and telephoned local
fish salesmen to try to find what vessel had been involved. Eventually
the *Heroine* was contacted and it was realised that it might have been
the *Antares*. Just before eleven o'clock that morning, a helicopter
found fish boxes and oil on the site and a full search of the area began.
The failure of the navy to make a full report, it was concluded, 'may
have contributed to the loss of life'. To the outside world, it looked like
another example of secrecy carried too far. Since the *Antares* was
'going about her legal business of commercial fishing and had no way
of knowing of the submarine's presence', the sole cause of the
collision, it was concluded, was 'a partial breakdown in the watch-
keeping structure and standards on board *Trenchant*'. Much stricter
controls on submarine movement were recommended by the inquiry,
and many were accepted by the navy.[68]

Though the position was now much better, there were still incidents. In September 1992 USS *Sturgeon* snagged the net of a fishing boats in the North Channel and the captain was disciplined for breaking the Clyde safety rules. In October 1999 a sonar cable towed by an SSN fouled the propeller of the ferry *Sound of Sleat* and did some damage. Submarine commanders were ordered to take more care in communicating with other vessels.[69]

In 1998 the Perisher Course consisted of six weeks of tactical training ashore, followed by a month of practical training in a nuclear submarine. The final phase consisted of four days of attacks on warships in the northern Irish Sea followed by two days in the waters around Arran. European Community regulations now prevent fishing on certain days, so these are used for submarine training.[70]

The Decline of Rosyth

Early in the 1980s Rosyth Dockyard seemed on the way up, with £200 million investment to cope with the Trident submarine programme and a support building for Type 42 destroyers. The old rival Chatham was finally closed in 1984 while Portsmouth was reduced in status to a 'naval base'. Devonport took on some of the nuclear refitting role, with £110 million of investment. A new synchro-lift was built at Rosyth to raise smaller warships, up to 1,646 tons, out of the water, replacing three floating docks and answering the old charge that the yard could not handle smaller vessels economically.

In 1987 the Royal Dockyard at Rosyth was privatised and operated by Babcock Thorne. From 1993 there was strong competition between Devonport and Rosyth for the remaining nuclear refit work in a reduced navy and the decision went in favour of the English yard. This was severely criticised by the Defence Select Committee of the House of Commons, who pointed out that the financial difference between the yards was actually very small, and other factors should have been taken into account. Nevertheless the navy ceased to use Rosyth as an operating base in 1995, transferring nuclear submarine refit work to Devonport. And the facility was sold to Babcock Thorne at a price of £20.5 million in 1996.

The Rosyth shore base HMS *Cochrane* remains in commission as an accommodation centre and a school for fire-fighting training. Rosyth is still used by the navy for decommissioning and storing nuclear submarines, including the *Dreadnought* and all the Polaris boats. Babcock Thorne's work includes refitting of naval vessels and it was guaranteed eighteen refits of major ships and forty-nine smaller ones over a twelve-year period. The Minor Warships Division works on mine warfare and offshore patrol vessels, while the large dry docks are used for fleet auxiliary vessels such as *Sir Bedivere*, of 5,500 tons, and for frigates and destroyers such as *Coventry* and *Newcastle*. The aircraft carrier *Illustrious* completed a £140 million refit at Rosyth in 2003.[71] There are many other jobs which would not have seemed suitable in the old dockyard – making joinery units for Planet Holly-wood in Amsterdam and producing carriages for the refurbishment of the London Underground, for example.[72]

The Navy in Scotland Today

With the closure of Rosyth as a Royal Dockyard, more facilities were shifted to Faslane. It became a naval base, rather than a submarine base, in 1996, making it equal to Portsmouth and Plymouth. The admiral commanding forces in the area, now known as Flag Officer Scotland, Northern England and Northern Ireland (FOSNNI, pronounced Fossninny), moved there in March 1996 when Pitreavie was closed down and is also base commander, so Faslane is now commanded by a rear-admiral, while Portsmouth and Plymouth only have commodores. A new Maritime Operations Centre had been set up and it was used to control its first major exercise, Joint Maritime Course (JMC) 961 that year. Warships of eight nations, including seventeen surface ships, three submarines and fifty-five aircraft, exercised over two weeks in the Clyde, Irish Sea and Hebrides. Similar exercises are held every year. The Third Mine Countermeasures Squadron is based at Faslane and conducts exercises in fields of sand-filled mines in Loch Fyne, Loch Long, the Sound of Jura and the Sound of Skye, while the training field near Campbeltown is regarded as 'the best MCM training area in Europe, if not the world'.[73]

Scottish submarine training has become increasingly important. HMS *Dolphin* at Fort Blockhouse, opposite Portsmouth, was the main home of the submarine service from its beginnings in 1901 until it closed down in 1999. *Navy News* reported, 'non-preference drafts are inevitable, and as the Trident force becomes an increasingly larger proportion of the submarine flotilla there will be an inevitable migration north.'[74] Basic submarine training was transferred to Ply-mouth and about a third of operational training takes place there, with the rest from Faslane. The attack submarines of the Third Flotilla were merged with the ballistic missile boats of the Tenth Squadron to form the First Submarine Squadron, consisting of four boats of the *Vanguard* class and five of the *Swiftsure* class.

Modern naval tasks are described in language which would not have been familiar to an earlier generation.

Embracing ambitious business targets swiftly became a key aim of FOSNNI's newly constituted Management Board. At over £188M, FOSNNI's share is the largest element of the overall Agency budget, and to this must be added a further £20M for the 2SL/CNH [Second Sea Lord, Commander-in-Chief of Naval Forces, Home] mandated tasks. With an area wide commitment to the highest safety standards, Total Quality Management (TQM), International Standards Organisation 9000 (ISO 9000) and Investors in People (IIP) accreditation are being pursued.[75]

Today the only Fleet Air Arm presence in Scotland is HMS *Gannet* at Prestwick, which since 1971 has been the base for a squadron of Sea King helicopters used in exercises in the area and in support of the submarines operating from Faslane. Other bases include the Royal Naval Armament Depots at Beith in Ayrshire and the older one at Crombie near Rosyth. Fairlie is used as a mooring and support depot and there are still refuelling facilities at Loch Striven and Loch Long, and a major NATO Armament depot in Glen Douglas. But the main naval activity in Scotland is support for the seaborne nuclear deterrent.

Chapter 16

The Nuclear Submarine Bases

The British Deterrent

The idea of the British nuclear deterrent was conceived soon after the first atom bombs were dropped in 1945. Its delivery system was to be provided by RAF Bomber Command, with its recent experience in the destruction of enemy cities. The three 'V-bombers' – the Vickers Valiant, Handley-Page Victor and Avro Vulcan – were built to specifications issued in 1946–8. They were originally designed to drop 'Blue Danube' nuclear bombs on a range of targets in the USSR. They were based exclusively in airfields in east-central England, where Bomber Command had operated against Germany. But three developments of the 1950s made the V-force look increasingly less credible, even as it came into service in 1955.

The first British nuclear device was tested in 1952, but the much more powerful hydrogen bomb was already on the way. Secondly, ballistic missiles now had the range to deliver a nuclear warhead from the Soviet Union direct to Britain and were unstoppable. Inertial guidance systems for the missiles proved surprisingly accurate. Britain was much closer to the threat than the United States and the 'four-minute warning' became proverbial, though eight minutes was claimed after the Ballistic Missile Early Warning System was set up at Fylingdales in Yorkshire in 1963. If the RAF deterrent force was to have any credibility, a large part of it would either have to be in the air at any given moment, or at instant readiness for take-off.

Thirdly, the development of the surface-to-air missile made the manned bomber very vulnerable. The Americans already had tens of thousands of Nike Ajax missiles in service by 1957, when the Soviets paraded their own missiles through Red Square on the fortieth anniversary of the October Revolution. Since they had just launched the first Sputnik to begin the Space Race, there were few who doubted that they could create an air defence system which would make life very difficult for the manned bomber.

Britain tried to develop her own ballistic missile, Blue Streak, which was cancelled in 1960. Meanwhile the RAF tried ground-based ballistic missiles. American Thor Intermediate Range Ballistic Missiles were acquired and placed in launchers in east-central England, near the V-bomber bases, but they could not be hidden underground, or put on mobile launchers like later missiles, so they offered a very soft target, and indeed a temptation for an enemy to get the first blow in.

In an attempt to counter this and prolong the life of the V-force, Britain began to develop a 'stand-off bomb' code-named Blue Steel, a missile to be launched from a manned bomber. The first version was intended to have a range of 100 miles, which would make it un-necessary for the bombers to go close to the Soviet cities. The developed version, it was hoped, might have a range of 600 or even 1,000 miles, which would make it unnecessary to penetrate Soviet territory to attack Moscow. But development fell behind schedule; even the first version was not ready by 1961, and costs were spiralling. By the time it entered service in 1963 the long-range version had been abandoned and the whole project had been overtaken by events.

The years from 1958 to 1963 were a time of extraordinary inter-national tension, as the world became aware of the vastly increased threat from the combination of hydrogen bomb and ballistic missile, and tension between East and West seemed to rise and fall with the seasons. Almost every year there was a major international crisis which appeared to bring the world to the brink. In May 1960 the Soviets shot down an American spy plane and stormed out of a summit meeting in Paris; in August 1961 they built the Berlin Wall and in October 1962 the world came closer than ever to nuclear war with the Cuban Missile Crisis.

For a time, Scotland seemed quite remote from this. Dounreay, a little-used wartime naval air station on the cliffs near Thurso, was chosen for Britain's first fast-breeder nuclear reactor in 1954, but at the time almost everyone was in favour of the peaceful uses of nuclear energy. Early in 1958 it had been suggested in the press that some of the American Thor missiles might be based there and protests came from several quarters, but it was announced that they would be sited in East Anglia, Yorkshire and Lincolnshire.[1] In 1960 John D. Drum-mond published his book *A River Runs to War* on the wartime role of the Clyde. He finished with an exchange between two locals:

'. . . Everything has been moved back to England, including our very own torpedo factory.' . . .

'Maybe there will be a call for us again,' they say.

'When some lunatic presses that button.'[2]

Unknown to Drummond, the notorious 'button' itself was about to arrive on the Clyde.

The US Navy in the Holy Loch

The missile-carrying nuclear submarine, known as the SSBN in the jargon of the US and later the Royal Navy, is still perhaps the most devastating weapons system yet devised by man. It can hide underwater for months at time and can launch several missiles (usually sixteen) which are almost unstoppable and each of which contains more destructive power than all the bombs dropped in the Second World War. The Polaris missile made its first flight tests in 1958.

Though the range of the submarines is practically unlimited, crews need to come ashore some time. On completing a sixty-day patrol within range of Soviet territory, the crew of a submarine could be sent home immediately and another crew could take over, getting maximum use from the expensive submarines and at the same time giving the seamen the largest amount of leave and home comforts. Highly skilled missile technicians were offered up to five time as much money in industry and would leave the navy if they could not spend time with their families. The range of the Polaris missile itself was only 1,500 miles in its early version. If the submarines had to return to the United States after each patrol in the operational area, then ten to fourteen days would be lost from each operational cycle, which would be taken out of the men's time at home. To get the best use from missiles targeted on the Soviet Union, the Americans needed a base in European waters.

During talks at Camp David in March 1959, President Eisenhower suggested to the British Prime Minister, Harold Macmillan, that a site in Scottish waters would be needed. Macmillan was cautious and noted in his diary, 'A picture could well be drawn of some frightful accident which might devastate the whole of Scotland.'[3] A site on the Clyde was mentioned casually, and Macmillan did not dissent at the time. In return, the British would be allowed to buy the American Skybolt air-launched missile to extend the life of the V-bomber force.

In November the Chief of Naval Operations of the US Navy, Admiral Arleigh Burke, wrote to the British naval representative in

Washington. 'It looks to us here as if basing a tender in the Gare Loch and the Clyde would be a most satisfactory way to the British and us, since it is a rather remote area and yet still fairly close to Prestwick. The tender would probably arrive about a year from now.' Prestwick Airport was important to the Americans because it was the only transatlantic airport in Scotland. Some of it was leased to the US Air Force as part of the lines of communication with Germany. In the days before automatic landing systems, its reputation for a fog-free environment made it particularly desirable.

The First Sea Lord, Sir Charles Lambe, was anxious to maintain good relations with the Americans and regarded it as 'of prime importance from the point of view of both our political and Service relations with the U.S. that we should not fail to meet their request for a base in U. K. Waters.'[4] Mountbatten (now the Chief of Defence Staff) had a rather complex attitude to nuclear missiles. As early as February 1959, when the first Polaris submarine was four months away from its launch, he was contacted by Arleigh Burke who wrote, 'The US Navy would strongly support the precept that we supply you with Polaris missiles (less warheads) at production cost. I am sure you understand, however, that such a decision can not be made by our Navy alone.'[5] Mountbatten believed that an independent British force was 'neither credible as a deterrent, nor necessary as part of the Western deterrent'. But already he was campaigning behind the scenes for the Royal Navy to acquire Polaris as part of an overall Western defence force.[6]

By March the following year Lambe was also in discussion with Burke about the possibility of getting Polaris around 1970, to replace the V-bombers. Lambe considered starting training Royal Navy personnel in Polaris by the summer of that year, and setting up a special body to develop the project.[7] However in June, the Secretary to the Admiralty, Sir John Lang, was rebuked by Playfair, the Permanent Secretary at the Ministry of Defence, when he took the idea too far. 'It is nonsense to suggest sending crews for training before we have decided whether or not we go in for Polaris.'[8] By this time the Macmillan government had staked a good deal of its political credibility on Skybolt. Polaris had many advantages, but it would involve starting from scratch with new submarines and a new base, whereas Skybolt only involved the purchase of the missiles. In 1960 the British Cabinet was told, 'There is little prospect on financial grounds of our being able to include the purchase of Polaris submarines in the defence budget for a number of years.'[9]

Meanwhile the concept of the Scottish Polaris base was being developed, under the code name of Lamachus. It was a replenishment anchorage, not a full-scale naval base, and shore facilities would be kept to an absolute minimum. Initially it would serve the first two Polaris submarines, the *George Washington* and *Patrick Henry*, but eventually the USN would have a force of forty-one and ten of these would operate from Scotland.

The British began a search for a site which was acceptable to both sides. Though Eisenhower had specified a Scottish base, the Welsh port of Milford Haven and the English one of Falmouth were looked at by the Admiralty, but rejected. Invergordon was also turned down. Loch Ewe was regarded as far too remote from any form of transport, and would involve a 'tortuous and difficult round journey'. If the American sailors were to be taken to the Clyde by sea, that would add two days to the turnaround. Perhaps if the helicopter had been a little more developed than it was in 1960, the option would have seemed more desirable. In any case, Loch Ewe could easily be blockaded by Soviet submarines operating in the international waters of the Minches and it was not secure from surprise submarine attack.[10] Harold Macmillan favoured a base at in Loch Linnhe and tried to persuade Eisenhower. 'From a security point of view, a robust population of three or four thousand Highlanders at Fort William is much more to my taste than the rather mixed population in the cosmopolitan city of Glasgow.' Eisenhower rejected this on the grounds that there was 'need for greater shore facilities for logistical support, more immediate access to open seas and international waters, and the need for comparative ease and safety of navigation.'[11]

Meanwhile a report was commissioned on four sites in the Firth of Clyde, largely from the point of view of nuclear safety. The Clyde in general was difficult.

> Hills rising to some 1,000 ft or more surround the lochs and much of the banks of the Clyde, and population centres are in general located on the coast and are backed by hills. Conditions in these towns cannot therefore generally be considered as favourable for the dispersal of airborne contamination in conditions of relative calm. Similarly, local conditions must at all times have a marked effect on dispersion of activity . . . Communications by road or rail are largely restricted to the river banks and sides of the lochs. The only rapid and practical connection between places on the north and south banks of the Clyde is by ferry steamer, taking 20 minutes or more for the single crossing. Places a few miles apart as the crow flies may be tens of miles apart by road. This situation could give rise to difficulties in the emergency arrangements necessary in the event of an accidental release of activity.

Of the individual sites, the channel between Largs and Cumbrae had 'the advantage of being closest to the open spaces in the lower reaches of the Clyde'. Though the report did not consider this at the time, it had the great advantage, to the Americans, of being only 30 miles by road from Prestwick Airport. But it was within half a mile of a town with a population of 7,800, according to the 1951 census. Another site slightly further away from Largs did offer some advantages, but the whole area had fatal snags which were not considered by the report. As the crow flies it is slightly closer to Glasgow than either Rothesay or the Holy Loch, and this would have been considered important in the event of either an accident or a nuclear attack. Of more immediate relevance, it was the only site on the east bank of the firth, and therefore easily accessible by road and rail. In view of the threat of mass civil disobedience, it was not considered any further.

Rothesay, recently vacated by the British Third Submarine Flotilla, was even worse from the safety point of view. The mooring buoys still existed, only 600 yards from the shore where 7,200 people lived. It might be possible to move the buoys further out, but only at the risk of losing the shelter offered by Rothesay Bay.

The Holy Loch was

> sheltered except from occasional north-west gales once or twice per year, and offers no navigational difficulties. The loch is fairly open to the south but the steep hills rise up directly from the north shore. The topography does not appear to favour undue concentrations at Dunoon of activities released to air in the loch, although in periods of calm such concentrations may persist immediately around the loch.

Rosneath, in the Gareloch, was already familiar to Eisenhower and Mountbatten, for they had disputed its possession in 1942. It was reported:

> The site is well sheltered and there is no navigational difficulty south of Rhu Point. There is no regular traffic into the Gareloch but the narrow entrance to the Gareloch at Rhu Point, requiring large ships to make a sweeping approach, would make it difficult to locate buoys elsewhere in Rosneath Bay to increase margins of safety.

It was concluded that Rothesay was the least suitable site, followed by a site close to the town of Largs. Rosneath was unsuitable, mainly because it was nearest to a major centre of population at Greenock. The Holy Loch had the disadvantage of being close to a thin line of population round the edges of the loch, but if these could be evacuated in the event of an emergency, then the problem would be solved. The report offered qualified support to the Holy Loch as a base.[12]

The other possible site, Faslane, was not specifically mentioned, though the report commented vis-à-vis Rosneath, 'Safety could be increased by moving up Gareloch, but this would lead to an increase in existing domestic problems, and is not considered further here.' Perhaps this was because it was already in use as the main British submarine base on the Clyde, though as yet it had no nuclear capabilities; perhaps, like Largs, it was too easy for demonstrators to get to, without any need for ferries.

There are signs that Harold Macmillan, despite his public reputation for 'unflappability', was becoming increasingly concerned about public opinion in general, and the Clyde base in particular. The Campaign for Nuclear Disarmament (CND) had been founded in 1958 to campaign peacefully against nuclear weapons and had spectacular success in its early stages. In April 1958, 25 per cent of people told opinion pollsters that they would approve 'if Britain gave up her H-bombs even if other countries did not do so'. Two years later, 33 per cent thought Britain should give up nuclear weapons entirely.[13] Meanwhile more militant wings, led by the Direct Action Campaign and the Committee of 100, organised civil disobedience. Mountbatten and Macmillan could see much to fear from this. The former had been Viceroy of India when Mahatma Ghandi's famous campaign led to independence. Macmillan had just completed a tour of Africa which had alerted him to the possibilities of a similar campaign in Britain's remaining colonies there. At this stage there was no real answer, either political or legal, to such campaigns. Too much leniency would allow the country to be disrupted; too much repression would play into the activists' hands.

The first crisis came on 14–15 June, with a flurry of meetings and telephone calls between government departments. In the morning of the 14th Harold Watkinson, Minister of Defence, briefed the First Lord and First Sea Lord on his recent visit to the US. Both he and the Prime Minister, it seemed, had been convinced about the value of Polaris and several options were talked about. But Macmillan, it was reported, was '*Not* happy to sanction Holy Loch as a base'. Lambe did not accept this, and at 9.30 next morning he wrote to Playfair to try to influence Watkinson in favour of the Holy Loch. But at 10.00 the Prime Minister was still adamant. In the afternoon the First Sea Lord was told, 'The Prime Minister and Foreign Secretary will not wear at any cost the proposal of a Polaris base in the Clyde, so close to Glasgow and therefore the Gareloch and Holy Loch are OUT.' The disadvantages of Loch Ewe were considered to be 'very great' but Loch Linnhe was still recommended. At 3.15 in the afternoon Lambe appeared to accept this, and telephoned the US naval attaché, giving him permission to tell Burke in Washington. But later in the afternoon Playfair had a meeting with the Prime Minister, who was apparently getting cold feet about a blank refusal to the Americans. Nothing was to be said until the following week, after alternative bases had been considered. The naval attaché was contacted. He had already spoken to Burke, but the latter was now asked to keep the matter confidential and not tell Eisenhower. The Holy Loch base was already causing confusion at the heart of the British government and the western alliance.[14]

By the 16th, the Minster of Defence was still unclear about what to do:

> We have not yet settled where the base should be. There are several places in Scotland which meet the principal requirements of the Americans (of which the principal one is an inlet with smooth and deep water) but they also want to be within easy reach of an airport, preferably Prestwick. The only places they have considered so far are the Gare Loch and the Holy Loch, which meet these requirements exactly. But they are both in a much visited part of the world, near Glasgow, and the political disadvantages of placing them there are obvious. I do not think that we can agree to them . . .[15]

Admiral Sir Caspar John, First Sea Lord since the early retirement of Charles Lambe in May, told one of his subordinates, 'We are up against a last minute political objection to the Holy Loch site which centres on potential anti H-bomb demonstrations which would be likely to take place from a community such as Glasgow.' He wrote to Playfair,

> My own view is that if we now deny the United States Navy the use of the Holy Loch there will be an almighty row, not only between the two navies but also, I should have thought, between the two governments. Personally I think it most probable that the Americans would decide not to base their submarines in this country at all, since the alternatives to the Holy Loch fall so far short of their requirements. This would wreck any prospect we may have of a joint Polaris venture.[16]

Certainly there were suggestions that the base might go to Bremerhaven instead, because the Americans wanted to show that they would not abandon mainland Europe in the event of a war, and because they found the Germans easier to work with. But civil service opinion in Britain dismissed this as bluff.

In Washington, Arleigh Burke was at a loss. None of the alternatives were suitable, for he needed an area with good family accommodation. Eisenhower attempted to console the British and wrote to Macmillan. 'Please be assured there was no misunderstanding at Camp David on the question of location. I mentioned only Scottish ports; all of our technical problems concerning specific locations have been handled on other intergovernmental levels.' Loch Linnhe, however, would not do and he still wanted the Gareloch. Macmillan wrote back,

> It would surely be a mistake to put down what will become a major nuclear target so near to the third largest and most overcrowded city in this country. As soon as the announcement was made, Malinovsky [the Soviet defence minister] would threaten to aim his rockets at Glasgow and there would not only be the usual agitation of the defeatists and the pacifists but also genuine apprehension among ordinary folk.[17]

But Macmillan was beginning to retreat. He had to admit that he had actually agreed to the Clyde at Camp David, and indeed Eisenhower had suggested the Gareloch, though the written record only mentioned a Scottish Base. At a meeting between the British Minister of Defence and his American counterpart on 6 July it was minuted that the Loch Linnhe proposal 'might have been misconstrued as an attempt to withdraw from the Camp David agreement . . . The PM had now said that he was quite ready to reconsider the Americans' original proposal for a base at Gareloch, if they so wished.' By the 12th, the Holy Loch proposal was being taken seriously by both sides.[18] By the 20th, it was considered acceptable and plans were made to make it 'saleable' to the Americans.[19] From Washington the British mission reported on 27 July:

> Many here think the Holy Loch has great disadvantages in the matter of shore accommodation and transport thereto . . . The US Navy is disturbed at the problem of transporting men from the Holy Loch to the shore for their accommodation and shore leave, particularly in winter, and the effect this may have on efficiency and morale. The Gareloch with its proximity to Helensborough [sic] and railroad and short sea passage ashore seems to them to have great advantages.[20]

An element of British control over the firing of missiles would had made the base more palatable to public opinion but the navy, always jealous of the control of its own weapons, did not back the government in this. When it was suggested to Sir Charles Lambe he wrote 'Monstrous!' in the margin of the report. Macmillan persevered, but the most Eisenhower would concede was that missiles would not be launched from within British territorial waters (i.e. the 3-mile limit) without consent; but that still meant that they could be launched in much of the Firth of Clyde south of the Cumbraes.[21]

By 4 August there were signs of an agreement on the Holy Loch and Eisenhower congratulated Macmillan on his 'helpful message' of 30 July. 'I am delighted that you have been able to reconsider the matter of facilities in Scottish waters and your people feel that they can work out some suitable position in the Clyde area.'[22]

The British Cabinet was informed of the latest situation in time for a meeting on 15 September. The Holy Loch had been accepted by the Americans after a 'discreet reconnaissance by a team of United States naval officers who expressed themselves as well satisfied with the site'. The base would have a full strength of nine submarines, with a maximum of three in port at once. There would be an element of UK control over operations, but not very much; besides the agreement about territorial waters, the US Government would take 'every possible step' to consult the British before firing missiles. The Americans offered little in return for the base. 'The US authorities have not been prepared to offer us a simple option to buy Polaris submarines as a *quid pro quo* for facilities we were providing in the Holy Loch.' This was to be linked to a general NATO agreement about joint deterrent forces, which was unacceptable to the British.[23]

Despite the unsatisfactory terms, the Cabinet agreed. Macmillan announced it formally on 1 November after the reopening of Parliament, amid 'violent objections from certain members of the community.' His memoirs suggest that by now he had regained his composure.

> I, at least, knew enough about these mysteries to realise that an atomic bomb is an uncommonly difficult thing to set off, since it needs a powerful explosion to detonate it. Moreover the safety devices built into the bomb are extremely sophisticated and effective. But many of the inhabitants of Glasgow and the West Coast of Scotland were led to believe that these horrible and destructive engines might explode with the ease of a Mills bomb or a fifth of November firework.[24]

On 8 November Macmillan tried to talk up the agreement with the Americans and told Parliament, 'I am perfectly satisfied that no decision to use these missiles will ever be taken without the fullest possible previous consultation.' Even this vague statement was too much for the Americans, who protested, and Macmillan was humiliated in the press.[25]

Public support for unilateral disarmament was now down to 20 per cent and the CND tide was ebbing. Macmillan's political position was vastly improved in the following month when the Labour opposition put down a motion criticising the government's defence policy and immediately split between disarmers and others. As Macmillan wrote, 'From all this confusion there followed at least one advantage – the decision to allow the American Polaris base in Scotland was now generally accepted' – among the political classes at Westminster, at least.[26]

Desmond Wettern, naval correspondent of the *Daily Telegraph* and an officer of the old school, wrote, 'Why Holy Loch was chosen was not disclosed since it lay miles from the open sea and even further from deep water where missile submarines would operate. In time of tension the Clyde approaches would be particularly vulnerable to enemy minelaying.'[27] But this misses the point about the new type of submarine. Its most important work was deterrence and it would have failed if war began on that scale. Commander N. F. Whitestone, also of the *Daily Telegraph*, saw advantages in the fact that the Clyde was then a busy waterway.

> Some critics have complained that the choice of such a busy focal area for shipping carries grave security risks, in that departures for patrol can be observed and individual submarines tracked. The reverse is true. A submarine can leave undetected at night, while the busy area is a help rather than a hindrance. What little noise the submarine may make in those conditions is soon merged with the incessant underwater pulsation and chatter of coastal shipping. There is no better 'get-away' than to get lost in the crowd.[28]

To be successful, the submarines had to be able to evade Soviet shadows in peacetime, and the topography of the Clyde was helpful here. There were many different exits, along the north or south of Ireland, through the Minches or the Kyles of Lochalsh, for example. Each of these involved passing through territorial waters, from which an unfriendly vessel could be excluded in peacetime.

Detailed safety plans were made for the new nuclear base. Early in 1961 the Clyde Public Safety Scheme was set up. It was confident that the ultimate accident was not going to happen. 'In no circumstances could a nuclear explosion (i.e. with a nuclear yield) occur in the submarine or tender, either from the submarine reactor or weapons.' There were three kinds of accident which needed to be considered. A gamma radiation from the hull of a submarine would only be dangerous within a radius of 35 yards from the reactor compartment;

the release of a cloud of iodine 131 would be dangerous within an angle of 30 degrees downwind of the reactor. Children 600 yards away might be at risk, unsealed food within half a mile would be contaminated and milk within 5.5 miles would be in danger. But

> The only accident which could lead to a radiological hazard to the public would be the ignition or explosion of the H.E. [high explosive] or solid propellant in one or more missile. This might lead to scattering of radio-active material in fragments by the force of the explosion, or the contaminated smoke due to the burning. The resulting alpha contamination would be expected to fall mainly in the sea, but some might reach the shore, particularly down wind.

Such an accident would spread radioactivity over about 500 yards. It would almost certainly sink the submarine or tender, but it was regarded as 'a very remote possibility'.[29]

The Arrival of USS Proteus

The depot ship USS *Proteus* had been built in California in 1941 and saw service in the closing stages of the Pacific War. During 1959–61 she was converted to be the first Polaris submarine tender, by cutting her apart and inserting a 44–ft section amidships, which included the area where the missiles would be serviced. The British Assistant Chief of Naval Staff visited her in October and was not impressed. It was a 'rough and ready' conversion and the accommodation was cramped.[30] The *Proteus* had a crew of 980 officers and men and a maximum of 500 families were expected to come with them. Unlike the crews of the submarines, they would be based permanently in Scotland.

The original plan was for the tender to arrive on 1 December 1960. Harold Macmillan wanted to 'play things reasonably long' and was not at all disappointed when it was delayed by a strike affecting the manufacture of spare missiles. This seemed likely to put it off until mid-December, so the Americans preferred to wait until after Christmas.[31]

At the end of 1960 there was conflict within the British government about how to handle her arrival. The Scottish Office wanted it to be done as quietly as possible; the Admiralty wanted a 'fanfare' to 'scoop the headlines'.[32] The Admiralty view prevailed, perhaps because the government wanted to impress the new President, John F. Kennedy, who was sworn in on 20 January 1961, and the Royal Navy made plans to produce favourable publicity. The Flag Officer at Rosyth wrote, 'Lamachus is a very big issue in Scotland, particularly in the Glasgow area, and we badly need some good counter-blast to the Unilateralists and Anti-Polaris elements, whose publicity at present is virtually unchallenged.' Just as important was the question of how to deal with demonstrations when USS *Proteus* finally arrived. This was a complex issue involving several authorities. The base was, of course, an American project, but the Royal Navy was deeply involved in several ways. Its close relationship with the US Navy caused it to persuade the government to accept the base, and once it had been agreed the Royal Navy was concerned to protect its guests from harassment and embarrassment. The US Navy was responsible for security on board its own ships, while the Admiralty Constabulary would protect the entrances to the piers and bases. The Royal Navy would guarantee the safe passage of the *Proteus* and later the submarines themselves, and for the actual arrival it offered to use naval launches, with two police constables on board each. The civil police, Argyll Constabulary, would be responsible for controlling demonstrations outside the base areas.[33]

Though support for CND was waning, direct action campaigns were more effective than ever. The Royal Navy made very detailed plans for the arrival of the *Proteus*, the press coverage and the control of the demonstrations both by land and sea. At the end of January the Americans proposed it should happen on Saturday 4 March, though the protesters believed it would be 18 February. The British authorities pointed out that a Saturday would allow the maximum numbers of demonstrators to gather, and persuaded the US Navy to advance it to Friday the 3rd.

By the end of January a copy of the demonstrators' plans had been given to the local police, who copied them on to the Admiralty Constabulary. A line of boats was to be ranged across the entrance to the loch if they could find enough, or failing that, between the two navigational buoys marking the entrance. Those in the centre of the line would be manned by 'direct actionists' – 'people who feel so strongly about the evil of atomic armaments they plan to remain in place even if ordered to move and thus risk arrest and imprisonment.' A few canoes had already been promised, but far more were needed.[34]

Tension began to build up in the days before the *Proteus*'s arrival. The London *Evening News* of 2 March featured a local taxi driver looking over the loch and quoted him as saying, 'I don't know whether to get rid of my taxi and buy an American car.' The local girls, it was said, waited in anticipation, the boys with apprehension. A lady who worked on Dunoon Pier spoke for many when she said, 'I shall feel unsafe from the moment that ship comes into the loch.' There were fears that the boat-building industry at Sandbank on the loch would be driven out of business. There was a certain irony in the fact that it had produced the *Sceptre,* the unsuccessful challenger for the Americas Cup in 1958.

The Captain in Charge, Clyde (Capic) made very detailed plans for the arrival on the 3rd. At 7.10 in the morning, two naval motor fishing vessels would leave Largs Pier carrying up to 100 press representatives carrying security passes. The *Proteus* would be off Cumbrae by 8.00 and the MFVs would make passes on her for the benefit of the photographers. At 9.20 the depot ship would be off Hunter's Quay at the entrance to the loch and would pass ropes to naval tugs. At 10.00 she would begin to secure to A1 Buoy off Kilmun. Meanwhile dignitaries would gather, often collected by naval boats from around the Clyde. Naval officers would be in full uniform, with swords and medals. Provosts of many towns would be picked up. The US Consul General and representatives from the Scottish Home Department would board the *Proteus* at 10.40 and a press conference would begin five minutes later, though it would be 11.00 before full telecommunication links were set up with the ship. The press would leave at 11.15 and Customs Officers would come on board at 2.00 in the afternoon. The social programme was to begin in the evening, with a reception in Queen's Hall, Dunoon, for 150 officers and enlisted men of the *Proteus.* The following evening there would be a public dance in Queen's Hall, and 300 enlisted men were invited by the Town Council.[35]

The navy's greatest concern was demonstrations by canoeists, for there were many places round the loch where small boats could be launched. The great leisure explosion was under way, and the development of plywood and fibreglass meant that many people could afford to buy or build canoes and sailing dinghies, but the demonstrators had not nearly enough to form a barrier across the loch as they had planned. Only three canoes and one dinghy appeared. The dinghy capsized and its crew was rescued and arrested. One of the canoes became waterlogged and the occupant was taken ashore. Three people in the two other canoes maintained complete passive resistance and were brought ashore on stretchers. The passage of the ship was not impeded.

Later Protests

Five days later the first Polaris submarine, USS *Patrick Henry*, arrived in the loch. One canoeist attempted to interfere with the berthing and was arrested. Another stayed well clear displaying anti-nuclear slogans, but was not apprehended.[36]

On 16 April, *Proteus* sailed to the North Channel for training. On the way out one canoeist succeeded on hanging on to her bows but had to let go when she reached 4 knots. On her return the following day, two demonstrators climbed up her side and one managed to stay in position for three hours, while a woman sat on her stern buoy but cause no hindrance. On 22 April the supply ship *Betelgeuse* arrived:

> One demonstrating dinghy and one canoe appeared. Two R.N. Launches in attendance, R.N. Officer, two Argyle [*sic*] Constables and one U.S. Navy swimmer embarked in each boat. Canoeist Chandler attempted to place himself in front of civilian tug ahead of BETELGEUSE proceeding at 5 knots down the Loch. On approach of Admiralty boat he took to the water and twice tried to swim into a suicidal position ahead of the ship or her tugs, the second of which was alongside the quarter. The U.S.N. Swimmer twice pulled him clear risking considerable personal danger.[37]

At Whitsun, 21 May 1961, the biggest demonstration of all was expected. The Direct Action Committee planned what it called a 'sea action'. For the navy the term carried overtones of a great battle, and they preferred to call it 'action by sea-borne demonstrators'. According to the campaigners' plans, which were shown to the authorities, 'demonstrators will leave from both sides of the Loch in a flotilla of small boats and attempt to board the Polaris vessels. If they succeed, they will attempt non-violently to obstruct the working of the ships. They will remain in occupation as long as possible.' All volunteers for the sea action had to be able to swim. The organisers would provide life-jackets, but 'would be most grateful if participants could either provide their own or purchase one from us. The cost price of the life-jackets is 39/- [£1.95] with a maximum buoyancy of 12 stone and 41/6 [£2.075p] with a maximum buoyancy of 16 stone.' The action would begin at 3.30 in the afternoon of the 21st, but other attempts would be made throughout the weekend and over a longer period if necessary.

The authorities met on 10 May to discuss their own plans. As well as Capic, the meeting was attended by three US Navy representatives, four British naval officers, the area police officer from Rosyth and the chief constables of Argyll, Renfrewshire and Greenock. The navy would provide four boats to patrol around *Proteus*, with a naval officer in charge and two constables on board as usual. The USN would provide twelve. Several others would be held in reserve and a 75 ft MFV would be available to Argyll Police for transporting arrested demonstrators to Dunoon. The action in the water would be fairly low-key. No steps would be taken to prevent boats approaching the *Proteus*. Any demonstrator who fell into the sea would be rescued; anyone who fell into the water while attempting to board *Proteus* would be rescued and arrested and demonstrators on buoys would be left there unless they attempted to tamper with the buoy or to paint slogans. Capic would be in charge of 'Afloat Operations'. The captain of the *Proteus* claimed that demonstrators would not be able to board his ship. Gangways would be raised, booms stowed and bridles greased. 'The use of fire hoses to prevent demonstrators painting slogans on the ship's side was agreed but fire hoses could not be used to prevent demonstrators approaching *Proteus*.'[38]

In the event, twelve canoes set out for the *Proteus,* while an oddly constructed houseboat was used by the demonstrators as a hospital ship and a 60 ft launch carried the CND flag. Local yachtsmen tried to obstruct the canoes and *The Times*, echoing the language of the protesters, reported, 'Marine skirmishing of this enthusiastic nature probably had not been seen in these parts since the Danes were here.'[39] Fire hoses were used rather more liberally than had been intended, and at one stage a British naval officer had to tell the Americans to stop when one canoe became waterlogged, causing danger to life. But the conservative press was delighted and the *Daily Mail* reported in large headlines, 'Hosepipe Victory – Holy Loch Americans Repel Polaris Boarders'. Macmillan did not share in the triumphalism and was still worried about public reaction. 'There was quite a lot of film shown on television of the Scottish Police handling the demonstrators. The action seemed unnecessarily vigorous.'[40] The American sailors were to be curbed for fear of a serious accident, and at a meeting on the 26th it was agreed that they would not use fire hoses again, but would apprehend demonstrators who boarded.[41]

In September the Committee of 100, which had taken over the leadership of the national campaign of civil disobedience, planned its greatest protest yet, with simultaneous demonstrations in Trafalgar Square and on the Holy Loch. The Minister of Defence was now in favour of a much tougher line:

> Nothing can do more harm to the relationships between the Americans and ourselves, for they just do not understand this sort of action, which no doubt will be widely publicised in the American press . . . The Committee of 100 has, I think, lost a great deal of public sympathy. We could now get away with more restrictive measures, both in Scotland and elsewhere.[42]

The government reacted by arresting more than a third of the committee's members and banning the Trafalgar Square demonstration. The organisers decided to defy the government's authority.

During the Holy Loch demonstrations of the weekend of 16–17 September, both sides were hit by bad weather. A force 8 gale blew up during Saturday and 400 demonstrators were stranded on a ferry which was unable to land at Dunoon; all services were cancelled during Saturday evening. Some of the demonstrators contented themselves by marching to the navy buildings at Greenock, where the US Navy stored some equipment, but the police were ready and headed them off. Meanwhile, a party of policemen was transferring from a tug to a fishing boat in the middle of the loch when they noticed that two of their number were missing. It transpired that they had been violently seasick in the toilets of the tug and had been accidentally locked in. They eventually arrived at the loch 'very much worse the wear than the others [*sic*].'

The first demonstrations took place on Saturday afternoon, when parties attempted to block the entrance to the US Navy's pier at Ardnadam on the south bank of the loch. The superior communication facilities offered by both the US Navy and the Royal Navy were a great help to the police, who were not so familiar with radio as they later became. There was concern about demonstrators trying to reach the ship and at 4.20 a swimmer was taken out of the water. He turned out to be an American sailor who had missed the boat and decided to swim to the ship. When Americans turned up at the gate there were cries of 'Ban the bomb', 'Go home, Yanks', 'Yankee filth' and 'Who dropped the first bomb?' The police cleared all demonstrators by 8.25 in the evening and arrested 289 people, most of whom were fined £10 with the option of sixty days' imprisonment.

The second wave of demonstrations began soon after six o'clock on Sunday morning, when a new group arrived at Ardnadam Pier, apparently much more determined and fanatical than the last, and led by the well-known campaigner Pat Arrowsmith. They divided into two groups, some sitting down in front of the gates and the others standing apart and offering encouragement by singing songs and chanting. A lady 'dressed in a white nightgown flowing in the strong wind' came out of a local hotel and pleaded with the demonstrators to stop chanting and singing their songs 'as she was about demented and could not sleep'. She got short shrift until Pat Arrowsmith ordered silence. When the American sailors began to arrive for duty they were obliged to climb over the heads of the sitters, which they found acutely embarrassing. Some tried to swing over the barbed wire, but cut their hands. A small party of British sailors arrived and they were less considerate. 'Jack effected entry over their heads without loosing [*sic*] any dignity and without care in manner of step.' Eventually the Admiralty Police called in a large contingent of civil police who arrested the sitters and cleared the area by 10.30. Though many of the more passive protesters remained on the roads round the Holy Loch, normal business had resumed by the early afternoon.

The police reports, compiled by Sergeant McColville of the Admiralty Constabulary at Rosyth, show signs of disorientation in the changing social climate of the 1960s. 'Young people and females' tended to be treated more lightly by the courts, but

> there was some difficulty in ascertaining the sex of some of the demonstrators. The female element sported masculine clothes and hair cuts whereas a large number of the apparent male side had coiffures with tight seated trousers. Since all had been shouting their voices had husky tones. No doubt the civil police sexed them by names.

The class system of the age was being challenged, and police were disconcerted to arrest people of 'good' education and accent. Arrested demonstrators were allowed to stay with their friends if they asked. On the other hand a press photographer with a long telephoto lens refused to move, and was 'carried off the road with his equipment, in an undignified manner, that is without the consideration offered to the demonstrators.' When an elderly lady with a black eye was spotted among the demonstrators, McColville commented that it had obviously been sustained some time before. 'She was a very well-spoken lady and it can only be assumed that the shiner was accidentally obtained.' Though most of the leaders of the demonstration seem to have come up from London, it was noted that the most insulting jeering was produced by men with Glasgow accents.[43]

Though the Holy Loch demonstration was a disappointment to its organisers in terms of numbers, 12,000 people attended the illegal demonstration in Trafalgar Square. It was the high-water mark of the anti-nuclear movement in the sixties. Moderates began to take fear about unconstitutional action, and some of the heat was taken out of the issue by the first Test Ban Treaty in 1963. By that time, protesters had found a different and more convenient site to hold their demonstrations, at Faslane.

In January 1963 the *Proteus*, a hasty conversion of an eighteen-year-old ship, was replaced by the new USS *Hunley*, recently launched as the first ship designed from the start as a ballistic missile submarine tender. She was far superior to the *Proteus* and was reported as having the most modern mess facilities afloat. Bagpipes played from one of the American tenders, but apart from that the ship slipped quietly to her mooring. In spring of the same year it was reported that the US Navy planned to moor up to four boats at a time in the loch, which exceeded the agreed number of three. The agreement was extended to allow four, but no more.[44] By December 1965 the *Hunley* had carried out 100 refits of submarines, representing sixteen and a half years of deterrent patrols.[45]

The base had a profound effect on the local economy, making Dunoon the town with the highest proportion of taxi drivers in Europe. It closed in 1992, after the end of the Cold War created a 'peace dividend' which allowed the closure of many military bases throughout the world. Moreover the new Trident missiles had a range of over 4,000 miles, which made an eastern Atlantic base much less necessary.

The British Polaris

By 1962 the RAF's hopes were pinned on the American missile Skybolt, which was still under development. It was an air-launched ballistic missile with a range of 1,000 miles. This too was cancelled in December, placing considerable strain on the Anglo-American 'Special Relationship' which was much valued by the government. Harold Macmillan met President John F. Kennedy at Nassau in the Bahamas and it was agreed that the British would be allowed to buy Polaris missiles, to be operated by the Royal Navy as the main British deterrent force.

In retrospect the decision in favour of Polaris seems almost inevitable. The V-bombers had been conceived when the hydrogen bomb and the ICBM were still dreams. Had the devastating effect of their combination been predicted, it is difficult to believe that Britain would have opted for manned bombers as the main deterrent force. The country has a land area about a fortieth of the United States and less than a hundredth of the USSR. In 1948 it might have been possible to consider basing the bombers somewhere in the British Empire. By 1963 most of the colonies had become independent, with varying amounts of rancour and bloodshed, and that was impossible. On the other hand, Britain had 6,000 miles of coastline, dozens of good harbours and immediate access to deep waters where a submarine could hide. Polaris's range of 2,500 miles (for the new A3 version) meant that it could be launched on Moscow or any of the great Soviet cities from anywhere off the British coast, or even 600 or 700 miles out into the deep waters of the Atlantic. Conversely, in an emergency it could be launched from British waters without any need for the submarines to go far from their bases.

Decisions still had to be made about the number of ships, the number of missiles each would carry and whether to buy from the Americans, to copy them or design a British version. On the question of the numbers of missiles Sir Solly Zuckerman, the government's chief scientific adviser, pointed out,

> The difference in cost of a 16-missile submarine is not very much higher than that of an 8-missile vessel. An analysis of US costs shows that approximately 70% of the total cost of the Polaris submarine goes into the hull, propulsion unit and navigational system; the sonar, launching equipment and fire control, plus torpedoes, take up another 12%.[46]

HMS *Neptune*

The detailed requirements for a new base were drawn up early in 1963. There were to be two main elements. The operational base would service the submarines and provide accommodation, stores and training for their crews. There would be a Royal Naval Armaments Depot nearby. It had to be at least 4,400 ft from the base for safety reasons, but no more than one hour's steaming away and should involve minimum diversion in the submarine's passage from the operating base to the open sea. It would be useful if the base was sited so that in an emergency the submarines could fire their missiles on their targets from within the base. It was suggested that 'there should be a choice of departure routes from the base, preferably with the cover provided by shipping lanes. The frequent presence of other own submarines is most important.' A good harbour was needed, with approaches which could be used by day and night, and water deep enough for the submarines to submerge in harbour.[47] Rosyth and Plymouth were still under consideration, but of the latter it was said 'the use of Devonport as an operating base for nuclear submarines would be tantamount to siting a land-based reactor in a populated area.'

Faslane scored well on all points, though perhaps not on the stipulation that 'Ideally, it is desirable that the operating base should be sufficiently remote from any other Polaris submarine base to provide that one nuclear explosion should not put both bases out of action.' Faslane was close to Coulport on Loch Long, and the Admiralty already owned a good deal of land for the Admiralty Hydro

Ballistic Research Establishment, where tests on underwater weapons were carried out.

The official history of the project states:

> Faslane had a number of desirable characteristics which caused it to be preferred to other possible sites, including the immediate availability of government owned land for the base itself and the armament depot which would need to be located close by. But, architecturally, it was not the easiest of sites to develop; the hills and the hardness of the rock (and, during the building phase, the high rainfall) gave rise to a number of persistent difficulties.[48]

According to a naval recruiting pamphlet,

> Among the factors that had to be considered were: accessibility by sea and by land, not too close to civilisation (we are better off than Dounreay and other nuclear power stations in this respect), but close enough to give reasonable amenities for families, nearness to potential operating areas, nearness to an armament depot and to local deep areas for diving, and on a railhead.[49]

Like the Holy Loch, Faslane was accessible by road and river from Glasgow and other major centres of population, but remote enough to be separate. Like the Holy Loch, it had easy access to deep water through a variety of exit routes. The SSNs of the Third Submarine Squadron could act as decoys and escorts. In any case it was later claimed that no British Polaris submarine was ever detected by the Soviets at sea.

On 24 April 1963 the Civil Lord of the Admiralty told the House of Commons:

> After careful consideration of all possible sites in the United Kingdom it has been decided that development of existing submarine facilities at Faslane in the Gare Loch offers on balance the greatest advantage for a Polaris operating base. A new armament depot will be constructed at Coulport, on the eastern shore of Loch Long, about 8 miles by road and 13 miles by sea from Faslane.

He gave several reasons for the choice:

> The operating base for the Royal Navy's Polaris submarines needs to be near deep water; to offer easy navigational access; and to be a short distance by sea from the associated armament depot.
>
> All the Royal dockyards fail in some degree to meet these basic requirements, but Rosyth will, of course, refit Polaris submarines as well as the nuclear hunter/killer submarines.

Work would start immediately and would be finished by 1968 at a cost of £20–25 million. When finished the base would employ 1,700 officers and men (including 1,200 to provide two crews for each submarine) as well as 400 civilians, half of them recruited locally.

Much had changed since 1960, when Harold Macmillan had been terrified of the political cost of a base so near Glasgow. In the House, protest was muted. The local MP, Thomas Steele, wanted to know if adequate housing and educational provisions had been made in his constituency. The member for Galloway wanted to know if the other old military port, Cairnryan, had been considered. On the whole the government was proud that it was creating work in a high-unemployment area of Scotland. Outside Parliament, the Scottish Trades Union Congress was meeting at Dunoon and it passed a resolution demanding the removal of the base at the Holy Loch and deploring the proposed new base. The growing Scottish Nationalist movement suggested that such a base would not be sited so close to an English city. Metal Industries, which leased part of the site as a shipbreaking yard, was unwilling to give up its tenure and stated, 'The great advantage of Faslane as a shipbreaking yard are the depth of approach, the depth alongside at low water and the length of the quays.'

Unlike traditional British submarine bases, the new one was not to rely on a depot ship. This had clearly been appropriate for the Americans in the Holy Loch, for that was not their main base, and their position there was not completely secure – a future left-wing government might order their removal. For the British, a shore base was needed for the mass of equipment associated with Polaris. Furthermore it offered much more space and comfort for the crews, and the unhappy experience with the *Maidstone* in the Gareloch showed how necessary this was in the modern navy. However the fixed base might have restricted operation had China, for example, emerged as the main nuclear threat rather than the Soviet Union. A new floating dock, AFD 60, was begun at Portsmouth and arrived at Faslane in 1966. The largest ever built in Britain, it was about 450 ft long and 96 ft broad to hold the new submarines. It was moored to a jetty at the southern end of the base.

By March 1964, the sites for all the different buildings had been agreed by all parties. The original programme of construction called for the 'beneficial occupation' of workshops and stores during the autumn and winter of 1966, limited support facilities for the first Polaris submarine by May 1967, the opening of the first of eleven accommodation blocks for ratings in August and the officers' wardroom and ratings' galley in September. All ratings' quarters were to be ready by the end of the year and full support was to be given to both submarine squadrons by March 1968. In addition to the construction work, nearly £5 millions worth of equipment was to be installed, of which three-quarters would come from the United States.[50]

The new base was a massive project, involving 2,000 workmen at its peak. Apart from the Polaris School which was separate in some respects, the base had three main areas. The first, the docks, had accommodation for two Polaris submarines, three conventional submarines and a frigate as well as the floating dock; the old berths of the Military Port were adapted for this. The second area was for accommodation and the third had administration and engineering facilities.

The main road, the A874, ran close to the lochside and through the centre of the site. This was a serious problem as the government had promised security equivalent to an American base. Fortunately Dunbarton County Council already wanted to remove two awkward bends in the road. They proposed a flyover, a fashionable concept at the time, but this would have done nothing for security and it was agreed to build a new road on the hill above the base.[51] Bunkers for warheads were already being built in Glen Douglas as part of a NATO project. The new base, HMS *Neptune,* was commissioned on 10 August 1967 and the first British Polaris submarine, HMS *Resolution,* was commissioned two months later.

The design of the Royal Naval Armament Depot at Coulport was based on the American facility at Bangor, Maine, but adapted for British requirements – particularly the very steep sides of the loch. It was able to fit or remove the warhead of one missile per day. It consisted of four main parts. The Special Security Area contained the actual warheads and their equipment. It was bounded by a double fence and access was controlled by the police through a single point. The explosives area contained conventional explosives such as torpedoes and Polaris detonators. The non-explosive area was used for offices, canteens and workshops, and the pier by the side of the loch for the unloading of supplies sent by coaster, and the arming of the Polaris submarines. The original plan was for it to be 950 ft long, to allow two submarines to berth at the same time as supply ships. This was too expensive and an 800 ft jetty was recommended by a working party.[52]

Two major changes of policy made it easier to set up a new naval base than in the 1900s. In the first place, the home port system had finally been abolished in 1957, when the First Lord of the Admiralty reported to Parliament, 'the drafting of general service ratings is now being centralised under a single authority, instead of being dispersed at the three home ports at Portsmouth, Devonport and Chatham.' A new centralised drafting authority began work in April that year. The navy was reducing in size, from 142,000 men and women in 1950 to 120,000 in 1958 and fewer than 100,000 in 1961. It was more reliant on specialised skills and there was no room for parallel training courses in three ports. Furthermore, modern transport meant that it was not so difficult to travel between Chatham and Portsmouth, for example, and the navy was now much more generous with travel expenses.

The other thing which made the new base more palatable to the seamen was the policy on married quarters. These had only been adopted after 1945, when the Labour government attempted to improve the position of the ordinary serviceman, as well as trying to equalise conditions between the army, navy and air force. Budgets of £1.5 or £2 million were provided in the annual Navy Estimates after 1947, initially for 'naval personnel serving abroad and at remote stations at home', but later in the home ports. In Helensburgh 240 married quarters were built after the Third Submarine Squadron moved to Faslane in 1957, but they were not enough. When Lieutenant CommanderGeoff Feasey was posted there in 1962 he found that 'until newcomers came to the top of the roster it was back to the old routine of finding rented accommodation wherever they could. Lise and I were relatively lucky. We rented a cottage converted from outhouses at Shandon, less than a mile from Faslane.' A year or so later, 'Moving to a married quarter was a great relief. We were in a semi-detached house and our neighbours on the detached side, the Commander S/M [Submarine] of the squadron, Peter and his wife Issy and their five sons became close friends.'[53]

Like the United States Navy a few miles away, the Royal Navy now placed great emphasis on family life, in contrast to its attitude earlier in the century. As Rear-Admiral (later Admiral of the Fleet Lord) Lewin commented in 1968, 'the greatest single factor is no longer the man but the man and his family, and the wife has the greatest effect on the re-engagement rate.'[54] Certainly the naval authorities were keen to boost Helensburgh as a desirable place to live:

> For a town of its size Helensburgh now offers an astonishing variety of entertainments.
>
> In addition to the usual Scottish hostelries there are:
>
> An Art Club, Wine Club (not for topers) Toastmasters Club, Horticultural Society, Flower Club, WVS, Library, Saltire Society (Scottish way of life), 35 mm Camera Club . . .

This contrasted with Barrow-in-Furness and Birkenhead where sailors might be posted while their ships were under construction. Barrow had 'very little surplus accommodation for single people' and sailors often had to live in a hutted camp. At Birkenhead 'the accommodation situation in this area is difficult.' The only advantage was the chance of a visit to Liverpool, still 'a thriving, rich seaport' and 'the home of certain well known musicians'.[55]

Right from the start the Polaris scheme was intended to have 500 houses for civilians, 270 for naval officers and 730 for ratings, the latter on the Churchill Estate in Helensburgh.[56] But again it was not enough; it was based on the standard expected from other naval establishments, but a higher proportion of the Faslane men were married.[57]

The last part of the original base to be completed was the Attack Teacher for training submarine commanders in torpedo attack. Soon after the base was planned, it was realised that the facilities of the *Maidstone* would eventually be phased out, while the old SAT on Bute was 65 miles away by road and was long out of date. It was planned to build a new one which would incorporate 'a digital computor [*sic*] manufactured by Messrs. Ferranti.'[58] It was finally opened in November 1970 when it was known as Faslane Massed Attack Teacher or FASMAT.[59]

The Clyde Submarine Base continued to grow throughout the sixties and early seventies. In 1967 it employed 1,265 servicemen and 990 civilians. By 1970 this had risen to 2,780 naval personnel and an estimated 2,320 civilians and by 1974 there were 3,100 service men and women and 2,800 civilians, making a total of nearly 6,000. As on board the individual ships, the technical nature of the work meant that there was little of the traditional pyramid structure. There were 144 senior officers in 1970, and 213 lieutenants and sub-lieutenants. There were 1,009 chiefs and petty officers, more than a third of the whole complement, and 1,412 junior rates, including leading seamen. The total of 2,778 included 82 women of the WRNS, of whom 1 was a senior officer, 6 were junior officers and 15 were chiefs and petty officers.[60]

The statistics of the project are impressive. The Polaris Project was estimated to cost £370 million and was described by the Ministry of Defence as 'the largest single industrial undertaking that this country has ever attempted within a given timescale'.[61]

As originally set up, the structure of the Clyde Submarine Base was complex. Commodore La Niece describes his responsibilities:

First there was overall charge of the base, which comprised all the facilities on the Gareloch at Faslane for supporting submarines and also

the Armament Depot at Coulport situated on the shore of the neighbouring stretch of water, Loch Long. The Naval Establishment which
was an integral part of the base had the ship name of HMS *Neptune*; I
was its Commanding Officer. Secondly all ships and submarines
operating within the Clyde Sub Area, which extended across the whole
of the West coast of Scotland, came under my operational command.
Thirdly across the Clyde at Greenock was a subsidiary Naval Base at
which was based the civilian manned Port Auxiliary Service comprising
a small armada of tugs, water boats, naval ferries and miscellaneous
other craft. Finally all other naval shore facilities in the Clyde Sub Area
came under Commodore Clyde's administration in varying degrees.
These included a NATO Armament Depot, a Boom Depot, a Torpedo
Range and various embryo War Headquarters such as at Inverkip on
the south side of the Clyde and at Aultbea on Loch Ewe.[62]

No fewer than twenty officers and civil servants reported directly to
the commodore. This was soon reduced so that he delegated most of
his responsibilities to the engineer captain, taking direct responsibility
for the captains of the two submarine flotillas.

Operating Polaris

Training of nuclear engineers started with a mock submarine nuclear
reactor in the experimental atomic power station at Dounreay in
Caithness. The crews of the first two submarines, *Resolution* and
Repulse, trained in the United States as the British facilities were not
ready. High standards were necessary because the submarine had to
be self-sufficient in all respects during a sixty-day patrol. Submarine
captains had nine weeks of training, including two on the navigational
system and five on the missiles. The Polaris systems officer, in charge
of the missiles, had a much longer course, thirty-seven weeks. The
highest trained of all was the senior rating of the Navigation Systems
Department, the chief radio electrical artificer, who would maintain
the Ship's Inertial Navigation System, a vital part of the operation. He
would train for forty-five weeks, while other artificers associated with
missiles and navigation would have courses of thirty-one weeks. Some
of the graduates of the American courses were chosen to become
instructors at Faslane.

The Polaris School was the first part of the Faslane base to open on
30 June 1966. It was 'A striking looking building, not unlike a
medieval fortress or keep, its construction is a modern architect's
dream, the entire exterior being clad in dark grey, heat-insulating

aluminium.'[63] It was air-conditioned to simulate the interior of a submarine and its 'keep' housed a travelling crane for lowering a demonstration missile into a tube. The school would train the crews for the third and fourth boat and any future boats, instruct replacement members of all crews and offer advanced and refresher courses for crews between patrols. It had eleven teaching rooms. It had rooms to simulate every department and aspect of submarine operation and maintenance, such as the Missile Control Centre, the Missile Compartment, the Guidance Laboratory and the Navaids Laboratory. At the top of the building was a lecture theatre with projection facilities.[64]

The deterrent force was different from other naval activities in many ways. It had nothing to do with the old naval principles of 'command of the sea', 'sea denial' or 'keeping the sea lanes open'. At the highest level, there were doubts about its role. Far from being delighted with the navy's vastly increased destructive power, Admiral of the Fleet Sir Caspar John confided in December 1962, 'A filthy week. This millstone of Polaris hung round our necks. I've been shying off the damned thing for 5½ years. They are potential wreckers of the real Navy and my final months are going to be a battle to preserve some sort of balance in our affairs.' He feared that the new submarines would cream off many of the better officers and technicians, and use up a large proportion of the naval budget.[65] When it was proposed to send out teams to extol the virtues of the new weapon, one staff officer wrote,

> Even in a narrow view of self-interest there could be dangers of talking ourselves into the state of self-hypnosis such as the RAF have had for years about the overriding importance of the V-bombers. They may have had good reason for getting into this frame of mind, since the strategic bombing concept could be regarded as the cornerstone of the case for a separate air force. The relationship of Polaris to the navy is, however, quite different. There is no need to over-emphasise the importance of Polaris in order to bolster the case for the continued existence of the Royal Navy.[66]

Among submarine officers, actual and potential graduates of the Perishers' Course delighted in seeking out and destroying enemy shipping and referred to surface vessels as 'targets'. A Polaris captain was expected to do the opposite, to hide for two months, well away from any shipping routes. For the lower deck, one of the main attractions of naval life was the prospect of visits to foreign ports; these never happened in the Polaris force, except for trips to naval bases in the USA for trials and training.

The navy was well aware of these problems and listed some of the potential doubts:

Why me? – POLARIS? You're joking . . . Three months at sea ˅ h no mail . . . And then to Faslane for life . . . Big ships nothing but flannel . . . Sit at the bottom for months on end . . . No runs ashore . . . won't be enough schools at Faslane . . . Married Quarters situation hopeless . . . Don't make me laugh . . .

It was denied that any of these comments was true, but there were many problems with recruiting which had to be addressed.

The routine is described by a naval pamphlet of 1966, intended to attract sailors to the Polaris fleet:

Each submarine will have two crews of 13 officers and 124 ratings. There will be a spare crew at Faslane as well (i.e. nine crews altogether). Patrols will last eight weeks . . . the submarine then returning to Faslane for a month to change over crews and maintain, after which the opposite crew will go to sea for eight weeks. NO ONE WILL EVER GO TO SEA FOR TWO PATROLS RUNNING. In two years the average person will do four patrols. The 'off patrol' crew will take leave due (standard leave rules apply), take refresher and advancement courses, break in the new boys, and work in the base at Faslane. It should be possible to tell a year in advance the exact dates of leave.[67]

In case anyone was put off by the poor reputation of the old base, the pamphlet claimed, 'the name is about all that is the same as the old Third Submarine Squadron Base. Out of the rubble and mud is rising £47,000,000 worth of new equipment, offices, amenities and houses.'

By the time the *Renown* entered service in 1969, the crew had been slightly increased to 13 officers and 131 men. Up to this time submarine captains had usually been lieutenant-commanders, but in view of the increased responsibility, SSBN captains were full commanders. Each was backed up by an executive officer who took charge of the day-to-day running and organisation of the ship and by a senior technical officer. There was a marine engineering officer, a weapons electrical officer and a Polaris systems officer, each with assistants. There were navigating, sonar, medical, supply and communication officers, all already qualified in submarines. The crew was divided into eight departments. The largest, 'seamen and miscellaneous', included a CPO coxswain who was the senior rating on board. Most of its 23 members were underwater control ratings who operated the sonar, steered the ship and operated its hydroplanes, or underwater weapons men to operate the six torpedoes. The Navigational Department was

452 *Shield of Empire*

surprisingly large, at 11 men, charged with operating and maintaining the Ships Inertial Navigational System which used gyroscopes to give a very precise position without reference to the outside world. The Communications Department had eight radio operators led by a chief radio supervisor. The Supply Department was more mixed and included stores assistants, writers (i.e. clerks), cooks and stewards to a total of 11. The three technical departments – Electrical, Marine Engineering and Polaris – were a long way from the traditional pyramid structure of service organisations, with a high proportion of artificers and mechanicians, rated as petty officers and chiefs. The Polaris Department, perhaps the most skilled of all, had only 2 men below the rank of leading seaman out of 19, and it had 5 chief petty officers. The Medical Department was the smallest, with 2 medical technicians and a leading medical attendant.[68]

During their two months on patrol, the crew members had little contact with home – only a forty-word 'familygram' every week, carefully edited to exclude any disturbing news. The submarine was not expected to break surface after leaving the Clyde, and would probably spend little time even using its periscope, though it had to come close to the surface to receive radio messages, probably daily. The passage of night and day would be marked only by the dimming of lights in operational areas during the hours of darkness above. Each submarine was on a war footing throughout the length of the patrol. Only the captain and navigating officer would ever know where they had been. Officers and men, apart from the captain and heads of department, usually kept watch for eight hours each day, and the navy was keen to encourage men to use their leisure wisely, to discourage boredom and dissension. A substantial library was carried. In the early days each patrol set off with a supply of fifty cinema films, nearly one for each day. In later years video recorders were used, but not all the films from private stocks were as wholesome as the Ministry of Defence would have wished. Until the rum ration was abolished in 1970, men were allowed one tot per day, instead of the more normal two. Air conditioning and the distilling of 10,000 gallons of water per day made the physical conditions more comfortable than on conventional submarines. Overcrowding was greatly reduced, but the boats were still cramped by any other standards. Junior ratings slept in three-tier bunks without enough room to sit up in bed; senior officers had single cabins. According to the recruiting pamphlet:

> Messing will be on a cafeteria system, with several choices of hot and
> cold dishes provided by four chefs. There is also a canteen, a washing

up machine and an ice-cream dispenser. Senior rates have a lounge and coffee bar over twice the size of a *Porpoise* class Petty Officers' mess, also bunk spaces on decks 2 and 3 and a dining hall. Junior rates have a recreation space abaft the fore ends, a dining hall on deck 2 and bunk space on deck 3.

A daily newspaper (with *Daily Mirror* cartoons) will be produced and a special news summary incorporating local news from the Faslane area.[69]

After the boat returned, there was still much work to do:

Very soon *Resolution* returned from patrol and all the departments swung into action. The procedure was generally always the same. The movement of Polaris submarines was highly classified and, with the exception of a limited number of officers, the first intimation of a return from patrol was when the submarine appeared at the entrance to the Clyde estuary. Included in the Port Auxiliary Service was a fast despatch boat which had started life as an RAF Rescue vessel. This despatch boat would take Captain SM 10 out to meet the returning submarine which would proceed direct to the jetty at Coulport to unload one or more missiles for routine inspection. At the Coulport jetty she was met by a contingent of Base Staff and the replacement crew. The families of the incoming crew were also allowed to attend. They had an uncanny knack of always being ready, despite the short notice. The replacement crew immediately took over and the patrol crew proceeded on leave. The work list was rapidly evaluated and the submarine came round to berth at Faslane for her maintenance period.[70]

Faslane and the Community

National Service was not yet ended when the Polaris project began and there were fears that the anti-nuclear movement might spread to the armed forces – there were incidents in the army and air force, but none in the navy, which used a far smaller number of conscripts. But the Admiralty Constabulary paid attention in 1963 when it received a copy of a crudely duplicated leaflet produced by 'Scots Against War' or SAW. Among other things it suggested that supporters 'invite troops to desert or stop serving. Find sympathetic soldiers to start *Anti War* cells in the forces. Send subversive literature to the army camps . . . The work on the Polaris Base at Faslane must be blocked by Trade Unions refusing to work.'[71]

It was normally assumed that a military base would create much work for local civilians, but this was less true of Faslane. Because of

the specialised scientific nature of the work, many of the civilian staff
were brought into the area from outside, including some of the 834
non-industrial civil servants employed in 1970. The base also employed 359 skilled workers in 1969, 60 per cent of them electrical or
mechanical fitters. The unskilled workers were fewer than in many
bases, but they included Danny McAteer the dockyard ratcatcher,
who became Convener of Shop Stewards. According to Commodore
La Niece, 'When he was not being goaded on by his engineering
colleagues, Danny was a likeable fellow, although conversation with
him was not easy since he spoke with an almost unintelligible Glasgow
accent.'[72]

A year or two before the Polaris project began Geoff Feasey had
found that Helensburgh was 'an exception to Scotland's proud
tradition of good schooling'.[73] Thomas Steele, the local MP, asked
if Dunbartonshire County Council would 'press ahead with the new
Hermitage Academy and primary schools on the Gareloch'. Commodore La Niece claimed that the naval personnel had a good effect on
local schooling:

> At the end of the summer my wife and I were invited to the Hermitage
> Academy, the local comprehensive school, she to present the prizes,
> myself to make the customary prize-giving speech. The school had
> 1,100 pupils and so, together with parents and staff, it was quite an
> assembly. Many of the pupils were children of the Clyde Submarine
> Base families. Academic standards had recently risen and this was
> attributed to the higher intellectual abilities of the naval invaders . . .
> Unrelated to education, the other undoubted effect was the increased
> spending power generated by the substantial additional numbers of
> base personnel; the local shops flourished as never before.[74]

The Trident Base

In the late 1970s the British government decided to adopt the Trident
nuclear missile system. This was controversial, not just because of a
revival of support for nuclear disarmament. The Trident missile,
designed for American needs, was much larger than Polaris and the
submarines to carry it had to be larger still. It was also decided that the
cost should be borne from the naval budget rather than the defence
budget as a whole, as had been done with Polaris. Trident became a
'cuckoo in the nest' in the eyes of some influential naval officers.

The adoption of Trident coincided with the new, hawkish policies
of Thatcher and Reagan which revived fears of a nuclear holocaust.

Peace camps were set up round the American cruise missile bases at Greenham Common and Molesworth in England and the idea soon spread to Scotland, where a camp was set up at Faslane. The cruise missiles, paid for by the Americans, were especially hated because they moved around the country and took the threat of nuclear retaliation with them. Trident was less dangerous in that sense, but it was costing the British taxpayer an enormous amount of money at a time of mass unemployment, and when health, education and social services were all being cut. The situation was never close to the terror of the early 1960s. Certainly there was a frisson of fear in some quarters when Reagan took over the American Presidency in 1981, but most people, on Clydeside and elsewhere, had become used to living 'in the shadow of the bomb.' There was a revival of CND and direct action campaigns, and the demonstrations continued into the new millennium, but by that time people were more likely to be concerned about green issues than the threat of world war.

The new Trident facilities at Faslane mainly involved the area north of the base, once occupied by Metal Industries. They had vacated the site in 1981, for shipbreaking in Europe had declined due to the falling price of scrap and increased health and safety regulations. The former occupation still caused a major problem, for tons of asbestos had been taken out of ships and dumped there. This had to be dealt with at considerable expense, and delayed the project for six months.

The most impressive part of the new construction was the shiplift, which would replace the floating dock. Housed in an 185 m long building, it used 92 hydraulic hoists to lift a 16,000-tonne submarine out of the water. Once inside it rested on 77 cradles and two 55-tonne cranes were available to lift assemblies in and out of it. The shiplift was first tested in June 1993, when a barge was filled with water to make up a weight of 12,500 tonnes and lifted out of the water. The old AFD60 of 1966, the last of 72 floating docks built for the Royal Navy and the last in service, was put up for sale in 1998.[75]

The Finger Jetty was built alongside the Shiplift Building. It provided a double-sided jetty so that two Trident submarines could lie alongside at once. Protection against the waves was provided by a floating breakwater round the jetty and the shiplift. Power for the whole complex was provided by two generators in the Northern Utilities Building, which could produce 6 megawatts of electricity between them, making the base independent of the National Grid if necessary. The Strategic Weapons Support Building housed equipment connected with the missiles, mostly the ballast cans – objects looking like giant Coke-tins would be placed inside the missile compartments when the tube was unarmed. There was also a General Service Building with facilities for the off-duty crews.

The Armament Depot at Coulport was reconfigured, for now it had to deal with the warheads only, not the actual missiles. Technically it was known as a 'green field' site, though that hardly seems appropriate for a steep hillside beside a loch. The main feature is a great floating pontoon of 88,000 tons, more than four times the size of the navy's aircraft carriers. It provides a covered space in which missile warheads can be installed and removed from the submarines away from prying eyes. It was constructed at Hunterston in Ayrshire and towed to Coulport in April 1992.[76] The first Trident submarine, HMS *Vanguard,* arrived there in July 1992 and the last Polaris boat, the *Repulse,* sailed to Rosyth for decommissioning in August 1996.

The statistics of the Trident project are even more impressive than those of Polaris. Each submarine displaces 16,000 tons, only 2,000 less than the current generation of British aircraft carriers, and HMS *Neptune* was expanded at a cost of £1.7 billion. Faslane cost more than £130 million to run in 1997–8 and Coulport cost more than £50 million. Modernisation continues, though the work on the domestic accommodation is given the most publicity. In 2003 a new hotel-style 'super mess' was opened, with *en suite* single rooms for all ratings. Eventually it will have total of 1,754 beds in 'the country's largest single military living accommodation'.[77]

The Trident boats offer slightly more comfort to the crews. Each rating has a bunk, one drawer and a cupboard, while an officer has an additional cupboard. There is piped music to each bunk, at the choice of the occupant. The captain has his own cabin, which is also used as an office and a meeting room when needed. The old three-part division of the Polaris boats, with accommodation forward, missiles amidships and engine aft, is blurred in Trident submarines, and some of the accommodation is amidships alongside the missile tubes. The sports officer of *Victorious* comments, 'Although the submarine design does not incorporate a gym, there is ample space in the missile compartment or "Rocket Shop" to improvise. We now have a range of exercise bikes, rowing machines and weights to suit most needs.'[78] Because submarines can be detected by the noises they make, special efforts were made to preserve silence, with motors being mounted on rubber rafts. This makes the interior very quiet, compared with the continuous hum of earlier submarines.

Ironically, the Cold War was over by the time the Trident submarines entered service, for the Berlin Wall fell in 1989 and the Soviet Union ceased to exist at the end of 1991. Supporters of the project might argue that the very building of the force was part of an arms race which forced the Soviet Union into bankruptcy. The Labour Party fought the elections of 1983, 1987 and 1992 on a programme of cancelling or decommissioning Trident, and lost each of them. New Labour has accepted the need for the missiles and the numerous doubts about its cost and real utility are no longer debated at that level. The new Labour Government made some modifications in its *Strategic Defence Review* of 1998. Only one submarine is now kept on patrol, with its missiles detargeted. It is at several days' notice for action, rather than minutes as in the Cold War. Because of the reduced pressure to maintain deterrent patrols, Trident submarines can occasionally take part in other activities and in November 1998 HMS *Vanguard* visited Gibraltar, giving the crew a 'run ashore' in which they received a tremendous welcome.[79] It is argued in naval circles that it would be dangerous to cut Trident crews any further because of the damage to morale, as there would always be a risk of having to order the remaining crews to do extra patrols in an emergency. For the moment the future of HMS *Neptune* seems secure, though Scottish independence would have an incalculable effect on the base and on the British nuclear deterrent. A future generation of missiles and submarines is already under consideration and is likely to provoke as much controversy as in the past.

The Past and the Future

It is interesting to speculate what the navy of an independent Scotland might look like. The Scottish National Party claims to be left of centre and it is strongly opposed to the Faslane base and to the 'illegal war' in Iraq. On the other hand it is against the merger or disbanding of historic regiments, and reducing the military infrastructure. It makes no specific mention of naval policy in its documents. Would an independent Scotland follow the Irish model of a very small navy? That country became independent in the aftermath of the First World War when anti-militarism was at its strongest, and it was desperately poor at the time. Scandinavian countries have tended to have much larger navies in recent times, especially after Norway was surprised by the Germans in 1940. A 1990s website on the Scottish Navy suggests a large force of fifty-six vessels, including four nuclear-powered submarines and eleven destroyers and frigates.[80] Interestingly, it does not suggest any names from the UK period of Scottish history, such as Duncan and Cochrane. This is rather different from the story of the Scottish regiments of the army, which won almost all their glory while fighting for the United Kingdom. Nor does it explain how such a large force could be justified. Scotland has no specific threat such as that posed by the Soviet Union, but it would have vital oilfields to protect. The division of the British navy would be a very difficult task during any agreement on independence, far harder than the army or air force. Perhaps these questions will never really be answered.

In the meantime, Scottish naval history seems to be going through a quiet phase. It is rather like the nineteenth century when wars were fought far away and there was no specific maritime threat, but offshore assets such as fishing or oil must be protected. It would be rash to predict how long this might continue.

The history of the Royal Navy in Scotland gives many lessons on British and world naval history; on the conflicts which have taken place, both in Scottish waters and much further afield; on the developing relationship between Scotland and the United Kingdom; on the importance of Scotland's geographic position in the world; and on the character and interests of the Scottish people. Scottish naval history is revealing and it is far from over.

Notes

1 Before the Union

1. See W. Stanford Reid, 'Sea-Power in the Anglo-Scottish War, 1296–1328', in *Mariner's Mirror*, vol. xlvi, pp. 7–23.
2. Norman MacDougall, *James IV*, Edinburgh, 1989, pp. 223–43, *passim*.
3. Register of the Privy Council of Scotland, 1604–7, vol. 7, 1885, p. 498.
4. *Ibid.*, 1625–7, Second Series, vol. 7, 1885, pp. 333–6.
5. *Ibid.*, pp. 362–3.
6. *Ibid.*, pp. 386–9.
7. N. A. M. Rodger, *The Safeguard of the Sea*, London, 1997, p. 402.
8. *Register of the Privy Council*, 1625–7, 2nd series, vol. 1, 1899, pp. 225–6, 470, 570, 627.
9. *Ibid.*, pp. 535–6, 571.
10. *Ibid.*, pp. 367–8, 364, 390–1, 489n, 571.
11. *Ibid.*, pp. 283–4, 436–7.
12. *Ibid.*, pp. 473–4, 582, 630.
13. *Ibid.*, pp. 441, 457–8, 459–63, 489–93.
14. M. C. Fissel, *The Bishops' Wars*, Cambridge, 1994, p. 5.
15. Fissel, p. 94n, Gilbert Burnet, *Memoirs of the Lives and Actions of James and William, Dukes of Hamilton*, 1677, p. 155.
16. *Calendar of State Papers, Domestic, Charles I*, vol. 14, 1639, 1873, pp. 163, 190.
17. Burnet, pp. 151, 157, 162, 169, 174, 179.
18. *Calendar of State Papers, Domestic, 1639*, op. cit., pp. 71, 97, 226, 240.
19. *Ibid.*, p. 278.
20. *Calendar of State Papers, Domestic, Charles I*, vol. 16, 1640, p. 112.
21. *Register of the Privy Council*, Second Series, vol. vii, 1638–43, 1906, pp. 171–2, 196, xxvi-xxviii.
22. *Calendar of State Papers, Domestic, Commonwealth*, vol. ii, 1650, 1876, pp. 204, 210, 236, 262.
23. Thomas Carlyle, *Oliver Cromwell's Letters and Speeches*, London, 1849, part v, p. 163.
24. *Calendar of State Papers, Domestic, Commonwealth*, 1650, op. cit., pp. 313, 321.
25. *Register of the Privy Council of Scotland*, Third Series, vol. ii, 1665–8, 1909, p. 141.
26. *Calendar of State Papers, Domestic, Commonwealth*, vol. iii, 1651, 1877, pp. 54, 485.
27. Scottish History Society, vol. 18, 1893–4, *Scotland and the Commonwealth*, ed. C. H. Firth, pp. 2–3.
28. *Ibid.*, pp. 16, 38, 332–4.

29. *Ibid.*, pp. 359, 361.
30. Scottish History Society, vol. 31, 1898–9, *Scotland and the Protectorate*, ed. C. H. Firth, pp. 412–4.
31. *Scotland and the Commonwealth*, pp. 140 and n, 238.
32. Colin Martin, 'The Cromwellian Shipwreck off Duart Point, Mull', *International Journal of Nautical Archaeology*, Vol 24, no 1, p. 17.
33. *Scotland and the Protectorate*, pp. 364, 96.
34. *Ibid.*, pp. 105, 175.
35. *Calendar of State Papers, Domestic, Commonwealth*, vol. v, 1652–3, 1878, p. 373.
36. Navy Records Society, vol. xiii, *The First Dutch War*, ed. S. R. Gardiner, vol. 1, 1898, p. 404.
37. *Register of the Privy Council of Scotland*, Third Series, vol. i, 1661–4, 1908, pp. 600, 606, 642.
38. *Register of the Privy Council*, Third Series, vol. ii, 1665–9, 1909, pp. 2, 15.
39. *Ibid.*, pp. 16–17, 30.
40. *Register of the Privy Council*, Third Series, vol. i, 1661–64, 1908, p. 607.
41. *Register of the Privy Council*, Third Series, vol. ii, 1665–69, p. 18.
42. *Aberdeen Council Letters*, ed. L. B. Taylor, Oxford, 1954–57, vol. iv, pp. 175–7, vol. v, pp. 139–40.
43. *Register of the Privy Council*, Third Series, vol. ii, 1665–69, pp. 90–2, 162, 194, 333.
44. Navy Records Society, vol. lxiv, *Journal of the Earl of Sandwich*, ed. R. C. Anderson, 1928, pp. 260–1.
45. Scottish History Society, vol. 14, *Diary of John Erskine of Garnock, 1683–1687*, ed. John M. Gray, 1891–2, pp. 120–1.
46. *Calendar of State Papers, Domestic, James II*, vol. i, Feb.–Dec. 1685, p. 202.
47. The transcription says 'Point of Cornwall' but this is unlikely. 'Point of Corsewall' is far more probable.
48. Navy Records Society, vol. xliv, *The Old Scots Navy from 1689 to 1710*, ed. James Grant, LLB, 1914, *passim*.
49. *Ibid.*, p. 53.
50. *Ibid.*, pp. 17, 71, *passim*.
51. *Ibid.*, esp. 55–61, 93–99, 106–8.
52. *Ibid.*, pp. 145, 148, 149.
53. *Ibid.*, p. 163.
54. *Ibid.*, p. 178.
55. *Ibid.*, pp. 49, 101, 109–111.
56. *Ibid.*, p. 218.
57. *Ibid.*, p. 333.
58. *Ibid.*, pp. 306–7.
59. *Ibid.*, pp. 257, 316–17.
60. Lord Belhaven's Speech in the Scotch Parliament, 1706, p. 3.
61. Quoted in T. C. Smout, *Scottish Trade on the Eve of Union*, London, 1963, p. 275.

2   Sea Power and the Jacobites

1. PRO SP 54/10, ADM 1/1826.
2. PRO SP 54/10.
3. Rear-Admiral H. W. Richmond, *The Navy in the War of 1739–48*, Cambridge, 1920, vol. 2, p. 16.
4. Bruce Lenman & John S. Gibson, *The Jacobite Threat, England, Scotland, Ireland, France: A source book*, Edinburgh, 1990, pp. 9, 90.

5. HMC, *Manuscripts of the House of Lords*, vol. viii, 1708–10, 1923, p. 6.
6. *Ibid.*, pp. 147–9.
7. HMC, *Calendar of the Stuart Papers at Windsor Castle*, vol. 1, 1902, pp. 218–21.
8. Lenman & Gibson, op. cit., p. 10.
9. HMC, *House of Lords Manuscripts*, vol. viii, op. cit., p. 4.
10. *Ibid.*, p. 41.
11. *Ibid.*, p. 140.
12. Navy Records Society, vol. 99, *The Vernon Papers*, ed. B. McL. Ranft, 1958, p. 45.
13. W. M. James, *The British Navy in Adversity*, London, 1926, pp. 255–6.
14. *Ibid.*, p. 256.
15. NRS, *Vernon Papers*, op. cit., p. 45.
16. Scottish History Society, Second Series Vol. 3, *Seafield Correspondence*, 1912, ed. James Grant, p. 457.
17. HMC, *House of Lords*, vol. viii, op. cit., pp. 156–.
18. Navy Records Society, vol. lxviii, *The Byng Papers*, ed. Brian Tunstall, 1931, vol. ii, p. 9.
19. *Ibid.*, p. 37.
20. HMC *House of Lords*, vol. viii, op. cit., p. 4.
21. *Extracts from the Records of the Burgh of Edinburgh, 1701–1718*, ed. Helen Armet, Edinburgh, 1967, p. 15.
22. NRS, *Vernon Papers*, op. cit., p. 46.
23. Scottish History Society, Second Series Vol. 11, 1913–14, *Letters of the Earl of Seafield*, ed. Hume Brown, p. 46.
24. James, *Adversity*, op. cit., p. 26.
25. John S. Gibson, *Playing the Scottish Card*, Edinburgh, 1988, p. 121.
26. PRO ADM 2/48, Scottish History Society, Third Series, vol. 25, *The Warrender Letters*, ed. Margarite Wood & William K. Dickson, 1935, p. 6.
27. PRO ADM 2/4.
28. NRS, vol. lxx, *Byng Papers*, vol. iii, 1933, pp. 73–7.
29. PRO ADM 8/1.
30. NRS *Byng Papers*, vol. iii, pp. 87–15.
31. PRO Adm 2/4.
32. SHS, *Warrender Letters*, op. cit., pp. 75–7.
33. *Ibid.*, p. lvii.
34. *Ibid.*, p. 101.
35. PRO Adm 1/182.
36. SHS, *Warrender Letters*, pp. 10, 93, 103.
37. C. S. Terry, *The Jacobites and the Union*, Cambridge, 1922, p. 8.
38. *Ibid.*, pp. 85–8.
39. SHS, *Warrender Letters*, op. cit., p. 11.
40. PRO ADM 51/79.
41. C. S. Terry, op. cit., p. 8.
42. HMC, *Stuart Papers*, op. cit., vol. 1, pp. 461–2.
43. *Ibid.*, p. 48.
44. *Ibid.*, p. 508.
45. *Ibid.*, p. 224.
46. *Ibid.*, pp. 488, 490.
47. *Ibid.*, p. 494.
48. *Ibid.*, vol. ii, 1903, p. 3
49. *Ibid.*, pp. 22–3.
50. *Ibid.*, p. 41.
51. NMM LOG/L/19

52. HMC, *Stuart Papers*, vol. ii, op. cit., p. 11.
53. Account of the battle from the log of the *Worcester*, NMM LOG/L/W 17.
54. *Historical Register*, vol. iv, pp. 279–85.
55. The Spalding Club, *Memoirs of George Keith, Earl Marischal*, ed. Thomas Constable, Aberdeen, 1863, p. 52.

3   The Navy and the 'Forty-Five'

1. PRO SP 54/14, f 17.
2. *Ibid.*, f 9.
3. *Ibid.*, f 74.
4. PRO SP 54/17, ff 71, 19, 9.
5. Sir James Fergusson, *Argyll in the Forty-Five*, London, 1951, pp. 11–1.
6. PRO ADM 1/148.
7. Navy Records Society, vol. 99, *The Vernon Papers*, ed. B. McL. Ranft, 1958, pp. 461–2.
8. *Ibid.*
9. Scottish History Society, Second Series, vol. 2, *Origins of the '45 and Other Narratives*, ed. W. B. Blaikie, 1909–10.
10. PRO SP 54/26.
11. *Ibid.*
12. *Ibid.*, f 15.
13. *Origins of the '45*, op. cit., p. 11.
14. *Report of the . . . Board of General Officers on . . . The Conduct, Behaviour and Proceedings of Lieutenant-General Sir John Cope*, Dublin, 1749, p. 4.
15. *Ibid.*, p. 54.
16. PRO ADM 1/51.
17. NRS, *Vernon Papers*, op. cit., p. 48.
18. *Ibid.*, pp. 491–2.
19. PRO ADM 1/51.
20. NMM ADM A/1976, f 5066 f.
21. NMM LOG/G/5.
22. PRO ADM 1/51.
23. NMM LOG/L/M 18.
24. Scottish History Society, vol. viii, 1890, *A List of Persons Concerned in the Rebellion*, ed. the Earl of Rosebery and Rev. Walter Macleod, p. 16.
25. PRO ADM 1/5288, from which most of the details of this account are taken.
26. PRO ADM 51/1042, 51/4214, SP 54/27, 54/29, 54/30, 54/31, 54/3.
27. Lord Elcho, *The Affairs of Scotland*, 1907, reprinted Edinburgh 1973, p. 36.
28. Elcho, *Affairs of Scotland*, op. cit., p. 41.
29. *Scots Magazine*, VIII, p. 8.
30. PRO 51/46.
31. Compiled largely from John S. Gibson, *Ships of the '45*, London, 1967, pp. 17–24, and from *Mariners' Mirror*, vol. 67, 1981, p. 17.
32. Elcho, *Affairs of Scotland*, op. cit., p. 41.
33. *Mariners Mirror*, op. cit., vol. 67, p. 17.
34. Quoted in *Ships of the '45*, p. 2.
35. Scottish History Society, vol. 22, 1895–6, *The Lyon in Mourning*, ed. W. B. Blaikie, vol. iii, p. 15.
36. *Ibid.*, p. 15.
37. *Ibid.*, p. 29.
38. Scottish History Society, vol. 20, 1894–5, *The Lyon in Mourning*, vol. i, pp. 163–5.

39. *Ibid.*, p. 301.
40. The most detailed account is in *The Lyon in Mourning*, vol. 1, pp. 329–31.
41. The French voyages are described in considerable detail in *Ships of the '45*, passim.
42. *The Lyon in Mourning*, op. cit., vol. i, p. 16.
43. *The Lyon in Mourning*, op. cit., vol. iii, p. 37.
44. James Ferguson and Robert Menzies Fergusson, *Records of the Clan and Name of Fergusson or Ferguson*, Edinburgh, 1895, pp. 246, 267–9, 274–.
45. Scottish History Society, vol. 21, 1895–6, *The Lyon in Mourning*, vol. ii, pp. 99, 253, vol. iii, op. cit., p. 12.
46. *The Lyon in Mourning*, vol. ii, p. 25.
47. *Ibid.*, p. 79.
48. *Ships of the '45*, op. cit., pp. 50–1.
49. *The Lyon in Mourning*, op. cit., vol. iii, pp. 86–8.
50. *The Lyon in Mourning*, op. cit., vol. i, p. 19.
51. *Ibid.*, p. 123.
52. PRO SP 54/38, ff 4a, 5a, 9.
53. *Ibid.*, f 64.

4   Scottish Officers

1. Navy Records Society, vol. xliv, 1914, *The Old Scots Navy*, ed. James Grant, pp. 353–88, passim.
2. The History of Parliament, *The House of Commons 1715–1754*, vol. ii, London, 1970, p. 99.
3. James Ralfe, *The Naval Biography of Great Britain*, London, 1828, vol. 1 p. 193.
4. Thomas, Tenth Earl of Dundonald, *The Autobiography of a Seaman*, Edinburgh, nd, p. 1.
5. Michael Lewis, *A Social History of the Navy*, London, 1960, p. 70.
6. Duke of Atholl, *Chronicles of the Atholl and Tullibardine Families*, vol. iv, Edinburgh, 1908, passim; Mrs Montagu, *Memorials of the Family of Wood of Largo*, London, 1863, passim.
7. Alexander Allardyce, *Memoir of Viscount Keith*, Edinburgh and London, 1882, pp. 11–12.
8. Sir William Fraser, *The Elphinstone Family Book*, Edinburgh, 1897, vol. i, p. 270.
9. R. P. Fereday, *The Orkney Balfours*, 1747–99, Oxford, 1990, p. 157.
10. *Chronicles of . . . Atholl and Tullibardine*, op. cit., vol. iii, p. 435.
11. *Autobiography of a Seaman*, op. cit., p. 10.
12. Janice Murray, ed., *Glorious Victory, Admiral Duncan and the Battle of Camperdown, 1797*, Dundee, 1997, pp. 26–7.
13. Basil Hall, *Fragments of Voyages and Travels*, London, 1865, vol. 1, pp. 260, 268.
14. A. and H. Tayler, *The Book of the Duffs*, vol. i, Edinburgh, 1914, pp. 260, 268.
15. Admiral Sir James Gordon, *Letters and Records*, London, 1890, p. 5.
16. John Charnock, *Biographia Navalis*, vol. vi, London 1798, pp. 34–7.
17. William R. O'Byrne, *A Naval Biographical Dictionary*, London, 1849, vol. i, p. 199.
18. BL Additional Ms 38042.
19. *The Book of the Duffs*, op. cit., vol. i, p. 249.
20. *Autobiography of a Seaman*, op. cit., p. 8.
21. *The Orkney Balfours*, op. cit., pp. 191–2, 246.
22. *The Book of the Duffs*, op. cit., vol. i, p. 249, vol. ii, p. 403.
23. BL Additional Ms 38043.

24. *The Book of the Duffs*, op. cit., vol. i, p. 260.
25. Navy Records Society, vol. xxxix, 1911, *Letters and Papers of Charles, Lord Barham*, vol. iii, pp. 389–91.
26. Ronald M. Sunter, *Politics and Patronage*, Edinburgh, 1986, pp. 51–2.
27. Col. R. H. Mackenzie, *The Trafalgar Roll*, London, 1913, pp. 180–6.
28. *Memoir of Viscount Keith*, op. cit., p. 13.
29. BL Additional Ms 38042.
30. *The Trafalgar Roll*, op. cit., pp. 38–45, 180–6, 122–8, 223–8.
31. *Book of the Duffs*, op. cit., vol. ii, p. 314.
32. *Biographia Navalis*, op. cit., vol. iii, pp. 15–17, 380–2.
33. *Chronicles of . . . Atholl and Tullibardine*, op. cit., vol. iv, pp. 148–9.
34. *Letters and Records*, op. cit., pp. 7–8.
35. *Book of the Duffs*, op. cit., vol. 1, p. 269.
36. *The Elphinstone Family Book*, vol. i, p. 270.
37. *Chronicles of . . . Atholl and Tullibardine*, op. cit., vol. iv, pp. 37–8.
38. *The Trafalgar Roll*, op. cit., p. 223.
39. *Chronicles of . . . Atholl and Tullibardine*, op. cit., vol. iv, pp. 37–8.
40. BL Additional Ms 38039.
41. The History of Parliament, *The House of Commons 1790–1820*, vol. iii, London, 1986, p. 636.
42. C. C. Lloyd, *Mr Barrow of the Admiralty*, London, 1970, p. 71.
43. *Correspondence of George, Prince of Wales*, ed. A. Aspinall, Cambridge, 1970, vol. v, pp. 208–9.
44. History of Parliament, *House of Commons*, vol. iii, p. 636.
45. BL Additional Mss 38042.
46. Michael Lewis, *A Social History of the Navy*, London, 1960, pp. 72–3.
47. Thomas Huskisson, *Eyewitness to Trafalgar*, Royston, 1985, pp. 78, 63.
48. *The Trafalgar Roll*, op. cit., pp. 173–86.
49. *Eyewitness to Trafalgar*, op. cit., pp. 78, 63.
50. John Marshall, *Royal Naval Biography*, London, 1823–35, vol. iv, p. 558.
51. Charnock, *Biographia Navalis*, op. cit., vol. 6, pp. 36n, 37n.
52. Michael Lewis, *A Social History of the Navy*, London, 1960, pp. 61, 69–73.
53. N. A. M. Rodger, *The Wooden World*, London, 1986, p. 340. BL Additional Mss 5725C, f 169.
54. *Wooden World*, op. cit., p. 111.
55. *Ibid.*, pp. 306–7.
56. *The Book of the Duffs*, op. cit., vol. 1, p. 263.
57. *Ibid.*, p. 265.
58. *Glorious Victory*, op. cit., p. 13.
59. *Ibid.*, p. 20.
60. Navy Records Society, vol. xxviii, 1904, *The Letters of Admiral Markham*, p. 398.
61. Reproduced in Lewis, *Social History of the Navy*, op. cit., p. l7.
62. *Extracts from the records of the Burgh of Glasgow*, vol. ix, 1796–1808, ed. Robert Renwick, Glasgow, 1914, p. 483.
63. *Glasgow Herald*, 11 November 1805.
64. *Newsletter of the 1805 Club*, October 1997.
65. John D. Comrie, *History of Scottish Medicine to 1860*, London, 1927, passim.
66. L Melville, *Life and Letters of Tobias Smollett*, 1721–71, London, 1926, p. 17.
67. Unpublished journal, photocopy in the author's possession.
68. Navy Records Society, vol. xci, *Five Naval Journals*, ed. H. G. Thursfield, 1951, p. 46.
69. Tobias Smollett, *Roderick Random*, 1899, Westminster and New York, vol. i, p. 124.

70. Unpublished Journal, op. cit.
71. NRS, *Five Naval Journals*, op. cit., p. 49, 47, 55.
72. Chaplain Richard Walter, *Anson's Voyage Round the World*, ed. Percy G. Adams, New York, 1974, p. 96.
73. B. Lavery, *The Royal Navy's First Invincible*, Portsmouth, 1988, p. 48.
74. Scottish History Society, Second Series, vol. 9, *Steuart's Letter Book*, 1915, ed. William Mackay, p. 455 and passim.
75. Major-General Andrew Burn, *Memoirs*, London, 1816, p. 10.
76. *Five Naval Journals*, op. cit., p. 24.
77. *Universal Dictionary of the Marine*, 1815 edition, revised by William Burney, reprinted New York, 1970, p. xiii.
78. *Ibid.*, p. xiv.
79. *Dictionary of National Biography*, vol. xxxiv, p. 402.
80. Portsmouth Records Series, *Records of the Portsmouth Division of Marines, 1764–1800*, ed. J. A. Lowe, Portsmouth, 1990, passim.
81. Navy Records Society, vol. 138, *Shipboard Life and Organisation 1831–1815*, ed. B. Lavery, 1998, p. 519.
82. Frederick Lewis Maitland, *Narrative on the Surrender of Buonaparte*, 2nd edition, London, 1826, p. 83

5 Naval Operations in Scotland

1. NMM ADM/A/1976, f 5066 ff.
2. *Extracts from the Records of the Burgh of Edinburgh 1701–1718*, ed. Helen Armet, Edinburgh, 1967, pp. 166, 191, 198, 36.
3. PRO SP 54/15, passim.
4. PRO SP54/23, f 5.
5. PRO ADM 1/178.
6. PRO Adm 1/178.
7. *The New Statistical Account of Scotland*, Edinburgh and London, 1845, vol. xiii, pp. 20–1.
8. G .V. C. Young and Caroline Foster, *Captain Francois Thurot*, Peel, p. 198.
9. Georges Lacour Gayet, *La Marine Militaire sous la regne de Louis XV*, Paris, 1902, vol. i, pp. 322–4.
10. Young and Foster, op. cit., pp. 123–5.
11. *Ibid.*, pp. 159–81.
12. John Robertson, *The Scottish Enlightenment and the Militia Issue*, Edinburgh, 1985, passim.
13. Murdoch Mackenzie, *Orcades, or a Geographic and Hydrographic Survey of the Orkney Islands*, London, 1750, p. 3.
14. *Ibid.*, *Nautical Descriptions of the West Coast of Great Britain*, London, 1776, pp. 30, 31, 4.
15. A. H. W. Robinson, *Marine Cartography in Britain*, Leicester, p. 196.
16. Navy Records Society, vol. lxix, *The Sandwich Papers*, ed. J. R. Barnes and J. H. Owen, vol. i, 1932, pp. 227–8.
17. Lincoln Lorenz, *John Paul Jones*, Annapolis, 1942, pp. 153–4.
18. J. H. Sherburne, *The Life and Character of John Paul Jones*, second edition, New York, 1851, p. 10.
19. PRO ADM 1/2392, 51/99.
20. PRO SP 54/4.
21. Navy Records Society, vol. lxxvii, *The Sandwich Papers*, ed. J. R. Barnes and J. H. Owen, vol. 4, 1938, p. 8.
22. *Ibid.*, pp. 84–5.

23. *Ibid.*, p. 91.
24. *Ibid.*, p. 86.
25. *Ibid.*, p. 100.
26. PRO Adm 1/52.
27. PRO Adm 8/7.
28. PRO Adm 1/52.
29. PRO Adm 1/53.
30. Navy Records Society, vol. lxi, *The Letters of Lord St Vincent*, ed. David Bonner-Smith, vol. ii, 1927, p. 36
31. Navy Records Society, vol. xxviii, *The Letters of Admiral Markham*, ed. Sir Clements Markham, 1904, p. 29.
32. *Correspondence of the Prince of Wales*, ed. A. Aspinall, Cambridge, 1970, vol. v, p. 20.
33. Navy Records Society, *Markham*, op. cit., p. 10.
34. Navy Records Society, vol. xxxix, *Letters of Lord Barham*, ed. Sir J. K. Laughton, 1911, vol. iii, p. 13.
35. NRS *Markham*, op. cit., p. 2.
36. NMM LOG/L/R/164
37. NMM KEI 28/86, 6 Jan 1804.
38. NMM KEI 28/79, 4 June 1804.
39. NMM KEI 28/86, 6 Jan 1804.
40. NRS, *Markham* op. cit., pp. 159–6.
41. NMM KEI 28/8.
42. NMM MLN/1.
43. Navy Records Society, vol. CX, *The Saumarez Papers: The Baltic, 1808–1812*, 1968, ed. A. N. Ryan, p. 6.
44. *Ralfe* iii, pp. 193–4.
45. NRS, *Saumarez*, pp. 141–2.
46. *Ibid.*, p. 232.
47. KEI/28/8.
48. PRO Adm 1/69.
49. *Ibid.*
50. *Ibid.*
51. *Ibid.*
52. PRO Adm 1/214.
53. *Ralfe*, pp. iv 44.
54. NMM MLN/1.
55. NMM MLN/1.
56. NMM MLN/1.
57. PRO ADM 1/69
58. James Ralfe, *The Naval Biography of Great Britain*, London, 1828, vol. iii, pp. 193–4.
59. NMM MLN/17.
60. 'Mariners Mirror', *The Journal of the Society for Nautical Research*, vol. xv, p. 42.
61. NMM KEI/28/8.
62. NMM MLN/1.
63. *Navy List*, 181.
64. NMM MLN/1.
65. PRO ADM 1/69.
66. PRO ADM 2/1329, 1489.

6 Naval Recruitment in Scotland

1. Navy Records Society, vol. xliv, *The Old Scots Navy*, ed. James Grant, 1914, pp. 371–2.
2. Admiralty Library, Corbett Manuscripts, vol. x.
3. Navy Records Society vol. 120, *Naval Adminstration, 1715–1750*, ed. Daniel Baugh, 1977, p. 11.
4. David Hume, 'Of Some Remarkable Customs' , in *Essays, Moral, Political and Literary*, ed. T. H. Green and T. H. Grose, London, 1875, vol. i, p. 38.
5. *Calendar of State Papers, Domestic, Commonwealth*, vol. xii, 1658–9, 1885, pp. 277–8.
6. *Diary*, ed. Robert Latham and William Matthews, vol. v, London, 1971, p. 16.
7. *The Parliamentary History of England*, vol. xi, 1739–41, col. 42.
8. *State Trials*, ed. T. B. Howell, London, 1812, vol. 18, cols 1326, 133.
9. PRO ADM 1/160.
10. PRO ADM 1/160.
11. Unpublished Journal, photocopy in the author's possession.
12. Thomas Trotter, *A Practical Plan for Manning the Navy*, Newcastle, 1819, pp. 15–16, 30–1, 37–38.
13. Photocopy in Dunfermline Public Library.
14. William Spavens, *The Narrative of a Chatham Pensioner*, 1796, reprinted London, 1998, p. 13.
15. Admiralty Library, Corbett Manuscripts vol. x.
16. John Nicol, *Life and Adventures*, 1822, reprinted London, 1937, p. 20.
17. PRO ADM 1/178.
18. *Ibid.*
19. *Ibid.*
20. PRO ADM 1/170.
21. PRO ADM 1/150.
22. PRO ADM 1/151.
23. David J. Hepper, *British Warship Losses in the Age of Sail, 1650–1859*, Rotherfield, 1994, pp. 40–1.
24. PRO ADM 1/68.
25. PRO ADM 1/57.
26. PRO ADM 1/1708.
27. PRO ADM 1/150.
28. *Ibid.*
29. *Ibid.*
30. PRO ADM 1/386.
31. PRO ADM 1/68.
32. PRO ADM 1/2220.
33. PRO ADM 1/689.
34. *Ibid.*
35. Photocopy in Dunfermline Public Library.
36. PRO ADM 1/2220.
37. PRO ADM 1/2221, 1/1509.
38. PRO ADM 1/1508.
39. PRO ADM 1/2220.
40. PRO ADM 1/1708.
41. Michael Fry, *The Dundas Despotism*, Edinburgh, 1992, p. 320.
42. PRO ADM 1/579.
43. *Ibid.*
44. PRO ADM 1/689.
45. NRS, vol. xxviii, *The Letters of Admiral Markham*, ed. Sir Clements Markham, 1904, p. 200.

46. M. J. Williams, unpublished PhD thesis, *The Naval Administration of the Fourth Earl of Sandwich, 1771–82*, Oxford University, 1962.
47. NRS, vol. lxxi, *The Sandwich Papers*, ed. Barnes and Owen, vol. ii, 1933, p. 76.
48. NMM MEL/2.
49. NMM MEL/2.
50. *Extracts from the Records of the Burgh of Glasgow*, vol. vii, 1781–95, ed. Robert Renwick, Glasgow, 1913, p. 601.
51. *Landsman Hay*, ed. M. D. Hay, London, 1953, p. 35.
52. *Life and Adventures,* op. cit., p. 179.
53. PRO ADM 1/2220.
54. PRO ADM 1/690.
55. PRO ADM 1/689.
56. *Ibid.*
57. *Ibid.*
58. Captain John Gourly RN, *On the Great Evils of Impressment*, London and Southampton, 1838, pp. 29–30.
59. PRO ADM 1/1707.
60. PRO ADM 1/690.
61. *Ibid.*
62. PRO ADM 1/2178.
63. PRO ADM 1.2178.
64. PRO ADM 1/1997.
65. Navy Records Society, vol. 119, *Manning Pamphlets*, ed. J. S. Bromley, 1974, p. 352.
66. M. Lewis, *A Social History of the Navy,* London, 1960, p. 120.
67. Navy Records Society, vol. 138, *Shipboard Life and Organisation*, ed. B. Lavery, 1998, p. 451.

7   Nineteenth-century Neglect

1. BL Additional Ms 38041.
2. John Vincent Barrie, *Alexander Maconachie of Norfolk Island*, Oxford, 1958.
3. BL Additional Ms 38041.
4. Admiralty, *Committee on Manning*, pp. 532–3, 14, 578–9.
5. *Letters of Queen Victoria*, ed. Arthur Christopher Benson and Viscount Esher, London, 1908, vol. iii, p. 151.
6. Lord Brassey, *Papers and Addresses*, London, 1894, vol. ii, p. 42.
7. *Sam Noble AB*, an Autobiography, London, c 1925, p. 73.
8. William R. Kennedy, *Hurrah for the Life of a Sailor*, Edinburgh and London, 1900, pp. 235–6.
9. Navy Records Society, vol. 131, *British Naval Documents 1204–1960*, ed. Hattendorf *et al*, 1993, p. 732.
10. W. J. Gordon, *A Chat about the Navy,* London, 1891, p. 14.
11. PRO ADM 116/1365
12. *The Caledonia Magazine*, December 1938, p. 22.
13. Anthony Carew, *The Lower Deck of the Royal Navy*, Manchester, 1981, p. 53, Bradshaw's *Guide*, 1863, p. 171.
14. Navy Records Society, vol. 138, *Shipboard Life and Organisation 1731–1815*, ed. B. Lavery, 1998, p. 15, vol. xxxviii, *The Barham Papers*, vol. ii, ed. Sir J. K. Laughton, 1910, p. 163.
15. Navy Records Society, vol. xci, *Five Naval Journals 1789–1817*, ed. H. G. Thursfield, 1951, p. 8.
16. H. Y. Moffat, *From Ship's Boy to Skipper*, Paisley, 1910, pp. 28–32.

17. Gordon Taylor, *The Sea Chaplains*, Oxford, 1978, pp. 385–8.
18. *Queen's Regulations and Admiralty Instructions*, 1879, pp. 206–7.
19. *Queen's Regulations, Addenda*, 1897, p. 33, Article 620.
20. *The Sea Chaplains,* op. cit., 385–8.
21. PRO ADM 1/26601.
22. *Hansard*, vol. 569, cols 391–4.
23. P. G. La Niece, *Not a Nine to Five Job*, Yalding, 1992, pp. 220–1.
24. H. J. Hanham, *Scottish Nationalism*, London, 1969, pp. 77, 131.
25. William McMillan, *Scottish Symbols*, Paisley, 1916, p. 222.
26. Quoted in Michael Lewis, *The Navy in Transition*, London, 1965, p. 195.
27. See Peter Hore, 'Lord Melville, the Admiralty and the Coming of Steam Navigation', in *Mariners Mirror*, vol 86, May 2000, pp. 157–72.
28. Marinell Ash, *This Noble Harbour*, Invergordon, 1991, pp. 179–80.
29. John Wells, *The Immortal Warrior*, London, 1987, p. 123.
30. Mrs Frederick Egerton, *Admiral of the Fleet Sir Geoffrey Phipps Hornby*, Edinburgh and London, 1896, p. 102.
31. *Ibid.*, p. 103.
32. *This Noble Harbour*, op. cit., 1991, p. 181.
33. *Phipps Hornby*, op. cit., p. 104.
34. *The Times*, 9 September 1863.
35. James Graham Goodenough, *Journal . . . With a Memoir, by his Widow*, London, 1876, p. 77.
36. A. B. Cunningham, *A Sailor's Odyssey*, London, 1951, pp. 45–6.
37. Sir E. R. Fremantle, *The Navy as I have Known It*, London, 1904, pp. 282, 285.
38. PRO ADM 120/45.
39. PRO ADM 120/20.
40. NMM MLN/17.
41. *The Navy as I Have Known It*, op. cit., pp. 291–2.
42. Frank C. Bowen, *His Majesty's Coastguard*, London, 1928, pp. 138–9.
43. *Coastguard Instructions*, 1911, p. 169.
44. PRO ADM 120/10.
45. *Hurrah for the Life of a Sailor*, op. cit., p. 237, *The Navy as I Have Known It*, op. cit., p. 286.
46. *The Navy as I Have Known It*, op. cit., p. 289.
47. Admiralty, *Committee on Manning*, 1852, p. 31.
48. *Report of the Naval Reserves Committee*, 1902, pp. 283–4.
49. *Royal Naval Reserve Regulations (Men)*, 1911, amendment pasted in copy in NMM Library.
50. *The Navy as I Have Known It*, op. cit., p. 286.
51. PRO ADM 120/45.
52. *Hurrah for the Life of a Sailor*, op. cit., p. 234.
53. James Graham, Sixth Duke of Montrose, *My Ditty Box*, London, 1952, pp. 133–4.
54. PRO ADM 120/45.
55. Angus Martin, *The Ring-Net Fishermen*, Edinburgh, 1981, reprinted 1996, pp. 10–12.
56. *Ibid.*, pp.18–9.
57. *Ibid.*, pp. 19–21, 24.
58. James R. Coull, *The Sea Fisheries of Scotland, an Historical Geography*, Edinburgh, 1996, p. 150.
59. PRO ADM 120/45.
60. James Hunter, *The Making of the Crofting Community*, Edinburgh, 1976, pp. 59–69.
61. *Ibid.*, pp. 150–4

62. I. M. M. MacPhail, *The Crofters' War*, Storn0way, 1989, pp. 190–1.
63. *The Making of the Crofting Community*, op. cit., p. 175.
64. PRO ADM 120/33.
65. Brassey's *Papers and Addresses*, op. cit., vol. ii, pp. 66–8.
66. *Ibid.*, pp. 67–8.
67. *Brassey's Naval Annual*, 1891, pp. 372–3.
68. Henry Baynham, *Men from the Dreadnoughts*, London, 1976, pp. 73–4.
69. PRO ADM 53/18336.
70. Navy Records Society, vol. cii, *Fisher Papers*, vol. i, ed. P. K. Kemp, pp. 12–15, 106.
71. First Lord's Statement, 1906–7, in *Brassey's Naval Annual*, 1906, p. 370.
72. *Hansard*, vol. 131, col. 1500.
73. *Brassey's Naval Annual*, 1888, p. 421.
74. *Brassey's Naval Annual*, 1909, p. 134.
75. *Naval Estimates*, 1892–3, in *Brassey's Naval Annual*, 1892, pp. 379, 362.
76. *My Ditty Box*, op. cit., p. 37.
77. *Ibid.*, pp. 133–41.
78. PRO ADM 120/45.
79. *Brassey's Naval Annual*, 1908, p. 113.

8   The First Scottish Bases

1. Statement of the First Lord of the Admiralty, 1894–5, in *Brassey's Naval Annual*, 1894, p. 430.
2. Hugh B. Peebles, *Warshipbuilding on the Clyde*, Edinburgh, 1987, p. 165.
3. Paul Kennedy, *The Rise and Fall of British Naval Mastery*, 3rd edition, London, 1991, p. 247.
4. Quoted in Admiralty, *Committee on Naval Works at Dover and Rosyth*, London, 1913, p. 150.
5. *Hansard*, vol. 131, col. 1496.
6. *Committee on Naval Works*, op. cit., p. 158–9.
7. Navy Records Society, vol. cii, *The Fisher Papers*, vol. i, ed. P. K. Kemp, 1960, p. xx.
8. *Committee on Naval Works*, op. cit., p. 152.
9. Quoted in Ruddock F. MacKay, *Fisher of Kilverstone*, Oxford, 1973, p. 419.
10. Lord Charles Beresford, *The Betrayal*, Westminster, 1912, p. 53.
11. *Hansard*, Fourth Series, vol. 173, col. 835.
12. *The Times*, 4 December 1907.
13. *Hansard*, Fourth Series, vol. 185 App. III p. 10.
14. *Ibid.*, cols 1393–4.
15. *Ibid.*, col. 1227.
16. *Ibid.*, col. 403.
17. *Ibid.*, App. III, p. 10.
18. *Ibid.*, col. 1378.
19. PRO ADM 1/8012.
20. *Ibid.*
21. PRO ADM 1/8352.
22. D. J. Munro, *Scapa Flow, a Naval Retrospect*, London, *c.* 1920, pp. 149, 151.
23. Sir Reginald Bacon, *The Life of Lord Fisher of Kilverstone*, vol. ii, London, 1929, p. 155.
24. *A Naval Retrospect*, op. cit., pp. 137–8.
25. PRO ADM 116/1365.
26. *Committee on Naval Works*, op. cit., pp. B2, B3.

27. *Ibid.*, p. 156.
28. D. K. Brown, *The Design and Construction of British Warships, 1939–45,* London, 1995, pp. 25–6, 34–5.
29. PRO ADM 116/1365.
30. Admiralty (Civil Engineer in Chief), *The Technical History and Index,* TH 47, *HM Dockyard, Rosyth, Notes on construction etc During Period of War,* London, 1920, p. 21.
31. William Scott-Bruce, *The Railways of Fife,* Perth, 1980, p. 180.
32. Phillip MacDougall, *Royal Dockyards,* Newton Abbot, 1982, p. 169.
33. *Hansard,* vol. 131, cols. 1501–2.
34. PRO ADM 1/8351.
35. PRO ADM 1/8352.
36. *A Naval Retrospect,* op. cit., pp. 141–2.
37. *Ibid.*, pp. 18–19, 35.
38. *Ibid.*, p. 144.
39. Quoted in Marinell Ash, *This Noble Harbour,* Invergordon, 1991, p. 187.
40. *Ibid.*, pp. 189–94.
41. PRO ADM 116/1380.
42. *Ibid.*
43. *Technical History,* TH 47, op. cit., p. 2.
44. *Ibid.*, p. 3.
45. *Ibid.*, p. 8.
46. PRO ADM 1/8474/267.
47. PRO ADM 116/1545.
48. *Ibid.*
49. *Technical History,* TH 47, op. cit., p. 4.
50. *Ibid.*, pp. 8–9, 3.
51. *Ibid.*, p. 19.
52. *Hansard,* vol. 166, col. 416.

9 The Grand Fleet and its Bases

1. Navy Records Society, vol. 128, *The Beatty Papers,* vol. i, ed. B. McL. Ranft, 1989, p. 118.
2. James Graham, Sixth Duke of Montrose, *My Ditty Box,* London, 1952, pp. 168–70.
3. Imperial War Museum, *Royal Naval Division, Roll of Honour,* London, 1991.
4. W. S. Galpin, *From Public School to Navy,* Plymouth, 1919, passim.
5. Marinell Ash, *This Great Harbour,* Invergordon, 1991, p. 29.
6. D. J. Munro, *Scapa Flow, a Naval Retrospect,* London, *c.* 1920, p. 223.
7. *Orkney Miscellany* vol. 4., pp. 60–1.
8. *This Great Harbour,* op. cit., pp. 35–6, 41.
9. PRO CAB 45/266.
10. Navy Records Society, *The Beatty Papers,* op. cit., vol. i, p. 83.
11. Lord Chatfield, *The Navy and Defence,* London, 1942, p. 121.
12. J. R. Jellicoe, *The Grand Fleet,* London, 1919, pp. 4–6.
13. *Ibid.*, p. 29.
14. Admiralty, *Naval Staff Monographs (Historical),* vol. x, *Home Waters,* Part II, 1924, pp. 40–1.
15. PRO ADM 137/1972.
16. Navy Records Society, *The Beatty Papers,* op. cit., vol. i, pp. 139, 141.
17. Quoted in *A Naval Retrospect,* op. cit., p. 205.
18. Navy Records Society, *The Beatty Papers,* op. cit., vol. i, p. 140.

19. *A Naval Retrospect*, op. cit., p. 187–9.
20. *Ibid.*, p. 222.
21. *Ibid.*, pp. 211–13.
22. Admiralty (Civil Engineer in Chief), *The Technical History and Index*, TH 37, *The Northern Base*, 1920, pp. 44–5.
23. Naval Staff Monographs, *Home Waters*, op. cit., vol. iii, 1924, pp. 51–2.
24. *A Naval Retrospect*, op. cit., p. 216.
25. Lockhart Leith, compiler, *History of British Minefields 1914–1918*, London, *c.* 1920, pp. 352–6a.
26. Technical History, TH 37, *The Northern Base*, op. cit., p. 45.
27. Sir Angus Cunningham Graham, *Random Naval Recollections*, Gartocharn, 1979, pp. 33–4.
28. PRO ADM 137/1972.
29. W. S. Hewison, *This Great Harbour*, Stromness, 1985, pp. 62ff, *Technical History*, TH 37, *The Northern Base*, op. cit., p. 46.
30. Technical History, TH 37, *The Northern Base*, op. cit., p. 36.
31. *This Great Harbour*, op. cit., p. 125.
32. Navy Records Society, *The Beatty Papers*, op. cit., vol. i, p. 447.
33. Technical History, TH 37, *The Northern Base*, op. cit., pp. 10–13.
34. Brown and Meehan, *Scapa Flow*, London 1968, p. 70.
35. Henry Baynham, *Men from the Dreadnoughts*, London, 1976, p. 116, Stephen King-Hall, *My Naval Life*, London, 1952, p. 109, *Technical History*, TH 37, *The Northern Base*, op. cit., p. 20.
36. *Men from the Dreadnoughts*, op. cit., p. 118.
37. *Technical History*, TH 37, *The Northern Base*, op. cit., p. 20.
38. *Ibid.*, pp. 21–8.
39. *Ibid.*, pp. 31–3.
40. *Ibid.*, pp. 4–10.
41. Navy Records Society, vol. cviii, *The Jellicoe Papers*, vol. i, ed. A. Temple Patterson, 1966, p. 126.
42. *The Grand Fleet*, op. cit., pp. 64–6.
43. *A Naval Retrospect*, op. cit., p. 216.
44. *Random Naval Recollections*, op. cit., pp. 43–5.
45. *Naval Life*, op. cit., p. 106.
46. *Random Naval Recollections*, op. cit., pp. 37–8
47. Navy Records Society, vol. 113, *The Naval Air Service*, ed. S. W. Roskill, 1969, p. 545.
48. *Technical History*, TH 37, *The Northern Base*, op. cit., pp. 45–6.
49. *Random Naval Recollections*, op. cit., p. 36, Stephen King-Hall, *A North Sea Diary*, London, *c.* 1930 p. 399, Navy Records Society, *The Beatty Papers*, op. cit., vol. i, p. 437.
50. *Journal of the Royal United Service Institution*, February 1923, p. 2.
51. From *The Influence of Sea Power upon History*, Oxford Dictionary of Quotations, fourth edition, Oxford, 1996, p. 442.
52. Sir Arthur Longmore, *From Sea to Sky*, London, 1946, pp. 55–6.
53. *My Naval Life*, op. cit., pp. 112, 114.
54. PRO ADM 218/1.
55. *From Sea to Sky*, op. cit., p. 62.
56. *My Naval Life*, op. cit., p. 140.
57. Dick Cronin, *Royal Navy Shipboard Aircraft Developments, 1912–1931*, Tonbridge, 1990, p. 38.
58. *Ibid.*, pp. 57–8, 61.
59. Norman Friedman, *British Carrier Aviation*, London, 1988, passim.
60. Vice-Admiral Richard Bell Davies, *Sailor in the Air*, London, 1967, p. 181.

61. Navy Records Society, *The Naval Air Service*, op. cit., p. 743.
62. Vice-Admiral Richard Bell Davies, *Sailor in the Air*, op. cit., p. 182.
63. Navy Records Society, *The Naval Air Service*, op. cit., pp. 561, 684.
64. PRO ADM 137/1170.
65. PRO ADM 137/1892.
66. *Ibid.*
67. PRO ADM 137/1217.
68. PRO ADM 137/1892.
69. Admiralty (Civil Engineer in Chief), *The Technical History and Index*, TH 10, *Admiralty Oil-Fuel Pipe-Line from the Clyde to the Forth*, 1919, passim, PRO ADM 53/56860.
70. PRO ADM 53/56860.
71. S. W. Roskill, *Admiral of the Fleet Earl Beatty*, London, 1980, p. 263.

10 The First Submarine War

1. Admiralty, *Naval Staff Monographs (Historical), Home Waters*, Part ii, 1924, p. 65.
2. *Ibid.*, pp. 42–4.
3. *Ibid.*, p. 63–4.
4. Brenda Girvin and Monica Cosens, *Log of HMS Gunner*, Granton, *c.* 1920, pp. 7, 17.
5. *Naval Staff Monographs (Historical), Home Waters*, Part II, pp. 127–8.
6. *Ibid.*, Part IV, 1926, pp. 135–8.
7. *Ibid.*, pp. 238–9.
8. *Ibid.*, pp. 241–2.
9. *Ibid.*, p. 244.
10. *Log of HMS Gunner*, op. cit., p. 7.
11. *Lloyds Register of Yachts*, 1913. Admiralty, 'Red list', Auxiliary Patrol, *Weekly Report of the Yacht Patrol Office*.
12. *Log of HMS Gunner*, op. cit., p. 55.
13. *Auxiliary Patrol List*, op. cit., 21 February 1917, passim.
14. *Naval Staff Monographs (Historical), Home Waters*, Part II, p. 113.
15. *Ibid.*, Part IV, p. 99–100.
16. *Ibid.*, pp. 95–9.
17. *Ibid.*, pp. 105–6.
18. *Ibid.*, Part VI, 1926, pp. 98–100.
19. *Ibid.*, Part IV, pp. 128–9.
20. *Ibid.*, pp. 249–50.
21. *Ibid.*, Part V, 1926, pp. 33–6.
22. *Ibid.*, pp. 36–8.
23. *Log of HMS Gunner*, op. cit., pp. 20–1.
24. *Naval Staff Monographs (Historical), Home Waters*, Part IV, p. 106.
25. Paul G. Halpern, *A Naval History of World War I*, London, 1994, p. 294 and passim.
26. *Naval Staff Monographs (Historical), Home Waters*, Part VI, p. 51.
27. *Ibid.*, Part V, pp. 115–19, 127–131.
28. *Ibid.*, Part VI, pp. 48–51, Jellicoe, *The Grand Fleet*, London, 1919, p. 267.
29. *Naval Staff Monographs (Historical), vol. x, Home Waters*, Part VII, 1927, pp. 24–35.
30. Lockhart Leith, compiler, *History of British Minefields 1914–1918*, London, *c.* 1920, p. 341.
31. *Ibid.*, p. 17.

32. *Ibid.*, pp. 56–8.
33. *Ibid.*, pp. 59–61, 80–1.
34. *Ibid.*, pp. 26–8, 31, 56, 57, 60. D. J. Lyon, *The Denny List*, Greenwich, 1975, vol. iii, pp. 669, 677.
35. Navy Records Society, vol. 128, *The Beatty Papers*, vol. i, ed. B. McL. Ranft, 1989, pp. 269, 271.
36. Quoted in Willem Hackman, *Seek and Strike*, London, 1984, p. 26.
37. Admiralty (Civil Engineer in Chief), *The Technical History and Index*, TH7, *The Anti-Submarine Division of the Naval Staff, December 1916 – November 1918*, pp. 40–2.
38. *Seek and Strike*, op. cit., p. 48.
39. *Ibid.*, pp. 64–8.
40. *Ibid.*, pp. 19–29, PRO ADM 218/1, 218/104.
41. PRO ADM 218/4.
42. *The Accident to 'K13'*, Address to the Greenock Association of Engineers and Shipbuilders, 4 March 1919.
43. Quoted in Don Everitt, *K-Boats*, reprinted Shrewsbury, 1999, p. 3.
44. *Ibid.*, pp. 76–106.
45. Patrick Abbott, *The British Airship at War, 1914–1918*, Lavenham, 1989, p. 75.
46. Admiralty (Civil Engineer in Chief), *The Technical History and Index,* vol. 8, *Scandinavian and East Coast Convoys*, p. 59.
47. *Ibid.*, pp. 4–5.
48. *Ibid.*, p. 34.
49. Navy Records Society, vol. 111, *The Jellicoe Papers*, ed. A. Temple Patterson, 1968, vol. ii, 223–4.
50. *Technical History and Index*, vol. 8, op. cit., p. 11.
51. *Ibid.*, pp. 78–80.
52. *Ibid.*, p. 11.
53. *Ibid.*, pp. 26–7.
54. *History of British Minefields*, op. cit., pp. 173–5.
55. *Ibid.*, pp. 176–7.
56. Admiralty (Civil Engineer in Chief), *The Technical History and Index,* vol. 45, *Minelaying Bases at Grangemouth, Dalmore and Glen-Albyn*, 1920, passim.
57. *History of British Minefields*, op. cit., pp. 178–203.
58. *Ibid.*, p. 202.
59. J. S. Cowie, *Mines, Minelayers and Minelaying*, Oxford, 1949, pp. 71–2.
60. Lord Wester Wemyss, *Life and Letters*, London, 1935, p. 392.
61. Navy Records Society, *The Beatty Papers*, op. cit., vol. I, pp. 562–74, *A Naval History of World War I*, op. cit., p. 448.

11   Lean Years

1. Von Reuter, *Scapa Flow*, translated by I. N. M. Mudie, London, 1940, pp. 33–4.
2. *Ibid.*, p. 37.
3. *Ibid.*, p. 86.
4. Lockhart Leith, compiler, *History of British Minefields 1914–1918*, London, *c.* 1920, pp. 346, 349, 353, 355–6.
5. Admiralty, Naval Staff, Intelligence Department, *German statement of Mines Laid by Surface Vessels and Submarines of the Flanders Command 1914–1918, c.* 1920, p. 48.
6. W. S. Hewison, *This Great Harbour*, Stromness, 1985, pp. 175–82.
7. Dan van der Vat, *The Grand Scuttle*, London, 1982, pp. 229–30.
8. Freiderich Ruge, *Scapa Flow 1919*, London, 1973, pp. 111–12.

9. Von Reuter, *Scapa Flow*, op. cit., p. 107.
10. Quoted in *The Grand Scuttle*, op. cit., p. 176.
11. *Ibid.*, p. 180.
12. PRO ADM 1/8546/326.
13. PRO ADM 116/2073.
14. PRO ADM 1/8543/298.
15. For example, A. J. Marder, *From the Dreadnought to Scapa Flow*, vol. III, London, 1966; N. J. M. Campbell, *Jutland: an Analysis of the Fighting*, London, 1986; Navy Records Society, vol. 124, *The Pollen Papers*, ed. Jon Sumida, 1984; Andrew Gordon, *The Rules of the Game*, London, 1996.
16. Ludovic Kennedy, *On my Way to the Club*, London, 1989, p. 33.
17. PRO ADM 1/8622/52.
18. PRO ADM 1/8662/122.
19. PRO ADM 1/17157.
20. PRO CAB/21/287.
21. *Hansard*, vol. 189, col. 854.
22. *Ibid.*, cols 854–5.
23. PRO ADM 1/8662/122.
24. A. B. Cunningham, *A Sailor's Odyssey*, London, 1951, pp. 111, 119–20.
25. C. R. Benstead, *HMS Rodney at Sea*, London, 1932, p. 153.
26. Lord Chatfield, *The Navy and Defence*, London, 1942, p. 220.
27. *On My Way to the Club*, op. cit., pp. 47–8.
28. *HMS Rodney at Sea*, op. cit., p. 15.
29. *A Sailor's Odyssey*, op. cit., p. 143.
30. *The Navy and Defence*, op. cit., p. 22.
31. John A. Gurr, *In Peace and in War*, Worcester, 1993, p. 16.
32. Anthony Hogg, *Just a Hogg's Life*, Chichester, 1993, p. 90.
33. *HMS Rodney at Sea*, op. cit., p. 10.
34. *Ibid.*, p. 11.
35. *In Peace and in War*, op. cit., p. 16.
36. *HMS Rodney at Sea*, op. cit., p. 99.
37. Anthony Carew, *The Lower Deck of the Royal Navy, 1900–39*, Manchester, 1981, pp. 70–1, 104, 112.
38. S. W. Roskill, *Naval Policy Between the Wars*, vol. ii, *The Period of Reluctant Rearmament, 1930–1939*, London, 1976, pp. 89–90.
39. Alan Eriera, *The Invergordon Mutiny*, London, 1981, pp. 54, 71.
40. *Ibid.*, p. 58.
41. Quoted in *Ibid.*, p. 61.
42. *Ibid.*, pp. 68–9.
43. NMM ELK/2.
44. *Naval Policy Between the Wars*, op. cit., vol. ii, p. 107.
45. *The Invergordon Mutiny*, op. cit., p. 87.
46. *Ibid.*, p. 97.
47. *Ibid.*, p. 101.
48. *Ibid.*, p. 128.
49. *Naval Policy Between the Wars*, op. cit., vol. ii, p. 11.
50. *Ibid.*, pp. 108–11.
51. *The Invergordon Mutiny*, op. cit., pp. 107–8.
52. *HMS Rodney at Sea*, op. cit., p. 172.
53. *The Invergordon Mutiny*, op. cit., p. 167.
54. *A Sailor's Odyssey*, op. cit., p. 153.
55. PRO ADM 116/3860.
56. PRO ADM 167/95.
57. PRO ADM 1/14705.

58. PRO ADM 1/9885.
59. PRO ADM 116/4490.
60. PRO ADM 1/9883.

12   The Second World War in the North

1. S. W. Roskill, *The War at Sea*, vol. 1, *The Defensive*, London, 1954, reprinted 1976, p. 67.
2. John Charles Jones, *From the Forecastle Mess Deck to the Wardroom*, Lewes, 1987, pp. 36–7.
3. PRO ADM 208/14.
4. *The War at Sea*, op. cit., vol. 1, pp. 36–7.
5. *Ibid.*, p. 97.
6. PRO ADM 116/5790.
7. *The War at Sea*, op. cit., vol. 1, p. 78.
8. PRO ADM 116/5790.
9. Quoted in Alexandre Korganoff, *The Phantom of Scapa Flow* , translated W. and D. M. Strachan, London, 1974, p. 180.
10. Gunther Prien, *I Sank the Royal Oak*, London, 1954, p. 184.
11. PRO ADM 199/158.
12. *The Phantom of Scapa Flow*, op. cit., p. 176.
13. PRO ADM 199/158.
14. *Ibid.*
15. Alexander McKee, *Black Saturday*, London, 1960, pp. 67–8.
16. *The Phantom of Scapa Flow*, op. cit., p. 177.
17. PRO ADM 199/158.
18. PRO ADM 1/11593.
19. Winston G. Ramsey, ed., *The Blitz Then and Now*, vol. 1, London, 1987, pp. 51, 68, 71–2, 76.
20. *Ibid.*, vol. 1, pp. 77–8.
21. PRO ADM 1/11922.
22. *Ibid.*
23. *The War at Sea*, op. cit., vol. 1, pp. 175–97.
24. D. K. Brown, ed., *The Design and Construction of British Warships, 1939–45*, London, 1996, vol. 3, pp. 96–7.
25. W. S. Hewison, *This Great Harbour*, Stromness, 1985, p. 310.
26. PRO ADM 1/4111.
27. PRO ADM 208/14.
28. *Ibid.*
29. Most of the above from PRO Adm 116/5790.
30. Ludovic Kennedy, *On My Way to the Club*, London, 1989, pp. 111–12.
31. D. A. Rayner, *Escort*, London, 1955, p. 148.
32. David Howarth, *The Shetland Bus*, London, 1951, pp. 6–7.
33. PRO ADM 199/373.
34. Sydney Hart, *Discharged Dead*, London, 1956, pp. 34, 38.
35. W. S. Chalmers, *Max Horton and the Western Approaches*, London, 1954, p. 72.
36. PRO ADM 199/279.
37. War Diary, PRO ADM 199/279.
38. John D. Drummond, *HM U-Boat*, London, 1958, p. 149.
39. PRO ADM 199/279.
40. Ewan Southby-Tailyour, *Blondie*, London, 1998.
41. Ewen Montagu, *The Man who Never Was*, London 1956, pp. 72–5.

42. C. E. T. Warren and James Benson, *Above us the Waves*, London, 1953, p. 26.
43. *Ibid.*, p. 34.
44. *Ibid.*, p. 113.
45. *Ibid.*, p. 110.
46. PRO ADM 1/22675.

13   The Clyde Convoy Base

1. Paul Kemp, *U-Boats Destroyed: German Submarine Losses in the World Wars*, London, 1997, p. 60.
2. David Kahn, *Seizing the Enigma: the Race to Break the German U-Boat Codes*, London, 1992, pp. 104–12.
3. PRO Adm 199/371, war diary.
4. Navy Records Society, vol. 137, *The Defeat of the Enemy Attack on Shipping*, Barley and Waters, ed. Eric J. Grove, 1997, p. 59. Plan 16 (2).
5. Admiralty, CB 04050, *Monthly Anti-Submarine Reports*, March 1943, Plate 5.
6. John Hood (ed.) *The History of Clydebank*, Carnforth, 1988, pp. 129–34.
7. PRO CAB 102/419.
8. C. B. A. Behrens, *Merchant Shipping and the Demands of War*, London, 1955, p. 151.
9. *War Memoirs*, London, 1934, vol. iii, p. 1244.
10. PRO CAB 102/419, p. 60.
11. PRO LAB 10/71.
12. PRO CAB 102/419.
13. PRO CAB 102/423.
14. PRO CAB 102/419.
15. *Ibid.*, Appendix 3.
16. PRO ADM 199/1.
17. Nicholas Monsarrat, *Life is a Four Letter Word*, vol. II, *Breaking Out*, London, 1970, pp. 92–3.
18. PRO Adm 1/13430.
19. *Ibid.*
20. Graeme Ogden, *My Sea Lady*, London, 1963, pp. 29–31.
21. PRO Adm 187/21.
22. *Ibid.*
23. PRO Adm 1/10577
24. John D. Drummond, *A River Runs to War*, London, 1960, p. 56.
25. *Monthly Anti-Submarine Reports*, 1942, pp. 60–2.
26. John Shields, *Clyde Built*, Glasgow, 1949, p. 157.
27. PRO Adm 199/646.
28. David W. Bone, *Merchantmen Rearmed*, London, 1949, p. 33.
29. PRO Adm 208/20.
30. Stephen W. Roskill, *The War at Sea*, vol. i, *The Defensive*, London, 1954, reprinted 1976, 1 pp. 457–9.
31. *Monthly Anti-Submarine Reports*, September 1940, Plate 5.
32. PRO Adm 187/10.
33. Chris Howard Bailey, *The Royal Naval Museum Book of the Battle of the Atlantic*, Stroud, 1994, pp. 5, 95.
34. PRO ADM 187 series, 'Pink Lists'.
35. Peter Coy, *The Echo of a Fighting Flower*, Upton upon Severn, 1989, p. 196.
36. PRO Adm 199/631.
37. Stephen W. Roskill, *The War at Sea*, vol. ii, *The Period of Balance*, London, 1956, pp. 91, 459–60.

38. Royal Institution of Naval Architects, *British Warship Design in World War II*, London, 1947, reprinted 1983, pp. 85–126.
39. *Merchantmen Rearmed*, op. cit., pp. 154, 196.
40. *My Sea Lady*, p. 33.
41. *Merchantmen Rearmed,* op. cit., p. 155.
42. Joseph H. Wellings, *On His Majesty's Service: Observations of the British Home Fleet*, ed. Hattendorff, Newport, 1983, p. 103.
43. *Merchantmen Rearmed*, p. 35.
44. Wellings, op. cit., p. 105.
45. PRO MT 63/93
46. PRO MT 63/193.
47. *Ibid.*
48. PRO CAB 102/419.
49. A. E. Jeffery, *The History of Scruttons*, London, 1970, p. 70.
50. *Ibid.*
51. PRO MT 63/204.
52. *Merchantmen Rearmed*, p. 188.
53. PRO Adm 199/11.
54. Transactions of the Institution of Engineers and Shipbuilders in Scotland, Paper no. 1108 by Sir Bruce G. White, *The Construction and Operation of the Military Ports on Gareloch and Loch Ryan*, 16 November 1948.
55. Mike Hughes, *The Hebrides at War*, Edinburgh, 1998, p. 21.
56. PRO CAB 102/836.
57. S. A. Kerslake, *Coxswain in the Northern Convoys*, London, 1984, p. 109.
58. PRO CAB 102/419.
59. Navy Records Society, vol. 137, *The Defeat of the Enemy Attack on Shipping*, Barley and Waters, ed. Eric J. Grove, 1997, pp. 233, 30–2.
60. *Ibid.*, p. 233.
61. Wellings, op. cit., p. 104.
62. *My Sea Lady*, op. cit., p. 34.
63. D. A. Rayner, *Escort*, London, 1955, pp. 73–4.
64. *Echo of a Fighting Flower*, op. cit., p. 16.
65. PRO CAB 102/419.
66. Roger Hutchison, *Polly*, Edinburgh, 1990.
67. PRO Adm 199/1443.
68. PRO Adm 199/11.
69. PRO DEFE 2/815.
70. Roskill, *The War at Sea*, op. cit., vol. ii, pp. 313–28.
71. PRO Adm 199/631.
72. Roskill, *The War at Sea*, op. cit., vol i, p. 89.
73. Robert Harling, *The Steep Atlantick Stream*, Bath, 1974, p. 28.
74. PRO Adm 199/631.
75. PRO Adm 1/1430.
76. C. P. Stephenson, *RAF Quickforce Operations, August 1940–October 1942*, *Ships Monthly*, March 1999, pp. 32–6.
77. PRO CAB 102/836.
78. Vice-Admiral Sir Peter Gretton, *Convoy Escort Commander*, London, 1964, p. 6.
79. *My Sea Lady*, op. cit., p. 31.
80. Drummond, *A River Runs to War*, op. cit., pp. 61–2.
81. *Life is a Four Letter Word*, vol. ii, op. cit., pp. 92, 94.
82. P. G. La Niece, *Not a Nine to Five Job*, Yalding, 1992, p. 29.
83. PRO Adm 199/659.
84. Derek Howse, *Radar at Sea*, London, 1993, pp. 343–4.

85. *Merchantmen Rearmed*, op. cit., p. 186.
86. Arnold Hague, *Convoy Rescue Ships 1940–1945*, Gravesend, 1998.
87. Drummond, *A River Runs to War*, op. cit., p. 122.
88. Wilem Hackman, *Seek and Strike*, London, 1984, pp. 244–6, 248–50, 306–9.
89. *My Sea Lady*, op. cit., p. 30.
90. *Random Naval Recollections*, Gartocharn, 1979, p. 232.
91. Paul Chapman, *Submarine Torbay*, London, 1989, p. 28.
92. *Life is a Four Letter Word*, op. cit., p. 93.
93. PRO Adm 199/631.
94. PRO Adm 219/485?
95. PRO Adm 199/631.
96. *Ibid.*
97. John Steele, *The Tragedy of HMS Dasher*, Glendaruel, 1995.
98. *Monthly Anti-Submarine Reports*, March 1945, pp. 3, 4.
99. *Ibid.*, June 1945, pp. 9–10.

14   Naval Training

1. A. H. Cherry, *Yankee RN*, London, 1951, p. 148.
2. *Ibid.*, p. 142.
3. PRO ADM 1/17573.
4. Dunstan Hadley, *Barracuda Pilot*, Shrewsbury, 1993, p. 86.
5. Amphibious Warfare Headquarters, *History of the Combined Operations Organisation, 1940–45*, London, 1956, pp. 152, 171.
6. Navy Records Society, vol. 122, *The Keyes Papers*, vol. iii, ed. Paul Halpern, 1980, pp. 91, 172.
7. PRO DEFE 2/815.
8. L. E. H. Maund, *Assault from the Sea*, London, 1949, p. 75.
9. PRO DEFE 2/815.
10. Paul Lund and Harry Ludlam, *The War of the Landing Craft*, London, 1976, pp. 15–16.
11. Bernard Fergusson, *The Watery Maze*, London, 1961, p. 324.
12. PRO DEFE 2/1430.
13. *Assault from the Sea*, op. cit., p. 107.
14. PRO DEFE 2/1319.
15. *The Diaries of Evelyn Waugh*, ed. Michael Davie, London, 1976, p. 489.
16. Peter Young, *Storm from the Sea*, London, 1989, pp. 22–3.
17. PRO DEFE 2/815.
18. *Diaries*, op. cit., p. 492.
19. *Ibid.*, p. 493.
20. *The War of the Landing Craft*, op. cit., pp. 16–17.
21. *Diaries*, op. cit., p. 492.
22. *The War of the Landing Craft*, op. cit., pp. 22–3.
23. Brian Macdermott, *Ships Without Names*, London, 1992, p. 28.
24. *Assault from the Sea*, op. cit., p. 109.
25. PRO DEFE 2/900.
26. *The Watery Maze*, op. cit., p. 228.
27. *History of the Combined Operations Organisation*, op. cit., p. 96.
28. Samuel Elliot Morrison, *History of United States Naval Operations in World War Two*, vol. xi, *The Invasion of France and Germany*, Oxford, 1957, p. 58.
29. Gifford, *Highlands and Islands*, op. cit., p. 255.
30. *The War of the Landing Craft*, op. cit., p. 82.
31. PRO ADM 1/14003.

32. *The War of the Landing Craft,* op. cit., p. 86.
33. *Ibid.,* pp. 82, 91.
34. *History of the Combined Operations Organisation,* op. cit., pp. 134–5.
35. *Ibid.,* p. 125.
36. *Ibid.,* pp. 141, 144–5.
37. *The Watery Maze,* op. cit., p. 324.
38. NRS, *Keyes* III, op. cit., p. 142.
39. *The Watery Maze,* op. cit., pp. 272–3.
40. *History of the Combined Operations Organisation,* op. cit., p. 64.
41. *The Watery Maze,* op. cit., p. 274.
42. *Ibid.,* p. 273.
43. PRO DEFE 2/815.
44. *The Watery Maze,* op. cit., pp. 350–1.
45. *Yankee RN,* op. cit., p. 143.
46. *Ibid.,* p. 146.
47. PRO ADM 1/12918.
48. PRO ADM 298/461.
49. *Yankee RN,* p. 148.
50. Richard Baker, *The Terror of Tobermory,* London, 1972, p. 17.
51. Chris Howard Bailey, *The Royal Naval Museum Book of the Battle of the Atlantic,* Stroud, 1994, pp. 12–13.
52. Paul Lund and Harry Ludlam, *Out Sweeps,* London, 1978.
53. PRO Adm 1/1325.
54. War Diary, PRO Adm 199/373.
55. Edward Young, *One of our Submarines,* London, 1952, p. 43.
56. *Ibid.,* pp. 115–27.
57. Keith Nethercoate-Bryant, *Submarine Memories,* Hadley, 1994, pp. 65–6.
58. Rebecca John, *Caspar John,* London, 1987, p. 74.
59. Gerard A. Woods, *Wings at Sea, A Fleet Air Arm Observer's War, 1940–45,* London, 1985, p. 131.
60. E. E. Barringer, *Alone on a Wide, Wide Sea,* London, 1995, pp. 39–40.
61. George E. Sadler, *Swordfish Patrol,* Wrexham, 1996, p. 40.
62. H. J. C. Spencer, *Ordinary Naval Airman,* Tunbridge Wells, 1992, p. 146.
63. *Alone on a Wide, Wide Sea,* op. cit., pp. 40, 42.
64. Ray Sturtivant and Theo Ballance, *The Squadrons of the Fleet Air Arm,* Tonbridge, 1994, p. 15.
65. Admiralty, *Fleet Air Arm,* London, 1943, p. 26.
66. Gordon Wallace, *Carrier Observer,* Shrewsbury, 1993, p. 23.
67. *Ibid.,* pp. 172–3.
68. *Ibid.,* p. 22.
69. Dunstan Hadley, *Barracuda Pilot,* op. cit., pp. 170–3.
70. *Ibid.,* p. 85.
71. John Hoare, *Tumult in the Clouds,* London, 1976, p. 66.
72. *Alone on a Wide, Wide Sea,* op. cit., p. 43.
73. Hugh Popham, *Sea Flight,* London, 1954, p. 49.
74. Norman Hanson, *Carrier Pilot,* Cambridge, 1979, p. 114.
75. *Ordinary Naval Airman,* p. 137.
76. *Carrier Pilot,* op. cit., p. 66.
77. *Ibid.*
78. PRO AIR 10/4038.
79. *Ordinary Naval Airman,* op. cit., p. 136.
80. Hoare, *Tumult in the Clouds,* op. cit., pp. 170–1.
81. *Squadrons of the Fleet Air Arm,* op. cit., p. 189.
82. From David Jefferson, *Coastal Forces at War,* Yeovil, 1996.

83. Admiralty, *His Majesty's Minesweepers*, London, 1943, p. 34.
84. Paul Lund and Harry Ludlam, *Out Sweeps!*, op. cit., p. 124.
85. *Ibid.*, p. 125.
86. Navy Records Society, vol. 137, *The Defeat of the Enemy Attack on Shipp.ing*, Barley and Waters, ed. Eric J. Grove, 1997, p. 186.
87. Sir Angus Cunningham Graham, *Random Naval Recollections*, Gartocharn, 1979, pp. 270–1.

15 Cold War and Cod Wars

1. *Brassey's Annual, the Armed Forces Yearbook, 19—*.
2. Sir Angus Cunningham Graham, *Random Naval Recollections*, Gartocharn, 1979, p. 271.
3. Viscount Cunningham of Hyndhope, *A Sailor's Odyssey*, London, 1951, p. 9.
4. Richard Holme, *Cairnryan Military Port, 1940–1996*, Wigtown, 1997.
5. PRO ADM 116/5272.
6. PRO ADM17157.
7. *Random Naval Recollections*, p. 108.
8. *Ibid.*, p. 315.
9. PRO ADM1/17164.
10. PRO ADM1/20626.
11. PRO ADM1/24397.
12. PRO ADM1/20626.
13. *Ibid.*
14. PRO ADM1/24397.
15. *Random Naval Recollections*, op. cit., p. 314.
16. *Ibid.*, pp. 316–17.
17. *Ibid.*, p. 315.
18. Most of the passage is taken from Ian Buxton and Ben Warlow, *To Sail No More*, Liskeard, 1997.
19. *Brasseys Annual*, op. cit., 1952, pp. 151–2.
20. PRO ADM1/19958.
21. PRO ADM1/24477.
22. Statement, paras 24, 27.
23. *To Sail no More*, op. cit., pp. 65–7.
24. PRO ADM 1/27147.
25. PRO ADM 205/176.
26. John Coote, *Submariner*, London, 1991, p. 17.
27. PRO ADM 116/6253.
28. PRO ADM 1/29247.
29. PRO ADM 1/29265.
30. PRO ADM 1/28659.
31. *Brasseys 1952*, pp. 111, 113.
32. *Brasseys 1953*, pp. 159–63.
33. *Brasseys 1954*, pp. 285–9.
34. PRO ADM 1/26857.
35. PRO ADM 258/79.
36. PRO ADM 1/27805.
37. PRO ADM 205/165.
38. PRO ADM 1/26777.
39. PRO DEFE 13/11, 7/2175.
40. PRO ADM 1/26777.
41. James Cable, *Britain's Naval Future*, London, 1983, p. 131.

42. *One Hundred Days*, London 1992, p. 44.
43. Coote, op. cit., p. 177.
44. *Ibid.*, pp. 156–7.
45. PRO ADM 1/25252.
46. Coote, op. cit., p. 17.
47. PRO ADM 1/24783.
48. PRO MT 82/28, POWE 61/133.
49. Geoff. Feasey, *Very Ordinary Officer*, Fisher, Australia, 1999, p. 208.
50. *Ibid.*
51. *Ibid.*
52. *The National Service Sailor*, Wivenhoe, 1993, pp. 120–3, 134–7.
53. Cammel Laird, *HMS Renown*, nd, 1969, Birkenhead.
54. *The Times*, 19, 20, 21 August 1970.
55. *Jane's Fighting Ships*, 1960–1, p. 297.
56. PRO ADM 1/29264.
57. *Ibid.*
58. Pamphlet, *Tay Division Royal Naval Reserve, 1861–1994.*
59. *RNR 100*, Commemorative Brochure, Liverpool, 2003, pp. 30, 34, 40.
60. *Ibid.*, p. 80.
61. PRO ADM 306/32.
62. *Ibid.*
63. Norman Storey, *What Price Cod?*, Beverley, 1992, pp. 19–20.
64. R. H. Osborne, 'The "Third Cod War"' in *Warship Supplement* no. 52, June 1978.
65. Hannes Jonsson, *Friends in Conflict: the Anglo-Icelandic Cod Wars and the Law of the Sea*, London, 1982, pp. 220–1.
66. Quoted in Christopher Harvie, *Fools' Gold*, London, 1995, p. 236.
67. *Warship Supplement* nos 128, 129, Rossman, *Nuclear Powered Submarine Incidents.*
68. Marine Accident Investigation Branch, *Report of the Chief Inspector . . . Into the Collision between the Fishing Vessel Antares and HMS Trenchant . . .*, London, 1992.
69. *Dunoon Observer*, 11 December 1999.
70. Ministry of Defence, *Broadsheet*, 1997–8, pp. 36–8.
71. *Broadsheet*, 2003–4, p. 38.
72. *RRD 2000*, August 1996.
73. *Broadsheet*, 1997–8, pp. 58–9.
74. *Navy News*, May 1998, p. 4.
75. *Broadsheet* 1997–8, p. 11.

16   The Nuclear Submarine Bases

1. *The Times*, 30 January, 24, 25, 26 February 1958.
2. John D. Drummond, *A River Runs to War*, London, 1960, p. 200.
3. Alistair Horne, *Macmillan*, vol. ii, 1957–1986, London, 1989, p. 276.
4. PRO ADM 205/222.
5. PRO ADM 205/163.
6. Phillip Zeigler, *Mountbatten*, London, 1985, pp. 560–1.
7. PRO ADM 205/163.
8. PRO ADM 205/222.
9. PRO CAB 129/102.
10. PRO ADM 1/27203.
11. PRO ADM 205/222.
12. *Ibid.*

13. Christopher Driver, *The Disarmers*, London, 1964, p. 99.
14. PRO ADM 205/222.
15. PRO ADM 1/27203.
16. PRO ADM 205/222.
17. *Ibid*.
18. PRO PREM 11/2941.
19. PRO ADM 1/27203.
20. PRO ADM 205/222.
21. *Ibid*.
22. PRO PREM 11/2941.
23. PRO CAB 129/102.
24. Harold Macmillan, *Pointing the Way*, London, 1972, p. 256.
25. Richard Lamb, *The Macmillan Years: The Emerging Truth*, London, 1995, p. 295.
26. *Ibid*., pp. 255–9.
27. Desmond Wettern, *The Decline of British Seapower*, London, 1982, p. 183.
28. *Brasseys Annual, The Armed Forces Year-Book*, London, 1966 p. 131.
29. PRO CAB 1/4012.
30. PRO ADM 205/163.
31. PRO ADM 205/222.
32. PRO DEFE 7/2176.
33. PRO ADM 1/27201.
34. *Ibid*.
35. *Ibid*.
36. *Ibid*.
37. *Ibid*.
38. *Ibid*.
39. 22 May 1961, p. 4.
40. PRO PREM 11/3969.
41. PRO ADM 1/27202.
42. PRO PREM 11/3969.
43. PRO Adm 1/27202.
44. PRO Adm 1/28174.
45. *Dictionary of American Naval Fighting Ships*, vol. v, Washington, 1970, reprinted 1979, p. 396.
46. PRO Adm 205/213.
47. PRO Adm 1/29039.
48. Peter Nailor, *The Nassau Connection*, London, 1988, p. 91.
49. Chief Polaris Executive, *Polaris and the Royal Navy*, London, 1966, p. 3.
50. PRO Adm 1/28887.
51. *Ibid*.
52. PRO Adm 1/29039.
53. Geoff Feasey, *Very Ordinary Officer*, Fisher, Australia, 1999, pp. 206, 213.
54. *Royal United Services Journal*, vol. 113, p. 217.
55. *Polaris and the Royal Navy*, op. cit., 1966, pp. 6–7.
56. *Brassey's Annual*, op. cit., 1966, p. 134.
57. *The Nassau Connection*, op. cit., p. 97.
58. PRO Adm 1/28885.
59. P. G. La Niece, *Not a Nine to Five Job*, Yalding, 1992. pp. 221–2.
60. John Short, Timothy Stone and David Greenwood, *Military Installations and Local Economies: A Case Study: The Clyde Submarine Base*, Aberdeen, 1974, Table 2, A9.
61. *Polaris and the Royal Navy*, op. cit., 1966, p. 1.
62. *Not a Nine to Five Job*, p. 208.

63. *Brassey's Annual,* 1966, p. 132.
64. PRO Adm 1/29143.
65. Rebecca John, *Caspar John,* London, 1987, p. 197.
66. PRO Adm 1/28838.
67. *Polaris and the Royal Navy,* op. cit., 1966, p. 1.
68. Cammel Laird, *HMS Renown,* nd, c 1969, Birkenhead.
69. *Polaris and the Royal Navy,* 1966, p. 3.
70. *Not a Nine to Five Job,* op. cit., p. 210.
71. PRO Adm 1/28966.
72. *Not a Nine to Five Job,* op. cit., p. 212.
73. *Very Ordinary Officer,* op. cit., p. 214.
74. *Not a Nine to Five Job,* op. cit., p. 218.
75. *Fairplay,* 22 Jan 1998, p. 4.
76. *Shipping Today and Yesterday,* October 1993, pp. 4–9.
77. Ministry of Defence, *Broadsheet,* 2003–2004, p. 39.
78. *Clyde-a-Scope, The Newspaper of HM Naval Base Clyde,* no. 3, Spring 1996, p. 11.
79. Ministry of Defence, *Broadsheet* 1999/2000, p. 29.
80. siol-nan-gaidheal.com.

Index of Ships

Dates are given when it is necessary to distinguish two or more ships of the same name. The launch date is given where known, otherwise the date of mention in the text.

SB = shore base commissioned as a ship

General Index

Operation Hammer 305
Operational training 370, 372–4
Operation Torch 343, 363–4, 387
Operation Wilfred 304–5
Orkney,16, 19, 23, 25, 40, 61–2,
  93, 107, 113, 120–1, 130, 144,
  146, 150, 169, 175, 204, 206,
  212, 214, 224, 238, 240, 244,
  249, 257–8, 262–3, 265, 268,
  270, 272, 275, 295, 297, 302–
  3, 308, 310, 377–8, 380, 401
Orkney Royal Garrison Artillery
  214
Ormonde, Duke of 34–6, 40, 42–3
Osborne House 203
Oslo 304
Ostend 30–1, 58–9, 110
Oughton, Sir James 115
Outline of Future Policy 397
overside discharge 333–5
Oxcars 205, 231–2, 238, 251, 400

Pantelleria 362
Para Handy 336
Parkestone Quay 254
Pearl Harbor, 230, 364
PO 218
Pembroke 178, 276–7
Parker, William 168
Paine, Thomas 138
Parker, Admiral Sir Hyde 117
Parliament, English 3, 11, 12, 26
Parliament, Scottish 18, 25–6, 43
Parliament, United Kingdom 35,
  70, 71, 83–84, 90, 107, 112,
  132–3, 144–5, 150–1, 154–6,
  174, 178–9, 182, 186–8, 194,
  197, 277, 282–3, 392, 396,
  421, 433, 444–6
Pay rates, naval 98, 135, 152, 153,
  166, 192, 282–8
Perishers' course 374, 404–5, 419–
  21, 450
Peterhead, 15, 36, 40–1, 44, 52,
  58–9, 111, 144, 239–40, 243,
  247, 249, 272, 301
Peter the Great, Tsar 70
Phipps Hornby, Captain Geoffrey
  160–1

Physicians, Scottish 96–9, 134
pirates, 28, 107, 142
Pitreavie Castle 393–4, 399, 403,
  413, 422
Pitt, William 84
Pittenweem 5, 30, 34, 38,
Place, Lieutenant, VC 318
Playfair 427, 430–1
Plymouth 28, 79, 103, 109, 139,
  145, 153, 159, 173–4, 178,
  219, 276, 282, 288, 218,
  320, 342, 361, 390, 416,
  422, 443,
Polaris missile 412, 426–7, 442
Polaris submarines 410, 427–8,
  433, 435, 437, 443, 444–6,
  453
Poole 418
Popham, Hugh 381
Port Bannatyne 317
Port Edgar 232–3, 272, 278, 373,
  384, 397, 414
Port Emergency Committee 325,
  334
Porterfield, George 8
Port Glasgow 198, 147, 398
Portree 109, 164, 166, 169, 170
Portsmouth 71, 75, 81, 89, 102,
  144, 153, 158, 160, 170, 172,
  178–9, 182, 185, 187, 188,
  192, 271, 273, 276, 288, 290,
  312, 315, 318, 359, 369, 374,
  375, 387, 390, 394, 397, 406–
  7, 412, 421–2, 445–7
Portsoy 130
Pottinger Captain, 19
press gangs 20, 74, 94, 96, 109,
  116, 131–44, 146–9, 153, 275
Pressing tenders 138–40
Preston 29, 39, 55
Prestongrange 104
Prestonpans, Battle of 50
Prestwick Airport 367, 403, 423,
  427, 429, 431
Prien, Gunther 297–8
Prince's Dock, Glasgow 323
Pringle, Captain Thomas 139
prize money 79080
privateering 2, 4–6, 11–3, 15, 19,